Financial Engineering

Second Edition

John F. Marshall

Vipul K. Bansal

Kolb Publishing Company
4705 S.W. 72nd Avenue   Miami, Florida 33155
(305) 663-0550   FAX (305) 663-6579

Dedication

For my mother Marian and my father Charles
with much love.

JFM

To my best friend and wife Archana
with love

VKB

About the Authors

Jack Marshall is Professor of Finance in the Graduate School of Business at St. John's University, New York. He is an author or coauthor of a number of books on derivative securities, risk management, and other aspects of financial engineering. These include *Futures and Option Contracting* (South-Western), *Understanding Swap Finance* (South-Western), *The Swaps Handbook* (New York Institute of Finance), and *The Swaps Handbook Supplements* (New York Institute of Finance). Jack is also a senior partner with Marshall & Associates, a New York-based financial engineering and consulting firm. Jack is the Executive Director of the American Association of Financial Engineers and an accomplished financial engineer in his own right. He is a frequent speaker at financial seminars, conferences, and symposia and a regular contributor to the financial literature. Jack holds the M.B.A., M.A., and Ph.D. degrees.

Vipul K. Bansal is Assistant Professor of Finance in the Colleges of Business at St. John's University, New York. In addition to this book, he is a coauthor of another book on financial engineering and a significant contributor to *The Swaps Handbook Supplements*. Vipul is an Associate with Marshall & Associates. He also serves as Associate Director of the American Association of Financial Engineers. Vipul is an accomplished financial engineer in his own right, having developed both new uses for swaps and new types of swaps. He is a frequent speaker at financial seminars and conferences and a regular contributor to the financial literature. Vipul holds the M.B.A. and Ph.D. degrees and is a Chartered Financial Analyst (CFA).

Contents

7   Measuring Risk: Advanced Topics, 147

8   Understanding Interest Rates and Exchange Rates, 181

9   Speculation, Arbitrage and Market Efficiency, 219

27 Legal Protections for Innovative Financial Products and Services, 687

Foreword

Financial engineering is the lifeblood of financial innovation—the process that seeks to adapt existing financial instruments and processes and to develop new ones so as to enable financial market participants to cope more effectively with the changing world in which we live. A book that captures the spirit of financial innovation and adequately explains the process of financial engineering and its rich harvest over the past two decades has long been overdue. This book does a remarkable job of filling the void.

A comprehensive book on financial engineering is an ambitious undertaking. This book is clearly written and it successfully bridges the interests of the practitioner and academic communities. Practitioners will find the conceptual background material presented in Chapters 4 through 11 very useful. Academics will find the institutional background material presented in each chapter that deals with innovative financial instruments and strategies equally informative. Given this background, both audiences will be able to appreciate better the detailed descriptions of innovative financial instruments and financial strategies that are skillfully presented in Chapters 12 through 25. The authors also do an excellent job of placing the subject of financial engineering in an international context. I think the final chapter, which deals with intellectual property protection, is one to which financial engineers will want to pay particular attention.

Financial innovation, as a discipline, has not, until recently, been taught as a formal component in MBA and doctoral programs in finance. Instead, each course, be it corporate finance, investments, commercial banking, or investment banking, has included some discussion of recent innovations as they pertain to those subjects. Due to time constraints and the amount of material that typically needs to be covered in those courses, financial engineering is only covered to the degree that a discussion of recent developments in finance complements the basic course content. In most cases, the closest we have come to formal study of financial engineering are the courses in derivative securities that many MBA and doctoral programs have introduced. But these courses tend to concentrate on standard applications of existing products rather than the creative development of new products, new uses for existing products, and new strategies for adding value.

The good news is that during the past few years leading institutions of higher learning have begun to elevate the examination of financial innovation to the level of formal study. These schools have introduced courses carrying titles such as "financial innovation," "financial engineering," "securities innovation," and so on. In addition, some courses that have carried the "futures and options" label or the "derivative securities" label have also evolved into broader studies of financial engineering. I expect that these developments represent the beginning of a trend, and I expect that most major academic programs in finance will soon have formal courses in financial engineering, if they do not have such courses already.

The major handicap to the formal study of financial engineering has been the lack of a well-structured and pedagogically sound textbook with sufficient rigor to serve as the cornerstone for such a course. This book fulfills that need. It is written at a level that enables it to appeal to most MBA students. Moreover, if supplemented by the primary references provided at the end of each chapter, this book could serve as an excellent foundation for a more advanced course in financial engineering.

The authors, whose past work in the area of innovative financial products and financial strategies is widely respected among both their practitioner and academic peers, have divided the book into five sections: (1) an introductory section that provides an interesting overview of financial engineering; (2) a background section that ensures that the reader will have the analytical tools necessary to appreciate the in depth discussion of financial engineering presented in subsequent chapters; (3) a financial instruments section that describes the principal securities innovations that have taken place within the past two decades; (4) a financial strategies section that provides a comprehensive look at the broad range of innovative financial strategies that have been developed in recent years to manage financial risk and maximize returns; and (5) a closing section that looks to the future, provides a global perspective, and discusses intellectual property protection. The chapters are not only well-written, but also loaded with practical examples and applications.

I particularly like the authors' critical look at financial innovations that did not succeed. A careful post mortem of a failed effort is often more useful to practitioners and academicians alike than is a recital of a litany of successes. In particular, often we learn more from the failure of one new product or strategy than we do from the success of another.

To end on a personal note, I have taught a course on financial innovation at Fordham University for several years. I have lamented the fact that I have been unable to find a book that I considered suitable for the course. In my desperation, I have even considered writing my own book. But thanks to Professors Marshall and Bansal I now have a textbook that I can not only use in my own courses, but also heartily recommend to others.

John D. Finnerty

Professor of Finance
Fordham University

General Partner
McFarland Dewey & Co.

Foreword

One of the most important attributes of a professional in any industry is to accept the responsibility of not only contributing to the expansion and further development of the techniques and the storehouse of knowledge for that profession, but also communicating knowledge, skills and techniques to both their fellow colleagues and new individuals entering the field.

The extremely diverse nature of financial engineering, the rapid pace of change and new development, as well as the day-to-day pressures of business make it virtually impossible for any one professional to accomplish the task of researching and preparing a book of this scope. Through the project, leading financial engineering professionals have taken advantage of the opportunity provided by Professors Marshall and Bansal to work together to create this excellent and far reaching book which represents the current state of the art of financial engineering.

Regardless of our official titles, job descriptions, or organizations with which are associated, those of us who are actively involved as practicing financial engineers tend to regard financial engineering as what *we* do. In my own case, this means the design and the development of new derivative securities and the applications of these ideas to solve funds-raising problems for major companies, governments, and supra-national agencies.

Like most practitioners, my time is very limited and I tend to read only that professional material that bears directly on my career. Not surprisingly, that material reinforces a somewhat narrow view of financial engineering. Usually, I applied the term to the creation or application of derivative securities. At the same time, I was aware that others were also using the term to describe altogether different sorts of financial activities. The creation of this book gives the financial engineering professional the opportunity to view our collective work in a broader context—as a science.

I was one of the many people that Jack and Vipul approached as they developed their outline for this book, and as they searched for resource material and support. I shared my thoughts with them, as did others at Bear Stearns. About two years later, I have now had the opportunity to preview the product of their long efforts. I can say unequivocally, that, as a consequence of having read this book, my view of what constitutes financial engineering is considerably broader. I enthusiastically endorse the broader definition and conceptualization espoused by the authors. While on a day-to-day basis what each of use do is surely financial engineering, we can now plainly see that what each other of us are doing is also financial engineering. We can also see how, collectively, our individual financial engineering activities constitute a science and broadly based profession. We seek to add value and we each know some of the ways to do that. However, unless we have the bigger picture and know what other financial engineers are doing, we cannot maximize the value we add.

This book ties together the pieces of the science of financial innovation that we are all coming to call financial engineering. Jack and Vipul have created a very valuable resource for everyone in this business and for everyone looking to understand this business. This book is informative, well-structured, and as near to complete as a single volume can get. Even more importantly, it stresses the ways in which a successful financial engineer must think and the ways that different specialists fit together to form a financial engineering team.

You cannot read this book without appreciating the authors' diverse backgrounds, which include experienced practitioners and rigorous academicians. The book, like the science it is all about, seeks to, and does, add value.

J. Michael Payte

Senior Managing Director Derivative Securities Bear, Stearns and Co., Inc.

Preface

We started planning this book in 1988, shortly after the term *Financial Engineering* first appeared in the finance literature. Since that time, it has been used more and more frequently in both academic and trade publications. The term is appealing because it accurately describes, for the first time, what a great many financial practitioners and financial theorists do. Unfortunately, or perhaps fortunately, those who have used the term have often used it very narrowly to describe very specific activities. At the same time, different people used it to describe different activities. This is also the case in other countries were the term has caught on. For example, in Japan, the word for financial engineering is *zaitech*. All of the usages, however, are captured under the broader meaning used in this book.

When we first set out to develop our outline for this book, we struggled for an accurate and properly encompassing definition of financial engineering. We began by contacting a long list of practitioners and academicians to discuss what the term meant to them. We were amazed and delighted by the interest that was shown in the project by virtually everyone we spoke to. We were invited in to sit down with the most senior people at many of the world's leading financial institutions. These experts gave most generously of their time and they shared their thoughts freely with us. We also conducted many interviews over the phone. These discussions, together with lengthy conversations we held with academicians, led us to repeatedly redefine, in our own minds, what financial engineering was. At each iteration our definition broadened. In the end, we could not improve on a definition offered by John Finnerty and this is the definition we use in this book (Chapter 1). For now, it is sufficient to state that financial engineering is the development and application of financial technology to solve financial problems and the creation of value by the identification and exploitation of financial opportunities.

After our first round of interviews, we drafted our first outline. It had 18 chapters. We shared this outline with a number of financial engineers and then held a second round of interviews. As a consequence of this second round, the outline grew to 23 chapters. We then conducted a third and final round of interviews before settling on our final outline which had the 27 chapters that make up this book. Despite the length of this book, we could not address every area and every topic that was identified as important by the people we interviewed. And, we could not possibly do complete justice to any one topic. We had to pick and choose and condense in a manner that we felt was pedagogically sound.

Some of those who reviewed earlier drafts objected to our inclusion of some very fundamental financial theory. However, when we proposed taking it out, others objected. In the end, we decided to leave it in as Chapters 4 and 5. The reader who is comfortable with this material can just glance through it and then move on without a serious loss of continuity.

In writing the book, there were certain important topics that we did not feel fully competent to address. At other times, others contributed so heavily to the development of the subject that we did not feel it appropriate to claim authorship. For these reasons, several of the chapters in this book have been authored or coauthored by others. We are deeply indebted to these people. Their contributions have undoubtedly added great value.

We have many people and many institutions to thank for their contribution to the final product. Some shared their thoughts, some provided resource material, some pulled strings to get us interviews, some wrote chapters or parts of chapters, some provided much needed financial resources, some provided us with a forum to test our material, and some reviewed chapters for us. All of these inputs were necessary and for all the help we say thanks. Thank you

Mike Barney (Seer Technologies)
Robert Bench (Price Waterhouse)
Andy Carron (First Boston Corporation)
Fred Casey (Bear, Stearns & Company)
Pat Catania (Chicago Board of Trade)
Judy Chan (Continental Bank)
Roy Cohen (Haas & McBryde International)
Ray Cullen (Merrill Lynch)
M.E. Ellis (St. John's University)
Bill Falloon (Corporate Risk Management Magazine)
John Finnerty (Fordham University)
Mike Finerty (Citibank)

Michael Fitzgerald (Continental Bank)
Debra Hardt (First Boston Corporation)
Tony Herbst (University of Texas)
Gene Johnson (University of Rhode Island)
Ken Kapner (Hongkong and Shanghai Bank, Ltd.)
Dilip Kare (University of North Florida)
Rick Klotz (First Boston Corporation)
Francis Lees (St. John's University)
Gilbert Leistner (Chicago Board of Trade)
Ken Leong (Bank of Tokyo)
Robert Mackay (Virginia Polytechnic Institute)
John Manna (St. John's University)
John McElravey (Federal Reserve Bank of Chicago)
Jim MeVay (Chase Manhattan Bank)
Jeffrey Mondschein (Continental Bank)
Bill Montgoris (Bear, Stearns & Company)
Ehsan Nikbakht (Hofstra University)
Steve Orme (Price Waterhouse)
Ed Paules (Continental Bank)
Carol Parish (Chase Manhattan Bank)
Christine Pavel (Citicorp)
Mike Payte (Bear, Stearns & Company)
Larry Quinn (Corporate Risk Management Magazine)
Giovanna Righini (Mitsubishi Bank)
Eb Scheuing (St. John's University)
Bob Schwartz (Mitsubishi Capital Market Services)
Bidyut Sen (Morgan Stanley & Company)
Timothy Shanovich (Continental Bank)
Randolph Sides (First Boston Corporation)
Justin Simpson (Morgan Stanley & Company)
Donald Smith (Boston University)
Charles Smithson (Chase Manhattan Bank)
Peter Trzyna (patent attorney)
Alan Tucker (Temple University)
Bob Willens (Lehman Brothers)
Kevin Wynne (Pace University)
Robert Yuyuenyongwatana (St. John's University)
Brad Ziff (International Swap Dealers Association)

A project like this would not have been possible without substantial financial resources. We would like to offer special thanks to those persons and institutions that saw enough merit in this project to dig into their pockets to support it. These include The Chicago Board of Trade, Continental Bank, The Business Research

Institute, Corporate Risk Management Magazine, and, especially, the St. John's alumni employees of Bear, Stearns and Company. We would also like to thank several institutions for sharing material with us. These include Ford Motor Credit Company, Sinochem International Oil Company Limited, Morgan Stanley & Company, The First Boston Corporation, Lehman Brothers, The Chicago Board of Trade, The Chicago Mercantile Exchange, The Chase Manhattan Bank, Citicorp, The Bank of Tokyo, The Financial Management Association, and the Federal Reserve Bank of Chicago. We would also like to thank Bernadette Garino and Marge Willaum for all their administrative help and the Colleges of Business of St. John's University for many forms of support. Lastly, we would like to thank the dozens of practitioners and academicians who shared their thoughts with us at various seminars and conferences over the last few years but who are not mentioned above because we failed to keep a list.

The effort behind this book led to more than just this book. It also led to the formation of the American Association of Financial Engineers. The Association seeks to network those persons, both academicians and practitioners involved in or interested in becoming involved in financial engineering. The Association is described in Chapter 3. (Interested persons may contact Jack Marshall, Executive Director, American Association of Financial Engineers.) The project also led to the launching of a new journal, *The Journal of Financial Engineering*.

This book is a little different from most in that it is somewhere between a professional guide and an academic text. This was our plan from the beginning. As a professional guide, it is aimed at those persons working in some aspect of financial engineering who need to have the bigger picture. As an academic text, it has been crafted to be pedagogically sound, sufficiently robust in theory and case studies, and well documented with respect to primary source literature. On this latter point, we have included, at the end of each chapter, a section entitled *References and Suggested Reading*. This material is provided for those readers who might require greater detail on some particular point or who are pursuing their own research.

We would be most interested in hearing your thoughts and any suggestions you have on how we might improve future editions of this book. Your comments should be addressed to the authors at St. John's University, Jamaica, New York, 11439.

Jack Marshall

Vipul Bansal

Chapter 1

An Introduction to Financial Engineering

Overview

The rapidity with which corporate finance, bank finance, and investment finance have changed in recent years has given birth to a new discipline that has come to be known as **financial engineering.** As with most disciplines in their early stages of development, the field of financial engineering has attracted people with an assortment of backgrounds and perspectives.

In preparing to write this book, we interviewed dozens of people including commercial bankers, investment bankers, corporate treasurers, corporate recruiters, financial engineers, financial analysts, and others. Many of these people are leading industry figures and respected authorities in their fields. As we met with more and more of these experts, we came to the conclusion that the term *financial engineering* means different things to different people. This is not surprising. The field is not yet very well defined

1

and each practitioner tends to view his or her own body of experience as the crux of that which constitutes the discipline. Each interview we conducted added some new dimension to our overall view and helped shape the final approach we decided to take in organizing this book. We are deeply indebted to all of those who shared their time and their thoughts with us. We are only sorry that space limitations and competing views have probably made it impossible for us to fully satisfy any one of them.

While we assume that most of our readers have considerable foundation in financial theory and quantitative technique, we expect that some may not. For the benefit of the latter but at the risk of insulting the former, we have chosen to include a brief review of some basic financial concepts. The more experienced reader will readily know what can be skipped without loss of continuity. We do not assume that our reader is familiar with the jargon of investment banking. For this reason, we will avoid burying the reader in market slang. We would be remiss, however, if we did not introduce the reader to relevant colloquialisms. We distinguish here between technical terms and colloquialisms. We will introduce technical language as we go along and then we will feel free to use the language in subsequent discussions. Colloquialisms, on the other, are nontechnical short-cuts which convey whole thoughts in a few words. They can easily lose a reader who is not familiar with the entire context in which they are used. On those occasions when we do employ a colloquialism, we will identify it as such.

In this chapter, we are going to define financial engineering and we are going to discuss the role of the financial engineer in modern business. We are also going to discuss some of the career opportunities available to prospective financial engineers and we are going to lay out the plan for the remainder of the book.

Because this chapter is meant to serve as a general introduction to financial engineering and its place in modern business, we will not define until later most of the instruments and the strategies which we mention, in passing, in this chapter. The reader unfamiliar with the terms we use in this chapter can rest assured that our failure to define them will be rectified before a deeper understanding is really required. Our goal here is to achieve a sufficient appreciation of where we want to go and why we want to go there as we work our way through the remainder of the book.

The Scope of Financial Engineering

We struggled for some time in an effort to come up with a definition of financial engineering which is capable of capturing the true scope of the discipline. In the end, we decided that we could not improve upon a definition offered by John Finnerty.[1]

> *Financial engineering involves the design, the development, and the implementation of innovative financial instruments and processes, and the formulation of creative solutions to problems in finance.*

The soul of Finnerty's definition is captured by the words *innovative* and *creative*. Sometimes this innovation and creativity involves a quantum leap in our thinking. This is the kind of creativity involved in the introduction of a revolutionary new product such as the first swap, the first mortgage-backed product, the first zero coupon bond, or the introduction of junk bonds to finance leveraged buy outs. At other times, it involves a novel twist on an old idea. This is the kind of creativity involved in the extension of futures trading to a commodity or a financial instrument not previously traded in a futures pit, the introduction of a swap variant, or the creation of a mutual fund with a new focus. At still other times, it involves the piecing together of existing products and processes to fit a particular set of circumstances. This latter dimension is often overlooked in animated discussions of financial engineering, but it is of at least equal importance. Examples include the use of existing products to reduce a firm's financial risks, to reduce the cost of a firm's financing, to gain some accounting or tax benefit, or to exploit a market inefficiency.

It is often difficult to distinguish between those innovations which truly represent quantum leaps and those which involve novel twists on old ideas. A ready example is that form of program trading which seeks to exploit price discrepancies between the cash market for equities and stock-index futures. The basic arbitrage strategy itself, i.e., buying (selling) the cash asset while selling (buying) a futures contract, is very old. In fact, it has been practiced in the grain trade for over a century. But, the extension of the strategy to encompass cash equities and stock-index futures required complex mathematical modeling, high-speed computing, and electronic securities trading in order to work. If we focus on the basic strategy, we must conclude that program trading was a novel twist on an old idea. If, on the other hand, we focus on the complex modeling, the development of the software, and the introduction of the computer linkages to make the whole thing work, we must conclude that program trading involved a quantum leap.

Financial engineering is not limited to corporate and institutional applications. Many of the most creative financial innovations in recent years have been directed at the retail, sometimes called the consumer, level. These include such things as adjustable rate mortgages, cash management accounts, NOW accounts, IRAs and Keoghs, and various new forms of life insurance.

While financial engineering is practiced at both commercial banks and investment banks, the activity, at least from the corporate end user's perspective, is more closely related to the traditional role of investment banks. Indeed, commercial banks involved in engineering solutions for corporate clients often regard their financial engineers as part of their investment banking operations. For this reason, we will often use the term *investment bank* loosely to include traditional investment banks, commercial banks involved in financial engineering, and other parties involved in structured deal-making and risk-management activities. We specifically exclude from this definition, however, financial engineers and financial engineering departments employed on the corporate side. We view the corporate side as the end user of the financial engineer's services; although we will, to a lesser degree, also consider retail-level end users.

From a practical perspective, financial engineers are involved in a number of important areas. These include corporate finance, trading, investment and money management, and risk management. In corporate finance, financial engineers are often called upon to develop new instruments to secure the funds necessary for the operation of large-scale businesses. This is not to say that traditional, off-the-shelf, instruments cannot accomplish the desired result. Quite often they can. But, at other times, the nature of the financing required or cost considerations dictate a special instrument, a collection of special features to be attached to an instrument, or a combination of instruments to be used in concert. This is where the financial engineer comes into the picture. He or she must understand the nature of the desired result and must piece together an appropriate solution. The frequency of innovation of this type is readily apparent to anyone browsing through the tombstones which appear daily in the financial pages of newspapers.

Closely related to financial engineering in corporate finance is financial engineering in mergers and acquisitions (M&A). Merger and acquisition teams engineer deals all the time. The most dramatic example of this engineering skill in recent years was the introduction of junk bonds and bridge financing to secure the funds necessary for takeovers and leveraged buyouts (LBOs). During the decade of the eighties alone, hundreds of billions of dollars of junk bonds were sold to finance hundreds of such deals.

Financial engineers are also employed in securities and derivative products trading. They are particularly adept at developing trading strategies of an arbitrage nature or quasiarbitrage nature. These arbitrage strategies can involve opportunities across space, time, instruments, risk, legal jurisdictions, or tax rates. Recent innovations involving arbitrage across space include linkages between futures exchanges so that trades made in U.S. markets can be offset by trades made in foreign markets. These global linkages are very exciting developments and have ushered in a new world of 24 hour trading. Numerous innovations in recent years have involved arbitrage across time. The best known example is probably program trading, but any situation in which the return from a strategy exceeds the cost of carry provides such potential and engineers continuously seek out such situations. Arbitrage across instruments explains many new developments which have given rise to "synthetic" instruments and "repackaging" of cash flows. Synthetic options, zero-coupon bonds, and collateralized mortgage obligation bonds (CMOs) are all examples of this kind of activity. Asymmetries in risk, asymmetries in market access, and asymmetries in tax exposure also create opportunities. These asymmetries explain the advent of swaps, much of the use of preferred stock, and the proliferation of special purpose partnerships.

Financial engineers have played a tremendous role in investment and money management. They have developed new investment vehicles such as "high yield" mutual funds, money market funds, sweep systems, and the repo market to mention just a few. The have also developed systems for transforming high risk investment instruments into low risk investment instruments through such ingenious devices as repackaging and overcollateralization.

Finally, financial engineers have been heavily involved in risk management. Indeed, most of the people we interviewed in preparing to write this book equated the terms *financial engineering* and *risk management*. This equating of concepts stems in part from the origins of the term *financial engineer*. It is generally agreed that the term *financial engineer* was introduced by London banks which began, in the mid-1980s, to build risk management departments consisting of teams of experts who would peddle structured solutions to corporate risk exposures. These teams took a new strategic approach to risk management. That is, they carefully examine *all* of the financial risks to which a firm is exposed. Some of the exposures are readily apparent to all, but some exposures are indirect and not at all apparent. Furthermore, risk exposures are sometimes offsetting and at other times mutually reinforcing. The teams work with the client firm to (1) identify the risks, (2) measure the risks, and (3) determine the kind of outcomes the firm's management would like to achieve. Everything up to this point constitutes analysis. Upon completion of the analysis, the team fires up its financial engineering skills. From a basket of existing products, including swaps, futures, rate caps, rate floors, forward rate agreements, and so on, the team will piece together a solution, sometimes called a structured deal, to achieve the desired outcome. This "building block" approach to risk management became the cornerstone of those financial engineers engaged in financial risk analysis and management. For their services, financial engineers sometimes charge engineering fees. But, more often, they earn their reward indirectly by executing the "deal" with the team's bank. The bank, in turn, is a market maker in many of the instruments employed in structuring the deal. As such, it profits from its bid-ask spread.

Before concluding this section on the scope of financial engineering, a few words are in order on the nature of the people involved in financial engineering. In a sense, financial engineers serve three roles: deal makers (marketers), idea generators (innovators), and loophole exploiters (outlaws). The deal makers structure a deal to serve the client's needs and then sell the client on the idea. The deal is the best one if and only if the deal accomplishes the client's objectives at the least possible cost with no hidden surprises. The innovators are the ones which create new products and processes. They often work with the deal makers to custom design a new product if the client's needs cannot be met with existing products and processes. The outlaws look to exploit loopholes. They are thoroughly versed in accounting and tax law and find ways to arbitrage asymmetries wherever they find them. Quite often, the activities of this latter group serve to expose loopholes. Were it not for the ability of the engineers to ferret out such loopholes, taxing authorities would often be unaware of them. As a general rule, when the exploitation of a loophole becomes general knowledge, legislation is eventually proposed to close it. But the adoption of legislation can be a slow process and the exploitation can go on for some time.

Successful financial engineers are always well versed in the areas of financial theory which are relevant to their trade and the mathematical relationships which make their deals work. They tend to grasp ideas quickly, and easily see through the details to the basic components of a structure. They also tend to be intellectual liberals who are encouraged to avoid the kind of "boxed" thinking which stifles creativity. Unlike most, they do not view the financial world as consisting of a set of givens. When told that something cannot be done, their first impulse is to ask why not. They tend to view every problem as a personal challenge.

Despite these general similarities, financial engineers are anything but clones of one another. Some are number crunchers who make discoveries and develop strategies through tedious and detailed examination of historical relationships and complex mathematical equations. These are the "quant jocks" of the trade. Others are opportunists. They look for exploitable situations and seize any opportunity which presents itself. They move quickly and decisively before prices have had an opportunity to change, before a necessary counterparty is lost, or before someone else with a better idea can think of it. The truly extraordinary of both groups are often described, in market slang, as "rocket scientists." In truth, however, a rocket scientist is often a duet (a rapid-fire opportunist working closely with a superb quant jock).

The Tools of Financial Engineering

Like any engineer, the successful financial engineer needs a toolkit. We find it convenient to divide the tools of the financial engineer into two broad categories: conceptual and physical. The **conceptual tools** involve the ideas and concepts which underlie finance as a formal discipline. Many of these conceptual tools are taught as part of modern finance curricula in graduate-level business programs. They are generally not, however, organized or presented in such a way as to readily lend themselves to a systematic study of financial engineering. Examples of the conceptual tools with which the engineer must be at home are valuation theory, portfolio theory, hedging theory, accounting relationships, and tax treatment under different forms of business organization.

The **physical tools** of the financial engineer include the instruments and the processes which can be pieced together to accomplish some specific purpose. At a very broad level, the instruments include fixed income securities, equities, futures, options, swaps, and dozens of variants on these basic themes. The processes include such things as electronic securities trading, public offerings and private placements of securities, shelf registration, and electronic funds transfer. By combining the physical tools in different ways, the financial engineer is able to custom design solutions to an incredible array of seemingly bewildering problems.

Financial Engineering Versus Financial Analysis

Most of the currently practicing financial engineers entered the field as some sort of financial analyst—although many may not have held the formal title of analyst. Indeed, many of those engaged in financial engineering still hold the official job title, or at least have a job description, that includes the word **analyst**. For this reason, it is important to distinguish between the role of the financial analyst and the role of the financial engineer.

A financial analyst is a person engaged in the practice of financial "analysis."**Analysis** is defined as the process or method of studying the nature of something in order to determine its essential features and their relationships. A financial engineer is a person engaged in the practice of financial "engineering." As we have already defined it, engineering is the process of formulating and implementing a new instrument, a new process, or a creative solution to a problem. The confusion between the roles of the analyst and the engineer stems from the fact that many analysts become involved in engineering without realizing it. This is particularly true at the corporate level. For example, the financial analyst is confronted with the task of deciphering a situation. In the process, the analyst comes to understand the situation. If a problem is involved, the analyst may be called on as the resident expert to offer a solution. The analyst may or may not be sufficiently trained, possess the intellectual skills, or have sufficient knowledge of available products to offer a viable solution. Nevertheless, in such a situation, most analysts will attempt to offer a solution. Without a sufficient knowledge base however, the solution offered may be far from optimal.

We have found it useful in distinguishing between an analyst and an engineer to employ an analogy. Consider the difference between the role of a geneticist and a genetic engineer. The geneticist is an expert at decomposing an organism's genetic material into its component genes and mapping the locations of these genes on the organism's chromosomes. The geneticist is akin to the analyst. That is, he or she examines the nature of the genetic material in order to understand its essential features and their relationships. The genetic engineer, on the other hand, takes this knowledge, together with certain physical tools, and extracts the genes of one organism for recombination in another organism. The end product is an altered organism or, in the extreme, an entirely new form of life. The genetic engineer is akin to the financial engineer. The upshot of the analogy is that the proper function of the analyst is to analyze while the proper function of the engineer is to create.

An example of the roles of the financial analyst and the financial engineer should reinforce the distinction. Consider a firm with a highly volatile cash flow stream. The firm would like to know (1) the sources of the volatility, and (2) how to remove the volatility. The firm hires a financial analyst to decompose the historic cash flow stream. Let's suppose that the analyst determines that the cash flow stream contains a secular trend, a seasonal component, an exchange rate component, and a small random component. Each component is measured and isolated. At this point the analyst has finished his work. He has explained the components of the firm's cash flow and the sources of the firm's risk. But, as important a step as the analysis is, the analysis alone does not solve the problem—i.e., the elimination of the volatility. It is time to bring in the financial engineer. The financial engineer picks up where the analyst leaves off. The financial engineer structures a solution to the volatility problem. The solution is likely to consist of several separate parts—each designed to eliminate one of the volatility components—hence, the term **structured solution.**

We do not mean to leave the impression that financial engineers do not need to understand financial analysis. Nor do we mean to leave the impression that the financial engineer can leave the financial analysis entirely to others—although this is sometimes the case. Rather, the financial engineer goes one step beyond that of the analyst. But, in order to do so, he or she must first understand financial analysis and be proficient at the appropriate methodologies.

Where Financial Engineering Fits In

Most of the financial engineering that makes the headlines—the revolutionary new products, trading strategies, processes to accomplish some end result, major financing deals, and so forth—takes place at the level of the financial institution, most often an investment bank or a commercial bank. These institutions pride themselves on the innovative minds they employ. They hire top talent, compete aggressively with one another to keep the talent, and put their people through extensive training programs. What's more, they never stop educating their people. They provide ongoing training programs to keep their employees current as to what is happening both in-house and at other "shops."

Despite the concentration of financial engineering talent at the top commercial and investment banks, financial engineers are also needed on the corporate side. There are several reasons for this. First, no one is in a better position to appreciate the concerns of a corporation's shareholders and creditors than those people most directly responsible for the firm's management. This appreciation becomes particularly important when there is more than one potential solution to a given problem. Different solutions may give rise to identical cash flow patterns and yet have very different qualitative effects. One must give serious consideration to these qualitative differences before selecting among the alternative solutions. An in-house financial engineer is often the best person to evaluate these concerns. Second, it is unfortunate to say, but it is nevertheless true, that some deals engineered by financial institutions on behalf of client firms are simply not in the best interests of the client firm—although they may be very profitable from the investment bank's perspective. An in-house financial engineer on the corporate side can intelligently consider the potential for negative ramifications from a particular proposal made to the firm.

While our discussion of financial engineering in this book will largely examine the subject from the investment bank's perspective, an appreciation of the corporate side is critical. We sincerely believe that readers of this book on the corporate side will be helped by a better understanding of the process of financial engineering and the pitfalls which exist for the corporate end user. Knowledge in the hands of an investment bank's financial engineers is at least equally useful when it is in the hands of the corporation's financial engineers. To help the corporate reader still further, we will take apart a number of deals which ultimately proved deleterious for the end user. This post-mortem approach is not meant to cast dispersions on the investment banks which put the deals together—although some questioning of skills is unavoidably implied. Rather, the purpose is to more fully appreciate what can go wrong with a structured deal in order to avoid falling into unforeseen traps with all the collateral damage that such traps entail.

The Financial Engineering Team

Financial engineers often work as part of a larger team. The elements of the team will vary depending on the nature of the engineering involved. Members of the team might include accountants, tax specialists, attorneys, underwriters, compliance officers, capital market personnel, traders, financial analysts, modeling groups, programmers, information services personnel, and so on. The exact combination will be tailored to fit the situation.

The important point to remember is that the financial engineer does not usually work alone. The extent of the expertise needed to handle a complex mix of financial, legal, and accounting and tax matters is usually beyond any single individual's knowledge base. The team approach provides the solution. All members of the team are carefully selected to work together efficiently and with the speed required by the situation. Communication is the key.

Productizing the Solution

Many of the most innovative new products trading in the capital markets and derivative instrument markets today originated as a financial engineer's solution to a particular client's needs. That is, the engineer devoted a considerable amount of time and energy to the development of a solution to fit a very specific client's situation. For these services, the engineer, or the engineer's bank to be more precise, charged the client a substantial engineering fee. The fee covers the engineer's time, the accounting and legal work, the execution costs, and the profit required by the bank—all of which can be very substantial. In such situations, the client must be large and the size of the transaction considerable in order to justify the cost. For obvious reasons then, this kind of engineering constitutes a low-volume high-margin design.

Once the time and energy has been expended to produce a customized design to satisfy a client's needs, the bank can often profit by recycling the solution. In many cases, the nature of the situation for which the design was engineered is unique or very nearly so. In such cases, there is little advantage to publicizing the design or to streamlining its delivery. It is better to reap the high margin afforded by the product from those few other situations for which it is reasonably appropriate or to shelve the design for later recycling should a similar usage arise. But, at other times, a design has a great many applications. Interest-rate and currency swaps (rate swaps) are such a situation. The initial design was very complex and required extensive engineering, reams of documentation, and innumerable hours of accounting and legal review. But, once all the bugs had been worked out, it was a relatively simple matter to reuse the basic design. Once the potential of the instrument was realized, energies were devoted to standardizing the product and streamlining its delivery. In the end, swaps became a well-defined instrument traded in a liquid dealer market. The bid-ask spread narrowed as the design was duplicated and dealers proliferated.

The process of taking a custom-designed solution to a client's problem, standardizing it, and streamlining its delivery is called **productizing** a solution. Productizing turns low-volume high-margin designs into high-volume low-margin products which are only profitable for those dealers which can deliver them very efficiently and which have the expertise to manage the associated risks. While swaps are the classic example of productizing in the 1980s, other examples abound: interest-rate caps, interest-rate floors, forward rate agreements, collateralized mortgage obligations, adjustable rate mortgages, and so on.

Career Opportunities for Financial Engineers

We will not say a great deal just yet about career opportunities for financial engineers. We will leave most of that topic to Chapter 3. Nevertheless, this brief overview of financial engineering should have suggested a great many potential career paths for the motivated student of financial engineering.

In brief, opportunities for innovative and creative individuals abound in the traditional arenas in which we would expect to find this type of talent. These, of course, are the investment banks and the commercial banks. This is particularly true of those institutions that have a global perspective. But do not overlook the corporate side. The modern corporation, particularly multinationals, have a crying need for the type of talent which has so long been siphoned off to the deal makers. These firms have become increasingly aware of the need for risk analysis and risk management, and for the ability to reduce financing costs by tapping nontraditional markets. Very few such firms, however, possess sufficient quantities of talent to fully evaluate the structured deals offered to them by competing financial institutions. Undoubtedly, the corporate demand for talent will increase dramatically in coming years. We remind the reader that while our focus in this book will be largely from the perspective of the investment banker, everything we have to say is equally applicable to the corporate-based financial engineer.

Careers in financial engineering do not generally start out as such. Instead, they usually begin as junior financial analysts and researchers. In time, the analyst might graduate to a corporate finance desk, a risk management department, a capital markets group, or another specialized area with a need for truly innovative thinkers.

The Plan of the Book

We want to make it very clear that this book is concerned with financial engineering *as a discipline*. Our primary interest is in the creative process which characterizes innovation and the kinds of thinking which are involved in problem solving. We will discuss the specific tools employed by financial engineers, including both those of a conceptual and those of a physical nature. But, this book is not intended to serve as the be-all and end-all of specific instruments employed by financial engineers. We will, for example, devote a chapter to futures and forwards, two chapters to options, and a chapter to swaps. These are the instruments which make up a class of products called derivative securities. But, we could not possibly provide a complete analysis of any one of these instruments in a single chapter or even in two. It is doubtful that an entire book the length of this one could adequately describe even one of the instruments employed by financial engineers. Instead, our goal will be to examine each of the instrument groupings at a more abstract level. For the interested reader, we will provide reference material which describes each product grouping and each conceptual tool in far greater detail than we can provide in this limited space. We will also provide information on how this material can be accessed. Collectively, the publications we suggest should be adequate to serve as the core of a financial engineer's library.

While we would have liked to have written every word in this book on our own, certain topics required exceptional expertise which we simply lacked. In those situations for which we did not feel adequate to the task or for which others had more to contribute, we sought help. As we go through the book we will give credit where credit is due. And it is due to many.

We have divided this book into five broad sections consisting of twenty-seven chapters. Section I, which consists of this introductory chapter and the next two, provides an overview of financial engineering.

Section II, which consists of Chapters 4 through 10, deals with the conceptual tools of the financial engineer. We discuss valuation relationships, risk measurement, and the logic involved in risk management. We also introduce a number of very useful practical tools which help us visualize the kinds of financial flows of interest to the financial engineer. These include such things as risk profiles, investment horizons, cash flow diagrams, and so on. Chapter 10 is a little different. It was contributed by friends at Chase Manhattan and Continental Banks and deals with the corporate treasurer's perspective.

Section III, which consists of Chapters 11 through 19, deals with the physical tools. These include the various instruments that are traded in the money markets, the capital markets, and the derivative securities markets. We separate the capital market instruments into debt instruments and equity instruments even though it is becoming increasingly difficult to tell the two apart. Indeed, hybrid instruments, which contain a combination of the features normally associated with money market instruments, capital market instruments, and derivative securities, blur the traditional distinctions completely. Chapter 19, which deals exclusively with hybrids instruments, was contributed by a friend at Morgan Stanley. Among the derivative securities examined in Section III are futures and forwards, options—including interest-rate caps and floors, and swaps—including currency swaps, interest-rate swaps, commodity swaps, and equity swaps.

In Section IV, which consists of Chapters 20 through 25, we consider processes and strategies. These include asset/liability management, hedging and related forms of risk management, arbitrage and the creation of synthetic instruments, and a variety of strategies to exploit tax asymmetries, capture value through synergism and divestiture, better manage liquidity, and so on.

Section V, which consists of Chapters 26 and 27 and which concludes the book, explores some important dimensions of financial engineering which, while already very important, will undoubtedly become even more important in the years to come. Specifically, we examine the ongoing trend toward globalization of the financial markets, the role played by technology, and the increasing use of product protection laws to safeguard financial innovations. Our look at globalization considers capital market integration and the internationalization of competition among financial and nonfinancial institutions. We also consider, to a modest degree, the changing nature of regulation and tax and accounting treatments. Our examination of technology focuses on the opportunities created by technology and telecommunications; and our examination of legal protections includes the role of patents and copyrights.

Summary

Financial engineering is the application of investment technology in an effort to solve financial problems. Financial engineers are employed by investment banks, commercial banks, a variety of other financial intermediaries, and nonfinancial corporations. Financial engineers are responsible for most financial innovation. It is difficult to overstate the importance of such innovation over the last fifteen years. Financial engineers must be trained in both the conceptual tools that constitute financial theory and in the physical tools that take the form of financial instruments and processes.

Financial engineering should not be confused with financial analysis. Analysts decompose structures in order to understand them. This is an important step in identifying the existence of a problem and in getting to its root cause. While this is a critical step in financial engineering, it is only the first step. The engineer uses his or her knowledge of the relevant theory, instruments, and processes together with his or her understanding of the problem to engineer a solution to the problem.

The solutions that financial engineers create are sometimes one-of-a-kind and have little recyclability. At other times, however, the solution has much wider applicability and can be productized. Productizing a solution tends to transform a solution from high-margin/low-volume nature to one of low-margin/high-volume.

Because financial engineers possess specialized sets of hard to come by skills, and because the speed of innovation has outpaced the ability of the market to produce competent financial engineers, financial engineers tend to be in short supply and high demand. Career opportunities seem exceptionally bright and the work is, undoubtedly, very rewarding.

Endnote

[1]See Finnerty (1988).

References and Suggested Reading

Black, F. and M. Scholes. "From Theory to a New Financial Product," *Journal of Finance*, pp. 399-412, May, 1974.

Brown, K.C. and D.J. Smith. "Recent Innovations in Interest Rate Risk Management and the Reintermediation of Commercial Banking," *Financial Management*, pp. 14-33, Winter 1988.

Finnerty, J.D. "Financial Engineering in Corporate Finance: An Overview," *Financial Management*, pp. 14-33, Winter 1988.

Miller, M.H. "Financial Innovation: The Last Twenty Years and the Next," *Journal of Financial and Quantitative Analysis*, pp. 459-471, December 1986.

Power, W. "Many of 1987's New Trading Products are Failing Despite Spirited Marketing," *Wall Street Journal*, p. 26, January 4, 1988.

Shirreff, D. "Down with Innovation," *Euromoney*, p. 23ff., August, 1986.

Silber, W.L. "The Process of Financial Innovation," *American Economic Review*, pp. 89-95, May 1983.

Van Horne, J.C. "Of Financial Innovation and Excesses," *Journal of Finance*, pp. 621-631, July 1985.

Chapter 2

Factors Contributing to the Growth of Financial Engineering

Overview

The explosive growth in financial engineering over the last two decades is consequence of a number of factors. Each of these factors has stimulated one or more aspects of financial engineering, made some form of financial engineering possible, or, when combined with other factors, formed an environment conducive to financial engineering. We will divide the factors into two groups. The first consists of those factors that characterize the environment in which the modern corporation operates. The **environmental factors** may be regarded as the factors external to the firm and over which the firm has no direct control but which are nevertheless of great concern to the firm because they impact the firm's performance. The second group consists of those factors that are internal to the firm and over which the firm has at least some control. We call these latter factors **intrafirm factors.**

The environmental factors include such things as increased price volatility, a general globalization of industry and financial markets, tax asymmetries, technological advances, advances in financial theory, regulatory change, increased competition, and transaction costs. The intrafirm factors include such things as liquidity needs, risk aversion among managers and owners, agency costs, greater levels of quantitative sophistication among investment managers, and more formal training of senior-level personnel.

In this chapter, we will describe these factors and consider some of the ways each has helped to dramatically increase the use of and the need for financial engineering. Our goal is to appreciate the forces at work in an effort to better understand the environment in which the modern financial engineer operates. This look at the environment will help us understand the kinds of innovative solutions for which the financial engineer strives.

The Environmental Factors

Environmental factors are those factors external to the firm but which nevertheless impact on the firm's performance. As already noted, the environmental factors include such things as price volatility, globalization of the markets, tax and accounting rules, technological developments, advances in financial theory, and so on. We will look at each of these factors in the several subsections that follow. Later in this book we will look at each of these factors in considerably greater depth.

Price Volatility

Financial engineers use the term *price* very broadly. A **price** is what one pays to acquire something of value or the use of something of value. The object having value may be a commodity, domestic financing (money), or a foreign currency. The concept of price is clear to most people when the focus of the discussion is on commodities. There is a price, for instance, to be paid for oil, wheat, cattle, lumber, an industrial or precious metal, and so on. The price one pays for the use of a unit of another's money is called an interest rate, and the price one pays in one's own currency for a unit of a different currency is called an exchange rate. Closely related to the notion of interest, as a price paid for the use of another's money, is the concept of an equity capitalization rate. An equity capitalization rate is the price which providers of equity capital expect to receive in exchange for providing equity capital to a firm. This latter price, however, is considerably more abstract than any of the others we will discuss and so we treat it separately.

Prices are determined by market forces. In the language of economics, consumers of things of value have "demands" for them and bid for them in the market while producers of things of value have supplies of them offer them for sale in the market. The collective interaction of the demands by consumers and the supplies by producers ultimately determine market clearing prices and quantities. If demands and supplies are relatively stable over time, then the market clearing price yesterday, the market clearing price today, and the market clearing price tomorrow will all be much the same. This is referred to as price stability. But, if demands and supplies for a thing of value change rapidly over a short period of time, then market clearing prices can change dramatically. This is referred to as **price volatility.** Price volatility has three dimensions: the speed of price change, the frequency of price change, and the magnitude of price change.

The classic economic explanation for price changes can be demonstrated by the use of demand and supply curves. Such curves are depicted in Exhibit 2.1 Panel A. In this portrayal, aggregate market demand is depicted as a downward sloping curve and aggregate market supply is depicted as an upward sloping curve. The intersection between these two curves represents the market clearing quantity (horizontal axis) and the market clearing price (vertical axis). If demand were to suddenly increase, as depicted in Exhibit 2.1 Panel B, then the market price must rise to re-establish a balance between supply and demand. Similarly, if supply were to suddenly decrease, as depicted in Exhibit 2.1 Panel C, then the market price must also rise to re-establish a balance between supply and demand. Sudden decreases in demand and sudden increases in supply would, of course, have just the opposite effects on price.

Despite the importance of price in determining the shapes of the demand and supply curves, there are a great many other factors that influence the positions of the demand and supply curves. It is these other factors that explain the kinds of shifts in demand and supply depicted in Panels B and C of Exhibit 2.1. These factors include such things as changes in the cost of production, changes in the prices of other goods, expectations about future demand and supply conditions, the size of the market, and so on.

Changes in the demand and supply influencing factors culminate in market adjustments through price changes. These price

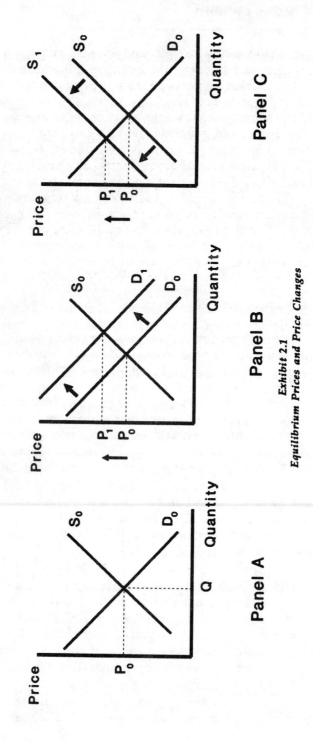

Exhibit 2.1
Equilibrium Prices and Price Changes

22

changes are themselves neither good nor evil; but they are necessary for the proper and smooth functioning of a market economy. More specifically, market responses through price changes are essential for rationing goods and allocating them to their most productive uses. At the same time, however, price changes expose individuals, producing firms, and governments to significant risks.

There is nothing particularly new about the nature of price formation to warrant significant financial engineering activity. What is new and what does warrant significant financial engineering activity is the increased speed, the increased frequency, and the increased magnitude of price changes in most markets since the mid-1970s. That is to say, since the mid-1970s, the commodity and financial markets have become much more volatile. Examples of this increased price volatility are depicted in Exhibit 2.2.

The explanation for this increased price volatility is not easy to pin down. To some degree, it is a product of (1) inflationary forces which disrupted the financial markets during the 1970s; (2) the breakdown of traditional institutions and international agreements; (3) the globalization of the markets; (4) the rapid industrialization of many underdeveloped countries; and (5) greater speed in acquiring, processing, and acting upon information.

Exhibit 2.2 Panel A
Exchange Rate Volatility
Composite of World Currencies vis-a-vis the Dollo

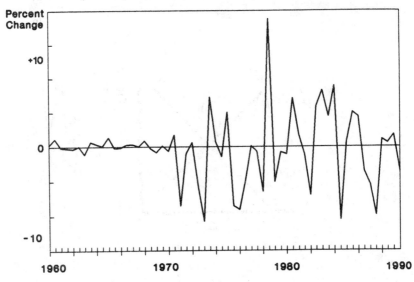

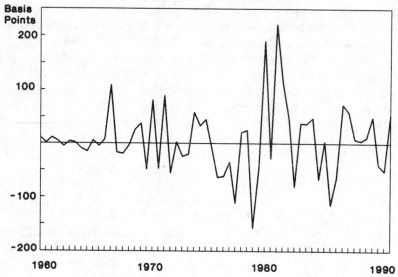

Exhibit 2.2 Panel B
Interest Rate Volatility
Yield Changes on Long-Dated Investment-Grade Debt
Composite for Selected Hard Currencies

Exhibit 2.2 Panel C
Commodity Price Volatility
Composite of Industrial Commodities (Dollars)

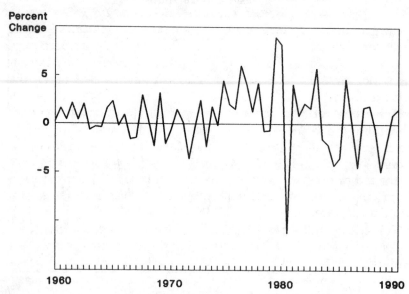

The inflationary spiral which began in the late 1960s and which accelerated through the 1970s caused major disruptions to market clearing processes. Worse, efforts to control prices by ill-conceived price controls interfered with the normal workings of the market and caused pressure-cooker situations that were often released with near explosive force. The breakdown of the Bretton Woods Agreement brought an end to the stabilizing role of fixed exchange rates and the gold convertibility of the dollar. The globalization of the markets and the rapid industrialization of many underdeveloped countries brought a new scale and dimension to the markets. Previously impoverished peoples suddenly became major sources of supply and major demanders of goods. They also discovered their economic muscle and some banned together to manipulate prices to their advantage. The oil price shocks of the 1970s and the 1980s were the most disruptive of these efforts at cartelizing the markets. The advent of telecommunications, and data processing brought information to the markets more quickly. Information, which might have taken weeks or months to significantly impact the markets in a bygone day, can now be fully felt in a matter of days, hours, and, often, just seconds.

As we noted earlier, the equity capitalization rate is a more abstract price than most others. In fact, there are two prices associated with equity. One is the price of the equity itself expressed as dollars per share. The other is the rate of return to an equity holder expressed in percent form. The rate of return to equity holders is a random variable in the sense that those who provide equity financing do not know in advance what rate of return their investment will ultimately provide. The rate consists of two parts: the first is the dividend rate and the second is the capital gain rate—both of which are uncertain until after the investment period has ended.

Although the rate of return to equity holders is uncertain, there is, at any given point in time, some market expectation of this rate of return. This market expectation is fairly easily estimated with the aid of present value arithmetic and the well-known capital asset pricing model. We call this expected rate of return the equity capitalization rate.

The equity holder is exposed to price risk because the price of corporate shares fluctuates—sometimes quite dramatically. To a considerable degree, equity price risk can be decreased by diversifying into a number of different stocks. But, diversification alone is not sufficient to completely eliminate the risk. In recent years, equity price volatility has been increased by a more rapid flow of information to the markets, a spate of takeover efforts, and a new form of spot-futures arbitrage known as program trading made possible by new financial products and new technology.

While some of the factors contributing to the increased price volatility of the 1970s and 1980s may be of a passing nature, others are more lasting. Even without the introduction of any new volatility stimulators—a dubious assumption—one cannot expect to see a return to the stable prices of the 1950s and 1960s. Those who are threatened by price volatility must accept this greater volatility as a fact of life and learn to manage the risks it poses.

Globalization of the Markets

There was a time when managers of U.S. corporations only had to deal with domestic economic concerns. What happened in the rest of the world was largely irrelevant. From the end of World War II until the early 1960s, the preeminence of the United States assured U.S. firms that little heed needed to be given to foreign producers. If anything, foreign markets were potential demanders of U.S. goods and suppliers of basic raw materials—little more. Indeed, for several decades, college economics courses found it quite convenient to simply assume away the foreign sector entirely.

In the 1960s, with long periods of near full employment and rapid advances in U.S. living standards, wage rate disparities between the U.S. and other countries led some U.S. firms, particularly larger ones, to look for ways to lower labor costs. Not surprisingly, many U.S. firms opened overseas production facilities or contracted out their production to foreign producers. Much of this effort was directed at those underdeveloped countries where labor was very cheap. As one would expect, overseas production began in those labor intensive industries that produced low-technology products which were easily transported. In time, however, as the labor forces of other countries became more highly skilled and as the wage differentials declined, overseas production spread to high-technology products.

At the same time, the war-ravaged economies of Europe and Japan were rebuilding and reemerged as major producers and exporters of quality goods. In time, they repeated the U.S. model and also began overseas production.

In addition to cheaper labor afforded by overseas operation, U.S., European, and Japanese firms eventually came to discover other benefits from geographically-dispersed operations. These included, at the very least, better access to raw materials, and reduced transportation costs.

As corporations globalized their production, they came to realize the potential benefits from globalizing their marketing efforts. They opened overseas subsidiaries to market their goods, entered joint ventures with foreign firms, and pressured their governments to provide export financing.

As the technology and commercial bases of the underdeveloped countries developed, homegrown entrepreneurs, often aided by their governments, began to develop their own domestic industries. In time, these firms became exporters in their own right. They set up marketing programs in the U.S. and other developed countries and shipped an ever increasing quantity of goods. As they developed, these countries demanded large quantities of U.S. machine tools and other high-tech capital goods.

Global production and marketing efforts led to the precursor of the multinational corporation. The premultinational is a firm with global production and marketing but which still depends on the capital markets of the country in which it is domiciled for its financing. True multinationals were born only after corporations learned to tap the capital markets of host countries. This effort at foreign financing was aided by the development of the Eurodollar market in the 1970s and the integration of the world's capital markets following the introduction of new financial instruments capable of bridging these formerly segregated markets. These financial instruments were themselves the products of truly revolutionary financial engineering.

Modern multinationals have little regard for national boundaries, and little allegiance to governments. They are truly global in scope. They produce, market, and obtain their financing wherever and however it best suits their long-run strategic plans. They can tap any developed financial market with near equal ease and are driven to do so by a desire to minimize costs and maximize reward.

Globalization has increased the size of markets and greatly enhanced competition. This has benefited consumers who obtain better quality merchandise at lower cost. But, it has also exposed the modern corporation to significant risks and, in many cases, cut profit margins. Increased size has also led to greater use of debt in capital structures which has contributed to an increasing reliance on leverage to enhance returns. The use of high degrees of leverage is of particular concern when other risks are considered. In particular, the multinational has considerable exposure to exchange-rate risks and interest-rate risks. These risks must be managed if the multinational is to successfully compete and prosper over the long haul. For the multinational, the volatility of exchange-rates discussed in the previous section simply cannot be ignored.

A development of particular importance was the emergence of Japanese financial institutions as major players in the global financial markets. For example, Japanese banks grew so rapidly that, by the mid 1980s, they occupied the top five slots in size among all the world's banks. Other Japanese financial institutions also played a major role. For example, Japanese pension funds brought tremendous increases in U.S. equity market transactional volume in the mid- to late 1980s when they aggressively engaged in various "dividend capture strategies" to convert capital gain income into dividend income. (The dividend capture strategy is discussed in more detail in later chapters, and the global dimensions of the banking community are discussed in Chapter 26.)

Tax Asymmetries

Much financial engineering is inspired by tax asymmetries. Tax asymmetries exist for a number of reasons: First, some industries are granted special tax exemptions and preferences in order to encourage their development and growth or to redirect their energies in particular directions. Second, different countries impose different tax burdens. This is further complicated by the fact that some countries tax domestic firms differently from foreign firms doing business within their borders. Third, the nature of their past performance has left some firms with sizable tax credits and write-offs which effectively eliminate any tax obligations for some years to come.

A tax asymmetry exists if two firms are subject to different effective tax rates. These asymmetries are often exploitable by clever financial engineers. Let's consider a simple example: In the United States, interest paid by one corporation to another is, in general, fully taxable at the level of the recipient corporation and fully tax deductible at the level of the paying corporation. Dividends on common and preferred stock owned by a corporation, on the other hand, are largely exempt from taxation at the level of the recipient corporation because the income from which the dividends are derived has, presumably, been taxed at the level of the paying corporation. In most situations, this exemption covers 80 percent of the dividends received. Now, suppose that Company A, which pays a marginal corporate income tax rate of 40 percent, can borrow funds at a cost of 10 percent. Company A borrows $10 million and uses it to purchase 8 percent preferred stock of Company B. That is, the preferred stock pays a fixed 8 percent dividend (as a percentage of its par value) which translates to $800,000 a year.

At first glance, these transactions do not seem to make much sense from Company A's perspective. After all, Company A is borrowing at 10 percent to invest at 8 percent. But, when the tax asymmetries are considered, the deal might make perfect sense. And it does in this case. The actual after-tax cost of Company A's borrowings is really only 6 percent because the interest paid is fully deductible and the firm's tax rate is 40 percent. At the same time, the firm's after-tax benefit from the dividends it receives amounts to 7.36 percent because 80 percent of the dividends are tax exempt and the remainder are taxed at 40 percent. This latter calculation is as follows:

$$\text{After-tax return} = 8\% - (8\% \times 20\% \times 40\%)$$
$$= 7.36\%$$

Now, let's take this example a step further. Suppose that Company B is only subject to a tax rate of 12 percent on its earnings due to tax incentives provided by its government to encourage growth in its industry. (For example, Company B might be in the alternative fuels business during a period when its government is trying to encourage the development and use of alternative fuels.) Might Company A be willing to borrow funds from Company B at an interest rate of 10 percent and then use the proceeds from this loan to buy Company B's preferred stock paying 8 percent? The answer is yes. For each $1 that Company B lends to Company A, Company B will receive $0.10 in interest. Of this, Company B will have $0.088 left after taxes. It will then pay Company A a preferred dividend of $0.08 for each $1 Company A has invested in Company B. Thus, Company B nets $0.008 on each $1 swapped in this way. At the same time, Company A has the benefits already described and so it nets $0.0136 on each dollar swapped.

It is clear that these two companies have arbitraged a tax asymmetry by entering into a swap of Company A's debt for Company B's equity. Both firms benefit, but not necessarily to equal degrees. These kinds of swaps carry certain risks for the involved parties. For example, what happens if Company B's tax rate rises or if Company A's tax rate declines? Or, what happens if Company A defaults on its debt to Company B? The first situation can be dealt with by including special provisions allowing one firm to call its debt while the other firm calls its preferred stock. The second situation can be dealt with by securing Company A's debt with the preferred stock of Company B which Company A holds.

The situation described above is not meant to be entirely realistic and we don't mean to suggest that it could necessarily be effected under current law, but the example does serve to illustrate the nature of exploitable tax asymmetries. It also illustrates another important point. Structured deals developed by financial engineers to exploit tax asymmetries are often one-of-a-kind. That is, they are made possible by the unique situations and surrounding financial circumstances peculiar to the individual firms involved.

It is important to appreciate that financial engineers do not assist firms in the evasion of taxes. Evasion of taxes is illegal. Rather, financial engineers that arbitrage tax asymmetries help firms to avoid taxes—a practice ruled by the courts to be a constitutionally guaranteed right. This kind of exploitation of tax asymmetries provides a partial explanation for interfirm debt/equity swaps which developed in the 1980s. The burden, of course, is carried by the government which suffers from diminished tax revenues and, consequently, can be expected to move to close these kinds of exploitable loopholes. Nevertheless, for the time it exists, it represents fertile ground for the financial engineer.

Technological Advances

A great deal of financial engineering has been motivated by technological breakthroughs. Many of these breakthroughs involve the computer. Advances in this area include the development of high speed processors, the introduction of powerful desk-top units, network systems, and enhanced methods of data entry. Closely related to advances in computer technology are advances in telecommunications. Breakthroughs in this area were, and continue to be, critical to certain forms of financial engineering but, because they go on behind the scenes, are not often appreciated except on those occasions when they break down. Improvements in communications allow for instantaneous worldwide conferencing, data transmission via hard-wired data lines, and transmission of information and data by satellite. At the same time, there were tremendous advances in software programs without which the computer and telecommunications advances would be nearly meaningless. One of the most important of such developments was the advent of spreadsheet programs which allow the modeling of complex financial deals. Indeed, prior to the introduction of microcomputers and spreadsheet software, an old Wall Street adage held that "three-way deals don't close." Yet, after the introduction of microcomputers and spreadsheet software, currency and interest-rate swap activity—the epitome of the three way deal—blossomed. Leaders in the industry give the microcomputer and spreadsheet software much of the credit.[1]

Consider just one of the many important financial engineering innovations made possible, in part, by advances in technology. In 1982 the old-line commodities exchanges engineered the first stock-index futures contracts. The first such contract was introduced by the Kansas City Board of Trade and was written on the Value Line Composite Index. Shortly thereafter, other exchanges introduced stock-index futures on the Standard & Poor's 500 Index (Chicago Mercantile Exchange), the New York Composite Index (New York Futures Exchange), and, some time later, the Major Market Index (Chicago Board of Trade).

The design and introduction of stock index futures was of course an important result of financial engineering. But, trading activity in these contracts remained relatively light until a number of other factors fell into place. These included the development of financial theory capable of explaining the proper valuation of stock index futures contracts—relative to the underlying cash index—and the introduction of an order matching computer system on the New York Stock Exchange—known as the Designated Order Turnaround (DOT) System.

With these tools in place, clever financial engineers worked out the elaborate mathematical relationships necessary to exploit discrepancies between the market price of the index futures and the fair value of these same futures. They then transformed these relationships into computer programs and enlisted the necessary hardware and data linkages to obtain a continuous feed of data and instantaneous order execution. In time, these programs became more and more sophisticated and by late 1985 and early 1986 had become a major force in the equities markets. The trading strategy, now known as *program trading* or *futures-cash arbitrage,* led to seriously misunderstood increases in short-run equity price volatility and, consequently, bitter debate over the economic implications of the trading strategy. More scholarly discussions, however, have generally concluded that program trading activity enhances the efficiency of stock price formation and, in fact serves as an information-transfer mechanism.[2]

The upshot of this brief discussion of program trading is that it demonstrates the essential linkage between much financial engineering activity and technological developments. It also demonstrates other important elements which have contributed to a rapid growth in financial engineering. The first is the importance of financial theory, most of which is developed by academicians. The second is the importance of those financial engineers commonly referred to as "quant jocks." These are the individuals who take the theory and, by painstaking examination of relationships and manipulations of data, work out useful speculative, arbitrage, and hedging strategies.

Technological developments have contributed to financial engineering in other important ways. Consider, for example, the relationship between technology and price volatility. As already noted, program trading has increased short-run price volatility in the equity markets as program trading transfers information from futures prices to stock prices. Other technological developments have increased price volatility as well. Consider, for example, "look-down" satellites which are capable of assessing world-wide crop developments. In bygone days, crop information filtered out of the world's grain growing regions very slowly. Reports were scattered and often contradictory, rumors abounded, and official forecasts and crop reports were notoriously inaccurate. Information about the true state of the world's potential harvests emerged only slowly. As a result, market prices changed slowly. Today, on the other hand, with the more accurate crop projections made possible by computer-enhanced assessments of growing regions and improvements in weather satellites, grain prices can respond very quickly to any new development. This better flow of information is manifested in more rapid and larger absolute changes in agricultural prices in the short-run.

Although more rapid movement to true long-run market-clearing prices is beneficial to the economy as a whole (because resources are more rapidly reallocated to their most productive uses and better rationed over time), the greater price volatility exposes producers and consumers of these commodities to greater price risk. Manifestations of this risk can easily destroy a business which is otherwise well-managed and well-run. Therein lies a role for the financial engineer. As mentioned earlier, the financial engineer can help a firm manage the price risks inherent in a market economy. To the extent that technological developments increase volatility, the risk-management role of the financial engineer becomes that much more important.

Advances in Financial Theory

Finance, as a formal discipline, is concerned with value and risk and no financial engineer can function effectively without a solid foundation in financial theory. This does not necessarily require formal academic training in finance, but formal training surely helps.

Finance derives from economics and most financial theorists have an extensive background in economic theory and technique. In particular, both financial theorists and empiricists are well versed in the modeling skills prized by economists. While finance evolved as an applied subdiscipline of economics, it eventually acquired sufficient distinction to stand alone. Indeed, many leading academic institutions have spun their finance departments off from their economics departments; but many others have chosen not to do so.

Finance is also closely associated with accounting and much financial engineering requires a solid foundation in accounting principals and accounting nuances. The link between the accounting and finance disciplines is so strong that it is also not unusual to find the two disciplines housed under the same academic departments.

For a very long time, financial practitioners had relatively little use for financial academicians. The old saw that "them that can do and them that can't teach," seemed to pervade their thinking. We believe that this long standing distrust of academicians traces to the economic roots of the finance discipline. Economists engage in elaborate modeling exercises which employ assumptions and reach conclusions which often have little "real-world" relevance—at least in the eyes of many practitioners. But, in fact, these exercises serve a number of very useful purposes. First, they train the mind to isolate that which is relevant to a modeling situation from that which is not. Second, they teach skills, both logical and mathematical, which are useful in deriving essential results from a set of starting assumptions. They also teach one to question every element in modeling—from the assumptions, through the derivations, and, finally, to the interpretations of the conclusions. These are important skills to possess for anyone engaged in financial engineering where a small error in an assumption, a faulty derivation, an erroneous conclusion, or an erroneous interpretation of a conclusion can all lead to a financial disaster.

There is no denying that the bulk of the conceptual tools in the modern financial engineer's tool kit were developed by academicians or by practitioners working closely with academicians. Consider just a few examples. At the heart of financial theory is the fundamental valuation relationship which holds that an asset's value is equal to the sum of the present values of all futures cash flows the asset will generate. This fundamental relationship was first recognized and explained by Irving Fisher in 1896. (Fisher also made many important later contributions to economic and financial theory.) Or consider the contributions of Benjamin Graham and David Dodd whose 1934 work on security valuation became the bible of the securities industry. Or consider the 1938 contribution of Frederick Macaulay whose work on duration and immunization gave rise to the tools now employed by nearly everyone engaged in asset/liability management. Or consider the 1952 work of Harry Markowitz whose portfolio theory contributions spawned modern portfolio analysis. Or consider the work of Leland Johnson and Jerome Stein in the early 1960s which extended portfolio theory to hedging and gave birth to modern hedging theory. Or consider the works of William Sharpe, John Lintner, and Jan Mossin which, collectively, created capital asset pricing theory—now a mainstay of modern security analysis. Or, consider the classic of the 1970s: the publication of the first complete option pricing model by Fischer Black and Myron Scholes in 1973. This model, including variants of it, has been used almost from the moment it was published to determine the fair value of put and call options. (Related models have been adapted to fit multiperiod interest-rate and exchange-rate options introduced in the late 1980s.) Or, finally, consider the late 1970s work of Louis Ederington which extended the earlier work of Johnson and Stein to the hedging of financial price risks with financial futures.

All of these individuals, and these are only a few of the many hundreds of possible examples, made seminal contributions to financial theory. And each piece of this theory is now part of the backbone that carries the modern financial engineer. What these contributors share is that they were all academicians or academically affiliated. Irving Fisher was with Yale, Benjamin Graham and David Dodd were with Columbia, Frederick Macaulay was with the NBER,

Harry Markowitz was with Rand, Leland Johnson and Jerome Stein were with Rand and Brown, respectively, William Sharpe was with University of Washington and Stanford, John Lintner was with Harvard, Jan Mossin was with Norway School of Economics and Business, Fischer Black and Myron Scholes were both with the University of Chicago, and Louis Ederington was with Georgia State.

The 1980s were no less productive. The period saw a flood of research that extended earlier theoretical work, examined new financial instruments and the performance of new financial markets, and took a very detailed and much needed look at risk management instruments and techniques. It was also during the decade of the 1980s that the financial services industry came to recognize the tremendous contributions to their profession made by the academic community. In recognition of this fact, industry increased funding for academic research considerably during the decade. (Indeed, this book was funded in large part by industry sources.) This type of partnership between industry and academia, which was once limited to the natural sciences, is healthy and shows all the signs of increasing in scope.

Regulatory Change and Increased Competition

Much of financial engineering activity in recent years has been fostered by an atmosphere of deregulation of industry and the encouragement of entrepreneurial experimentation. Deregulation has fed competition and forced once protected industries to become more efficient or to close down and thus release their resources to more productive ends. This has had a number of related impacts that have encouraged financial engineering.

Consider first commercial and investment banking. Commercial banking and investment banking activities in the United States were separated in 1933 by the Glass-Steagall Act. This act grew out of a generally held belief that the widespread failure of banks in the early 1930s was due, at least in part, to losses suffered on securities underwriting and other investment banking activities. These activities were financed, in large part, by the funds of bank depositors who had little understanding of how their deposits were to be used by their bank. In passing the Glass-Steagall Act, Congress hoped that, by separating the deposit taking and loan making activities (commercial banking) from the underwriting and securities trading activities (investment banking), future systemic failures could be avoided.

The Glass-Steagall Act probably made sense at the time it was enacted. And, in conjunction with other regulatory measures adopted at or about the same time, it undoubtedly did a lot to restore confidence in the banking system.[3] But as technology, the state of knowledge, foreign competition, and risk management techniques all evolved, the regulatory structure became a burden around the neck of the more aggressive firms in the industry. Banks needed to grow in order to provide services on a scale demanded by their customers. They also needed to grow in order to compete effectively with very large foreign banking institutions. This meant handling both the commercial banking and the investment banking needs of its corporate customers on the asset side, and handling both the savings and the investment needs of its depositors on the liabilities side. Growth itself dictated a need to end the prohibitions against interstate banking introduced in 1927 by the McFadden Act and the prohibitions against multi-branch banking adopted by many states to protect local banking institutions.

There was a time when industrial corporations were extremely loyal to their investment banks, and investment banks employed what essentially amounted to an honor system not to steal, at least not overtly, each other's clients. But the increasing competitive pressures on the industry in the 1980s and the re-introduction of commercial banks into investment banking in the 1980s ended this peaceful coexistence. Banks began to undercut one another's fee structures in an effort to lure away the more lucrative customers. And many corporations, concerned about their bottom lines, abandoned long standing relationships with their investment bankers to benefit from more advantageous fee structures.

In an effort to better compete and to keep existing clients, investment banks went on an innovation binge. That is, they understood that if all they were going to do was underwrite standard off-the-shelf type instruments, such as stocks and bonds, they would have to bid aggressively on a competitive basis for clients and profit margins would be cut to the bone. But, if they could engineer unique instruments to fit their clients' needs, then they increased the probability that clients would stay with them on a negotiated basis—a prospect that offered considerably greater reward for the investment bank. Once a new instrument is introduced, however, it does not take long for competitors to copy the instrument or, at the very least, to pirate its more appealing features. Thus, a competition to innovate new products developed, and the 1980s became the decade of the new product blizzard.

Some of the new products introduced were genuinely beneficial in the sense that they could accomplish the same end at less cost, or they accomplished some objective which could not be accomplished with existing products. In the language of finance, we would say that the former makes a market more efficient and the latter makes a market more complete. But, much of the innovation was innovation with no genuine purpose other than welding a client to a specific investment bank. To the degree that the client firm really did not understand the product which was engineered on its behalf, it was entering a financial minefield. It is unfortunate to say, but nonetheless true, that many of the financial products innovated in the 1980s blew up in the faces of the client firms soon after they were issued. We will discuss specific examples in later chapters.

There are two other considerations which need to be addressed before we leave the subjects of regulation and competition. These are breadth of services provided and economies of scale. Small banks simply cannot provide the same breadth of financial services as can large banks. This suggests that large banks have a competitive advantage over small banks in attracting new depositors and borrowers. In addition, the nature of banking is such that there are significant economies of scale. Economies of scale exist whenever the per unit cost of providing a service or producing a good decreases as the number of units of that service provided or that good produced increases.

The increased competitive pressures coupled with the 1980s atmosphere of deregulation led to efforts to repeal much of the regulation heaped on the industry during previous decades and, where unsuccessful, led to efforts to circumvent existing regulation. Helped along by massive failures in the thrift industry and a government need for banking industry assistance, many of these efforts bore fruit. Prohibitions against interstate banking broke down, commercial banks became increasingly involved in investment banking activities, and nonbank firms entered banking and other financial services areas. At the heart of all of these activities were creative people, many of them financial engineers.

The Cost of Information and the Cost of Transacting

Competition among investment banks increased the transactional nature of investment banking. At the same time, the cost of information, on which many transactions feed, and the cost of transacting itself, declined significantly during the decade of the 1980s— continuing a trend which was already well established by the close of the 1970s. The 1980s trends in information and transaction costs were largely an outgrowth of the enormous technological developments of the last two decades that we highlighted earlier. Many financial engineering activities, particularly those involving arbitrage and those involving multi-instrument structured deals, are dependent on minimizing transaction costs and the costs of acquiring information.

To get some idea of the degree to which these costs have declined, consider something as simple as a large stock transaction—a 10,000 share block for example. The per share cost of transacting a share of say $100 stock has declined from something on the order of $1.00 at the start of the 1970s to under 2 cents by the start of the 1990s. Consider then an arbitrage strategy which seeks to exploit say a $0.25 pricing discrepancy between an instrument trading in one market and a related instrument trading in another market. Under 1970s transaction cost levels, an arbitrage opportunity does not exist and no financial engineering activity will be undertaken to exploit the price discrepancy. But, under 1990s transaction cost levels, an arbitrage opportunity does exist and financial engineers will expend considerable time and energy to develop an appropriate trading strategy.

Consider some of the innovations which have reduced transaction costs over the years. First, from the investor's perspective, we have witnessed the development of a "third" and a "fourth" market for block trades by institutions, electronic trading for computer order matching, and the emergence of an efficient discount brokerage business for the small investor. From the issuer's perspective we have seen a dramatic decline in flotation costs through such innovations as extendable notes, shelf registrations, and the increased competition brought about by the re-introduction of commercial banks into investment banking.

Intrafirm Factors

The factors that we have considered thus far have all contributed in their own way to the rapid growth in financial engineering activity. And, as we noted earlier, these factors are all environmental in the sense that they are largely external to the firm. We now turn our attention to the intrafirm factors. The intrafirm factors include such things as liquidity needs, risk aversion among managers and owners, agency costs, greater levels of quantitative sophistication among investment managers, and more formal training of senior-level personnel.

Liquidity Needs

Liquidity has many faces and many meanings in finance. The term itself is often used to refer to the ease with which an asset can be converted to cash, the ability to put cash to work, or the ability to raise cash in a hurry. At other times, it refers to the degree to which a security's value will deviate from par as economic conditions, particularly interest rates, change. At still other times, the term is used to refer to the degree to which a market can absorb purchases and sales of a security without imposing excessive transaction costs. Indeed, the liquidity of a market is often measured by the size of the bid-ask spread. The narrower the bid-ask spread, the more liquid is the market.

Both corporations and individuals have liquidity needs and concerns and many of the financial innovations pioneered over the last 20 years have targeted these needs and concerns. Some innovations were designed to provide easier access to cash while others were designed to make it easier to put temporarily unneeded cash to work. Examples include money market funds, money market accounts, sweep accounts, electronic funds transfer and electronic payment systems, the development and rapid expansion of the commercial paper and certificate of deposit markets, and the development of the repo market. Other innovations have sought to create long-term securities whose values do not deviate to nearly the same degree as the values of traditional fixed-coupon notes and bonds, common stock, and fixed-rate preferred stock. Examples of such new instruments include floating rate notes, adjustable rate preferred stock, adjustable rate mortgages, real yield securities, and floating rate rating-sensitive notes. Still other innovations have sought to improve liquidity by adding depth to a market. Sometimes this takes the form of standardizing a formerly nonstandard instrument, at other times it means structuring the instrument in such a way that it can more easily trade in a well-defined secondary market, and sometimes it means adding credit enhancements so that a high-risk instrument will appeal to investors with low risk tolerance. Examples of these latter innovations include such things as the introduction of mortgage passthroughs, collateralized mortgage obligations (CMOs), and repackaging and overcollateralizing of high-risk assets such as automobile receivables and junk bonds.

Risk Aversion

It is considered a fundamental tenet of financial theory that rational individuals have an aversion to financial risk. This does not imply that individuals are unwilling to bear risk. Rather, it is understood to mean that individuals are only willing to bear risk if they are adequately compensated for doing so. We will examine the concept of risk aversion more formally in later chapters. For now, we need only consider some of the innovations which attempted to enhance the value of the firm or the utility of the individual investor by either reducing the risk inherent in an instrument or by the creation of an instrument which can be used to manage risk.

Some of the innovations discussed in the preceding section which dealt with liquidity concerns also have risk-limiting capability and, therefore, overlap this section. For example, collateralized mortgage obligation bonds provide a vehicle by which individuals and institutions can invest in the residential mortgage market without having to be overly concerned about the prepayment risk which otherwise characterizes direct investment in mortgages or mortgage passthrough certificates. Or, consider adjustable-rate debt or adjustable-rate preferred stock. These instruments are not nearly as price sensitive to changes in the general level of interest rates as equivalent maturity fixed-coupon instruments. Thus, these instruments expose their holders to considerably less risk.

As interesting and as important as the above noted developments were, the heart of financial innovation directed at the individual's and the firm's aversion to risk during the last two decades has been the introduction of very efficient risk management instruments and the design of sophisticated risk management strategies. Among the instruments introduced during the last two decades are interest-rate futures and interest-rate options, stock-index futures and stock and stock-index options, currency futures and currency options, over-the-counter contracts such as forward rate agreements and forward exchange agreements, and a whole array of swap products including interest-rate swaps, currency swaps, commodity swaps, and equity swaps. Among the risk management strategies developed or improved over the last two decades are asset/liability management techniques—including various forms of duration and immunization strategies, better risk assessment and measurement techniques—including both the quantification of price risks via volatility measures and graphic representations via risk profiles, and the development and improvement of hedging strategies—including duration-based, regression-based, and dollar-value based techniques. We will discuss all of these instruments and all of these techniques in later chapters.

Although corporate managers have become increasingly aware of their risk exposures, studies done in the mid-1980s have shown that these same managers are also uncomfortable with the instruments of modern risk management.[4] They often fail to understand the nature of the instruments, the uses of the instruments, and the costs associated with the instruments. As price volatility has increased over the years and as management and shareholders have become more aware of the perils posed by this volatility, corporations have sought to recruit personnel with risk-management training and risk-management experience. This has created a serious shortage of such persons. Business schools have, for the most part, been slow to recognize the need for formal risk management training but many are now scrambling to fill the void with carefully focused courses. Until the gap can be closed, the corporate sector must depend on consultants—many of whom are associated with financial institutions offering structured solutions.

Agency Costs

A concept introduced in 1976 by Michael Jensen and William Meckling explains another motivating force behind much financial engineering.[5] The concept is called **agency costs** and, in its simplest form, it refers to the fact that the structure of modern corporate ownership and control is such that corporate managers simply do not always have the best interests of the firm's owners at heart.

For a publicly held firm with a broad ownership base involving many thousands of small shareholders, the firm's management can easily become unresponsive to the wishes of the shareholders. Management can, with the cooperation of the firm's board of directors, write itself excessively lucrative contracts—often including termination bonuses and performance bonuses based on very short-run measures of firm performance. These measures can result in a management which sacrifices long-run growth and stock price maximization for short-run accounting profits and concomitant bonanzas for themselves. The costs to the firm from this separation of ownership and control (the agency relationship) are generally not readily apparent and are difficult to measure, but the market for the firm's stock will often tell the tale.

It is very hard to explain much of the merger and acquisition (M&A) activity and the leveraged buyout (LBO) activity, particularly the latter, that reshaped American industry in the 1980s on the basis of anything other than agency costs. Consider the LBO: Why, for example, would a firm's management be willing to pay $80 a share for the stock of the firm when the market would otherwise only price it at $50 a share? Clearly, in such situations, management perceives value that the market does not perceive. But how would the firm change if management bought it? The ready answer is that management would cut costs, reorganize the firm, and divest the firm of operations which do not fit into its own strategic plan. How does management benefit? Well, quite simply, by assuming ownership, management eliminates the agency relationship and, presumably, most of the costs which that relationship entails. In the end, management expects that the elimination of these costs will produce a per share value in excess of $80 and this excess accrues to the firm's new owners. Many would respond to this argument by pointing out that there are other sources of value in such a reorganization including the ability of the firm to concentrate on its strengths and to enjoy the synergisms which certain acquisitions might provide. But, this argument overlooks the fact that management could just as easily, perhaps more easily, secure these gains without first acquiring ownership. Thus, the gains are derived from a reduction in agency costs.

Many of the financial innovations of the 1980s were due, at least in part, to their ability to reduce agency costs. LBOs are, as already demonstrated, a clear example. But securing the capital to make LBOs possible required new forms of financing. This need inspired still other innovations including Drexel's creation of a LBO-driven junk bond market.

Quantitative Sophistication and Management Training

Critics have often chided business schools as machines which produce carbon copy managers. Indeed, numerous articles appearing in the press over the years, have heralded the coming end of business schools (B-schools) and their MBA programs.[6] But time has repeatedly proven these predictions to be wrong. Business school graduates are at the heart of modern business. They have the formal training, the analytical skills, and the conceptual tools to manage modern large-scale enterprises. They are increasingly represented at the top echelons of today's corporations, and they understand the need for quantitative sophistication and solid foundations. Industrial corporations, commercial banks, investment banks, and institutional investment houses all compete aggressively for each year's crop of these talented high potential people. It is from this same group that the financial engineers are, for the most part, born. They speak the language and they understand the needs of business.

In very few areas is quantitative sophistication more important than in the investment arena. Not surprisingly, institutional investors—including mutual funds, insurance companies, pension funds, trust managers, and securities dealers and arbitragers—have expended considerable sums acquiring and training competent personnel. These people wear their "quant jock" labels very proudly and rightly so. They decipher complex situations through tedious mathematical manipulations and, in so doing, are often able to enhance returns by a respectable number of basis points. Indeed, if the portfolio under management is sufficiently large, just a few additional basis points can be sufficient to justify considerable effort.

Accounting Benefits

Many of the financial innovations of the last few years have been directed at improving a firm's financial statements. That is, the deals engineered have changed the appearance of the financial statements which can have a positive effect on a firm's short-run earnings or can enhance the various measures of a firm's creditworthiness. Examples of this kind of activity include the defeasance of a firm's debt and debt for equity swaps. But, there is real debate among academics and practitioners alike as to whether these engineering activities actually add any value to the firm.[7] Many, it would seem, produce short-run benefits, with commensurate rewards for management, but at the sake of long-run performance.

Innovative Products of the Last Twenty Years

To this point in this chapter, we have briefly considered the factors that have contributed to the explosive growth in financial engineering over the last 20 years. In so doing, we have mentioned in passing many of the innovative products, processes, and strategies designed by engineers. But, we have hardly scratched the surface. The several pages which follow provide a compendium of innovative products and processes introduced during this period.[8] In addition, for each product, process, or strategy, the factors responsible for its development are provided. The list is, of course, not complete and never could be. But it is nevertheless very instructive. This list was compiled by Finnerty (1988).

Exhibit 2.3A Finnerty's Compilation

Factors Primarily Responsible for Financial Innovations

Innovation	Factors Primarily Responsible[*]	Innovation	Factors Primarily Responsible
	Consumer-Type Financial Instruments		
Broker cash management accounts	7	Money market mutual funds	6,7
Municipal bond funds	2,4,6	Money market accounts	6,7
All-saver certificates	6,7	NOW accounts	6,7
Equity access account	1,6,8	Bull/Bear CDs	2
Debit card	2,7,11	IRA/Keogh accounts	1,6
Tuition futures	4,8	Universal or variable life insurance	1,7,8
Variable or adjustable rate mortgages	7	Convertible mortgages or reduction option loans	2,7
	Securities		
Deep discount/zero coupon bonds	1,4,7	Stripped debt securities	1,4,7
Floating rate notes	4,5,7	Floating rate, rating sensitive notes	3,4,5,7
Floating rate tax-exempt notes	4,5,7	Auction rate notes/debentures	2,3,4,7
Real yield securities	2,4,5,8	Dollar BILS	4,7
Puttable-extendible notes	2,3,4	Increasing rate notes	3
Interest rate reset notes	3	Annuity notes	11
Extendible notes	2,4	Variable coupon/rate renewable notes	2,4,6
Puttable/adjustable tender bonds	2,4,7	Variable duration notes	4,7
Euronotes/Euro-commercial paper	2,4	Universal commercial paper	4
Medium term notes	2	Negotiable CDs	2,5
Mortgage-backed bonds	4	Mortgage pass-throughs	2,4,5
Collateralized mortgage obligations	2,4,5	Stripped mortgage-backed securities	4
Receivable-backed securities	4,5	Real estate-backed bonds	4,5
Letter of credit/surety bond credit support	4,11	Yield curve/maximum rate notes	4,6,7
Interest rate swaps	4,6,7	Currency swaps	4,6
Interest rate caps/floors/collars	4,7	Remarketed reset notes	2,3,4
Foreign-currency-denominated bonds	4,7	Eurocurrency bonds	7
Dual currency bonds	4,6	Indexed currency option notes/	
Commodity-linked bonds	4,6,8	Principal exchange rate linked securities	4,6,7
Gold loans	4,8	High-yield (junk) bonds	2,5,7,9
Exchange-traded options	4,9	Foreign currency futures	4,9,11
Interest rate futures	4,7,9	Stock index futures	4,8,9
Options on futures contracts	4,7,9	Forward rate agreements	4,7
Warrants to purchase bonds	4,7	Adjustable rate preferred stock	1,4,5,6,7
Convertible adjustable preferred stock	1,4,5,7	Auction rate preferred stock	1,4,5,7
Remarketed preferred stock	1,4,5,7,11	Indexed floating rate preferred stock	1,4,5,7
Single point adjustable rate stock	1,2,4,5,7	Stated rate auction preferred stock	1,3,4,5,7
Variable cumulative preferred stock	1,2,3,4,5,7,	Convertible exchangeable preferred	1,2,10
Adjustable rate convertible debt	1,10	Zero coupon convertible debt	1,11
Puttable convertible bonds	3,4,7	Mandatory convertible/equity contract notes	1,6
Synthetic convertible debt	1,10	Exchangeable auction preferred	1,2,4,5,7
Convertible reset debentures	3	Participating bonds	3,4
Master limited partnership	1	Additional class(es) of common stock	11
Americus trust	4,6	Paired common stock	4
Puttable common stock	3,4,10		
	Financial Processes		
Shelf registration	2,6,7	Direct public sale of securities	2,6
Discount brokerage	2,6	Automated teller machines	2,11
Point-of-sale terminals	11	Electronic security trading	2,11
Electronic funds transfer/		CHIPS (same day settlement)	7,11
automated clearing houses	7,11	Cash management/sweep accounts	7,11
	Financial Strategies/Solutions		
More efficient bond call strategies	7,9	Debt-for-debt- exchanges	1,7,10
Stock-for-debt swaps	1,7,10	In-substance defeasance	1,7,10
Preferred dividend rolls	1	Hedged dividend capture	1
Leveraged buyout structuring	1,9,11	Corporate restructuring	1,9,11
Project finance/lease/			
asset-based financial structuring	4		

[*]Notation: 1, tax advantages; 2, reduced transaction costs; 3, reduced agency costs; 4, risk reallocation; 5, increased liquidity; 6, regulatory or legislative factors; 7, level and volatility of interest rates; 8, level and volatility of prices; 9, academic work; 10, accounting benefits; and 11, technological developments and other factors.

Exhibit 2.3B Finnerty's Compilation

Selected Common Equity Innovations

Security	Distinguishing Characteristics	Risk Reallocation/ Yield Reduction	Enhanced Liquidity	Reduction in Agency Costs	Reduction in Transaction Costs	Tax Arbitrage	Other Benefits
Additional Class(es) of Common Stock	A company issues a second class of common stock the dividends on which are tied to the earnings of a specified subsidiary.						Establishes separate market value for the subsidiary while assuring the parent 100% voting control. Useful for employee compensation programs for subsidiary.
Americus Trust	Outstanding shares of a particular company's common stock are contributed to a five-year unit investment trust. Units may be separated into a PRIME component, which embodies full dividend and voting rights in the underlying share and permits limited capital appreciation, and a SCORE component, which provides full capital appreciation above a stated price.	Stream of annual total returns on a share of stock is separated into (i) a dividend stream (with limited capital appreciation potential) and (ii) a (residual) capital appreciation stream.				PRIME component would appeal to corporate investors who can take advantage of the 70% dividends received deduction. SCORE component would appeal to capital-gain-oriented individual investors.	PRIME component resembles participating preferred stock if the issuer's common stock dividend rate is stable. SCORE component is a longer-dated call option than the ones customarily traded in the options market.
Master Limited Partnership	A business is given the legal form of a partnership but is otherwise structured, and is traded publicly, like a corporation.					Eliminates a layer of taxation because partnerships are not taxable entities.	
Puttable Common Stock	Issuer sells a new issue of common stock along with rights to put the stock back to the issuer on a specified date at a specified price.	Issuer sells investors a put option, which investors will exercise if the company's share price decreases.		The put option reduces certain agency costs associated with a new share issue that are brought on by informational asymmetries.			Equivalent under certain conditions to convertible bonds but can be recorded as equity on the balance sheet so long as the company's payment obligation under the put option can be settled in common stock.

Exhibit 2.3C Finnerty's Compilation

Selected Convertible Debt/Preferred Stock Innovations

Security	Distinguishing Characteristics	Risk Reallocation/ Yield Reduction	Enhanced Liquidity	Reduction in Agency Costs	Reduction in Transaction Costs	Tax Arbitrage	Other Benefits
Adjustable Rate Convertible Debt	Debt the interest rate on which varies directly with the dividend rate on the underlying common stock. No conversion premium.					Effectively, tax deductible common equity. Security has since been ruled equity by the I.R.S.	Portion of the issue carried as equity on the issuer's balance sheet.
Convertible Exchangeable Preferred Stock	Convertible preferred stock that is exchangeable, at the issuer's option, for convertible debt with identical rate and identical conversion terms.				No need to reissue convertible security as debt—just exchange it—when the issuer becomes a taxpayer.	Issuer can exchange debt for the preferred when it becomes taxable with interest rate the same as the dividend rate and without any change in conversion features.	Appears as equity on the issuer's balance sheet until it is exchanged for convertible debt.
Convertible Reset Debentures	Convertible bond the interest rate on which must be adjusted upward, if necessary, by an amount sufficient to give the debentures a market value equal to their face amount 2 years after issuance.			Investor is protected against a deterioration in the issuer's financial prospects within 2 years of issuance.			
Debt with Mandatory Common Stock Purchase Contracts	Notes with contracts that obligate note purchasers to buy sufficient common stock from the issuer to retire the issue in full by its scheduled maturity date.					Notes provide a stream of interest tax shields, which (true) equity does not.	Commercial bank holding companies have issued it because it counted as "primary capital" for regulatory purposes.
Exchangeable Auction Preferred Stock	Auction rate preferred stock that is exchangeable on any dividend payment date, at the option of the issuer, for auction rate notes, the interest rate on which is reset by Dutch auction every 35 days.	Issuer bears more interest rate risk than a fixed-rate instrument would involve.	Security is designed to trade near its par value.		Issuance of auction rate notes involves no underwriting commissions.	Issuer can exchange notes for the preferred when it becomes taxable.	Appears as equity on the issuer's balance sheet until it is exchanged for auction rate notes.
Synthetic Convertible Debt	Debt and warrants package structured in such a way as to mirror a traditional convertible debt issue.					In effect, warrant proceeds are tax deductible.	Warrants go on the balance sheet as equity.
Zero Coupon Convertible Debt	Non-interest-bearing convertible debt issue.					If issue converts, the issuer will have sold, in effect, tax deductible equity.	If holders convert, entire debt service stream is converted to common equity.
Variable Rate Renewable Notes	Coupon rate varies monthly and equals a fixed spread over the 1-month commercial paper rate. Each quarter the maturity automatically extends an additional quarter unless the investor elects to terminate the extension.	Coupon based on 1-year termination date, not on final maturity.			Lower transaction costs than issuing 1-year note and rolling it over.		Designed to appeal to money market mutual funds, which face tight investment restrictions.
Warrants to Purchase Debt Securities	Warrant with 1–5 years to expiration to buy intermediate-term or long-term bonds.	Issuer is effectively selling a covered call option, which can afford investors opportunities not available in the traditional options markets.					
Yield Curve Notes and Maximum Rate Notes	Interest rate equals a specified rate minus LIBOR.	Might reduce yield relative to conventional debt when coupled with an interest rate swap against LIBOR.					Useful for hedging and immunization purposes because of very long duration.
Zero Coupon Bonds (sometimes issued in series)	Non-interest-bearing. Payment in one lump sum at maturity.	Issuer assumes reinvestment risk. Issues sold in Japan carried below-taxable-market yields reflecting their tax advantage over conventional debt issues.				Straight-line amortization of original issue discount pre-TEFRA. Japanese investors realize significant tax savings.	

Security	Distinguishing Characteristics	Risk Reallocation/Yield Reduction	Enhanced Liquidity	Reduction in Agency Costs	Reduction in Transaction Costs	Tax Arbitrage	Other Benefits
Puttable Bonds and Adjustable Tender Securities	Issuer can periodically reset the terms, in effect rolling over debt without having to redeem it until the final maturity.	Coupon based on whether fixed or floating rate and on the length of the interest rate period selected, not on final maturity.		Investor has a put option, which provides protection against deterioration in credit quality or below-market coupon rate.	Lower transaction costs than having to perform a series of refundings.		
Puttable-Extendible Notes	At the end of each interest period, the issuer may elect to redeem the notes at par or to extend the maturity on terms the issuer proposes, at which time the note holder can put the notes back to the issuer if the new terms are unacceptable. Investors also have series of put options during initial interest period.	Coupon based on length of interest interval, not on final maturity.		Put options protect against deterioration in issuer's credit standing and also against issuer setting below-market coupon rate or other terms that might work to investor's disadvantage.			
Real Yield Securities	Coupon rate resets quarterly to the greater of (i) change in consumer price index plus the "Real Yield Spread" (3.0% in the first such issue) and (ii) the Real Yield Spread, in each case on a semi-annual-equivalent basis.	Issuer exposed to inflation risk, which may be hedged in the CPI futures market.	Real yield securities could become more liquid than CPI futures, which tend to trade in significant volume only around the monthly CPI announcement date.		Investors obtain a long-dated inflation hedging instrument that they could not create as cheaply on their own.		Real yield securities have a longer duration than alternative inflation hedging instruments.
Receivable Pay-Through Securities	Investor buys an undivided interest in a pool of receivables.	Reduced yield due to the benefit to the investor of diversification and greater liquidity. Significantly cheaper for issuer than pledging receivables to a bank.	More liquid than individual receivables.		Security purchasers could not achieve the same degree of diversification as cheaply on their own.		
Remarketed Reset Notes	Interest rate reset at the end of each interest period to a rate the remarketing agent determines will make the notes worth par. If issuer and remarketing agent can not agree on rate, then the coupon rate is determined by formula which dictates a higher rate the lower the issuer's credit standing.	Coupon based on length of interest period, not on final maturity.	Designed to trade closer to par value than a floating-rate note with a fixed interest rate formula.	Investors have a put option, which protects against the issuer and remarketing agent agreeing to set a below-market coupon rate, and the flexible interest rate formula protects investors against deterioration in the issuer's credit standing.	Intended to have lower transaction costs than auction rate notes and debentures, which require periodic Dutch auctions.		
Stripped Mortgage-Backed Securities	Mortgage payment stream subdivided into two classes, (i) one with below-market coupon and the other with above-market coupon or (ii) one receiving interest only and the other receiving principal only from mortgage pools.	Securities have unique option characteristics that make them useful for hedging purposes. Designed to appeal to different classes of investors; sum of the parts can exceed the whole.					
Stripped Treasury or Municipal Securities	Coupons separated from corpus to create a series of zero coupon bonds that can be sold separately.	Yield curve arbitrage; sum of the parts can exceed the whole.					
Variable Coupon Renewable Notes	Coupon rate varies weekly and equals a fixed spread over the 91-day T-bill rate. Each 91 days the maturity extends another 91 days. If put option exercised, spread is reduced.	Coupon based on 1-year termination date, not on final maturity.			Lower transaction costs than issuing 1-year note and rolling it over.		Designed to appeal to money market mutual funds, which face tight investment restrictions, and to discourage put to issuer

Security	Distinguishing Characteristics	Risk Reallocation/ Yield Reduction	Enhanced Liquidity	Reduction in Agency Costs	Reduction in Transaction Costs	Tax Arbitrage	Other Benefits
Floating Rate, Rating Sensitive Notes	Coupon rate resets quarterly based on a spread over LIBOR. Spread increases if the issuer's debt rating declines.	Issuer exposed to floating interest rate risk but initial rate is lower than for fixed-rate issue.	Price remains closer to par than the price of a fixed-rate note of the same maturity.	Investor protected against deterioration in the issuer's credit quality because of increase in coupon rate when rating declines.			
Floating Rate Tax-Exempt Revenue Bonds	Coupon rate floats with some index, such as the 60-day high-grade commercial paper rate.	Issuer exposed to floating interest rate risk but initial rate is lower than for fixed-rate issue. Effectively, tax-exempt commercial paper.				Investor does not have to pay income tax on the interest payments but issuer gets to deduct them.	
Increasing Rate Notes	Coupon rate increases by specified amounts at specified intervals.	Defers portion of interest expense to later years, which increases duration.		When such notes are issued in connection with a bridge financing, the step-up in coupon rate compensates investors for the issuer's failure to redeem the notes on schedule.			
Indexed Currency Option Notes/ Principal Exchange Rate Linked Securities	Issuer pays reduced principal at maturity if specified foreign currency appreciates sufficiently relative to the US dollar.	Investor assumes foreign currency risk by effectively selling the issuer a call option denominated in the foreign currency.					Attractive to investors who would like to speculate in foreign currencies but cannot, for regulatory or other reasons, purchase or sell currency options directly.
Interest Rate Caps, Floors, and Collars	Investor who writes an interest rate cap (floor/collar) contract agrees to make payments to the contract purchaser when a specified interest rate exceeds the specified cap (falls below the floor/falls outside the collar range).	Seller assumes the risk that interest rates may rise above the cap (fall below the floor/fall outside the collar range.					
Interest Rate Reset Notes	Interest rate is reset 3 years after issuance to the greater of (i) the initial rate and (ii) a rate sufficient to give the notes a market value equal to 101% of their face amount.	Reduced (initial) yield due to the reduction in agency costs.		Investor is compensated for a deterioration in the issuer's credit standing within 3 years of issuance.			
Interest Rate Swaps	Two entities agree to swap interest rate payment obligations, typically fixed rate for floating rate.	Effective vehicle for transferring interest rate risk from one party to another. Also, parties to a swap can realize a net benefit if they enjoy comparative advantages in different international credit markets.					Interest rate swaps are often designed to take advantage of special opportunities in particular markets outside the issuer's traditional market or to circumvent regulatory restrictions
Medium-Term Notes	Notes are sold in varying amounts and in varying maturities on an agency basis.	Issuer bears market price risk during the marketing process.			Agents' commissions are lower than under-writing spreads.		
Mortgage Pass-Through Certificates	Investor buys an undivided interest in a pool of mortgages.	Reduced yield due to the benefit to the investor of diversification and greater liquidity.	More liquid than individual mortgages.		Most investors could not achieve the same degree of diversification as cheaply on their own.		
Negotiable Certificates of Deposit	Certificates of deposit are registered and sold to the public on an agency basis.	Issuer bears market price risk during the marketing process.	More liquid than non-negotiable CDs.		Agents' commissions are lower than underwriting spreads.		

Exhibit 2.3D Finnerty's Compilation

Selected Debt Innovations

Security	Distinguishing Characteristics	Risk Reallocation/ Yield Reduction	Enhanced Liquidity	Reduction in Agency Costs	Reduction in Transaction Costs	Tax Arbitrage	Other Benefits
Adjustable Rate Notes and Floating Rate Notes	Coupon rate floats with some index, such as the 91-day Treasury bill rate.	Issuer exposed to floating interest rate risk but initial rate is lower than for fixed-rate issue.	Price remains closer to par than the price of a fixed-rate note of the same maturity.				
Auction Rate Notes and Debentures	Interest rate reset by Dutch auction at the end of each interest period.	Coupon based on length of interest period, not on final maturity.	Designed to trade closer to par value than a floating rate note with a fixed interest rate formula.	Interest rate each period is determined in the marketplace, rather than by the issuer or the issuer's investment banker.	Intended to have lower transaction costs than repeatedly rolling over shorter maturity securities.		
Bonds Linked to Commodity Price or Index	Interest and/or principal linked to a specified commodity price or index.	Issuer assumes commodity price or index risk in return for lower (minimum) coupon. Can serve as a hedge if the issuer produces the particular commodity.					Attractive to investors who would like to speculate in commodity options but cannot, for regulatory or other reasons, purchase commodity options directly.
Collateralized Mortgage Obligations (CMOs) and Real Estate Mortgage Investment Conduits (REMICs)	Mortgage payment stream is divided into several classes which are prioritized in terms of their right to receive principal payments.	Reduction in prepayment risk to classes with prepayment priority. Designed to appeal to different classes of investors; sum of the parts can exceed the whole.	More liquid than individual mortgages.		Most investors could not achieve the same degree of prepayment risk reduction as cheaply on their own.		
Commercial Real Estate-Backed Bonds	Nonrecourse bonds serviced and backed by a specified piece (or portfolio) of real estate.	Reduced yield due to greater liquidity.	More liquid than individual mortgages.				Appeals to investors who like to lend against real estate properties.
Credit-Enhanced Debt Securities	Issuer's obligation to pay is backed by an irrevocable letter of credit or a surety bond.	Stronger credit rating of the letter of credit or surety bond issuer leads to lower yield, which can more than offset letter of credit/ surety bond fees.					Enables a privately held company to borrow publicly while preserving confidentiality of financial information.
Dollar BILS	Floating rate zero coupon note the effective interest rate on which is determined retrospectively based on the change in the value of a specified index that measures the total return on long-term, high-grade corporate bonds.	Issuer assumes reinvestment risk.					Useful for hedging and immunization purposes because Dollar BILS have a zero duration when duration is measured with respect to the specified index.
Dual Currency Bonds	Interest payable in US dollars but principal payable in a currency other than US dollars.	Issuer has foreign currency risk with respect to principal repayment obligation. Currency swap can hedge this risk and lead, in some cases, to yield reduction.					Euroyen-dollar dual currency bonds popular with Japanese investors who are subject to regulatory restrictions and desire income in dollars without principal risk.
Euronotes and Euro-commercial Paper	Euro-commercial paper is similar to US commercial paper.	Elimination of intermediary brings savings that lender and borrower can share.			Corporations invest in each other's paper directly rather than through an intermediary.		
Extendible Notes	Interest rate adjusts every 2-3 years to a new interest rate the issuer establishes, at which time note holder has the option to put the notes back to the issuer if the new rate is unacceptable.	Coupon based on 2-3 year put date, not on final maturity.		Investor has a put option, which provides protection against deterioration in credit quality or below-market coupon rate.	Lower transaction costs than issuing 2 or 3-year notes and rolling them over.		

The Changing Face of the Securities Industry

Financial engineering activity is heavily concentrated in the financial services industry and it has been particularly strong in that subset of the financial services industry known as the securities industry. The securities industry has both helped shape financial engineering and been itself transformed by financial engineering. As a result, the securities industry has changed considerably over the last two decades. Consider for example how the sources of the industry's revenue have changed since the early 1970s.

In 1972, well over half of the industry's revenue was derived from commissions. Today, less than a fifth of the industry's revenue is derived from this source. On the other hand, in 1972 only about 10 percent of the industry's revenue was derived from transactions (capital gains). Today, about 30 percent comes from this source. When one considers that the profit margins on transactions have been squeezed considerably by competition and increasingly efficient markets, it is remarkable how much more dependent the industry has become on transactional sources of revenue. Indeed, the changing financial landscape and the slimmer profit margins have created an industry which can be, and which has been, described as "transactionally driven." This is important to keep in mind as we examine the birth of new products and the mechanisms used to deliver the products to the end users.

Summary

Financial engineering over the last 20 years has been driven by both environmental factors which are external to the firm and by intrafirm factors which are those that are internal to the firm. The environmental factors include increased price volatility in most market sectors, a general globalization of the markets, tax asymmetries, developments in technology, advances in financial theory, regulatory change, increased competition, and reductions in information and transaction costs. The intrafirm factors include the liquidity needs of business, the risk aversion of managers and owners, reduced profit margins, agency costs, greater levels of quantitative sophistication among investment managers, and more formal training of senior-level personnel.

While lulls in the pace of financial innovation will likely occur, financial engineering is unlikely to disappear. The forces that have given birth to this profession will continue to drive it. There are both great opportunities to be seized and great pitfalls to be avoided. As we work our way through this book we will be looking for both.

Endnotes

[1]See the Forward by Robert Schwartz in *The Swaps Handbook: Swaps and Related Risk Management Instruments*, Kapner and Marshall (1990).

[2]See, for example, Grossman (1988), Hill and Jones (1988), Edwards (1988), Merrick (1987), and Fremault (1989).

[3]This is not a universally held view. Some economic historians hold that the Act was unnecessary and without merit.

[4]Two studies which have shown this lack of understanding of risk management instruments and techniques are Block and Gallagher (1986) and Booth, Smith, and Stolz (1984).

[5]See Jensen and Meckling (1976).

[6]See, for example, Lee (1986).

[7]See, for example, McCullum (1987) and Hand and Hughes (1990).

[8]This list of innovative products and processes first appeared in Finnerty (1988) and is reproduced here with permission.

References and Suggested Reading

Black, F. and M. Scholes. "The Pricing of Options and Corporate Liabilities," *Journal of Political Economy*, 81, pp. 637-659, 1973.

Block, S.B. and T.J. Gallagher. "The Use of Interest Rate Futures and Options by Corporate Financial Managers," *Financial Management*, Autumn, 1986.

Booth, J.R., R.L. Smith, and R.W. Stolz. "The Use of Interest Rate Futures by Financial Institutions," *Journal of Bank Research*, Spring, 1984.

Ederington, L. "The Hedging Performance of the New Futures Markets," *Journal of Finance*, pp. 157-170, 1979.

Edwards, F.R. "Studies of the 1987 Stock Market Crash: Review and Appraisal," Columbia Center for the Study of Futures Markets: WP#168, 1988.

Finnerty, J.D. "Financial Engineering in Corporate Finance: An Overview," *Financial Management*, Winter, 1988.

Fisher, I. *Appreciation and Interest*, American Economic Association Third Series, August, 1896.

Fremault, A. "Stock Index Futures and Index Arbitrage in a Rational Expectations Model," Columbia Center for the Study of Futures Markets: WP#195, 1989.

Graham, B. and D. Dodd. *Securities Analysis*, New York: McGraw-Hill Book Company, Inc., 1934.

Grossman, S.J. "An Analysis of the Implications for Stock and Futures Price Volatility of Program Trading and Dynamic Hedging Strategies," *Journal of Business*, 61, pp. 275-298, 1988.

Hand, J.R.M. and P. Hughes. "The Motives and Consequences of Debt/Equity Swaps and Defeasance: More Evidence that it Does Not Pay to Manipulate Earnings," *Journal of Applied Corporate Finance*, 3(3), pp. 77-81, 1990.

Hill, J.M. and F.J. "Jones Equity Trading, Program Trading, Portfolio Insurance, Computer Trading and All That," *Financial Analysts Journal*, July-August, pp. 29-38, 1988.

Jensen, M.C. and W.H. Meckling. "Theory of the Firm: Managerial Behavior, Agency Costs and Ownership Structure," *Journal of Financial Economics*, 3(4), pp. 505-360, 1976.

Johnson, L. L. "The Theory of Hedging and Speculation in Commodity Futures," *Review of Economic Studies*, 27(3), pp. 139-151, 1960.

Kapner, K.R. and J.F. Marshall, *The Swaps Handbook: Swaps and Related Risk Management Instruments*, New York: New York Institute of Finance, 1990.

Lee, S. "What's with the Casino Schools?" *Forbes*, 138(6), September 22, pp. 150-158, 1986.

Lintner, J. "The Valuation of Risk Assets and the Selection of Risky

Investments in Stock Portfolios and Capital Budgets," *Review of Economics and Statistics*, 1965.

Macaulay, F.R. *Some Theoretical Problems Suggested by the Movement of Interest Rates, Bond Yields, and Stock Prices in the United States Since 1856*, New York: National Bureau of Economic Research, 1938.

Markowitz, H. "Portfolio Selection," *Journal of Finance*, pp. 77-91, March, 1952.

McCullum, J.S. "Our Las Vegas Style Financial Markets: Madness or Marvelous," *Business Quarterly*, 52(1), pp. 20-23, Summer 1987.

Merrick, J.J. "Volume Determination in Stock and Stock Index Futures Markets: An Analysis of Arbitrage and Volatility Effects," *Journal of Futures Markets*, 7, pp. 483-496, 1987.

Mossin, J. "Equilibrium in a Capital Asset Market," *Econometrica*, pp. 768-783, 1966.

Sharpe, W.F. "Capital Asset Prices: A Theory of Market Equilibrium Under Conditions of Risk," *Journal of Finance*, pp. 425-442, 1964.

Stein, J. "The Simultaneous Determination of Spot and Futures Prices," *American Economic Review*, 51(5), pp. 223-235, 1961

Chapter 3

The Knowledge Base of the Financial Engineer

Overview

In this chapter, which is misleadingly short, we examine the knowledge base of the modern financial engineer. We would like to be able to spell out a specific course of study and say that anyone who successfully completes it would qualify as a financial engineer. Unfortunately, things are not as simple as that.

Financial engineers are involved in many types of financial activity and the specific knowledge base required of one financial engineer may be quite different from that required of another. There are, however, certain areas of knowledge and certain types of skills that are useful in many financial engineering applications, and we concentrate on these. By this introductory discussion of the knowledge base of the modern financial engineer, we hope the reader will better understand our motivation for including the various chapters which follow. In particular, it will help to explain the chapters on the conceptual tools of the financial engineer, which make up Section II of this book, and the chapters on the instruments used by financial engineers, which make up Section III of this book.

Theory

The financial engineer must be well grounded in theory. In all cases, this will include basic economic and financial theory with advanced financial theory in applicable areas. Basic economic and financial theory includes such topics as the sources of value and wealth, measures of value and return, methods for identifying risk exposures, the various measures of risk and the applicability of each, basic portfolio theory, basic hedging theory, basic option pricing theory, relationships between risk and return and investor satisfaction, the sources of agency costs, and such other topics as are routinely covered in well-designed finance degree programs.

Because financial engineers usually specialize, they will also require advanced knowledge of theory in narrowly focused areas. Those involved in portfolio design, for example, will require advanced study in investment analysis, portfolio management, and asset allocation. Those involved in risk management will need more extensive study in methods of risk measurement and risk management. Both of these groups, and many others besides, will require advanced knowledge of option pricing theory.[1] Those involved in mergers and acquisitions will need more extensive study in capital budgeting techniques, agency costs, and accounting and tax rules. Those involved in corporate finance will need more extensive study in asset/liability management, and so on.

As markets have become more global in scope, financial engineers are increasingly required to design solutions or develop strategies that involve multiple currencies. This requires a knowledge of exchange rate theory and interest rate theory, and the relationships between the two.

Mathematical and Statistical Skills

Most successful financial engineers have a thorough grounding in mathematics and statistics, although the extent of skills in these areas varies greatly from one financial engineer to the next. Some financial engineers concentrate their efforts in areas where little more than simple arithmetic is required. This is typical, for example, of those financial engineers involved in tax arbitrage. While little advanced mathematics and statistics is required in this work, a very thorough grounding in accounting and tax and at least some study of business law is typically required. Some financial engineers, on the other hand, must possess advanced mathematical and statistical skills. This is typically the case, for example, in work involving the measurement of financial risk exposures and the design of hedging strategies. Indeed, advanced mathematical and statistical skills are nearly always required when option strategies are employed. Modern option pricing theory makes extensive use of stochastic calculus—a skill only mastered by hard work.[2] Advanced mathematical and statistical skills are also often a prerequisite for successful product innovation and trading strategy design.

Mathematical skills typically include a knowledge of calculus, linear and nonlinear optimization techniques, the uses of logarithms and exponential functions, and the ability to work with formulas, equations, and graphs. Statistical skills typically required include some knowledge of distribution theory, the ability to measure basic statistical parameters like means, standard deviations and correlation coefficients, a knowledge of regression and correlation techniques, and familiarity with analysis of variance techniques and their uses.[3] Basic skills in these areas are often sufficient, but some financial engineering work requires considerably greater levels of sophistication in both mathematics and statistics. These more advanced skills are possessed by the "quant jock" subset of financial engineers. Most financial engineering teams will have at least one such resident expert.

Modeling Skills

Many areas of financial engineering require advanced modeling skills. Other areas require only modest modeling skills. But all areas require at least some modeling skills. We define *modeling skill* as the ability to distill out the critical elements of a complex situation in order to separate that which is relevant from that which is not. Modeling is a necessary step in the analysis of problems and in the testing of potential solutions to problems.

There are many different ways to model, and different financial engineers use different approaches. Some approaches are very intuitive while others are very rigorous and structured. Many, for example, use the sorts of modeling skills taught in economics courses. In such an approach, one starts out with a set of assumptions, derives relationships, and then reaches conclusions. This form of modeling may make use of advanced mathematical techniques or it may be very graphical. In recent years, this sort of modeling has been adapted to spreadsheets. Spreadsheet software allows one to examine with lightning speed how a model's conclusions change with changes in the underlying assumptions. This testing of outcome sensitivity to changes in assumptions is called **sensitivity analysis.** When spreadsheets are used, sensitivity analysis is often referred to as "what if" analysis.

Product Knowledge

All areas of financial engineering require product knowledge. This does not mean that all financial engineers need to be thoroughly versed in all financial products. With the tremendous proliferation of financial products in recent years, it is doubtful that anyone currently alive is thoroughly versed in all of them. But the financial engineer does need to be thoroughly versed in those financial instruments and processes that are useful in designing solutions to the kinds of problems in which he or she deals. For example, financial engineers working in corporate treasury need to be thoroughly familiar with those tools widely used to achieve short-term and long-term financing objectives. Financial engineers working in risk management need to be well versed in derivative products (sometimes called derivative securities). And, financial engineers working in financial planning need to be well versed in retail level financial products.

One area in which the talents of financial engineers are heavily utilized is arbitrage involving replicating portfolios. It can be shown, and we will do so in great detail later, that almost any security can be replicated by a combination of other securities. Determining the combination (portfolio) of instruments necessary to exactly replicate the target security can be a complex mathematical and statistical exercise. The portfolio which replicates the target security is called a **synthetic security.** The purpose for replicating the target security might be as simple as a desire to achieve a certain form of financing at lower cost or as complex as arbitraging a pricing discrepancy between the real security and the synthetic security.

Knowledge of Relevant Technology

At the broadest level, relevant technology includes economic and financial theory, mathematical and statistical techniques, product knowledge, computer and telecommunications hardware, and computer software. Indeed, at this level, financial engineering can be defined, and has been defined, as the application of financial technology to the solution of problems in finance. But, in this section, we are using the term **technology** more narrowly to refer only to those elements that we routinely associate with a lay usage of the term—i.e., the computer and telecommunications hardware and the software that drives them.

Technology has revolutionized modern finance. It has made it possible to perform millions of calculations, called instructions, per second. Indeed, major investment houses often measure their potential for successful trading by the number of MIPS (millions of instructions per second) at their disposal. MIPS levels in the hundreds or even the thousands are not uncommon.

But all the technology in the world will do little good unless the financial engineer knows how to use it. Financial engineers have encouraged their MIS (management information systems) personnel to develop ways to channel market data directly into computer applications software (requiring the "digitizing" of data), and to develop easy-to-use applications software and automatic market-tracking software. For example, with appropriate "real-time" data flows and appropriate software, an options trading house can literally track every single stock and every single option on every single stock simultaneously, and immediately identify any option that is overvalued or undervalued relative to the underlying stock. This, of course, requires an appropriate option pricing (valuation) model.

Spreadsheets, the microcomputers that run them, and the networking of microcomputers to allow the sharing of information have dramatically increased the speed with which financial engineers can analyze situations and formulate their responses. Similarly, **applications software**—premodeled software that can calculate the solution to complex financial problems with minimal input on the part of the user—is proliferating. This type of software was, until quite recently, very expensive and only available on mainframe computers. What is more, it was difficult to use—often requiring a knowledge of computer programming languages and/or complex JCL syntax. Today, such software has become relatively inexpensive and is readily available for microcomputers. It has also become much easier to use. Program designers have learned the importance of being user friendly. One such program, which we found very useful, is *A-Pack: An Analytical Package for Business.*[4]

This package, which is typical of modern applications software, offers the user hundreds of the financial, statistical, and mathematical techniques most often used in financial engineering and financial analysis. All of these techniques are selected from fully integrated menus that make any desired technique extremely easy to access. We used this package extensively in developing this text. With little "work" on our part, we generated solutions to all sorts of complex problems in just a few minutes. By combining the appropriate techniques, we found very few problems that were so unique that *A-Pack* could not take us a long way toward a solution. Software like this, once priced in the thousands of dollars, is now available for just a few hundred.[5]

Accounting, Tax and Legal

Many areas involving financial engineering require specialized accounting, tax, or legal expertise. While it can surely not hurt for a financial engineer to possess this knowledge himself or herself, it is not unusual for the financial engineering team to include corporate accountants, tax accountants, corporate lawyers, and securities lawyers. Financial engineering teams, often working out of merger and acquisitions departments, typically have such skills readily available. Such people are usually not, themselves, the financial engineer, but they are available to the financial engineer as a resource. As we work our way through this book, it should be readily apparent where and when these specialized skills would be called upon.

Despite the occasional need for specialists, financial engineers generally require at least some background in accounting, tax law, and business law. If nothing else, such background is essential if one is to communicate effectively with the appropriate experts on the team.

The American Association of Financial Engineers

During 1990 and early 1991, the authors of this book worked with leading practitioners and academicians involved in financial engineering to form a professional association of financial engineers. The Association, known as the American Association of Financial

Engineers, or AAFE, was chartered in 1991. It provides a vehicle by which financial engineers can network with one another. The Association, a nonprofit corporation, is dedicated to serving its members. Membership in AAFE is opened to those persons actively engaged in the practice of financial engineering, those persons who contribute to the theoretical underpinnings of financial engineering, those persons engaged in the formal study of financial engineering, and those persons interested in a possible career in financial engineering.

Among AAFE's current planned activities, as enunciated in its funding proposal, are (1) research and dissemination of information, 2) interaction and communication, 3) member support services, 3) industry support services, 4) education, and 5) long range planning. Many of the activities of the Association shall be carried out by the Center for the Advancement of Financial Engineering to be funded by the Association's corporate sponsors.

Parties interested in AAFE membership can contact the senior author at the address below.

John F. Marshall, Ph.D.
Executive Director
American Association of Financial Engineers
Graduate School of Business
St. John's University
Jamaica, NY 11439

Summary

Financial engineers are not clones of one another, and the skills required of one are not necessarily the skills required of another. While almost all financial engineers have a good foundation in economic and financial theory, basic accounting, basic mathematics and statistics, and at least some modeling skill, others have much greater levels of skill in one or more of these areas. Modern financial engineers must be versed in the relevant technology and understand how it is used in their profession. Some will use it extensively and others only occasionally.

Financial engineers often function as part of a team. This requires good interpersonal skills and the ability to communicate effectively. These skills become particularly important when a financial engineer must consult with a specialist in one of the many areas that impinge on the work of the financial engineer.

Endnotes

[1] For a good primer on options see the books listed below by Kolb (1991) and Marshall (1989). For a more advanced treatment see the books listed below by Ritchken (1987) and Jarrow and Rudd (1983).

[2] A good primer on stochastic calculus and its application in option pricing can be found in Ritchken (1987).

[3] A good, although somewhat advanced, text on statistical technique, is Mood, Graybill, and Boes (1973).

[4] *A-Pack: An Analytical Package for Business* is published in both an educational edition (Kolb Publishing, Miami, Florida) and a professional edition (MicroApplications, 516-821-9355, FAX: 516-744-1225.) The hundreds of tools in this package are grouped by discipline. The Master Menu brings up the various disciplines which include Financial Analysis, Investment Analysis, Mathematical Analysis, Operations Research, and Statistical Analysis. The selection of a discipline brings up a grouping of tools that logically fall within that discipline. Each subsequent menu narrows down the choice until the appropriate tool is found.

[5] For example, the educational edition of *A-Pack* is priced under $40 and the professional edition is priced under $200.

References and Suggested Reading

Jarrow, R.A. and A. Rudd. *Option Pricing*, Homewood, IL: Irwin, 1983.

Kolb, R.W. *Options: An Introduction*, Miami, FL: Kolb Publishing, 1991.

Marshall, J.F. *Futures and Option Contracting*, Cincinnati, OH: South-Western, 1989.

Mood, A.M., F.A. Graybill, and D.C. Boes. *Introduction to the Theory of Statistics*, New York: McGraw-Hill, 1973.

Ritchken, P. *Options: Theory, Strategy, and Applications*, Glenview, IL: Scott Foresman, 1987.

Chapter 4

Valuation Relationships and Applications

Overview

In this chapter, we examine the valuation relationships that are the foundation of all financial analysis and financial engineering. They are usually the first financial concepts introduced in any first-level finance course. These same relationships are ordinarily reviewed at the start of almost every advanced finance course. They are so fundamental to the logic of finance that, among financial engineers, the concepts and relationships are taken as axiomatic.

Given the very fundamental nature of the concepts discussed in this chapter and the next, and the general level of sophistication of our readership, we were tempted to skip this material altogther—believing that our readers could fill in the missing pieces when the need arose. At least one of our academic reviewers shared this view. We were encouraged, however, by some of our industry reviewers to include it. They argued that not all those who enter financial engineering do so from a traditional finance track and, for these latter individuals, a review of the basics might be helpful. Quite obviously, we have accepted this argument. Those readers thoroughly familiar with present and future value arithmetic and its applications can skip this chapter. Those readers who are not might also want to consider some of the reference material listed at the end of this chapter for a more detailed discussion of these topics.

Cash Flows

Every investment opportunity can be fully described by the cash flows that it generates. A **cash flow** is simply a payment made or received. Cash flows have three important characteristics. The first is the size or the amount of the cash flow. The second is the direction of the cash flow. And the third is the timing of the cash flow.

Cash flows can be in any currency. Americans will typically think in dollars, Germans in Deutschemark, and Japanese in yen. The denomination of the currency is, however, completely irrelevant to the logic of the analysis. (To enhance the reader's ability to think globally, we will vary the currencies used in our examples in later chapters. For now we will usually use dollars.) Payments received are often called cash inflows, and payments made are often called cash outflows. Cash outflows represent costs.

The full set of cash flows that describe a particular investment are often called the cash flow stream or the payment stream. In this book, we will tend to use the term **cash flow stream**. A cash flow stream may be known with certainty or it may not be known with certainty. The more certain is the cash flow stream, the less risk that is associated with the investment opportunity. For purposes of establishing our foundation concepts, we will assume throughout this chapter that the cash flows are all known with certainty. We will relax this assumption in later chapters.

Consider now two investment opportunities, denoted A and B, that provide cash flows beginning one year from today and ending four years from today. These cash flows appear in Table 4.1. For the moment, we ignore the cost of these two opportunities.

Table 4.1
Cash Flows for Two Investment Opportunities

Investment A		Investment B	
Time	Amount	Time	Amount
1	$500	1	$900
2	600	2	600
3	700	3	500
4	800	4	400
Total	$2600	Total	$2400

Investment A provides a greater total cash flow than does Investment B. Assuming equal initial costs, Investment A provides a greater absolute profit (or, equivalently, a smaller loss) than does Investment B (in an accounting sense). But this *does not mean* that Investment A is superior to Investment B in a financial sense.

Time Value

The financial value and the accounting profit of the cash flows represented by Investments A and B above are not equal because financial valuation explicitly considers the time value of cash flows while accounting profit does not. That is to say, time has a value and this value must be explicitly considered when evaluating cash flows. Time is taken into consideration by "discounting" the cash flows to common temporal equivalents. These temporally-standardized values are called **present values**.

To discount cash flows to their present values, we need a discount rate. In the langauge of economics, the appropriate discount rate is simply the opportunity cost of money to the party considering the investment. For example, since the cash flows are known with certainty (by our earlier assumption), it would not be inappropriate to use the yield currently afforded by a safe investment, such as Treasury securities of an appropriate maturity, as the discount rate. The yield afforded by the Treasuries may be viewed as the opportunity cost of putting our money into Investments A and B.

The procedure for calculating the present value of a cash flow is complicated just slightly by the fact that we need to take compounding into consideration. This is so because monies received can be and should be reinvested (if not used for consumption purposes). We will denote the cash flow to be received at time t by CF_t and we will denote the discount rate to be applied to the cash flow occurring at time t by k_t. The present value of this cash flow is then given by Equation 4.1a or, equivalently, by Equation 4.1b.

$$PV = \frac{CF_t}{(1+k_t)^t} \qquad (4.1a)$$

$$= CF(t) \cdot (1 + k_t)^{-t} \qquad (4.1b)$$

It is not necessary for the discount rate applied to each cash flow to be the same. Indeed, there are very good reasons to believe that cash flows to be received at different points in time should be discounted at different rates. Nevertheless, we will assume the same discount rate applies to all cash flows for purposes of the examples that follow.

Let's suppose that the yield on Treasuries of the appropriate maturity is 10 percent. We would calculate the present value of the first cash flow associated with Investment A as follows:

$$PV = \frac{500}{(1.1)^1} = 454.55$$

The present value of the second cash flow associated with Investment A is calculated similarly:

$$PV = \frac{600}{(1.1)^2} = 495.87$$

This process is repeated until all the cash flows have been calculated. The full set of cash flows for Investments A and B together with their present values is depicted in Table 4.2.

Table 4.2
Discounted Cash Flows at 10%

Investment A			Investment B		
Time	Amount	Present Value	Time	Amount	Present Value
1	$500	454.55	1	$900	818.18
2	600	495.87	2	600	495.87
3	700	525.92	3	500	375.66
4	800	546.41	4	400	273.21
Total	$2600	$2022.75	Total	$2400	$1962.92

Each cash flow has some present value. Since the present value of each cash flow is directly comparable, as each has the same temporal reference (the present), they may be summed. Summing the present values is the key to determining overall valuation. The sum of the present values is usually represented using summation notation. The standard formulation is given by Equation 4.2.

$$PV = \sum_{t=1}^{n} CF_t \cdot (1 + k_t)^{-t}$$

(4.2)

Equation 4.2 requires that the present value of each cash flow be separately determined and then the individual present values summed. As we can see from Table 4.2, this renders a valuation for Investment A of $2022.75 and a valuation for Investment B of

$1962.92. We need to interpret these numbers. The present value of Investment A tells us that we should be willing to pay *up to* $2022.75 for that invesment opportunity *but no more than $2022.75*. Similarly, the present value of Investment B tells us that we should be willing to pay *up to* $1962.92 for that investment opportunity *but no more* than $1962.92.

At this point, it is reasonable to ask about the cost. Most often, but not always, the cost of an investment opportunity takes the form of a single cash outlay that is made up front (at time 0). Let's suppose that both investments are available at time zero at a cost of $1200. Since the present value of $1200 in hand must be $1200, we can readily see that any time zero cash flow, whether an outflow such as cost, or an inflow such as income, must have a present value equal to itself. Thus, such a value is directly addable (if positive) or deductable (if negative) from the sum of the present values already obtained.

The difference between the sum of the present values of the cash flows and the time-zero cost is called a **net present value**. Net present values, often denoted NPVs, are very useful for analyzing and comparing investment opportunities. The NPV of Investment A, for example, is $822.75, and the NPV of Investment B is $762.92. Clearly, Investment A is superior to Investment B.

The time value analysis we have been doing thus far is called **present value arithmetic** because it takes sums to be received at future points in time and discounts them to their present value. Sometimes, however, we want to take values in the opposite direction. That is, we have a present sum to invest and we would like to know what it will be worth at some point in the future if it earns some annual rate of interest. These types of time value problems are called **future value** or **terminal value** problems. The future value, denoted FV, of a given starting sum, denoted PV (since the starting sum at time zero is the present value at time zero) is given by Equation 4.3.

$$FV = PV(1+r)^t \qquad (4.3)$$

The value r in Equation 4.3 denotes the interest rate and the value t denotes the number of periods forward in time that we wish to project the value. The rate of interest in Equation 4.3 serves the same purpose as the discount rate in Equation 4.1. Indeed, if you examine Equations 4.1b and 4.3 closely, and you substitute PV for CF in 4.1b, you will realize that they are really the same equation.

The only real difference is the negative sign before the number of periods in the present value equation and the positive sign before the number of periods in the future value equation. This difference in sign is easily explained. Present value problems take future sums *back* to their present values and, hence, have negative signs, while future value problems take present sums *forward* to their future values and, hence, have positive signs.

Once one recognizes the identity of the present value and the future value formulations, it becomes unnecessary to distinguish between discount rates and interest rates. Indeed, in most areas of financial practice we dispense with the distinction and simply refer to the two collectively as the **yield**. Similarly, we can dispense with the distinction between present value arithmetic and future value arithmetic and simply refer to them collectively as **valuation arithmetic**.

Sensitivity Analysis of Time Value

One of the very interesting aspects of net present value as a measure of investment performance is that the measure is very sensitive to changes in the discount rate. That is, even if the cash flows are known with certainty, the NPV of an investment will fluctuate if the discount rate fluctuates. For example, consider what happens to the NPV of Investments A and B if the discount rate is 25 percent rather than 10 percent. The new present values together with the old are depicted in Table 4.3.

Table 4.3
Present Values at 10% and 25%

	Investment A				Investment B		
Time	Amount	PV at 10%	PV at 25%	Time	Amount	PV at 10%	PV at 25%
1	$500	454.55	400.00	1	$900	818.18	720.00
2	600	495.87	384.00	2	600	495.87	384.00
3	700	525.92	358.40	3	500	375.66	256.00
4	800	546.41	327.68	4	400	273.21	163.84
Total	$2600	$2022.75	$1470.08	Total	$2400	$1962.92	$1523.84
	NPV	822.75	270.08		NPV	762.92	323.84

By deducting the initial $1200 cost to obtain the NPVs at a 25 percent discount rate, we find that Investment A has a NPV of $270.08 and Investment B has a NPV of $323.84. Thus, at a 10 percent discount rate, Investment A is clearly superior to Investment B, but

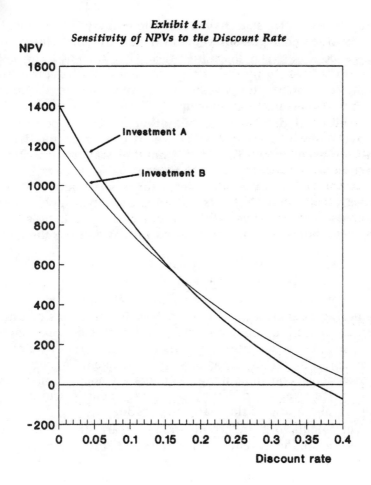

Exhibit 4.1
Sensitivity of NPVs to the Discount Rate

at a 25 percent discount rate, Investment B is clearly superior to Investment A.

This comparison of two investment opportunities NPVs under different discount rate assumptions is useful for illustrating the role of sensitivity analysis in financial engineering. Sensitivity analysis is, quite simply, an explicit consideration of the sensitivity of financial outcomes to changes in underlying assumptions.

The example also serves to demonstrate the inverse relationship between discount rates and present values. Notice that the present values of both investment opportunities cash flows declined as the discount rate rose from 10 percent to 25 percent. Another useful approach, which we shall have reason to employ later in this book, is to consider how present values (or net present values) change across a continuum of discount rates. This kind of thing is most easily illustrated by means of a graph. Exhibit 4.1 depicts the net present value curves for Investments A and B as the discount rate rises from 0 percent to 40 percent.

Exhibit 4.1 demonstrates one other important point as well. An investment is attractive whenever it can be acquired for less than its present value. To put this another way, an investment is attractive whenever it has a net present value greater than zero. This is not to imply that an investment is unattractive if its NPV is exactly zero, only that it is not an exceptional opportunity. Investments with negative NPVs should clearly be avoided unless there are other, nonfinancial, reasons for considering them.

Applications

The number of uses for the valuation arithmetic we have been considering is enormous. It is used to price all forms of financial securities including common stock, preferred stock, bonds, mortgages, and real estate deals. It is also used in corporate finance to make capital budgeting decisions; by investment bankers to value takeover deals; and in banking to generate amortization schedules and to price swaps and other risk management instruments. And these are just a few of the many applications.

The calculations underlying valuation are straightforward but tedious. Before the advent of computers and software packages, the only way to lessen the tedium of the calculations was to resort to tables. A number of different types of tables were prepared to provide the present and future values of $1 under various yield assumptions and various time period assumptions. In their simplest form, these tables provided present and future values for integer rates (1 percent, 2 percent, 3 percent....) and whole time periods (1, 2, 3,.....). The problem with these tables was that very few "real world" problems fell neatly into the whole-rate/whole-period categories. The only reasonable solutions avaliable were either to have a much more detailed set of tables (which took the form of books of tables) or to employ an approximation technique called interpolation. This latter approach was widely taught (and still is) in many business schools. The student is shown a mathematical procedure that finds an intermediate point between two whole rates or two whole periods.

$$(1 + k_t)^{t/m}$$

The problem with interpolation is that it is a linear technique applied to a nonlinear relationship. Thus, by definition, it produces an error with a distinct bias. While some finance professors argue that this error is small and can be ignored, in fact, on large transactions a small per-dollar error can translate into a lot of money. Furthermore, many modern arbitrage activities are driven by an effort to take advantage of very small price discrepancies between the *market* value and the *fair* value of one or more instruments. Fair value is interpreted as the present value of a cash flow stream given knowledge of the discount rate. Small errors can lead to serious distortions as to the profitability of these strategies.

The kind of error introduced by interpolation is illustrated in Exhibit 4.2. The exhibit depicts the present value of $1000 to be

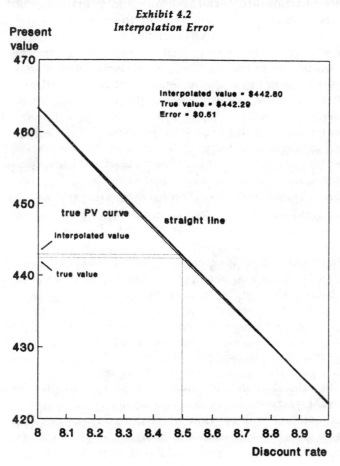

Exhibit 4.2
Interpolation Error

received in 10 years at a discount rate of 8 percent and again at 9 percent. The curve connecting the points represents the true present values of $1000 to be received in 10 years at all discount rates between 8 percent and 9 percent. Notice that the actual relationship between discount rates and present value is nonlinear. Now suppose that we are interested in the present value at a discount rate of 8.5 percent. Because 8.5 percent does not appear on short-form tables, we obtain the present value by interpolating from the known 8 percent and the known 9 percent values. As depicted, the interpolation finds the mid-point on a straight line between the 8 percent value and the 9 percent value. This mid-point misses the true value by the amount indicated.

The upshot of this simple demonstration is that neither tables nor interpolation are perfect solutions to valuation problems. The financial engineer must understand the underlying relationships and must be able to work with the formulas associated with them.

Early attempts to deal with the tedium of the present and future value computations led to a number of specialized equations that greatly simplified the number of calculations involved—provided that certain specific criteria are met. Three such equations are particularly useful. These are the present value annuity relationship, the future value annuity relation, and the constant growth model valuation relationship.

The present value annuity (PVA) relationship provides a short cut for determining the present value of a cash flow stream provided that the following conditions are satisfied: First, the cash flows must take the form of an annuity (an annuity is a series of equal-size payments made at equal intervals in time). Second, the first payment must be due one period from the present. Third, there must be a finite number of payments. Finally, the periodic discount rate must be the same for all cash flows. When all these conditions are satisfied, the present value formula given by Equation 4.2 reduces to Equation 4.4.

$$PVA = CF \cdot \frac{1 - (1+k)^{-n}}{k} \tag{4.4}$$

The annuity condition and the requirement that the discount rate be the same for all cash flows allows us to drop the time subscript on CF and k. Note that while Equation 4.4 does not look any less complex than Equation 4.2, in an application situation it is far superior. For example, suppose that the number of cash flows in

Equation 4.2 is 40; that is n=40. Equation 4.2 would require a total of 40 separate computations and then a final summation to arrive at the present value. Equation 4.4 will produce an identical result with only one computation.

The second special case involves a future value annuity (FVA). In this case, we are interested in the future value of a series of equal-size contributions to an investment instrument paying a fixed rate of interest over the entire life of the instrument. The payments must be spaced at equal intervals in time and the first payment must be due to be made one period from the present. We are interested in the value of the cash flow stream at the time of the last contribution. When all these conditions are satisfied, the future value of the cash flow stream is given by Equation 4.5.

$$FVA = CF \cdot \frac{(1+r)^n - 1}{r}$$
(4.5)

The final special situation involves a series of cash flows in which the cash flows are growing at a fixed per period rate, denoted here by g, the cash flows are expected to continue indefinitely (without end), the cash flows will occur at equal intervals in time, and all the cash flows are discounted at the same rate. When these conditions are satisfied, the present value of the cash flow stream is given by Equation 4.6.

$$PV = \frac{CF_1}{k - g}$$
(4.6)

The present value formulation in Equation 4.6 is sometimes called the constant growth model. The only cash flow that needs to be entered is the one that is due one period out, denoted above by CF_1.

There is one special case of Equation 4.6 that it would be useful to address. This occurs when the growth rate g is zero. When g is zero, the cash flows associated with the constant growth model take the form of a perpetual annuity. In these cases, Equation 4.6 reduces to Equation 4.7.

$$PV = \frac{CF}{k}$$
(4.7)

The perpetuity valuation model is very useful for valuing such perpetual annuities as fixed-dividend preferred stock. It is also useful for valuing perpetual fixed-coupon debt. The latter has not been issued in significant quantitites in U.S. capital markets, but it has been issued and well-received in European capital markets.

Spreadsheets

One of the great boons to financial analysis and financial engineering has been the introduction and widespread adoption of spreadsheet software. The popular packages—such as Lotus 1-2-3 (Lotus Development Corporation) and Excel (Microsoft)—have similar structures and capabilities. They allow the user to examine and price complex cash flow patterns with remarkable ease and speed. They also lend themselves to very efficient exercises in sensitivity analysis.

We will not dwell on the use of spreadsheets except to say that few financial engineers would willingly part with these useful tools. Much of the modeling we have done for later chapters of this book, as well as the valuation analysis depicted in Exhibit 4.1, were done using spreadsheets.

Compounding

Many, if not most, valuation situations involve compounding. In such situations, the cash flows are received more frequently than the period on which the interest rate or the discount rate is defined. Interest rates (and discount rates) are most often stated on a period of one year. The frequency of compounding is sometimes explicity stated and at other times is simply understood from the context. For example, a mortgage rate is stated on an annual basis but the mortgage payments are usually made monthly. A Treasury bond's coupon rate is stated on an annual basis but the coupons are paid semiannually. Many money market mutual funds declare and pay dividends (interest) daily even though the dividend rate is stated as an annual rate. The list of possible examples is endless.

The point is that the financial engineer must take the effect of compounding on valuation into consideration. We will briefly consider the implications of compounding and the necessary adjustments to our valuation equations.

Suppose we are considering a rate of interest of 10 percent (call this the nominal rate). If the interest is paid once a year at the end of the year, then the **effective annual rate** (sometimes called the **simple rate of interest**) is indeed 10 percent. But suppose that the interest is paid twice a year (semiannually). That is, one-half the interest (5 percent) is paid after six months and one-half is paid at the end of one year. What effect would this have on the effective rate of interest? To appreciate the effect, we need to simply understand that the interest paid at the end of the first six months will itself earn interest during the second six months and, therefore, the effective rate of interest will be higher than 10 percent. The more frequent the compounding, the greater will be the effective rate. The relationship between the effective rate of interest, denoted here by *ER*, the nominal rate of interest, denoted here by *NR*, and the number of compoundings, denoted here by *m*, is given by Equation 4.8.

$$ER = \left(1 + \frac{NR}{m}\right)^m - 1$$

(4.8)

It is easily demonstrated that the effective rate of interest increases as *m* gets larger. This is depicted in Exhibit 4.3.

While the effective rate of interest gets larger with more frequent compounding, you will notice that it is increasing at a decreasing rate. That is, as the number of compoundings increases, the effective rate of interest is approaching a constant (the curve is flattening out). This constant is the effective rate of interest under continuous compounding. You cannot get the effective rate of interest under continuous compounding using Equation 4.8 because, under continuous compounding, *m* is infinity. But, you can get it using Equation 4.9.

$$ER = exp(NR) - 1$$

(4.9)

In Equation 4.9, *exp*(.) denotes the "exponential function." This is the value "e" raised to the power NR. Fortunately, it is easy to get this value. All scientific calculators and most business calculators have this function. On calculators, the exponential function is usually denoted e^x. For example, if we enter 10 percent (.1) and then press e^x, we obtain the value 1.1051709. From this value, we subtract 1 (as in Equation 4.9), to arrive at an effective rate of interest of 10.517 percent. This is the limiting value that the curve in Exhibit 4.3 is approaching.

It is customary to state the compounding assumption when quoting an interest rate unless the frequency of compounding is understood from the context. For example, we often hear reference to a "semiannual rate" (often denoted sa). This means an "annual rate of interest compounded semiannually." Similarly, the phrase a

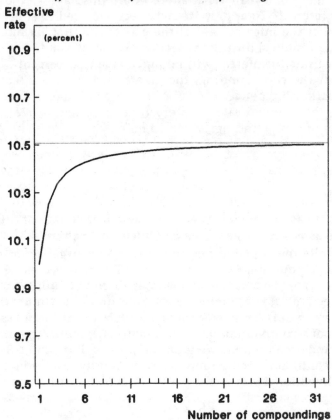

Exhibit 4.3
Effective Rate of Interest & Compounding

"quarterly rate" is interpreted to mean an "annual rate of interest compounded quarterly." Of course, the phrase an "annual rate of interest" means an "an annual rate of interest compounded annually."

As already mentioned, the frequency of compounding is sometimes understood from the context. For example, in the United States, bond yields are quoted on a "bond basis" which assumes semiannual compounding—unless specifically stated otherwise. (Bond basis and other yield quotation conventions are described in later chapters.) Thus, when a bond trader says "the bond is yielding 8.5 percent," he or she means that the bond is yielding a semiannual rate of 8.5

percent. In Europe, however, bond yields are quoted as annual rates rather than as semiannual rates. It takes the beginner some time to appreciate these conventions.

Absolute Valuation Versus Relative Valuation

The valuation arithmetic we have been describing is used to determine the "absolute" value of an investment. An equally important concept which we will take up again when we examine arbitrage, is that of "relative value." Absolute value describes the dollar (or other currency unit) value of an investment opportunity. Relative value, on the other hand, considers the value of an investment opportunity relative to other investment opportunities. It is quite possible and indeed quite common for an asset to have a high absolute value and simultaneously to have a low relative value or vice versa.

Let's consider a simple example. Suppose that a bond is currently selling at a premium to its par value (a premium bond). To make the example more concrete let's suppose that the bond is priced at 108 percent of par. This may be the highest price at which this bond has ever traded and one must conclude that it has a high absolute value. But, if current bond yields suggest that other bonds of equivalent risk and maturity to this bond are trading at even higher prices (lower yields), then the bond has a low relative value. In such a situation, a bond trader might purchase the bond, which is perceived as undervalued, and sell the other bonds, which are perceived as overvalued.

The concept of relative value is critically important in many trading situations, like the one just described, but it is also critically important in financing situations. For example, a corporate treasurer in need of financing can obtain financing in a great many ways. Several of these ways may be nearly equivalent in terms of the cash flow streams they entail. But one financing alternative may have a lower cost than the others and, therefore, have greater relative value to the firm.

These arguments suggest two things. First, as important as absolute value is in making investment and financing decisions, relative value is at least equally important. Second, we need a way to calculate and compare the relative values or relative costs of various financial alternatives. We will examine such measures later in this book.

Summary

All investment and financing decisions give rise to cash flows. These cash flows occur at different points in time and, consequently, are not directly comparable or combinable. But, the cash flows can be temporally-standardized by converting them to present values with the aid of appropriate discount rates. Once the cash flows have been converted to their present values, they can be summed to determine the current value of the investment or financing alternative. This sum is called the instrument's present value. Present values may be thought of as "fair" values.

Present values are sensitive to the choice of a dicsount rate and there is an inverse relationship between present values and discount rates. That is, as the discount rate rises the present value declines. Closely related to the concept of present value is the concept of future value. While present value arithmetic allows us to convert future cash flows to their current values, future value arithmetic allows us to determine the future or terminal value of current sums.

Although the term **interest rate** is often used to describe the rate used to take monies forward in time, there really is no difference between a discount rate and an interest rate, and practitioners often use the term **yield** in lieu of either.

There are a great many applications of valuation arithmetic. The calculations are often tedious but they lend themselves to spreadsheet solutions. For this, and other reasons, spreadsheets have become indispensable to modern financial engineers.

Compounding plays an important role in determining the effective rate of interest on an investment. All other things being equal, the more frequent the compounding, the greater is the effective rate of interest for any given nominal rate of interest. As the frequency of compounding increases, the effective rate of interest approaches a limiting value which is the rate achieved under continuous compounding. The notion of continuous compounding is very important in financial modeling and we take it up again in later chapters.

It is important to distinguish between absolute value and relative value. By relative value we mean the value of one currently available financial alternative relative to another.

Suggested Reading

Brown, S.J and Kritzman, M.P. *Quantitative Methods for Financial Analysis*, Homewood, IL: Dow Jones-Irwin, CFA, 1987.

Kolb, B.A. and R.F. DeMong, *Principles of Financial Management*, 2nd ed., Plano, TX: Business Publications, Inc., 1988.

Rao, R.K.S. *Financial Management: Concepts and Applications*, New York: Macmillan, 1987.

Van Horne, J.C. *Financial Management and Policy*, 8th ed., Englewood Cliffs, N.J.: Prentice Hall, 1989.

Weston, J.F. and T.E. Copeland *Managerial Finance*, 8th ed., Chicago, Dryden, 1986.

Chapter 5

Measuring Return

Overview

In this chapter, we discuss a number of concepts pertaining to the measurement of return. Specifically, we will examine holding period yields and rates of return. Following this, we consider the importance of measuring return on an after-tax basis. We then extend the discussion begun in the last chapter, which contrasted the measurement of return on an effective basis with measurement under continuous compounding. We also introduce the concept of an investment horizon and we briefly consider its importance for financial decision making. Knowledge of the conceptual tools introduced in this chapter will be of importance to us later when we consider the work of the engineer and take an in-depth look at more advanced concepts. We have tried to illustrate our points in this chapter, as in the other chapters of this book, with concrete, practical examples involving the engineer at work. Finally, we will use this chapter to introduce the concept of **utility**. We introduce utility first in order to get that important term out of the way.

At first glance, the measurement of return seems a simple matter. But, in fact, it often is not—particularly if the cash flows are uncertain. For purposes of introducing return, we will continue to assume that the cash flows associated with an instrument or an investment are known with certainty, and we will put off until later the complications introduced by risk, except to make some general remarks regarding the relationship between risk and utility.

As with the last chapter, most of the topics discussed in this chapter involve very basic conceptual tools. For this reason, we regard this chapter as largely one of review. Most readers with an academic background in finance can skip the first few sections without worry. Those with a more modest background, however, should read the entire chapter.

Utility

It is standard operating procedure in all modern economic analysis to assume that people make decisions in such a fashion as to achieve outcomes that maximize their utility. Utility is the economist's term for the satisfaction that comes from the consumption of goods and services. Although utility is difficult to measure, there is no denying its existence.

Economists, including financial theorists, assume that each individual possesses a set of preferences that are, at any given point in time, well-defined in a mathematical sense. Because they are well-defined mathematically, these preferences can be expressed in functional form and such a function is called, not surprisingly, a **utility function**. Economists ascribe a number of important properties to utility functions. If a person's utility function possesses these properties, then the economist describes the function as "well behaved" and describes the person possessing it as "rational." To be well behaved, utility functions must possess three specific properties. These are (1) insatiability, (2) diminishing marginal utility, and (3) diminishing marginal substitutability. While the terms are a little arresting, their meanings are straightforward and intuitively appealing.

Insatiability refers to the inability of an individual to ever be fully satisfied. That is, no matter how much of a consumable good or service an individual possesses, he or she always wants more. Economists do not actually take this behavior literally. Instead, they interpret it at a more general level. That is, no matter how many goods and services an individual possesses, he or she will always enjoy a gain in utility from additional goods and services. It is easier to appreciate this behavior in a financial setting. Wealth makes the purchase and consumption of goods and services possible and it follows that the more wealth one possesses, the more utility one enjoys. We therefore conclude that people have an insatiable desire to acquire wealth.

Diminishing marginal utility refers to the fact that as people acquire more and more units of a particular consumable good, each additional unit of that good provides a smaller increase in total utility. Even when broadened to include all goods and services, this property will usually hold. In a financial context, it implies that each additional dollar of wealth acquired enhances total utility but each dollar adds less to total utility than the previous dollar.

The final property of well-behaved utility functions is diminishing marginal substitutability. Diminishing marginal substitutability means that as each additional unit of a particular good or service is acquired, that good becomes less satisfying relative to other goods and services. When applied in a financial context, this property has certain important implications. For example, as additional wealth becomes available, a person is more and more likely to find leisure time more attractive and is consequently more willing to sacrifice wealth for leisure time.

At this point, it would be helpful to define **return,** even if only loosely. Return is a *change* in the quantity of wealth. This change can be expressed in terms of monetary units (profit) or as a percentage of initial wealth (rate). Since wealth provides utility by making consumption possible, it follows that individuals associate utility with return because return augments wealth. This is an unambiguous conclusion—return means more wealth, more wealth means more consumption, and more consumption means more utility. On the other hand, in order to achieve a return, it is usually necessary to temporarily part with some liquidity. Thus, there is a price to be paid to earn return. The price takes the form of a postponement of consumption. For this reason, an investment intended to earn a return may be regarded as an exchange of current consumption for a potentially greater level of later consumption. This brings up an important and often neglected point. All other things being equal, in most cases for most people, the present value of the utility associated with the immediate consumption of a given quantity of wealth is greater than the present value of the utility associated with the later consumption of that same quantity of wealth. In simple terms, immediate satisfaction is preferred to the expectation of later satisfaction, all other things being equal.

There is a direct connection between the concept of utility and the concept of present value. For example, suppose that utility is related to wealth by the following function (which possesses the important properties of all utility functions and in which U denotes the number of "units of utility" and $ln()$ denotes the natural logarithm): $U = ln(\text{Wealth})$. Now suppose that the investor possesses $100 of current wealth. Then, the investor has 4.605 units of utility. Suppose now that the investor is asked to part with his or her wealth for a period of one year. At the end of the one year period, the investor will get back the $100—no more and no less. We know the investor's utility must decline because $100 to be received in one year has less present value than $100 in hand now. That is, the utility of the present value of $100 to be received in one year is less than the utility of $100.

The question that immediately arises is then "how much additional wealth does one need to acquire over the period of the investment in order for the present value of the utility associated with the terminal wealth to be just equal to the present value of the utility associated with the initial starting wealth?" The answer will vary tremendously from individual to individual which demonstrates the uniqueness of utility functions and helps to explain why people will discount the present value of future cash flows at different rates. People who may be described as "spendthrifts" are simply people who apply a very high discount rate to consumption. People who may be described as "frugal" are people who apply a very low discount rate to consumption. This helps explain why some people save a high percentage of their disposable income while others do not save at all. It also has application for financial engineers who design savings/investment plans for individuals.

There is one final property of well-behaved utility functions that is not always explicitly mentioned in *economic* discussions of utility. This property is very important however in understanding the behavioral implications of utility functions in a financial setting. The property is called **risk aversion**. In financial analysis it is generally held that rational people are risk averse. That is, all other things being equal, risk diminishes utility.

Risk aversion derives from the diminishing marginal utility property of utility that we discussed above. Nevertheless, it is worth noting explicitly as it plays a very important role in financial decision making. For now, we will note that risk can be thought of as a "good" in the same sense as any economic good, except that it provides disutility instead of utility.

Although all rational people will behave as though they have well-behaved utility functions, very few will actually think in terms of the utility implications of the decisions they make. This does not mean that they do not consider utility; rather, it means that they do so innately—without any specific need to think about it. It is also important to realize that there are an infinite number of variations of utility functions (preference sets) that are equally well behaved in the sense that they satisfy all of the aforementioned properties. For example, while all rational individuals will be averse to financial risk, not all will be equally risk averse. Some, for example, will be exceedingly averse to risk and not be willing to take a small risk even when the potential reward for doing so is large. Such people are generally described as financially "conservative." Others will only be modestly averse to risk and, if offered a reward for bearing risk, will choose to take risk even when the potential reward for doing so is small. Such people are referred to as financially "aggressive." Most people, of course, fall between these two extremes.

Economists and financial theorists have developed elaborate and very useful mathematical and graphical approaches for explaining the relationships between utility, return, and risk. These forms of analysis are most often used to explain portfolio choices and portfolio sequencing. We return to these subjects in later chapters.

Measuring Return: Profit versus Rates

It is important for the modern financial engineer to think of currencies very generally and not to focus too narrowly on the dollar. For this reason, we prefer phrases like "monetary units" to specific monetary forms like dollars, pounds, or yen. Nevertheless, terms like monetary unit are awkward and so we will use specific currencies in our examples. We will add the global view by varying the currencies. (We do this more in later chapters than in this one.)

There are two distinct, but related, approaches to measuring return. The most natural for most people is to speak in terms of **profit**. Profit is simply the difference between the number of dollars (or other monetary units) afforded by the investment at the end of the investment period and the number of dollars expended to acquire the investment at the start of the investment period. The second approach is to convert profit returns to percentage form and express them as **rates of return**. The latter method of measurement has distinct advantages in analytical work, but the former is still necessary for accounting and tax purposes.

The most serious problem with using profit as a measure of return is that this measure ignores the scale of the investment required to earn the return and it ignores the length of the investment period over which the return is earned. For example, what does a profit of $500 mean if we do not know the size of the initial investment necessary to earn it? A $500 profit on an investment of $1000 is one thing, and a $500 profit on an investment of $1 million is quite another. Similarly, a $500 profit earned over 1 year is something quite different from a $500 profit earned over a period of 10 years.

There are other problems as well. For example, many investments involve assets that lose value over time. In some cases, this loss of value is due to physical deterioration or obsolescence of the asset. Examples include such physical assets as buildings, machinery, and vehicles; endowed assets such as oil and coal deposits; and intangible assets such as patents, copyrights, and licenses. In other cases, the loss of value results from a *paydown* of the principal balance—a form of value decline characteristic of many financial assets. A conventional residential mortgage, for example, returns a portion of the starting principal with each monthly payment. How should these declines in the value of assets be accounted for? Logic, of course, suggests that the losses of value experienced should be used to offset a portion of the cash flows generated by the assets. This explains such important accounting concepts as depreciation, depletion, and amortization. But how much of a cash flow should be chargeable toward the loss of value in any given reporting period? These are issues that have been repeatedly addressed by Congress and the Financial Accounting Standards Board (FASB). The rules periodically change with concomitant effect on the size and the timing of profit.

Regardless of the applicable rules for accounting for the loss of value over time, the *total profit over the life of an investment* (assuming it is held to the end of its accounting life) *will be the same.* Nevertheless, the timing of the profits will be affected by the state of the applicable rules. And, as we demonstrated in the last chapter, the timing of cash flows (of which profit is a portion) has a significant impact on present value.

The upshot is that profit, as a measure of return, is deficient because it ignores the size of the initial investment, the timing of returns, and the impact of accounting conventions on the value of cash flows. All of these reasons suggest the need for a measure of return that expresses return on a percentage basis.

The standard method for measuring return on a percentage basis is to convert profits or (more inclusively) cash flows, to a rate of return. The term *rate of return* is often misused and needs some clarification. First, a rate of return should always be stated on an annual basis. If we wish to state the return in percentage form and not be specific as to the length of the period involved or to use a period of arbitrary length, then the percentage return should be called a **holding period yield**. A rate of return is, therefore, a holding period yield for a period of one year. (In a later chapter, we will examine the relationship between holding period yields stated on periods of one length and holding period yields stated on periods of different lengths.)

The best way to compute a rate of return for an investment with known cash flows is to calculate the internal rate of return on the investment using a period that corresponds to the frequency of the cash flows, and then to convert this rate to an effective annual rate of return using the procedure described in the last chapter. The internal rate of return is a measure closely related to present value. To demonstrate the concept, consider an investment that requires an initial cash outlay of $2000 at time zero and then returns $500 every six months for three years. There is no residual terminal value because the periodic payments have amortized the original investment. The full set of cash flows are depicted in Table 5.1.

Table 5.1
Cash Flows from an Amortizing Investment

Time (in years)	Payment Number	Cash Flow
0	0	(2,000)
0.5	1	500
1.0	2	500
1.5	3	500
2.0	4	500
2.5	5	500
3.0	6	500

Now recall from the last chapter that we can compute net present value (NPV) of the initial investment by employing Equation 5.1. (Since the cash flows take the form of an annuity, we could use the annuity formula instead to get the present value of the cash flows occurring during periods 1 through 6, but we want to stay at a more general level here.)

$$NPV = \sum_{t=1}^{6} PV_{CF_t} - Cost \qquad (5.1)$$

$$= \sum_{(t=1)}^{6} 500 \cdot (1+k)^{-t} - \$2000$$

The value k is the discount rate used to obtain the present value of a future sum. By varying k, we vary NPV. This is depicted graphically in Exhibit 5.1.

Exhibit 5.1
NPV Curve for Finding IRR

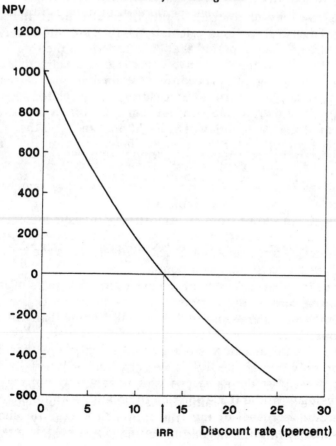

It is always true that as the discount rate rises, the NPV declines. Thus, the NPV curve has a downward slope. Now notice that there is one discount rate at which the NPV is exactly zero. As it happens, this discount rate is 12.978 percent. We can now define the internal rate of return. The internal rate of return, often denoted IRR, is the discount rate that makes an investment's NPV exactly zero. Thus, this investment has an internal rate of return of 12.978 percent.

There is, however, one serious misrepresentation that needs to be corrected. The cash flow periods involved in the calculation of the internal rate of return were six months in length and not one year. Thus, the rate 12.978 percent is a six-month IRR. We must convert this six-month rate to an annual rate of return using the logic of compounding that we discussed in Chapter 4. The calculation, given below by Equation 5.2, yields an effective annual rate of return. In Equation 5.2, *ER* denotes the effective rate of return that we are after and *m* denotes the number of periods in one year.

$$ER = (1 + IRR)^m - 1 \qquad (5.2)$$

$$= (1 + .12978)^2 - 1$$

$$= 27.64\%$$

The investment's annual rate of return, expressed as an effective rate of return is now seen to be 27.64 percent. If we prefer to express the rate of return as a semiannual rate, we would simply multiply the six-month IRR by two and then refer to the resultant value as a semiannual rate of return. In this case, the semiannual rate of return is 25.96 percent.

As a side note, the rate of return calculated above is sometimes called a **yield** or a **yield to maturity**. This latter terminology, however, is generally applied when the investment takes the form of a fixed-income security such as a bond.

There are some criticisms of the use of internal rates of return for comparing alternative investments. One criticism is that there are cases in which there is more than one IRR value that will make a NPV equal to zero. These cases only occur, however, when the cash flows in the cash flow stream change sign more than once. Even then, only one of the IRR values obtained will usually make economic sense. For these reasons, this is generally not regarded as a serious flaw of the IRR approach to obtaining a rate of return.

A second criticism of the IRR approach is that the method implicitly employs an assumption that may not hold in practice.

Specifically, the method assumes that any and all cash flows received will be reinvested to earn a rate equal to the IRR. In practice, of course, it is usually impossible to know what future investment opportunities will be like and so the reinvestment rate assumption can fail. Most theorists and practitioners will note this concern and then ignore it. This is a position with which we agree. If the present set of opportunities afford an IRR of some calculated percent, and if the present set of opportunities are not in some way extraordinary, then there is just as much reason to believe that future investment rates will be higher than those available today, as they will be lower than those available today. In such situations, the IRR is an unbiased statistic even if the reinvestment rate assumption fails.

The preceding line of argument begs the question, how should one measure return if the internal rate of return is not an unbiased estimate of the reinvestment rate? There are several situations in which this can occur. We need to consider two of them. The first occurs if the reinvestment rate is expected to be either higher or lower than the internal rate of return. It is considered particularly important if the reinvestment rate is expected to be *lower* than the internal rate of return. In this situation, we estimate what the reinvestment rate will be. We then assume that all return earned on the investment will be reinvested at the expected reinvestment rate. With this assumption, we can estimate the expected terminal value of the investment. Finally, we can use the internal rate of return formula to determine what annual rate of return would equate the beginning value with the expected terminal value. This rate is called the **realized compound yield**. A special case of the realized compound yield, used in a capital budgeting context, is the **modified internal rate of return**, in which the assumed reinvestment rate is the firm's cost of capital.

The second case involves situations in which the source of the cash flow stream might be terminated prior to its scheduled maturity. A callable bond is an example of this. If the bond issuer can call the bond at a specific price, called the **call price,** prior to its maturity, then the bond's yield to maturity may not be an accurate measure of its return. In these situations, we calculate the internal rate of return on the assumption that the bond *will* terminate prematurely on the call date and will pay the call price. The internal rate of return calculated in this way is called the instrument's **yield-to-call.** Investment analysts—particularly those working in fixed-income securities—will then focus on the *lower* of the yield-to-maturity and the yield-to-call. The lower of these two values is sometimes called the **promised yield.**

Rates of Return—Before and After Taxes

There is one more issue to address before we move on. It involves tax considerations. There are two different ways to take taxes into consideration when calculating rates of return. Which one should be used depends largely on the nature of the situation. Consider the simplest situation first. Suppose that there are two nonamortizing instruments currently available for purchase and both are selling at par (face value). One is a corporate bond and pays a coupon of 12 percent. The other is a municipal bond and pays a coupon of 10.5 percent. For simplicity, assume that the bonds have the same maturity and are of the same credit quality.

Since the bonds are currently selling at par, the rates of return they provide are equal to their coupon rates. Based on risk considerations alone, the corporate bond is a better investment since it affords a higher rate of return with no greater risk. But, this ignores taxes. The coupon interest received by the holder of a municipal bond is exempt (for most holders) from federal taxation and may also be exempt from state and local taxation. The coupon interest received by the holder of a corporate bond is, on the other hand, fully taxable (for most holders). This difference in tax treatment of interest can have a profound effect on the attractiveness of an investment opportunity. In these cases, we can convert the before-tax rate of return, denoted r_b, to an after-tax rate of return, denoted r_a, using Equation 5.3. In Equation 5.3, mt denotes the marginal tax rate that applies to the interest earned by the particular investor involved.

$$r_a = r_b \cdot (1 - mt) \tag{5.3}$$

Consider the after-tax rates of return associated with these two bonds for two different investors. Suppose that the first investor is in a 30 percent marginal tax bracket (federal, state, and local combined) and the second is in a 10 percent bracket. Using Equation 5.3, we can compute the after-tax rates of return for both investors. These are summarized in Table 5.2.

Table 5.2
After-Tax Equivalents of Before-Tax Returns

	Before Tax Rate of Return	After Tax Rate of Return Investor 1 (mt = 30%)	Investor 2 (mt = 10%)
Corporate	12.00%	8.40%	10.80%
Municipal	10.50%	10.50%	10.50%

Clearly, what really counts in any investment is the disposable income that the investment provides. Thus, it is the after-tax return we are concerned about. For Investor 1, the superior investment is clearly the municipal bond. For Investor 2, the superior investment is the corporate bond. (A critic of the different tax treatments of the interest on different issuers' instruments would be inclined to point out the negative implications of these differing tax treatments on the efficient allocation of resources. It is not, however, the purpose of this book to analyze the economic merits of fiscal and tax policies.)

The second approach is more general and it is best applied to those situations involving profit and loss statements (P&L). The procedure involves the computation of the after-tax cash flows associated with an investment followed by the generation of an IRR using the after-tax cash flows. The procedure also illustrates the noncash nature of certain P&L expense items such as depreciation and depletion. The resultant IRR is an after-tax value. To illustrate the procedure, suppose that a firm invests $1000 in a new fixed asset having a depreciable life of three years and generating cash flows for four years. The asset will be depreciated using a straight-line method and each year's depreciation is $333.33.[1] The investment will give rise to earnings before depreciation and taxes (EBDT) of $500 each year and the firm is in a flat 25 percent tax bracket. The calculation of the after-tax cash flows appear in Table 5.3.

Table 5.3
Calculation of After-Tax Cash Flows
(straight-line depreciation)

	Year 1	Year 2	Year 3	Year 4	Total
EBDT	500.00	500.00	500.00	500.00	
Less depreciation	333.33	333.33	333.33	0.00	
= EBT	166.67	166.67	166.67	500.00	
Less taxes	41.67	41.67	41.67	125.00	
= EAT	125.00	125.00	125.00	375.00	
Plus depreciation	333.33	333.33	333.33	0.00	
= after-tax cash flow	458.33	458.33	458.33	375.00	1750.00

We now use the cash flows above to generate the internal rate of return just as we did for the investment described in Table 5.1. The only difference is that these cash flows are stated on an annual basis and, consequently, the resultant IRR does not require an additional step to annualize. As it happens, the IRR associated with these cash flows is 27.764 percent.

Let's now assume that instead of using a straight-line method of depreciation, we use an accelerated method. Suppose that this method allows us to depreciate 45 percent of the asset the first year, 35 percent the second year, and the remaining 20 percent the third year. The after-tax cash flows are recalculated in Table 5.4.

Table 5.4
Calculation of After-Tax Cash Flows
(accelerated method of depreciation)

	Year 1	Year 2	Year 3	Year 4	Total
EBDT	500.00	500.00	500.00	500.00	
Less depreciation	450.00	350.00	200.00	0.00	
= EBT	50.00	150.00	300.00	500.00	
Less taxes	12.50	37.50	75.00	125.00	
= EAT	37.50	112.50	225.00	375.00	
Plus depreciation	450.00	350.00	200.00	0.00	
= after-tax cash flow	487.50	462.50	425.00	375.00	1750.00

If you examine the after-tax cash flows at the bottom of Table 5.4 and compare them to the after-tax cash flows at the bottom of Table 5.3, you will observe that they have the same 4-year total. But, also observe that the timing of the individual cash flows has been affected by the choice of depreciation methods. If we re-compute the IRR using the after-tax cash flows, we find that the after-tax rate of return is 28.335 percent. This compares favorably with the 27.764 percent rate of return we obtained using straight line depreciation.

The preceding discussion leads to several interesting conclusions. First, the attractiveness of many investment strategies is significantly affected by the applicable tax and accounting rules. The reason for this is that these rules impact not just the *absolute amount of taxes* but also the *timing of tax obligations*. This explains many of the tax-sheltered investment strategies that were engineered in the 1970s and early 1980s to exploit depreciation rules. For example, by organizing itself as a partnership, a firm could pass its losses on to its partners on a *pro rata* basis. By investing only a small sum of the partners' own money in such ventures and then borrowing the rest, the partnership could purchase large quantities of depreciable assets (such as rental properties). Then, by employing accelerated methods of depreciation, the firm could generate large accounting losses that passed directly to the partners. The partners, in turn, could use these losses to offset other income. Such strategies proved very attractive to high-bracket individuals and huge sums of money were eventually channeled into such sheltering schemes. The more successful partnerships could sometimes generate as much as $7 in accounting losses for each $1 invested by the partners.

Ideally, such partnerships would ultimately sell the assets they had purchased to recoup the investment and pay off the creditors. Of course, if the assets were sold for anything above their depreciated value, the partnership had a gain that then became taxable income to the partners. But, this gain would come many years after the losses and, thus, the strategy allowed the partners to exploit the time value of the deferred taxes. Multiple unit residential properties and commercial real estate were the ideal kind of assets for this strategy. They held their value very well, were good collateral for bank loans, and generated income to help offset operating expenses and carrying costs. Agricultural ventures, oil and gas operations, and leasing deals were also attractive for this purpose and partnerships blossomed to exploit the opportunities. In many cases, the desire to acquire assets for tax-sheltering partnerships often led to inflated market prices. It is often contended, for example, that tax-sheltering schemes, created by financial engineers, contributed to excessive commercial real estate prices and excessive commercial real estate development during the mid-1980s. (This is another example, of course, of a misallocation of resources brought about by quirks in the tax codes.)

It is not surprising that many financial engineers concentrate their talents on finding loopholes in the tax laws and accounting rules that allow for the creation of value (or, more accurately, the transfer of value) by altering the timing of cash flows. It is also not surprising that Congress has repeatedly sought to close these loopholes with the result that the tax codes have become ever more complex. The Tax Equalization and Fiscal Responsibility Act of 1986 (TEFRA) effectively dampened the usefulness of the tax-sheltering approach described above by imposing limits on the losses a partner can take relative to the amount of investment the partner has made in the partnership. The financial engineers that we called "outlaws" in Chapter 1 essentially play a cat-and-mouse game with regulators. This game has given rise to a formal theory of the interaction of financial engineering and regulatory reform called the **regulatory dialectic.** The regulatory dialectic was first described by Edward Kane.[2] John Finnerty summarized this regulatory dialectic quite nicely as "a cyclical process in which the opposing forces of regulation and regulatee avoidance adapt continuously to one another."[3]

Another interesting point worth noting is that depreciation, depletion, and amortization of intangible assets are non-cash expenses. That is, accounting rules allow the firm to take a charge against earnings but this charge does not actually involve a cash expenditure on the part of the firm. The non-cash nature of depreciation, depletion and amortization allow the firm to have wide disparities between after-tax profit in a given year and after-tax cash flow in that year since cash flow is defined as after-tax profit plus non-cash expenses.

Many financial engineers devote their talents to finding ways to postpone taxes. While there is a natural tendency to focus these strategies on high tax rate individuals and firms, many strategies and instruments have been introduced to provide these opportunities for smaller players including the average individual. Tax-postponement is, for example, the logic that underlies such savings and investment plans as individual retirement accounts (IRAs), Keogh plans, and 401K plans. Let's consider the benefits of such a plan.

Suppose that an individual who pays a flat tax rate of 25 percent has the choice of investing $2000 of *gross* income each year into a regular savings account yielding 8 percent or into an IRA account yielding the same 8 percent. Deposits made to the IRA account are tax deferred until the individual withdraws the money. To keep things simple, let's suppose that the individual makes a single contribution to the plan each year on his birthday from age 21 to age 65 and then withdraws all the funds on his 65th birthday. If he invests his $2000 of gross income into the regular plan, he only deposits $1500 because that is all that he has left after paying the 25 percent tax. At the end of each year he must also pay 25 percent of the 8 percent interest he earned and thus the after-tax rate is only 6 percent. On the other hand, at age 65, when he withdraws all of his money, he has no further taxes to pay. We can use a future value annuity formula to find out how much he will have on his 65th birthday. The future value annuity formula is given by Equation 5.4 and the calculation follows immediately.

$$FVA = PMT \cdot \frac{(1+r)^n - 1}{r}$$

(5.4)

$$FVA = \$1500 \cdot \frac{(1 + 0.06)^{45} - 1}{0.06}$$

$$= \$319,115$$

Now consider the outcome if he invests his $2000 of gross income into the IRA plan. Since the contribution is made to an IRA, the $2000 is not subject to taxation in the year in which the contribution is made, nor is the interest earned subject to tax at the end of each year. Thus, he contributes the full $2000 each year and he earns 8 percent annually. The calculation is:

$$FVA = \$2000 \cdot \frac{(1 + .08)^{45} - 1}{0.08}$$

$$= \$733,010$$

However, at the time the funds are withdrawn, the individual must pay the 25 percent tax. After the tax has been paid, he has $579,757.50 left. Thus, saving in a regular account, in which income is taxed each year, results in terminal spendable wealth of $319,115 while saving in an identical, but IRAed, account results in a terminal spendable wealth of $579,757.50. This is an improvement of almost 82 percent.

Just as the tax-sheltered partnership engineered for the wealthy increases wealth largely by affecting the timing of taxes, the IRA is the everyday man's tax shelter and it also increases wealth by affecting the timing of taxes. Keogh and 401K plans serve a similar purpose.

Like tax-sheltered partnerships, IRAs eventually had a significant impact on tax collections. In response, Congress limited access to IRAs, as part of TEFRA, by placing income limitations and employment-connected pension plan limitations on would-be IRA contributors.

As we have seen, financial engineers can enhance wealth by devising strategies for tax deferral. But they can also enhance wealth by devising ways to pass income from high taxpaying organizations (or individuals) to low tax paying organizations (or individuals). In an earlier chapter, we demonstrated one way that this can be accomplished by passing dividend income from a low tax corporation to a high tax corporation. This is possible because intercorporate dividend payments are largely exempt from taxation at the level of the recipient corporation. Similar strategies have been devised for individuals. Probably the most frequently utilized prior to TEFRA was to pass interest and dividend income from high-tax rate parents to low-tax rate children. Another strategy, designed for wealthy individuals and still applicable in some cases, is to "skip a generation" when bequeathing wealth. Again, the goal of these strategies is to lessen the tax liability or to affect the timing of the tax liability.

Rates of Return and Compounding

In the last chapter we discussed the role of compounding when interest rates are stated on an annual basis. We saw that, for a given nominal rate of interest, the more frequent the compounding the greater is the effective rate of interest. We also demonstrated that the limit to the benefits of compounding occurs when compounding is continuous. In this case, the effective rate of interest can be obtained by employing the exponential function so that the effective rate (ER) is related to the nominal rate (NR) by ER = exp(NR) − 1 where exp(.) denotes the exponential function.

The same considerations apply to holding period yields (HPYs) and to rates of return (as special cases of holding period yields). There are times when we have a series of observations on wealth and we would like to compute the successive holding period yields. For example, suppose that we start with $100 of wealth invested in some security with all income from the security immediately reinvested in additional units of the same security. Each month we make an observation on the value of our position. This value is our end-of-month wealth. The end-of-month wealth for each of the first six months from a series of observations is reported in Table 5.5.

Table 5.5

Month	End-of-Month Wealth	Return Relative	HPY (Effective)	HPY (Continuously Compounded)
0	100	—	—	—
1	110	1.1000	10.000%	9.531%
2	105	0.9545	−4.545%	−4.652%
3	95	0.9048	−9.524%	−10.008%
4	115	1.2105	21.053%	19.106%
5	125	1.0870	8.696%	8.338%
6	115	0.9200	−8.000%	−8.338%

$$HPY = exp(HPY_c) - 1$$

The effective holding period yield is found by taking the change from one period to the next and dividing by the starting value. That is, in the first period, the effective holding period yield is (110 − 100) ÷ 100 or 10 percent. For the second period, it is (105 − 110) ÷ 110 or −4.545 percent, and so on. Another way to get these same results is to divide the wealth at the end of one period by the wealth at the end of the preceding period and then subtract 1 from the quotient. The ratio of wealth in one period, denoted W(t+1), to wealth in the preceding period, denoted W(t), is often called the return relative. The return relative is also known as the value relative and the wealth relative. The return relative for period *t*, denoted below by R(t), is given by Equation 5.5. The effective holding period yield is then given by the return relative minus 1.

$$R(t) = \frac{W(t+1)}{W(t)} \qquad (5.5)$$

The holding period yield continuously compounded (HPY$_c$) is found by taking the natural logarithm of the return relative. On most hand-held calculators, the natural logarithm is denoted *ln x* or *log$_e$*. Thus, if we enter the return relative for the first period and press *ln x* we obtain the value 9.531 percent. An equivalent way to obtain the same result is to take the natural log of wealth in period t+1 and subtract the natural log of wealth in period *t*. When calculated in this way, the result is often called the *first difference of logs*. This relationship is given by Equation 5.6.

$$HPY_c = ln\,(W(t+1)) - ln\,(W(t)) \qquad (5.6)$$

It is important to understand that the value 10.000 percent (as an effective HPY) and the value 9.531 percent (as a continuously compounded holding period yield) are the same even though they do not look the same. That is, the effective holding period yield that is equivalent to a 9.531 percent holding period yield continuously compounded is 10.000 percent.

One might reasonably ask why we need to be so concerned about both effective rates and rates continuously compounded if either can be used to measure the performance of an investment? Why not just use one or the other? The answer is a bit complex and involves statistical properties. It becomes important when an investment's return is risky. Under very reasonable assumptions, holding period yields measured on an effective basis have a distribution that is closely related to the lognormal distribution. The lognormal distribution, unlike the normal distribution, does not have nice symmetry and its statistical properties are difficult to work with. On the other hand, effective yields are very easy to interpret because their meaning is intuitively obvious. Holding period yields continuously compounded are normally distributed, or very nearly so, (under reasonable assumptions) and have all the nice statistical properties of that familiar symmetric distribution. For this reason, the continuous measure is the measure of choice in analytical work and its properties are widely exploited by academicians in their modeling exercises and by the quant jocks who need to know the precise statistical properties of investment outcomes. Unfortunately, yields measured in this way are not intuitively easy to understand. By recognizing the relationship between the effective measure and the continuous measure, we can exploit the symmetry of the distribution of the latter and the intuitive ease of understanding of the former. We will have further use for these relationships when we consider risk and its measurement in the next chapter.

A brief review of the properties of the holding period yield continuously compounded and the lognormal distribution is presented in the appendix to this chapter.

Investment Horizons

A very important consideration for financial engineers that work with, or for, investment managers is the investment horizon. The investment horizon is defined as the period of time until the planned liquidation of a position and the use of the proceeds. There are times when the investment horizon is known with a high degree of certainty—such as when a parent is saving for a child's college education or for retirement at a known age. At other times, the investment horizon is highly uncertain. Such situations occur when the investor takes a position with the expectation of holding the position until such time as the occurrence of a specific event—the timing of which is unknown. Money held for rainy day purposes is a good example.

Both the length of an investor's horizon and the degree of certainty associated with the horizon are critically important in making intelligent investment decisions. Unfortunately, these factors are often seriously neglected in most work involving investment analysis and portfolio management.

There is one other aspect of the investment horizon worth

discussing at this stage as we will have use of it later. There are times when an investment requires a firm commitment of funds with no opportunity for portfolio revision until the very end of the investment horizon. For example, suppose an investor agrees to purchase some non-assignable private-placement five-year debt. Because the debt is nonassignable (not transferable), the investor is locked into this investment for the full five years. A similar result would occur if the investor would encounter prohibitive transaction costs from liquidating an investment prior to some specific maturity date. In portfolio situations such as this, the investor's portfolio problem is a one-time problem involving a single-period. The length of the single period corresponds to the length of the investment horizon (in this case, five years).

There are other times when an investor has a specific horizon but is free to revise his or her portfolio periodically. For example, suppose that an investor has a five-year investment horizon and his portfolio consists of a high-risk equity fund and a low-risk money market fund. Suppose now that, at the beginning of each new year, the investor is free to re-evaluate his situation and change the mix between his high-risk and low-risk assets. In such a situation, the portfolio problem is multi-period in nature. In this situation, the investor must make repeated portfolio mix (sometimes called asset allocation) decisions. Such a problem is basically one of portfolio sequencing. That is, we are asking the question what is the optimal sequence of portfolios as the investor moves from a horizon of five years down to one year? This problem involves a five-year horizon consisting of five successive single periods, each of one year in length. This difference is best illustrated by a comparative time line. Such a time line appears as Exhibit 5.2.

Exhibit 5.2
Multiperiod versus Single-Period Investment Horizons

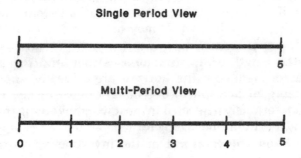

The investment horizon dimension to financial engineering is not new but it has only recently begun to attract considerable attention. It requires some appreciation of how return and risk are perceived by individuals as their investment horizons grow shorter. The issue is clearly of concern to engineers involved in the management of pension portfolios and other horizon-sensitive investment vehicles. We will postpone further discussion of the horizon dimension until after we have considered risk—the subject of our next chapter.

Summary

We have seen that investment returns can be measured in terms of raw dollars (or other currency units) or as percentage rates. Dollar profit is very appealing, but less analytically useful than percentage rates. We have also seen that the rather abstract economic concept of utility is closely related to the far less abstract financial concept of present value. Utility functions and their properties are important in much financial work. They explain how investors and other financial operatives make their decisions. Present value concepts also work quite well in explaining the same behaviors. Which we choose to use depends on which concept is most easily adapted to a given situation.

We have also seen how return is measured and the assumptions that underlie the various measures of return. The most often used measure of return is the internal rate of return, called the yield to maturity in most fixed-income analysis. But, in certain situations, it may be more appropriate to use a realized compound yield or a yield to call in lieu of an internal rate of return. We have also seen that we must distinguish between returns measured before taxes and returns measured after taxes. Not only must we consider applicable tax rates in making financial decisions but we must also consider the timing of tax obligations. Much of financial engineering strives to do nothing more than change the timing of such obligations.

Finally, we have seen that the length of the investment horizon and the frequency of compounding are also critically important in understanding return and we have seen that it is often important, for analytical purposes, to measure rates of return on a continuously compounded basis rather than on an effective basis. Continuous returns, while difficult for most people to understand at an intuitive level, have nicer statistical properties than do effective returns.

Endnotes

[1]This is a simplification. Accounting rules provide for special adjustments for the first year in which an asset is placed in service. These rules are subject to change and we ignore them here and elsewhere in this chapter. Additionally, the accelerated rates employed in this chapter are not meant to be indicative of actual rates, but rather to illustrate certain concepts.

[2]See Kane (1977, 1981, 1984).

[3]See Finnerty (1988).

References and Suggested Reading

Finnerty, J.D. "Financial Engineering in Corporate Finance: An Overview," *Financial Management*, pp. 14-33, Winter, 1988.

Haley, C.W. and L.D. Schall *The Theory of Financial Decisions*, 2nd ed., New York: McGraw Hill, 1979.

Kane, E.J. "Good Intentions and Unintended Evil: The Case Against Selective Credit Allocation," *Journal of Money, Credit and Banking*, pp. 55-69, February, 1977.

Kane, E.J. "Accelerating Inflation, Technological Innovation, and the Decreasing Effectiveness of Banking Regulation," *Journal of Finance*, pp.355-367, May, 1981.

Kane, E.J. "Technology and Regulatory Forces in Developing Fusion of Financial Services Competition," *Journal of Finance*, pp. 759-772, July, 1984.

Appendix

The Lognormal Distribution, Return Relatives, and Holding Period Yields

John F. Marshall, Ph.D.

The concepts of lognormal distributions, return relatives, and holding period yields are particularly important in the derivation of option pricing models. They are also important for understanding portfolio analysis—particularly in a multi-period context—and other areas of great importance to financial engineers. While we cannot possibly explore any of these concepts in depth in this short appendix, we can review some of the important properties of the lognormal distribution and how it relates to return relatives and holding period yields. Some of the uses will become apparent later.

We will begin by denoting the return relative obtained by dividing the beginning wealth at time B by the ending wealth at time E by $R(B,E)$. Consider a simple example, suppose that an investor purchases a nonpayout asset at time 0 for a price of $P(0)$ and holds it until time T, at which time it is priced at $P(T)$, then the return relative $R(0,T)$ is given by $P(T)/P(0)$. Alternatively, for a payout asset, we could assume that any periodic income provided by the asset is immediately reinvested in additional units of the same asset so that the ending value of the investment fully reflects the value of all income generated. If we denote the beginning period investment value by $P(0)$ and the ending period investment value by $P(T)$, then we still have the same formulation—i.e., $R(0,T)$ is still given by $P(T)/P(0)$.

We will assume that price $P(0)$ is known at time time 0 but that $P(T)$ is not known at time 0. Thus, as perceived at time 0, $P(T)$ is a random variable. This implies that $R(0,T)$ is also a random variable.

The holding period yield for a period of length T, stated as an effective rate and denoted below by $r(T)$, is related to the return relative $R(0,T)$ by:

$$r(T) = R(0,T) - 1, \qquad (5.A.1)$$

and the continuous holding period yield for a period of length T and denoted below by $r_c(T)$ is related to the return relative by:

$$r_c(T) = ln(R(0,T)). \qquad (5.A.2)$$

Recalling that *exp(.)* is the inverse function of *ln(.)* it follows that r(T) and $r_c(T)$ are related as follows:

$$r(T) = exp(r_c(T)) - 1 \qquad (5.A.3)$$

$$r_c(T) = ln(1+r(T)) \qquad (5.A.4)$$

Since the return relative is a random variable, it follows that both r(T) and $r_c(T)$ are random variables.

The Distribution of P(T), R(0,T), r(T) and r_c(T)

We need to know a little more about the distributional properties of the four random variables we have encountered: P(T), R(0,T), r(T), and $r_c(T)$.

Under the assumptions that the stochastic price-change generating process is stationary and that successive price changes are mutually independent, prices of assets traded in competitive markets should have a lognormal distribution.[1] If so, the return relative should have a lognormal distribution, the effective holding period yield should have a lognormal distribution shifted left by 1.0, and the continuous holding period yield should have a normal distribution.[2]

Although the underlying assumptions cannot be expected to hold precisely in all real world situations, the distributions described might nevertheless be expected to hold reasonably well as first approximations for assets traded in competitive auction-type markets. For long holding periods, this does, generally, seem to be the case.[3] Given this evidence, we will assume that the distributions described hold perfectly across the entire spectrum of possible holding periods and investment horizons.

As random variables with lognormal and normal distributions respectively, r(T) and $r_c(T)$ are each completely described (statistically speaking) by their mean and variance. These two distributions are depicted in Exhibits 5.A.1 and 5.A.2, respectively.

Unfortunately, since the lognormal distribution is asymmetric, it is difficult to use its statistical parameters to estimate confidence intervals or to conduct tests of hypotheses. The solution is to convert the mean and variance of the lognormally distributed r(T), denoted by $\mu(T)$ and $\sigma^2(T)$ respectively, to the statistically equivalent mean and variance of the normally distributed $r_c(T)$, denoted $\mu_c(T)$ and $\sigma_c^2(T)$ respectively. Once so converted, the analysis can be con-

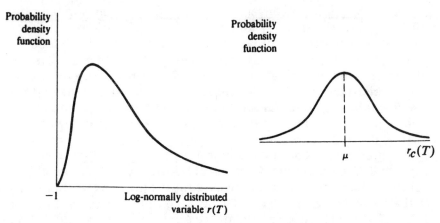

Exhibit 5.2a
The Distribution of r(T) (Log-Normal)

Exhibit5.2b
The Distribution of $r_c(T)$ (Normal)

ducted in terms of $r_c(T)$. In the case of confidence interval estimation, the mean and variance of $r_c(T)$ can be used to find an upper and lower bound for $r_c(T)$ at whatever level of confidence is desired. These can then be transformed back to their effective holding period yield equivalents to provide the confidence interval for the effective holding period yield.

We can move between the mean and variance of r(T) and the mean and variance of $r_c(T)$ by employing the following relationships:[4]

$$\mu_c(T) = 2 \cdot ln\{1 + \mu(T)\} - \tfrac{1}{2} \cdot ln\{\sigma^2(T) + (1 + \mu(T))^2\} \tag{5.A.5}$$

$$\sigma_c{}^2(T) = ln\{1 + (\sigma(T)/(1 + \mu(T)))^2\} \tag{5.A.6}$$

We may move in the opposite direction as follows:

$$\mu(T) = exp\{\mu_c(T) + \tfrac{1}{2} \cdot \sigma_c{}^2(T)\} - 1 \tag{5.A.7}$$

$$\sigma^2(T) = exp\{2 \cdot \mu_c(T) + 2 \cdot \sigma_c{}^2(T)\} - exp\{2 \cdot \mu_c(T) + \sigma_c{}^2(T)\} \tag{5.A.8}$$

It would clearly help to run through a complete example. Suppose that the effective holding period yield for a 5-year investment horizon has been estimated to have a mean of 0.40 and a variance of 0.36 (the standard deviation is therefore 0.60). We would like to estimate the 90% confidence interval for the effective holding period yield.

First, we need to convert $\mu(T)$ and $\sigma^2(T)$ to their normally distributed equivalents $\mu_c(T)$ and $\sigma_c^2(T)$ using Equations 5.A.5 and 5.A.6. The calculations provide the values 0.2522 and 0.1686 for $\mu_c(T)$ and $\sigma_c^2(T)$ respectively. Thus, we conclude that $r_c(T)$ is distributed normally with a mean of 0.2522 and a variance of 0.1686. The standard deviation for this same random variable is then 0.4106. A 90% confidence interval for a normally distributed random variable is given by its mean plus and minus 1.64 standard deviations.[5] That is, the 90% confidence interval is given by $\mu_c(T) \pm 1.64\, \sigma_c(T)$, which produces a continuous holding period yield confidence interval of 0.9256 (upper bound) to -0.4212 (lower bound). To give these values a more intuitive meaning, we must now convert them back to their effective equivalents. This is accomplished using Equation 5.A.3. That is, the upper bound of the effective yield, denoted $r(T)_u$, and the lower bound of the effective yield, denoted $r(T)_l$, are computed as:

$$r(T)_u = exp\,(r_c(T)_u) - 1 \quad \text{and} \quad r(T)_l = exp\,(r_c(T)_l) - 1$$

Thus, the 90% confidence interval for the effective holding period yield has an upper bound of 1.5234 or 152.34% and a lower bound of -0.3437 or -34.37%.

There are a number of other important properties of return measures, but we postpone an examination of these until later.

Endnotes

[1]For a fuller discussion of the lognormality of prices, return relatives, and holding period yields, see Marshall (1989) and Aitichison and Brown (1957).

[2]Ibid.

[3]Granger and Morgenstern (1970) review the empirical evidence through 1970 on the distributional properties of securities prices. Later work confirmed earlier findings for other classes of assets. Specifically, security returns exhibit skewness and leptokurtosis. In most cases, however, these departures from the assumed behaviors are not so serious as to invalidate the lognormal and normal distributions, for effective and continuous returns, respectively, as a first approximation in most cases.

[4]See Aitchison and Brown (1957).

[5]For normal distributions, confidence intervals are symmetrically distributed around the mean. The parameters given are for a 90 percent confidence interval and can be found on normal distribution tables.

References

Aitchison, J. and J.A. Brown. *The Lognormal Distribution,* Cambridge, MA: Cambridge Press, 1957.

Granger, C.W.J. and O. Morgenstern. *Predictability of Stock Market Prices*, Lexington, MA: Heath, 1970.

Marshall, J.F. *Futures and Option Contracting*, Cincinnati, OH: South-Western, 1989.

Chapter 6

Risk: Portfolio Considerations, Investment Horizons, Leverage

John F. Marshall and Kevin J. Wynne

Overview

The financial performance of most firms is affected, to some degree, by changes in one or more financial prices. These prices include interest rates, exchange rates, commodity prices, and stock prices. A firm that employs floating-rate financing or that holds floating-rate assets, for example, will be affected by a change in interest rates. A domestic firm that sells its products in foreign markets will be directly affected by fluctuations in the exchange rate between its currency and that of its foreign market. A firm in the manufacturing sector will be affected by changes in the market prices of its raw materials and/or the prices of its finished goods. An equity mutual fund will be affected by changes in stock prices. And so on. Fluctuations in financial prices are, clearly, a source of significant risks. These risks are called, collectively, price risks.

John F. Marshall is Professor of Finance, Graduate School of Business, St. John's University, New York. Kevin J. Wynne is Associate Professor of Finance, Lubin Schools of Business, Pace University, New York. Parts of this chapter are adapted from the authors' recent work in portfolio theory, Marshall and Wynne (1990a, 1990b).

A firm does not have to be directly involved in a market in which prices are changing to be affected by the changing prices. For example, a retailer may not employ debt financing at all and may hold no rate-sensitive assets. Yet, it may have considerable exposure to interest-rate risk. If the retailer's sales are sensitive to interest rates, then the firm will suffer a loss of sales should interest rates rise. Such a situation is typical of the housing, automobile, and durable goods industries in which buyers often finance their purchases.

As a second example, consider a manufacturer that purchases all of its inputs domestically and sells its output domestically. At first glance, such a firm would not seem to be affected by fluctuations in exchange rates. But, if the firm has foreign competitors that sell their products in the firm's domestic market, then fluctuations in exchange rates will affect the prices of the competitors' products and, through this effect, impact the firm's sales. Similarly, an increase in the price of one commodity can affect the prices of other commodities by shifting demand toward, or away from, those other commodities as consumers try to substitute one commodity for another. Consider, for example, the situation of a livestock producer that feeds its livestock corn. Suppose that a fungus seriously damages wheat crops with the result that wheat prices rise. The livestock producer is not directly affected by the rise in wheat prices. But, as some of the wheat consumers respond to the increase in wheat prices by substituting corn for wheat, the demand for corn increases and corn prices rise. This example serves to highlight the fact that exposure to price risks may be direct or indirect and indirect exposures are just as real, but usually harder to measure, as direct ones.

Most successful firms are adept at dealing with their core business risks. Core business risks involve such things as the choice of technology in production, the method of delivering goods and services to clients, ongoing research and development efforts, etc. But price risks are a type of environmental risk. That is, they are caused by events that occur outside the firm. Manifestations of this risk can wreak havoc on even the best managed and most efficient of producers. For this reason, it is not sufficient to only manage core business risks; price risks must be managed as well.

In this chapter, we consider the source of price risk, the measurement of price risk, and the utility implications of risk. We also introduce portfolio theory and consider how risk behaves as diversification of the portfolio increases. Finally, we consider the implications of the length of the investment horizon on risk. Other aspects of risk measurement and risk management are considered in the next chapter.

Volatility: The Source of Price Risk

Price risk is defined as the potential for a future price to deviate from its expected value. A deviation from an expected price is not necessarily for the worse. Indeed, if expectations are unbiased, beneficial deviations are just as likely as detrimental ones. Nevertheless, we define any deviation from the expected value as a manifestation of price risk. When we want to limit our definition of risk to injurious outcomes, we refer to risk as downside risk. For now, we concentrate on price risk.

The definition of price risk suggests a way to measure it. Since price risk takes the form of deviations from expected values, the more volatile the prices, the more price risk the exposed parties will bear. This volatility can be quantified with the aid of well-defined statistical measures. The most often used of these measures are the variance and the standard deviation. The standard deviation is the square root of the variance and, so, if you know one of these values, you also know the other. Indeed, it has become common practice to equate the terms **volatility** and **standard deviation.** Many financial institutions, for example, use the term **volatility unit** or **vol** to mean one standard deviation.

The definition of price risk also suggests a way to deal with it. Since price risk represents the potential for actual prices to deviate from expectations, one can try to improve the accuracy of the expectations. For example, suppose that we have a series of market forecasts, in the form of forward prices, and a corresponding series of realized prices. Sample values are given in Table 6.1. The forward prices may be viewed as the value expected by the market (expected value).

Table 6.1
Market Forecasts versus Realized Prices

Time	Market Forecast One Period Out	Actual Price One Period Later	Deviation
1	145	152	−7
2	163	158	5
3	156	175	−19
4	164	180	−16
5	188	151	37
		Total	0

Observe first that the deviations sum to zero, which suggests that, on average, the market's forecast is unbiased. But notice also that the market forecast has missed the mark each time, as represented by the individual deviations. Clearly, there is some price risk in relying on the market for one's forecasts. One solution, it would seem, is to make better forecasts than the market.

Beginning in the early 1970s, market prices became progressively more volatile. This was demonstrated in Chapter 2 for exchange rates, interest rates, and commodity prices. The behavior of exchange-rate volatility is repeated in Exhibit 6.1.

Exhibit 6.1
Exchange Rate Volatility
Composite of World Currencies vis-a-vis the Dollar

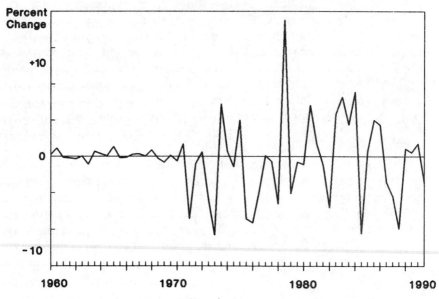

Corporations, banks, and other institutions initially responded to the increased volatility by hiring more economists to forecast prices. This intense utilization of the economics profession led to a spate of advances in forecasting theory and forecasting models. Volatility tapered off somewhat in the mid-1980s but, for most prices, volatility never returned to its pre-1970s level. During much of this period, many assets lacked well-developed forward (futures) markets for comparative market forecasts. As time went on, however, more forward markets were introduced. And, as market forecasts became increasingly available, a frustrating, and at first surprising, picture began to emerge. Market forecasts tended to outperform individual economists' forecasts. This is not to say that individual economists did not sometimes come closer to correctly forecasting the future price but, rather, that they could not do so consistently enough to produce a lower forecast volatility than that produced by the market.

Today there is a well-advanced theory to explain this phenomenon. The theory, called the **efficient markets hypothesis,** holds that the market may be viewed as a great gatherer and channeler of information. Each market participant gathers and processes information but none has a complete picture. That is, each participant possesses a subset of the total relevant information and its importance. By buying and selling, the individual market participants register their private forecasts in the market and channel their private information into the market price. Through this process, the market price comes to reflect *all* available information. The collective wisdom embodied in the market then produces a better forecast than that which can be produced by any individual economic prognosticator.

The upshot is that forecasting, regardless of the individual forecaster's talents, is not a solution in and of itself to the price-risk problem. If price risk cannot be eliminated by forecasting, then the only remaining solution is to manage the price risk. This is the strategy that has emerged as advances in theory, development of new instruments, and technological improvements converged to make risk management practical and cost effective. The development of risk management theory and techniques has, as one might expect, been accompanied by a cutback in the number of economists employed by industry and a dramatic increase in the demand for experienced risk managers.

Expressing Price Risk In Percent Form

As already noted, price risk is most often measured with the aid of a well-understood statistic called standard deviation. We will, for the present, work in terms of the square of this value called the variance. In order to compute the variance of a price, we need a series of observations on the price in question. Consider the series of observations on the price of copper that appears below in Table 6.2. Notice that the price of copper has been trending higher as these observations were being made.

Table 6.2
Copper Price Series

Observation	Copper Price (cents per pound)
1	49.65
2	49.85
3	49.70
4	51.25
5	51.10
6	53.30
7	54.20
8	55.10
9	54.90
10	55.65

There is a serious problem, however, with using the variance of price in analytical work. The problem is that "raw" price series are usually not stationary. This means that the mean and the variance are changing as the price level changes. What is more, we are really less interested in the variance of price than we are in the variance of price changes. Unfortunately, the series of price changes is often not stationary either. The simplest way to correct this problem is to re-express the price change series as a return series. We do this using the approach discussed in the last chapter. You will recall that we can express the periodic returns as effective holding period yields or as holding period yields continuously compounded. Once we have one, we can easily convert it to the other. For now, we will convert the price series to effective holding period yields. This is done by dividing each successive observation by the preceding observation and deducting 1. The calculation of the return for period t, denoted $r(t)$, is given by Equation 6.1 and the return series itself appears in Table 6.3.

$$r(t) = \frac{\text{Price}(t+1)}{\text{Price}(t)} - 1$$

(6.1)

Table 6.3
Copper Price and Return Series

Observation	Copper Price (cents per pound)	Return Series (percentages)
1	49.65	0.4028
2	49.85	−0.3009
3	49.70	3.1187
4	51.25	−0.2927
5	51.10	4.3053
6	53.30	1.6886
7	54.20	1.6605
8	55.10	−0.3630
9	54.90	1.3661
10	55.65	—

A return series has several advantages over a price series for analytical purposes. First, by converting the price series to a percentage return series, we make different price series more directly comparable. Second, the return series is more stable in the sense that its mean and variance are more likely to be stationary than the mean and the variance of the raw price series. This is not to imply that a return series is necessarily a statistically stable series. Indeed, numerous empirical studies dating back to the 1960s have shown that return series for assets traded in competitive markets exhibit deviations from the kind of stable distributions we like to work with in statistics.[1] On the other hand, the deviations are *usually* not so significant as to invalidate the results of analysis conducted under the assumption of distributional stability. Furthermore, when treated in the context of a diversified portfolio, the deviations from stable distributions are further mitigated.

The computation of the mean and variance of the return series in Table 6.3 is straightforward. In the case of the mean, we simply sum the return observations and divide by the number of observations. The variance is a little more complicated. For this calculation, we first subtract the previously computed mean from each of the individual observations in the return series. We then individually square each of the resultant differences. We then sum these squared values and divide the sum by the number of observations less one. These calculations are given in Equation 6.2 and 6.3 respectively.

$$\mu = \frac{\Sigma\, r(t)}{n} \tag{6.2}$$

$$\sigma^2 = \frac{\Sigma\, (r(t) - \mu)^2}{n-1} \tag{6.3}$$

The statistics generated using Equations 6.2 and 6.3 represent a **sample mean** and a **sample variance**, denoted here by μ (mu) and σ^2 (sigma squared) respectively. That is, they are not necessarily the true mean and the true variance for the entire population from which the ten observations were drawn. If the returns series is stationary, then the larger the number of observations from which the sample mean and the sample variance are generated, the more likely that the sample values will be very close to the true population values. This suggests that the accuracy of empirical results can be enhanced by using larger series—a fact not lost on the quant jocks. No one calculates means or variances manually anymore except when working with very small sample sizes. For this purpose, most people use a spreadsheet, a statistical software package, or a pre-programmed calculator.[2]

One final point on variance. Once we have obtained the variance by the calculation above, we then take its square root to get the sample standard deviation. The sample standard deviation is then used in most subsequent analysis. In the case above, the mean, variance, and standard deviation (all expressed in percentage form) are 1.2872, 2.3659, and 1.5382, respectively.

In the last chapter, we looked at return under the assumption that the cash flows associated with an investment are known with certainty. While that is the case for some cash flow sources—such as fixed-income securities held to maturity—it is not the case for all cash flow sources. More often than not, investments, including the production of goods to be sold in competitive markets, give rise to returns that are risky. Consequently, it has become common practice in financial work to use the term **return** or **expected return** to mean the **mean percentage return** associated with a position and to use the term **risk** to mean the **standard deviation of the percentage return** associated with a position. It is also standard practice to express these returns on a period of one year, irrespective of the actual holding period. When this is done, it is appropriate to refer to the expected return as the **mean rate of return** and to refer to the risk measure as the **standard deviation of the rate of return**. As we will argue shortly, however, this treatment may not be appropriate if the investment horizon is longer or shorter than one year.

The Mathematics of Portfolio Analysis

In the discussion that follows, we do not necessarily define the holding period to be one year in length and so we avoid referring to return as an annual rate of return. All returns are understood to be percentage returns. Nevertheless, we do assume the returns are single-period—we are just not specific as to the length of that single period. For the time being, we assume away the existence of a riskless asset.

A portfolio is simply a collection of assets. Each asset in the portfolio has an associated mean return and an associated variance of return. In addition, for each pair of returns, there is an associated correlation coefficient. The correlation coefficient of returns measures the degree of linear correlation between the two returns. The correlation coefficient must lie in the range of +1 and -1. At either extreme we have perfect correlation. When we have perfect correlation, the fluctuations in one asset's return are perfectly predictable in terms of the fluctuations in the other asset's return. When the correlation is +1, the returns are said to be perfectly positively correlated and when the correlation is -1, the returns are said to be perfectly negatively correlated. Of course, all asset returns are perfectly positively correlated with themselves.

When the correlation of returns is between the values +1 and -1, we say that the returns are less than perfectly correlated. At the midpoint between the extreme values, where the correlation is zero, we say the returns are uncorrelated.

In order to distinguish between the different assets in a portfolio, we need to add appropriate subscripts to our notation and we need to add notation for the correlation coefficient. We denote the percentage return on asset i by r_i, the mean of r_i by μ_i, and the variance of r_i by σ_i^2. We will denote the correlation between the returns on asset i and asset j by $\int_{i,j}$ (rho).

As with means and variances, correlation coefficients are calculated with the aid of spreadsheets, statistical software, and pre-programmed calculators. To calculate a correlation coefficient, we must first calculate the covariance between the two returns. The covariance between the return on asset i and asset j is denoted by $\sigma_{i,j}$. The calculation of $\sigma_{i,j}$ is given by Equation 6.4 and the correlation coefficient is computed from the covariance and the standard deviations by Equation 6.5.

$$\sigma_{i,j} = \frac{\Sigma(r_i(t) - \mu_i) \cdot (r_j(t) - \mu_j)}{n-1} \tag{6.4}$$

$$\Gamma_{i,j} = \frac{\sigma_{i,j}}{\sigma_i \cdot \sigma_j} \tag{6.5}$$

We now possess all of the statistical tools necessary to generate the mean percentage return and the variance of the percentage return for a portfolio of assets. We will denote the portfolio return by r_p, the mean portfolio return by μ_p, and the variance of portfolio return by σ_p^2. The only remaining decision to make is to how to weight the different assets that are to be included in the portfolio. We will denote the weight on asset i by w_i and we will assume that there are n assets included in the portfolio. The weights we use must sum to 1 (100%). (If the weights sum to anything less than 1, it implies that we are allowing some wealth to sit idle.) The portfolio values are related to the individual return parameters (means, variances, and correlation coefficients) by Equations 6.6, 6.7, and 6.8, respectively.[3]

$$r_p = \Sigma w_i \cdot r_i \tag{6.6}$$

$$\mu_p = \Sigma w_i \cdot \mu_i \tag{6.7}$$

$$\sigma_p^2 = \sum_i^n \sum_j^n w_i \cdot w_j \cdot \sigma_i \cdot \sigma_j \cdot \Gamma_{i,j} \tag{6.8}$$

The portfolio return r_p and the portfolio mean return μ_p are easily understood. Both are weighted averages of the corresponding individual asset values. The variance of return σ_p^2 is considerably more complex. It is the sum of a series of products (each of which involves five terms). The first two terms in the product are the respective weights, the second two terms are the standard deviations, and the last term is the correlation coefficient. These products are calculated for each combination of i and j. In total, there will be $n \times n$ or n^2 such products in the final summation.

Equation 6.8 can be simplified and the number of calculations involved reduced by recognizing two things. First, when i and j are the same, then the term $w_i \cdot w_j \cdot \sigma_i \cdot \sigma_j \cdot \Gamma_{i,j}$ reduces to $w_i^2 \cdot \sigma_i^2$. This is so because the correlation of any return with itself is, by definition, 1.

Second, when i and j are different, the terms $w_i \cdot w_j \cdot \sigma_i \cdot \sigma_j \cdot \Gamma_{i,j}$ and $w_j \cdot w_i \cdot \sigma_j \cdot \sigma_i \cdot \Gamma_{j,i}$ are identical and need only be included once if we simply double their value at the end. Employing these two relationships, we can re-write Equation 6.8 as Equation 6.9.

$$\sigma_p{}^2 = \sum_i^n w_i{}^2 \cdot \sigma_i{}^2 + 2 \cdot \sum_{i>j}^n \sum^n w_i \cdot w_j \cdot \sigma_i \cdot \sigma_j \cdot \Gamma_{i,j} \qquad (6.9)$$

$$(1) \qquad\qquad\qquad (2)$$

While the two different ways of representing portfolio variance will produce identical values, there is a distinct advantage to using Equation 6.9. By decomposing the variance in this fashion, we can more easily see that portfolio risk consists of two distinct parts. The first, labeled (1), is the risk associated with the individual variance terms alone. This risk is called unsystematic risk (sometimes called specific risk). The second component of risk, labeled (2), is the risk associated with the correlations between the returns on the assets included in the portfolio. This risk is often called systematic risk (sometimes called market risk).

The importance of distinguishing between unsystematic and systematic forms of risk is that these two types of risk behave very differently as the number of assets included in the portfolio gets larger. Assuming that the different assets included in the portfolio are weighted approximately equally, $w_i = 1/n$, then, as the portfolio gets larger, the unsystematic risk gets progressively smaller (in the language of statistics, we say that it asymptotically approaches zero). The behavior of unsystematic risk is depicted in the Exhibit 6.2.

Systematic risk, on the other hand, behaves quite differently. As the number of assets included in the portfolio gets larger, the systematic risk converges to the average of all the covariances for all pairs of assets included in the portfolio. The behavior of the systematic component of risk as the number of assets included in the portfolio gets larger is depicted in Exhibit 6.3.

The unsystematic and systematic behaviors must, of course, be combined to fully appreciate the consequences of diversification on total portfolio risk. This is depicted in Exhibit 6.4. Notice that the decline in the unsystematic component of risk outweighs the increase in the systematic component (provided that at least some of the correlation coefficients are not +1).

The behaviors of unsystematic and systematic risk highlight a number of salient points. First, as long as asset returns are not perfectly

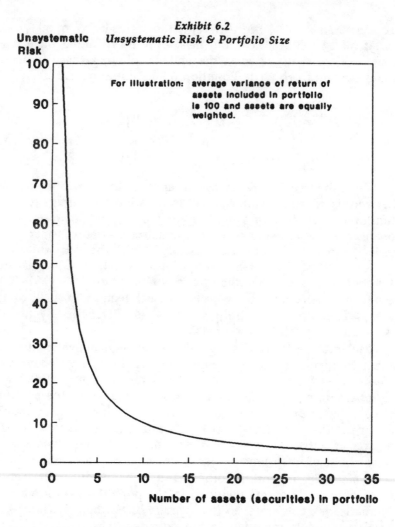

Exhibit 6.2
Unsystematic   *Unsystematic Risk & Portfolio Size*
Risk

positively correlated, diversification of a portfolio reduces the portfolio's variance (risk) without any concommitant reduction in the mean return. (This, together with the risk-averse nature of investors, explains why diversifiaction has been called the "only free lunch in economics.") Second, in a well-diversified portfolio, unsystematic risk can be discarded because it tends to zero anyway. The key here is the phrase "well-diversified." There is considerable disagreement as to how many assets it takes for a portfolio to be well-diversified. Some analysts are happy with 15 while others require at least 60. The general rule of thumb is 30. Finally, since

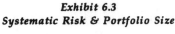

Exhibit 6.3
Systematic Risk & Portfolio Size

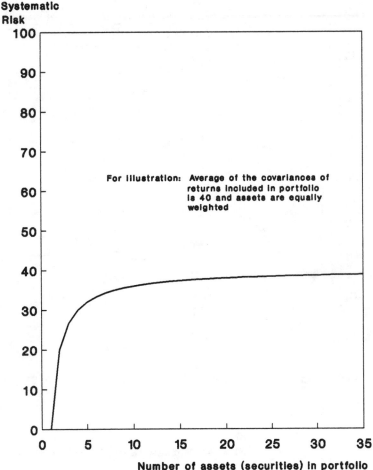

Number of assets (securities) in portfolio

systematic risk does not disappear with diversification, it must be dealt with and managed. Fortunately, extensions of portfolio theory have made this a relatively simple matter—at least in the case of stock portfolios.

The portfolio theory we have elucidated above is at the heart of many of the activities of financial engineers. For example, it is the foundation on which the capital asset pricing model (CAPM) was built. This model of stock price behavior is a very useful one for determining the fair return that should be provided by a security

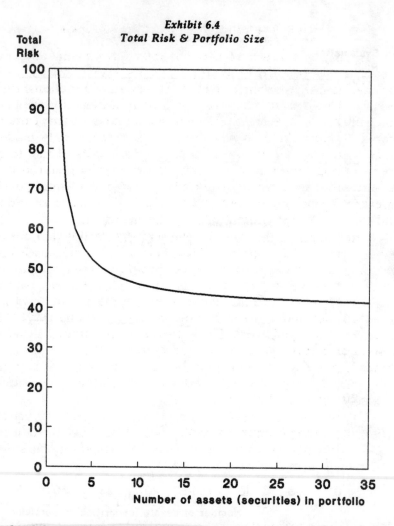

Exhibit 6.4
Total Risk & Portfolio Size

based solely on that security's contribution to a portfolio's systematic risk. It is also the heart and soul of hedging theory. A **hedge,** is a position taken to offset the price risk associated with some other position (called the cash position). A hedge is only effective to the degree that the returns on the hedging instrument and the returns on the cash position are correlated. The more highly correlated are these returns (whether positive or negative), the more effective will be the hedge. (This application of portfolio theory is considered in more detail in the next chapter.)

Risk Aversion and Portfolio Analysis

In Chapter 4, it was argued that an important tenet of financial theory is that rational individuals are risk averse. That is to say, rational people (those with well-behaved utility functions) dislike risk. But, we also said that not all individuals are equally risk averse. Some are very risk averse and unwilling to bear even small amounts of risk to earn above average returns. Others are only modestly risk averse and are willing to bear large amounts of risk to earn above average returns. We refer to the former as financially conservative and the latter as financial aggressive. We would now like to examine this willingness to bear risk a little more analytically and to do so in the context of portfolio theory.

First, suppose that we plot the set of portfolios that, for each level of return, have the least risk. This set of portfolios is called the minimum variance set. It can be shown that the minimum variance set of portfolios has a quadratic form and graphs as a parabola. The efficent set of portfolios is that subset of the minimum variance set which lies above the minimum variance portfolio (MVP). This is depicted in Exhibit 6.5. These portfolios are plotted in what is called **risk/return space** (with mean return on the vertical axis and standard deviation of return on the horizontal axis). At any given point in time, the prevailing efficient set of portfolios may be viewed as a given state of the world.

Suppose we employ the quadratic equation given by Equation 6.10 and only focus on those portfolios that lie above the minimum variance portfolio in order to map a typical efficient set. The efficient set is depicted in Exhibit 6.6.

$$\sigma_p{}^2 = 0.01 - 0.2 \cdot \mu_p + 2 \cdot \mu_p{}^2 \qquad (6.10)$$

Any well-behaved utility function will give rise to indifference curves that look similar to those depicted in Exhibit 6.7. An indifference curve is a set of risk/return combination that provide exactly the same utility. Thus, the risk/return combination associated with Portfolio A and the risk/return combination associated with Portfolio B provide the same amount of satisfaction (utility) because they lie along the same indifference curve. Notice that while Portfolio B is more risky than Portfolio A, the loss in utility from the greater risk is compensated for by the greater return. The full set of indifference curves that describes an individual's utility function is called an indifference map. Notice that utility increases as the

Exhibit 6.5
Minimum Variance Set

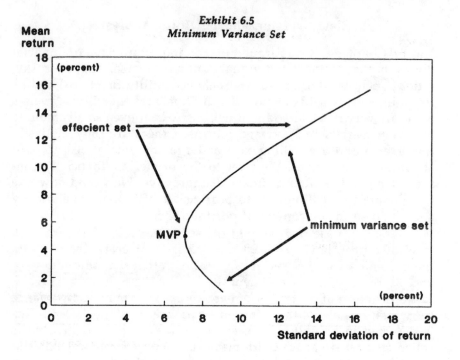

Exhibit 6.6
Efficient Set of Portfolios

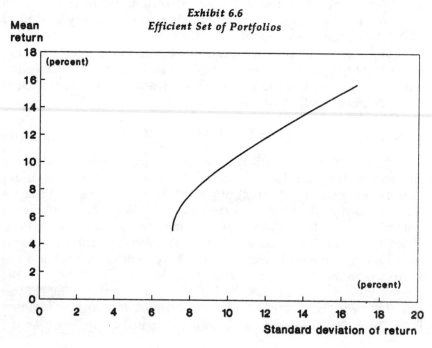

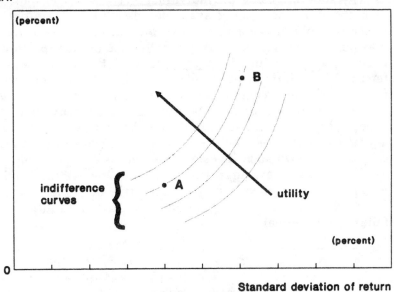

Exhibit 6.7
The Investor's Indifference Map

Exhibit 6.8
The Investor's Optimal Portfolio

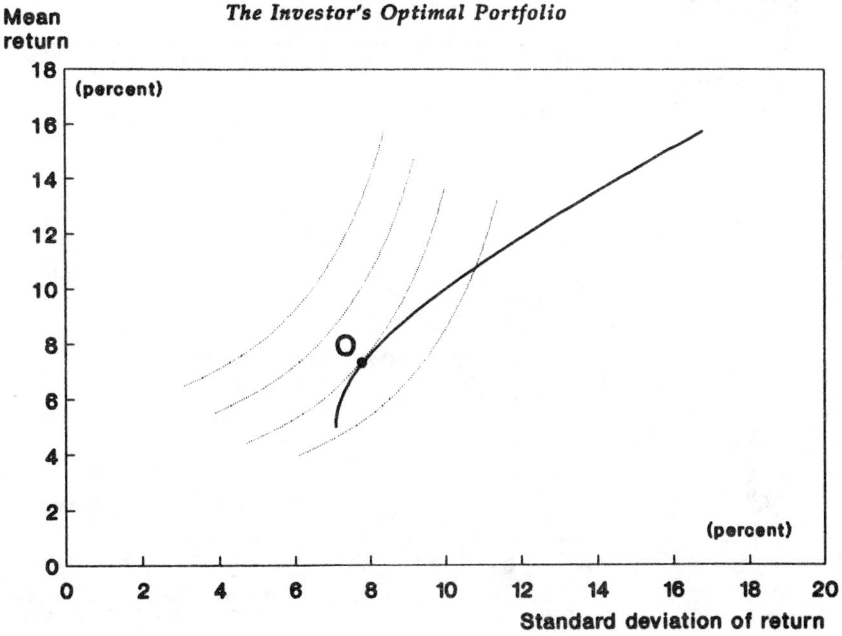

investor moves from one indifference curve to the next in a North-westerly direction.

By superimposing the individual's very personal indifference map on the efficient set of available portfolios, we can determine which portfolio maximizes the investor's utility. The portfolio that maximizes the investor's utility is called the optimal portfolio and it occurs at the point of tangency between the individual's indifference map and the efficient set of portfolios. The optimal portfolio found by this approach is depicted in Exhibit 6.8 as Portfolio O.

The analysis above can be used to explain why some people choose very conservative portfolios and other people choose very aggressive portfolios. The answer lies in the slope of their indifference curves. Two such investors are contrasted in Exhibit 6.9. Investor 1 picks a very aggressive portfolio (high return, high risk) while Investor 2 picks a very conservative portfolio (low return, low risk). Both are behaving rationally yet they find different portfolios to be optimal.

Exhibit 6.9
Comparative Optimal Portfolios

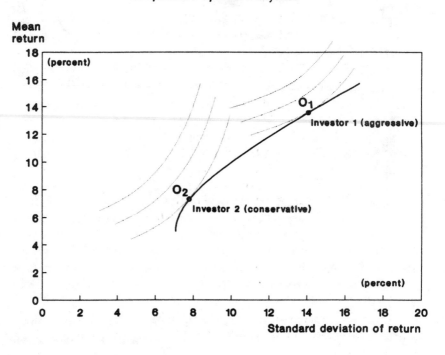

Role of the Investment Horizon (The Time Dimension)

To this point, we have assumed that the portfolio is held for a single period. We will now relax that assumption in order to add a multi-period dimension to portfolio analysis. This added dimension is necessary to understand how an investor's optimal portfolio can be expected to change as the investor's investment horizon grows shorter. There is one complication, the quadratic utility function, that we employed to generate indifference curves is a single-period approach and is not easily extended to a multi-period context. We get around this problem by employing an optimization criteria which we call drawdown. Drawdown criteria has been shown to be consistent with the way investors actually choose their portfolios and it is consistent with utility criteria.

Financial theorists and practitioners have largely ignored the importance of the length of the investment horizon when engaging in portfolio analysis and when making portfolio selections. Ignoring the length of the investment horizon, however, is only appropriate if either (1) the optimal portfolio is independent of the length of the investment horizon, or (2) all investors share a common horizon and this horizon exactly coincides with the span of time over which returns are defined. The second of these possibilities is easily ruled out on the face of it. The first is more difficult to reject but it can nevertheless be rejected.

In this section, we demonstrate that the level of risk associated with a given portfolio is not the same for all investors. That is, different investors considering the same portfolio will perceive different degrees of risk. This difference in perceptions is not an illusion but rather a function of the relationship between the riskiness of the portfolio and the length of the investor's horizon. In general, the longer an investor's horizon, the less risky is a given single-period portfolio. Thus, all other things being equal, a long-horizon investor will appear to be more risk tolerant than a short-horizon investor. Risk is then largely a matter of perception and perception is a function of the length of the investment horizon. (The use of the term *perception* is not meant to imply "unreal." Rather, it is meant to connote the fact that different people looking at the same thing can and will see it differently, but all views are nevertheless very real.)

In order to appreciate the importance of the length of the investment horizon and how utility-maximizing investors can be expected to behave as their horizons change, we need to examine the mathematics of multi-period portfolio analysis. We could simplify the presentation by conducting our analysis in terms of continuous returns, but this would depart from our earlier treatment of the return parameters (mean and variance) and it would alter the nature of the statistical distributions. For these reasons, we will make our presentation using effective returns.

Elements of a Multi-Period Model

We assume that time is broken into discrete periods of equal length. We call these single-periods. A length-T investment horizon is one which involves T successive nonoverlapping single-periods. The length of the horizon may be regarded as the time to the planned use of investment proceeds for consumption purposes. We will denote the length-T return relative, i.e., ending period wealth relative to beginning period wealth, by R(T). We assume the single-period return relatives are lognormally distributed and that the distributions of successive return relatives are stationary and mutually independent, or, at least, are perceived as such by the investor. We denote the mean and variance of the length-T return relative by $\mu_R(T)$ and $\sigma_R^2(T)$, respectively.

We denote the effective length-T return by r(T). We denote the mean and variance of r(T) by $\mu(T)$ and $\sigma^2(T)$ respectively. The multi-period return parameters are related to the single-period return parameters by Equations 6.11 and 6.12.[4]

$$\mu_R(T) = \mu_R(1)^T \text{ and } \mu(T) = \mu_R(T) - 1 \tag{6.11}$$

$$\sigma^2(T) = \sigma_R^2(T) = [\mu_R(1)^2 + \sigma^2(1)]^T - \mu_R(1)^{2T} \tag{6.12}$$

The single-period portfolio parameters are given by Equations 6.13 and 6.14. These are expressed here in terms of return relatives rather than the more customary effective rates of return.

$$\mu_{R,p}(1) = \Sigma w_i \mu_{R,i}(1) \tag{6.13}$$

$$\sigma_p^2(1) = \Sigma \Sigma w_i \cdot w_j \cdot \sigma_i(1) \cdot \sigma_j(1) \cdot f_{i,j} \tag{6.14}$$

The multi-period portfolio parameters are obtained from the single-period portfolio parameters by combining Equations 6.11 and 6.13 to get portfolio return and by combining Equations 6.12 and 6.14 to get portfolio variance. How we combine these equations however, depends on whether or not we assume periodic rebalancing.

Since different assets provide different returns, the weighting scheme selected for the portfolio will change of its own volition. Rebalancing implies periodic adjustment of the portfolio to re-establish the original weighting scheme. We assume that the original portfolio weighting scheme is re-established at the beginning of each new single period. Under this assumption, the multi-period return parameters are given by Equations 6.15 and 6.16.

$$\mu_{R,p}(T) = \mu_{R,p}(1)^T \tag{6.15}$$

$$\sigma_p^2(T) = [\mu_{R,p}^2(1) + \sigma_p^2(1)]^T - \mu_{R,p}(1)^{2T} \tag{6.16}$$

The rebalancing assumption assures the stationarity and mutual independence of the portfolio return relatives across all single-periods. This, in turn, assures that the multi-period portfolio return relative has an approximately lognormal distribution as perceived at the time of initial portfolio selection.[5]

The Multi-Period Efficient Set

The single-period minimum variance set of risky market portfolios is identical to the multi-period minimum variance set under the assumptions already made irrespective of the length of the investment horizon. All portfolios which are efficient for a single-period investment horizon are efficient for a multi-period investment horizon. Additionally, some portfolios that are single-period inefficient (but still on the single-period minimum variance set) can be multi-period efficient.

In order to have a fully specified function to illustrate the concepts which follow, consider an efficient set of portfolios in which portfolio variance and expected portfolio return are related as in Equation 6.17.

$$\sigma_p^2(1) = .03 - 0.625 \cdot \mu_p(1) + 5 \cdot \mu_p(1)^2 \tag{6.17}$$

Selected values from the single-period minimum variance set (in terms of the standard deviation of return) together with the corresponding portfolio values for the five-period minimum variance set appear in Table 6.4. The portfolios which are efficient are marked by an asterisk. The five-period values were generated using Equations 6.15 and 6.16.

Table 6.4
Minimum Variance Portfolios

Portfolio	Single-Period		Five-Period	
	$\mu_p(1)$	$\sigma_p(1)$	$\sigma_p(5)$	$\mu_p(5)$
1	0.000	0.173	0.000	0.399
2	0.010	0.156	0.051	0.371
3	0.040	0.114	0.217	0.302
4	0.050	0.106	0.276	0.291
5	0.055	0.104	0.307	0.290*
6	0.060	0.102	0.338	0.292*
7	0.065	0.102*	0.370	0.298*
8	0.070	0.104*	0.403	0.307*
9	0.200	0.324*	1.488	1.616*
10	0.265	0.464*	2.239	3.040*

We can see that while Portfolios 5 and 6 are not single-period efficient they are five-period efficient. As the investment horizon becomes longer, more of the single-period minimum variance portfolios become multiperiod efficient. The full single-period efficient set of portfolios is depicted in Exhibit 6.10.

Exhibit 6.10
Single-Period Minimum Variance Set and Efficient Set

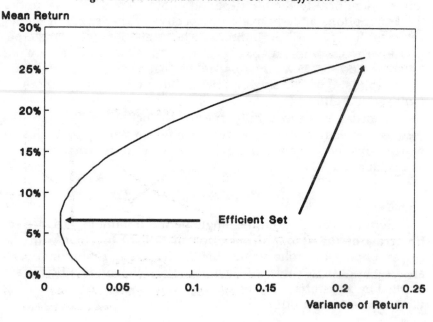

An Intuitive Demonstration of the Importance of the Investment Horizon

Suppose that the optimal portfolio for an investor with a single-period investment horizon is Portfolio 7 in Table 6.4. This portfolio has a single-period mean return of 6.5 percent and a single-period standard deviation of 10.2 percent. Now compare Portfolio 7 to Portfolio 10, which has a single-period mean return of 26.5 percent and a standard deviation of 46.4 percent.

Next, suppose we compute the 90 percent confidence interval of return outcomes for both Portfolios 7 and 10 over a continuum of investment horizons from zero to 50 periods. The confidence interval when measured over a continuum of investment horizons has been called a **confidence channel.**[6] Selected values for both portfolios are reported in Table 6.5. The confidence channel for Portfolio 7 is depicted in Exhibit 6.11.

Exhibit 6.11
Confidence Channel: Upper Bound, Mean, Lower Bound

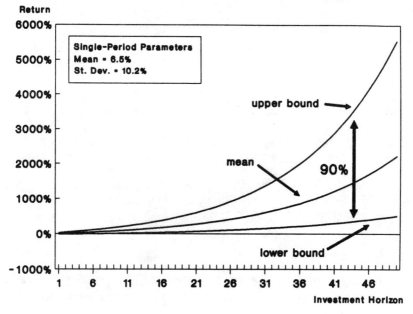

Consider the worst case scenario (lower bound for each port-folio) in Table 6.5. While the lower bound for the more risky Portfolio 10 is a worse result than the lower bound for the less risky Portfolio 7 for an investment horizon of length 14 or less, the lower bounds are equal somewhere between horizons of lengths 14 and 15. At any investment horizon of length 15 or more, the worst case scenario of the more risky Portfolio 10 is preferable to the worst case scenario of less risky Portfolio 7. It would appear that any rational risk-averse investor could be expected to show an increasing preference for riskier Portfolio 10 the longer was his or her investment horizon.

Table 6.5
Confidence Channel: 90%

$\mu_p(1) = 6.5\%$ $\sigma_p(1) = 10.2\%$ $\mu_p(1) = 26.5\%$ $\sigma_p(1) = 46.4\%$

(Portfolio 7)   (Portfolio 10)

Investment Horizon	Upper Bound	Mean	Lower Bound	Upper Bound	Mean	Lower Bound
1	0.241	0.065	−0.095*	1.132	0.265	−0.339
2	0.405	0.134	−0.101*	2.226	0.600	−0.384
3	0.566	0.208	−0.094*	3.614	1.024	−0.393
4	0.732	0.286	−0.079*	5.409	1.561	−0.383
5	0.906	0.370	−0.059*	7.738	2.239	−0.362
6	1.090	0.459	−0.036*	10.756	3.098	−0.332
14	3.088	1.415	0.254*	97.973	25.870	0.239
15	3.424	1.572	0.302	125.911	32.991	0.363*
16	3.785	1.739	0.353	161.324	41.998	0.502*
42	31.291	13.083	3.171	60326.766	19399.015	29.589*
43	33.649	13.998	3.368	74921.266	24540.019	33.727*
44	36.174	14.973	3.575	92998.184	31043.389	38.445*
45	38.878	16.011	3.793	115378.748	39270.153	43.826*
49	51.740	20.884	4.781	272076.275	100561.428	74.117*
50	55.541	22.307	5.060	336785.533	127210.471	84.559*

This example suggests that investors should show an increasing preference for less risky single-period portfolios as their horizons shorten and confirms the conclusions of a number of empirical studies.[7]

Drawdown Criterion

The intuitive demonstration of the role played by the invest-ment horizon in the preceding section suggests a very practical approach to building a more formal model of portfolio optimization in a multi-period context. The approach hinges on a selection criterion which has been called **drawdown criterion.**[8]

Drawdown criterion is a logical extension of the notion of a confidence channel. The lower bound of a confidence channel, as that term has been defined above, represents the maximum drawdown, as a percentage of initial investment capital, that might occur and the temporal frame within which this drawdown might occur for a specified level of confidence. This level of confidence is translated to a level of significance by recognizing that drawdown criterion focuses on downside risk only. Thus, the lower bound of a 90 percent level of confidence translates to a drawdown curve at a 5 percent level of significance. *In drawdown criterion, we define the optimal single-period portfolio as that portfolio which, if repeated each period for the entire investment horizon, maximizes expected return subject to the specified acceptable drawdown (loss) of initial investment capital at the terminal point of the investment horizon.* As noted earlier, this criterion is more consistent with the way people actually seem to think about risk/return trade-offs than is the more generally accepted but very abstract utility criterion.[9]

While the mathematics of drawdown criterion is a bit complex because of the lognormality of portfolio return, the methodology readily lends itself to an iterative computer solution. A quadratic programming approach is first used to isolate the single-period efficient set. Using the multi-period equations discussed earlier, the single period efficient set is then used to generate the multi-period efficient set. Finally, by wrapping a binomial search algorithm around the multi-period efficient set, the optimal multi-period portfolio can be found for any given set of drawdown parameters. We then look back to the single-period efficient set to identify the single-period portfolio which, if held for T successive periods, gives rise to the optimal multi-period portfolio. This portfolio is then the optimal single-period portfolio for the length-T investment horizon. The drawdown criterion parameters are 1) the length of the investor's horizon (a state variable), 2) the maximum acceptable drawdown as a percent of initial investment capital, and 3) the investor-specified level of significance.

The Optimal Portfolio in the Absence of a Riskless Asset

In this section, we apply the drawdown selection criterion to see how the optimal single-period portfolio changes as the investment horizon grows shorter. We assume that there is no risk-free asset available and that the optimization criterion does not change as time passes. We continue with the parameter values already selected. Since the criterion is defined to hold *perceived* risk constant (maximum acceptable loss of 10 percent of investment capital at a 5 percent level of significance), any change in portfolio selection must represent a change in risk perception.

Using the approach described in the preceding section, we obtain the optimal single-period portfolios for the minimum variance set given by Equation 6.17 and the drawdown parameters specified earlier. The optimal single-period portfolios for the same investor for 5-period, 4-period, 3-period, 2-period, and 1-period horizons are summarized in Table 6.6 and the optimal portfolios are depicted in single-period risk/return space in Exhibit 6.12. (Note that in Exhibit 6.12 risk is measured in terms of portfolio variance rather than standard deviation.)

Table 6.6
Optimal Single-Period Portfolios

Horizon Length	Mean	Variance	Standard Deviation
5	15.5%	0.05327	23.08%
4	13.5%	0.03675	19.17%
3	12.0%	0.02689	16.40%
2	10.5%	0.01949	13.96%
1	9.5%	0.01575	12.55%

The table and the exhibit make it quite clear that as time passes and the investor's horizon grows shorter, the investor will find it desirable to move from a more risky (more aggressive) single-period portfolio to a less risky (more conservative) single-period portfolio. Casual observation of such behavior has long led financial planners to believe that investors tend to become more risk averse as they age. This, however, is not necessarily a correct interpretation. Our investor, for example, *did not* become more risk averse. Indeed, his criterion for optimal portfolio selection never changed at all. Nevertheless, he *was* observed to select progressively less risky portfolios. This leads us to conclude that the investor's perception of the riskiness of any given single-period portfolio changes, and correctly so, as his or her horizon grows shorter. This is not to say that investors do not become more risk averse with age, only that it is *not necessary* for an investor to become more risk averse to observe

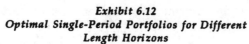

Exhibit 6.12
Optimal Single-Period Portfolios for Different
Length Horizons

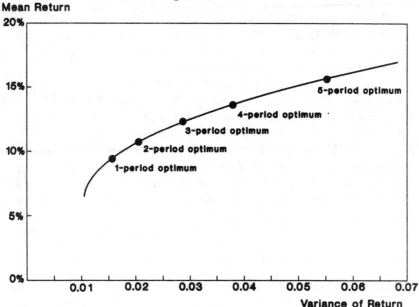

a gradual shift from more to less risky portfolios with the passage of time.

The Riskless Asset

All of the portfolio analysis we have considered thus far has assumed away the existence of a riskless asset. In the absence of a riskless asset, the efficient set of portfolios has a concave shape when drawn in a standard risk/return space. If all investors share the same investment horizon, then the existence of a riskless asset changes the shape of the efficient set. The concave efficient set becomes linear. The reason is simple. The presence of the riskless asset affords investors the opportunity to formulate portfolios consisting of a diversified portfolio of risky assets and the risk-free asset. The diversified portfolio of risky assets is called the **market portfolio.** The new portfolio problem then becomes one of choosing the appropriate combination of the market portfolio and the risk-free asset. This is depicted in Exhibit 6.13.

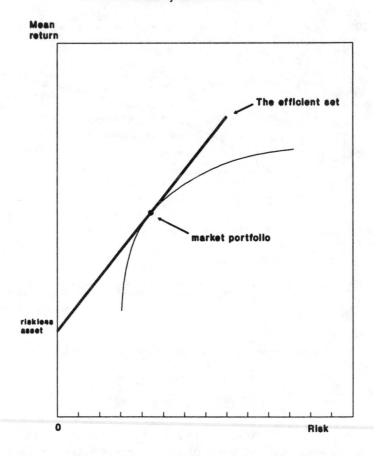

Exhibit 6.13
*The Efficient Set of Portfolios
In the Presence of a Riskless Asset*

The linearity of the efficient set under the existence of a risk-free asset led to advances in portfolio theory and the emergence of the capital asset pricing model (CAPM).[10] In that very useful model, the required return on a security is a function of the systematic risk associated with the security, the expected return on the market portfolio (denoted below by r_m), and the rate of return on the risk-free asset (denoted below by r_{rf}). While not perfect, the model has proven to provide good forecasts of actual portfolio returns and is widely used by financial practitioners. The key ingredient is the measure of systematic risk. Systematic risk is measured using what is called a **beta coefficient** (denoted by β). The actual model is given by Equation 6.18. In Equation 6.18, the required rate of return on Security X (denoted r_x) is determined with the aid of the beta coefficient on Security X (denoted β_x).

$$r_x = (r_m - r_{rf}) \cdot \beta_x + r_{rf} \qquad mx + b \qquad (6.18)$$

Beta coefficients can be estimated several different ways with nearly identical results. The most widely used approach is to run a simple linear regression. In regression analysis, we employ historical data to obtain the best possible estimate of the linear relationship between two or more variables. To generate the beta coefficient for Security X, we would regress the excess rate of return on Security X against the excess rate of return on the market as a whole. An excess rate of return is simply the difference between the return on the asset (or market) and the risk-free rate of return for the same period. The beta coefficient is then the slope of the regression line. This is depicted in Exhibit 6.14.

Exhibit 6.14
Estimating Beta Coefficients via Regression Analysis

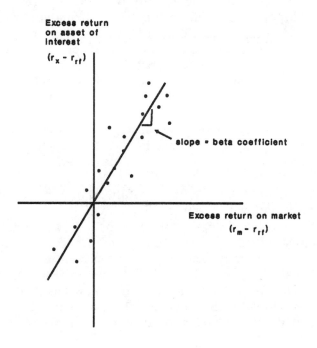

To generate a beta coefficient, one needs a proxy for the "market." This is generally taken to be one of the popular stock indexes. Most often it is the Standard & Poor's Index of 500 stocks (S&P 500). The beta coefficient can also be shown to be equal to the ratio of the covariance of the return on the security in question and the return on the market as a whole (denoted here by $\sigma_{x,m}$) to the variance of the return on the market as a whole (denoted here as σ_m^2). That is, the beta coefficient for Security X is given by Equation 6.19.

$$\beta_x = \frac{\sigma_{x,m}}{\sigma_m^2}$$

(6.19)

We can estimate the beta coefficients of the individual securities to be included in a portfolio or we can measure the beta coefficient for the portfolio as a whole. The portfolio beta (denoted β_p) is related to the individual security betas (denoted β_i, for security i) by Equation 6.20.

$$\beta_p = \Sigma \, w_i \cdot \beta_i$$

(6.20)

There are two problems with the analysis we have been describing. The first is that the validity of the CAPM rests, in part, on the assumption that all investor's share a common investment horizon. This is, of course, blatantly untrue. The second is that no market proxy is capable of capturing all possible investment assets. We typically use a U.S. stock index as the proxy because we are most often interested in the return on a U.S. stock. But, the true universe of investment assets includes a great many things besides stocks. For example, the investor can also purchase bonds, commodities, currencies, foreign securities, real estate, collectibles, and so on. No one, however, has yet managed to devise a "market" portfolio that encompasses all possible classes of investment assets.

While the limitations on the usefulness of a stock index as a proxy for the market as a whole is rather self-evident, the implications of heterogenous investment horizons is less obvious so let's take a moment to consider its importance. It is *impossible* to define a riskless asset without also specifying the investor's investment horizon. To see this, we need to first define what it means for an asset to be riskless. A riskless asset is one that will provide a known return without any possible deviation. That is, there is zero variance associated with the percentage return. For example, suppose that an investor has a horizon of one month. If the investor purchases a one-month T-bill (which is sold at a discount from its face value) and holds it to maturity, then the investor knows in advance precisely what the return will be since the T-bill will be redeemed for its face value upon maturity. There is no variance so there is no risk. Clearly, a one-month T-bill to an investor with a one-month horizon is a risk-free asset. But is a one-month T-bill a risk-free asset to an investor with a two-month horizon? Such an investor would purchase the T-bill today and hold it until it matures in one month. At that time, he would invest it in another one-month T-bill. This is called a rollover. But, does the investor know today what rate will prevail on one-month T-bill's one month from today? Clearly not. And, since the investor must rollover the T-bill for the second month, there is some variance to the return from a one-month T-bill strategy. Thus, a one-month T-bill is not risk-free for a two-month investor. Consider now an investor with a two-week horizon. A two-week investor who purchases a one-month T-bill must sell the T-bill two weeks prior to its maturity. While the value of the bill at maturity is known, its value two weeks prior to maturity is not known and so the rate of return has positive variance. Thus, a one-month T-bill is only risk free for an investor with a one-month investment horizon.

T-bills are short-term zero coupon bonds. (Zero coupon bonds are discussed in detail in Chapters 16 and 17.) For now, we only want to make the point that a risk-free instrument is only risk free for an investor with an investment horizon that exactly matches the maturity of the instrument. What is more, to be risk free, the instrument must be a zero coupon bond. (Coupon bearing instruments are never completely risk free unless the coupon payments received are used to meet commitments on the holder's liabilities).

As a side point, when risk-free assets are introduced, the behavior of the optimal portfolio, with respect to the passage of time, is similar to what it is before the introduction of risk-free assets. That is, the optimal single-period portfolio becomes less single-period risky as the investor's investment horizon grows shorter. The only difference is that this behavior characterizes the overall portfolio (risky market portfolio plus risk-free asset) rather than just the risky market portfolio. Another way to describe this is to say that the investor reduces his or her use of leverage as the investment horizon shortens. Leverage is discussed in the next section.

Long and Short Positions and the Role of Leverage

When an investor believes that an asset's value will rise, he or she will be tempted to purchase the asset for resale at a higher price later. The purchase of an asset gives rise to a **long position** in the asset. While many people find it difficult to understand, it is just as easy to profit from a belief than an asset will decline in value. In this case, the asset is sold first and repurchased later (hopefully at a lower price). The sale of an asset that one does not currently own is called a **short sale**. A short sale gives rise to a **short position**. It is important to distinguish between a **short sale** and a **sale**. In a sale, one is selling what one already owns. In a short sale, one is selling what one does not own.

Short sales of equity and debt securities are accomplished by borrowing the securities needed for the sale with the promise to return the securities to the lender at a later date. (There are well-developed mechanisms in place to facilitate the borrowing of securities for purposes of short sales. Some of these are discussed in a later chapter.) With derivative securities, the asset to be sold does not have to be borrowed in order to be sold short. Instead, the very act of selling it creates it. Futures and options are examples of these types of assets.

In both long and short positions, the motivation is to make a profit. And, in both cases, the source of the profit is the sale of an instrument at a price higher than the purchase price. The only real difference is that in a long position the purchase comes first and the sale second while in a short position the sale comes first and the purchase second.

Leverage is a magnification of potential financial return with an associated magnification of financial risk. The purpose of leverage is to increase return without increasing the size of one's investment. There are many ways to obtain leverage. The three most widely used are to (1) buy assets using borrowed money (buying stock on margin is an example), (2) holding levered contracts rather than cash assets (futures are an example), and (3) purchasing contingent claims (options are an example).

When we calculate return, we need to be able to account for leverage and the side of the market we are on. The calculation of holding period yield that we previously used ignores leverage and assumes long positions. Equation 6.21 provides a more general way of calculating holding period yield.

$$r(T) = D \cdot L \cdot (R(T) - 1) - C \qquad (6.21)$$

The term $R(T)$ in Equation 6.21 is the familiar return relative. It is equal to the value of the asset at time T divided by the value of the asset at time 0. L is a leverage multiplier. A leverage multiplier is the number of times return is magnified by the use of leverage as compared to a straight cash investment. D denotes a dummy variable that takes on the value +1 if the investor is long and -1 if the investor is short. Finally, C denotes the cost of carrying a position expressed as a percentage of the total investment. The cost of carry can be negative or positive. It is typically positive with leverage created by borrowing money for a securities purchase but it is negative for leverage created using futures contracts. (In the latter case, margin can be posted in the form of interest-bearing securities.)

Equation 6.21 will work equally well for positions that are levered using margin, futures, or options as the source of the leverage. Consider a simple scenario. Suppose that a stock is currently selling at $20 and an investor purchases it using 50 percent borrowed money. The borrowed money comes from his broker who charges 10 percent annually. The position is a long position so the dummy variable takes the value +1. Half the purchase price is borrowed so the leverage multiplier is 2. Now, let's suppose that after six months the investor sells the security for $23.50. The value relative is then 1.175 and C is one-half year's interest on one half of the purchase price or 0.025 (2.50 percent). Equation 6.21 then suggests that the holding period yield on this investment is 0.325 or 32.5 percent.

It is important to appreciate the effect that the use of leverage has on risk. Suppose that the selling price is $20 (unchanged from the purchase price). Then the unleveraged investor who paid cash for the security would break even. But, the levered investor does not break even. Indeed, he would suffer a loss of 2.5 percent. The effects of one-half year two-for-one leverage with a 10 percent annual carrying cost (one half borrowed money) under different terminal values for the security are depicted in Exhibit 6.15. As the leverage multiplier increases, the effects of leverage are, of course, magnified even further.

This concludes our introduction to risk. In this chapter, we have tried to capture some of the risk concepts having general applicability in finance. The next chapter considers more advanced concepts in the measurement and management of risk. It also focuses the examination to more clearly reflect the concerns of financial engineers.

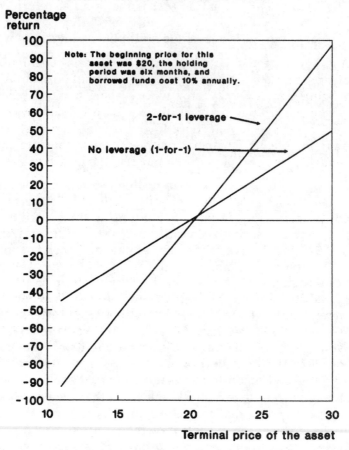

Exhibit 6.15
The Effects of Leverage on Return & Risk

Summary

The source of risk is return volatility. Risk is defined as the potential for return to deviate from an expected or mean value. The potential for returns to deviate from expected values is measured with the aid of variances and standard deviations.

Investment assets are usually not held alone. Instead, investors hold a collection, called a portfolio, of assets. It is possible for the individual assets in the portfolio to be individually risky and yet for the overall portfolio to have a low risk character. The keys are (1) the degree to which the different assets included in the portfolio are correlated with one another, (2) the signs (+ or -) on those correlations, and (3) the weights assigned to the different assets included in the portfolio.

A long neglected but extremely important consideration in portfolio modeling is the length of the investment horizon. All other things being equal, an investor with a short horizon will find a given risky portfolio more risky than will an investor with a long horizon. This suggests that those financial engineers that structure portfolios for clients (financial planners) must consider not only the client's degree of risk aversion but also the length of the client's horizon.

There is no such thing as an asset that is risk-free for all investors if we define risk as the potential for deviation from an expected return. The reason is simple. Different investors have different horizons. In most cases, the risk-free asset for an investor is that zero coupon bond having a maturity equal to the investor's horizon. Any other instrument is not completely risk free.

Leverage plays a significant role in much of financial engineering. If leverage is to be employed, the role of leverage must be factored in when developing a strategy to address any type of investment problem. Leverage is considered more carefully in Chapter 12 when futures contracts are examined and it is considered again in Chapter 22 in the context of leveraged buyouts.

Endnotes

[1]See, for example, Rozelle and Fielitz (1980) and Kryzanowksi and To (1987).

[2]Any good statistical package can generate sample means, sample variances, and sample correlation coefficients. We used *A-Pack: An Analytical Package for Business* for the calculations employed throughout this text. *A-Pack* was discussed in Chapter 3.

[3]These portfolio relationships were first demonstrated by Markowitz (1952).

[4]These relationships were first identified by Tobin (1965). Formal proofs may be found in Marshall (1989).

[5]For a formal proof of this proposition, see Aitchison and Brown (1957).

[6]The term "confidence channel" was coined by Marshall (1989).

[7]In particular, see Lloyd and Haney (1980) and Lloyd and Modani (1983). Others who have looked at this issue include Reichenstein (1987), McEnally (1985), and Bernstein (1976)

[8]Variants of the drawdown criterion used here have long been used in the futures industry in developing trading strategies. The version employed in this paper is more formally defined than most and has nice statistical properities. Its use is also consistent with traditional utility criteria long used in the selection of optimal portfolios at a theoretical level.

[9]This has been shown by Zelney (1982).

[10]The capital asset pricing model was the result of work by Sharpe (1964), Lintner (1965), and Mossin (1966). The model and its uses are very well described in Sharpe and Alexander (1990).

References and Suggested Readings

Aitchison, J. and J.A. Brown. *The Lognormal Distribution*, Cambridge, MA: Cambridge Press, 1957.

Bernstein, P.L. "The Time of Your Life," *Journal of Portfolio Management*, Summer 1976.

Gressis, N., G.C. Philippatos, and J. Hayya. "Multiperiod Portfolio Analysis and the Inefficiency of the Market Portfolio," *Journal of Finance*, vol 31, September 1976.

Kryzanowksi, L. and M.C. To. "The E-V Stationarity of Security Returns: Some Empirical Evidence," *Journal of Banking and Finance*, vol 11(1), pp. 117-136, 1987.

Lintner, J. "The Valuation of Risk Assets and the Selection of Risky Investments in Stock Portfolios and Capital Budgets," *Review of Economics and Statistics*, 1965.

Lloyd, W.P and R.L Haney. "Time Diversification: Surest Route to Lower Risk," *Journal of Portfolio Management*, Spring 1980.

Lloyd, W.P. and N.K. Modani. "Stocks, Bonds, Bills, and Time Diversification," *Journal of Portfolio Management*, Spring 1983.

Markowitz, H. "Portfolio Selection," *Journal of Finance*, 7, March 1952.

Marshall, J.F. *Futures and Option Contracting*, Cincinnati, OH: South-Western, 1989.

Marshall, J.F. and K.J. Wynne. "Time Diversification: A Multi- Period Model," Center for Applied Research, Working Paper #88, March, 1990a.

Marshall, J.F. and K.J. Wynne. "The Proper Treatment of the Investment Horizon in Portfolio Selection Problems: GPH Versus MW," Business Research Institute, Working Paper #WP90S-1, March, 1990b.

McEnally, R.W. "Time Diversification: Surest Route to Lower Risk?," *Journal of Portfolio Management*, Summer, 1985.

Mossin, J. "Equilibrium in a Capital Asset Market," *Econometrica*, pp. 768-783, 1966.

Reichenstein, W. "On Standard Deviation and Risk," *Journal of Portfolio Management*, Winter 1987.

Rozelle, J.P. and B.D. Fielitz. "Stationarity of Common Stock Returns," *Journal of Financial Research*, vol 3(3), pp. 229-242, 1980.

Sharpe, W.F. and G.J. Alexander. *Investments*, Englewood Cliffs, NJ: Prentice Hall, 1990.

Sharpe, W.F. "Capital Asset Prices: A Theory of Market Equilibrium Under Conditions of Risk," *Journal of Finance*, pp. 425-442, 1964.

Tobin, J. "The Theory of Portfolio Selection," in *The Theory of Interest Rates*, F. Hahn and F. Breechling, eds., London: Macmillan, 1965.

Zelney, M. *Multiple Criteria in Decision Making*, New York: McGraw-Hill, 1982.

Chapter 7

Measuring Risk: Advanced Topics

Overview

In the last chapter, we introduced a number of concepts associated with risk and its measurement. These included (1) the use of variance and standard deviation as logical measures of risk; (2) important elements of portfolio theory including systematic and unsystematic risk, efficient portfolios, and optimal portfolios; (3) the relationships between the length of the investment horizon, risk perception, and optimal portfolio selection; (4) the use of beta as a measure of the systematic component of risk; and, (5) the role of leverage.

In this chapter we continue with our examination of price risk and its measurement, and we begin to look at ways to manage this important form of risk. Among the ways to manage risk which we briefly consider are the purchase of insurance, asset/liability management, and hedging. Our main focus in the management of risk is on hedging, but we can do little more than introduce the logic of hedging and some of the related concepts in this one chapter. In the process, however, we will see the connection between hedging theory and portfolio theory. We will return to the subject of hedging repeatedly as we work our way through the book.

Measuring Exposure to Price Risk

Knowledge of the existence of a price risk is not sufficient to manage it. The risk manager also needs to know the degree of exposure to the price risk. Two different firms can have an exposure to the same price risk but the extent of the exposures can be quite different. Consider two firms: The first is a passenger airline and the second is a large lawncare company. Both firms employ oil derivatives in their business. The airline uses kerosene (jet fuel) to fuel its planes and the lawncare firm uses gasoline to power its mowers. Both firms have an exposure to a change in oil prices because both kerosene and gasoline will fluctuate in price with the price of oil.

As it happens, expense for fuel represents 38 percent of the airline's operating costs and 4 percent of the lawncare firm's operating costs. Thus, a change in the price of oil will dramatically influence the financial performance of the airline but may have only a very modest effect on the lawncare firm's performance.

The first step after measuring the volatility of a price is then to measure the firm's exposure. This is done by constructing separate risk profiles for each price risk to which the firm is exposed. A **risk profile** is a specification of the relationship between a performance measure and price. Sometimes we find it convenient to use price changes from the current price level instead of the price. Performance is usually plotted on the vertical axis and price, or price change, is plotted on the horizontal axis. These alternative forms of the risk profile are depicted in Exhibit 7.1, Panels A and B respectively. Notice that when a risk profile employs price changes from expected values, as in Panel B, the risk profile will pass through the origin.

The performance measure most often used in developing risk profiles is a change in the present value of the firm's cash flows. The change in value measure is particularly useful when the goal of exposure measurement is to neutralize the risk. Let's consider an example. A U.S. financial corporation has just acquired $12 million of five-year fixed-rate assets (loans) paying a semiannual rate of 10 percent. It has financed these assets with floating-rate liabilities. Specifically, the liabilities take the form of six-month commercial paper. This paper will be rolled over every six-months for five years. The first paper issue required a paper rate of 7 percent and the firm expects that this is a good estimate of future paper rates.

Exhibit 7.1
Risk Profiles—Alternative Forms

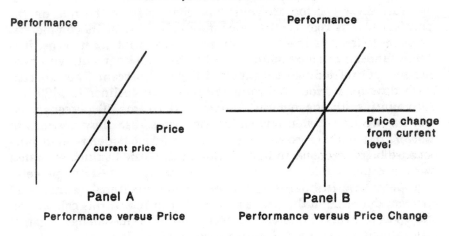

Panel A	Panel B
Performance versus Price	Performance versus Price Change

The difference between the payments the firm will receive at 10 percent and the payments the firm will make at 7 percent represents a cash flow stream from the firm's business as a finance company. Under current expectations and a semiannual discount rate of 10 percent, the firm concludes that the cash flow stream has a present value of $1,389,913. The calculation, which uses the present value arithmetic discussed in Chapter 4, is illustrated in Table 7.1

Table 7.1.
Calculating the Present Value of an Expected Cash Flow Stream

Period	Known Expected Cash In	Cash Out	Net Cash Flow	Discounted Value (at 10%)
1	$600,000	$420,000	$180,000	$171,429
2	600,000	420,000	180,000	163,265
3	600,000	420,000	180,000	155,491
4	600,000	420,000	180,000	148,087
5	600,000	420,000	180,000	141,035
6	600,000	420,000	180,000	134,319
7	600,000	420,000	180,000	127,923
8	600,000	420,000	180,000	121,831
9	600,000	420,000	180,000	116,030
10	600,000	420,000	180,000	110,504
			Total Value	1,389,913

Now consider how the value of the firm would change if commercial paper rates suddenly increase by 1 percent. The firm's *initial* net cash flow (period 1) would not change since the rate on the firm's assets is fixed at 10 percent and the cost of its commercial paper financing is fixed at 7 percent for the first six months. It is the refunding rate six months out that rises to 8 percent, with each subsequent refunding now expected to cost 8 percent. The expected cash flow for periods 2 through 10 therefore declines to $120,000. Discounting all the net cash flows at the same 10 percent used earlier, we find that the value of the firm's cash flow declines to $983,751. Thus, a 1 percent rise in commercial paper rates results in a $406,162 decrease in that portion of the firm's value associated with this particular financing. This seemingly modest one percentage point rise in interest rates can be seen to translate into a 29 percent decrease in the firm's value. We can repeat this calculation for all new levels of interest rates and plot the value changes against the rate changes to get the firm's risk profile. The risk profile for this firm, with respect to changes in the commercial paper rate, is depicted in Exhibit 7.2. This profile is downward sloping because an increase in rates leads to a decrease in value and vice versa.

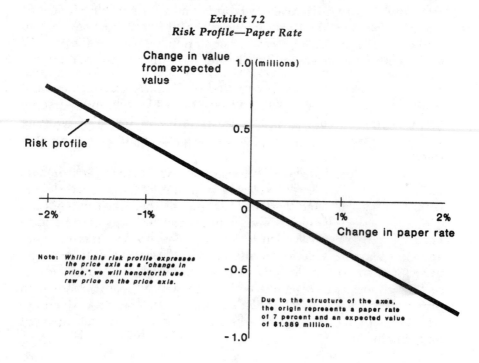

Exhibit 7.2
Risk Profile—Paper Rate

Change in value from expected value

1.0 (millions)

0.5

Risk profile

-2%   -1%   0   1%   2%

Change in paper rate

Note: While this risk profile expresses the price axis as a "change in price," we will henceforth use raw price on the price axis.

-0.5

Due to the structure of the axes, the origin represents a paper rate of 7 percent and an expected value of $1.389 million.

-1.0

Risk profiles, like the one above, can be drawn for any price exposure. This can be an exposure to interest rates, exchange rates, any of hundreds of commodity prices, and even stock prices. Risk profiles are useful for several reasons. First, the very act of developing risk profiles forces those exposed to give serious thought to the existence of the exposures. Second, without a serious effort to measure the exposures, it is impossible to efficiently manage them. Finally, the nature of the exposures and the shape of the risk profiles might suggest appropriate risk management techniques.

Managing Risk

There are three different, but related, ways to manage financial risks. The first is to purchase **insurance**. Insurance, however, is only viable for the management of certain types of financial risks. Such risks are said to be insurable. The second approach is **asset/liability management**. This approach involves the careful balancing of assets and liabilities so as to eliminate net value changes. Asset/liability management is most often used in the management of interest-rate risk and exchange-rate risk. The final approach, which can be used either by itself or in conjunction with one or both of the other two, is **hedging**. Hedging involves the taking of offsetting risk positions. It is very similar to asset/liability management but while asset/liability management, by definition, involves on-balance sheet positions, hedging usually involves off-balance sheet positions. This distinction between asset/liability management and hedging is important but often overlooked. In fact, many people consider asset/liability management strategies forms of hedging and vice versa. For our purposes, it is worth maintaining the distinction.

Later in the book we will examine the financial instruments used by risk managers. The more important of these are swaps, futures, forwards, and options. All four of these instruments are off-balance sheet contracts and, hence, hedging tools. But, because hedging tools are often used to take up where asset/liability management leaves off, or as an alternative to asset/liability management, it is important to look at this activity as well. Insurance is of less importance to us but we will say a few words about it in order to be clearer as to which risks are insurable and which are not. We will look at insurance, then asset/liability management and, finally, hedging.

Insurance

An **insurable risk** is a risk to which many firms (or individuals) are exposed, for which manifestations of the risk are not highly correlated among those exposed, and for which the probability of a manifestation of the risk is known with a high degree of certainty. Insurable risks include such risks as death, loss from fire, loss from theft, liability, and medical expense. Consider the case of fire. Damage from fire results in financial loss and the risk of fire is therefore a financial risk.

The financial risk to which the firm is exposed from fire is a function of the probability of the firm experiencing a fire and the value of the assets at risk. The risk of losses from fire is an insurable risk because many firms experience a similar exposure and these individual exposures have a near zero correlation. That is, the probability of a fire at Firm A is the same whether or not Firm B experiences a fire.[1] Additionally, while we cannot say that Firm A will or will not experience a fire, we do know with great certainty the statistical likelihood (probability) that Firm A will experience a fire. The latter is established through careful actuarial studies.

For simplicity, suppose that there are 1000 identical firms each with a net worth (equity) of $2 million. Each is subject to the same 2 percent probability of a fire. Should a fire occur at any of the firms, the loss will average $5 million (in terms of replacement cost of assets and lost business). For any of the firms, a fire would be devastating—wiping out all equity and leaving unpaid debts. Thus, not only are the owners of these firms exposed to a financial risk from fire but so are the firms' creditors.

The amount of the exposure, per year, can be obtained by multiplying the probability of a fire (2 percent) by the loss resulting from fire ($5 million). The exposure is then $100,000. Now, suppose that an insurance company offers to cover any fire losses at any of the firms for an annual premium of $120,000. The excess covers administrative costs and profit for the insurer. If a fire occurs, the insurer pays out $5 million. If a fire does not occur, the insurer benefits by the amount of the premium.

For the insured firms, the payment of the insurance premium, even if in excess of the amount of the exposure, may be money well spent. First, the risk-averse nature of both the firms' owners and managers suggest that they will be willing to pay, up to a point, for the removal of the risk. In the language of economics, we say that they enjoy a utility gain from risk reduction. Second, the firms' creditors will view the firms as more creditworthy if they minimize their risks. If they are more creditworthy, the creditors may be willing to extend credit to the firms at lower cost. This reduced financing cost offsets, to some degree, the cost of the insurance.

While the insurer has assumed the risk of all of the individual firms, it is, itself, not at significant risk because the individual risks of fire were not highly correlated. That is, the risks are unsystematic in nature. If we assume zero correlation, a reasonable approximation in this case, the insurer's *per firm risk* is quite small. This is a rather simple application of portfolio theory. Since the risks are independent of one another, the premiums received from all the firms tend to offset the payments to the firms that do experience a fire. The more policies the insurer writes, the greater the degree to which the premiums and policy payouts are offsetting. From the insurer's perspective, its average per-firm risk decreases with each new firm added to its policy base. The average per-firm risk to the insurer is given by Equation 7.1.

$$PFR = \frac{IFE}{\sqrt{N}}$$

$$(7.1)$$

PFR: denotes average per-firm risk to insurer
IFE: denotes the individual firm's exposure
N: denotes the number of identical firm's insured

Another way to look at this is to consider the insurer's risk per dollar of premiums received. The relationship between the number of firms insured and the insurer's per-dollar risk exposure is depicted in Exhibit 7.3.

Insurance works because the insurer's risk, when spread across a large policy base, is a small fraction of the insured's risk. The keys to the principal of insurance then is the independence of the individual exposures and the spreading of the risk across a large policy base. The latter is called, in the language of statistics, the law of large numbers. In a sense, insurers are practicing arbitrage. Instead of arbitraging across space or time, however, they are arbitraging across risk.

There are two problems with removing risks by insuring them. First, the introduction of an intermediary, the insurer, suggests that the cost of insurance will exceed its expected monetary value. The insurer, after all, must cover its own administrative costs and its owners expect to earn a reasonable profit. Second, not all risks are

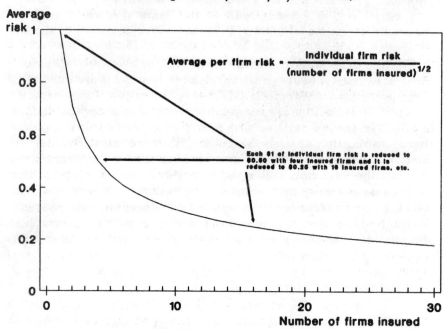

Exhibit 7.3
Insurer's Average Risk Exposure (per firm insured)

insurable and price risks are generally not insurable. The reason is simple, the financial performances of firms with an exposure to the same price risk are not independent of one another. In fact, they lie at the opposite end of the statistical spectrum—they are nearly perfectly positively correlated. That is, if one firm experiences financial injury from a manifestation of the risk, all similarly exposed firms will experience financial injury from a manifestation of the risk. This would be like insuring firms against fire while knowing that if one policyholder experiences a devastating fire, all policyholders will experience a devastating fire. In such a situation, insurance has no meaning. Should the insurer be required to pay off on all policies simultaneously, it could not possibly do so and so the insurance is useless. And this is precisely the case in price risk. If the yield curve shifts upward for example, all firms experience a similar increase in the cost of funds. If the dollar weakens, all firms with an exposure to the dollar are impacted. If the price of corn falls, all corn farmers will suffer.

Asset/Liability Management

Asset/liability management is an effort to minimize exposure to price risk by holding the appropriate combination of assets and liabilities so as to meet the firm's objectives (such as achieving a stated earnings target) and simultaneously minimize the firm's risk. The key to this form of risk management is holding the *right* combination of on-balance sheet assets and on-balance sheet liabilities.

Asset/liability management is most highly developed for managing interest-rate risk. Indeed, few discussions of this approach to risk management are conducted in any other context. But asset/liability management can be used and is often used in the management of exchange-rate risk, commodity-price risk, and stock-price risk. In the case of equity mutual funds, the fund itself is at no risk from stock price fluctuations because, by construction, asset/liability management works perfectly to balance the claims of the funds' shareholders against the value of the funds' assets.[2] Despite its applicability to other forms of price risk, we will limit our look at asset/liability management to the management of interest-rate risk and exchange-rate risk.

The first users of asset/liability management techniques were pension funds. Banks, insurance companies, savings and loans, and finance companies soon followed suit. The following example discusses how a pension fund uses asset/liability management.

Pension funds are exposed to considerable interest-rate risk and it was this risk that the funds needed to manage. A pension fund sells policies to clients. These policies can take a variety of forms. One of the most popular in use today are **guaranteed investment contracts** or **GICs**. GICs guarantee a fixed stream of future income to their owners, i.e., the policyholders, and constitute liabilities of the pension fund. The proceeds obtained from the sale of these policies are invested, by the fund, in financial assets that provide a return for the fund. Fluctuations in market interest rates, however, can and will cause the return on the firm's assets to deviate from the return promised to the fund's policyholders. For example, if rates decline the fund might find itself investing future cash flows in assets that are yielding an insufficient return to meet the fund's obligations—as represented by the claims of the policyholders. An alternative, but equivalent, way to look at this problem is to consider the market value of the firm's assets and the market value of the firm's liabilities. While these values should initially be the same, they may not be equally sensitive to changes in interest rates. Thus, a fluctuation in rates may impact the value of the fund's assets more than the value of the fund's liabilities, or vice versa. The risk is then that the fund's liabilities might be underfunded at the time the fund is due to pay off.

Ideally, asset/liability management should strive to match the timing and the amount of cash inflows from assets with the timing and the amount of the cash outflows on liabilities. An asset portfolio constructed to precisely match cash flows is called a **dedicated portfolio**.[3] Unfortunately, it can be extremely difficult, if not impossible, to precisely match cash flows. Furthermore, even when it can be done, it may be too expensive or may require the fund to pass up more attractive investment opportunities. The solution is to forget about matching cash flows and to concentrate instead on the value of the fund's assets and the value of the fund's liabilities and to make the value difference completely interest-rate insensitive. The selection of assets so as to minimize the rate sensitivity of the difference between asset and liability values is called, in the context of asset/liability management, **portfolio immunization**. The concept of immunization and the strategy for implementing it were first developed by F.M. Redington in a paper published in 1952.[4]

Since the goal of immunization is to make the asset/liability mix insensitive to interest-rate fluctuations, the logical starting point for an immunization strategy is the measurement of interest-rate sensitivity. The most widely used measure of interest-rate sensitivity was developed in 1938 by Frederick Macaulay and is called duration. Actually, duration is a relative measure of a debt instrument's interest-rate sensitivity. In its original form, duration is calculated as a weighted-average of the time to the instrument's maturity. The weights are the present values of the individual cash flows divided by the present value of the entire stream of cash flows. The weights, denoted here by w(t), are then multiplied by the time at which the cash flow will occur (t/m) (where t denotes the number of the cash flow and m denotes the number of cash flows per year). The products are then added to get duration. The duration calculation is given as Equation 7.2. This representation of the duration calculation produces a duration value measured in years.

$$D = \sum_{t=1}^{m \cdot T} w(t) \cdot (t/m)$$

$$(7.2)$$

The duration value is often modified by dividing by 1 plus the instrument's yield (y) divided by the number of cash flows per year (m). This **modified duration**, denoted below by D*, is given by Equation 7.3.

$$D^* = \frac{D}{(1 + y/m)} \tag{7.3}$$

The concept of duration is closely related to the concept of a risk profile. To see this, consider the relationship between the present value of a debt instrument and the instrument's yield. This is depicted in Exhibit 7.4.

Exhibit 7.4
Relationship Between a Risk Profile and Duration

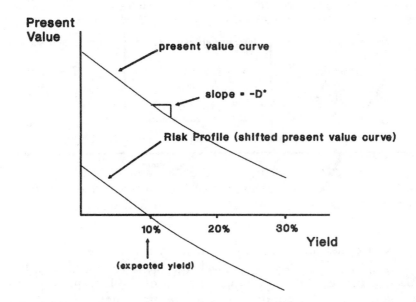

It can be shown, though we will not do so here, that the negative of the slope of the value curve in Exhibit 7.4 is the instrument's modified duration.[5] If we subtract the starting present value from the new present value to get a change in present value, will not affect the slope of the value curve because we have merely shifted the vertical axis. However, once we have shifted the axis, we have, by our earlier definition, a risk profile. Thus, we see that, at least in the context of interest rates, modified duration is the slope of the risk profile.

Let us now compare the risk profiles associated with holding three different debt instruments. The first is a long-maturity instrument, the second is an intermediate-maturity instrument, and the third is an overnight-money instrument. The latter instrument refers to money that is lent overnight at the overnight money rate and then re-lent at the next day's overnight money rate. Think of this as an instrument with a floating rate of interest that is reset daily (as close to continuously as is currently practical). The risk profiles associated with these three instruments are depicted in Exhibit 7.5.

Exhibit 7.5
Interest-Rate Risk, Maturity, and Duration

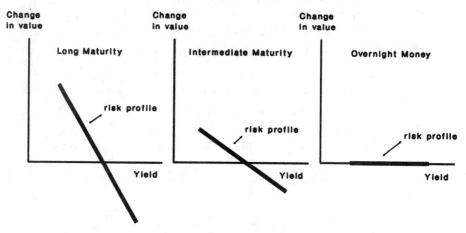

Notice that the long-maturity instrument has the steepest risk profile. The risk profile of the cash instrument is absolutely flat. This is consistent with the long duration of the long-maturity instrument and a zero duration for the overnight-money instrument. This suggests that the concept of duration is useful in the same way as a risk profile—it can be used to assess the extent of an interest-rate exposure.

An interesting property of duration is that the duration of a portfolio of assets is a weighted average of the durations of the individual assets included in the portfolio when the instruments' weights are taken to be the market values of the instruments divided by the entire market value of the portfolio. (This type of weighting is called **value weighting**.) This duration property of asset and liability portfolios is the key to immunization strategies. In the immunization strategy developed by Redington, the fund manager determines the duration of the firm's liabilities and then selects two assets with different durations. Finally, the manager determines the weights on the two assets in the asset portfolio so that the portfolio has a duration that matches precisely the duration of the liabilities. Those who employ immunization strategies generally use the original (Macaulay) duration, but the modified duration can also be used. We employ the latter.

Let's consider a simple example. Suppose that the pension fund sells a new policy that commits the fund to pay $100 each year for the next 15 years. The cash flows of the liability stream, together with their discounted values (using a 10 percent discount rate) and their contributions to duration (products), look as depicted in Table 7.2. We see that the liability stream has a present value of $760.61 and a modified duration of 5.708.

Table 7.2
The Calculation of Modified Duration

Time	Cash Flow	Discounted Value of Cash Flow	Weight	Product
1	100	90.909	0.120	0.120
2	100	82.645	0.109	0.217
3	100	75.131	0.099	0.296
.	.	.	.	.
.	.	.	.	.
.	.	.	.	.
15	100	23.939	0.031	0.472
	Total	760.608	1.000	6.279

Modified Duration = 6.279 ÷ 1.1 = 5.708

The problem for the fund is how to invest the $760.61 proceeds from the sale of the policy to earn a return of at least 10 percent while assuring itself that the assets in which the fund invests will have a value at least equal that of its liabilities at each and every point in time in the future. Suppose now that the fund has two instruments in which it can invest. The first is a 30-year Treasury bond paying a coupon of 12 percent and selling at par. The second is six-month T-bills yielding 8 percent (bond equivalent). The bond has a modified duration of 8.080 years and the bill has a modified duration of 0.481.[6]

Fluctuations in yields will, of course, cause both the fund's assets and liabilities to fluctuate in value. For the immunization strategy to be completely effective, the fluctuations in the value of the asset portfolio must precisely match the fluctuations in the value of the liability portfolio. This means weighting the bond and the bill in such a fashion as to produce a portfolio duration precisely equal to the duration of the liabilities. The weights must, of course, sum to 1.0. The model is given by Equations 7.4 and 7.5 where w_1 and w_2 are the weights on the bond (instrument 1) and the bills (instrument 2) respectively. D_1 and D_2 are the corresponding durations and D_L denotes the overall duration of the liabilities.

$$w_1 \cdot D_1 + w_2 \cdot D_2 = D_L \tag{7.4}$$

$$w_1 + w_2 = 1 \tag{7.5}$$

Substituting the known duration values into Equation 7.4 and solving renders the appropriate weights. The solution is illustrated in Table 7.3.

Table 7.3
The Determination of Immunizing Portfolio Weights

$$w_1 \cdot 8.080 + w_2 \cdot 0.481 = 5.708$$

and $w_1 + w_2 = 1$ implying that $w_2 = 1 - w_1$

substituting for w_2:
$$w_1 \cdot 8.080 + (1 - w_1) \cdot 0.481 = 5.708$$

finally, solving for w_1:
$$w_1 = 68.79\%$$

The solution for w_1 implies that the solution for w_2 is 31.21 percent. Thus, we conclude that the pension fund should invest 68.79 percent of the proceeds it received from the sale of its policies in the 30-year bond and 31.21 percent in the six-month bill. This translates into a current investment of \$523.23 in bonds and \$237.38 in bills.

Now consider what happens if the yield curve moves upward by 10 basis points. This movement represents a parallel shift in the yield curve. The liabilities are now discounted by 10.1 percent instead of 10, the bond is discounted by 12.1 percent instead of 12, and the bill is discounted at 8.1 percent instead of 8. The old values and the new values are depicted in Table 7.4.

Table 7.4
Performance of the Immunized Portfolio

		Assets	
	Pension Liabilities	30-Year Bond	6-Month Bill
Old value	760.61	523.23	237.38
New value	756.29	519.03	237.26
Change in value	−4.32	−4.20 +	−0.12 = −4.32

Notice that the change in the value of the fund's assets (−$4.32), obtained by combining the value change in the bond and the value change in the bill, is precisely equal to the value change in the fund's liabilities. Thus, the immunization strategy has successfully protected the fund from a ten basis point change in asset and liability yields. In addition, this portfolio is "profitable" in the sense that the return on the assets exceeds the 10 percent cost of the liabilities. Had this not been the case, the fund would not have offered the policy for sale. The return on the fund's portfolio is computed as the weighted average of the return on the individual assets. In this case, the calculation is: (68.79% × .12) + (31.21% × .08) = 10.75%.

There are three problems with the immunization approach described above. First, the duration values are only reliable for short periods of time. That is, as time passes, the durations of the individual assets and the duration of the liabilities change and these changes are not equal for all the instruments involved. Thus, a weighting scheme that works perfectly today will probably not work perfectly tomorrow. This is not to say that it will not work well tomorrow, only that it will not work as well as it does today; and, with each passing day, the weighting scheme becomes less reliable. The second problem is that durations also change with changes in yields and these duration changes are not necessarily the same for all the instruments. Thus, for small changes in yield, the duration matching strategy will work very well. But for large changes in yield, the duration matching strategy will work less well. Both of these problems, however, are easily solved. The solution is to re-compute the durations frequently, recalculate the weights, and adjust the portfolio accordingly.[7]

The third problem with the simple duration matching strategy described here concerns the assumption that all movements of the yield curve take the form of parallel shifts. This is simply not the case. Shorter-term rates are more sensitive than longer-term rates; the rates on different types of instruments have different sensitivities, even if they have the same maturities; and the same types of instruments with the same maturities may have different sensitivities due to different degrees of default risk.

A very workable solution, however, is to adjust the size of the asset positions on the basis of the historical relationship between the yield changes on the liabilities and the yield changes on the assets. That is, if we assume that there is a proportionality to the yield change on the liabilities and the yield change on the assets, then we can measure this proportion using historical data. The statistical procedure used for this purpose is linear regression. In this procedure we regress the past changes in the yield of the liabilities against the past changes in the yield of the 30-year bond. The resultant coefficient is the required proportion. We call this coefficient the **yield beta**. The regression is given by Equation 7.6 in which y_L denotes the yield change on the liabilities and y_b denotes the yield change on the bond, and β_y denotes the yield beta that represents the proportionality factor.

$$y_L = \beta_y \bullet y_b \qquad\qquad (7.6)$$

We then measure a yield beta for the liabilities and the six-month bill using the same procedure. Once we know the yield betas, we can adjust the duration model so as to account for nonparallel shifts in the yield curve.

There are more sophisticated immunization models, but none has been shown to be consistently superior to Redington's original model (with the adjustments we have noted) and so we do not go into these any further.[8] We should note that the risk profile for the pension fund, i.e., its value changes with respect to changes in interest rates, will be perfectly flat if the portfolio weighting was done correctly. (We consider the subject of duration again in the next chapter.)

Now consider the asset/liability management approach as it can be applied to the management of exchange-rate risk. We use a U.S. bank with global operations as the basis of our example. The bank makes loans to corporations worldwide. These loans are usually made in the currency of the borrower. Thus, a loan made to a British firm is usually made in British pound sterling (BPS). A loan made to an Italian firm is usually made in Italian lira (ITL), and so on. These loans are recorded on the bank's books as assets. But some of the assets are denominated in sterling, some in lira, and some in other currencies.

Now, suppose that the bank raises the funds that it lends to these firms by borrowing dollars in the U.S. These dollars are then converted, at the prevailing spot exchange rate, to the currency of the lending. The borrowings are recorded as dollar liabilities of the bank.

The bank described in this example has a serious currency mismatch in its asset/liability structure. The bank's balance sheet, for example, for one day's activity at the end of the day of that activity, might look something like that depicted in Table 7.5.

Table 7.5
Global Bank's Balance Sheet (one day activity)
(all values in millions)

Assets		Liabilities	
Loans (sterling)	2.50	Demand deposits (dollars)	3.51
Loans (lira)	1480.00	CDs (dollars)	11.48
Loans (dollars)	12.40	Other time deposits (dollars)	2.70
		total liabilities	17.69

Exchange Rates: USD/BPS = 1.6550
USD/ITL = 0.0007785
USD/USD = 1.0000

At the current exchange rates, the bank's assets have a current dollar-value equivalent of 17.69 million. This is to be expected since the value of the assets and the value of the liabilities should be equal at the moment they are created—which is what Table 7.5 depicts. But, suppose that the dollar strengthens over the next few weeks. For example, suppose that the USD/BPS rate declines to 1.6385 and the USD/ITL rate declines to 0.0007625. In such a case, the value of the bank's assets, when translated to their dollar-value equivalent, is significantly below the value of its liabilities: 17.62 million versus 17.69 million. The difference, 0.07 million will show up as a translation loss and will be reflected in the bank's equity account (not shown here).

The asset/liability management of this bank's exchange-rate exposure is conceptually quite simple. The bank should borrow lira to fund lira loans and the bank should borrow sterling to fund sterling loans. Dollar borrowings should be reserved for funding dollar loans. By matching the currency denomination of liabilities to the currency denomination of the assets, the bank eliminates a large portion of its exchange-rate exposure. A simplified breakdown of the bank's balance sheet by currency appears as Table 7.6.

Table 7.6
Global Bank's Balance Sheet (by currency) (one day activity)
(all values in millions)

Assets		Liabilities	
Sterling			
Loans	2.50	Demand deposits	1.30
		Time deposits	1.20
total BPS assets	2.50	total BPS liabilities	2.50
Lira			
Loans	1480.00	Demand deposits	330.00
		Time deposits	1150.00
total ITL assets	1480.00	total ITL liabilities	1480.00
Dollar			
Loans	12.40	Demand deposits	3.56
		Time deposits	8.84
total USD assets	12.40	total USD liabilities	12.40

The asset/liability **currency-matching** strategy does not completely eliminate the bank's exchange-rate exposure. The bank still bears the risk associated with the ultimate repatriation of its profits from its global activities. This exposure is very small, however, compared to the unmatched strategy depicted in Table 7.5.

For institutions with exchange-rate exposures, which includes global banks like the one above and multinational corporations, there are usually interest-rate exposures as well. These can also be managed with immunization techniques. For example, the global bank could use the currency-matching strategy to solve its exchange-rate exposure and, within each currency, use an immunization strategy to manage its interest-rate exposure—just as the pension fund did.

As a closing point to this section on asset/liability management, we should mention that immunization strategies and currency-matching strategies are not necessarily the best way to manage interest-rate risk and exchange-rate risk. Such strategies often require the sacrifice of better, more profitable, opportunities. For this reason, hedging strategies can sometimes prove superior. Such strategies are discussed in the next section.

Hedging

Although closely related to asset/liability management and often used in conjunction with asset/liability management, hedging is a distinct activity. A hedge is a position that is taken as a *temporary substitute* for a later position in another asset (liability) or to protect the value of an existing position in an asset (liability) until the position can be liquidated. Most hedging is done in off-balance sheet instruments. The instruments most often used for hedging are futures, forwards, options, and swaps. It is important to note, however, that a hedge can take the form of an on-balance sheet position. This is often the case, for example, when swap dealers hedge their swaps in Treasury bonds and bills. The key, in this case, is the temporary nature of the cash market hedge.

We will discuss the hedging instruments in later chapters. For now, we need to focus on the underlying theory of hedging rather than the instruments used to hedge.

Consider once again the standard risk profile. For illustration, we will consider a West German firm's exposure to exchange-rate risk. This firm's long position in dollars stems from a $500,000 T-bill it owns that matures in 30 days. The risk profile appears as Exhibit 7.6. Note that value change, which, for consistency, we will henceforth call "profit," is on the vertical axis and price, in this case the DEM/USD 30-day forward exchange rate, is on the horizontal axis.

The upward sloping nature of this risk profile suggests that the German firm's exposure stems from a long forward position in dollars. That is, an increase in the DEM/USD 30-day forward rate represents a strengthening of the dollar vis-a-vis the deutschemark. The German firm benefits from any such strengthening. On the other hand, the German firm will suffer financially from any weakening of the dollar.

The slope of the risk profile suggests something about the extent of the German firm's exposure but it does not tell the whole story. The other consideration is the degree of volatility of the DEM/USD exchange rate. This volatility is measured, as we argued earlier in this chapter, by the standard deviation of the exchange rate (price). Suppose that one standard deviation, for a 30-day period, is 0.0625 DEM/USD and that the exchange rate is approximately normally distributed. Given this knowledge, we can translate the exchange-rate risk into a dollar exposure risk. This is depicted in the three panels of Exhibit 7.7

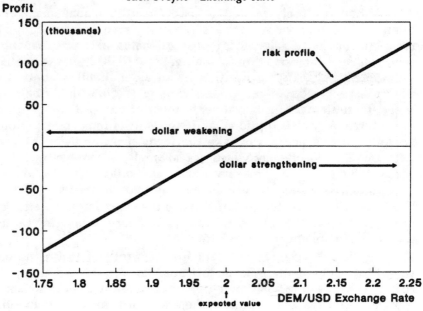

Exhibit 7.6
Risk Profile—Exchange Rate

Exhibit 7.7
Panel A

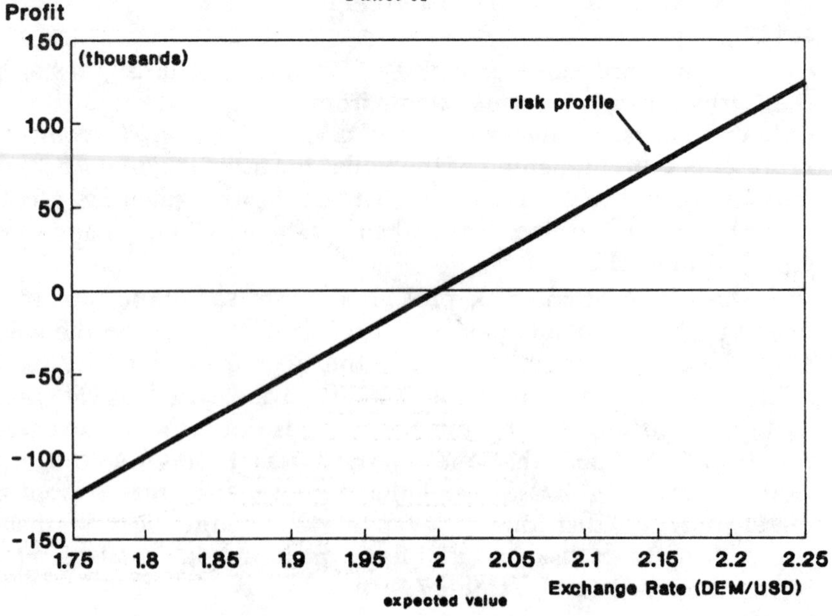

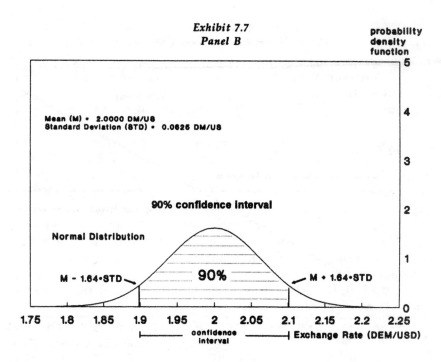

Exhibit 7.7
Panel B

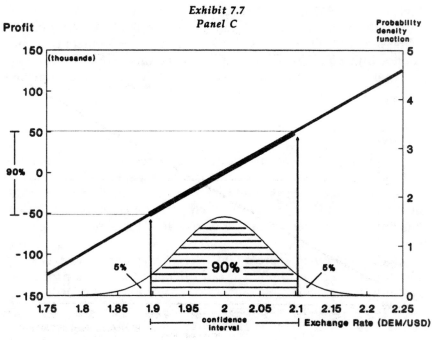

Exhibit 7.7
Panel C

This three panel approach is easy to understand. Panel A is the same risk profile depicted in Exhibit 7.6. Panel B depicts a normal distribution for the 30-day forward exchange rate. By using the properties of the normal distribution, we can make confidence interval statements, conduct hypothesis tests, and determine the probabilities of the exchange rate falling outside of any specific range.

A **confidence interval** is a range of values symmetrically distributed around the expected value that captures a specified probability for the actual outcome. The probability is called the **confidence level** and the range of values is called the confidence interval. For example, a 90 percent confidence interval is given by the range that begins with the expected value plus 1.64 standard deviations and ends with the expected value less 1.64 standard deviations. A 95 percent confidence interval is given by the expected value plus 1.96 standard deviations to the expected value less 1.96 standard deviations. In statistical work, the expected value is often called the mean. We will suppose that the mean exchange rate, as represented by the current 30-day forward rate, is 2.0000 DEM/USD.

To return to Panel B, since the mean is 2.0000 and a standard deviation is 0.0625, the 90 percent confidence interval is [1.8975, 2.1025]. This is calculated as the mean (2.0000) less 1.64 × 0.0625 to the mean (2.0000) plus 1.64 × 0.0625. Panel B depicts this confidence interval. Now, if we superimpose the confidence interval in Panel B on the risk profile in Panel A, we can determine the 90 percent confidence interval for the firm's profit. This is depicted in Panel C. We conclude that, for this firm, the 90 percent confidence interval for value change is the range DEM −51,250 to DEM 51,250.

The nice feature of this approach to assessing risk exposure is that the standard deviation of the price change, for whatever price being considered, is the same for any and all firms. The risk profile, on the other hand, is unique to each firm. By combining the two, we convert a standard measure of risk to a firm-specific measure of risk.

There are other, more quantitative, ways to look at this same relationship.[9] For example, we can calculate the firm's profit risk by multiplying the size of the position in the foreign currency by the standard deviation of the exchange rate. (Recall that an exchange rate is just a price.) This is given by Equation 7.7.

$$\text{Profit Risk} = \text{Size of Position} \quad \times \quad \begin{array}{c} \text{Standard Deviation} \\ \text{of the Price} \\ \text{(price risk)} \end{array} \qquad (7.7)$$

For our German firm, this is:
$$= \text{USD } 500{,}000 \times 0.0625 \text{ DEM/USD}$$
$$= \text{DEM } 31{,}250$$

The value DEM 31,250 is then the profit risk, stated in terms of a standard risk measure (one standard deviation or one unit of volatility), that is specific for this firm. This firm-specific profit risk can be converted to a confidence interval by using the same properties of the normal distribution. For example, the 90 percent confidence interval is the mean, now equal to zero, plus and minus 1.64 times 31,250 (a standard deviation). This interval covers all values from DEM –51,250 to DEM +51,250. It can be seen that this is the range of values on the vertical axis covered by the bolder portion of the risk-profile depicted in Panel C of Exhibit 7.7 and it is also equal to the range of profit values we generated using the first approach.

As already defined, a hedge is a position taken as a temporary substitute for another position or a position taken to protect the value of another position until the first position can be terminated. While the position to be hedged gives rise to a **risk profile**, the hedge itself gives rise to a **payoff profile**. Payoff profiles and risk profiles are actually the same thing. The latter term is used to emphasize the risk associated with holding a cash market position and the former is used to emphasize the profit/loss potential associated with holding the hedge instrument. The hedge eliminates risk if the risk profile and payoff profile are mirror images of one another.

Consider Exhibit 7.8. This exhibit depicts the payoff profile for a short position in 500,000 30-day forward dollars. The German firm in the preceding illustration arranged this forward contract through a German bank. That is, the firm agreed to the sale of $500,000 for delivery in 30 days. The agreed price on this exchange is 2.0000 DEM/USD. If the dollar's value rises, the German firm stands to lose on its forward contract with the German bank. If the dollar's value falls, the German firm stands to benefit on its forward contract with the German bank.

Observe that in a payoff profile, "profit" is usually placed on the vertical axis. Nothing is lost, however, if "profit" is interpreted as a value change. This representation makes the risk profile and

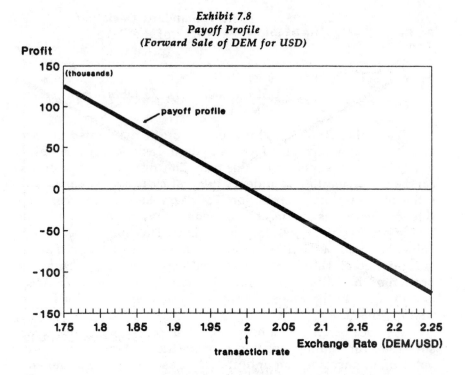

Exhibit 7.8
Payoff Profile
(Forward Sale of DEM for USD)

the payoff profile directly comparable. As we mentioned before, however, we will henceforth refer to "value changes" as profit. Profit, in this sense, is any value deviation from the expected value.

Notice that the German firm's payoff profile on the forward position with the bank and the risk profile on its forward position from its T-bill are mirror images of each other. These are depicted on the same graph in Exhibit 7.9, Panel A. Since, a payoff profile is itself a risk profile, the forward position with the bank represents a second risk exposure, but one that is opposite that of the original exposure. This offsetting of risks is the key to successful hedging. A hedge creates a second risk equal to, but opposite, that of the original exposure. The two exposures are then offsetting and the end result is no net risk. This is depicted by the flat exposure line, representing net risk, in Panel B of Exhibit 7.9.

The approach taken above considers any deviation from the expected outcome to be a manifestation of price risk. When management wishes to hedge this risk in this way, forward contracts,

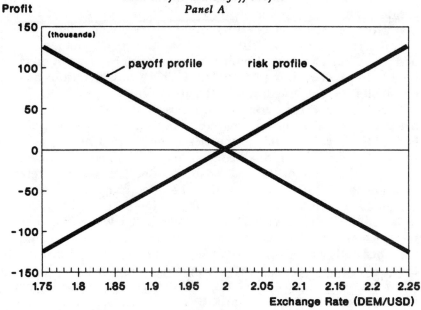

Exhibit 7.9
Risk Profile and Payoff Profile
Panel A

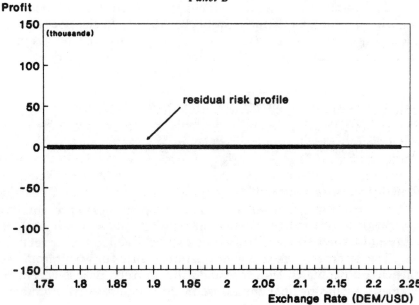

Exhibit 7.9
Residual Risk Profile
Panel B

futures contracts, and swaps can be used to formulate the hedge. But, often, management only wants to formulate a hedge to cancel the downside risk. That is, management wants to construct a hedge that protects the firm from unfavorable price changes but that still permits the firm to benefit from favorable price changes. Such hedges can be engineered with the use of options and options coupled with other hedging instruments. These considerations and instruments are examined more carefully in later chapters.

There are three hedging considerations that need to be addressed before closing this chapter. The first involves the size of a hedge, the second involves the effectiveness of a hedge, and the third involves the cost of a hedge. The size of a hedge is measured relative to the size of the cash position to be hedged. This relative measure is called the hedge ratio. The effectiveness of a hedge is measured by the degree to which the hedge reduces the price risk to which the firm is exposed. The forward hedge we used to manage the German firm's exposure to exchange-rate risk seems to have been perfectly effective, and indeed it was. But not all hedges are that perfect. Sometimes a hedge eliminates some of the risk but not all of the risk. The cost of a hedge is the degree to which the hedge reduces the firm's expected profit.

Size of the Hedge

The number of units of the hedging instrument necessary to fully hedge one unit of the cash position is called the **hedge ratio**. For example, if on average it takes two units of 5-year T-note futures to offset the risk exposure from one unit of corporate debt, then the hedge ratio is 2:1. (We discuss methods for calculating hedge ratios in the next chapter and we examine hedging in much more detail in Chapter 21. In addition, the reader may want to consult some of the reference material listed at the end of this chapter.[10]) For the remainder of our discussion, we assume that the correct hedge ratio is always used.

Measuring Hedge Effectiveness

The degree of correlation between two prices represents the closeness with which their movements track one another. The correlation is measured with the aid of a statistic called the **correlation coefficient**. (The concept of a correlation coefficient was introduced in the last chapter.) We will denote the correlation coefficient by $\int$ (rho). Assuming that the appropriate hedge ratio is employed,

the risk that remains after a hedge is placed is called **basis risk.**
The relationship between basis risk (when measured as a variance)
and price risk (when measured as a variance) is given by Equation
7.8.[11]

$$\text{Basis risk} = (1 - \digamma^2) \cdot \text{Price Risk} \qquad (7.8)$$

Notice that Equation 7.8 employs the square of the correlation
coefficient rather than the correlation coefficient. This squared value
is called the **coefficient of determination.** It is an exact measure
of the percentage of the original risk that is removed by the hedge.
For example, suppose $\digamma^2$ is 0.87, then the hedge will reduce the
price risk by 87 percent. Of course, 13 percent of the original risk
will remain. This remaining part is the basis risk. For obvious reasons, the coefficient of determination is the most often used measure
of hedge effectiveness.

Hedgers are often interested in the source of basis risk. By
better understanding its source, one gains insights into how to construct better hedges. Basis risk exists because the cash price and
the price of the hedging instrument are not perfectly correlated.
This is so because the demand and supply conditions in the cash
market may evolve somewhat differently than the demand and supply conditions in the market for the hedging instrument. The prices
cannot, ordinarily, stray too far from one another without giving
rise to arbitrage opportunities. But the prices can stray to some
degree without giving rise to profitable arbitrage opportunities and
so some basis risk will exist. Consider, for example, a corporate
investor's efforts to hedge his or her planned 3-month commercial
paper issue in 3-month T-bill futures contracts. The bills and the
paper have the same maturity and their rates tend to track each
other fairly closely—although paper rates are always at a premium
to bill rates. The tracking isn't perfect as illustrated in Exhibit 7.10
and so the firm that hedges its planned paper issues in bill futures
will bear some basis risk.

Cost of a Hedge

The final consideration to be addressed before closing this
chapter is the cost of a hedge. There is a great deal of literature on
the subject of the cost of hedging. The general consensus is that
hedging is relatively cheap but not free. There are two good reasons
not to expect hedging to be costless. First, the risk that hedgers
seek to shed when they take on a hedge must be borne by the

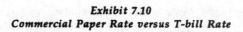

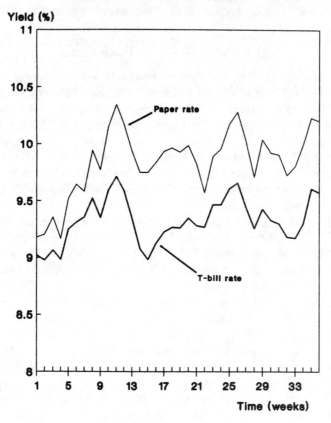

Exhibit 7.10
Commercial Paper Rate versus T-bill Rate

counterparty to the hedge contract. If the counterparty is another hedger with a mirror image exposure, then *both* hedgers enjoy some benefit and we would not expect either to have to compensate the other. But, more often, the counterparty to the contract is a speculator—particularly when the hedging instrument is a futures contract. The speculator is taking a position in order to earn a speculative profit. If speculation is privately costly to the speculator (resources expended) and if speculators are risk averse, then we would expect speculators to require compensation for their risk-bearing services. To the extent that speculators are compensating for risk bearing, hedgers must bear the cost. The second reason for expecting hedging not to be costless is the presence of transaction costs. Every trade involves some transaction costs in the form of a commission, a bid-ask spread, or both.

Although hedging is not costless, not all hedges will be equally costly. It may be, due to inefficiencies in the market, that one type of hedge is less costly than another. Furthermore, the relative costs may change from one day to the next so that the cheaper hedge today might not be the cheaper hedge tomorrow. The prudent hedger compares the cost of alternative hedging strategies before committing to one.

The upshot of these closing remarks is that the hedger must consider both the effectiveness of the hedge and the cost of the hedge. Together, these factors determine the **efficiency of the hedge.** Efficient hedges are those that provide maximum risk reduction per unit of cost. From among the set of available efficient hedges, the hedger must select the optimal one. The **optimal hedge** is that which maximizes the hedger's utility—as this term is used in economics. Consider the five hedges depicted in Exhibit 7.11.

Exhibit 7.11
Efficient Versus Inefficient Hedges

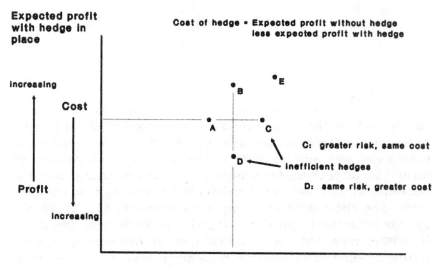

Notice that Hedge C is *inefficient* compared to Hedge A because Hedge C is less effective than Hedge A at the same cost. Notice also that Hedge D is inefficient compared to Hedge B because Hedge D is more costly than Hedge B while only equally effective. The efficient hedges then are Hedges A, B, and E.

The hedger who derives positive utility from reducing risk and negative utility from paying the cost must choose a hedge so as to balance these competing considerations. The hedge that maximizes the user's utility is then the optimal hedge. Importantly, the optimal hedge for one hedger may not be optimal for another hedger. This is a reflection of the individual's own, very personal, utility function. The selection of a hedge must consider these differences.

There has been some confusion in recent literature concerning the meaning of the terms **effectiveness, efficiency**, and **optimality**, as these terms have been applied to hedging theory. The distinctions become exceedingly important when composite hedging is considered. A **composite hedge** is a hedge that involves more than one hedging instrument—as opposed to a simple hedge which involves a single hedging instrument. The advantage of composite hedging is that such a hedge can reduce the basis risk otherwise associated with simple hedges. This is a direct application of portfolio theory to hedging. (We examine composite hedging more carefully in Chapter 21.)

Summary

Price risk is the potential for a future price to deviate from its expected value. Price risk itself is measured with the aid of a statistic called variance or, its square root, which is called standard deviation. It is quite common to refer to a standard deviation as a volatility unit or a vol.

Price risks exist independently of individual firm's exposures. But, individual firms are exposed to price risks. The extent of an exposure, however, will vary considerably from one firm to another. Such exposures must be identified and measured. There are a number of useful and well-established tools for measuring the extent of a firm's exposure to a price risk. One useful way is to use a risk profile. A risk profile is a graphic depiction of the relationship between the change in a firm's value (which we will henceforth call profit) and the changing price that gives rise to this profit. With the aid of a distributional assumption, such as the assumption that a price is normally distributed, we can convert the price risk to a profit risk. That is, we can determine a particular confidence interval so that we know the range of values that profit may assume with any desired degree of confidence.

Financial risks, of which price risk is just one form, can be managed in several ways. Some financial risks can be managed by the purchase of insurance. Risks that can be managed in this way are said to be insurable. Most price risks, however, are not insurable. For these risks, the sophisticated manager will employ either or both asset/liability management techniques or hedging strategies. These approaches are very closely related but the former usually involves on-balance sheet positions and the latter usually involves off-balance sheet positions.

Asset/liability management techniques are most highly developed for the management of interest-rate risk. Two such techniques are cash flow matching strategies and immunization strategies. Asset/liability management is also used to manage exchange-rate exposures. In this case, we attempt to match our assets and our liabilities in each currency.

Although very useful, asset/liability management is not a complete answer to the exposure problem. In many cases, an asset/liability approach to risk management will result in the loss of more attractive investment or financing alternatives. In addition, asset/liability management strategies often take some time to implement. In either case, the manager should consider hedging strategies. A hedge is a position taken as a temporary substitute for a position in a cash asset (liability) or to offset the risk associated with holding a cash asset (liability) until the position is liquidated. The instruments most widely used for hedging are futures contracts, forward contracts, options contracts, and swaps. Collectively, these instruments are often called derivative securities.

Endnotes

[1]In the language of statistics, we would say that the marginal and conditional probabilities are the same.

[2]Technically, the shareholders of a mutual fund have an equity interest in the fund and, therefore, their claims are not liabilities. But, the concept is the same. The value of the assets is fixed in relation to the value of the claims on those assets. In this case, the value is fixed by defining, on a daily basis, a "net asset value" (NAV) for the fund's shares. The NAV is equal to the per share

value of the fund's holdings less the per share value of the fund's liabilities.

[3]For a more detailed discussion of dedicated portfolios, see Hodges and Schaefer (1977) and Liebowitz (1986a, 1986b, 1986c)

[4]See Redington (1952).

[5]See Schaefer (1986)

[6]These duration values were determined using the financial analytics package *A-Pack*. A more detailed discussion of A-Pack can be found in the footnotes to Chapter 3.

[7]Any adjustment in the size of positions will have an effect on profitability. For example, the adjustment might result in an increase in 30-year bond holdings and a decrease in six-month bill holdings, or the adjustment might require a less-than-full investment of the proceeds from the sale of policies— allowing the fund to direct the remaining proceeds elsewhere.

[8]For further discussion of the empirical performance of the Redington model versus other, more sophisticated models, see Schaefer (1986).

[9]For a thorough discussion of the theory of hedging together with the mathematical detail, see Marshall (1989), Chapter 7 with applications in later chapters.

[10]Ibid., Chapters 7, and 10 through 13.

[11]This relationship was first shown by Johnson (1960).

References and Suggested Readings

Brown, K.C. and D.J. Smith, "Recent Innovations in Interest Rate Risk Management and the Reintermediation of Commercial Bank Lending," *Financial Management*, 17(4), Winter 1988.

Hodges, S.D. and S.M. Schaefer, "A Model For Bond Portfolio Improvement," *Journal of Financial and Quantitative Analysis*, 12(2), pp. 243-260, (1977).

Johnson, L.L. "The Theory of Hedging and Speculation in Commodity Futures," *Review of Economic Studies*, 27(3), pp. 139-151, (1960).

Liebowitz, M.L. "How Financial Theory Evolves into the Real World- Or Not: The Case of Duration and Immunization," *Financial Review*, 18(4), pp. 271-280, (1983).

————"Total Portfolio Duration: A New Perspective on Asset Allocation," *Financial Analysts Journal*, 42(5), pp. 18-29, (1986a).

————"The Dedicated Bond Portfolio In Pension Funds — Part I: Motivations and Basics," *Financial Analysts Journal*, 42(1), pp. 68-75, (1986b).

————"The Dedicated Bond Portfolio In Pension Funds — Part II: Immunization, Horizon Matching, and Contingent Procedures," *Financial Analysts Journal*, 42(2), pp. 47-57, (1986c).

Marshall, J.F. *Futures and Option Contracting: Theory and Practice*, Cincinnati, OH: South-Western, (1989).

Redington, F.M. "Review of the Principle of Life Office Valuations," *Journal of the Institute of Actuaries*, 18, pp. 286-340, (1952).

Schaefer, S. M. "Immunization and Duration: A Review of Theory, Peformance and Applications," in *The Revolution in Corporate Finance*, J.M. Stern and D.H. Chew (eds.), Oxford, UK: Blackwell, (1986).

Wade, R. E. "Managing a Negative Gap in a Rising Interest Rate Environment," *Financial Managers' Statement*, 9(4), 33-37 (July 1987).

Chapter 8

Understanding Interest Rates and Exchange Rates

Overview

Financial engineers are often called upon to devise ways to transform the character of debt obligations. Sometimes this means transforming a fixed-rate obligation to a floating-rate obligation in the same currency. At other times, it means transforming an obligation in one currency to an obligation in another currency. Anyone with a serious interest in financial engineering must, therefore, have an understanding of the factors that determine interest rates and exchange rates and must have an appreciation for the risk exposures associated with fluctuations in these rates.

This chapter starts with a discussion of interest rates and the cash flows associated with debt instruments. The various forms of risk associated with debt instruments and some of the tools used to manage these risks will also be introduced in this chapter.

Following the discussion of interest rates, the related topics of exchange rates and exchange-rate risks will be examined. Much of this examination concerns the determinants of spot and forward exchange rates. Our primary objective is to help the reader understand how exchange rates are related to interest rates (and vice versa), the risks that variations in these rates pose for borrowers and others involved in the international markets, and how interest-rate and exchange-rate discrepancies may be exploited for profit. All of these topics will prove important in our later discussions of the physical tools, the processes developed, and the strategies employed by modern financial engineers. It is important to note that we use the terms **debt markets** and **credit markets** synonymously to refer to the markets for debt securities.

Debt Instruments: The Basics

A debt instrument is a promissory note that evidences a debtor/creditor relationship. In such a relationship, one party borrows funds from another party. The borrowing party promises to repay the borrowed funds together with interest. The borrowing party is the debtor and the lending party is the creditor. The promissory note is satisfied when the borrowing party's obligations have all been met.

A debt instrument may be marketable or nonmarketable. Marketable debt instruments are considered **securities**. When the debt instrument takes the form of a security, the borrower is called the **issuer**. The issuer sells its securities to the lender who is called an **investor** or **holder**. All securities sold as part of the same issuance are called, collectively, an **issue**.

Some marketable debt securities, such as corporate bonds, require a neutral third party to oversee the issue. In these cases, the promissory note takes the form of an indenture. An **indenture**, which is called a trust deed in the United Kingdom, is an agreement that details all applicable terms and that appoints a trustee to serve as the neutral third party between the issuer and the holders of the securities. The provisions of the indenture designed to protect the holders of the securities are called **protective covenants**.

The length of time until the debt instrument matures is called its **term to maturity** or, more simply, its **term**. Debt instruments having maturities of less than one year (when issued) are often lumped together under the heading of money market instruments. Those with maturities of a year or more are generally considered capital market instruments. The line of demarcation between money market and capital market instruments has become progressively more fuzzy and many professionals in the industry prefer looser language, such as short-term, intermediate-term, and long-term debt.

Most debt instruments call for a fixed rate of interest that is paid periodically: semiannually or annually, for example. The fixed rate of interest, which is always stated on an annual basis, is called the **coupon rate** and the payment itself is called the **coupon**. Some debt instruments, however, require a periodic resetting of the interest rate to reflect changes in market conditions. Such instruments constitute **floating-rate** or **adjustable-rate** debt.

Some debt instruments provide for periodic payments that include both interest and principal. Others only require periodic payment of interest. Still others require no payments of either interest or principal until such time as the instrument matures. (In this book, the payments associated with a debt instrument are called cash flows and the collection of cash flows is referred to as the cash flow stream.)

When an instrument requires that each payment include some principal as well as interest in such a fashion that the principal is gradually repaid over the life of the instrument, the instrument is said to be **amortizing**. Residential mortgage debt is an example of amortizing debt. When the instrument provides for the full repayment of principal in a lump sum at maturity, with interim payments limited to interest, the instrument is said to be **nonamortizing**. Conventional bonds are examples of nonamortizing debt. When no payments of any kind are required until the instrument matures, the instrument is called a **zero coupon bond** or, more simply, a **zero**.

The Coupon

In the case of fixed-rate debt, the debt instrument's coupon is fixed at the time of issuance. The size of the coupon is determined by a number of factors. These include (1) the general market conditions for debt of the maturity involved, (2) the creditworthiness of the issuer, (3) the tax status of the issue, (4) the value of any collateral offered to support the issue, and (5) any special features that might be included in the issue's indenture.

Since debt securities issued by the United States Treasury (called Treasury securities or simply Treasuries) include a near continuum of maturities out to 30 years, are of the highest quality, and are extremely liquid, the rates afforded by Treasuries are the logical starting point for setting coupon rates on other instruments. Beginning then with the prevailing Treasury rate for a given maturity, a premium will be added in order to reflect the relative riskiness of a particular new issue. This rate will then be adjusted up or down depending on the tax status of the issue. All other things being equal, the more heavily taxed is the income provided by an instrument, the higher the coupon the instrument must carry to attract investors. Thus, fully taxable corporate issues will carry higher coupons than tax-exempt municipals of similar maturities and risks. The provision of collateral reduces the financial injury to holders of an instrument in the event of a default by the issuer. The greater the value of collateral and the more liquid the collateral, the more secure the holders of the instrument are, and the smaller the coupon necessary to sell the issue.

Some of the special features that affect the size of the coupon include callability, conversion, and sinking funds. **A call provision** grants the issuer the right to call back the issue on or after the **call date**. In the event that the call provision is exercised, the holder will receive the **call price**. The call price is equal to the instrument's par value plus a call premium specified in the indenture. An instrument is **convertible** if it can be converted, at the discretion of the holder, into some other asset of the issuer. In the case of corporate issuers, this asset is usually common stock. Call provisions are unattractive to potential investors and thus increase the coupon necessary to sell an issue. Conversion features are attractive to potential investors and thus reduce the coupon necessary to sell an issue. Both call and conversion features are forms of options. (We discuss these features in an option's context in Chapter 14.)

A **sinking fund** is a mechanism that provides for the gradual retirement of a debt issue. Sinking funds take one of two general forms. In the first, which is the most common in use today, the issuer must periodically repurchase a specified portion of the outstanding issue. These repurchases may be accomplished by either or both partial calls and outright market purchases—depending on the terms of the indenture. In the second, the issuer makes periodic payments to a dedicated account, supervised by a trustee. The proceeds of this account are used to retire the issue at maturity. Bonds with sinking fund provisions are known, colloquially, as **sinkers**. In general, sinking funds reduce the level of uncertainty for the holders of the issue and thereby reduce the size of the coupon required to sell the issue. However, the extent to which uncertainty is reduced depends largely on the type of sinking fund employed.

Valuation of Debt Instruments

The valuation of debt instruments is an exercise in the mathematics of present value. That is, the cash flows that the instrument will provide to the investor must be discounted to their present values. The cash flows are discounted at what is called the instrument's yield. The sum of these present values is then the current market price of the instrument. Symbolically, the yield is the value y that satisfies Equation 8.1.

$$\sum_{t=1}^{m \cdot T} \frac{CF(t)}{(1 + y/m)^t} = \text{Current market price} \qquad (8.1)$$

The left hand side of Equation 8.1 discounts the successive cash flows, denoted CF(t), at the rate of y, and then sums these discounted values. The value m denotes the frequency of the payments. If the payments are made annually, then m is 1; if the payments are made semiannually, then m is 2; and so on. The frequency of the payments is important. When the payments are made semiannually, the yield is understood to be quoted on the assumption that it is compounded twice a year (semiannually). This is called a **semiannual rate** but it is still stated on an annual basis. As a general rule, there is only one value of y that will solve Equation 8.1. The yield can be found using the same type of algorithm used to compute an internal rate of return in Chapter 4.[1] The process can be sped up a bit by recognizing that the coupon payment portion of the cash flow stream represents an annuity.

It should be readily obvious from Equation 8.1 that there is an inverse relationship between bond prices and bond yields. This is simply another manifestation of the inverse relationship between present values and discount rates discussed in Chapter 4.

Two small points are in order before moving on. First, different bonds have different par values. To avoid confusion when comparing debt instruments that have different par values, it is customary to quote the prices of debt instruments as a percentage of their par values. Thus, a $1000 par value bond priced at $967.50 would be quoted at 96.75. The decimal portion of this value (.75) might be quoted as a fraction based on thirty-seconds or eighths. For example, Treasury bonds are usually quoted in thirty-seconds of a percentage point. In such a case, 96.75 would be reported as 96²⁴⁄₃₂, i.e., 96 and 24 thirty-seconds. Bond prices are usually quoted on an "and interest" basis.[2] That is, the price *does not* include the interest that has accrued on the bond. The accrued interest is calculated separately and the purchaser pays the seller the accrued interest in addition to the agreed purchase price. The accrued interest is calculated using standard interest-accrual formulas and is then added on to the purchase price. There are several interest-accrual formulas and which applies depends upon the type of bond. For example, Treasury bonds accrue interest on an **actual over 365 day** basis while corporate bonds accrue interest on a **360 over 360 day** basis. Thus, Treasury bonds accrue one day's interest each day with interest calculated as if a year consists of 365 days. Corporate bonds, called **corporates**, accrue and pay interest on the assumption that the year consists of 360 days and each month consists of 30 days. Thus, February pays two days extra interest while the 31st day of a month having 31 days is a "bad day" in the sense that no interest accrues on that day.

The second point we need to make involves basis points. Yield changes and interest-rate spreads are usually quoted in basis points. A **basis point (bp)** is one one-hundredth of one percent (0.01%). One hundred basis points is, therefore, one percentage point. In market slang, basis points are sometimes called "beeps."

The mathematics of yield measurement are the same whether measuring the yield of a nonamortizing debt instrument, such as a bond, or an amortizing instrument, such as a mortgage. The concept of yield is one of the most important concepts in fixed-income security analysis. It is important to understand, however, that different instruments have different yields. As indicated earlier, the yield, like the coupon at the time of initial issue, is explained by the market conditions associated with the maturity of the instrument, by the creditworthiness of the issuer, by the quantity and the quality of any collateral provided, and by various other features specific to the bond. Of the many factors that influence an instrument's yield, the two most important are the instrument's maturity and the riskiness of the issue. The next two sections examine these issues.

The Yield Curve

We focus on the role of maturity by holding default risk constant. This is most easily done by limiting ourselves to conventional coupon-bearing Treasury securities. We use Treasury securities because this is the only class of securities widely regarded as completely free of default risk. Each bond of a given maturity is priced by the market and this price can be transformed, by the arithmetic we have already described, into a yield. We can then plot these yields against maturity. The relationship between yield and maturity is called the **term structure of interest rates**. When graphed, the term structure is called a **yield curve**. A yield curve can be plotted in either of two ways. The first is to fit a smooth curve to the observations on yield. The second is to connect every observation in a point-by-point plot. A yield curve of the former type is depicted in Panel A of Exhibit 8.1 and a yield curve of the second type is depicted in Panel B of Exhibit 8.1.

Exhibit 8.1
Panel A
Fitted Yield Curve

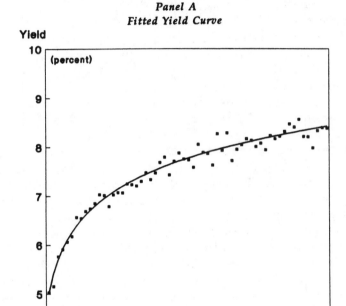

Notice that the yield curve depicted in Panel A of Exhibit 8.1 is upward sloping. This is considered normal and is called an **ascending** or **upward sloping** yield curve. There are several compet-

Exhibit 8.1
Panel B
Point-by-Point Plot of Yield Curve

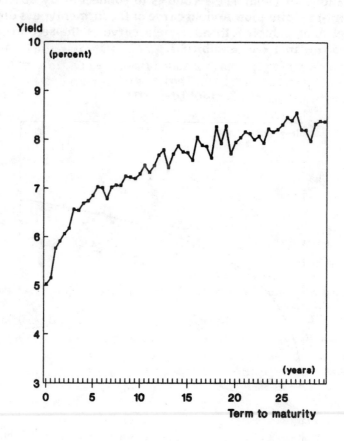

ing, although not mutually exclusive, explanations for the shape of
the yield curve. First, long-term yields (yields on long-term instruments) should reflect market expectations of successive future short-
term rates since an alternative to holding a long-term instrument
is to hold a series of successive short-term instruments. If this is
the only determinant of long-term rates, then long-term rates should
be the geometric average of expected future short-term rates. This
explanation for the shape of the yield curve is called the **expectations
theory.** Under the expectations theory, an upward sloping yield

curve is explained by the expectation of higher future short-term rates.

The second explanation for the shape of the yield curve is called the **liquidity premium theory**. The liquidity premium theory holds that since, as we will demonstrate shortly, long-maturity instruments are more price sensitive than are short-maturity instruments, holders of long-term instruments are exposed to more price risk from a general change in the level of interest rates than are holders of short-term instruments.

The final theory, called the **segmented markets theory** or **segmentation theory**, argues that there are reasons to believe that demand and supply conditions for different maturities are different and that these maturity-specific demand/supply conditions are the determinants of yields. This theory views the debt markets as a continuum of individual, separate maturity markets. The problem with this theory, at least in its pure form, is that it fails to allow for arbitrage between maturities. Nevertheless, there are undoubtedly maturity-specific demand and supply considerations and they must certainly have some effect on yields. Most players in the credit markets have concluded that all three explanations for term structure play a role, but that the relative importance of each varies with market conditions.

The yield curve is not static. It is continuously changing in response to evolving credit market conditions. Occasionally, the curve will shift up or down. Such shifts, however, are usually not parallel. Rather, the short-maturity end of the curve (short-end) might shift by more than the long-maturity end (long end). During periods of monetary tightening by the Federal Reserve, for example, the entire curve will typically move higher but the short end will move by a greater amount—this results in a flattening, or even an inversion, of the yield curve. Such an inversion is depicted in Exhibit 8.2.

Investment Risks in the Debt Markets

There are a number of risks associated with holding a debt instrument. These include interest-rate risk, default risk, reinvestment risk, call risk, prepayment risk, and purchasing power risk. We will briefly consider each of these in a few moments. First, however, some general observations about risk must be made.

As we discussed in Chapter 6, any financial risk consists of two basic components called systematic risk and unsystematic risk. The systematic component of risk represents the degree to which

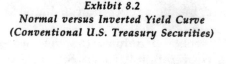

Exhibit 8.2
Normal versus Inverted Yield Curve
(Conventional U.S. Treasury Securities)

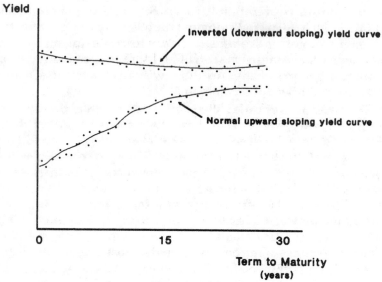

manifestations of the risk are associated with more general market behaviors. The unsystematic component of risk represents the degree to which manifestations of the risk are independent of more general market behaviors.

The various types of risk associated with holding debt instruments also have systematic and unsystematic components. The systematic component of a risk to which the holder of a debt instrument is exposed is the degree to which that instrument's value fluctuates with the values of other debt instruments. The unsystematic component is the degree to which the value changes in the debt instrument are independent of the value changes in other debt instruments.

The importance of the distinction between systematic and unsystematic components of risk has to do with the management of risk. Unsystematic risk disappears with diversification. That is, the greater the degree of diversification in a portfolio, the less unsystematic risk one will find. Systematic risk, however, does not disappear with diversification and must, therefore, be managed by other means.

A more specific examination of the forms of risk associated with holding debt instruments follows.[3]

Interest-Rate Risk

Interest-rate risk is examined first because this form of risk usually dominates the other risks associated with holding debt instruments. Interest-rate risk is the risk that evolving market conditions will bring about a change in interest rates. Since yields on existing instruments must respond to reflect prevailing interest rates, a change in the level of interest rates will mean a change in market values for existing debt instruments. Manifestations of interest-rate risk are broadly felt since a change in market conditions that leads to an upward or downward shift in the yield curve will influence most debt securities similarly and simultaneously.

Interest-rate risk is of great significance to both issuers and holders of debt instruments. For issuers, changes in interest rates effect the cost of funds and may effect the return on rate-sensitive assets. The latter is particularly important if the return on the assets is used to meet the interest expense on the issuer's liabilities.

As mentioned earlier, long-term instruments are more price sensitive to changes in interest rates than short-term instruments. This point is very important and worth some elaboration. Suppose we have five instruments that have maturities of six months, one year, two years, five years, and twenty years, respectively. Each instrument is initially priced at par, that is, the yields and the coupons match, and each instrument pays a semiannual coupon. Consider the effect on the prices of these instruments from a 20 basis point parallel upward shift in the yield curve. This parallel shift in the yield curve is depicted in Exhibit 8.3 and the resultant values and value changes are reported in Table 8.1.

Table 8.1
Debt Instrument Maturity and Price Sensitivity

Maturity (Years)	Coupon	Initial Yield (%)	Initial Price	New Yield (%)	New Price	Price Change
0.5	7.000	7.000	100.000	7.200	99.903	−0.097
1.0	7.750	7.750	100.000	7.950	99.811	−0.189
2.0	8.250	8.250	100.000	8.450	99.639	−0.361
5.0	8.750	8.750	100.000	8.950	99.208	−0.792
20.0	9.375	9.375	100.000	9.575	98.233	−1.767

Note: The prices and price changes are reported per $100 of face (par) value.

Exhibit 8.3
Parallel Shift in the Yield Curve

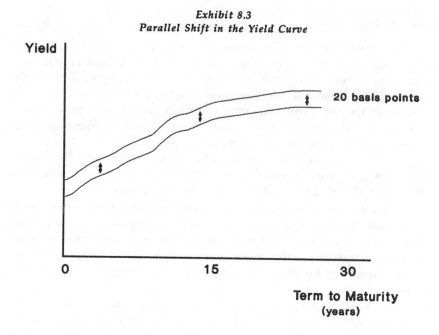

The values of the bonds, both before and after the 20 basis point change in yield, are calculated using Equation 8.1. Now consider the column labeled "Price Change." Notice that the instrument with six months to maturity declined in value by $0.097 for each $100 of face value as a result of the 20 basis point increase in yields. Notice also that the bond with 20 years to maturity declined in value by $1.767 for each $100 of face value as a result of the same 20 basis point increase in yields. *The 20 year bond declined in value by more than 18 times as much as the bond with 6 months to maturity.* Thus, we see that the longer the maturity, all other things being equal, the more price sensitive a debt instrument is to a change in its yield.

The price changes discussed above measured the change in bond values for a 20 basis point change in yields. Bond traders and others involved in interest rate risk management need to know very precisely how changes in yield will effect prices. There are a number of related measures that are used for this purpose. The three most widely used are **duration**, the **dollar value of a basis point**, and the **yield value of a thirty-second.**

Duration and Convexity

We have demonstrated that the longer a debt instrument's maturity, all other things being equal, the more sensitive is its price to changes in its yield. Maturity, however, is not the only factor that influences a debt instrument's price sensitivity to yield changes. Four other factors also play a role. The other factors are (1) the size of the instrument's coupon, (2) the frequency of the coupon payments, (3) the speed with which the loan principal amortizes, and (4) the instrument's present yield.

In 1938, Frederick Macaulay developed a measure of price sensitivity to yield changes that incorporates all the factors that influence price sensitivity.[4] This measure is known as duration. We introduced the concept of duration in Chapter 7, but we expand a little here. Assuming equal basis point changes in yield (i.e., a parallel shift in the yield curve), two debt instruments that have identical durations will have identical interest-rate sensitivities. Further, the ratio of two debt instruments' durations is an accurate measure of their relative price sensitivities to equivalent yield changes when such price sensitivity is stated on a percentage basis. Duration, which is measured in years and denoted here by D, is a weighted average-time-to-maturity of an instrument. The weights are the ratios of the present values of the future cash flows (including both interest and principal) to the current market price of the instrument. The current price of the instrument is, of course, the sum of the present value of all future cash flows associated with the instrument. The duration formula is given by Equation 8.2.

$$D = \sum_{t=1}^{m \cdot T} w_t \cdot \frac{t}{m}$$

(8.2)

$$\text{where } w_t = \frac{CF(t) \cdot (1 + y/m)^{-t}}{\sum CF(t) \cdot (1 + y/m)^{-t}} \qquad t = 1, 2, 3, \ldots, m \cdot T$$

CF(t):   Cash flow during period t.
   y: Present yield on instrument.
  m: The number of payment periods per year.
   T: The number of years covered by the cash flow stream.

Let's consider the duration calculation for a simple bond. Consider the two-year bond in Table 8.1. It has a coupon of 8.250 percent and an initial yield of 8.250 percent—so it is priced at par. The duration calculation for this bond, which reveals a duration of approximately 1.88 years, is shown in Table 8.2.

Table 8.2
Duration Calculation

t value	Cash Flow	Discounted Value of Cash Flow	Weight w(t)	Time (t/m)	Product w(t) · (t/m)
1	$4.125	3.961	0.0396	0.5	0.0198
2	$4.125	3.805	0.0381	1.0	0.0381
3	$4.125	3.654	0.0365	1.5	0.0548
4	$104.125	88.580	0.8858	2.0	1.7716
	Totals	100.000	1.00000	Duration =	1.8843

The durations for all the bonds in Table 8.1 are listed in Table 8.3.[5]

Table 8.3
Comparative Durations

Maturity (Years)	Coupon	Initial Yield (%)	Initial Price	Duration (Years)	Modified Duration
0.5	7.000	7.000	100.000	0.50	0.48
1.0	7.750	7.750	100.000	0.98	0.94
2.0	8.250	8.250	100.000	1.88	1.81
5.0	8.750	8.750	100.000	4.15	3.98
20.0	9.375	9.375	100.000	9.38	8.96

Notice that Table 8.3 also includes a modified duration. Modified duration was discussed in Chapter 7. Modified duration, denoted here by D^*, is related to the Macaulay duration by Equation 8.3.

$$D^* = \frac{D}{(1 + y/m)}$$

(8.3)

Duration has a great many theoretical as well as practical applications. The interested reader can get some idea of the many applications by consulting the "References and Suggested Reading" section which appears at the end of this chapter.

Consider one such application, compare the duration of the 20-year bond to the duration of the 5-year bond. Notice that the 20-year bond has a duration that is approximately 2.25 times that of the 5-year bond. This means that the yield change necessary to cause a 1 percent decline in the market value of the 5-year bond will cause a 2.25 percent decline in the market value of the 20-year bond. Duration ratios, like the one we just used to compare the above two bonds, provide a measure of relative price sensitivities in terms of percentage changes in value. To convert these values to dollar terms, we must multiply the duration ratio by the ratio of the bonds' prices. This adjusted duration ratio (ADR) will prove important shortly. It is given by Equation 8.4.

$$ADR = \frac{D_{20\text{-yr}}}{D_{5\text{-yr}}} \times \frac{P_{20\text{-yr}}}{P_{5\text{-yr}}} \tag{8.4}$$

Since both of these bonds were priced at par the price ratio is 1.0. This will, of course, usually not be the case. Since it happens to be the case here, however, we can say that the yield change just sufficient to cause a $1 change in the value of the 5-year bond would cause a $2.25 change in the value of the 20-year bond.

It would be instructive to consider the relationship between a bond's Macaulay duration and its term to maturity. The relationship will depend on whether the bonds examined are selling at a discount from par (called discount bonds), at par (called par bonds), or above par (called premium bonds). The extreme form of a discount bond is a zero coupon bond since it pays no periodic coupon at all. The relationship between the Macaulay duration and term to maturity for these four categories of bonds is depicted in Exhibit 8.4. For purposes of the illustration, the coupon is assumed to be 8 percent for all the bonds except the zeros. For the premium bonds, the yield is assumed to be 6 percent and for the discount bonds the yield is assumed to be 10 percent.

It has long been known that, all other things being equal, the duration of an instrument will change as the instrument's yield changes. Until the 1980s, however, not much thought was given to these changes other than to point out that one needed to periodically recalculate durations and modify the hedge ratios or asset/liability mix accordingly. During the latter half of the 1980s, however, considerable interest developed in predicting changes in duration.[6] The importance of this can be made clear by way of an example. Suppose that a corporate treasurer has developed an asset portfolio—using duration modeling—so as to match the asset portfolio duration to the liability portfolio duration. If yield rises, how do the two portfolio durations change? If

Exhibit 8.4
Duration vs. Term
Discount Bonds, Premium Bonds, Par Bonds, Zeros

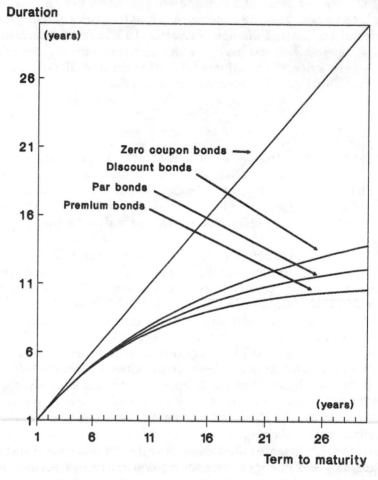

the durations change by equal amounts, then the asset/liability mix is still correct. But, if the asset portfolio duration increases or decreases by more or less than the liability portfolio duration, then the asset/liability mix is no longer correct.

The key to understanding how durations change is the concept of **convexity**. If we plot the present value (PV) of an instrument against the instrument's yield, the negative of the slope of this present value curve is the duration of the instrument. This

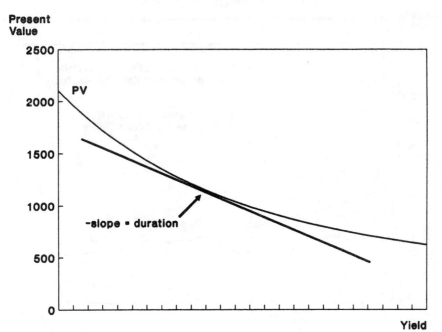

Exhibit 8.5
Relationship between Duration and the PV Curve

is depicted in Exhibit 8.5. (The slope of the straight line drawn tangent to the PV curve is the slope of the PV curve at the point of tangency.)

We see that the PV curve is convex, meaning that the slope is continuously changing. Convexity measures the *rate of change* in the slope. The greater the rate of change, the more the duration changes as yield changes. Measuring convexity has become important in many areas involving risk management. For now, however, just consider the PV curve of the asset portfolio and the PV curve of the liability portfolio depicted in Exhibit 8.6. Notice that they have the same initial duration (denoted D_1). After a yield increase, we see that the asset portfolio has a greater duration than the liability portfolio (denoted D_2). Had we known that the asset portfolio's duration was more convex than the liability portfolio's duration, we could have predicted this change and planned for a modification of either the asset mix or the liability mix to compensate for it.

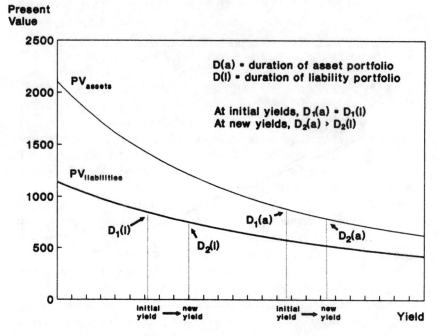

Exhibit 8.6
Effects of Convexity on Asset/Liability Management

Dollar Value of a Basis Point:

Closely related to duration as a measure of interest rate sensitivity is the **dollar value of a basis point**, denoted DV01 (read "dollar value of a zero one") or DVBP. (The dollar value of a basis point is sometimes called the price value of a basis point and denoted PV01 or PVBP. It is also sometimes called the present value of a basis point). An instrument's DV01 is the amount of value change per $100 of face value that will occur if yields change by one basis point. The DV01 values for the five bonds in Table 8.1 appear in Table 8.4.

Table 8.4
Comparative DV01s

Maturity	Yield	Price	DV01
0.5	7.000	100.000	0.00483
1.0	7.750	100.000	0.00945
2.0	8.250	100.000	0.01809
5.0	8.750	100.000	0.03980
20.0	9.375	100.000	0.08953

The DV01s in Table 8.4 were obtained by calculating the price of the instruments at their actual yields, recalculating the prices at yields one basis point higher than their actual yields, and then taking the difference between the two prices. Consider for a moment the DV01 of the 5-year and the 20-year bonds. The 5-year bond has a DV01 of 0.03980 while the 20-year bond has a DV01 of 0.08953. The ratio of the DV01s provides a relative measure of the dollar value changes that are associated with equivalent changes in yield. Thus, the 20-year bond is 2.25 times as price sensitive to yield changes as is the 5-year bond. This is exactly the same result we got from the duration calculation (after multiplying by the price ratio). We see then that DV01s and durations provide similar information and have many of the same applications. For the remainder of this discussion, we consider DV01 only.

Those involved in the management of interest-rate risk often have positions in instruments of different maturities. A position in an actual instrument is called a **cash position.** Some of these cash positions may be long positions while others are short positions. Clearly, a short position in one debt instrument is a partial hedge for a long position in another debt instrument.

Unfortunately, knowledge of the instruments' DV01s is not sufficient, in and of itself, to effectively manage interest-rate risk. The reason is simple. The DV01 measures the dollar value change that results from a single basis point change in yield. But, not all yield curve shifts are parallel and, hence, not all yields change by the same number of basis points. To deal with this problem, risk managers typically convert all interest-rate exposures to some **baseline** or **benchmark** equivalent. This is usually an instrument on which a futures contract is written. For example, the baseline instrument might be the 20-year Treasury bond or the 10-year Treasury note. Next, the historic yield changes for the cash instrument in which the firm has a position is regressed against the corresponding historic yield changes for the baseline instrument to get a yield beta. The yield beta measures the number of basis points the yield of the cash instrument is likely to change for each 1 basis point change in the yield of the baseline instrument. For example, suppose that a bond trader has a long position in $2,000,000 (face value) 15-year bonds of Issuer X. The bonds have a DV01 of 0.0792. The baseline 20-year Treasury bond has a DV01 of 0.0884. Finally, the yield beta (β_x) of the 15-year bonds of Issuer X is 0.84. Then the DV01 hedging model can be used to determine the face value of the baseline instrument which is *risk equivalent* to this long position. The DV01 model is given by Equation 8.5, in which FV denotes face value. Face value is also called par value.

$$FV_b = FV_x \times \frac{DV01_x}{DV01_b} \times \beta_x$$

(8.5)

$$FV_b = 2,000,000 \times \frac{0.0792}{0.0884} \times 0.84$$

$$= 1,505,158$$

From this calculation, we see that the long position in $2,000,000 of Issuer X's bonds is equivalent to a long position in $1,505,158 of baseline T-bonds.

Suppose that the firm also has a short position in $1,800,000 (face value) of 9-year notes of Issuer Y. Using the DV01 model, these notes are found to be equivalent to a short position in $1,066,500 of baseline Treasury bonds. By converting all positions to the same baseline equivalent, the risk managers can accurately assess the degree to which the firm's various exposures are offsetting. For example, the risk managers sum the baseline equivalent of the long position in Issue X with the baseline equivalent of the partially offsetting short position in Issue Y to obtain a net exposure *equivalent* to a long position in $438,658 of the baseline security. Since a futures contract on the baseline security exists, the risk manager can hedge by taking a *short* position in the futures. In this case, each 20-year Treasury bond futures covers $100,000 of face value bonds. Thus, to fully hedge, the risk manager needs a short position in approximately 4.4 futures.

Yield Value of a Thirty-Second

The yield value of a 32nd (YV32) is another method of measuring an instrument's interest-rate sensitivity. The yield value of a 32nd is simply the number of basis points the instrument's yield must change in order for the instrument's price to change by 1/32 of a percentage point. It provides the same kind of information as a duration and a DV01, but, unlike duration and DV01, it is *inversely* related to volatility. That is, the greater is an instrument's YV32, the less sensitive is the instrument's price to changes in yield.

A 32nd of a percent is 0.03125 percent. Since the two-year

bond in Table 8.4 had a DV01 of 0.01809, it must have a YV32 of 1.727. That is, the instrument's yield must change by 1.727 basis points for the instrument's price to change by 0.03125 percent. Similarly, the 20-year bond in Table 8.4 has DV01 of 0.08953 and, hence, has a YV32 of 0.349. The relationship between the yield value of a 32nd and the dollar value of a basis point is given by Equation 8.6.

$$YV32 = \frac{0.03125}{DV01} \qquad (8.6)$$

Default Risk

Default risk is the risk that the borrower will fail to make timely payments of interest and/or principal on its debt. Most issuers of debt securities have their debt rated by debt rating agencies. As a general rule, underwriters will not handle unrated issues. The two principal rating agencies are Moody's and Standard & Poor's. The rating systems of these two rating agencies are similar but not identical. The best grade is the top investment grade (Aaa or AAA, respectively) and the poorest grade is for those bonds that are already in default. The higher the rating, the lower the yield an instrument will provide. A decade ago, very few issuers could sell debt that had a less than investment-grade rating. But this has changed dramatically during the last decade as speculative grade (also called **high yield** or **junk**) issues have become a major source of finance for those involved in takeovers and leveraged buyouts. The dramatic change in the volume of this type of debt is illustrated in Exhibit 8.7.

Default risk is not a hedgeable risk, but investors can manage it in several ways. One way is to enhance the creditworthiness of the borrower by insisting on collateral. Another way is to limit the size of the position in any one issuer's debt.

Default risk is largely unsystematic in nature and, hence, it can be greatly reduced by diversification. In a well-diversified high-yield portfolio, the risk premium on high-yield debt tended to exceed the default rate on the debt during most of the 1980s. The difference represents an excess premium, i.e., an excess of that necessary to compensate for risk. This changed dramatically during the final two years of the decade. The excess premium on high-yield corporate debt for the period is depicted in Exhibit 8.8.

The serious deterioration of the junk bond market during the late 1980s and into 1990 led to charges of unethical behavior on the

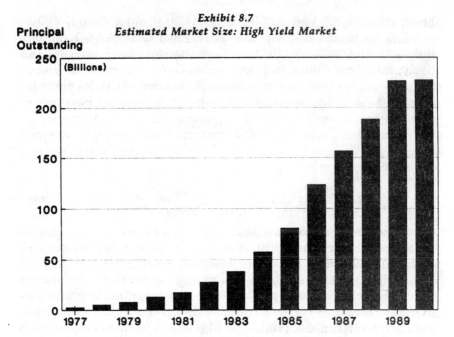

Exhibit 8.7
Estimated Market Size: High Yield Market

Source: First Boston Corporation, High Yield Handbook 1991

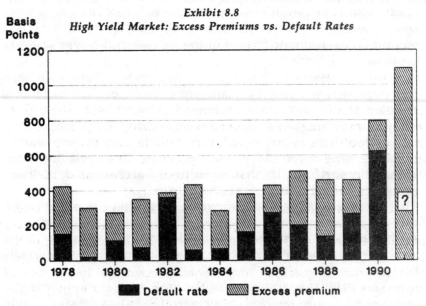

Exhibit 8.8
High Yield Market: Excess Premiums vs. Default Rates

Source: First Boston Corporation, High Yield Handbook 1991

part of a number of people. In particular, Michael Milken, a Drexel Burnham Lambert employee who is credited with single-handedly creating a junk bond market as a vehicle to finance mergers and acquisitions, was shown to have selectively cited portions of studies of speculative grade bond performance in his sales efforts. He provided data for periods in which speculative grade bonds outperformed "safer" investment vehicles and conveniently neglected periods during which they seriously underperformed.[7] Investment managers who accepted Milken's pitch appear not to have examined Milken's data sources with sufficient care.

Reinvestment Risk, Call Risk, and Prepayment Risk

Reinvestment risk, call risk, and prepayment risk are closely related forms of risk. When an investor purchases a debt instrument that has a known yield, the investor takes the risk that the instrument's value will fluctuate in response to changes in its yield. This is the interest-rate risk we discussed earlier. However, if the investor purchases an instrument with a maturity that is identical to his or her investment horizon, then these fluctuations in value are really quite irrelevant. Regardless of interim changes in value, the instrument will ultimately be redeemed for its full face value (par) and, thus, for this investor, interim fluctuations are not very important. But if the investment provides periodic income, such as coupon payments, then there is still a risk that the terminal wealth will deviate from initial expectations. The concept of yield implicitly assumes that income generated by an investment can be reinvested to earn the same rate. But if yields are fluctuating, the investor may very likely find that the reinvestment rate differs from the yield that prevailed at the time the instrument was purchased. These reinvestment rates might be higher or lower than the purchase-time yield and so the terminal wealth may deviate from the expectation held at the time of the instrument's purchase. The deviations from expected terminal wealth that result from fluctuations in the reinvestment rate are called **reinvestment risk**.

Call risk and **prepayment risk** are the risks that the issuer will choose to repay the loan principal before maturity. In the case of callable bonds, the issuer can choose, at its discretion, to call the bond on or after the call date. If a bond is called, the holder gets the call price as specified in the bond's indenture. In the case of mortgages debt, the mortgagor usually has the right to prepay the mortgage balance at any time. The mortgage balance is the portion of the principal that has not amortized plus any accrued interest. In both a call and a prepayment, the holder of the debt instrument receives proceeds sooner than expected and, presumably, sooner than desired. This premature receipt of funds forces the investor to look for an avenue to reinvest.

A debt instrument is most likely to be called or prepayed when interest rates have declined. Lower interest rates provide an incentive for the issuer to issue new debt at the prevailing lower rates and to use the proceeds to pay off the existing debt. This tendency for calls and prepayments to occur when rates decline implies that the investor will find that the available investment alternatives after a call or a prepayment are usually poorer than they were at the time of the original investment. It is for these reasons that call risk and prepayment risk are closely related to reinvestment risk.

One way to avoid reinvestment risk is to invest exclusively in securities that are not callable or prepayable and that do not provide periodic coupons. Noncallable zero-coupon bonds are such an instrument. (The relationship between zero-coupon bond maturities, risk, and the length of investment horizons was discussed in Chapter 6.)

Purchasing Power Risk

The last form of risk we consider is **purchasing power risk.** This is the risk that the terminal wealth from an investment will have less purchasing power than the investor expected at the time of the instrument's purchase. This form of risk is associated with any investment that is not indexed to the rate of inflation. Although some debt instruments have coupons that are indexed to various measures of inflation, debt with indexed coupons are not common in the United States. They are more common in Europe. Floating-rate debt, however, is, in a sense, inflation indexed. As we will argue later in this chapter, interest-rates tend to reflect inflationary expectations. Thus, a change in inflationary expectations should be accompanied by a change in interest rates. Floating-rate debt should then adjust to offer a greater nominal rate of interest when inflationary expectations are high, and a lower nominal rate of interest when inflationary expectations are low.

Exchange Rates: The Basics

An exchange rate (or foreign-exchange rate) is the number of units of one currency that can be purchased (exchanged) for one unit of another currency. An exchange rate is therefore the price of one currency stated in terms of another currency. This price is determined by a number of related factors, including (1) the general price level for goods in the two countries, (2) the expected rates of inflation in the two countries, (3) the rates of interest in the two countries, and (4) the degree to which the governments of the two countries restrict trade and/or manipulate exchange rates involving their currencies for economic or political gain.

There are actually two different kinds of exchange rates: spot and forward. Spot exchange rates are the rates of exchange for immediate payment and delivery of a currency.[8] A typical exchange rate quote for deutschemarks (DEM) in terms of dollars (USD) would be 1.4555 DEM/USD. This means that one U.S. dollar will purchase 1.4555 deutschemarks for immediate delivery. Forward exchange rates are current rates of exchange for deferred delivery of a currency. Deferred delivery means that the price of the currency is agreed to now, but the delivery and payment for the currency will not occur until some specified later date. Forward exchange rates are stated in exactly the same way as spot rates but the length of the delivery deferral must be added. For example, the 30-day forward rate for deutschemark in terms of dollars might be 1.4552 DEM/USD 30-days.

The difference between the forward rate and the spot rate is called a **forward premium** if the forward rate is above the spot rate, and a **forward discount** if the forward rate is below the spot rate. In the example above, the 30-day forward deutschemark for dollar rate is at a discount to the spot rate (1.4552 DEM/USD as opposed to 1.4555 DEM/USD). In the case of this particular exchange rate, a forward discount has been the historic norm. This is generally attributed to the lower rate of inflation in West Germany than in the United States. We will ignore this historic relationship in some of the examples that follow in order to illustrate certain pertinent points. In addition, the recent opening of the Eastern block may alter the forward to spot relationship and thus render the historic relationship less meaningful.

The DEM/USD exchange rate could also be expressed as a USD/DEM exchange rate. When we express the rate as USD/DEM it is said to be in **American terms**. When we express it as DEM/USD it is said to be in **German terms**. The rate USD/DEM is the mathematical reciprocal of DEM/USD. The same is true for all other exchange rates.

The markets for both spot and forward foreign exchange are called **currency markets** or **foreign exchange markets** and are known in the trade as FOREX or FX markets. These markets are made, for the most part, by banks, with the banks acting as both dealers and brokers in currencies.

The foreign exchange markets are very liquid for the major hard currencies. While trading is decentralized, with each dealer/broker maintaining its own trading room and associated facilities, dealers and brokers are tied together electronically and the markets are very competitive and very efficient.

Banks, corporations, institutional investors, and private individuals often have commitments in currencies that differ from their domestic currency. These commitments may require exchanges of currencies at a single later date or at a series of later dates. For example, a British bank might make a 60-day dollar loan to an American borrower. The British bank made the loan by taking British pound sterling (BPS) deposits and converting them, at the spot rate, to dollars. The American borrower will repay the dollars, together with interest, in 60 days. Thus, the British bank knows the number of dollars to be received 60-days forward. Or a German automaker might agree to sell cars to an American distributor for a specified number of dollars. The agreement might require the autos to be delivered and payment to be made in 90 days. Thus, the German firm knows the number of dollars to be received 90-days forward. In both of these situations, the receiver of dollars does not really want dollars. The British bank wants pounds and the German automaker wants deutschemarks. Both the bank and the automaker have "long" forward positions in dollars.

Both the bank and the automaker just described can deal with their forward dollar positions in a variety of ways. The simplest way is to wait until they receive the dollars and then convert the dollars to their domestic currency at the prevailing spot rate. The trouble with this strategy is that the spot rates that will prevail 60 or 90 days forward are not known at the time of the initial transactions; that is, at the time the British bank makes its loan to the American firm, and at the time the German automaker agrees to sell cars to the U.S. distributor. It is quite possible, indeed it is highly probable, that the spot exchange rates will have changed from their initial levels by the time of the final currency conversions. If the dollar weakens between the time of the initial agreements and the time of the final exchanges, the British bank and the German automaker could find themselves with serious losses on what seemed like profitable transactions.

Fluctuations in exchange rates are the source of exchange-rate risk. This is the kind of risk to which both the British bank and the German automaker were exposed. When such a risk exists, it is often prudent to **hedge** the risk.

It is important at this point to distinguish between foreign currency transactions and foreign currency translations. For accounting purposes, it is often necessary or desirable to restate profits and losses (as well as balance sheet values) in another currency. Such restatements are referred to as foreign exchange translations. Actual exchanges of currencies, on the other hand, represent foreign exchange transactions.

The Determinants of Exchange Rates

In free markets, changes in exchange rates are determined, more than anything else, by changes in interest rates and inflationary expectations. The role of interest rates is explained by the concept of **interest-rate parity** and the role of inflation is explained by the concept of **purchasing-power parity**. These two explanations are, in turn, related to one another by the **Fisher Equation**. Since this is not meant to be a formal treatise on exchange rate theory, we will keep the discussion short and relatively nonquantitative. The reader interested in a more formal treatment of these topics should see the suggested reading at the end of this chapter.[9]

Interest-Rate Parity

Suppose that the nominal rate of interest for some given maturity in Country X is higher than the nominal rate of interest in Country Y for instruments that have comparable risk. Suppose further that the spot and forward exchange rates of Currency X for Currency Y are identical. Then investors with surplus funds in Country Y have an incentive to convert their Currency Y to Currency X at the current spot exchange rate. The Currency X obtained from this translation can then be invested in Country X at Country X's higher rates. The debt instrument purchased, however, will mature at a known future date and the Country Y investors, therefore, have unwanted long forward positions in Currency X. To eliminate the risk associated with these long forward positions in Currency X, the Country Y investors can contract forward to convert their future Currency X back to Currency Y. The Country Y investor who engages in this related series of transactions will earn a higher return than the Country Y investor who invests domestically at lower rates. Yet, because the investor has hedged his exchange-rate risk, the higher return is achieved without bearing greater risk.

Let's run through a more concrete example. Suppose that an American investor observes that six month (182 day) U.S. Treasury securities are currently yielding 8.20 percent while six-month (182 day) West German government securities are yielding 9.30 percent. The spot exchange rate of deutschemark for dollars is 1.9550 and the 182-day forward exchange rate is also 1.9550. The investor has $100,000 that he plans to invest in 182-day U.S. Treasury securities. After observing the higher yield on West German securities, however, he decides to convert his dollars to deutschemark and then invest these deutschemark in West German securities. At the current spot exchange rate, $100,000 will purchase DEM 195,500. If the deutschemarks are invested at 9.30 percent for 182 days (half a year), the American investor will have DEM 204,691.75 in 182 days. The interest portion is calculated as DEM 195,500 x 9.3% x 182/360. Thus, if the investor engages in this strategy, he will have a long position in 204,691.75 182-day forward deutschemark the moment he purchases the German securities. To hedge this, he would sell DEM 204,691.75 182-days forward for dollars at the current 182-day forward rate. This will yield $104,701.67. If the American investor invested his $100,000 in U.S. securities, on the other hand, he would only have had $104,145.56. For this American investor, the German investment, with the appropriate hedge, is clearly superior to the straight U.S. investment.

The strategy we have just described is actually a sophisticated and widely practiced form of arbitrage called **covered interest arbitrage**. In this strategy, the investor borrows funds in one country, converts the funds to the currency of another country at the prevailing spot exchange rate, lends the currency obtained at the prevailing interest rates in that country, and simultaneously contracts in the forward foreign-exchange market to convert the future proceeds from this lending back to his own currency. The proceeds at delivery can then be used to repay the original lending source. For example, suppose that the American investor, whom we will now call an arbitrager, had borrowed the $100,000 he used for the transaction in the U.S. at a cost of 8.20 percent. As before, the German investment, coupled with the currency transactions, will provide a terminal value of $104,701.67. After repaying the sum he borrowed and the interest (a total of $104,145.56), the arbitrager will have a riskless profit of $556.11. What's more, this profit was earned without any actual investment of the arbitrager's own funds. (The covered interest arbitrage strategy just described is illustrated schematically in Exhibit 8.9.)

Exhibit 8.9
Schematic of Covered Interest Arbitrage

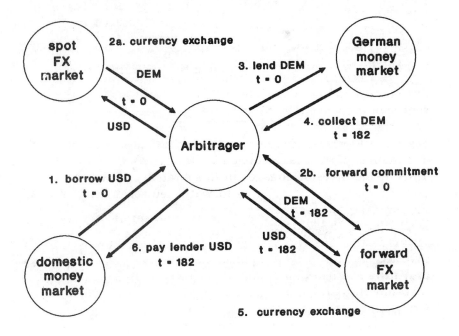

Continuing with the example, consider what happens if this covered interest arbitrage activity becomes widespread. The sales of dollars (for deutschemarks) in the spot market will depress the value of the dollar relative to the value of the deutschemark. Thus the spot exchange rate of DEM for USD will decline. At the same time, the forward sales of deutschemarks for dollars will cause the forward exchange rate of DEM for USD to rise. The spot and forward rates will eventually reach an equilibrium in which no further riskless arbitrage profits are possible. Assuming no change in the 182-day interest rates on the U.S. and German securities, we might find that the equilibrium is reached when the spot DEM/USD rate is 1.9495 and the 182-day forward rate is 1.9599. (We leave it to the reader to prove that no riskless arbitrage profits are possible at these exchange rates.)

The spot and forward rates arrived at in the preceding example do not represent a unique solution to the exchange rate equilibrium. Other combinations of spot and forward exchange rates will also yield a result in which arbitrage profits are not possible. Nevertheless, it is clear that competition among investors to earn the highest returns possible on their money, and competition among arbitragers to exploit interest rate and exchange rate discrepancies are responsible for maintaining logical relationships between spot and forward exchange rates.

The interest-rate parity theorem is summarized by Equation 8.7. In Equation 8.7, $E_{y,x}$ denotes the spot exchange rate; $E_{y,x}(D)$ denotes the D-day forward exchange rate; and $r_y(D)$ and $r_x(D)$ denote the interest rates on comparable risk instruments having maturities of D days.

$$\frac{E_{y,x}(D)}{E_{y,x}} = \frac{1 + r_y(D)}{1 + r_x(D)} \qquad (8.7)$$

Purchasing-Power Parity

The interest-rate parity theorem explains the relationship between spot and forward exchange rates in terms of interest-rate differentials between countries. Once the spot rate is known, for example, the forward rates are all determined by relative interest rates. The theory does not, however, explain why the spot rate is what it is. And without some means of determining the spot rate, the forward rates cannot be determined.

The current spot rate is explained by the concept of purchasing-power parity, which, in turn, is derived from a theorem called the **law of one price.** The law of one price argues, quite simply, that the price of a good in one country cannot exceed the price of the good in another country by more than the cost of transporting the good between the two countries. If it should, merchants, acting in the role of arbitragers, would buy the good in the cheaper market, transport it to the higher-priced market, and then resell it. Included in the transportation cost is a normal profit for the merchant and the cost of converting the good from the standard of the originating country to the standard of the destination country (if the two standards differ). The theory obviously assumes that there are no artificial barriers to trade. The law of one price is stated algebraically in Equation 8.8.

$$P_y = P_x \cdot E_{y,x} + Z_y \quad \text{where} \ -T_y \leq Z_y \leq T_y \qquad (8.8)$$

Equation 8.8 says that the price of the good in Country Y, stated in terms of Currency Y (P_y), must be equal to the price of the good in Country X stated in terms of Currency X (P_x) times the spot exchange rate of Currency Y for Currency X, denoted here as $E_{y,x}$, plus a stochastic component, Z_y, which is bounded by the cost of transportation stated in terms of Currency Y (T_y). Anytime the prices of the goods between the two markets deviate from the law of one price, arbitragers will become active. The arbitragers' purchases will bid the price up in the lower-priced market and the arbitragers' sales will drive the price down in the higher-priced market.

Now, suppose we average this law of one price relationship over all the goods that trade in the two countries. If we do so, the stochastic component, which averages zero, will disappear. If we use a common base period, the "averaged" values may be interpreted as price indexes. In this form, the relationship is known as purchasing-power parity and is given by Equation 8.9.

$$\tilde{P}_y = \tilde{P}_x \cdot E_{y,x} \tag{8.9}$$

In Equation 8.9, $\tilde{P}_y$ and $\tilde{P}_x$ denote the price indexes in Country Y and Country X respectively. We can manipulate the price indexes to obtain an expression for the spot exchange rate. This is given by Equation 8.10.

$$E_{y,x} = \frac{\tilde{P}_y}{\tilde{P}_x} \tag{8.10}$$

From Equation 8.10, we see that the spot exchange rate between the currencies of two countries should be a reflection of the relative price levels in the two countries.

Purchasing-power parity helps explain why the spot exchange rate is what it is, and interest-rate parity helps explain why the forward rates are what they are given the spot rate. If price levels determine spot rates, however, shouldn't we expect expectations of future changes in the price level (inflation) to influence forward rates? The answer is a decided yes! But the influence is felt through interest rates. To see this, we need to consider one last relationship—the Fisher Equation.

The Fisher Equation

The **Fisher Equation**, named for Irving Fisher (an important economist of the late 19th and early 20th centuries), argues that nominal interest rates are related to real interest rates by Equation 8.11.

$$r_{y,n}(D) = r_{y,r}(D) + i_{y,e}(D) \qquad (8.11)$$

Equation 8.11 states that the nominal rate of interest in Country Y for a maturity of D days, denoted here by $r_{y,n}(D)$, equals the required real rate in Country Y for that number of days, denoted here by $r_{y,r}(D)$, plus the expected change in the price level in Country Y over that number of days, denoted here by $i_{y,e}(D)$. (The latter is, of course, just the expected rate of inflation in Country Y.) The theory is predicated on the assumption that lenders and borrowers formulate their lending and borrowing plans on the basis of real rates of interest. In its modern form, the theory is also usually taken to assume that investors form rational expectations of future rates of inflation.

Together, interest-rate parity, purchasing-power parity, and the Fisher Equation form a complete and workable explanation for the structure of spot and forward exchange rates. Although we will not do so here, it can also be shown, by combining Equations 8.7 and 8.11, that the real rate of interest should be equalized across all countries (assuming no artificial constraints on the flow of capital or the flow of goods). We leave this to the reader. We note however, that the equations suggest, and practice proves, that an increase in inflationary expectations will lead to a weakening of a currency's value vis-a-vis other currencies and that an increase in real rates of interest for a currency will lead to a strengthening of that currency's value vis-a-vis other currencies.

Other Factors Influencing Exchange Rates

Our discussion of the determination of spot and forward exchange rates has focused, primarily, on the roles played by interest rates and inflation rates. Other factors also play a role—partly because they influence interest rates and inflation rates, and partly because they have a direct influence on the demand for or the supply of a currency. Currency traders watch these other factors very carefully. They know when each economic statistic is due to be released and they try to predict the values that are to be reported. Examples of these important factors include such things as the growth rate of gross national product (GNP), the size of trade surpluses and deficits, capital flows between countries, central bank interventions, monetary policy decisions, fiscal policy decisions, unemployment rates, and so on.

Comparative Yield Curves

The modern financial engineer must be able to move among

currencies and instrument maturities with the same fluidity that water seeks its own level. If a U.S. based financial engineer can raise funds more cheaply in short-term deutschemark debt than long-term dollar debt, then he or she should sell short-term deutschemark debt. If the funds obtained by the sale of the debt can be more profitably employed in the purchase of long-term yen-denominated assets than in short-term dollar-denominated assets, then he or she should buy the long-term yen assets. Both positions give rise to interest rate and exchange rate risks but these risks are manageable by hedging strategies that employ innovative combinations of futures, forwards, swaps, and options.

Just as the domestic yield curve has always been important to the domestic corporation with its traditional, but antiquated, domestic focus, the global engineer must be familiar with the yield curves for all currencies in which he or she might deal. In closing this chapter, we leave the reader with the yield curves (from two years to ten years) for the dollar, the deutschemark, the yen, and the pound, as they existed on 5 October 1991 (Exhibit 8.10). Examine the curves carefully and appreciate the differences. Ask yourself the open ended question, what opportunities, disguised though they

Exhibit 8.10
Comparative Yield Curves
U.S., West Germany, Japan, U.K.

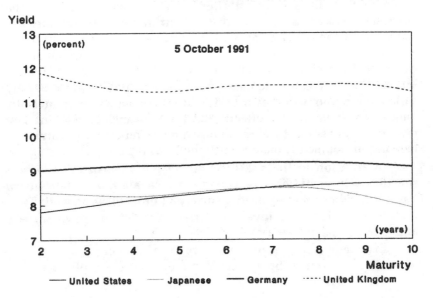

might be, am I looking at? This is one of the questions the financial engineer is always asking.

Summary

A debt instrument represents a debtor/creditor relationship. The most basic features of these instruments include the instrument's coupon, its term to maturity, its yield, and the process by which the debt will be amortized. Debt instruments often include special provisions that are written into the contract's indenture. Some of these special provisions are callability, convertibility, and sinking funds.

A debt instrument's value is determined with the aid of present value arithmetic. Ignoring the specialty provisions that influence value, the value of a debt instrument is simply the sum of the present value of all futures cash flows that the instrument is expected to provide. The instrument's yield plays a critical role in this discounting process because it serves as the discount rate.

A yield curve is a graphic depiction of the relationship between a debt instrument's yield and its term to maturity when all other yield-influencing factors are held constant. Other factors that influence yield include various types of risk, particularly default risk, tax status, and the provision of collateral. We observed that the price sensitivity of a debt instrument to changes in its yield is largely a function of the instrument's maturity. But we also argued that price sensitivity is influenced by the instrument's coupon, the present yield of the instrument, and the frequency of the coupon payments. The influence of all four sensitivity-influencing factors are captured by a single measure known as duration. An equivalent, but more intuitive, way to measure price sensitivity is via a measure called the dollar value of a basis point. From this latter measure, we can construct a very effective hedge by translating all interest-rate risk exposures to a common denominator in the form of a baseline instrument.

In addition to the risk stemming from an instrument's price sensitivity to yield changes, called interest-rate risk, a debt instrument can expose its owner to a variety of other risks as well. These include default risk, reinvestment risk, call risk, prepayment risk, and purchasing power risk.

Exchange rates represent the price of one currency in terms of another currency. Spot rates represent the price of a currency for immediate delivery and forward rates represent the price of a currency for later delivery. Currencies trade in foreign exchange markets, which are known in the trade as FOREX or FX markets. For the most part, these markets are made in an over-the-counter-like setting by major banks.

In completely free markets, spot rates are explained, at least in theory, by a relationship known as purchasing-power parity. Forward rate premiums (or discounts) are explained by a relationship known as interest-rate parity. Finally, the relationship between interest rates and expected rates of inflation is explained by the Fisher Equation.

Just as fluctuations in interest rates expose borrowers and lenders to interest-rate risk, so do fluctuations in exchange rates expose those with currency positions to exchange-rate risk. These risks need to be hedged and very sophisticated strategies exist for the hedging of these risks—most of which involve the use of such derivative products as futures, forwards, and/or swaps.

Endnotes

[1]Many inexpensive financial calculators have built in algorithms for finding a bond's yield. Additionally, many popular software packages have routines capable of solving for bond yields. We used *A-Pack*. See the footnotes to Chapter 3.

[2]Bonds that are in default and income bonds, whose coupon payments vary with the financial fortunes of the issuer, are exceptions. They are quoted on a "flat" basis. When a bond is quoted flat, the purchase price is understood to include accrued interest.

[3]The reader who would like to delve more deeply into systematic and unsystematic risks and the measurement of these risks should see Marshall (1989), Chapter 6.

[4]See Macaulay (1938).

[5]These durations were calculated using *A-Pack*.

[6]See Klotz (1985).

[7]See *Wall Street Journal*, November 20, 1990, "Milken Sales Pitch on High-Yield Bonds is Contradicted by Data."

[8]As a practical matter, immediate delivery is understood to mean two business days in the case of currencies.

[9]In particular, see Marshall (1989), Chapter 11.

References and Suggested Reading

A-Pack, Miami, FL: Kolb Publishing, 1991.

Arak, M., L. S. Goodman, and J. Snailer. "Duration Equivalent Bond Swaps: A New Tool," *Journal of Portfolio Management*, (Summer 1986), pp. 26-32.

Bierwag, G. O., G. G. Kaufman, and C. Khang. "Duration and Bond Portfolio Analysis: An Overview," *Journal of Financial and Quantitative Analysis* (November 1978), pp. 671-679.

Bierwag, G. O., G. G. Kaufman, and A. Toevs. "Duration: Its Development and Use in Bond Portfolio Management," *Financial Analysts Journal* (July/August 1983).

Bierwag, G.O., G.G. Kaufman, and A. Toevs (eds.). *Innovations in Bond Portfolio Management: Duration Analysis and Immunization*, Greenwich, CT: JAI Press, 1983.

Booth, G.G., J. E. Duggan, and P.E. Koveos. "Deviations from Purchasing Power Parity, Relative Inflation, and Exchange Rates: Recent Experience," *The Financial Review*, 20(2) (May 1985), pp. 195-218.

Gay, G.D. and R. W. Kolb. "Removing Bias in Duration Based Hedging Models: A Note," *Journal of Futures Markets*, 4:2 (Summer 1984), pp. 225-228.

Grove, M. A. "On Duration and the Optimal Maturity Structure of the Balance Sheet," *The Bell Journal of Economics* (Autumn 1974).

Gushee, C. H. "How to Hedge a Bond Investment," *Financial Analysts Journal* (March/April 1981), pp. 41-51.

Hicks, J.R. *Value and Capital*, Oxford: Claredon Press, 1939.

Khang, C. "Bond Immunization when Short-term Rates Fluctuate More than Long-term Rates," *Journal of Financial and Quantitative Analysis* (December 1979).

Klotz, R. *Convexity of Fixed Income Securities*, Salomon Brothers, New York, October 1985.

Leibowitz, M. L. "The Dedicated Bond Portfolio in Pension Funds— Part II: Immunization, Horizon Matching and Contingent Procedures," *Financial Analysts Journal*, (March/April 1986), pp. 47-57.

Macaulay, F. R. *Some Theoretical Problems Suggested by the Movement of Interest Rates, Bond Yields, and Stock Prices in the United States since 1856*, New York: Columbia University Press for the National Bureau of Economic Research, 1938.

Maloney, K. J. and J. B. Yawitz. "Interest Rate Risk, Immunization, and Duration," *Journal of Portfolio Management* (Spring 1986), pp. 41-48.

Marshall, J.F. *Futures and Option Contracting: Theory and Practice*, Cincinnati: South-Western, 1989.

Chapter 9

Speculation, Arbitrage, and Market Efficiency

Overview

Much of financial engineering is intended to exploit mispriced assets, aberrant price relationships, and other market inefficiencies. Exploiting these opportunities requires speculation and arbitrage. On the other hand, market efficiency is itself a product of speculation and arbitrage.

Among the general populace, speculation and arbitrage are much misunderstood. Many people associate these activities with efforts to unfairly or maliciously exploit producers and consumers. But, with only rare exceptions, nothing could be further from the truth. Speculation and arbitrage provide a great many direct and indirect benefits to both producers and consumers. Indeed, it would not be overreaching to say that a modern market economy could not possibly function very well without these activities.

Unfortunately, it is the negative view of speculation and arbitrage (and financial engineering more generally) that is more widely, but mistakenly, held—and often at the upper reaches of government. Examples of this misunderstanding abound. Consider, for example, the numerous attacks made on that index/futures arbitrage activity known as program trading, or the numerous attacks made on junk bond financing of leveraged buyouts. Or, consider the attacks made on the oil industry for the immediate rise in gasoline prices following the Iraqi invasion of Kuwait in August and September of 1990. The oil industry was castigated by many, including members of the House and Senate (and some economics and finance professors who should have known better). It made little difference that oil industry spokespersons were able to demonstrate that the immediate jump in the price of gasoline was necessitated by the hedging of oil inventories by oil companies (a basic financial engineering activity associated with good risk management). It was also of no matter that a well-understood principle of economics known as the **law of one price** dictated this outcome. Indeed, deviations from the law of one price are regarded among economists as indicative of market imperfections. The fact that prices did respond to the invasion as quickly as they did should have been applauded as a confirmation of the law of one price and efficiently functioning world markets. Clearly, it is important for the financial engineer to understand the broader market context in which his or her activities are conducted if he or she is to be a legitimate and positive spokesperson in an often poorly informed and sometimes hostile environment.

In this chapter, we take a brief look at price determination in a market economy, and how the signals provided by prices guide resource allocation. We then examine the activities of speculators and arbitragers and we examine how these activities interact to produce efficient markets.

The Market Mechanism at Work

A market economy consists of thousands of individual markets in which goods and services are exchanged. Consumers have demands for goods and services and producers have supplies of goods and services (the output of their production). Consumers come to the markets to purchase goods in order to satisfy their demands and producers come to the markets in order to sell their output.

Consumers obey a fundamental economic law known as the **law of demand**. The law of demand states that the quantity of a good demanded is inversely related to its price. Producers, on the other hand, obey an equally fundamental law known as the **law of supply**. The law of supply states that the quantity of a good supplied is directly related to its price. If most individual consumers and most individual producers obey the applicable laws, then the laws will hold in the aggregate. These fundamental laws are usually illustrated in introductory economics courses, by means of a simple demand and supply graph. Such a graph is depicted in Exhibit 9.1. A basic understanding of the laws of demand and supply are essential to understanding the work of financial engineers, and so we take a moment to review the concepts and their implications for price determination.

The intersection of the supply curve (S) and the demand curve

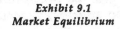

Exhibit 9.1
Market Equilibrium

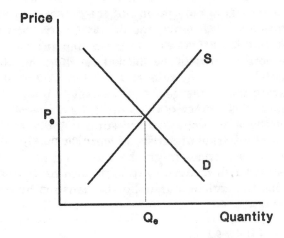

(D) represent the **market clearing** or equilibrium price on the vertical axis and the **equilibrium quantity** on the horizontal axis. This is the one price at which both the consumers' demands and producers' supplies are satisfied. All other things being equal, markets will always tend toward their equilibrium price. The reasoning is simple. At any price below the market clearing price, there will be excess demand. This excess demand will cause consumers to bid against one another for available supplies. The aggressive bidding will drive prices up. At any price above the market clearing price, there will be excess supply. Producers unable to sell their output at the current price will undercut the price and so prices will fall. Only at the marketing clearing price will there be neither excess demand nor excess supply. Thus, in sum, competitive market pressures will always drive prices to market clearing levels.

Price is not the only determinant of consumers' demands and producers' supplies. Many other factors play a role as well. In the case of demand, these include such things as consumers' tastes and preferences, the prices of other consumable goods and services, interest rates (especially for durable goods often purchased on credit), the number of consumers, consumers' disposable income, expectations about the future, and so on. In the case of supply, these other factors include such things as the prices of other producable goods and services, the prices of inputs, the state of technology, the number of producers, expectations about the future, and so on.

When a change occurs in any of the demand or supply influencing factors *other than price*, the demand curve or supply curve shifts. Such a shift, called a **change in demand** or a **change in supply**, temporarily upsets the market equilibrium. Market forces are immediately set in motion and, within a short time, a new market clearing price emerges. A price change brought about by a shift in demand is depicted in Exhibit 9.2 Panel A and a price change brought about by a shift in supply is depicted in Exhibit 9.2 Panel B. If the market under study were the market for soybeans, then a rise in corn prices might be the cause of the behavior in Panel A (as livestock feeders shift from corn to soybeans). An increase in fertilizer prices might be the cause of the behavior in, Panel B.

Exhibit 9.2
A Shift in Demand
Panel A

Exhibit 9.2
A Shift in Supply
Panel B

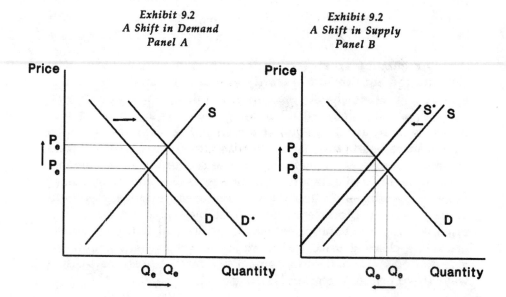

While markets tend toward their equilibrium values, each market is nevertheless in a continuous state of flux. To paraphrase an old saying, the one great constant in economics is change. Environmental conditions, credit market conditions, tax laws, technology, foreign competition, and so forth, are such that change is inevitable. As change occurs, information is generated and this information is fed to the players in the market. Much of this information has a direct bearing on the supply of or demand for goods and services. Demand curves shift, supply curves shift, and prices change.

The very pretty pictures that we draw to depict supply and demand are useful for understanding the process at work. But, they are not very useful for purposes of making real world market decisions. Economists often leave students with the impression that they can go out and "look" at the demand and supply curves. But they cannot. As real as these relationships are, they are not directly observable. All that is observable is the current market price and the set of all past prices. Future prices are not now known and will not be known with certainty until such time as the future becomes the present.

While future prices are not presently observable, they are nevertheless very important. A farmer planting a crop today is very much concerned about the price that will prevail at harvest; a corporation planning a public offering of its debt two months out is very concerned about the interest rates that will prevail at the time its issue comes to market; a multinational corporation with profits to repatriate in three months time is very concerned about the exchange rate three months hence, and so on. It is this uncertainty that creates a need for speculators.

Because all that is presently observable is a set of prices, consumers and producers must make consumption and production decisions on the basis of those prices. In the words of Adam Smith, prices serve as an "invisible hand" that guides producers and consumers in their daily economic decisions. Prices are both an input to the decision making and a consequence of that decision making. It is through this ongoing process that resources are allocated toward their most useful ends. A producer, for example, that observes input and output prices that could lead to profitable production of one good but unprofitable production of another good, is guided by those prices to reduce or cease production of the unprofitable good, and undertake or to increase production of the profitable good.

When markets are first observed, particularly those that are highly organized, they always seem to the uninitiated to be very chaotic places with little rhyme or reason. But, in actuality, they are very responsive mechanisms by which producers and consumers keep a hand on the pulse of the economy. They provide a flow of information, in the form of prices, that cannot be duplicated by any form of central planning authority—and many have tried. Markets are adaptable, flexible, and responsive, and this, more than anything else, is the engine that drives successful economies.

The efficiency of the market system depends critically on the efficiency with which prices accurately reflect all available information, and the honesty with which that information is represented by prices. Consumers and producers who take their cues from the markets must have faith that the prices are fair to all, and truly representative of underlying economic conditions. It is in this capacity that the role of the speculator is critically important.

Speculation

Speculation involves contemplation of the future, formulation of expectations, and taking of positions in order to profit. From this definition, we see that speculators are basically forecasters who act upon their forecasts in order to earn a return. The speculator *does not* see himself or herself as having *control* over prices. Rather, prices are determined by the interaction of supply and demand. The "fair" price is the price that balances the supplies provided by producers with the demands of consumers. Similarly, prices in the future are determined by the supply and demand conditions that prevail in the future. Thus, speculation is largely a matter of forecasting the evolution of supply and demand. Successful forecasting depends on the acquisition of superior information and/or the ability to interpret information and its implications better than others.

While the definition of speculation is readily applicable to traditional commodity speculation, it is also readily applicable to speculation in financial instruments and currencies. For example, the prices of debt instruments (bonds, notes, and so on) are determined by the interaction of the demand for loanable funds (by those with a deficiency of funds) and the supplies of loanable funds (provided by those with a surplus of funds). To be sure, the activities of the Federal Reserve and central banks impact the price of loanable funds. But, this impact itself occurs through these institutions' influence on supply and demand. Similarly, exchange rates (prices of currencies in terms of each other) are determined by the relative supplies and demands for the currencies involved.

In an ideal market economy, each speculator, like each consumer and each producer, is very small relative to the market as a whole and no individual speculator, consumer, or producer exerts enough market power to bring about a change in prices on his or her own. Thus, the speculator is a forecaster and not a manipulator. If prices rise when the speculator is long or fall when the speculator is short, then the speculator profits from a correct forecast. If prices fall when the speculator is long or rise when the speculator is short, then the speculator suffers a loss from an incorrect forecast. Clearly, the nature of speculation is such that to earn speculative rewards, speculators must bear risk.

The real world of markets is, of course, not as perfect as basic economic theory would have us believe and sometimes, for whatever reasons, an individual or a group acquires the power to manipulate a market. Such individuals are not speculators. They are market manipulators. By definition, a **manipulator** is one who uses his or her private power to bring about a rise or a fall in prices in such a fashion as to produce personal gain at the expense of others who are not party to the manipulation. Manipulation of markets is inherently evil in the sense that it undermines confidence in the pricing system and interferes with the efficient allocation of resources. It is not surprising then that manipulators try very hard to disguise themselves as something other than manipulators—usually as speculators. As a consequence, those injured by market manipulation often mistakenly blame speculators. (Ivan Boesky's and Michael Milken's market shenanigans are recent cases in point, and highlight the need for clear ethical standards for those who deal in the markets at any level.)

Speculators also get bad press when they reap honest profits. The nonspeculator hears tails of speculators who made "windfall" gains because they were long oil when oil prices rose, or short the stock market at the time of the equities market collapse. The nonspeculator concludes that the speculator's gain came at his, the nonspeculator's expense because he, the nonspeculator, is paying higher prices for gasoline or heating oil, or his retirement stock portfolio has less market value. The nonspeculator is often unable to distinguish cause from effect. The speculator who was long oil did not cause the price of oil to rise, irrespective of the extent of his personal profit from the occurrence. He gathered information and analyzed the information which led him to conclude that the price of oil would rise in order to clear the market. On the basis of the analysis, he bought oil. The speculators who lose money, and there are typically many more of these, do not get much press and their losses do not carry the same weight as the profits to the winners in the minds of the nonspeculators.

While the buying and selling activities of individual speculators rarely have more than a negligible impact on market prices, the cumulative or aggregate effect of speculator buying and selling can have a very significant effect. This is not, however, bad. Speculators buying and selling activities are in response to their information acquisition and analysis, and any price changes that subsequently result should represent movements toward market clearing. In the absence of speculation, market prices would respond more slowly to changing market conditions and delays would mean less efficiency in resource re-allocation.

There are many arguments that can be made in favor of the activities of speculators and many different ways to make the same arguments. We would like to make just a few of these. First, by gathering information, analyzing it, and taking positions, speculators (in the aggregate) bring information to the market and they help the market to properly evaluate the information. By this process, speculators assist the markets in what is often called the market's **price discovery** function. Others are then free to use the price information in their production/consumption decisions. Thus, the speculators' efforts to profit lead to better resource allocation at any given point in time.

Second, speculators help to allocate resources across time. This is particularly necessary for those goods that are harvested during short periods of time, but the stocks of which must last for much longer periods of time. Agricultural commodities are very good examples of these types of goods. In the absence of speculation, harvest supplies would overwhelm the markets and cause prices to be very low. Later, when all production had been consumed, prices would suddenly rise. Producers who sell at harvest would get little for their effort but would nevertheless produce again because of the high prices which prevail at the time of planting. But, speculators, understanding the historic pattern of prices, will tend to buy up the commodity when it is plentiful and cheap and hold it in storage until such time as it is scarce and dear. After the price has risen, speculators will release their stored stocks. The effect of this activity is to raise prices at harvest by introducing speculative demand, and to lower prices during the post harvest period by introducing speculative supply. These pricing patterns with and without speculation are depicted in Exhibit 9.3.

Exhibit 9.3
Temporal Pattern of Prices

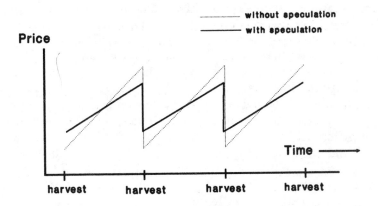

The final argument we will make involves the risk-bearing nature of speculation. We have, in earlier chapters, argued that producers and others often have a need to hedge. They do this by taking offsetting positions in related instruments—such as futures, forwards, options, and swaps. When a hedger is in need of a long position in a futures or other risk management contract, from whom will he or she buy it? And if a hedger is in need of a short position in a futures or other risk management contract, to whom will he or she sell it? There is, of course, the possibility that a hedger in need of a long position can obtain a contract from another hedger in need of a short position. Unfortunately, there tends, at any given time, to be a preponderance of hedgers on one side of the market. The slack must be taken up by someone else—someone willing to bear the hedger's risk. These people are the speculators. In this regard, they perform the vital economic service of risk bearing. And, for this service, they deserve some reward. Thus, one may view the profits that accrue to speculators as a reward for providing risk-bearing services.

Importantly, the notions of speculative profits as a reward for successful forecasting and speculative profits as a reward for risk bearing are not mutually exclusive and indeed are actually supportive. For example, hedgers' sales of risk management contracts tend to depress the prices of those contracts. Speculators then forecast that prices will go up and they buy the contracts. Prices subsequently rise as hedgers offset their risk management contracts upon termination of their cash positions and speculators profit from the rise in prices. By creating a vehicle by which producers can hedge price risk, speculators encourage production. The greater quantities of goods that are consequently produced result in lower prices for consumers. Society as a whole is, therefore, a major beneficiary of speculation.

At this point, it would be appropriate to return to the oil price shock of 1990 stemming from the Iraqi invasion of Kuwait which we touched on in the overview to this chapter. When that incident occurred and the price of gasoline immediately rose—despite the fact that the gasoline then in storage was refined from oil purchased prior to the shock—the oil industry was condemned for price gouging. This condemnation is ludicrous and suggests a certain market naivete. After all, if supplies of oil suddenly shrink, isn't it desirable that rationing by the market, through price, commence immediately? The faster prices reflect the new "realities," the faster resources can be re-allocated. This is a manifestation of the ability of markets to guide resources, by way of the market's invisible hand, to their most productive end.

Speculative Methods

It is often said that there are as many different speculative methods as there are speculators. While there is undoubtedly a grain of truth in this, speculative methods of price analysis are generally divided into two broad categories called **fundamental analysis** and **technical analysis**. These two schools of thought are not mutually exclusive. Nevertheless, users of one usually shun the other.

Fundamental analysts examine all information that bears on the fundamental economic relationships—supply and demand—that ultimately determine all prices. They gather information on domestic and foreign production, read government reports, try to interpret federal reserve policy, estimate input costs and usage rates, monitor technological developments, and so on. From this information, they attempt to determine what the correct market clearing price is. A current price below the market clearing price represents an **undervalued** asset and a current price above the market clearing price represents an **overvalued** asset. Undervalued assets are purchased and overvalued assets are sold.

This same approach is applied to commodities, stocks, debt securities, and currencies. In the case of a stock, the fundamental analyst examines the sources of a firm's earnings and the prospects for earnings to change. Firm earnings (and the affiliated disbursements to shareholders) are the source of a stock's value. Based on the analyst's assessment of future earnings, he or she can determine a present value for the stock's price. If the stock is currently selling for less than its present value (also called a fair value and analogous to a market clearing price) then it is undervalued and should be purchased. If the stock is currently selling for more than its present value, then it is overvalued and should be sold.

Fundamentalists' methods range from simple intuitive analysis of information to extremely elaborate and quantitatively sophisticated econometric models. As a general rule, the forecasting approach employed by these speculators takes a long view of the market. That is, fundamentalists are prepared to wait a considerable time for the market price to move to its fair value. This contrasts with the technical approach, which tends to take a much shorter view.

Technical analysis takes a very different approach to forecasting future prices. The technical analyst, or technician, accepts that the fundamental approach is founded on solid theory, but maintains that it is very difficult, if not impossible, to do successfully in practice. The technician argues that the fundamentalist simply cannot gather enough private information to consistently outperform the market. Instead, the technician focuses on one specific type of information called **transactions data.** Transactions data is any information associated with the record of past transactions (including the most recent ones). Transactions data consists of such things as trade prices, trading volume and open interest, short interest, specialists positions, odd-lot transactions, and so on.

The technician examines the transactions data for patterns that have predictive value. That is, the technician searches through long histories of transactions data for patterns or **formations** which have repeatedly occurred in the past and which have, frequently, been followed by some specific directional movement. Then, by examining very recent and current price behavior, the technician tries to find similar formations and to take a position based on those formations prior to the often encountered subsequent price movements.

The technician's faith in the existence of patterns of activity revealed slowly over time hangs on the technician's belief that prices move in identifiable trends. It is not at all clear why such trends should exist, but a number of plausible arguments have been made. These include (1) the gradual, rather than rapid, dissemination of information (as in the case of the development of a drought, or a failure in a firm's product that might lead to an expensive recall); (2) the tendency of market psychology to swing only slowly in a new direction; (3) the tendency of a "herd instinct" to dominate investor psychology; and (4) the access of some market participants to information before the general market.

Technicians have a variety of methods and varying horizons. Some limit their activities to visual chart-type methods that employ bar and point-and-figure charts. Others use computer-based models that have been "optimized" by systematic search procedures. Still others operate by a "seat-of-the-pants" approach—buying at the first sign of an up-move and selling at the first sign of a down-move. Some technicians take a long-term approach, trying to exploit a long-term or primary trend. But most take a much shorter view of the market looking to capture short- to intermediate-term trends.

Arbitrage

Arbitrage is the simultaneous taking of positions in two or more markets in order to exploit a valuation discrepancy between the pricing of assets in the different markets. Thus, unlike speculation which seeks profit from a change in price levels, arbitrage seeks profit from a discrepancy in price relationships. (We examined one form of arbitrage, called covered interest arbitrage, in Chapter 8.)

In the academic world, arbitrage is often defined as an effort to earn a riskless profit without investment by simultaneous activities in multiple markets. This **academic,** or **pure** arbitrage as it is also called, is sometimes possible, but, more often, real world arbitrage involves risk and at least some modest investment.

The earliest forms of arbitrage were arbitrage across space, called **spacial** or **geographic arbitrage,** and arbitrage across time, sometimes called **temporal arbitrage.** In spacial arbitrage, the arbitrager attempts to sell an asset in a market in which it is relatively rich and to simultaneously buy it in a market in which it is relatively cheap. The funds obtained from the sale in the rich market are used to finance the purchase in the cheap market and so the arbitrage is made without investment. Since the two sides of the transaction are effected simultaneously, the arbitrage is also riskless. In practice, the funds from the sale are not always immediately available and some very short-term interim investment is often necessary. Additionally, the prices at which the trades are actually made may vary a little from quotes prevailing at the time the arbitrage is undertaken. This gives rise to some risk, although this risk is very modest relative to that borne by speculators.

Spacial arbitrage is profitable whenever the difference between the asset's selling price and purchase price is sufficiently great to cover any transportation costs associated with moving the asset between the two markets, any transaction costs associated with effecting the transactions, and any conversion costs associated with converting the asset from the standard in one market to the standard in the other market (if the delivery standards differ).

Temporal arbitrage requires the purchase (or sale) of an asset at the present time and the simultaneous commitment to sell (or purchase) the asset at a later time. For example, a grain elevator might purchase corn in the spot market (paying for it with borrowed funds) and simultaneously sell a forward contract to deliver the corn three months out. At the appointed time, the corn is brought out of storage and delivered. The proceeds received from the sale are then used to repay the borrowed funds together with interest. If the forward price and the spot price differ by enough to cover the cost of three months storage and three months interest, then the arbitrage will be profitable. The sum of the storage costs and interest expense, less any convenience yield provided by the physical corn, is called the **cost of carry.** Thus, if the difference between a forward price and a spot price exceeds the cost of carry, the temporal arbitrage is profitable. Temporal arbitrage, when applied to agricultural commodities as in the case just described, is sometimes called a carrying charge hedge.

Profitable arbitrage opportunities are sometimes partly spacial in nature and party temporal in nature and they sometimes involve multiple currencies. The latter condition would arise whenever the purchasing and selling markets are in different countries. A simple and very logical equation describes the overall relationship between two prices and allows for multiple currencies. This appears below as Equation 9.1.

$$P_i(T) = P_j(t) \cdot E_{i,j} + G(t,T) + Z_i \qquad (9.1)$$

where $-W_{i,j} \le Z_i \le W_{i,j}$

Equation 9.1 says that the forward price of the asset in market i (priced in currency i) is equal to the spot price of the asset in market j (priced in currency j) times the spot exchange rate of currency i for currency j, plus the cost of carry from the present to later delivery, denoted $G(t,T)$, plus a stochastic component, denoted Z_i, which must lie within a range determined by the sum of the transportation, transaction, and conversion costs, denoted here by $W_{i,j}$. Both $W_{i,j}$ and $G(t,T)$ are stated in terms of currency i. Equation 9.1 is the key to understanding a great deal of arbitrage activity by financial engineers. It is a full-form version of the the law of one price which was discussed in Chapter 8. (We return to Equation 9.1 in Chapter 23 when we examine modern arbitrage in greater detail.) The relationship is depicted graphically in Exhibit 9.4.

Exhibit 9.4
The Law of One Price

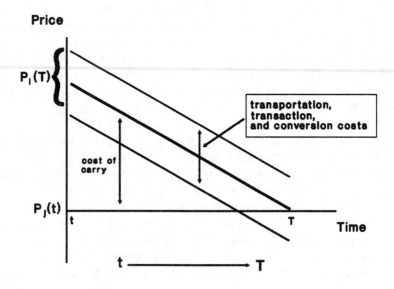

Other forms of arbitrage seek to exploit price discrepancies across risk, across instruments, and across maturities. We will consider each of these very briefly.

Insurance, which exploits the benefits associated with portfolio diversification, is an example of arbitrage across risk. In these forms of arbitrage a party sells its own low-risk debt to raise funds to purchase high-risk assets. While the individual assets are high risk, when combined into a properly diversified portfolio, the overall character can be very low risk. Thus, the insurer can demand a high premium for a policy and finance its own operations through low-risk debt. While it earns a high return on its high-risk assets it only pays a low cost for its own financing. Other examples are the **overcollateralization** of high risk junk bond portfolios to give them a low-risk character, and the emergence in recent years of a re-insurance industry used by insurers to spread their own risk.

Arbitrage across instruments has been one of the most exciting of the many forms of arbitrage in recent years. In this form of arbitrage, several assets or instruments are combined to produce one or more instruments having a very different character from the original. This is the process by which synthetic instruments are created. The process can also work in reverse. That is, one instrument can be disassembled to produce a series of instruments, each of which has properties different from that of the original instrument. There are many examples of this kind of arbitrage. An example of an instrument with a long history is the pooled investment vehicle. In this application, an intermediating entity, such as a mutual fund, is established. The mutual fund sells shares in itself to investors. The mutual fund then pools the investors funds and purchases a diversified portfolio of assets which afford the investor a degree of diversification and professional management that the investor is not capable of achieving on his or her own.

More recent examples of arbitrage across instruments include the creation of pooled mortgage securities, such as mortgage pass-throughs; the creation of zero coupon bonds by stripping coupon bonds; and the creation of collateralized mortgage obligations (CMOs) by **tranching** pooled mortgages. Other examples include the creation of synthetic futures from options, and the creation of synthetic put options from call options. All of these involve the creation of synthetic instruments which can be traded against real instruments.

The final form of arbitrage that we will briefly address is arbitrage across maturities. This is particularly appropriate when the instruments involved are debt securities. Swaps and forward rate agreements are particularly useful in this regard. For example, a firm can raise funds by selling short-maturity commercial paper, say 182-day paper. Every six months, this paper is rolled over for another 182 days. With each rollover the new paper is sold at the prevailing 182-day paper rate. This gives the financing a floating-rate character. The firm can now use the funds to purchase long-maturity debt of another issuer. This strategy is viable as long as the yield curve is upward sloping and stationary. But, if the yield curve shifts, the firm could find itself stuck with low return assets financed by high cost liabilities. The solution is to convert the floating-rate liabilities to fixed-rate liabilities by means of an interest rate swap. If the swap is consummated at the time the fixed-rate assets are purchased, the firm can lock-in the difference between the return on its fixed-rate assets and the cost of its transformed, and now fixed-rate, liabilities. If this difference is positive, the arbitrage is viable.

Financial engineers have been very active in all aspects of arbitrage. Critical to their activities are the fundamental relationships among the prices of assets having different risk, different maturity, different temporal, and different spacial characteristics.

Efficient Markets: Friend or Foe

Some years ago academicians proffered a theory which became known as the **efficient markets hypothesis**.[1] The efficient markets hypothesis maintains that market pressures brought about by intense competition among speculators and arbitragers to exploit information and aberrant price relationships will insure that competitive markets are, at all times, informationally efficient. That is, all market prices fully and timely reflect all available information. As such, it is not possible to earn a return in excess of a fair return commensurate with the risks involved.

The efficient markets hypothesis has been the subject of intensive and often heated debate and the subject of innumerable empirical investigations. From the late 1960s through the early 1980s, academicians repeatedly reported on scientific studies which could find no evidence of exploitable market opportunities.[2] The investment community, however, never accepted the efficient markets hypothesis. To do so it seemed would be to reject the very foundation on which their profession rests.

In the early 1980s, two respected academicians persuasively

rebutted the underlying logic of the efficient markets hypothesis.[3] They argued that it was inconsistent to believe that market efficiency could be the product of speculation and arbitrage, which are privately costly activities, and yet to also believe that speculation and arbitrage would not be rewarded. If there were no reward for speculation and arbitrage, then these activities would cease. And if they ceased, how could the markets continue to be efficient?

The question of market efficiency, or lack thereof, is critically important to financial engineers. Much of financial engineering over the last decade has sought to develop new instruments and new strategies to exploit price discrepancies. Clearly, this engineering should have and would have failed if markets were perfectly efficient.

The solution, which was also offered by the academicians noted above, is to accept that there is an equilibrium degree of inefficiency. That is, there is enough inefficiency, at least on occasion, to provide a return to speculation and arbitrage, but not so much inefficiency that the return is excessive. Thus, there is an incentive to develop new instruments and new strategies that can better (more effectively) exploit what inefficiencies exist. More sophisticated tests applied to the markets over the last few years have indeed found subtle, although usually very temporary, exploitable opportunities.[4]

There is no doubt that speculation and arbitrage make prices more efficient, and there is also no doubt that financial engineering with its stress on innovative new ways to exploit inefficiencies have themselves contributed to making the markets more efficient. But efficiency is not the friend of the financial engineer—at least not most of the time. As markets become ever more efficient, fewer exploitable opportunities remain and ferreting out those that do requires even more effort. This has led to the age of the quant jock to whom we have made reference in earlier chapters. Quant jocks employ sophisticated quantitative techniques, build elaborate valuation relationships, and sift through enormous quantities of data in their unending search for exploitable opportunities. When they find one, they quickly turn their resources, or those of their firm, to it and, in the process, they help to eliminate it. While this is not the intent, it is the inevitable result.

When stock index futures contracts were first introduced, there were enormous and very frequent opportunities to earn profits from cash/futures arbitrage. But, as financial engineers worked out the complex mathematics and developed the necessary number-crunching software and turned their theories to practice, the pricing discrepancies between the cash indexes and the index futures prices were gradually arbitraged away. Discrepancies between fair value basis and actual basis once ranged to 200 "points." Today, these value discrepancies rarely exceed 10 points before program trading strategies kick in and eliminate them. Similarly, when swaps were first introduced, swap dealers could easily earn up to 150 basis points on a pair of matched swap. Today, it is difficult to earn even 10 basis points.

The upshot of this discussion is that financial engineers detest efficient markets, yet their activities spawn new forms of speculation and arbitrage which are the driving forces behind market efficiency. We conclude, therefore, that financial engineers are largely responsible for making and keeping markets efficient. The financial engineer's struggle is to continuously search for new opportunities, new ways to trade, and an ever larger scale on which to trade to exploit ever shrinking margins.

We return to the subject of arbitrage in Chapter 23 (and a few other places later in this book). We will take a detailed look at a fuller form of Equation 9.1 and how that equation can be translated into profitable trading opportunities.

Summary

Speculation and arbitrage are absolutely critical to the smooth functioning of a market economy. By their buying and selling activities, speculators and arbitragers are instrumental in attaining market clearing prices. These prices drive the invisible hand that allocates economic resources.

Speculation, arbitrage, and other forms of financial engineering activity are very much misunderstood and sometimes condemned by the very people who stand to benefit the most from a smoothly functioning and efficient market machine. There is a need for financial engineers to be forceful advocates of their profession and to correct misunderstandings in a clear and positive manner whenever the opportunity arises. They must see their individual narrowly-focused activities in the broader context of market economics and the role the markets play in achieving ever higher standards of living for all citizens.

Speculators and arbitragers are instrumental in the efficient allocation of resources across both space and time. In a more modern context, they also assist in the efficient allocation of resources across risk and instruments. The methods employed by individuals in their private search for profit are as varied as the people who undertake the activity. Nevertheless, the methods can be grouped. In the case of speculators, most use either a fundamental or a technical approach. The former concentrates on supply/demand developments and basic measures of intrinsic value. The latter seeks to exploit trends and historic patterns in transactions data.

While speculators and arbitragers seek to profit by exploiting inefficiencies in the market, the end result of their activities is to make the markets more efficient.

Endnotes

[1] See Fama (1965).

[2] The first major survey paper on the subject which summarized all literature through 1970 was published by Fama (1970). Most of this research dealt with the behavior of stock prices. Subsequent literature focused on commodity prices. For a partial review of the latter see Marshall (1989, Chapter 9).

[3] This argument was first made by Grossman and Stiglitz (1980).

[4] See, for example, Reinganum (1981) and Keim (1983).

References and Suggested Reading

Basu, S. "The Investment Performance of Common Stocks in Relationship to Their Price Earnings Ratio: A Test of the Efficient Markets Hypothesis," *Journal of Finance*, 32(3) (1977), pp. 663-682.

Fama, E.F. "The Behavior of Stock Prices," *Journal of Business*, 38(1) (January 1965).

Fama, E.F. "Efficient Capital Markets: A Review of Theory and Empirical Work," *Journal of Finance*, 25(2) (May 1970).

Grossman, S. and J. Stiglitz. "On the Impossibility of Informationally Efficient Markets," *American Economic Review* (June 1980).

Keim, D.B. "Size-Related Anomalies and Stock Return Seasonalities: Further Empirical Evidence," *Journal of Financial Economics*, 12(1) (1983), pp. 13-32.

Marshall, J.F. *Futures and Option Contracting: Theory and Practice,* Cincinnati: South-Western, 1989.

Reinganum, M.R. "Misspecification of Capital Asset Pricing: Empirical Anomalies Based on Earnings Yields and Market Values," *Journal of Financial Economics*, 9(1), (March 1981).

Chapter 10

The Corporate Treasurer's Perspective: Reading Between The Lines

Judy A. Chan, Michael E. Fitzgerald, Jeffrey M. Mondschein, Timothy
T. Shanovich, and Charles W. Smithson

Overview

Risk management—one of the most important areas requiring
the skills of financial engineers—is a four step process: (1) identify
the risks to which the firm is exposed, (2) quantify the exposures,
(3) determine the form of the outcomes sought, and (4) design or
engineer a strategy to transform the risk exposures to the desired
form.

The financial literature has dealt extensively with steps 2, 3
and 4, and these are addressed thoroughly elsewhere in this text.
But, very little attention has been paid to the initial identification
of price risks. This is unfortunate. Unless the existence of a price
risk is established, how can one possibly hope to manage it?

---

*This chapter is adapted from a series of articles which were entitled "Reading Between the
Lines" and published in the September/October 1989, November/December 1989, and March/
April 1990 issues of Corporate Risk Management. At the time the articles first appeared,
all the authors worked in risk management at Continental Bank. Charles Smithson is currently
at The Chase Manhattan Bank.*

In this chapter, we demonstrate how a corporate treasurer can utilize the firm's financial statements and the footnotes that accompany those statements to uncover the firm's **strategic risks**. Strategic risks are those price risks which bear directly or indirectly on the firm's performance. While the strategic or price risks that impact the firm directly are usually easily recognized, those that impact indirectly can be very difficult to spot.

We also begin to suggest strategies for managing the risks that we uncover. In the process, we introduce a number of the financial instruments that are described in much greater detail later in this book. Do not be put off if instruments that are mentioned in passing are not adequately explained in this chapter. The problem will be rectified in the next section of the book. We have also included a brief explanation of how spreadsheet modeling can be used to quantify a firm's various strategic exposures—particularly useful when the exposures are complex and/or partially offsetting.

Why Risk Management?

The primary reason for using risk management is simple. In the 1970s the world became more risky. The increased risk first became apparent, and was most dramatic, in the foreign exchange markets following the breakdown of the Bretton Woods Agreement. It wasn't long, however, before increased price volatility showed up among interest rates and commodity prices. Examples of these volatility patterns are depicted in Exhibits 10.1, 10.2, 10.3, and 10.4.[1]

So why risk management? The answer is obvious. Managing a business in a highly volatile environment is like navigating a ship on stormy seas. Just imagine the difficulties a treasurer would have trying to map out a secure financial course for a corporation with unpredictable spikes in exchange rates, interest rates and commodity prices. Just as the danger of capsizing is ever-present for a ship in turbulent weather, a firm is just as likely to "go under" due to frenzied price shifts which drain cash flow, decrease stock price, and erode a competitive position.

To calm the choppy seas and keep the firm sailing smoothly, risks must be identified and managed. Identification is the first step and much of the information the treasurer needs can be found in the firm's annual report. The *Letter to Shareholders*, the *Statement of Consolidated Income*, the *Statement of Consolidated Changes in Financial Position*, and the *Consolidated Balance Sheet*, all contain clues as to

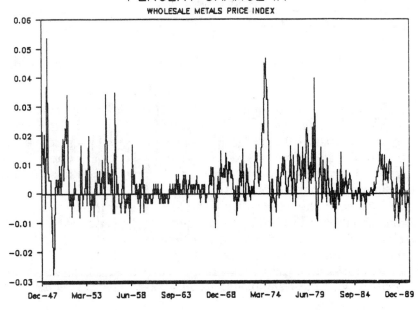

Exhibit 10.1
Interest Rate Volatility

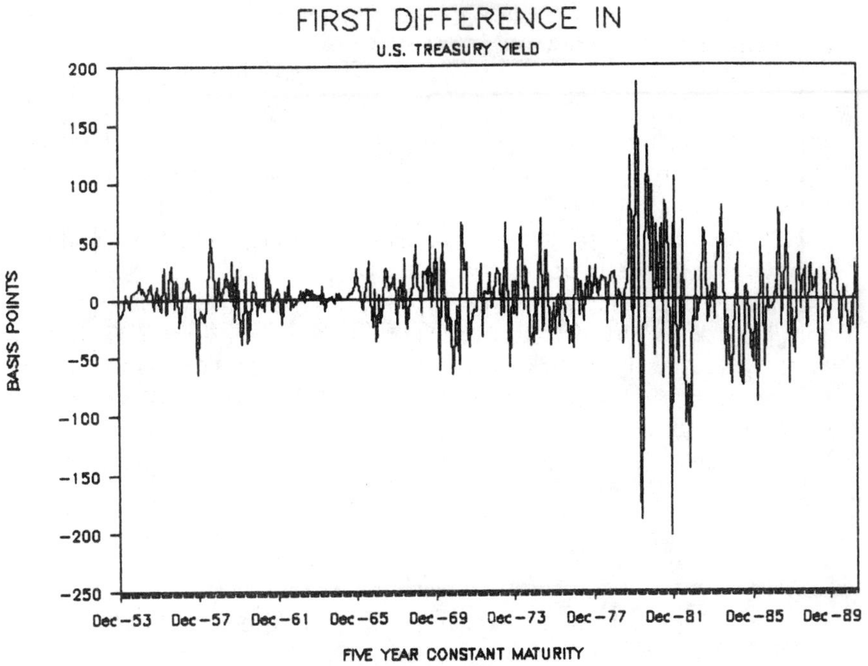

FIRST DIFFERENCE IN
U.S. TREASURY YIELD

FIVE YEAR CONSTANT MATURITY

Exhibit 10.2
Commodity Price Volatility: Metals

PERCENT CHANGE IN
WHOLESALE METALS PRICE INDEX

Exhibit 10.3
Commodity Price Volatility: Petroleum Products

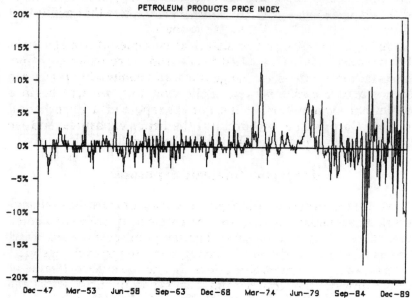

Exhibit 10.4
Exchange Rate Volatility: Yen/USD

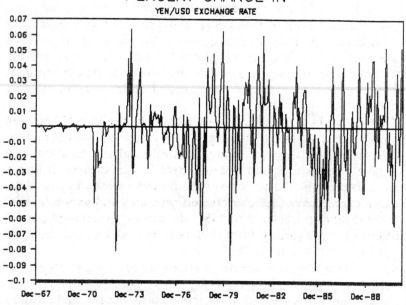

where risk management may be effective. Our goal is to learn to read the financial statements for clues—an exercise that might best be described as "reading between the lines."

We begin by noting a few historical examples of strategic risks and their consequences for actual firms. And we consider how fluctuations in interest rates, exchange rates, and commodity prices can influence a corporation's value. Following this, we will begin a more formal examination of the annual report of a hypothetical firm, XYZ Corporation, to ferret out the firm's exposures, and we will suggest some possible risk management solutions.

Identifying Strategic Exposures

We use the term **strategic exposures** to encompass the exchange rate risk, the interest rate risk, and the commodity price risks noted above.[2] These risks may manifest themselves in several ways. First, a firm has a strategic exposure if changes in foreign-exchange rates or interest rates or commodity prices change the expected value or *real* cash flows of the firm. Second, changes in financial prices can have an impact on the value of a firm via transactions not yet booked. These types of strategic exposures can be described as **contingent exposures**. Finally, changes in exchange rates, interest rates and commodity prices can influence a firm's sales and market share. Thus, **competitive exposures** are also a form of strategic risk.

The increased volatility of financial prices which surfaced in the 1970s led more companies to recognize their strategic exposures too late—only after these exposures put them into financial distress or out of business. In many cases, the corporation faced a contingent transaction exposure, arising from a mismatch in its revenues and expenses.

One example is Laker Airlines which, in the late 1970s, was doing well—so well that its existing fleet of aircraft could not handle the volume of British vacationers.[3] Freddie Laker's solution was to buy five more planes and finance them in U.S. dollars. It was a great idea except that the airline's revenues were mostly in pounds—creating a currency mismatch between revenues and expenditures. When the dollar appreciated in 1981, the airline's increased pound liabilities (after converting from dollars to pounds) forced the company to file for bankruptcy.

Consider a second example, this one involving a strategic exposure that was competitive in nature. Throughout the early 1980s, a strong dollar hurt Caterpillar. As the dollar strengthened relative to the yen, the price of Caterpiller's equipment rose relative to Komatsu's, a Japanese competitor, giving Komatsu a competitive pricing advantage.[4]

Could the management of Laker or the management of Caterpillar have protected their firms from the strategic risks they faced and, if so, what clues might they have had that Laker and Caterpillar had strategic exposures in the first place?

The Letter to Shareholders

To answer these questions, we now turn to our hypothetical firm. While the strategic exposure problems of Laker and Caterpillar became apparent in a strong dollar market, our hypothetical firm, XYZ, is experiencing diminished cash flows because of the weak purchasing power of the dollar.[5] How do we know this? Well, we have taken a look at XYZ's annual letter to its shareholders.

The contingent nature of some strategic exposures implies that they do all show up as accounting exposures. They may not appear in the accounting statements or even in the footnotes to the accounting statements. A company's letter to its shareholders in its annual report often contains clues, as demonstrated in this one from the Chairman of the Board and Chief Executive Officer of XYZ Corporation. In this case, the letter reiterates some of the exposures identified in its accounting statements, but it also mentions some contingent and competitive exposures. The letter to the shareholders appears as Exhibit 10.5.

Exhibit 10.5
Letter to Shareholders —
XYZ Corporation, 1988

Pursuing total quality is key to creating value—value for our shareholders, for our customers, and for our employees.

This Year's Results

The year's results met our challenging financial goal of maintaining the Corporation's steady growth. Our products show excellent improvements in sales worldwide with an increase in sales of 22 percent over last year.

Corporate earnings, however, declined to an unsatisfactory level due, largely, to unexpected *sharp increases in the cost of copper* and fierce competition which inhibited recovery of these costs. In addition to the increased cost of raw materials, we have continued to experience price increases on intermediate products; and a significant portion of our problems can be laid at Washington's doorstep. Over the past three years, the dollar lost almost one-fourth of its value relative to the yen as the dollar fell from 168 yen per dollar in 1986 to 144 yen in 1987 and 128 yen in 1988. Since XYZ sources a significant number of components from Asia, this decline in the value of the dollar has hit us hard.

In response to the severe foreign currency moves seen over the past several years, we have stepped up efforts to increase productivity and cut costs.

Tempered Optimism

Our longer-term outlook, while optimistic, is tempered by the knowledge that we face substantial challenges: the need to increase customer expectations, competitive pressures on margins, and substantial marketing costs. Furthermore, Washington's failure to negotiate down Japan's (and others') protective tariffs has severely limited our ability to recoup the high expense of our imports from export revenue.

Only the strongest performers will survive in the highly competitive years ahead, and we intend to be one of them. To do so, we must provide high-quality products and service that exceed our customers' expectations, instill a people-oriented culture throughout the company, and implement the most cost-efficient operating and business processes.

If we focus on these priorities, if we concentrate on our core values, and if we apply ourselves diligently to the basics of running the business, we will maintain our momentum and will perform strongly in the years ahead.

For the Board of Directors
March 30, 1989

Chairman of the Board and Chief Executive Officer

As a side note, the problems at XYZ are not unusual. An excerpt from Caterpillar's Letter to Shareholders in its 1982 annual report reads "...the strong dollar is a prime factor in Caterpillar's reduced sales and earnings..." Like Caterpillar, XYZ also faces transaction and contingent exposures: A weak dollar has made its input costs more expensive—and they may become even more expensive in the future.

Clearly, XYZ's chairman and CEO has recognized the effects of strategic exposures that have brought about cash flow problems, decreased profits, and increased the competitive threat. Although sales are up, XYZ appears to be sinking from sharp increases in the costs of major Japanese components, higher prices for raw materials, and closed markets due to protective tariffs.

The principals at XYZ are feeling the pinch. While going forward with "high quality products and services" is fine, it won't manage XYZ's strategic exposures. What can the firm do to avoid serious cash flow problems and, potentially, bankruptcy? The answer is **hedge**.

The firm can hedge its currency exposure using foreign-exchange forwards, futures, swaps, caps, or collars. (These instruments are discussed in later chapters.) The firm could reduce swings in cash flows by hedging the volatility of raw material prices. Commodity futures and/or commodity swaps could be used for this purpose. And, the firm should hire, or develop an ongoing relationship with, a risk management specialist to measure and hedge strategic exposures. This expertise can help the firm react quickly to changing market conditions.

Statement of Consolidated Income

A more revealing analysis of a firm's risk can be done with the aid of the firm's statement of consolidated income and its statement of changes in financial position found in its annual report. The analysis usually starts with the question, How do we know if our firm is exposed to financial price risk? In particular, managers want to determine the degree to which the value of the firm is sensitive to changes in interest rates, sensitive to changes in foreign-exchange rates, and sensitive to fluctuations in commodity prices. To look at the changes over time, a treasurer needs a movie, rather than a snapshot. In the jargon of finance, to look at the changes in the firm, one needs to look at **flows** rather than **stocks**. The income statement and statement of changes in financial position provide such flows. We will look at the income statement first.

The Consolidated Income Statement for XYZ appears below as Exhibit 10.6.

Exhibit 10.6
Statement of Consolidated Income

XYZ Corporation

Statement of Consolidated Income
(in millions of U.S. dollars, except per share data)

	Fiscal Year Ended 11/30/88	11/30/87
Net Sales	12,595	10,313
Costs and Expenses:		
Costs of Goods Sold	7,808	5,672
Selling, Administrative & General Costs	3,230	3,106
Interest Expense	463	403
Pension Expense	80	69
Foreign Currency Expense	232	206
Depreciation	113	103
Total Costs and Expenses	11,926	9,559
Income from Continuing Operations Before Taxes	669	754
Income Taxes (U.S. & Foreign)	122	176
Income from Continuing Operations	547	578
Income Per Share—Continuing Operations	$8.29	$8.76
Discontinued Operations After Taxes	34	—
Net Income	581	578
Net Income Per Share	$8.81	$8.76
Average Number of Common Shares	66	66

Notes: 1. **Cost of Goods Sold**: In 1988, the average price of electrolytic copper rose
to 122.66 cents per pound from 84.80 cents per pound in 1987. Since copper
is a primary input to producing XYZ's products, this 45 percent increase in
copper prices had a significant impact on cost of goods sold.

When risk management professionals examine an income statement, they first look at the state of the core business—the demands
for the firm's products and the pattern of costs—to provide a view
of the current financial health of the firm. From this baseline, they
can identify the financial risks which could jeopardize (or enhance)
the firm's financial condition. To accomplish this evaluation, the risk
management professional asks a number of questions. He or she gets
answers, or at least some indication of the answers, with the aid of
accounting data and financial ratios. Examples appear below:

Question: What is the state of the market for the firm's output?
Is core business expanding or eroding?

Indicators: Annual change in net sales, inventory turnover.

Question: How are costs changing relative to income?

Indicators: Gross profit margin, selling and administrative costs, general costs.

Question: Are there foreign-exchange exposures that could put the firm in jeopardy?

Indicators: What currencies does the firm buy/sell in? What percentage of the firm's inputs are foreign sourced? What percentage of the firm's output is sold overseas?

Question: How well is the firm carrying its debt? Are there year-to-year changes in the levels of debt or to the firm's sensitivity to interest rate changes?

Indicators: Times interest earned, debt to capitalization ratio.

Question: Are there problems with the firm's tax situation?

Indicators: Are there tax loss carry forwards or tax credits? Is XYZ an alternative minimum tax payer?

Using these guidelines, let's examine XYZ's income statement and compare the firm's performance in 1988 and 1987. Notice first that sales are doing well: Net sales have increased about 22 percent. And, even after adjusting for a 4 percent inflation rate in 1988, XYZ has experienced a real increase in output of 18 percent. Also notice that the sales force is not letting any grass grow under its feet—the inventory turnover ratio (cost of goods sold divided by average inventory) has increased from 12.2 in 1987 to an astounding 17.3 in 1988.

With such an increase in sales, many firms have had trouble keeping their people motivated—with sales increasing, the staff often begins to take life too easy. But, the income statement suggests that no one at XYZ is living "high on the hog." Selling, administrative and general costs have risen only 4 percent—a much smaller percentage than the increase in sales and about equal to the rate of inflation—indicating that the sales reps continue to fly coach and stay in Motel 6, while the office staff watches the paper clips.

Despite this good news, something is clearly wrong in production and in finance: Cost of goods sold increased dramatically, rising from 55 percent of net sales in 1987 to 62 percent of net sales in 1988. A footnote to the financial statement addressed this increase, noting that most of this increase was attributable to an increase in the price of copper—a primary input to the production of XYZ's output. The average price of electrolytic copper rose to 122.66 cents per pound from 84.80 cents per pound in 1987. Since copper is a primary input in producing XYZ's products, this 45 percent increase in copper prices had a significant impact on cost of goods sold.

Interest expense was also up (by 15 percent). (The source of this increase in interest expense will be discussed when we look at the statement of change in financial position.) With this increase in interest expense, service on the firm's debt is becoming troublesome. For example, times interest earned (operating profit divided by annual interest expense) has declined from 2.87 in 1987 to 2.44 in 1988. (Calculated here as *income from continuing operations before taxes + interest expense* divided by *interest expense.*)

As the value of the dollar continued its decline in 1988, XYZ's foreign currency expense increased markedly. The CEO of XYZ mentioned this problem explicitly in his letter to the shareholders, as he complained about Washington's monetary policies and about U.S. trade policies: Recall his words, "...And a significant portion of our problems can be laid at Washington's doorstep. Over the past three years, the dollar lost almost one-fourth of its value relative to the yen, as the dollar fell from 168 yen per dollar in 1986 to 144 yen in 1987 to 128 yen in 1988. Since XYZ Corporation sources a significant number of its components from Asia, this decline in the value of the dollar has hit us hard..."

The combined effect of these adverse developments was a substantial deterioration in the firm's performance. XYZ's net profit margin fell from 5.6 percent in 1987 to 4.6 percent in 1988.

Statement of Changes in Financial Position

The indications of strategic risks to look for in the statement of changes in financial position are more subjective than what we looked for on the income statement. However, we will note that risk management professionals tend to stress four areas: the quality of earnings, pension fund policies, structure of the firm's financing, and liquidity.

Quality of earnings: It is not enough to know that the firm is accumulating funds. A firm can be accumulating funds while it is going out of business. Hence, the question: Are the earnings of the firm the result of ongoing operations, or, do the earnings reflect short-term fixes?

Pension fund policies: Who manages the pension fund? What are the policy guidelines? What does the portfolio contain?

Structure of the firm's financing: How much debt exists? How does the size of the debt compare with the market value of the equity? How is the debt structured? (i.e., fixed-rate, floating-rate debt, convertible debt, etc.)

Liquidity: How much liquidity does the firm retain to deal with unexpected cash needs?

XYZ's Statement of Changes in Financial Position is depicted in Exhibit 10.7.

Exhibit 10.7
Statement of Changes in Financial Position

XYZ Corporation

Statement of Changes in Financial Position
(in millions of U.S. dollars)

	Fiscal Year Ended 11/30/88	11/30/87
Funds Provided (Used) by Operations:		
Net Income	581	578
Depreciation	113	103
Deferred Income Tax	67	58
Accounts and Notes Receivable	(56)	(40)
Deferred Pension Plan Costs	50	40
Accounts Payable - Trade	38	29
Funds Provided by Operating Activities	793	768
Funds Provided by Discontinued Operations	9	—
Funds Provided by Extraordinary Items	3	—
Total Funds Provided By Continuing Operations	805	768
Funds Provided (Used) by Investment Activities:		
Special Pension Funding	(37)	(25)
Total Funds Provided by Investment Activities	(37)	(25)
Funds Provided (Used) by Financing Activities:		
Short Term Debt Incurred	51	19
Short Term Debt Paid	(149)	(82)
Long Term Debt Paid	(220)	(142)
Dividend Paid	(122)	(120)
Total Funds Provided by Financing Activities	(440)	(325)
Increase in Cash and Short Term Investments	(6)	8
Net Increase (Decrease)	322	426

Notes: 1. **Discontinued Operations:** During the second quarter of 1988, XYZ sold its Ohio assembly operation to reduce operating costs and eliminate duplication of work responsibilities. Funds provided by this discontinued operation after taxes amounted to $9 million.

2. **Extraordinary Items:** A favorable judgement for XYZ was found after several years of dispute over a matter of unfair competition. The suit was initiated by XYZ against ABC in 1986. An award in the amount of $3 million was granted by the Appellate Court to XYZ during the first quarter of 1988.

3. **Retirement Benefits:** XYZ increased funds allocated to the special pension account to offset losses in the internally managed fixed-income portfolio. The special pension fund is protected by internal policy which determines the funding requirements.

4. **Short-Term Financing:** During the third and fourth quarters of fiscal year 1988, the management of XYZ saw it necessary to add $24.9 million in floating rate, short-term debt to the total debt outstanding. Total floating rate, short-term debt for the year amounted to $38.5 million while total fixed-rate debt equalled $12.5 million.

We can now apply these questions to XYZ's Statement of Changes in Financial Position. When we do, we discover a number of interesting things. First, the quality of earnings has declined. By comparing the 1988 financials with those for 1987, we can see that XYZ posted an increase in *net income* (from $578 million to $581 million). But, these aggregate figures disguise the fact that the *quality* of XYZ's earnings declined in 1988. The gain in total funds is derived from two one-time, nonoperational transactions. As recorded in the footnotes to the financial statements, XYZ benefited in 1988 from the sale of a facility. Specifically, during the second quarter of 1988, XYZ sold its Ohio assembly operation to reduce operating costs and eliminate duplicated work responsibilities. Funds from this discontinued operation, after taxes, amounted to $9 million. The second one-time nonoperational transaction involved the settlement of a lawsuit. A favorable judgement for XYZ Corporation was found after several years of dispute over a matter of unfair competition. The suit was initiated by XYZ against ABC Corporation in 1986. An award of $3 million was granted by the Appelate Court to XYZ during the first quarter of 1988.

There also seems to be a pension management problem. A special pension funding was required in 1988. According to a footnote to the financial statements, this special funding was required due to losses on the pension portfolio. XYZ Corporation increased funds allocated to the special pension account to offset losses in the internally managed fixed-income portfolio. The special pension fund is protected by internal policy which determines the funding limits. Since the losses occurred in the fixed income portfolio, these losses were themselves, most likely, the result of rising interest rates.

The structure of XYZ's financing has changed. As indicated in the *funds provided (used) by financing activities* section, XYZ incurred $51 million in additional short-term debt in 1988. (The footnotes indicate that most of this was of a floating rate nature.) Because the market value of its shares declined in 1988 and it issued no new shares in 1988, this increase in debt means that XYZ's debt/equity ratio has risen.

We can also see that XYZ's liquidity has deteriorated. In addition to a deterioration in its ability to collect its receivables, not shown here, the statement indicates that the cash and short-term investment holdings of XYZ decreased in 1988.

As one would expect, the problems at XYZ did not go unnoticed by debt rating agencies. As a consequence, in 1988 XYZ got an unfavorable review in Standard & Poor's *CreditWeek*. Specifically, the review stated, in part, "Credit implications are revised to negative from "developing" on XYZ Corporation's "A" senior debt and "A-" subordinated debt ratings...."

A Little Financial Engineering Can Go A Long Way

Having examined some of the problems at XYZ, we can now turn our attention to some discussion of possible solutions. These solutions are only suggested here as most of the instruments that would be employed have yet to be discussed. At the very least, however, this should whet the reader's appetite for a more thorough discussion of the instruments used by financial engineers. We consider the potential solutions for the interest rate exposure, the foreign exchange exposure, the commodity price exposure, the tax problems, and the pension fund problems.

The Interest Rate Dimension

With its current mix of fixed and floating rate debt, XYZ suffers when interest rates rise; so, this firm might well be interested in protection from rate increases. Several widely used risk management instruments can provide this insurance: interest-rate swaps—XYZ pays fixed and receives floating; interest rate caps—XYZ receives a payment if the interest rate rises above the cap level; or interest rate collars—XYZ receives a payment if the interest rate rises above the cap level but XYZ makes a payment if the interest rate falls below the floor level.

While these alternatives are viable, XYZ's current credit problems suggest that XYZ might be better off if it lowered its current interest expense via a swaption (an option on a swap). In its current position, XYZ will gain if rates fall; using a swaption, XYZ can trade this potential gain for a lower rate today. Or, XYZ might wish to lower the probability of default—and, thereby, improve its bond ratings—via one of the hybrid debt instruments. For example, XYZ might replace some of its floating rate debt with reverse floating rate debt—i.e., debt on which the coupon rate moves inversely with the floating rate index. This will offset its current exposure to increases in rates. (Hybrid securities are discussed in Chapter 19.)

As the firm becomes more conversant with risk management tools, the XYZ Corporation may want to fine tune its interest rate exposure by determining the **optimal duration** for its debt. To accomplish this, it is necessary for XYZ to determine not only the duration of its debt but also the duration of its liabilities—a feat that is more difficult to accomplish for a manufacturing firm than for a financial firm. (Asset/liability management is discussed more fully in Chapter 20.)

The Foreign Exchange Dimension

Because it sources such a sizeable portion of its input components from Asia, XYZ is hurt when the dollar weakens relative to the yen. To manage this exposure, XYZ may wish to enter into a currency swap in which XYZ receives cash flows in yen and pays cash flows in dollars. However, it is somewhat more likely that XYZ would prefer to use a currency option—XYZ would receive payments if the value of the dollar falls below an agreed-upon level. And, since XYZ is concerned about a stream of payments over time, rather than a single payment at a point in time, an average rate option would be more appropriate than an option on the spot exchange rate. Such an option pays if the average spot rate over a specified period of time is above some pre-specified level.

The Commodity Price Dimension

Until recently, XYZ's exposure to copper prices could only be hedged in futures contracts (traded on the COMEX and LME). To hedge its short-term exposure to changes in the value of its copper inventory, XYZ could *sell* copper futures. At the same time, to hedge its longer-term exposure to copper prices on the copper it has not yet purchased but which it will eventually need, XYZ could *purchase* copper futures. Today, however, XYZ has an alternative to futures. It could hedge in a copper swap. Such swaps have been gaining popularity as a hedging instrument since a favorable ruling by the Commodity Futures Trading Commission in 1989 granted such contracts legal standing. XYZ could also hedge in a copper cap or a copper collar. A copper cap would pay XYZ whenever the price of copper rose above a specified level. A copper collar would also pay XYZ when copper rose above a specified cap level but would require that XYZ pay when the price of copper fell below a specified floor level.

We could get even more inventive. For example, XYZ could lever its copper exposure to reduce its current interest rate risk. This could be accomplished via a hybrid debt instrument that replaces some of the firm's floating rate debt with debt having an interest rate indexed to copper prices. With such a loan XYZ would, at the outset, pay a below market coupon but, if the price of copper fell, the coupon would rise. Hence, this loan provides XYZ with the opportunity to monetize today its potential for gain should copper prices fall. This is equivalent to selling synthetic long-dated put options on copper. (Synthetic securities are discussed in Chapter 23.)

The Tax Dimension

Because XYZ's interest expense is large and volatile, its pre-tax income is also volatile. Hence, if interest rates are high—and pre-tax income is therefore low—XYZ is likely to be unable to use its other tax shields (e.g., its tax loss carry forwards and tax credits). There are at least two solutions to this problem: (1) XYZ could sell the tax shield it cannot use to another firm by issuing auction rate preferred stock, and (2) XYZ could increase the likelihood of being able to use its tax shields by hedging its interest rate exposure as outlined above. (Tax-driven deals are discussed more fully in Chapter 24.)

The Pension Portfolio Dimension

Because XYZ's problems seem to arise when interest rates rise, the simplest solution is for XYZ to purchase an interest rate cap. When interest rates rise, XYZ will receive a payment which will at least partially offset the losses on the portfolio.

In the longer run, however, the managers of XYZ may want to take a more careful look at the portfolio itself to determine if the portfolio contains embedded option positions, either long or short. If the portfolio has an inherent embedded short option position say, on interest rates, the manager of the portfolio can purchase an interest rate cap or floor to manage the exposure. On a happier note, if the portfolio has an inherent embedded long option position, the manager of the portfolio can sell the embedded option to enhance current yield on the portfolio.

Analyzing the Balance Sheet

We have looked at management's letter to shareholders, the firm's income statement, and the firm's statement of changes in financial position. We now turn to the balance sheet to see what it says about strategic exposures. The balance sheet, and some of its accompanying notes, is depicted as Exhibit 10.8.

Exhibit 10.8
Consolidated Balance Sheet

XYZ Corporation

Consolidated Balance Sheet

In Millions   November 30, 1988

Assets		Liabilities & Shareholders' Equity	
Current Assets		**Current Liabilities**	
Cash and Short-Term		Accounts Payable	$ 686
Investments	$ 213	Notes Payable	493
Receivables, Net	314	Accrued Liabilities	650
Prepaid Expenses	136	Other Current Liabilities	236
Deferred Income Tax Benefit	67	**Total Current Liabilities**	**2,065**
Inventories	452	**Long Term Debt**	**1,115**
Total Current Assets	**1,182**	**Deferred Income Taxes**	**388**
Property, Buildings & Equipment		**Other Liabilities**	**374**
Property	937		
Buildings	1,363		
Equipment	3,052		
Construction in Progress	166	**Shareholders' Equity**	
Total Prop, Bldgs, Equip		Preferred Stock	234
at cost	5,518	Common Stock	788
Less Accumulated		Retained Earnings	1,434
Depreciation	(1,876)	Less Common Stock	
Total Net Prop, Bldgs, Equip	**3,642**	in Treasury	(394)
Other Non-Current Assets	**189**	Cumulative Foreign	
Other Assets		Currency Adjustment	(8)
Intangible Assets	65		
Investments in Affiliates		**Total Shareholders' Equity**	**2,054**
(foreign & domestic)	629		
Miscellaneous Assets	289		
Total Other Assets	**983**	**Total Liabilities and**	
Total Assets	**$5,996**	**Shareholders' Equity**	**$5,996**

Notes: 1. **Principals of Consolidation:** The Consolidated financial statements include the accounts of XYZ Corporation, a holding company, and its domestic and foreign subsidiaries at the close of our fiscal year which occurred on 11/30/88. Due to the dissimilar nature of its operations, XYZ's wholly owned finance subsidiary is included here on the equity basis. Hereafter XYZ Corporation will be known as the "Parent Company,"...

2. **Inventories:** The LIFO method is used to value all inventories. Copper, a primary raw material for the manufacture of the firm's principal products, is a major component of raw materials inventory....

3. **Income Taxes:** The provision for income taxes is based on pretax financial income which differs from taxable income. Differences generally arise because certain items, such as depreciation and write-downs of certain assets, are reflected in different time periods for financial and tax purposes. At XYZ, we chose to use the flow-through method of accounting for investment tax credits. This method enables a firm to recognize investment tax credits as a reduction of income tax expense in the year the qualified investments were made. The statutory federal income tax rate for 1987 and 1988 was reduced by the Tax Reform Act of 1986. However, the effective income tax rate for 1987 actually increased due to the repeal of the investment tax credit (although some credits were allowed in 1986 under the transition rules) and a higher capital gains rate.

4. **Foreign Currency Translation:** The local currency of the foreign subsidiary is the functional currency. The rate of exchange in effect on the date of the balance sheet is used to translate the value of the assets and liabilities. Operating results are converted to U.S. dollars by averaging the prevailing exchange rates during the period. Gains or losses due to currency translations over the period have been captured in a special retained equity account.

5. **Retirement Benefits:** Employees of domestic and foreign operations participate in a non-contributory pension plan which is based on the number of years of service. Funding of the plan is done in accordance with SFAS 87 and is also based on long-range forecasts of planned financial assets, expected return on plant assets, tax considerations,....

6. **Foreign Operations:** Sales from consolidated foreign operations were 15.5% of the total sales in 1988.

7. **Cash and Short-Term Investments:** Figures for cash and short-term investments consist of commercial paper, loan participations, certificates of deposit, and bankers acceptances. The wholly owned finance subsidiary, XYZ Finance, purchases nearly all notes receivable resulting from domestic operations. Foreign subsidiaries sell certain receivables to a non-affiliated finance company.

8. **Preferred Stock:** In 1985, the Parent Company issued 2,340,000 shares of adjustable rate cumulative preferred stock at face value of $100 per share. The annualized dividend rate for the initial dividend periods ended 1/15/86 and 4/15/86 was 10%. Thereafter, dividends have been set quarterly at an annualized rate of 1.85% less than the highest of the U.S. Treasury three-month, 10-year or 20-year maturity rates, which rate may not be less than 6.75% nor greater than 14%.

XYZ isn't an organization on the ropes—yet. But, it could soon be. The company's current ratio (current asset, divided by current liabilities) is just 0.57. Which means that the firm could only pay about half of its short-term debt by converting its most liquid assets to cash. A more desirable ratio would be in the range of 1.5 to 2.0. Its quick ratio (which excludes inventory, prepaid expenses and deferred income tax benefits in the measurement of liquidity) is only 0.25. A more desirable range would be 0.75 to 1.0.

At the same time, XYZ is leveraged enough to raise the eyebrows of rating agencies. With a significant amount of overhanging debt, default could be triggered either by a reduction in sales revenues or by an increase in financial costs (interest rates, foreign exchange, or commodity prices). The traditional solution to XYZ's problem is to reduce the amount of debt in its capital structure, replacing debt with equity. For instance, XYZ might replace some debt with preferred stock. The firm might discover, however, that it cannot sell equity—either preferred or common—at acceptable prices, particularly if the company is on analysts' sell lists.

Alternatively, XYZ could reduce the volatility of its pre-tax income. For example, it could enter into an interest rate swap in which the company pays fixed and receives floating. With this contract in place, the loss XYZ would suffer if rates rose, from its balance sheet exposure, would be offset by the funds received from its swap counterparty. Conversely, when interest rates declined and XYZ became cash rich, it would make payments to its swap counterparty.

Again, we should ask questions when looking at the balance sheet. For example, is the return from investments in domestic and overseas affiliates making the firm vulnerable to movements in interest rates and exchange rates? Are interest rate options embedded in retained earnings? Does the firm have exposures to commodity prices? Are there potential leverage concerns? Is debt paid in the same currency as that received on the firm's receivables? Are there investment tax credits and tax loss carry forwards that can be accessed via risk management instruments? At the risk of some overlap and redundancy, let's briefly consider these questions.

XYZ's balance sheet shows that the company has $629 million invested in both foreign and domestic affiliates. Given the importance of maintaining the company's asset base in the face of high leverage, XYZ may want to hedge those investments with any number of instruments—caps, forwards, and options, among them.

The balance sheet also suggests that there are embedded options in the firm's retained earnings. Specifically, the firm has 2,340,000 shares of adjustable rate preferred stock outstanding which it issued in 1985.

XYZ's balance sheet also reveals the exposure to copper prices, referring, in a footnote, to "copper, a primary component for the manufacture of the latest design...and is among inventory." While the balance sheet does not tell us whether the firm's debt is paid in the same currencies as those received when it collects on its receivables, a little digging on management's part can answer this question.

Finally, let's address the subject of tax credits and carry forwards. Leveraged companies such as XYZ should be doing everything possible to reduce their tax burden and preserve cash, and one way to do this is via tax planning. It is essential for XYZ to use its investment tax credits (ITCs) and tax loss carry forwards (TLCFs). The balance sheet suggests that the company might take advantage of both ITCs and TLCFs. Investment tax credits have been recorded as reductions of income taxes during the year allowable assets are placed into service. Discontinued subsidiaries have tax loss carry forwards and additional after-tax changes from these discontinued operations have been recorded.

Derivative products such as swaps can create an environment in which management can plan more adequately for using ITCs and TLCFs that otherwise might go unused. (This is demonstrated in later chapters.) Derivatives, for example, can do this by removing income stream volatility. If a firm has a volatile pre-tax income because of changes in exchange rates, interest rates, or commodity price (where the income stream changes significantly year-to-year or quarter-to-quarter), a firm may not be able to use the tax credits or carry forwards during the current fiscal year but may have to wait until the following year. By smoothing out the income stream, then, the tax credits and carry forwards can be used immediately. Given the time value of money, the immediate use of tax preference items is preferred to the later use of tax preference items. Additionally, ITCs and TLCFs may evaporate during the following year due to time limitations.

Consider another question we might wish to ask while looking at the balance sheet: Does the company have foreign exchange exposure? Or, more narrowly, we might ask (1) does it have a net translation exposure? (2) does it have a long-term foreign exchange exposure? and (3) does it hold receivables with a foreign exchange sensitivity?

XYZ's balance sheet suggests that the company may face significant foreign exchange exposures—both translational and transactional exposures. Highly leveraged companies should be concerned about net asset translation exposures, which in XYZ's case, consist of manufacturing facilities in Ireland, Spain, Italy, and Taiwan. Failure to hedge this exposure may have an immediate adverse effect on the cost of raising capital. Longer-term exposures may impact the cost of capital as well.

Because foreign sales make up only 15.5 percent of the company's total sales, XYZ may be less concerned about foreign exchange rates. Nevertheless, exchange rate fluctuations may affect the company's ability to compete against foreign manufacturers. A treasurer may think, "As long as I can adjust my end selling price for adverse changes in exchange rate fluctuations, I have no exposure." But, companies often are exposed because they don't or can't react quickly enough. For example, most companies use a bulletin system for posting their prices and by the time they get around to making changes to their posted price, a year may have gone by. In the interim, competitors may enter XYZ's domestic market, pricing their products lower because exchange rates run in their favor.

One of the least obvious areas of exposure on XYZ's balance sheet can be found under the retirement benefits footnote. The company's balance sheet states that employees of both domestic and foreign operations "participate in noncontributory pension plans." If those payments are funded out of the parent company, the company may want to hedge the payments because, like other transaction costs, the company knows when they will happen and what the amounts of the transactions will be.

XYZ may wish to repatriate profits made through its overseas operations in the form of dividends, royalties or intercompany transfers. The case for such repatriation is especially strong in countries where the company forecasts a continuing decline in the value of the local currency. With an ongoing dividend and royalties payments programs, XYZ may be able to estimate both the timing and the amount of money to be transferred and can hedge appropriately.

Finally, while companies traditionally hedge only those profits remitted to the parent, they may want to consider hedging the portion of the profits that they do not remit. The argument for doing so is especially compelling for companies close to a ratings downgrade, those highly leveraged, and those thinking of using stock in making future acquisitions, either domestically or abroad.

We would like to point out a few other interesting facts revealed by our examination of XYZ's balance sheet and the footnotes to the balance sheet. First, XYZ's current assets include $213 million in cash and short-term investments which include commercial paper, loan participations, certificates of deposit and bankers' acceptances. The company should be concerned about possible yield erosion on these instruments and may want to protect itself by purchasing interest rate floors. (Interest rate floors and their uses are discussed in Chapter 15.)

Because XYZ is in a volatile industry where sales decline as interest rates rise, its earnings per share are highly sensitive to interest rate movements. As rates rise, its debt service will be higher, and XYZ will have less cash available to cover other costs.

We also observe that XYZ has a finance subsidiary. We should ask whether or not the subsidiary is effectively managing its gap. This is important because the finance subsidiary purchases receivables from domestic operations, it must fund those purchases, presumably through long-term debt. The subsidiary must either close or manage the resulting interest rate funding/lending gap. If foreign subsidiaries, selling receivables to a nonaffiliated finance company, are paid in the local currency, XYZ may want to hedge part or all of the currency risk, regardless of whether those funds are repatriated to the parent. Why? Because rate moves may impact the subsidiary's liquidity or tax position in the local currency.

Our last question before closing is, are there hidden interest rate exposures in the capital structure? Corporations often have hidden exposures in their capital structure that they tend to forget about. Many times these exposures result from the preferred stock that companies issue. XYZ has issued two types of preferred stock having different characteristics. First, it has issued adjustable rate preferred stock which pays interest tied to some interest rate index. (This was discussed earlier.) Second, XYZ has issued dividend-constrained preferred stock which specifies that the dividend payout will fall within a specified range—in the case of XYZ, this range is 6.75 percent and 14 percent. The net result is that the dividend-constrained preferred stock which XYZ has issued contains an embedded collar. That is, XYZ has written a collar.

Modeling a Firm's Exposures

We have seen that a careful examination of a firm's financial statements can take us a long way toward identifying a firm's strategic exposures. Such an examination requires more than just reading the lines on the financial statement. We must also read between the lines and this includes a careful reading of the footnotes.

As useful as this exercise has been for appreciating the gold that is buried in financial statements, it has not really focused on how to quantify the many exposures. Indeed, many of the exposures were themselves, to some degree, offsetting. For example, when a firm holds some floating rate asset and some floating rate liabilities (whether intentional or not) these exposures are partially, and may be wholly, offsetting. If a firm holds some floating rate assets and some inverse-floating rate assets, these too are partially, and may be wholly, offsetting. To the extent that these offsetting positions were not planned, they are sometimes called **natural hedges.**

When we conduct a thorough risk analysis, we must take all of the exposures into consideration. We must also assess the degree to which different exposures are offsetting and this requires a careful quantification. Given our discussion thus far, one would probably conclude that this is a very difficult task. At a conceptual level, however, it is not difficult at all—thanks to the advent of electronic spreadsheets.

The process, which employs **what if or sensitivity analysis,** requires us to build a financial model of the income statement. In the model, we explicitly incorporate the financial prices that have been identified in our examination of the financial statements as representing exposures for the firm. The current values of the financial prices are entered into a separate section of the spreadsheet called an **assumptions block.** The rest of the statement is then tied to the assumptions block in a fashion that represents the actual structural relationships between the firm's cost and revenue entries. In this modeling exercise, we must also take care to include the value changes in the firm's assets and liabilities because it is the *real* value changes we want to hedge—not just the accounting values.

Consider how this is done: Suppose that we determine that sales are functionally related to the prime rate, the yen/dollar exchange rate, and the price of our product. If we can give a precise functional form to the relationship between sales and these "financial prices," then we can build this relationship into our financial model. Similarly, we can examine the effect of interest rates on receivables, payables, adjustable rate preferred stock, and so on. Each of these relationships is carefully and judiciously built into the model.

After all income and value change influencing factors have been built into the model, we can begin the process of examining how a change in a financial price affects the firm's value (or income, if we are limiting ourselves to that variable). For example, after beginning with the current values of interest rates, exchange rates, and commodity prices, we can change each of these prices (one at a time) and examine how the firm's income is affected. Through this analysis, we can determine the firm's precise risk profile with respect to each of the financial prices.

A number of corporations have begun making analyses like this. Merck & Company, for example, starts with its strategic plan net income, derived with the use of forecasted local currency earnings and exchange rates likely to prevail over the coming year.[6] The model generates alternative exchange rates by quarter, which it then applies to forecasted local currency earnings, producing alternative U.S. dollar net income. By looking at the resulting distribution of net income, Merck has a measure of its foreign exchange exposure.

This type of analysis presents one major problem. Doing it requires a great deal of closely held data. If an outside analyst wants to look at the company's exposures—or if the managers of XYZ want to look at the exposures of its competitors—the measurements must be made on market valuations alone.

The upshot of these closing remarks is that there is no substitute for careful analysis when measuring a firm's strategic exposures. Without accurate measurement there cannot be effective management.

Endnotes

[1]These exhibits are updates from those that first appeared in Rawls and Smithson (1989)

[2]These definitions are borrowed from Rawls and Smithson (1989).

[3]See Business Week (1982) and Millman (1988).

[4]For more details, see Hutchins (1986)

[5]XYZ Corporation is a truly fictional firm. A wide variety of firms can experience the kinds of exposures discussed here. We have chosen not to give XYZ a fixed identity, in order to discourage the reader from associating a certain risk management technique or a certain risk exposure with a particular industry. We encourage

the reader to think about the different industries which may have exposures similar to those discussed here.

[6]See Rawls and Smithson (1990).

References and Suggested Reading

Business Week. "How Sir Freddie Shot Himself Down" (February 22, 1982).

Millman, G. "How Smart Competitors are Locking In The Cheap Dollar," *Corporate Finance* (December 1988).

Rawls, S.W. and C.W. Smithson. "The Evolution of Risk Management Products," *Journal of Applied Corporate Finance,* 4(1) (1989), pp. 18-26.

Rawls, S.W. and C.W. Smithson. "Strategic Risk Management," *Journal of Applied Corporate Finance,* 2(4) (1990), pp. 6-18.

Hutchins, D. "Caterpillar's Triple Whammy," *Fortune* (October 27, 1986).

Chapter 11

Product Development

Eberhard E. Scheuing and Eugene M. Johnson

Overview[1]

Financial engineers use off-the-shelf financial products to achieve specific objectives. They also assist in the development of new financial products when existing products are unsuitable or too cumbersome to accomplish a given objective, or when the structure of the new product is such that it will create new opportunities for the innovating firm or for the firm's clients.

New products may be the result of a concerted and very formal new product development effort or they may result from productizing the solution to a specific client's needs. This latter possibility was discussed in Chapter 1 and we do not dwell on it further except to say that, once a decision has been made to productize a solution, the same sequence of steps described in this chapter as part of the new product development effort should be followed.

In this chapter, we distinguish between **products** and **strategies,** both of which involve financial engineering. Products are

Eb Scheuing is Professor of Marketing in the Graduate School of Business at St. John's University, New York. He has authored or coauthored 19 books and several hundred articles on various aspects of marketing and product development. Gene Johnson is Professor of Marketing at the University of Rhode Island. He has authored numerous articles and coauthored several books on product development and marketing.

goods and services that are sold to clients. Strategies are in-house trading techniques designed to exploit market inefficiencies or to accomplish specific objectives of the firm. Strategies may be sold outright or consulting services involving the transfer of strategies may be sold. When this is done, the strategies become products of the firm. We will generally distinguish between products sold to customers and strategies employed in-house.

Much of our understanding of financial innovation is an outgrowth of research into product development in the consumer goods manufacturing sector. It is only in recent years that specialists in product development have become interested in financial products. It is not surprising, therefore, that models of financial innovation are closely related to models of product development more generally.

While relatively short, this is nevertheless an ambitious chapter from a financial engineering perspective. We begin by defining the concept of a product and by distinguishing between goods and services. Following this, we describe a normative model of new product development that takes us through the various stages of product development from need recognition to final delivery. Lastly, we review the major classes of financial instruments as a prelude to a fuller description of the physical tools of the financial engineer that begins with the next chapter.

Products Defined

Products are combinations of tangible and intangible benefits that provide satisfaction of end users' needs or wants. Products may take either of two forms—goods or services. A **good** is a product having a tangible character in the sense that it is ownable and transferable. This tangible character also makes it possible to inventory goods and to separate production from delivery. A **service,** on the other hand, is a product that is largely intangible in nature. It is created in the process of delivery and ceases to exist at the end of the delivery—although the benefits derived from the service may continue after the service itself has terminated. Because services are not tangible, they are not ownable or transferable in the same way that goods are ownable and transferable. For the same reason, they cannot be inventoried or distributed through intermediaries.

While intangible in nature, the provision of most services is not possible without the use of tangible goods. The goods used in the provision of a service may be of a supporting or a facilitating nature. Supporting goods are tangible items used by the service performer in providing the service and facilitating goods are tangible items used by the buyer in the course of consuming the service. As a general rule, services are performed as called for and represent a one-on-one relationship between the service provider and the service purchaser.

To make the distinction between services and goods clear, consider a recent innovation in banking. In order to give customers better access to their funds and to reduce the cost of providing tellers, banks and thrifts have introduced automated teller machines (ATMs). These machines allow customers to access cash from their accounts and to obtain cash advances on their credit lines at any time of the day or night whether at their home institution or away on travel. Ready accessibility to cash is clearly a service, but its provision requires supporting goods such as the ATM machine and the telecommunications and computing systems that drive it. At the same time, obtaining cash from an ATM system involves the use of a facilitating good (the bank card or credit card). Other examples of financial services include underwriting, risk management, asset allocation, and bridge financing.

Tangible goods used by financial engineers often take the form of financial instruments. Shares of stock, bonds, futures, options, swaps—all of these are "goods" in the sense that they are ownable and transferable. When we speak of financial products in this text, we are including both the financial instruments that are goods in and of themselves, and the services made possible with the aid of supporting goods.

A Model for New Product Development

Successful new products rarely emerge by mere happenstance. Rather, they tend to be the outgrowth of an appropriately designed structure and a carefully orchestrated process. Unfortunately, not all financial institutions have made the organizational and marketing changes required to establish procedures that will provide for a constant flow of profitable product innovations. In sharp contrast, leading consumer goods companies have systems in place that create, test, and introduce new products at a vigorous pace. The financial industry needs similar systems to take advantage of market opportunities and to meet competitive challenges. Rather than reinvent the process, financial institutions can benefit from the vast experience gained by consumer goods manufacturers.

The model presented here for new product development involves 15 steps grouped into four stages: direction, design, testing, and introduction. It is the outgrowth of a study of earlier models and conversations with product managers. The model was subsequently subjected to empirical scrutiny using a survey of members of the Financial Institutions Marketing Association. The overall model is illustrated in Exhibit 11.1.

Exhibit 11.1
Normative Model of New Product Development

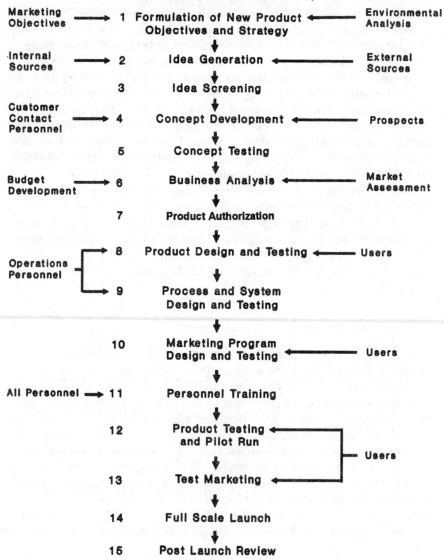

Directions

At the outset of the new product development process, senior management must chart the course of the effort and give it clear direction. This stage includes three individual steps: (1) formulation of new product objectives and strategy, (2) idea generation, and (3) idea screening.

Driven by a sense of urgency and a perceived need for a "quick fix," many firms jump right into idea generation. Doing this is akin to lifting anchor without first determining the desired destination. The course of the ship then becomes the result of whim and happenstance.

In contrast, a well-conceived and carefully implemented new product development process begins with a precise *formulation of the objectives and strategy* governing the effort. Of course, this direction is not conceived in a vacuum. It is the outgrowth of the firm's marketing objectives which, in turn, are derived from the corporation's objectives and the basic mission of the business. As a result, a well-designed new product strategy drives and directs the entire product innovation effort and imbues it with effectiveness and efficiency. The key question for product innovators is, what business are we in? The answer to this question provides the focal point for the development process.

New product development should be driven by one or more of four basic strategies. These are depicted in the new product strategy matrix in Exhibit 11.2.

Exhibit 11.2
New Product Strategy Mix

Markets / Offerings	Existing Buyers	New Buyers
Existing Services	*share building*	*market extension*
New Services	*line extension*	*new business*

The first strategy option is one of share building. This strategy aims to sell more existing products to current customers or clients of the firm. It is often implemented in the form of a newly found aggressiveness in style, such as discount pricing. The second strategy is called market extension and involves an effort to extend existing products to new customers. Neither of these first two strategies gives rise to financial innovation nor calls upon the skills of the financial engineer unless the extension involves an innovative new use. The third strategy is line extension. This strategy attempts to develop new products to be marketed to existing customers. This strategy is common in mature industries and involves the leveraging of a valuable asset, namely the current customer base. For instance, credit card issuers try to cross-sell insurance and other services to their cardholders, or investment bankers offer swaps to their existing capital market clients who formerly limited their purchases to underwriting services.

The final option is a new business strategy. This is the riskiest of the four fundamental strategies because it involves entering uncharted territory where the company cannot capitalize on any existing strengths. The failure rate is high.

While new product development strategy has to take into account environmental constraints and opportunities, *idea generation* can also draw on a number of external sources for inspiration. Suppliers of product components, agents, competitors, and end users are all important input sources. For example, home equity loans, which have transformed the nature of much consumer borrowing were inspired by environmental stimuli. In this case, the environmental stimuli took the form of changes in the tax law. Internal search, consultations, and brainstorming can also significantly add to the idea pool.

Once the ideas that are consistent with the firm's product development strategy have been identified, they must be subjected to a first, and relatively crude, sorting procedure that separates the more promising from the less meritorious ideas. Although this preliminary *idea screening* tends to be largely judgemental in nature, care should be taken not to reject an idea out of hand just because it is unusual. Although feasibility and profitability are the key considerations at this point, other factors may play a role, depending upon the circumstances.

Design

Steps four through eleven in the model comprise the design stage. They involve designing and refining a new product as well as its delivery system and marketing program. In *concept development*, the surviving ideas are expanded into full-fledged concepts with the help of input from prospects and the financial institution's own customer contact personnel. A concept is a description of a potential new product. A typical concept statement would include a description of a problem that a prospective user might experience, the reasons why the new product is to be offered, an outline of its features and benefits, and the rationale for its purchase.

Buyers responses to product concepts are examined during *concept testing*. A concept test of a new product is a research technique designed to evaluate whether prospective users (1) understand the idea of the proposed service, (2) react favorably to it, and (3) feel it offers benefits that answer unmet needs. This research step helps eliminate ideas that find little buyer interest while it simultaneously assists in shaping the feature and benefit bundles of attractive concepts.

For the few product proposals that have passed prior checkpoints, *business analysis* represents a comprehensive scrutiny of the business implications of each concept. This step encompasses both a complete market assessment and the drafting of a budget for the development and introduction of each proposed new product. The purpose is to develop recommendations to top management concerning which new product ideas should be implemented. A crucial decision point occurs at the *product authorization* step, when top management commits corporate resources to the implementation of a new product idea.

The next step is the conversion of the new product concept into an operational entity. This requires first the development of the operational details of the product itself, called *product design and testing*—an activity that should involve both the input of prospective users and the active cooperation of operations personnel who will ultimately be delivering it. Intimately interwoven with the design of the product is the design of its *delivery process and system*. All of these components have to be developed and tested in concert. The delivery mechanism that is very much part of the nature of the product itself has to be installed, refined, and debugged in order to ensure smooth delivery upon introduction.

During this portion of the process, the introductory *marketing program* has to be formulated and tested in conjunction with prospective users. To complete the design phase of the process, all employees have to be familiarized with the nature and operational details of the new product. This step constitutes *personnel training* and it is critical to the success of the product. All too often a new product fails because the firm's personnel have not been properly trained to sell and deliver the product. For instance, one commercial bank's answer to the Cash Management Account got off to a shaky start because branch personnel had not been adequately trained and, consequently, did not fully understand the new product. They were unable to explain it to interested customers who had been stimulated to inquire about the product by an effective advertising campaign.

Testing

Product *testing* is used to determine potential customers' acceptance of the new product while a *pilot run* ensures its smooth functioning. This step builds on knowledge and insights gained during the concept testing step earlier in the development process. The goal is to make any necessary refinements to the product and its marketing mix as a result of customers' reactions to the product offered.

Test marketing examines the saleability of the new product and field tests its marketing program in a few branches of the firm or with a limited sample of customers. In addition to testing further the market reaction to a product, test marketing allows management to evaluate alternative marketing mix options. For example, different prices may be charged to assess the impact of price on product demand. Completion of test marketing is followed by a review and final changes in the marketing effort.

A large life insurance company used testing to evaluate a new retired life reserve policy it had developed for corporate customers. A key feature of this new product was a provision for the continuation of group coverage past retirement. To test this provision and the new policy, the firm met with selected independent agents who would be responsible for selling the new product. In addition to obtaining valuable feedback that resulted in technical changes, the testing helped to get the new policy off to a fast start by informing key agents about the new product prior to its market introduction.

Introduction

With the delivery system and marketing program in place and thoroughly tested, the company now initiates the full-scale launch of the new product, introducing it to its entire market area. This step is followed by a *post launch review* aimed at determining whether the new product objectives are being achieved or whether adjustments are called for. Even after all aspects of the new product and its marketing mix are carefully tested, market conditions may require further modifications.

Instrument Preview

In the next several chapters, we will be looking at the various financial instruments that comprise the physical tools of the financial engineer. Before beginning a detailed look at the instruments, however, it will help to have an overview of all the instruments. The reason for this is that it is difficult to discuss any one instrument without some knowledge of the other instruments that share its world.

The financial instruments we will consider may be divided into four broad classes: equities, debt, derivatives, and hybrids. Equities represent ownership interests in a business firm. The most often discussed form of equity is common stock. But other forms exist as well and, from a financial engineering perspective, are at least equally important. For example, limited partnership interests constitute equity in limited partnerships. Equity interests are sold by corporations and partnerships in order to provide the equity financing—a necessary ingredient in any business organization.

Debt instruments represent a debtor/creditor relationship evidenced by some form of promissory note. That is, the borrower (debtor) has signed a binding obligation to repay borrowed principal together with interest under a schedule provided in the promissory note. Failure to make payments as required constitutes default. Debt instruments are sold by business firms, governments, and individuals to finance purchases and to increase leverage.

Debt instruments are often lumped together with preferred stock into a larger category called fixed-income securities. However, with the rapid growth of floating rate debt, the term fixed-income securities no longer accurately describes all forms of debt. Conventional preferred stock is accurately described as a fixed-income security because its dividend is fixed in the same sense that the coupon on a conventional bond is fixed. But, new forms of preferred stock have recently been engineered that pay a floating or adjustable dividend and, hence, not all preferred stock can accurately be described as fixed income.

Derivative instruments are instruments whose value is derived from that of other assets, called underlying assets. The most important types of derivative instruments are futures contracts, forward contracts, options contracts (including both single-period and multi-period options), and swaps. Futures contracts and forward contracts are contracts for deferred delivery of the underlying asset. While forward contracts are tailor-made to meet the idiosyncratic needs of the end user and trade over-the-counter in dealer-type markets, futures contracts are highly standardized instruments that trade on futures exchanges in auction-type markets. Futures and forwards can be used to speculate on the direction of a price, hedge price risk, and to arbitrage between the cash and the deferred delivery markets.

Whereas futures and forward contracts are binding on both the purchasers and the sellers, options contracts are only binding on the sellers (called writers). That is, the owner of an option has the right, but not the obligation, to do something. Most often, this right entitles the option holder to buy or sell some number of units of the underlying asset at a specified price for a defined period of time. Options can be used to hedge downside risk or to speculate on the direction of price. They can also be used to arbitrage markets.

Swaps are relatively new derivative instruments making their first appearance in the early 1980s. In the ten years that followed, the notional volume of these instruments grew so rapidly as to dwarf the growth of any other market in financial history. Yet, swaps cannot and would not exist in the absence of other financial markets including the debt markets and the futures markets. Swaps have also spurred the growth of related instruments including multi-period options and forward rate agreements. As simply put as possible, a swap is an agreement between two parties calling for the first party to pay a fixed price (based on some underlying quantity of assets) to the second party in exchange for the second party paying a floating (market determined) price to the first party. Swaps are widely used to reduce financing costs and to hedge risks, but they have other uses as well.

Critical to understanding derivative instruments are the cash flow diagrams and the payoff profiles associated with them. That is, there is a series of cash flows between the parties to derivative instruments and/or there is a payoff profile associated with a position in a derivative instrument. Understanding derivative instruments is largely a matter of understanding these cash flows and the payoff profiles. For these reasons, any discussion of derivative instruments will rely heavily on graphics to illustrate concepts.

Hybrid instruments are instruments that are not perfectly classified into any of the other categories because they possess properties from more than one category. For example, some debt instruments have option components, others have an equity component, and still others have both an equity and an option component. Hybrid instruments have become a very important category of asset in recent years and much financial engineering has been devoted to it.

There are two categories of assets that have been neglected in the discussion above and to which we do not devote individual chapters. These are the currencies and the commodities. Currencies were adequately discussed in Chapter 8 and further discussion would be largely redundant. What yet needs to be said will be incorporated in the chapters on futures, options, and swaps. Commodities are another matter. The traditional commodities include such groupings as the grains and oilseeds, foodstuffs, livestock and poultry, industrial materials, precious metals, and oil and petroleum products. Parties holding cash positions in commodities or who have future need for, or supplies of, commodities are exposed to price risk. These risks can be and need to be managed. For some years, it has been possible to hedge these risks in futures, forwards, and options; and, recently, it has become possible to hedge certain forms of commodity price risk in commodity swaps. Rather than devote valuable space explicitly to commodities, we will incorporate our comments on the management of commodity price risk in our discussion of futures, options, and swaps.

Endnotes

[1]Parts of this chapter are condensed from two of the authors' other publications, Scheuing (1989, Chapter 16) and Scheuing and Johnson (1989), respectively.

References

Scheuing, Eberhard, E. *New Product Management*, Columbus, OH: Merrill, 1989.

E.E. Scheuing and E.M. Johnson. "A Proposed Model for New Services Development," *The Journal of Services Marketing*, 3(2) (Spring 1989), pp. 25-34.

Chapter 12

Futures and Forwards

Overview

Futures and forwards are contracts made between two parties that require some specific action at a later date. Most often, this action takes the form of a delivery of some underlying asset. For this reason, these contracts are often described as contracts for **deferred delivery.** This definition distinguishes between contracts for later delivery and contracts for immediate delivery. The latter constitute spot contracts. The spot and forward markets together constitute the **cash markets.**

Futures contracts differ from forward contracts in several important ways. First, futures contracts trade on futures exchanges while forward contracts trade in over-the-counter dealer-type markets. Second, futures contracts are highly standardized, with all contract terms, except price, defined by the exchange on which they trade. Forward contracts are negotiated between the contracting parties with all contract terms subject to mutual agreement. Third, a clearing association stands between the parties to a futures contract. As a result, counterparties' identities are irrelevant. In a forward contract, each party is directly responsible to the other and, consequently, the identities of the counterparties are critically important. Fourth, futures markets (in the United States) are regulated by the Commodity Futures Trading Commission (CFTC). Regulations are very specific and detailed. Forward markets, in general, are not regulated. Fifth, the financial integrity of the futures markets is protected by requiring each party to a contract to post a performance bond called **margin**. Through a daily **mark-to-market** process, with corresponding transfers of margin, each party to a contract is assured of the other party's performance. No such market-wide systematic margining requirement is employed in the forward markets. Consequently, market makers in the forward markets tend to limit their contracting to parties who are well-known to them. Finally, the institutional structure of futures contracts makes them very easy to terminate via simple offsetting transactions. Forward contracts are much more difficult to terminate—in fact, termination is often not possible.

This chapter takes a closer look at the futures and forward markets. Its goal is to help the reader understand the instruments and their uses.

Futures

Futures are highly standardized contracts that call for either deferred delivery of some underlying asset or a final cash settlement based on some clearly defined rule. These contracts trade on organized futures exchanges with a clearing association that acts as a middleman between the contracting parties. The contract seller is called the **short** and the contract purchaser is called the **long**. Both parties post a performance bond, called margin, that is held by the clearing association. The clearing association may hold traders' margins itself or it may hold margins indirectly by way of clearing members. Margin transfers, called **variation margin**, are made daily in response to a mark-to-market process based on daily settlement prices.

Each futures contract has an associated month that represents the month of contract delivery or final settlement. Individual contracts are identified by their delivery month. Examples would include "December corn" and "July T-bills." All contracts on the same underlying asset, that trade on the same exchange, and that have the same delivery month are identical and constitute a **futures series**. Thus, all December corn contracts on the Chicago Board of Trade (CBOT) are part of the December series in corn. October corn contracts are part of the October series. To distinguish between two series, traders often refer to the sooner-to-deliver contract as the **front month** and the later-to-deliver contract as the **back month**.

The soonest-to-deliver contract is often called the **nearby contract.** Contracts are also sometimes distinguished by reference to the "less forward" and the "more forward" delivery months.

Margin requirements vary by the nature of the position held. If the position is a speculation without any type of risk-mitigating position, the margin can run as high as 5 to 7 percent of the contract's value. If the position is a speculation but the speculator is long one series and short another (called a **spread**), margin can be as little as 1 to 3 percent of contract value. If the position represents a hedge, margin will typically be in the 2 to 4 percent range.

The oldest futures exchange in the United States is the Chicago Board of Trade. For over a hundred years, the CBOT's market was limited to agricultural futures—mostly grains and the soybean complex. But, with the increased volatility in the financial markets demonstrated in Chapter 10, the CBOT, and other futures exchanges, began to make markets in financial futures. Today, there are financial futures on debt instruments, called **interest-rate futures,** foreign-exchange rates, called **currency futures,** and stock market averages, called **stock-index futures.**

Financial futures differ from commodity futures in several ways. Probably the most important is that many financial futures are not **deliverable** in the traditional sense. To make this clear, it is important to understand the delivery process associated with commodity futures. When a contract is deliverable, the actual delivery is restricted to a narrow delivery period. Within the bounds of the delivery period, the actual time of delivery is left to the discretion of the short. That is, the short notifies the clearing association that delivery will be made. The clearing association then assigns the delivery to a long. The long makes payment and the short turns over warehouse receipts that evidence ownership of the stored commodity.

Although the delivery process works, it is of limited use for two reasons. First, if the long or short is a hedger, the commodity hedged might not be exactly the same as that specified in the futures contract. Thus, if the hedger is short, the physical commodity held by the hedger might not be acceptable for delivery. (The physical commodity or other underlying asset is often called **actuals.**) If the hedger is long, the commodity to be delivered might not be exactly what the hedger needs. The second reason is that the delivery takes the form of a transfer of warehouse receipts from an approved warehouse. But only a limited number of warehouses are approved and they may not be conveniently situated.

For these and other reasons, very few futures contracts are actually delivered. Instead, hedgers take positions in futures as a *temporary* substitute for later cash market transactions. For example, a commodity producer who expects to harvest 5000 units in July, will short July futures covering 5000 units of the commodity. Later, in July, when the producer harvests his crop, the commodity is sold in the local cash market and the futures contract is terminated by an offsetting transaction. This procedure allows the producer to hedge efficiently without actually using the futures market for any transactions in actuals. By holding the short position in futures while awaiting harvest, the producer "locks in" a harvest price. This converts the hedger's price risk to a much smaller basis risk. **Basis risk** is the risk that the cash price and the futures price at harvest, July in this case, will differ by more or less than some expected amount.

The fact that very few futures contracts are actually delivered led many exchanges to consider eliminating the delivery feature altogether. To date, this has not happened in commodity futures. But, many of the financial futures were created as non-deliverable instruments. The stock-index futures and some of the interest-rate futures are examples. In lieu of delivery during a defined delivery period, these contracts are settled in cash on a specific final-settlement date. Stock-index futures, for example, are settled in cash on the third Friday of the contract month. The final settlement amount is determined by the value of the underlying stock-index at the time of the final settlement. Thus, final settlement is simply another mark-to-market where the final settlement price is the actual index value.

Some financial futures that do provide for delivery offer the short more than one instrument to deliver. Treasury bond futures are an example. These futures allow the short to select any of a number of different T-bond series for the delivery. Adjustment rules are required to equalize the values of the permissible delivery instruments. Nevertheless, at any given point in time, one approved delivery instrument may be cheaper to deliver than another. This has led to a great deal of study of the **cheapest-to-deliver** instruments. Studies have shown that T-bonds behave differently when they are the cheapest-to-deliver than when they are not.[1] Anyone involved in the government securities markets must consider these behaviors.

Traders continuously monitor the various deliverable T-bonds in order to determine which is the cheapest-to-deliver. As one bond moves into cheapest-to-deliver status and another bond moves out of cheapest-to-deliver status, profitable trading opportunities can arise. One bond, for example, may be the cheapest to deliver today while another may be the cheapest to deliver tomorrow. Strategies that exploit the cheapest-to-deliver status of a bond are forms of arbitrage—but they are not necessarily riskless. There are many option-like strategies, for example, that can be used to exploit relative value differentials created as individual bonds move into and out of the cheapest-to-deliver status. Table 12.1 depicts the cheapest-to-deliver Treasury bond on the CBOT's T-bond futures contract on October 13, 1988. Notice that, at the current futures price, the cheapest-to-deliver bond is the bond with a coupon of 7.25 percent and maturing in 2016. If, however, the yield on the T-bond futures were to decline by 33 bps, then the cheapest-to-deliver instrument would be the bond paying a 10.375 percent coupon and maturing in 2012.

Table 12.1
Treasury Bond Futures
(October 13, 1988)

	At Current Market	After 33 bp Decline
Futures Price	89-04	92-14
Cheapest Deliverable	TSY 7.25s '16	TSY 10.375s '12

Source: The First Boston Corporation

In addition to their uses as hedging instruments, futures are also extremely efficient as speculative instruments. Margin requirements are a small percentage of contract value and this gives the speculator considerable **leverage**. A small percentage change in a futures price will result in a large percentage change in the value of the speculator's margin. Futures speculators look for this type of leverage. In addition to the leverage afforded by futures, speculators like these instruments because the transaction costs are very small relative to contract value, and the markets are symmetric. The symmetry involves the ease with which either a short or a long position can be taken. Not all markets facilitate short positions as easily as do futures markets.

A final point involving margin is in order. Margin, as the term is used in futures, is a performance bond—not "equity" in the sense that margin is equity in stock and bond markets. Because its function is to guarantee performance, margin need not be tendered in the form of cash and only very small players would tender margin in the form of cash. Larger market players meet their margin requirements with T-bills or other forms of security. This feature is important because T-bills are interest-bearing assets. When the true purpose of margin is appreciated and margin is tendered in interest-bearing form, it is appropriate to view futures markets as markets in which a position can be taken without investment. For this reason, futures positions are **off-balance sheet**. That is, they do not appear on either the asset side or the liabilities side of a balance sheet.

The role of the clearing association in futures contracting is very important. Futures trades involve two private parties usually acting through an agent on the floor of the exchange called a **floor broker**. Neither party, as a general rule, knows the identity of the opposing party to a trade. The very instant that the trade is made, however, the obligations of the two parties are replaced by matched obligations to the clearing association. That is, the long's obligation to the contract seller is replaced by an obligation to the clearing association and the clearing association assumes the short's obligation to the long. Similarly, the original short's obligation to his counterparty is replaced by an identical relationship with the clearing association. This intermediating role of the clearing association frees both parties to a futures contract from any need to know the opposing party's identity and from any worry about the financial integrity of the other party. The clearing association, on the other hand, is protected from price risk by the fact that it is always long and short an identical number of contracts; and, it is protected from counterparty credit risk through the margining system.

There is much literature on the pricing performance of futures markets. Most academic literature has concluded that futures prices are **informationally efficient**. In the extreme, an efficient market is one in which prices *fully and instantaneously* reflect the value of all relevant information. In the case of futures prices, this would imply that futures prices are unbiased estimates of future spot prices and efficient indicators of true value given all known supply/demand influencing information. If correct, this theory would suggest that futures are a costless hedging instrument for those with a need to hedge price risk whether the price involved is a commodity price, an interest rate, an exchange rate, or a stock index. As discussed in detail in Chapter 9, there are very good reasons to reject the notion of markets that are both continuously and perfectly efficient. It is much more reasonable to believe that futures prices differ from expected future spot prices by an amount equal to an equilibrium risk premium. The amount of this risk premium depends on the imbalance between the needs of short hedgers and long hedgers and the willingness of speculators to bear risk.[2]

Futures are widely used to hedge price risks. These include commodity-price risk, equity-price risk, interest-rate risk, and exchange-rate risk. Our first example of hedging with futures involves an interest-rate exposure.

Suppose that it is currently May 15 and an industrial corporation's board is trying to decide whether or not to build a new production facility. The firm has a top investment grade rating and the firm's chief financial officer (CFO) would like to raise $50 million in new long-term debt capital. Specifically, the firm would sell 30-year mortgage bonds. In selling the idea to the firm's board, the CFO has argued that the current corporate yield curve for top investment grade bonds suggests that the firm can sell its debt at par if it is willing to pay a coupon of 9.75 percent. Unfortunately, several months will pass between the time the board approves the plan and the time the bonds can actually be sold. During this period, the firm's investment bank will undertake the required due diligence investigation, file the offering with the SEC, wait for approval from the SEC, and put together the underwriting syndicate.

The CFO has had bad experiences as a result of **offering lags** after approval of new security issues by the firm's board. On one occasion, interest rates increased by 80 basis points between the time of the decision to go ahead with a financing and the actual public offering. The rise in rates increased the firm's cost of funds and demonstrated the extent of the interest-rate exposure associated with offering lags. The CFO assures the board that she can hedge the offering and greatly reduce the firm's interim exposure to shifts in the yield curve. On the strength of her word, the board approves the project and the financing plan.

The CFO notifies the firm's investment bank that the offering is a "go." The investment bankers say that the offering will be ready in three months (August). The CFO calculates her hedge requirements using a dollar value basis point (DV01) model.[3] She chooses T-bond futures as the hedging instrument.

Suppose that 30-year investment grade corporate bonds have a yield beta of 0.45 and, at an assumed yield of 9.75 percent and selling at par, have a DV01 of 0.096585. The T-bond futures, written on 20-year 8.00 percent T-bonds, in which the firm will hedge happen to be selling at par (100) and have a DV01 of 0.098891. (Note, the actual calculation of the DV01 for a T-bond futures is discussed in Chapter 21.) To hedge the yield until the offering, the CFO calculates the hedge requirement using Equation 12.1.

$$FV_h = FV_c \times \frac{DV01_c}{DV01_h} \times \beta_y \qquad (12.1)$$

FV_h and FV_c denote the face value of the hedging instrument and the face value of the cash instrument (the firm's 30-year bond), respectively; $DV01_h$ and $DV01_c$ denote the dollar value of a basis point for the hedging instrument and the cash instrument, respectively; and β_y represents the yield beta.

Substituting for the values in Equation 12.1, the CFO finds the face value of the T-bonds required to hedge the offering to be $21.98 million.

$$FV_h = \$50 \text{ Million} \times \frac{0.096585}{0.098891} \times 0.45$$

$$= \$21.98 \text{ Million}$$

The CFO translates the face value of the hedge into the required number of futures (N_f) using Equation 12.2. That is, the face value of the required hedge is divided by the face value of a single T-bond futures FV_f ($0.1 million).

$$N_f = \frac{FV_h}{FV_f} \qquad (12.2)$$

$$= \frac{\$21.98 \text{ M}}{\$0.1 \text{ M}}$$

$$= 219.8 \text{ futures}$$

Thus, the CFO sells 220 August T-bond futures.

To check that this was the correct course of action, consider what happens to the firm if corporate yields rise by 80 basis points by the time of the actual offering so that the firm commits itself to pay a semiannual coupon of 10.55 percent. The firm will then pay $200,000 more interest every six months than it would have paid had rates stayed at 9.75 percent. This $200,000 semiannual sum is found by multiplying $50 million by 80 basis points, and then by multiplying the product by 0.5 (since this is a semiannual amount). Using the new 10.55 percent coupon to discount this stream over a 30-year period produces a present value of $3.618 million. This means that the increase in yield, and therefore the increase in the coupon the firm must pay to sell its bonds at par, costs the firm the equivalent of \$3.618 million. This sum is found using present value annuity arithmetic.[4]

Now consider the return on the firm's short position in 220 T-bond futures. If the corporate yield rose by 80 basis points, the T-bond yield should have risen by about 178 basis points. This is the information conveyed by the yield beta. What effect does this increase in T-bond yield have on the firm with a short position in T-bond futures equivalent to \$22 million of T-bonds? The answer is obtained using the same bond valuation arithmetic discussed in Chapter 4 and repeated here as Equation 12.3. The present value of the bond, denoted PV_{bond}, is found as the sum of the present values of the individual cash flows, denoted $CF(t)$, using the bond's yield, denoted y, as the discount rate.

$$PV_{bond} = \sum_{t=1}^{2N} CF(t) \cdot (1 + \tfrac{y}{2})^{-t} \qquad (12.3)$$

The equation above indicates that the T-bonds decline from par to about 84.495 percent of par. On \$22 million of T-bond equivalents, this is equal to a market value change of about \$3.411 million (the calculation appears below). Since bond values decline and the firm is short, this value accrues to the firm. Thus, while the actual issue of bonds by the firm costs the firm \$3.618 million *more* than expected, the hedge *offsets* \$3.411 million of the additional cost. The hedge therefore reduces the impact from yield changes considerably.

Profit on hedge = VPT × NOP × TPP × NF

VPT: Value per tick (\$31.25)
NOP: Number of points by which price changed
     (100 − 84.495 = 15.505)
TPP: Ticks per point (32)
 NF: Number of futures (220)

Profit = \$31.25 × 15.505 × 32 × 220
       = \$3,411,000

A reasonable question to ask at this point is why wasn't the hedge perfect? That is, the loss of \$3.618 million on the cash market commitment is only partially offset by the \$3.411 million profit on the hedge. The answer is simple. The DV01 model provides a very accurate and effective hedge for relatively small changes in yields (1 basis point at a time). As the yields change, the DV01s of the

T-bond and the corporate bond both change but not necessarily by equal percentage amounts. Thus, as yields rise or fall from the level at which the DV01s were calculated, the hedge becomes progressively less precise. This is not really a serious problem. In practice, a hedge can be periodically adjusted to reflect these DV01 changes. Only the hedger who fails to periodically recalculate and adjust is likely to experience the kind of "less than full offset" experienced by this hedger. A handy rule of thumb used by some risk managers is to recalculate the hedge after each 5 basis point change in yields. Periodic recalculation and adjustment of the size of the hedge introduces some additional cost in the form of transaction costs and back-office resources. From a purely practical perspective, any hedge strategy must consider these costs.

Ignoring the recalculation suggested above, let's now consider how the hedge performs in terms of the risk profiles and payoff profiles described in Chapter 7. Exhibit 12.1 depicts the firm's risk profile with respect to yield changes (over the period encompassed by the offering lag). Performance on the vertical axis is measured as the change in the present value of the future coupons the firm will have to pay starting with a coupon of 9.75 percent. We will call this performance measure **profit**.

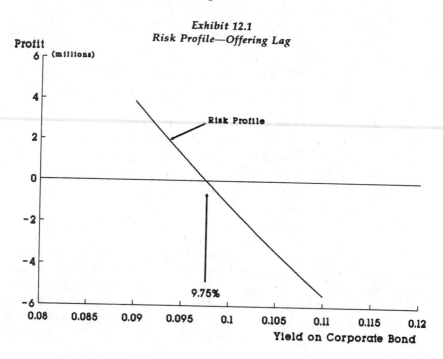

Exhibit 12.1
Risk Profile—Offering Lag

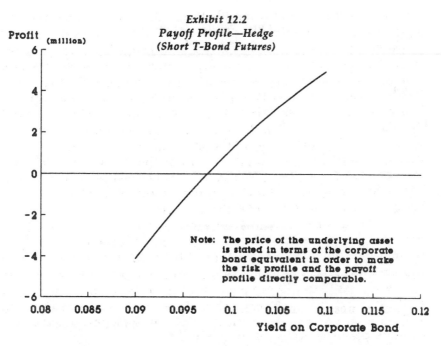

Exhibit 12.2
Payoff Profile—Hedge
(Short T-Bond Futures)

Note: The price of the underlying asset is stated in terms of the corporate bond equivalent in order to make the risk profile and the payoff profile directly comparable.

The payoff profile from the hedge is depicted in Exhibit 12.2 assuming no adjustments to the hedge as yields change. Notice that we have defined the horizontal axis as the yield on the corporate bond rather than the yield on the T-bond. We made this adjustment, using the yield beta, in order to make the firm's risk profile and the payoff profile from the firm's futures hedge directly comparable.

Combining Exhibits 12.1 and 12.2, we obtain the residual risk profile from the hedge. This is depicted in Exhibit 12.3.

If the hedge were adjusted after each 5 basis point change in yields, the payoff profile would look like that depicted in Exhibit 12.4. The unadjusted payoff profile is also depicted in Exhibit 12.4 to facilitate comparison.

Combining Exhibits 12.1 and 12.4, we get the residual risk profile for the hedger who recalculates and adjusts the hedge frequently. This is depicted in Exhibit 12.5. Notice that this "fine tuning" of the hedge has a favorable impact on residual risk and may be worth the extra effort.

The commercial firm in this example needed to hedge against the possibility of a rise in the level of interest rates. To do so, the hedger took a *short* position in interest-rate futures. This point will

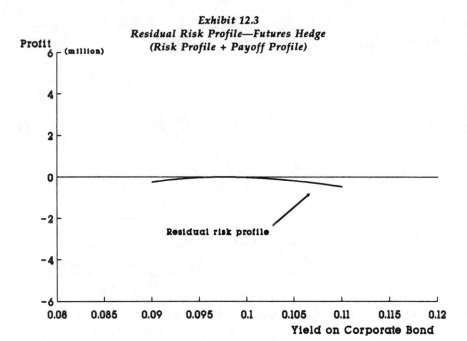

Exhibit 12.3
Residual Risk Profile—Futures Hedge
(Risk Profile + Payoff Profile)

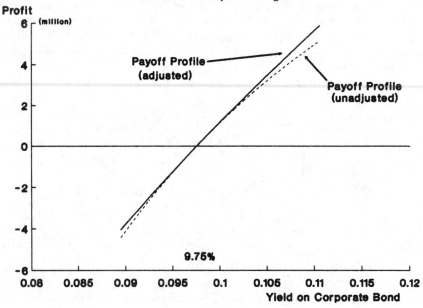

Exhibit 12.4
Payoff Profile of Adjusted Futures Hedge
(relative to unadjusted hedge)

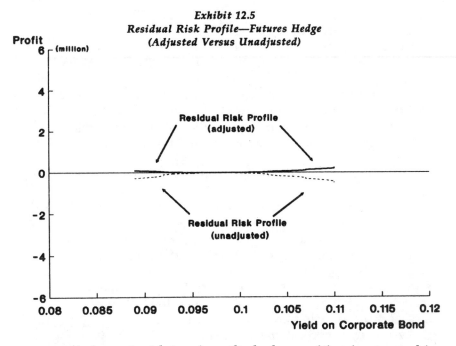

Exhibit 12.5
Residual Risk Profile—Futures Hedge
(Adjusted Versus Unadjusted)

prove quite important later since the hedge position is reversed in certain types of forward contracts.

Exchange-rate risk is more easily managed than interest-rate risk. The reason is simple. The currency hedge is a direct hedge rather than a cross hedge. A **direct hedge** is a hedge in which the cash position that is the subject of the hedge is virtually identical to the asset underlying the hedging instrument. This was not the case in our previous example in which corporate bonds were hedged in T-bond futures. Corporate bond hedging in T-bond futures is an example of **cross hedging**. (A cross hedge is discussed more fully in the next section.) The currency units of a given country are standardized. Thus, 1 currency unit of Country X to be received at some future point in time is identical to every other currency unit of Country X to be received at that same point in time.

This logic seems to suggest that the optimal hedge ratio is 1:1 in a direct hedge. That is, one unit of currency would be hedged in one unit of currency futures. Although a 1:1 hedge ratio is somewhat naive, it is often used in direct hedging and it will *usually* work *reasonably* well.[5] For the time being, we will use a 1:1 hedge ratio in currency hedging.

The leading futures exchange for currency contracts is the International Monetary Market or IMM. The IMM is an affiliate of the Chicago Mercantile Exchange or CME. The IMM's currency contracts are very important because they are widely used by swap dealers, foreign exchange dealers, and other market makers in non-exchange derivative instruments to hedge their positions and to engineer new products or product variants. The IMM also makes a market in Eurodollar futures that, as we will see later, play an important part in determining the pricing of a swap-related over-the-counter instrument called a forward rate agreement.

Forwards

If futures are so effective as hedging instruments, why would anyone want to hedge in forwards? The answer is a bit complex. Since forward contracts are not standardized, the end users can tailor-make the contracts to fit very specific needs. This makes forward contracts better suited for certain purposes. Another reason is that futures contracts do not exist on all commodities and all financials. Furthermore, even when they do exist, the futures standard and the actuals may differ in one or more significant ways.[6] In these cases, the best the futures hedger can do is engage in a cross hedge. A cross hedge involves a hedge in a futures written on a commodity or a financial instrument that differs in a meaningful way from the futures standard. As already noted, our hedging of corporate bonds in T-bond futures in the preceding section is an example of a cross hedge, and, as it happens, a fairly effective one.

There are times when a good cross hedge in futures is not possible. In these situations, the hedger should consider forwards. But even when a futures hedge does exist, the hedger might want to consider forwards as the hedging instrument. This has traditionally been the case when the subject of the hedge is an exchange-rate exposure. The forward markets in currencies are the most highly developed of all the forward markets. These markets are made by large banks—particularly those with a global view. Most forward transactions in these markets are interbank, but banks can and do effect transactions on behalf of nonbank clients.

Consider the example of a U.S. importer that needs to hedge an exposure to fluctuations in the yen/dollar exchange rate. We will denote the Japanese yen by JPY. On July 12, the importer enters a contract to buy merchandise from a Japanese manufacturer for the sum of JPY 256,450,000. At the time, the spot exchange rate of yen for dollars is 143.50 JPY/USD. The terms of trade, however, require the importer to make the payment on October 28 (which is 107 days later). The importer could purchase the yen immediately in the spot market and hold the yen until payment is required; but the importer does not want to tie up its capital in this way. At the same time, the importer cannot afford to run the risk of a significant change in the JPY/USD exchange rate, so the importer must consider his hedging alternatives.

There are futures contracts on the yen traded on the International Monetary Market (IMM) but only four delivery months are traded. These are March, June, September, and December. The U.S. importer could hedge in the September futures and, when these mature, go unhedged until October. Or, the importer could hedge in the December futures and lift the hedges in late October. Neither of these alternatives is optimal as each exposes the importer to some risk. In the first alternative, the importer is exposed to the risk of being unhedged for over a month. In the second alternative, the importer is exposed to some extra basis risk from the timing mismatch between the hedge and his actual needs.

A case like this is ready made for a forward contract. The importer can negotiate a 107-day forward yen-for-dollar purchase involving 256.45 million yen at the bank's 107-day forward yen/dollar rate (suppose that this is 142.15 JPY/USD). The importer is now hedged and the hedge horizon matches his requirements perfectly. Fluctuations in the yen/dollar exchange rate no longer need concern him.

There are other good reasons for hedging in forwards rather than futures. One is the different accounting treatment afforded to futures and forwards in some countries. (This will be addressed in the next section.) Another reason is the potential for a mismatch between the length of the hedger's hedging horizon and the maturity date of the futures. Futures typically have rather short lives. They only go out as far as two years and many do not go out that far. Even when futures are available for more distant delivery dates, these tend to be very illiquid and the consequent cost of transacting in them is high. Until recently, forward contracts have rarely run as long as a year. A hedger with longer-term needs was simply out of luck. But, in recent years, long-dated forward contracts have evolved for interest rates and exchange rates. These long-dated forwards are made possible, as we will show later, by an ability to synthesize forwards from swaps and vice versa.

Long-dated forward contracts in commodities are also possible, but these are usually negotiated directly between producers and end users. For example, major food processors often have multi-year contracts with farmers for the purchase of the latter's crops.

A final solution for the hedger with a long horizon is a swap. Swaps, whether they be interest-rate swaps, currency swaps, or commodity swaps, may be viewed, and often are viewed for modeling purposes, as a series of forward contracts. We will not dwell on swaps in this chapter, however, since swaps are discussed in Chapter 13.

In the next section, we examine a specific type of forward contract called a **forward rate agreement**. Forward rate agreements, or FRAs, have become very important in global banking. In the appendix to this chapter, we have taken the liberty of discussing two other potentially important instruments. One is a very special type of futures contract called a Euro-rate differential futures, or diff. The other is a special type of forward contract called a foreign exchange agreement, or FXA.[7] These latter two instruments are a bit complex and can be skipped without a loss of continuity. We encourage readers who feel up to the challenge, however, to read through the appendix.

Forward Rate Agreements (FRAs)

Forward rate agreements, or FRAs, are a type of forward contract originally introduced by banks in 1983. They originated in London, and British banks remain the principal market makers (dealers). New York banks, however, are rapidly catching up.

In a forward rate agreement, the two contracting parties, which we will call counterparties, agree on some interest rate to be paid on a "deposit" to be received (or made) at a later date. The size of the deposit, called the **notional principal**, together with the agreed upon **contract rate** of interest and the value of the **reference rate** of interest prevailing on the contract settlement date, serve to determine the amount to be paid or received in the form of a single cash settlement. The notional principal (deposit) itself, however, is not actually exchanged. The actual amount paid or received is determined in two steps. In the first step, we take the difference between the reference rate on the contract's settlement date and the agreed contract rate, and then multiply this difference by the notional principal and the term of the deposit (because rates are always stated on an annual basis). The second step discounts the sum obtained in the first step using the reference rate as the rate of discount.

The resultant present value is the sum paid or received. We will explain the purpose of the discounting shortly. The reference rate is most often LIBOR, but it can just as easily be the prime rate, the T-bill rate, or any other well-defined rate that is not easily manipulated.

A party that is seeking protection from a possible increase in rates would *buy* FRAs. Such a party is sometimes called the **purchaser**. A party that wants protection from a possible decline in rates would *sell* FRAs. Such a party is sometimes called the **seller**. Note that these hedge positions are the exact opposite of the hedge positions that would be employed if hedging in futures. This difference in hedge positions is a source of some initial confusion for those experienced in futures who subsequently enter the FRA market.

The difference between the futures and FRA hedging positions is explained by a difference in the pricing conventions used in futures and FRAs. Interest-rate futures are quoted in terms of a dollar price that is stated as a percentage of par. FRAs, on the other hand, are quoted in terms of yield. Since prices and yields are inversely related, a long position in a futures contract behaves like a short position in an FRA and vice versa. This quirk in the futures/forwards conventions dates back to the origins of interest-rate futures. To make financial futures more appealing to the traditional commodity futures trader, the futures exchanges decided to trade futures on a price basis rather than a yield basis. While trading bond and note futures on the basis of price is consistent with the trading practices in the cash markets for these intermediate- to long-term instruments, it is not consistent for short-term instruments that trade on the basis of yield. That is, T-bill futures, Eurodollar futures, and CD futures trade on the basis of price while the cash versions of T-bills, Eurodollar deposits, and certificates of deposit trade on the basis of yield. Since prices are inversely related to yields, the hedging strategies that employ futures appear to be reversed—relative to hedging strategies employing forwards—but, in fact, they are not.

Because forwards are not as standardized as futures, a much wider range of rates can be quoted by dealers. Conventions are, of course, required to avoid confusion. The quote convention in the FRA market is to identify the point in time when the deposit is to commence and the point in time when the deposit is to terminate. For example, the phrase "three month against nine month LIBOR" means a six-month LIBOR deposit to commence in *three* months and to terminate in *nine* months. In industry shorthand, this FRA would be denoted "3 × 9" and read "3 by 9."

We can now explain the purpose of the discounting in the calculation of the FRA settlement sum. Unlike other contracts, including swaps, that are cash settled **in arrears** (i.e., at the end of a settlement period), FRAs are cash settled at the beginning of their term. For example, if a dealer and a client enter into a LIBOR-based three month against nine month (3 × 9) FRA, the cash settlement would be effected three months out, which corresponds to the beginning of the six-month term. In order to make a cash settlement effected at the beginning of a period equivalent in value to a cash settlement effected at the end, the ending value must be discounted.

The following example illustrates the above scenario. Suppose a U.S. bank needs to lock in an interest rate for a $5 million six-month LIBOR-based funding that commences in three months. That is, in three months the bank will lend $5 million to a client for a period of six months. The client, however, needs a rate commitment from the bank immediately. The bank, on the other hand, cannot commit itself to a rate unless it can lock in the cost of its funds. The bank approaches a FRA dealer. At the time, six-month LIBOR (the spot rate) is quoted at 8.25 percent. The bank asks the dealer for a quote on three month against nine month LIBOR. The dealer offers a rate of 8.32 percent. That is, the FRA dealer is offering a six-month LIBOR deposit at a rate of 8.32 percent to commence in three months. The U.S. bank accepts (entering as contract buyer). Based on this rate, the U.S. bank offers its client a rate of 8.82 percent on its borrowing from the bank. The bank arrived at this figure by using its own in-house lending rule for its best-rated customers of LIBOR plus 50 bps. That is, the bank adds 50 basis points to its cost of funds (LIBOR) to allow for profit and to cover its credit risk.

What happens now? Suppose that interest rates rise substantially so that at the time the FRA is due to settle (three months), six-month LIBOR is at 8.95 percent. The bank then obtains $5 million of LIBOR deposits in the Eurodollar market at a rate of 8.95 percent and lends these funds to its corporate client for six-months at its commitment rate of 8.82 percent. Clearly, the bank loses money on the actual lending. The amount of profit or loss on the actual lending to the customer is determined by Equation 12.4.[8] Notice that the "six-month" term is given by 182/360. The reason for this is that LIBOR is quoted on a money market basis. In money market basis, the rate assumes that a year has 360 days, but it pays interest on the actual number of days in the term. This is sometimes referred to as **actual over 360.** (The different numbers of days employed in different yield conventions is discussed in Chapter 16.)

Profit/loss = (Rate received − Rate paid) × Principal × Term

$$= (8.82\% - 8.95\%) \times \$5 \text{ million} \times 182/360 \qquad (12.4)$$

$$= -\$3,286.11$$

Despite the loss on the lending, the bank comes out ahead because it was hedged. The hedge brings a positive cash flow (profit) to the bank. The calculation is given in Equation 12.5.

Hedge profit/loss = D × (RR − CR) × NP × Term $\qquad (12.5)$

$$= 1 \times (8.95\% - 8.32\%) \times \$5 \text{ million} \times 182/360$$

$$= \$15,925$$

In Equation 12.5, RR denotes the reference rate, CR denotes the FRA contract rate, and NP denotes the notional principal. The value D is a dummy variable with the value +1 if the counterparty is the FRA purchaser and −1 if the counterparty is the FRA seller. The purpose of the dummy variable is simply to give the hedge outcome the right sign, i.e., "+" if a profit and "−" if a loss. The sum obtained by Equation 12.5 must still be discounted in order to arrive at the amount paid or received. This is done using Equation 12.6—remember that the reference rate serves as the discounting rate and must be adjusted to reflect the six-month nature of the deposit term.

$$\text{Amount received/paid} = \frac{\text{Hedge profit/ loss}}{(1 + (RR \times 182)/360)} \qquad (12.6)$$

$$= \frac{15,925}{(1 + 0.04525)}$$

$$= \$15,235.59$$

The bank's overall profit (or loss) is then obtained by summing the profit/loss on the lending and the profit/loss on the hedge. In this case, this is $12,639. Notice that the bank's overall profit or loss is found using the hedge profit/loss ($15,925) rather than the amount received/paid on the hedge ($15,236). This is important because the lending profit/loss and the hedging profit/loss are realized at the same point in time (in a present value sense) but the lending profit/loss and the amount received/paid on the hedge are received at different points in time (again in a present value sense).

The hedger bank in this example hedged by "buying" an FRA. As was noted earlier, had this same bank wanted to hedge in futures, it would have "sold" the appropriate number of futures contracts.

Notice in the example used to illustrate the FRA process that the bank that purchased the FRA did not actually take delivery of the deposit. Instead the bank and the FRA dealer settled up-front in cash for a sum dictated by Equations 12.5 and 12.6. The bank then met its deposit needs by purchasing deposits in the Eurodollar cash market. This procedure is analogous to lifting a futures hedge through an offsetting transaction and then transacting in the cash market. It differs however from the traditional use of forward contracts as physical delivery instruments. This cash settlement feature then distinguishes FRAs (and, as we will see shortly, forward exchange agreements) from forward contracts more generally.

There is one other important reason why a user might prefer a forward contract to a futures for hedging purposes. This is the different accounting treatments of profits and losses on futures and forwards in some countries. In the U.S., accounting conventions are defined by the Generally Accepted Accounting Principles or GAAP. Under GAAP rules, profits and losses on speculative positions in futures are treated as though they were realized during the accounting period in which they accrued. That is to say, a mark-to-market process is applied for accounting purposes. However, if the futures position is part of a clearly identified **micro-hedge**, that is, the futures position is matched against a specific asset or liability (cash position), then the profit or loss can be amortized over the same period as the profit or loss on the cash position. This option is generally not available for a **macro-hedge**. The latter would involve a hedge taken to offset any net risk associated with the hedger's overall asset/liability mix. (It should be stressed that the accounting treatment of profits and losses on futures hedges is still a gray area.) Forward rate agreements are generally not, at this point in time, required to be marked-to-market for accounting purposes.

In the case of a macro-hedge, in which futures are marked-to-market on a daily basis but forwards are not, there can be clear accounting advantages to hedging with forwards. For a futures hedger, the profits (or losses) on the futures are largely offset by losses (or profits) on the underlying cash position. However, because the losses (or profits) on the cash position are not realized until the cash position is closed, the losses (or profit) might easily occur during a different accounting period than that of the profits (or losses) on the hedge. These different accounting treatments of futures profits and cash market profits can result in accounting-profit volatility which, in turn, can make the hedge appear more risky than it really is. It can also have unwanted, although temporary, tax effects. Because FRA profits (or losses) need not be marked-to-market, these accounting distortions may not occur when hedging in FRAs.

To see this accounting problem a little more clearly consider again the example of the bank using the FRA to hedge its lending commitment to its corporate client. We will treat this as a macro-hedge, even though in practice it may not be. Suppose the bank enters the FRA as contract purchaser on 15 October 1991 with settlement due on 15 January 1992. This is a 3 × 9 FRA, so the "deposit" commences on 15 January and matures on 15 July (but it is nevertheless cash settled on 15 January). Since there is no mark-to-market, all profit on the FRA is realized in 1992. This corresponds to the year in which the losses on the cash lending are realized. The end result is that the bank shows a net profit of $12,639 on its overall position for 1992 and $0 for 1991.

Now suppose instead that the bank hedges in futures (by selling Eurodollar futures) and achieves an identical overall performance. But, on 31 December 1991, the futures price is such that the bank has a mark-to-market profit for the year of $32,639. And in 1992 the bank has a futures profit of –$20,000. Over the two years, the bank earns the same $12,639 profit but investors see greater volatility in the bank's performance. In addition, if the bank hedges in futures it will pay substantial income taxes in 1991. Although a large portion of these taxes can be recovered in 1992, the time value of the money paid in taxes in 1991 is still lost.

It is important to appreciate that the scenario of large taxes in 1991 with some tax recovery in 1992 is only one possible outcome of the mark-to-market process. It could just as easily have gone the other way and worked to the advantage of the bank. But in either case, the mark-to-market process increases accounting-profit volatility and this is unattractive.

It is worth noting that there has been increasing regulatory and accounting interest in recent years in extending the mark-to-market principle to all derivative instruments and, potentially, to cash instruments as well. It is not clear however, whether or not this interest will culminate in uniform accounting treatment of all financial positions.

The FRA market is largely an **interbank** dollar-denominated market. That is, the bulk of transactions are bank-to-bank and most transactions involve dollars. There is relatively little involvement on the part of investment banks, but investment bank involvement seems to be increasing. The size of transactions has increased considerably since the contracts were first introduced and transactions involving notional principal of $50 million or more are not uncommon. In the early days, dealers typically quoted rates for every three month and every six month period up to one year. But broken dates are now common and long-dated forwards are also common. The latter can extend out to several years. A partial listing of one broker's quotes from 1 December 1989 is depicted in Table 12.2. The contract rates (rate) represent the "last" rather than a bid or an ask.

Table 12.2
FRA Rates—Cash & IMM Dates
(1 December 1989)

Part I: Non-IMM (Cash)

3-Months	Rate	6-Months	Rate	9-Months	Rate
1 × 4	8.28	1 × 7	8.10	1 × 10	8.05
2 × 5	8.09	2 × 8	7.98	2 × 11	7.99
3 × 6	7.90	3 × 9	7.86	3 × 12	7.92
4 × 7	7.77	4 × 10	7.79	6 × 15	7.95
5 × 8	7.74	5 × 11	7.79		
6 × 9	7.68	6 × 12	7.78		
7 × 10	7.68	7 × 13	7.82		
8 × 11	7.73	8 × 14	7.89		
9 × 12	7.74	9 × 15	7.94		

Part II: IMM

IMM Contract		FRA	Rate	FRA	Rate
DEC-89	91.64	0 × 3	8.360	6 × 9	7.640
MAR-90	92.23	0 × 6	8.147	6 × 12	7.765
JUN-90	92.36	0 × 9	8.083	6 × 15	7.955
SEP-90	92.26	0 × 12	8.116	6 × 18	8.121
DEC-90	91.98	3 × 6	7.770	9 × 12	7.740
MAR-91	91.87	3 × 9	7.780	9 × 15	7.958
JUN-91	91.74	3 × 12	7.868	9 × 18	8.125
SEP-91	91.65	3 × 15	8.026	9 × 21	8.286

Part I of Table 12.2 depicts a "snapshot" of non-IMM FRA rates for one broker as they appeared at about 4 PM (EST) on 1 December 1989. The broker is providing rates for sequential three-month FRAs, six-month FRAs, and nine-month FRAs. The table is not complete because this broker also provided dates beyond those indicated and provides rates for twelve-month FRAs as well. As noted earlier, these FRAs are identified by notation such as "w × y" where w indicates the time of commencement (in months) and y indicates the time of termination (in months). Thus, the FRA identified as 1 × 4 commences exactly 1 month from the spot date and terminates exactly 4 months from the spot date (FRAs follow Eurodollar date conventions).

Part II of Table 12.2 depicts IMM FRAs. IMM FRAs are FRAs that are priced off the IMM's Eurodollar futures contracts and that use **IMM settlement dates.** For example, at the time this "snapshot" was taken, the December 1989 IMM contract was priced at 91.64, which implies that the market's expectation of the three-month Eurodollar rate (LIBOR), to commence on the settlement date of the IMM contract, was 8.36 percent—calculated as 100 − 91.64. Since the "snapshot" was taken in December, the three-month FRA that commenced in December 1989 and terminated in March 1990 is denoted 0 × 3. The IMM 0 × 3 FRA has a rate of 8.36 percent. Similarly, the March 1990 IMM contract is priced at 92.23 implying a rate of 7.77 percent. The corresponding FRA is the FRA that commences in 3 months and terminates in 6 months and would be described as 3 × 6. The reader will observe that the IMM 3 × 6 FRA rate is indeed 7.77 percent.

Three-month IMM Eurodollar futures can be used to price longer maturity Eurodollar-based financial instruments. This is accomplished by calculating the implied longer-maturity rate from a sequence of shorter-maturity rates (the actual calculation is demonstrated shortly). The set of implied prices generated in this way is called the **Eurodollar strip.** The IMM FRAs were introduced to "piggy-back" off this strip. The FRAs that are priced off the Eurodollar strip use IMM settlement dates and are themselves called **strips.**

It is now typical to use three month Eurodollar futures to price six-month, nine-month, and twelve-month FRAs. The three-month strip has already been demonstrated. For this strip, the contract rate is simply the LIBOR rate implied by the appropriate Eurodollar contract.

The pricing of strips longer than three months is more difficult to explain. Remember that the rates implied by Eurodollar contracts are market expectations of three-month LIBOR but stated on an annual basis. For example, the implied rate for March 1990 was 7.77 percent. But, this rate only applies for three months. The actual return for the three-month period would be 91/360 times 7.77 percent or 1.96408 percent. (As noted earlier, we must take into consideration the actual number of days in the period.) An investor in three-month Eurodollars would therefore earn 1.96408 percent for his three-month deposit. This deposit could then be rolled over for another three months at the new three-month LIBOR rate. This could be repeated over and over again. The result is that the rate is compounded four times a year. We know that an annual rate of 7.77 percent compounded four times a year is not the same as an effective annual rate of 7.77 percent and not the same as an annual rate of 7.77 percent compounded twice a year. To find an equivalent rate for a six-month FRA, a nine-month FRA, or a twelve-month FRA, this compounding must be taken into consideration.

As in our first example, let's suppose we want to price a six-month FRA off the three-month IMM Eurodollar contracts. Suppose further that this FRA is to commence in six months and terminate in twelve months, so it is a "6 × 12." Since the current time is December 1989, six months out is June 1990. The two three-month periods involved are then the ones that begin in June 1990 (and end in September 1990) and September 1990 (which takes us to December 1990). Part II of Table 12.2 indicates that the JUN-90 IMM contract is at 92.36, implying a three-month LIBOR of 7.64 percent which is equivalent to a three-month return of 1.93122 percent (7.64 × 91/360). Denote this value by JUN. The SEP-90 IMM contract is at 92.26, implying a three-month LIBOR of 7.74 percent which is equivalent to a three-month return of 1.9565 percent (7.74 × 91/360). Denote this value by SEP. The implied six-month LIBOR rate can now be found using the formula given by Equation 12.7.

$$\text{6–M LIBOR} = [((1 + \text{JUN}) \times (1 + \text{SEP})) - 1] \times 360 / 182 \qquad (12.7)$$

In this particular case, the calculation is:

$$\text{6–M LIBOR} = [((1.0193122) \cdot (1.019565)) - 1] \times 360 / 182$$

$$= 7.765 \text{ percent}$$

The value 7.765 percent is identical to the price of the 6 × 12 month IMM FRA depicted in Part II of Table 12.2. The rate 7.765

percent is interpreted as the implied six-month LIBOR with semi-annual compounding.

The same calculation can be done to price a one-year strip. For example, suppose we want to calculate a 9 × 21—that is, a one-year strip that commences in September 1990 and terminates in September 1991. We would use the SEP-90, DEC-90, MAR-91, and JUN-91 IMM contracts for this purpose. The calculation is:

$$\text{12-M LIBOR} = [((1+\text{SEP}) \times (1+\text{DEC}) \times (1+\text{MAR}) \times (1+\text{JUN})) - 1] \times \frac{360}{364}$$

$$= [(1.019565 \times 1.0202727 \times 1.0205508 \times 1.0208794) - 1] \times \frac{360}{364}$$

$$= 8.286 \text{ percent}$$

The values SEP, DEC, MAR, and JUN are calculated in the same manner as before (i.e., 91/360 × annual rate). In this case, the calculation yields one-year LIBOR of 8.286 percent. This is identical to the contract rate in Part II of Table 12.2 for the 9 × 21 FRA. The one-year rate is interpreted as the contract rate on one-year LIBOR using annual compounding.

In 1985, the British Bankers' Association published standardized terms for FRAs. These terms are known as the "FRABBA terms" and they have become the standard, unless specifically stated otherwise, for all interbank FRAs among London banks. Similar standardization efforts have occurred in the U.S.

Forward rate agreements have a number of uses. In addition to their use as a hedging vehicle, they can be used by banks to arbitrage among related instruments. For example, the bank can arbitrage FRAs against futures, or FRAs against swaps, or FRAs against cash deposits.

Like swaps and futures, FRAs are off-balance sheet transactions. That is, they do not appear on either the asset side or the liabilities side of the balance sheet. Before the adoption of the Federal Reserve's revised capital guidelines in January of 1989, these instruments, like swaps, presented banks with the opportunity to increase earnings without inflating the balance sheet. By avoiding an inflation of the balance sheet and thus avoiding negative consequences in terms of additional capital requirements, the bank could enhance its return on equity. These considerations, however, have changed somewhat with the adoption of the new guidelines.

Because FRAs are not marked-to-market with variation margin transfers, the parties to an FRA are exposed to more risk than are parties to futures contracts. This point was made earlier. As a result, the FRA market tends to be limited to institutions with strong credit. Some risk, nevertheless, remains. For now, however, suffice it to say that the exposure, at any point in time, is equal to the replacement cost of the forward should the counterparty default. That is, the exposure is the amount the FRA dealer would have to pay as a front-end fee to secure a replacement FRA with identical terms to the one in default.

All of the illustrations involving futures and forwards have been cast in the context of hedging. While risk management is very important and, perhaps, the dominant component of financial engineering, we would be remiss not to at least mention the speculative uses of these instruments. Both futures and forwards can be used to speculate on the direction of financial prices, including interest rates. A speculator, for example, who believes that rates will rise can speculate on this belief by either selling interest-rate futures or by buying forward rate agreements. Once the position has been taken, the speculator can offset the position by taking an equal-but-opposite position. The speculator would want to offset the position once his or her expectations were realized or if the expectations changed in such a way as to no longer warrant the position.

It is important to appreciate that futures and forward positions do not have to be held until they are actually delivered or cash settled. Offsetting positions can be taken. This is particularly important to speculators who must be nimble in an ever changing interest-rate environment. The highly standardized nature of futures contracts makes futures easier to offset than tailor-made forward contracts, but both can be offset.

FRAs and Swaps

Swaps and forwards, particularly swaps and FRAs, are closely related. In fact, a swap can be viewed as a series of forward contracts. For example, the cash flow stream of a three-year semiannual fixed-for-floating interest-rate swap can be replicated by simultaneously entering six sequential forward rate agreements that each span six months.

This ability to replicate swaps from forwards means that there is the potential to create synthetic swaps from forwards. A **synthetic instrument** is an instrument that is created by combining other instruments so as to replicate the real instrument's cash flow stream. Synthetic instruments are created and used for a variety of purposes.

The most obvious are to reduce the cost of hedging by creating synthetic hedging instruments when the synthetic instrument is more cost effective than the real hedging instrument, and to arbitrage between the synthetic instrument and the real instrument.

Less immediately obvious, but just as real, is the opportunity to use swaps to synthesize forwards. For example, a swap dealer might enter a two-year interest-rate swap as fixed-rate payer and might simultaneously enter a one and one-half year swap as fixed-rate receiver. These swaps are not perfectly matched and so the swap dealer has a residual position. But the residual position is equivalent to an 18 month against 24 month FRA. The swap dealer could then sell an appropriate FRA, acting as an FRA dealer, to earn the bid-ask spread and simultaneously cover his residual risk from the mismatched swaps.

The point is that FRAs, like futures contracts, may be viewed as substitutes for swaps but, in many instances, are just as appropriately viewed as complements to swaps. Clearly, there are economies of scale for swap dealers who also make markets in FRAs and related instruments. (We examine swaps in the next chapter.)

Summary

Futures and forward contracts are contracts that allow users to hedge price risks by locking in prices on instruments that are to be delivered (or cash settled) in a single transaction. The payoff profiles associated with these instruments suggest that their hedging uses are best suited to hedging against price risk—as opposed to downside risk only. That is to say, the user of these instruments will profit if prices move favorably but suffer losses if prices move unfavorably.

Futures contracts are highly standardized instruments. Forward contracts are much more tailor-made but many forward markets have evolved a degree of standardization that approaches that of futures contracts. Futures markets are made by futures exchanges and trading takes place through a dual auction system on the floor of the futures exchange. The markets tend to be liquid with narrow bid-ask spreads. Forward contracts are traded in OTC-type markets by dealer banks. They tend to be less liquid than futures and characterized by larger bid-ask spreads. Because they are less standardized, however, a wider range of contract options are possible.

The integrity of a futures market is maintained by requiring all parties to a contract to post a performance bond called margin.

The margin is held by a clearing association that guarantees performance on all contracts. No system-wide margining is employed in the forward markets. As a result, participation in these markets tends to be limited to strong credits or to those who are in a position to offer collateral.

The markets for interest-rate and exchange-rate contracts have grown rapidly in recent years. Futures contracts are written on T-bills, Eurodollars, CDs, T-bonds, T-notes, mortgage instruments and other debt instruments. Some of these are cash settled contracts while others are deliverable. Currency futures exist for all major currencies. Foreign exchange markets are very highly developed and large banks make both spot and forward markets in currencies. Banks also make forward markets on interest-rates in the form of forward rate agreements or FRAs. If adjusted for the difference in the timing of the cash settlement, FRAs may be viewed as single-period swaps.

The most recent innovations in the futures and the forward markets are the advent of Euro-rate differential futures, which allow for the hedging of interest-rate differentials between short-term interest rates in different currencies, and forward exchange agreements, which allow for the hedging of changes in exchange-rate differentials. These instruments are similar in concept and have similar uses. They are discussed in the Appendix.

Forwards, futures, and swaps are simultaneously substitutes for and complements to one another. There are clear economies of scale for firms that make markets in swaps to also make markets in forward contracts in currencies and forward rate agreements.

Endnotes

[1]For discussion of the role played by cheapest-to-deliver bonds, see Livingston (1984), Meisner and Labuszewski (1984), and Kolb (1988). For an excellent discussion of the embedded options associated with cheapest-to-deliver bonds and strategies for exploiting the value of these embedded options, see Dominguez and Brauer (1988).

[2]For more detailed analysis of the cost of hedging and the interplay between the demand and supply of futures contracts, see Marshall (1989), Chapters 7 though 9.

[3]The dollar value basis point model (DV01) is the most widely used model for determining the size of a hedge by institutions which hedge fixed-income securities in futures. This model is discussed

in this book in Chapter 8. The academic literature, on the other hand, prefers to use duration-based models. It has been shown that these two approaches to hedging fixed-income securities, if adjusted to reflect the yield beta, produce identical hedge ratios. See Marshall (1989), Chapter 12.

[4]The present value annuity formula is given as follows:

$$PVA = PMT \times \left[\frac{1 - (1 + y/m)^{-n \cdot m}}{y/m} \right]$$

where, in this case, PMT, the periodic annuity payment, is $200,000; y, the annual discount rate (yield), is 10.55 percent; m, the number of payments per period (compoundings), is 2; and n, the number of years, is 30. This calculation was discussed in Chapter 4.

[5]A 1:1 hedge ratio in a direct hedge ignores the convergence of the futures and the spot prices. This convergence has been shown to have an effect on the risk minimizing hedge ratio. This important but subtle point is addressed in Chapter 21 by Herbst, Kare, and Marshall.

[6]The terms *actuals, physicals,* and *cash* are used interchangeably to refer to a physical commodity or financial instrument, as distinguished from a derivative instrument (such as a futures, a forward, or an option) which is written on the cash instrument.

[7]Forward exchange agreements (FXAs) are not widely used in the United States but they are popular in London.

[8]To call the result of this calculation "profit" is actually a misnomer as costs in addition to interest expense must be considered to arrive at profit. The value obtained is more correctly called "net interest," but, we will continue to refer to it as profit to be consistent with the hedging theory offered elsewhere in this book.

References and Suggested Reading

Arak, M. and L.S. Goodman. "Treasury Bond Futures: Valuing the Delivery Options," *Journal of Futures Markets,* 7(3) (1987), pp. 269-286.

Bank for International Settlements. *Recent Innovations in International Banking,* 1986.

British Bankers' Association, *Forward Rate Agreements: FRABBA Terms,* 1985.

Chew, L. "FRAs: Managing the Gap," *Risk,* 2(8) (1989).

Dominguez, N. and J. Brauer. "Strategies: Taking Advantage of De-

Dominguez, N. and J. Brauer. "Strategies: Taking Advantage of Delivery Options in Treasury Futures Contracts," First Boston, Derivative Products Group (October 18, 1988).

Grannan, L. "Futures: DIFFs Make All The Difference," *Risk*, 2(8) (1989).

Grossman, S.J. and J.E. Stiglitz. "On the Impossibility of Informationally Efficient Prices," *American Economic Review* (June 1980).

Hume, J. G. "Remaining Calm in Troubled Markets: The Growth of Risk Hedging Vehicles," *Journal of Commercial Bank Lending*, 7:7 (December 1984), pp. 36-44.

Kawaller, Ira G. "Hedging with DIFFS," *Market Perspectives: Topics on Options and Futures* (Chicago Mercantile Exchange), 7(3) (June/July 1989).

Kolb, R.W. *Understanding Futures Markets*, 3d ed., Miami, FL: Kolb Publishing, 1990.

Kuhn, B.A. "A Note: Do Futures Prices Always Reflect the Cheapest to Deliver Grade of a Commodity," *Journal of Futures Markets*, 8(1) (1988), pp. 99-102.

Livingston, M. "The Cheapest Deliverable Bond for the CBT Treasury Bond Futures Contract," *Journal of Futures Markets*, 4(2) (1984), pp. 161-172.

Marshall, J.F. *Futures and Option Contracting: Theory and Practice*, Cincinnati, OH: South-Western, 1989.

Meisner, J.F. and J.W. Labuszewski "Treasury Bond Futures Delivery Bias," *Journal of Futures Markets*, 4(4) (1984), pp. 569-577.

Nadler, D. *Eurodollar Futures/Interest Rate Arbitrage*, Quantitative Strategies Group, Shearson, Lehman, Hutton (April 1989).

Appendix:
Euro-rate Differential Futures and
Forward Exchange Agreements

There are two recent innovations in the deferred delivery market that we would do well to take a brief look at (we will treat them together as they have similar uses). One is a type of futures contract and the other is a type of forward contract. The futures contracts, called **Euro-rate differential futures** contracts, trade on the Chicago Mercantile Exchange (CME)—a U.S. futures exchange sometimes called the "Merc." These contracts can be used as hedging instruments when the risk exposures stem from changes in the interest-rate differential between a dollar-based interest rate and a nondollar-based interest rate. The forward contracts, called **forward exchange agreements**, are marketed by European banks, but are not, as yet, widely used in the U.S. They can be used as hedging instruments when the risk exposures stem from changes in exchange-rate differentials. A discussion of Euro-rate differential futures follows first.

A Euro-rate differential futures contract or, as it is known in market jargon, a "diff," is a futures contract tied to the differential between a three-month nondollar interest rate and three-month LIBOR. These contracts can be used to hedge rate differential exposures between currencies. Diffs were introduced on 6 July 1989 and, as of this writing, three contracts were available: dollar/sterling diffs, dollar/mark diffs, and dollar/yen diffs. A diff is ultimately cash settled for a sum based on the difference between USD three-month LIBOR and some other interest rate. For example, if USD 3-M LIBOR is at 9.45 and DEM 3-M LIBOR is at 6.20 at the time the March dollar/mark diff is due to settle, then the diff would be priced at 96.75—which is calculated as 100 less the difference between USD LIBOR and DEM LIBOR, i.e., 100 – (9.45 – 6.20). Note that all values are understood to be percentages. Suppose now that it is currently January and the March mark/dollar diff is currently priced at 96.90. This would suggest that the market currently expects the differential between USD LIBOR and DEM LIBOR to be 3.10 percent at settlement in March. By contract design, each basis point has a value of $25 (this is the same value as a basis point on a Eurodollar futures contract on the IMM). Thus, if you were to buy this diff at 96.90 (go long) and hold the diff to final settlement at 96.75, you would suffer a loss of 15 basis points worth $25 each for a total loss of $375. The calculation is $(96.75 - 96.90) \times 100 \times \$25$.

The diffs can be used to: (1) lock in or unlock interest-rate differentials when funding in one currency and investing in another; (2) hedge exposures associated with nondollar interest-rate sensitivities; (3) manage the residual risks associated with running a currency swap book; and (4) manage the risks associated with ever changing interest-rate differentials for a currency dealer.

Consider a simple example. Suppose that the treasurer of a U.S.-based corporation with a subsidiary in West Germany funds the subsidiary with short-term deutschemark borrowings. For simplicity, assume that the firm is able to borrow at DEM 3-M LIBOR. The treasurer occasionally rolls over the firm's debt if the funding need still exists. Now suppose that it is currently early August and the treasurer determines that he will need to rollover the firm's current 18 million deutschemark funding. Suppose further that the current dollar/deutschemark exchange rate is 0.7545. At this rate, the deutschemark funding has a dollar value of $13,581,000. The current debt matures in September. The treasurer could simply wait until September and take his chances with spot DEM LIBOR or he could hedge in dollar/mark diffs. He observes that the IMM's September 3-M Eurodollar contract is currently priced at 90.75 implying a market expectation of 9.25 percent for USD 3-M LIBOR in September. At the same time, the September mark/dollar diff is priced at 97.25. At current prices, the treasurer could lock in a DEM 3-M LIBOR rate of 6.50 percent. This is calculated as $(100 - 90.75) - (100 - 97.25)$ or, more simply, as 97.25 less 90.75. To effect this hedge, the treasurer will sell an appropriate number of September Eurodollar futures and buy the same number of September mark/dollar diffs. The treasurer can then hold these contracts until the actual time of the rollover. At that time, the treasurer can borrow deutschemarks at the prevailing DEM LIBOR rate. Assuming no serious manifestations of other risks, such as basis risk, the profit/loss on the diff and Eurodollar contracts will be just sufficient to offset any rise/fall in the DEM 3-M LIBOR rate.

As with any hedge, an important consideration is the calculation of the correct hedge ratio. This is rather straightforward with diffs. We begin by determining the dollar value of a basis point on the cash position. For example, the firm in the example above would calculate the DV01 of its funding requirement (the cash position) as follows:

$$DV01 = \$13.581 \text{ million} \times 0.01\% \times \frac{91}{360}$$

$$= \$343.30$$

Since, by contract construction, the dollar value of a diff basis point and a Eurodollar basis point are both $25, the number of futures contracts needed is $343.30 + $25 or approximately 14.

Diffs are still very new and the full range of uses is only beginning to be discovered. Trading volume in diffs has been light, but that is typical for some time after the introduction of a completely new type of futures contract. It will be a few years before we know whether or not diffs have found a permanent home in the modern financial marketplace. We now turn our attention to the over-the-counter counterpart to diffs.

Forward exchange agreements or FXAs were intended, by the financial engineers who created them, to be to the forward foreign-exchange market what FRAs had become to the forward Eurocurrency market. They allow parties to hedge movements in exchange-rate differentials without entering a conventional currency swap. From a conceptual perspective, an FXA combines two notional forward foreign-exchange contracts into a single instrument. At the termination of the agreement a single payment is made by one counterparty to the other based on the direction and the extent of movement in the exchange-rate differential. These contracts can be used to (1) hedge a form of exchange-rate risk, (2) to use a bank's foreign-exchange limits more efficiently, (3) to speculate on the direction of exchange-rate differentials, and (4) to engage in various types of arbitrage, such as that between FXAs and currency futures, FXAs and currency swaps, and FXAs and actual currency positions. Because interest-rate differentials and exchange-rate differentials are closely related (as we demonstrated in Chapter 8) the difference between diffs and FXAs is not as great as the definitional distinctions suggest.

Forward exchange agreements have the same advantages and disadvantages relative to diff futures that FRAs have relative to interest-rate futures, so we will not waste time repeating the comparisons. Instead, we will concentrate on an example of the use of an FXA and the calculation of the cash settlement amount.

The cash settlement formula is given by Equation 12.8.[9] The actual settlement amount indicated by Equation 12.8 is determined on what is called the **calculation date**, which occurs a few days prior to the settlement date.

$$\text{Settlement amount} = D \times NP \times \left(\frac{(SD - SC) + (FD - FC)}{(1 + ((R \times N) + (100 \times Y)))} - (SD - SC) \right) \quad (12.8)$$

where NP: Notional principal
SD: Near forward exchange rate at time of contracting
SC: Spot exchange rate at settlement
FD: Contract forward points
FC: Settlement forward points
R: LIBOR (expressed in percentage form but reported as a number rather than as a percentage, i.e., 9.5 percent is entered as 9.5)
N: Actual number of days between the two exchanges (i.e., period covered by the agreement)
Y: Number of days in the year, which may be 360 or 365 depending on the custom in the contractual currency.
D: Represents a dummy variable having the values +1 (if the counterparty is the contract purchaser) or −1 (if the counterparty is the contract seller).

Before proceeding to the example, the terms above need to be clarified. The notional principal is the amount of principal on which the final cash settlement will be based. As with FRAs, the notional principal is not exchanged.

There are a number of exchange rates involved in the determination of the cash settlement amount and so it is important to be very clear as to which rate is which. Let's denote the time of initial contracting by the letter c, the time of the first (near) forward exchange by the letter t, and the time of the second (far) forward exchange by the letter T. Then we can denote any exchange rate we like by using the letter E to mean an "exchange rate" together with two subscripts: the first represents the current time and the second representing the time of the forward transaction. For example, the notation $E_{t,T}$ would denote the exchange rate at time t for a transaction that will take place at time T. Since time T follows time t, $E_{t,T}$ denotes a forward rate. When the two subscripts are the same, as in $E_{t,t}$, the exchange rate is a spot rate. At time c, we know $E_{c,c}$, $E_{c,t}$, and $E_{c,T}$ but we do not know $E_{t,t}$ and $E_{t,T}$. The latter two are, however, known at the time of contract settlement. The settlement date is the same date that the near forward comes due.

We can now define the terms in Equation 12.8 using the notation we defined above:

$$SD = E_{c,t} \quad FD = E_{c,T} - E_{c,t}$$

$$SC = E_{t,t} \quad FC = E_{t,T} - E_{t,t}$$

Now let's consider an example. It is currently 6 January 1991 and a U.S.-based customer has approached an FXA dealer looking for a three month against nine month deutschemark-for-dollar FXA having notional principal of DEM 5 million. Specifically, the customer wishes to buy three-month deutschemarks and sell nine-month deutschemarks. The dealer's current set of "dollar for deutschemark" (USD/DEM) exchange rates are given in Table 12.3.

Table 12.3
FXA Dealer's Exchange Rates USD/DEM*
(6 January 1991)

Date for Value	type	Rate	Notation
8 January 1991	spot	0.40917	$E_{c,c}$
8 April 1991	forward (near)	0.40404	$E_{c,t}$
8 October 1991	forward (far)	0.40016	$E_{c,T}$

*Note: The standard two-day settlement is assumed.

The dealer and its customer enter the FXA with the dealer as contract seller and the customer as contract buyer (the convention is that the purchaser of the near forward, who is also the seller of the far forward, is considered the contract purchaser). Three months later on the contract's calculation date, 6 April 1991, the bank calculates the amount of the cash settlement based on the prevailing forward rates and six-month USD LIBOR. This amount will be paid *to* the customer if positive and paid *by* the customer if negative. The dealer's rates on the calculation date appear in Table 12.4.

Table 12.4
FXA Dealer's Exchange Rates USD/DEM
(6 April 1991)

Date for Value	type	Rate	Notation
8 April 1991	spot	0.37807	$E_{t,t}$
8 October 1991	forward	0.37258	$E_{t,T}$

6-M USD LIBOR: 8.00 percent.

The components of Equation 12.8 can be generated using the definitions for SD, SC, FD, and FC that we introduced before. These are:

$$SD = 0.40404 \qquad FD = 0.40016 - 0.40404 = -0.00388$$
$$SC = 0.37807 \qquad FC = 0.37258 - 0.37807 = -0.00549$$

The dummy variable is +1 since the customer was the contract buyer, the notional principal is DEM 5 million, LIBOR is 8.00 percent, the number of days involved is 183, and the number of days in the year is 360 in this case. Substituting these values into Equation 12.8 produces the cash settlement amount of $2,732.18. Since this sum is positive, *the bank* pays the customer the settlement amount.

An FXA contract exactly reproduces the cash flows associated with conventional cash market transactions. This is the key to understanding how these instruments can be used to hedge and arbitrage other positions. Suppose that on 6 January 1991, the customer had simply bought a three-month forward contract and sold a nine-month forward contract as two separate cash market transactions. How would the cash flows have looked from the customer's perspective? The answer is illustrated in Table 12.5.

Table 12.5
Cash Flows Associated with Two Cash Market Transactions
Effected on 6 January 1991

Date	DEM	USD	Relevant Exchange Rate
8 April 1991	5,000,000	(2,020,200)	0.40404 DEM/USD
8 October 1991	(5,000,000)	2,000,800	0.40016 DEM/USD

Now consider the cash flows associated with the FXA. In addition to the cash flow resulting from the FXA settlement, the customer would purchase deutschemarks on 6 April 1991 (for 8 April settlement) as a spot transaction and would sell deutschemarks forward on 6 April 1991 for settlement on 8 October 1991. The first of these two transactions would require the expenditure of $1,890,350 and the second would result in the receipt of $1,862,900. These sums are based on the exchange rates given in Table 12.4. The customer would also borrow (or lend) a sum in dollars equal to the difference between the dollar amount of the October transaction if made in April and the dollar amount of the October transaction if made in January, discounted for the appropriate number of days at 6-M LIBOR. This borrowing (or lending) is required to offset the movement in the spot rate between January and April. These cash flows are summarized in Table 12.6.

Table 12.6
Cash Flows Associated with FXA (as adjusted)

Date	DEM	USD	Origin of Payment
8 April 1991	5,000,000	(1,890,350)	Spot transaction DEM for USD
		(132,582.18)	Dollar amount of lending
		2,732.18	FXA settlement amount
	5,000,000	(2,020,200)	
8 October 1991	(5,000,000)	1,862,900	Forward transaction USD for DEM
		137,900	Lent funds returned + interest
	(5,000,000)	2,000,800	

Now compare the net cash flows from the cash market transactions in Table 12.5 and the net cash flows from the FXA and associated transactions in Table 12.6. Clearly, the FXA has replicated the conventional cash transactions perfectly.

FXAs are more difficult to understand than FRAs because they involve more variables. The FRA involved only two interest rates: the contract rate and the value of the reference rate on the settlement date. The FXA, on the other hand, involved six rates: two spot exchange rates, three forward exchange rates, and one interest rate. In addition, unlike the FRA whose cash settlement amount is a function of a change in *rates*, an FXA's cash settlement amount is largely a function of a change in *rate differentials*. As noted earlier, FXAs are not widely used by U.S. banks.

Endnote

[9]This version of the FXA settlement formula is taken from Midland Bank. We have added a dummy variable D to make it clearer as to who pays whom.

Chapter 13

Swaps

Overview

In all the history of financial markets, no markets have ever grown or evolved as rapidly as have the swap markets. This is a testament to the efficacy and flexibility of the instruments, the resourcefulness and the professionalism of the new breed of financial engineers, and the increased appreciation by financial managers of the importance of financial risk management in a volatile interest rate, exchange rate, and commodity price environment. Swaps are now used by industrial corporations, financial corporations, thrifts, banks, insurance companies, world organizations, and sovereign governments.

Swaps are used to reduce the cost of capital, manage risks, exploit economies of scale, arbitrage the world's capital markets, enter new markets, and create synthetic instruments. New users, new uses, and new swap variants emerge almost daily. Most people with some exposure to swaps believe that swaps are exceedingly complex instruments. In reality, this seeming complexity is more in the extensive documentation needed to fully specify the contract terms and the myriad of specialty provisions that can be included to tailor the swap to some specific need.[1]

In this chapter, we present a simple graphic illustration of the basic or "plain vanilla" swap in the form of cash flow diagrams. By visually depicting the pattern of cash flows associated with swaps and the ways that swaps meld with cash market transactions, one can easily see how a desired end result is achieved. We then apply this basic model in three different settings: (1) an interest rate swap to convert a fixed-rate obligation to a floating-rate obligation; (2) a currency swap to convert an obligation in one currency to an obligation in another currency; and (3) a commodity swap to convert a floating price to a fixed price. In a later chapter, we will use this same model to demonstrate an equity swap. Before presenting the swap model, however, a brief history of the swap product will put the instruments in perspective. We also take a brief look at swap variants and swap pricing.

History of the Swap Product

The first currency swap was engineered in London in 1979. During the two years that followed the market remained small and obscure. This obscurity ended when, in 1981, Salomon Brothers put together what is now the landmark currency swap involving the World Bank and IBM. The stature of the parties gave long-term credibility to currency swaps.

It was a short step from currency swaps to interest rate swaps. Like the currency swap, the first interest rate swap was engineered in London. This took place in 1981. The product was introduced to the United States the following year when the Student Loan Marketing Association (Sallie Mae) employed a fixed-for-floating interest rate swap to convert the interest-rate character of some of its liabilities.

Once established, the market for currency and interest rate swaps grew rapidly. From under $5 billion in combined notional principal outstandings at the end of 1982 the market grew to over $2.5 trillion by the end of 1990.

The financial institutions that originated the swap product first saw themselves in the role of brokers. That is, they would find potential counterparties with matched needs and, for a commission, would assist the parties in the negotiation of a swap agreement. The brokering of swaps proved more difficult than originally envisioned because of the need to precisely match each individual contract provision. It wasn't long, however, before these institutions realized their potential as dealers. That is, they could make a more liquid market by playing the role of a counterparty. This was possible because of the existence of a large cash market for U.S. Treasury debt and well-developed futures markets in which the swap dealers could hedge their resultant exposures.

By 1984, representatives from leading dealer banks (commercial banks and investment banks) began work on standardizing swap documentation. In 1985 this group organized itself into the International Swap Dealers Association (ISDA) and published the first standardized swap code. The code was revised in 1986. In 1987, the standardization efforts of the ISDA culminated in the publication of standard form agreements. These contracts are structured as master agreements. As such, all subsequent swaps entered by the same counterparties are treated as supplements to the original agreement. Standardization of documentation dramatically reduced both the time and the cost of originating a swap.

Commodity swaps were first engineered in 1986 by The Chase Manhattan Bank. But, no sooner was the mechanism for commodity swaps in place than the Commodity Futures Trading Commission (CFTC) cast a cloud over the product by questioning the legality of the contracts. The intervention of the CFTC brought that agency into direct conflict with the ISDA and a lengthy battle ensued. At the same time, those banks already involved in commodity swaps moved the bulk of their activity overseas.

In July of 1989, the CFTC issued a favorable policy statement on commodity swaps. The agency decided to grant the contracts a "safe harbor," provided that certain criteria were met. These criteria were of little consequence as, for the most part, they reflected current industry practice. By the end of 1989 the volume of commodity swap outstandings was nearly $8 billion. While still small in comparison to interest rate and currency swaps, there appears to be tremendous potential for this market.

A Note on Rate Conventions

Interest rate and currency swaps are often discussed together—in which case they are collectively called **rate swaps.** Since the inception of rate swaps, the floating-rate side has most often been tied to the London Interbank Offered Rate known by the acronym LIBOR. LIBOR is the rate of interest charged on interbank loans of Eurocurrency deposits. While it is rarely made explicit, LIBOR is understood to be a quote on dollar deposits (Eurodollars). But non-dollar LIBORs are also quoted. Deutschemark LIBOR, for example, would be denoted DEM LIBOR. All references to LIBOR in this chapter and elsewhere in this book are references to dollar LIBOR unless specifically indicated otherwise.

LIBOR quotes are available for various terms including one-month deposits (1-M LIBOR), three-month deposits (3-M LIBOR), six-month deposits (6-M LIBOR), and one-year deposits (1-Y LIBOR). Regardless of the length of the deposit, LIBOR, like all interest rates, is quoted on an annual basis. There are two complications, however, which we need to point out. To determine the *effective annual rate* corresponding to a given term deposit, we need to take into consideration the number of days in a six-month period and the number of compoundings per year. As we noted in the last chapter, LIBOR, by convention, is quoted "actual over 360." That is, the interest rate is stated as though the year has 360 days, but interest is actually paid every day. The effect of this is to raise the effective rate of interest. For example, if 6-M LIBOR is quoted at 8.00 percent, we would expect that the six-month periodic rate is 4 percent. But, in fact, one would earn $182/360 \times 8.00$ percent rather than 0.5×8.00 percent. Thus, the periodic rate is 4.0444 percent. During the second half of the year, one would earn a periodic rate of $183/360 \times 8.00$ percent for a periodic rate of 4.0667 percent.

The second complication stems from the fact that the interest earned during the first half of the year would itself earn interest during the second half of the year. That is, compounding raises the effective annual rate of interest. To get the effective annual rate, we must take the compounding into account. This is done below:

$$ER = [(1.040444) \times (1.040667)] - 1$$

$$\approx 8.276 \text{ percent}$$

We see then that the effective annual rate corresponding to a 6-M LIBOR quote of 8 percent is about 8.276 percent.

The reason that this is important is that the fixed-rate side of a rate swap, called the **swap coupon**, is most often quoted as a bond equivalent yield (BEY) (also called a coupon equivalent yield). Bond equivalent yields are calculated on the basis of a 365-day year with quotes stated **actual over 365**. This differing treatment implies that LIBOR rate differentials and swap coupon differentials are not directly comparable. In order to properly compare them, they must first be adjusted for the differing number of days on which the two rates are quoted. Most often, this adjustment takes the form of a simple multiplication of a rate differential by 365/360 (when going from LIBOR to BEY) or 360/365 (when going from BEY to LIBOR).

This adjustment is only correct, however, if the payment frequencies on the two sides (**legs**) of the swap are the same—i.e., they are both made quarterly, or both made semiannually or both made annually.

The floating-rate side of a swap need not be tied to LIBOR. It can be tied to some other readily identifiable rate that is not easily manipulated by an interested party. The rate can and often is tied to a rate index or based on an average of observations on a short-term rate or a rate index. Frequently used rates include certificate of deposit, commercial paper, T-bill, Fed funds, and the Twelfth District cost of funds. Nevertheless, the floating-rate side of most rate swaps are LIBOR-based.

The Structure of a Swap

All swaps are built around the same basic structure. Two parties, called counterparties, agree to one or more exchanges of specified quantities of underlying assets. We call the quantities of underlying assets in a swap the **notionals** in order to distinguish them from physical exchanges in the cash markets, which are called **actuals.** A swap may involve one exchange of notionals, two exchanges of notionals, a series of exchanges of notionals, or no exchanges of notionals. Most often, a swap involves one exchange of notionals at the commencement of the swap and a reexchange upon the swap's termination.

The notionals exchanged in a swap may be the same or different. Between the exchanges of notionals, the counterparties make payments to each other for the use of the underlying assets. The first counterparty makes periodic payments at a fixed price for the use of the second counterparty's assets. This fixed price is called the swap coupon. At the same time, the second counterparty makes periodic payments at a floating (market determined) price for the use of the first counterparty's assets. This is the basic or "plain vanilla" structure. By modifying the terms appropriately and/or adding specialty provisions, this simple structure can be converted to dozens of variants to suit specific end user needs. For purposes of illustration, we shall call the first counterparty Counterparty A and the second counterparty Counterparty B.

It is very difficult to arrange a swap directly between two end users. A much more efficient structure is to involve a financial intermediary that serves as a counterparty to both end users. This counterparty is called a **swap dealer,** a **market maker,** or a **swap**

bank. The terms are used interchangeably. The swap dealer profits from the bid-ask spread it imposes on the swap coupon.

The cash flows associated with a typical swap are illustrated in Exhibits 13.1, 13.2, and 13.3. Exhibit 13.1 depicts the initial exchange of notionals, which is optional in the sense that it is not required in all swaps; Exhibit 13.2 depicts the periodic usage payments; and Exhibit 13.3 depicts the reexchange of notionals, which, like the initial exchange of notions, is optional in the sense that it is not required in all swaps.

Exhibit 13.1
Swap: Initial Exchange of Notionals (optional)

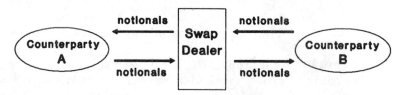

Exhibit 13.2
Swap: Periodic Usage or Purchase Payments (required)

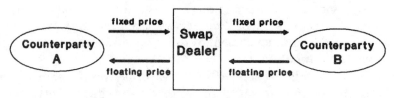

Exhibit 13.3
Swap: Reexchange of Notionals (optional)

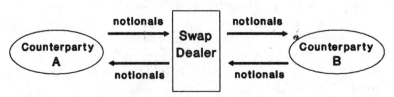

A swap by itself would generally not make much sense. But swaps do not exist in isolation. They are used in conjunction with appropriate cash market positions or transactions. There are three such basic transactions: (1) obtain "actuals" from the cash market, (2) make (receive) payments to (from) the cash market, or (3) supply actuals to the cash market. These possibilities are summarized in Exhibit 13.4. The cash markets depicted in Exhibit 13.4 may be the same or different.

Exhibit 13.4
Cash Market Transactions

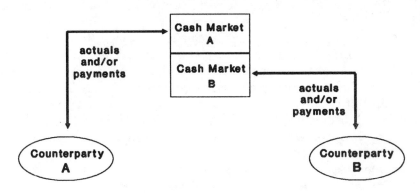

By combining the cash market transactions with an appropriately structured swap, we can engineer a great many different outcomes. For the moment, we will only look at the most basic of these. We will examine interest-rate swaps first, then currency swaps and, finally, commodity swaps. As already noted, the first two are sometimes lumped together and called rate swaps.

Interest Rate Swaps

In **interest rate swaps** the exchangeable notionals take the form of quantities of money and are consequently called **notional principals**. In such a swap, the notional principals to be exchanged are identical in amount and involve the same currency. As such, they can be dispensed with—which explains the origin of the term *notional*. Furthermore, since the periodic usage payments, called interest in this case, are also in the same currency, only the value differential needs to be exchanged on the periodic settlement dates.

Interest rate swaps are often motivated by a desire to reduce the cost of financing. In this case, one party has access to comparatively cheap fixed-rate funding but desires floating-rate funding while another party has access to comparatively cheap floating-rate funding but desires fixed-rate funding. By entering into swaps with a swap dealer, both parties can obtain the form of financing they desire and simultaneously exploit their comparative borrowing advantages. For example, suppose that Party A is in need of 10-year debt financing. Party A has access to comparatively cheap floating-rate financing but desires a fixed-rate obligation. For purposes of illustration, assume that Party A can borrow at a floating rate of six-month LIBOR + 50 bps or at a semiannual (sa) fixed rate of 11.25 percent. As it happens, Party B is also in need of 10-year debt financing. Party B has access to comparatively cheap fixed-rate financing but desires a floating-rate obligation. For purposes of illustration, assume that Party B can borrow fixed rate at a semiannual rate of 10.25 percent and can borrow floating rate as six-month LIBOR. As it happens, Party A desires fixed-rate funding and Party B desires floating-rate funding.

The swap dealer stands ready to enter a swap as either fixed-rate payer (floating-rate receiver) or as floating-rate payer (fixed-rate receiver). In both cases, the dealer's floating rate is six-month LIBOR. Under its present pricing, if the dealer is to be the fixed-rate payer, it will pay a swap coupon of 10.40 percent (sa). If the dealer is to be the fixed-rate receiver, it requires a swap coupon of 10.50 percent (sa).

The financial engineers working for the swap dealer suggest that Party A issue floating-rate debt and that Party B issue fixed-rate debt and that they both enter into swaps with the swap dealer. Party A, now called Counterparty A, enters a swap, with the swap dealer acting as floating-rate payer; and Party B, now called Counterparty B, enters a swap, with the swap dealer acting as fixed-rate payer. While there are no exchanges of notional principals in these swaps, there are still three types of exchanges if we include the borrowings in the cash market. The full set of cash flows is illustrated in Exhibits 13.5, 13.6, and 13.7. Exhibit 13.5 depicts the initial borrowings in the cash markets; Exhibit 13.6 depicts debt service in the cash markets and the cash flows with the swap dealer; and Exhibit 13.7 depicts the repayment of principals in the cash market.

Examine Exhibit 13.6. Notice that Counterparty A pays LIBOR + 50 bps on its cash market obligation and receives LIBOR from the swap dealer. The LIBOR portions of these payments are, there-

Exhibit 13.5
Interest Rate Swap with Cash Market Transactions
(initial borrowing of principals)

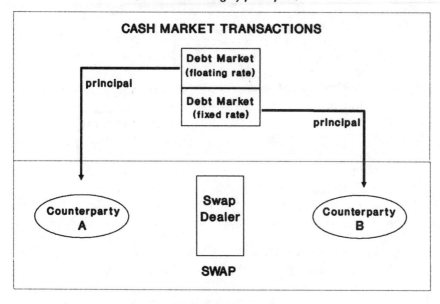

Exhibit 13.6
Interest Rate Swap with Cash Market Transactions
(debt service with swap payments)

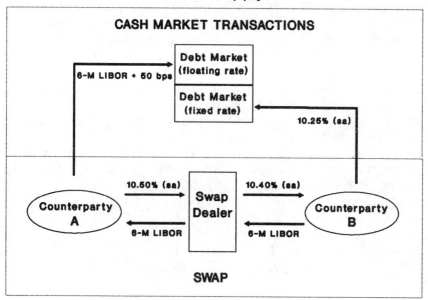

Exhibit 13.7
Interest Rate Swap with Cash Market Transactions
(repayment of principals)

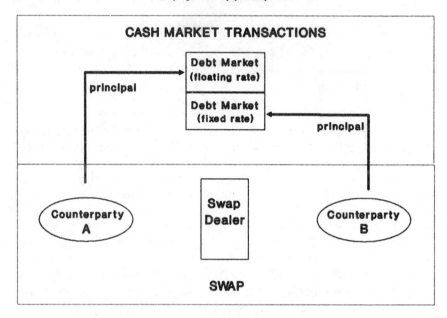

fore, offsetting. The only remaining obligation of Counterparty A is to pay the swap dealer 10.50 percent. Thus, Counterparty A's final cost is approximately 11.00 percent. This is an approximation because, as noted earlier, the 50 basis point LIBOR differential is not directly comparable to the fixed rate. It must first be adjusted by multiplying by 365/360. After this adjustment, we see that the real cost to Counterparty A is closer to 11.01 percent. Since direct borrowing of fixed rate in the cash market would have cost Counterparty A 11.25 percent, it is clear that Counterparty A has benefited by 24 basis points by employing the swap.

Counterparty B is paying a fixed rate of 10.25 percent on its cash market borrowing and receiving 10.40 percent from the swap dealer. Thus, Counterparty B is ahead by 15 basis points. In addition, Counterparty B is paying the swap dealer LIBOR. Thus, the total cost of Counterparty B's debt is approximately LIBOR – 15 basis points (even after adjusting the differential by 360/365). Had Counterparty B borrowed floating rate directly, it would have paid LIBOR. Thus, we find that the swap has saved Counterparty B 15 basis points.

As a side point, notice that the swap dealer earns 10 basis points for its services in making a liquid swap market. This 10 basis points is the difference between the swap coupon received from Counterparty A and the swap coupon paid to Counterparty B.

Interest rates swaps have many important uses besides lowering the cost of financing. We will be examining many of these uses in the strategies section of this book.

Currency Swaps

In a **currency swap**, the currencies in which the principals are denominated are different and, for this reason, usually (but not always) need to be exchanged. A currency swap is viable whenever one counterparty has comparatively cheaper access to one currency than it does to another. To illustrate, suppose that Counterparty A can borrow deutschemark for seven years at a fixed rate of 9.0 percent and can borrow seven-year dollars at a floating rate of one-year LIBOR. Counterparty B, on the other hand, can borrow seven-year deutschemark at a rate of 10.1 percent and can borrow seven-year floating-rate dollars at a rate of one-year LIBOR. As it happens, Counterparty A needs floating-rate dollar financing and Counterparty B needs fixed-rate deutschemark financing.

The financial engineers working for a swap dealer that makes deutschemark-for-dollar currency swaps work out a solution. The dealer is currently prepared to pay a fixed-rate of 9.45 percent on deutschemarks against dollar LIBOR and it is prepared to pay dollar LIBOR against a fixed-rate of 9.55 percent on deutschmarks. The counterparties borrow in their respective cash markets—Counterparty A borrows fixed-rate deutschemarks and Counterparty B borrows floating-rate dollars—and then enter a swap. Exhibit 13.8 depicts the initial borrowings in the cash markets and the initial exchange of notional principals at the commencement of the swap. Exhibit 13.9 depicts the debt service in the cash markets and the exchanges of interest payments on the swap. Exhibit 13.10 depicts the reexchange of notional principals upon the termination of the swap and the repayment of the cash market borrowings.

Notice that while Counterparty A borrows deutschemarks, the swap converts the deutschemarks to dollars. Notice also that these dollars have a floating-rate character with a net cost of approximately LIBOR – 45 basis points. This represents a 45 basis point savings over a direct borrowing of floating rate.[2] Similarly, Counterparty B borrows dollars but uses the swap to convert the dollars to

Exhibit 13.8
Currency Swap with Cash Market Transactions
(initial borrowings and exchanges of notional principal)

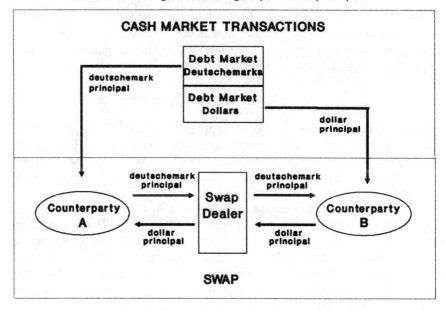

Exhibit 13.9
Currency Swap with Cash Market Transactions
(debt service with swap payments)

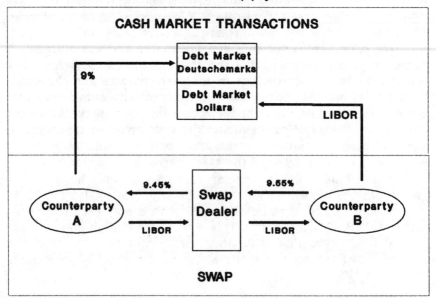

Exhibit 13.10
Currency Swap with Cash Market Transactions
(repayment of actuals and reexchanges of notional principal)

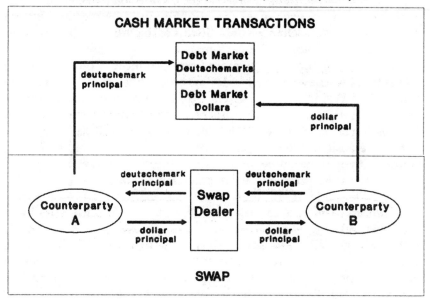

deutschemarks. These deutschemarks have a net cost of 9.55 percent. This represents a 55 basis point savings over a direct borrowing of fixed-rate deutschemarks. Thus, we see that a swap can be used with the appropriate cash market transactions to convert both the currency denomination of a financing and the character of the interest cost.

The plain vanilla currency swap described above is often called an **exchange of borrowings.** The reason for this terminology is readily evident from an examination of the cash flow diagrams. In particular, examine Exhibit 13.8. Notice that each counterparty to the swap borrows funds in its respective market and then "exchanges" those borrowings for the borrowings of the other counterparty—hence the name.

Commodity Swaps

The final type of swap we will look at is a commodity swap. In a **commodity swap,** the first counterparty makes periodic payments to the second at a per unit fixed price for a given quantity of some commodity. The second counterparty pays the first a per unit floating price (usually an average price based on periodic observations of the spot price) for a given quantity of some commodity. The commodities may be the same (the usual case) or different. If they are the same, then no exchanges of notionals are required. If they are different, exchanges of notionals could be required but, as a general rule, no exchanges of notionals take place—all transactions in actuals take place in the cash markets.

Consider a simple case, a crude oil producer (Counterparty A) wants to fix the price he *receives* for his oil for five years—his monthly production averages 8,000 barrels. At the same time, an oil refiner and chemicals manufacturer (Counterparty B) wants to fix the price he *pays* for oil for five years—his monthly need is 12,000 barrels. To obtain the desired outcomes, they enter swaps with a swap dealer but continue their transactions in actuals in the cash markets.

At the time these end users enter their swaps, the price of the appropriate grade of crude oil in the spot market is $15.25 a barrel. Counterparty B agrees to make monthly payments to the dealer at a rate of $15.30 a barrel and the swap dealer agrees to pay Counterparty B the average daily price for oil during the preceding month. At the same time, Counterparty A agrees to pay the swap dealer the average daily spot price for oil during the preceding month in exchange for payments from the dealer at the rate of $15.20 a barrel. As can be seen in Exhibit 13.11, these payments have the effect of fixing the price of crude oil for *both* the oil producer and the oil refiner.

Exhibit 13.11
Commodity Swap with Cash Market Transactions

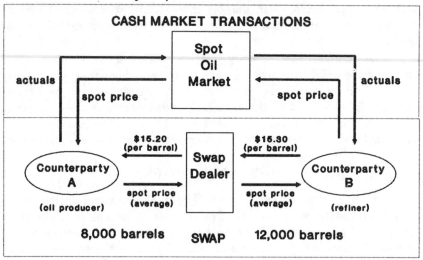

The difference in the notional quantities in these two swaps raises an interesting point. If Counterparty A and Counterparty B had attempted a swap with each other directly, it would have failed since the parties have different notional requirements. But, by using a swap dealer, both swaps are viable. The swap dealer can offset the risk from the mismatched notionals by entering a third swap as fixed-price payer on 4000 barrels. And, until an appropriate counterparty can be found, the swap dealer can hedge in futures.

Variants

There are two basic ways to create a swap variant. The first is to enter two separate commitments. Both might be swaps or only one might be a swap. For example, by entering a fixed-for-floating dollar-based interest rate swap as floating-rate receiver and simultaneously entering a fixed-for-floating dollar-for-deutschemark currency swap as floating-rate payer, a counterparty can convert a fixed-rate dollar obligation to a fixed-rate deutschemark obligation. (If both floating legs are tied to LIBOR, then this particular combination is called a **circus swap**.)

The circus swap is depicted in Exhibits 13.12, 13.13, and 13.14. Only the interest flows are shown in these exhibits and only those flows between Counterparty A and the swap dealer. In Exhibit 13.12, we see a fixed-for-floating dollar-for-deutschemark currency swap between Counterparty A and the swap dealer. In this example, Counterparty A is floating-rate payer (fixed-rate receiver). In Exhibit 13.13, we see a fixed-for-floating dollar-based interest rate swap between Counterparty A and the swap dealer. In this swap, Counterparty A is the fixed-rate payer (floating-rate receiver). The end result, after cancellation of the two floating-rate sides, is that the fixed-rate deutschemark obligation has been converted to a fixed-rate dollar obligation. This is what is depicted in Exhibit 13.14.

Exhibit 13.12
Deutschemark-for-Dollar Currency Swap

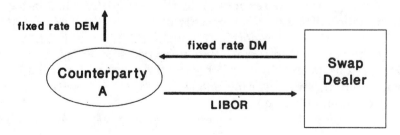

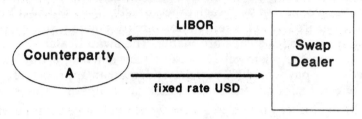

Exhibit 13.13
Fixed-for-Floating Interest Rate Swap

Exhibit 13.14
Circus Swap: Fixed-for-Fixed Currency Swap

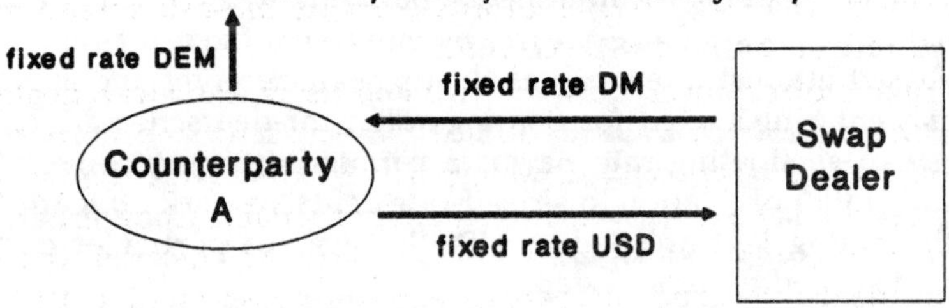

As another example of creating a variant by combining swaps with other swaps or with other instruments, a floating-rate paying counterparty to an interest rate swap might also enter a multi-period interest-rate option, such as an interest rate cap. The cap has the effect of placing a ceiling on the floating rate that might, at any given time, have to be paid. (We discuss interest rate caps and we demonstrate the use of interest rate caps together with swaps in Chapter 15.)

The second way to create a swap variant is to alter the terms of the swap itself. There are a great many ways by which a swap can be tailored to suit some specific end user need. For example, while the notionals are normally nonamortizing over the life of a swap, they can be made amortizing; swap agreements can be written with options to extend or to shorten their maturities (called the swap's **tenor**); swaps can be entered with delayed setting of the swap coupon; and so on.[3]

The point of this discussion is that all swap structures are predicated on the same basic model. By varying the terms of a swap, by combining swaps, or by combining swaps with other instruments, a great many novel structures can be engineered. Nevertheless, all swaps can be easily understood if reduced to their elemental components.

Swap Dealer's Role

The explosive growth in swaps would not have been possible without the transformation of swap brokers into swap dealers. The swap dealer stands ready to enter a swap as a counterparty and, with equal willingness, to play the role of fixed-rate payer or fixed-rate receiver. The swap dealer profits from its bid-ask spread on the fixed-rate side (the swap coupon).

Unlike a direct swap between two end users, the swap dealer does not need to match all terms of the first swap with Counterparty A to the second swap with Counterparty B. Moreover, the swap dealer does not have to have an immediately available Counterparty B in order to enter a swap with Counterparty A. The trick is for the swap dealer to keep the overall exposure associated with its swap book properly hedged. That is, the swap dealer strives to maintain a balanced book, but, in so far as any imbalances exist, the swap dealer will hedge them.

In order to hedge effectively, swap dealers need a liquid debt market trading a very low-risk form of debt and having a continuum of maturities. The one debt market that meets all of these requirements is the market for U.S. Treasury debt. Thus, if a swap dealer enters an interest rate swap as fixed-rate payer against 6-M LIBOR, it simply shorts the appropriate quantity of six-month T-bills and uses the proceeds to purchase intermediate- or long-term Treasury notes or bonds. Consider an example: A swap dealer is approached by a client firm in need of a $25 million fixed-for-floating interest rate swap having a five-year tenor. The client wants to be the floating-rate payer (fixed-rate receiver). The swap dealer agrees to pay the client 9.26 percent (sa) on $25 million in exchange for the client paying the dealer 6-M LIBOR on $25 million. This is depicted in Exhibit 13.15.

The swap dealer immediately hedges by selling $25 million (face value) of T-bills and uses the proceeds from this short sale to purchase $25 million (face value) of five-year Treasury notes. This is depicted in Exhibit 13.16. The swap dealer is now hedged. As a practical matter, the swap dealer will generally hedge in Treasury

Exhibit 13.15
Cash Flows Between Counterpart 1 and Swap Bank

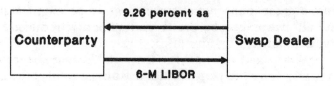

($25 million notional principal)

futures, but cash market hedges, as depicted here, can be used. Notice that the hedge leaves the swap dealer with some basis risk on the floating-rate side. The dealer is receiving LIBOR and paying the T-bill rate. To the degree that the changes in LIBOR and the changes in the T-bill rate are not perfectly correlated (and they are not), there is some basis risk.

Exhibit 13.16
Cash Flows After Offset in Government Securities Market

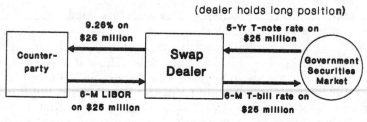

When the swap dealer identifies a matched swap, or at least matches a portion of the notional principal on the first swap, the dealer will lift an appropriate portion of its hedge in Treasuries (or Treasury futures). Thus, by continuously adjusting its cash or futures market positions, the swap dealer can effectively run a swap book without becoming overly concerned about matching individual swaps.

The use of the Treasury markets to hedge a swap book helps

explain why swap dealers price swaps the way they do. Swaps, particularly long-dated swaps (those with tenors of two years or more), are usually priced as a spread over Treasuries of equivalent average life.[4] For example, the swap dealer might make a market in five-year fixed-for-floating interest rate swaps with an ask price (dealer receives fixed rate) of the five-year Treasury note rate plus 62 basis points and a bid price (dealer pays fixed rate) of the five-year Treasury note rate plus 52 basis points. Thus, both prices are expressed as a spread over Treasuries of equivalent average life. Short-dated swaps, i.e., those with a tenor of two years (sometimes three years) or less, are often priced off the IMM's Eurodollar strip using a procedure akin to that used for pricing FRA contracts. This procedure was described in Chapter 12.

As already mentioned, interest rate options and currency options are often used in conjunction with swaps to create interesting structures. In the next two chapters we consider options and their uses.

Summary

A swap is an agreement between two counterparties in which the first agrees to make fixed price payments to the second while the second agrees to make floating price payments to the first. Swaps were a truly revolutionary example of financial engineering. In the first eleven years after their introduction, the notional outstandings of these instruments went from virtually nothing to over two and a half trillion dollars (year end 1990).

Swaps have many uses. They can be used to hedge multiperiod price risks, to reduce the cost of financing, to enter new markets, and to create synthetic instruments. Swaps are marketed by swap dealers who offer their products to banks, nonbank financial corporations, thrifts, nonfinancial corporations, and sovereign governments. The three most common types of swaps are interest rate swaps, currency swaps, and commodity swaps. While not discussed in this chapter, equity swaps have also recently been introduced. (Equity swaps are discussed in Chapter 23.)

The simplest swaps—essentially the forms first developed—are now referred to as the "plain vanilla" forms. Since their introduction, however, dozens of variants have evolved to serve specific, sometimes one-of-a-kind needs. Swap variants can be created by modifying the terms of the swap itself or by combining a swap with some other instrument. The other instrument is often a multiperiod option.

Swap dealers warehouse swaps and run a swap book. They seek to match their swap book in order to remove the risk associated with holding unmatched swaps. Until swaps can be matched, however, they are hedged. The hedging can occur in the cash markets or in other derivative products including futures and forwards. The dealer seeks to profit from its bid-ask spread. Dealer spreads have narrowed dramatically over the years as competition in the industry has transformed swaps from low-volume high-margin products to high-volume low-margin products.

Endnotes

[1]The reader interested in a more detailed discussion of swaps and their uses, swap variants, swap pricing, swap documentation, and the management of a swap portfolio should see Marshall and Kapner [1990]. The reader interested in these topics and the relationship between swaps and other derivative instruments should see Kapner and Marshall [1990].

[2]For purposes of this example, we are assuming that deutschemark interest differentials and dollar interest differentials are directly addable. We also assume that fixed-rate differentials and floating-rate differentials in the same currency are directly addable. Neither of these treatments is technically correct but little is lost in employing these treatments for purposes of illustrating the concepts involved. The necessary adjustments are fully described in Kapner and Marshall [1990].

[3]Ibid.

[4]Swaps are priced off Treasuries. Treasuries are nonamortizing instruments. The average life of a nonamortizing instrument is identical to its maturity. The same is true for nonamortizing swaps. But swaps that amortize have average lives that are shorter than their maturities. For this reason, we match average lives rather than maturities when determining the correct Treasury instrument to use as the basis of the pricing.

References & Suggested Reading

M. Arak, A. Estrella, L. Goodman, and A. Silver. "Interest Rate Swaps: An Alternative Explanation," *Financial Management* (Summer 1988), pp. 12-18.

D. Aspel, J. Cogen, and M. Rabin. "Hedging Long Term Commodity Swaps with Futures," *Global Finance Journal* (Fall 1989), pp. 77-93.

J. Bicksler and A. Chen. "An Economic Analysis of Interest Rate Swaps," *Journal of Finance* (July 1986), pp. 645-655.

S. Felgren. "Interest Rate Swaps: Use, Risk, and Prices," *New England Economic Review*, Federal Reserve Bank of Boston (November 1987), pp. 22-32.

A. Herbst. "Hedging Against Price Index Inflation with Futures Contracts," *Journal of Futures Markets* (Winter 1985), pp. 489-504.

J. Hull. *Options, Futures and Other Derivative Securities*, Englewood Cliffs, NJ: Prentice Hall, 1989.

K. Kapner and J. Marshall. *The Swaps Handbook*, New York: New York Institute of Finance, 1990.

J. Marshall, V. Bansal, and A. Tucker. "Swaps as a Cash Management Tool," working paper, St. John's University (March 1991).

J. Marshall and K. Kapner. *Understanding Swap Finance*, Cincinnati, OH: South-Western, 1990

J. Marshall and A. Tucker. "Equity Derivatives: The Plain Vanilla Equity Swap and Its Variants," working paper, St. John's University (February 1991).

Y. Park. "Currency Swaps as a Long-Term International Financing Technique," *Journal of International Business Studies* (Winter 1984), pp. 47-54.

C. Smith, C. Smithson, and L. Wakeman. "The Evolving Market for Swaps," *Midland Corporate Finance Journal* (Winter 1986), pp. 20-32.

C. Smith, C. Smithson, and L. Wakeman. "The Market for Interest Rate Swaps," *Financial Management* (Winter 1988), pp. 34-44.

A. Tucker. *Financial Futures, Options, and Swaps*, St. Paul, MN: West Publishing, 1991.

S. Turnball. "Swaps: A Zero Sum Game," *Financial Management* (Spring 1987), pp. 15-22.

L. Wall. "Interest Rate Swaps in an Agency Theoretic Model with Uncertain Interest Rates," working paper No. 86-6, Federal Reserve Bank of Atlanta (July 1986).

L. Wall and J. Pringle. "Alternative Explanations of Interest Rate Swaps," working paper No. 87-2, Federal Reserve Bank of Atlanta (April 1987).

Chapter 14

Single-Period Options: Calls and Puts

Overview

The instruments we will be discussing in this chapter and the next differ from other financial instruments in that they are all, in some sense, options. An option is a contract between two parties in which one party has the *right but not the obligation* to do something—usually to buy or sell some underlying asset.

The concept of an option is quite general. The best known types are calls and puts. A **call option** grants its purchaser the right (but not the obligation) to buy some underlying asset while a **put option** grants its purchaser the right (but not the obligation) to sell some underlying asset. Only the purchaser of the call or put has a right without an obligation. The contract seller has an absolute obligation.

Calls and puts are not the only types of options. For example, many bonds have option-like features. The two most frequently encountered of these features are the **conversion feature** associated with convertible bonds and the **call feature** associated with callable bonds. A **convertible bond** is a bond in which the bondholder has the right, but not the obligation, to convert the bond into some other asset of the issuer. A **callable bond** is a bond in which the issuer has the right, but not the obligation, to call the bond (for redemption) prior to maturity.

Since rights without obligations have value, the option purchaser must expect to pay the option seller for the option or option-like feature. That is, one does not get value without giving value. In the case of calls and puts, the price paid for the option takes the form of a flat up-front sum called a **premium**. In the case of a convertible bond, the bond purchaser gets the option-like feature as a part of the bond and pays for the option indirectly in the form of a reduced coupon. That is, the bondholder pays par at issue but accepts a coupon below market for the life of the bond. Thus, payment for the option is made in installments over the life of the bond.

The call feature on a bond is a little trickier to understand. The bondholder owns the bond but the bond issuer owns the option. Thus, when an investor purchases the bond from the issuer, he or she simultaneously sells the issuer an option. For this option, the issuer pays the bond purchaser. In this case, the payment takes the form of an above-market coupon—relative to a noncallable bond—for the life of the bond and, so again, payment for the option is made in installments over the life of the bond.

There are many other types of options and option-like features associated with financial instruments. In this chapter, we are going to focus on the oldest and simplest types of options, namely calls and puts, and, more briefly, on the option-like features sometimes associated with bonds. All of these options are **single-period options** in the sense they cover one defined period of time. In the next chapter, we take up multiperiod options.

Option pricing is one of the most mathematically complex of all applied areas of finance. The first complete option pricing model (OPM) was developed by Fisher Black and Myron Scholes and published in 1973. The original Black/Scholes model was limited as to the types of options it was capable of valuing, the types of assets on which the options were written, and the nature of the price behavior describing the underlying asset as it moved through time. Subsequent research built on the original Black/Scholes model and dozens of OPM variants eventually emerged to handle other types of options, other types of underlying assets, and other types of price behaviors. In most cases, the derivation of option pricing models rests on the mathematics of stochastic calculus and a presentation of such models without a solid background in these sophisticated quantitative tools would be confusing at best.[1] This is not a serious problem, however, as the calculations necessary to ascertain the fair market values of options have been automated and software for such purposes is available for both mainframe and microcomputers.[2] For these reasons, we will not examine the mathematics of option pricing models.

Calls and Puts: The Basics

A call option grants its purchaser, called the **option holder,** the right to purchase a specified number of units of some underlying asset from the option seller. The option seller is called the **option writer** or, sometimes, the **option grantor.** This right is good for some specified period of time, called the **time to expiration** or the **time to expiry.** The precise date on which the option right expires is called the **expiration date.** The price at which the option holder may purchase the underlying asset from the option writer is called the option's **strike price** or **exercise price.** The option writer is said to be **short the option** and the option purchaser is said to be **long the option.** For the rights bestowed by the option, the option purchaser pays the option seller a one time up-front fee called the option premium.

A put option has an identical definition except that the option purchaser has the right to sell ("put") the underlying asset to the option writer. This sale, if the option purchaser elects to exercise the option, is made at the option's strike price.

Calls and puts can be one of two types: European or American. (The terms explain the origins but are no longer geographically meaningful.) A **European option** is an option that can only be exercised during a very limited exercise period near the end of the option's life. An **American option,** on the other hand, can be exercised at any time from the moment it is created until the time it expires. In either case, once an option expires, it is worthless if it has not been exercised. The difference between European and American options is depicted in Exhibit 14.1.

In order to fully identify an option, several things must be specified. These include the underlying asset, whether the option is a call or a put, the strike price of the option, the expiration date of the option, and, if the option trades on more than one exchange, the exchange on which the option trades. For example, a call option on IBM stock, having a strike price of $100 and that expires in November would be identified as an "IBM November 100 call." In

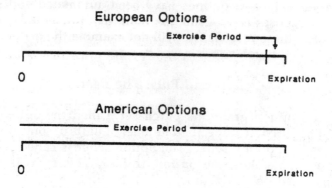

Exhibit 14.1
Exercise Periods: European vs. American

this case, the exchange is the Chicago Board Options Exchange or CBOE. Not all options trade on an options exchange, and, as we will see in the next chapter, some of the most important options for risk management purposes are traded in over-the-counter dealer-type markets.

For any underlying asset on which options are written, there will be multiple options trading. For example, Table 14.1 lists some of the options on IBM stock as they appeared in *The Wall Street Journal* on Friday, 1 December 1989. These prices were the "last trade of the day" prices for these options on Thursday, 30 November 1989. We have deliberately limited the list to two strike prices below the closing price of IBM (90 and 95) and to two strike prices above the closing price of IBM (100 and 105).

Table 14.1
Option Premiums
1 December 1989

| IBM | strike | ———Calls——— | | | ———Puts——— | | |
		DEC	JAN	APR	DEC	JAN	APR
97½	90	8⅜	9¼	11¼	¼	⅝	1⅝
	95	3⅝	5½	7⅞	⅝	1¹¹⁄₁₆	3¼
	100	¾	2⁹⁄₁₆	5⅛	2¾	3¾	5¼
	105	³⁄₁₆	1	3⅛	7⅛	7⅝	8⅜

The structure of Table 14.1 is typical of the way options prices are reported, whether in the financial press or on a computer screen. The calls are listed first and the puts are listed second. The expiration months are listed horizontally and the strike prices are listed vertically. The value 97½, which appears directly under the name of the underlying asset (IBM), is the closing price of the underlying asset on the same day.

Option prices are always quoted and reported *per unit* of underlying asset, regardless of the number of units of underlying asset covered by the option. For example, the price of the IBM December 90 call is $8⅜ or $8.375. This represents the option price per unit of stock covered by the option. Since the option covers 100 shares of stock, the actual price of this option is $837.50. Different options cover different numbers of units of the underlying asset. (Equity options, however, typically cover 100 shares of stock.) For this reason, it is less confusing if each option is treated as if it covers just one unit of the underlying asset. This is also the reason why the per unit pricing convention has been adopted in actual trading. Nothing is lost by this treatment.

Almost all stock options and most other put and call options traded in the United States expire on the third Friday of the expiration month. That is, the December 1989 options expired on the third Friday of December 1989, which happened to be 15 December 1989. The actual date of expiration is very important as it can range anywhere from the 15th of the month to the 21st of the month. As we will see shortly, a large part of an option's value is derived from the time remaining to maturity. A few days can make a big difference in this value.

Listed options, that is, those options listed on an exchange, are cleared through a **clearing house.** All listed stock options and most other listed options in the United States are cleared through the Option Clearing Corporation (OCC) located in Chicago. An option clearing house serves the same function in options trading that a clearing association serves in futures trading. That is, the clearing house guarantees performance on each option and, for this reason, the clearing house may be viewed as long to all shorts and short to all longs. As with futures, the clearing house holds margin to assure performance by the option writers. Option purchasers do not post margin as they have no obligations once they have paid the option premium.

Since OTC options are not traded on exchanges, they are not

cleared through a clearing house. Instead, each party to the contract must know the other party and must have faith in the other party's ability to perform. Nevertheless, dealers in these markets may require margin or collateral from option writers to minimize the risk from a failure to perform.

Options have value for two entirely different reasons. The fair value of an option, i.e., the fair premium, is the sum of these two component parts. The two components of value are called **intrinsic value** and **time value.** Additional terminology will be explained in the following paragraphs. This terminology will help the reader understand the value components. In order to make the components more intuitive, we will assume, for the time being, that the options we are talking about are of the American variety.

An option can be **in-the-money, at-the-money,** or **out-of-the-money.** Which of these terms applies depends on the relationship between the current price of the underlying asset and the strike price of the option. For a call option, the option is in-the-money if the price of the underlying asset exceeds the strike price of the option. It is at-the-money if the price of the underlying asset exactly equals the strike price of the option. Finally, it is out-of-the-money if the price of the underlying asset is below the strike price of the option. The relationships between monieness and price are reversed for put options. These relationships are summarized in Table 14.2.

Table 14.2
Monieness and Options

Relationship	Calls	Puts
A > S	in-the-money	out-of-the-money
A = S	at-the-money	at-the-money
A < S	out-of-the-money	in-the-money

Notes: A denotes the current price of the underlying asset
        S denotes the strike price of the option

To make this notion of monieness clearer, let's apply the rules in Table 14.2 to the IBM options in Table 14.1. The IBM 90 calls and the IBM 95 calls are in-the-money because, at 97.50, the price of the underlying asset, IBM stock, is above the strike price of these options. The IBM 100 calls and the IBM 105 calls are out-of-the-money because the price of the underlying asset is below the strike prices of these options. For the IBM puts, the situation is reversed.

The IBM 90 puts and the IBM 95 puts are out-of-the-money because the strike prices of these options are below the price of the underlying asset. The IBM 100 puts and the IBM 105 puts are in-the-money because the strike prices of these options are above the price of the underlying asset.

Options that are very far into the money are said to be **deep-in-the-money**. Similarly, options that are very far out of the money are said to be **deep-out-of-the-money**. Options that are in or out of the money but not by very close to the money are said to be **near-the-money**.

An option's intrinsic value is either (1) the amount by which it is in-the-money, or (2) zero, whichever is greater. In terms of mathematical functions, this relationship can be written using a MAX function. A MAX function, for "maximum," is simply a function that selects the largest value from a set of values. The appropriate MAX function for describing an option's intrinsic value is given by Equation 14.1.

$$\text{Intrinsic value} = \text{MAX[in-the-money, zero]} \qquad (14.1)$$

Since the conditions for a put to be in-the-money are exactly opposite those for a call to be in-the-money, the MAX functions are slightly different for calls and puts. These appear below.

Intrinsic value
Call   MAX[A-S, 0]
Put   MAX[S-A, 0]

For example, if the underlying asset has a price of 60 and the strike price is 55, then the call is in-the-money by 5, which is larger than zero, so the call's intrinsic value is 5. At the same time, the put is out-of-the-money by 5, which can be viewed as another way of saying in-the-money by –5. So the put's intrinsic value is 0 since 0 is greater than –5.

The logic underlying intrinsic value is very intuitive. Suppose that a call option with a strike price of 55 is commanding a premium of *less* than $5 when the underlying asset is priced at 60. Suppose, for example, that the option is priced at $3. What will happen? Since we have assumed an American-type option, this call can be exercised at any time. Arbitragers will see a riskless profit opportunity and exploit it. In this case, the arbitrage strategy is to buy the call for $3 and exercise it immediately. This requires that the arbitrager pay the call writer $55 (the strike price) to get a unit of the underlying asset. The total cost of the underlying asset to the arbitrager is therefore $58: $3 for the option and $55 to exercise it. But, since the underlying asset is trading for $60, the arbitrager can immediately resell the underlying asset acquired through the exercise of the option. This sale brings $60. The **buy-to-exercise** strategy thus nets the arbitrager a $2 profit. This profit is the difference between the price at which the underlying asset is sold ($60) and the cost of acquiring the underlying asset ($3 + $55).

The buy-to-exercise strategy is a riskless strategy that requires no investment on the arbitrager's part. The arbitrage does not require any investment because the arbitrager pays for the option and pays the option writer the exercise price from the proceeds of a short sale of the underlying asset. A short sale, in this case, means that the arbitrager borrowed the underlying asset and used the borrowed asset to make delivery on his sale in the cash market. The short sale of the underlying asset is then covered by the underlying asset acquired through the exercise of the option. (A short sale is "covered" when the party that borrowed the asset returns it to the party that lent it.) The strategy is riskless because all transactions are executed simultaneously at known prices.

Since the strategy is riskless and requires no investment (a classic example of pure arbitrage), many arbitragers will recognize the profit opportunity and behave similarly. Since the strategy requires the purchase of the call option, we can expect that the cumulative effect of this buying by arbitragers will bid up the price of the option until the option no longer affords an arbitrage profit. This of course happens at a price of $5. The option therefore must have a value of at *least* $5 and this is its intrinsic value. This is precisely the sum suggested by Equation 14.1.

Intrinsic value places a floor on the total value of an option. But can the option have a value greater than its intrinsic value and, if so, why? The answer is yes, the option can and usually will have a total value greater than its intrinsic value. The difference between the total value and the intrinsic value is called time value. Time value, like intrinsic value, is easily understood at an intuitive level.

Suppose that a call option has an intrinsic value of $5 and that it is priced at $5, as in the case we examined a moment ago. Next, suppose that the option has six months left before its expiration.

What can happen in the next six months? If the price of the underlying asset declines, the intrinsic value will decline but cannot go below zero. Thus, the most the holder of this option can lose is the amount by which it is in-the-money. If the price of the underlying asset declines by $5, i.e., from $60 to $55, we lose the full intrinsic value. If it declines by $10 (to $50), or $15 (to $45), or any other amount greater than $5, we still only lose the $5 intrinsic value. Suppose, instead, that the price of the underlying asset rises. If it rises by $5, our intrinsic value increases to $10. If it rises by $10, our intrinsic value increases to $15, and so on. We can readily see that there is an asymmetry here. The loss of intrinsic value from a downside price movement is strictly limited whereas there is no limit to the upside potential. It is this asymmetry between the up and down sides that gives an option value beyond its intrinsic value.

How much in excess of intrinsic value will someone be willing to pay for this upside potential? This can be readily determined by looking at some actual option prices. Consider again Table 14.1. Notice that IBM was priced at $97.50 on 30 November 1989 and that the December 95 call was priced at $3.625 (3⅝). Since this option was in-the-money by $2.50 but the option was commanding a premium of $3.625, the excess value was $1.125. Now look at the January 95 call. Notice that it was commanding a premium of $5.50 (5½). Thus, it had excess value of $3.00. Finally, look at the April 95 call. It was commanding a premium of $7.875 (7⅞), which represented excess value in the amount of $5.375. These three call options were identical except for the *time remaining until they expired*. Clearly, the longer the time until expiration, the greater the excess value. But why? The answer is simple. The excess value represents a monetary value placed on the *option's potential to become more valuable before it expires*. The longer the time until expiration, the greater is this potential. It is not surprising then that the excess value we have been describing is called time value. The relationship between time value and time is depicted in Exhibit 14.2 and the relationship between the fair value of an option, the option's intrinsic value, and the option's time value is given by Equation 14.2.

Total value (premium) = Intrinsic value + Time value   (14.2)

Before moving on, other factors that influence an option's time value must be considered. Since time value is a price placed on

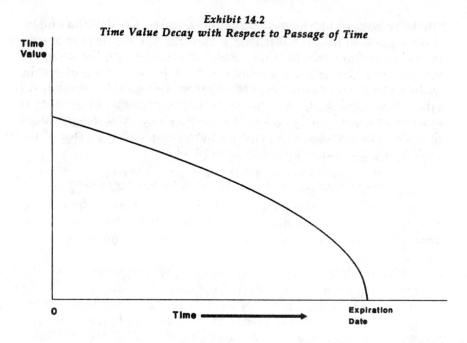

Exhibit 14.2
Time Value Decay with Respect to Passage of Time

potential, the question we need to ask is "what are the factors that influence potential?" Clearly, time remaining to expiration is one important factor, but it is not the only one. Suppose that the underlying asset's price has never changed over the last five or ten years. Is it likely to change significantly over the near future? Probably not. Does the option have much potential to become more valuable? Clearly not. Would you be willing to pay a sizable sum for this potential? Certainly not. But suppose that the underlying asset's price has fluctuated dramatically over the last few years. Does the option have potential now? Clearly it does. The point then is that time value is a function not only of time but also of the volatility of the price of the underlying asset. We measure this volatility using a well known statistical measure called standard deviation. We will call a standard deviation a **volatility unit** or a **unit of volatility** just as we did when we first introduced these terms in Chapter 6.

What other factors influence time value? One is the current price of the underlying asset itself. This price has two opposing impacts on time value. If the option is deep out-of-the-money, then there is very little potential for the underlying asset's price to change enough to put the option significantly into the money and we would not be willing to pay very much for time value. On the other hand, if the option is deep-in-the-money then the intrinsic value is considerable and we will have to risk a large sum to get the potential we are after. This risk is an important factor and we will not be willing to pay very much beyond intrinsic value for the option. All other things being equal then, we would expect that time value is at a maximum when the option is at-the- money. And this is indeed the case. The relationship between time value and the price of the underlying asset is depicted in Exhibit 14.3.

Exhibit 14.3
Time Value as a Function of the Price of the Underlying Asset

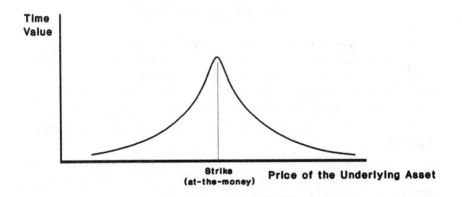

There are two other factors that influence time value. One is the strike price of the option and the other is the current level of interest rates. The strike price of the option is obviously important because it, together with the price of the underlying asset, determines whether the option is *in* or *out* of the money. The role played by interest rates is a bit more complicated. Call options can be viewed as a substitute for a long position in the underlying asset with the advantage that call options provide leverage. An investor can also get leverage, however, by borrowing some of the funds necessary for the direct purchase of the underlying asset. The higher the interest rate, the more attractive the call option alternative. Thus, we would expect the time value of call options to increase as interest rates increase. By the same token, we would expect the value of put options to decrease as interest rates increase.

Option pricing models must capture all of the effects that have been described. As already noted, the most widely used of the various option pricing models was first developed by Fisher Black and Myron Scholes and is referred to as the Black/Scholes option pricing model or OPM. This model was designed to determine the fair market value of a European-type call option on a nonpayout asset. Many variants of the original model have been developed to fit special situations. Examples include European-type put options on non-payout assets, American-type options on nonpayout assets, options on payout assets, options on futures contracts, and so on.[3]

Payoff Profiles

One of the best ways to understand the risk management and other financial engineering uses of options and option-like instruments is to examine the **payoff profiles** associated with them. We discussed payoff profiles in Chapter 7 and we used the concept to illustrate the outcomes of futures hedges in Chapter 12. In the case of options, payoff profiles are often called **profit diagrams**.

A payoff profile depicts the profits and losses from a position in an instrument *as of some specific point in time*. In the case of call and put options, payoff profiles are *usually*, but not always, depicted as of the time of the option's expiration. This is the last moment of the option's life before it expires. At that time, the option has no remaining time value and so the option's value is entirely explained by its intrinsic value.

Let's consider the payoff profile for a call option first. The first step in the construction of a payoff profile is the construction of a value diagram. Suppose that, at some time prior to expiration, the call commands a premium of C dollars. This premium represents the sum the option purchaser pays for the option. At expiration the option will have a value of A-S or zero, whichever is greater, where A denotes the value of the underlying asset and S denotes the strike price. For any value of A equal to or less than S, the option is worthless. For each $1 by which A exceeds S, the option's terminal value increases by $1. The value diagram then looks like that depicted in Exhibit 14.4.

Now recall that the option purchaser paid C dollars for this call option. The payoff profile is then the value diagram in Exhibit

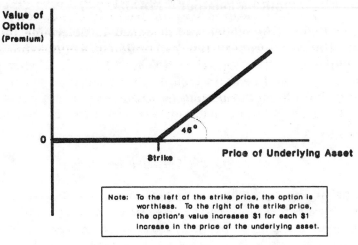

Exhibit 14.4
Value Diagram for a Long Call
(at expiration)

14.4 shifted *down* by the amount paid for the option. The profit function is given by Equation 14.3.

$$\text{Profit on long call} = \text{MAX}[A\text{-}S, 0] - C \qquad (14.3)$$

This profit is illustrated by the payoff profile depicted in Exhibit 14.5.

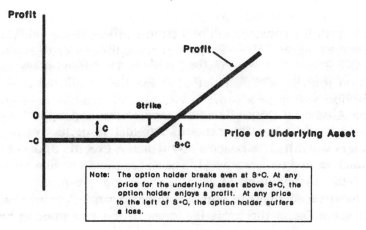

Exhibit 14.5
Payoff Profile for a Long Call
(at expiration)

By the same process, we can construct the payoff profile for a put option. The profit for a long put is given by Equation 14.4.

$$\text{Profit on long put} = MAX[S-A, 0] - P \qquad (14.4)$$

In Equation 14.4, P denotes the premium paid for the put. The payoff profile that corresponds to this profit function is depicted in Exhibit 14.6.

Exhibit 14.6
Payoff Profile for a Long Put
(at expiration)

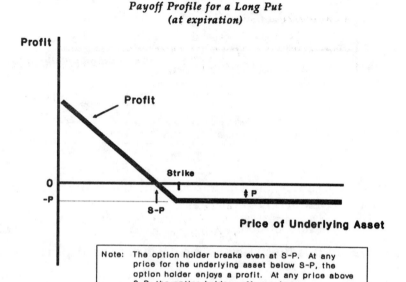

Note: The option holder breaks even at S-P. At any price for the underlying asset below S-P, the option holder enjoys a profit. At any price above S-P, the option holder suffers a loss.

The payoff profiles for option writers are the mirror images of the payoff profiles for option purchasers. This symmetry is explained by the fact that option trading (ignoring transaction costs) is a **zero-sum game**. That is, the profits to the winners exactly equal the losses to the losers. The payoff profiles for option writers are depicted in Exhibits 14.7 and 14.8.

Options are very often combined to develop elaborate strategies. Most of these strategies are devised for speculative purposes but, quite often, special needs will make one of these strategies useful to a hedger.[4]

The most frequently used of the combination strategies are the straddle, the vertical spread, the horizontal spread, the diagonal spread, and the butterfly spread. In a **straddle**, the option

Exhibit 14.7
Payoff Profile for a Short Call
(at expiration)

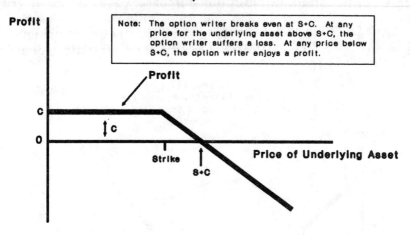

Note: The option writer breaks even at S+C. At any price for the underlying asset above S+C, the option writer suffers a loss. At any price below S+C, the option writer enjoys a profit.

Exhibit 14.8
Payoff Profile for a Short Put
(at expiration)

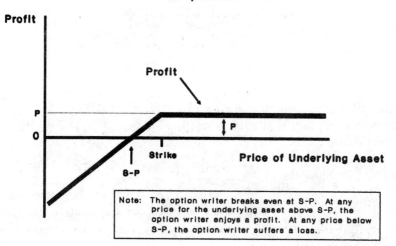

Note: The option writer breaks even at S-P. At any price for the underlying asset above S-P, the option writer enjoys a profit. At any price below S-P, the option writer suffers a loss.

purchaser buys (or sells) *both* a call and a put on the *same* underlying asset with the *same* strike price and the *same* expiration date. For this straddle, the option purchaser pays the option writer a sum equal to the cost of the two options, $C+P$. The payoff profile associated with this long straddle strategy is depicted in Exhibit 14.9. The payoff profile for the short straddle is depicted in Exhibit 14.10.

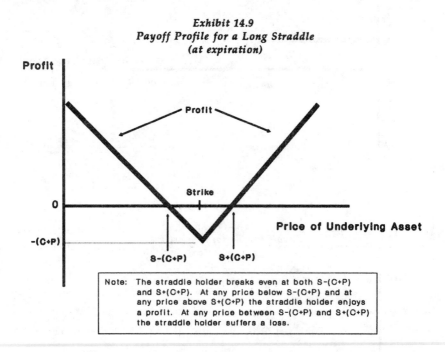

Exhibit 14.9
Payoff Profile for a Long Straddle
(at expiration)

Note: The straddle holder breaks even at both S−(C+P) and S+(C+P). At any price below S−(C+P) and at any price above S+(C+P) the straddle holder enjoys a profit. At any price between S−(C+P) and S+(C+P) the straddle holder suffers a loss.

Notice the peculiar V shape of a straddle's payoff profile. The profile suggests that such a strategy is useful for speculating on volatility rather than on direction. That is, the long straddle shows a positive payoff regardless of the direction of movement in the underlying asset's price. All that is required for a profit to be realized is that there be sufficient movement away from the strike price. The opposite is true for a short straddle.

A speculator who purchases a straddle is sometimes said to be **long volatility** (or **long vols** in market parlance). The terminology stems from the fact that the speculator who is long a straddle will profit from an increase in volatility. Similarly, a speculator who is short a straddle is said to be **short volatility** (or **short vols**).

For risk management purposes, these straddle strategies would

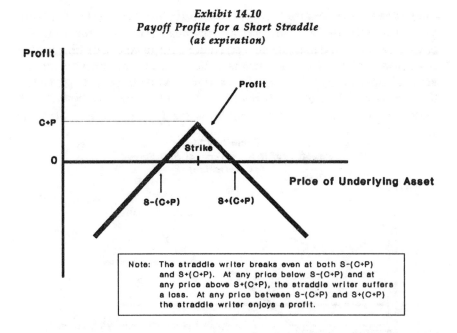

Exhibit 14.10
Payoff Profile for a Short Straddle
(at expiration)

Note: The straddle writer breaks even at both S-(C+P) and S+(C+P). At any price below S-(C+P) and at any price above S+(C+P), the straddle writer suffers a loss. At any price between S-(C+P) and S+(C+P) the straddle writer enjoys a profit.

be of interest to a firm with a volatility exposure. A volatility exposure is an exposure in which the firm will suffer a negative result from *any* movement away from the current price level. A firm with such an exposure can hedge it by purchasing a straddle with a strike price equal to the current price of the underlying asset. The opposite would hold for a firm that would suffer if there is *not* a movement away from the current price. Such an exposure could be hedged by writing a straddle.

A **spread** is a combination of options that involves the purchase of one option and the sale of another where both options are of the same class. That is, both options are calls or both options are puts. The payoff profiles associated with spreads are nearly identical whether we use calls or puts so we will not distinguish between them.

There are a number of different types of spreads. **Vertical spreads** are spreads across strike prices. The term *vertical spread* comes from the traditional vertical listing of strike prices as we showed in Table 14.1. In the vertical spread, we buy a call (or a put) with one strike price and simultaneously sell a call (or a put) having a different strike price. The expiration month and the underlying asset for the two options in the vertical spread are identical. If we buy the lower strike option and sell the higher strike option, the spread is called a **vertical**

bull spread. For example, we could buy the Dec IBM 90 call for 8.375 and sell the Dec IBM 95 call for 3.625. The *net* premium *paid* is then 4.75. If we sell the lower strike option and buy the higher strike option, then the spread is called a **vertical bear spread.** A vertical bear spread with the same two IBM calls used to illustrate the vertical bull spread will result in a *net* premium *received* of 4.75. Payoff profiles for these two strategies are depicted in Exhibit 14.11 and 14.12.

Exhibit 14.11
Payoff Profile for a Vertical Bull Spread
(at expiration)

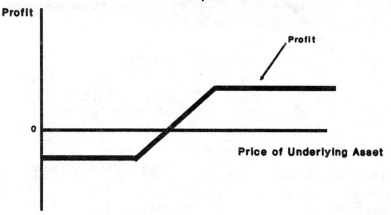

Exhibit 14.12
Payoff Profile for a Vertical Bear Spread
(at expiration)

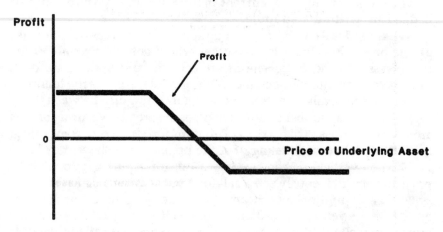

Horizontal spreads are spreads across expiration months. In these spreads, we sell an option that has one expiration month and buy an option having a different expiration month. Both options have the same strike price and are written on the same underlying asset. The spread is called a **horizontal bull spread** if we buy the back month and sell the front month. For example, we could buy the Jan IBM 95 call and sell the Dec IBM 95 call. The spread is called a **horizontal bear spread** if we buy the front month and sell the back month. Using the same two options and continuing the example, the horizontal bear spread would require that we buy the Dec IBM 95 call and sell the Jan IBM 95 call. The payoff profiles for these two horizontal spread strategies are depicted in Exhibits 14.13 and 14.14.

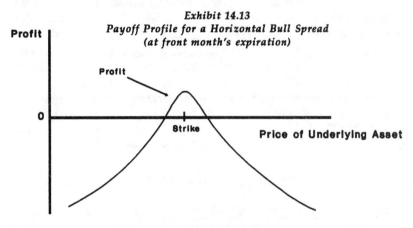

Exhibit 14.13
Payoff Profile for a Horizontal Bull Spread
(at front month's expiration)

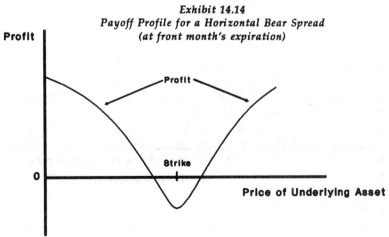

Exhibit 14.14
Payoff Profile for a Horizontal Bear Spread
(at front month's expiration)

Notice the similarity of the payoff profile for the horizontal bull spread depicted in Exhibit 14.13 and the payoff profile for the short straddle depicted in Exhibit 14.10. Also notice the similarity of the payoff profile for the horizontal bear spread depicted in Exhibit 14.14 and the payoff profile for the long straddle depicted in Exhibit 14.9. These similarities suggest that horizontal spreads can be used in a fashion similar to straddles to hedge volatility exposures.

Diagonal spreads are spreads across both the strike price and the expiration month. That is, they are vertical and horizontal at the same time. For example, we might buy the Dec IBM 95 call and sell the Jan IBM 100 call. A **butterfly spread** involves four options that are *all* calls or *all* puts. All four options have the same expiration month and are written on the same underlying asset. One option has a high strike price, one has a low strike price, and two have the same strike price, which is between those of the high strike and low strike. The two middle strike options are sold and the two end options are purchased. For example, we might buy the Dec IBM 90 call and the Dec IBM 100 call and sell two Dec IBM 95 calls. This strategy can also be reversed. The reverse strategy, which consists of buying the two middle strikes and selling the two end strikes, is called a **reverse butterfly** or a **sandwich spread**. We will not draw the payoff profiles for either diagonal spreads or butterfly spreads.

Hedging with Options

Having developed the payoff profiles for the more popular option strategies, let's consider the outcomes for a firm in need of a hedge that chooses to use an option as the hedging instrument. We will use the example of a CFO whose board has authorized the public offering of $50 million of 30-year bonds to fund the construction of a new production facility. This is the same example used to illustrate the use of interest-rate futures as hedging instruments in Chapter 12. At the time the CFO received authorization, the corporate yield curve for investment grade bonds suggested that the firm could float an issue at par if it agreed to pay a coupon of 9.75 percent. Unfortunately, there is an estimated three-month lag between authorization by the board and the actual issuance of the securities. During these three months, the firm is exposed to the risk that yields might rise and the offering will have to be sold with a coupon above 9.75 percent.

In Chapter 12, we examined how the firm's interest-rate risk could be hedged using interest-rate futures. The firm's risk profile, the payoff profile, and the residual risk profile (formed by combining the risk profile and the payoff profile) are repeated as Exhibits 14.15, 14.16, and 14.17 respectively.

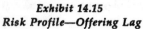

Exhibit 14.15
Risk Profile—Offering Lag

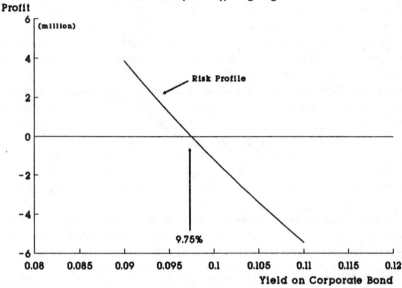

Exhibit 14.16
Payoff Profile—Short T-Bond Futures

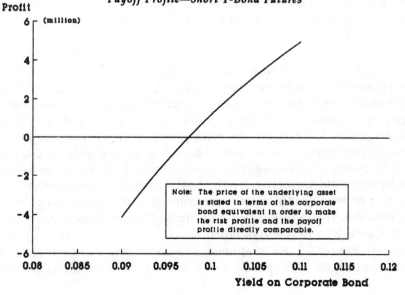

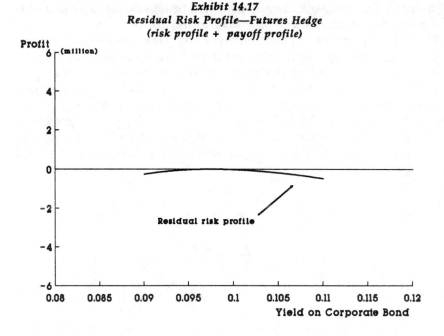

Exhibit 14.17
Residual Risk Profile—Futures Hedge
(risk profile + payoff profile)

As it happens, the CFO believes that interest rates are more likely to fall than rise in the coming months. (Her past experience at predicting interest rate movements has been reasonably good—she's been batting about 600.) Nevertheless, the size of this offering is such that the interest-rate exposure must be hedged against an adverse upward movement in rates. She decides to hedge this offering in options.

Since the firm will suffer financially from any increase in rates, the CFO needs a hedge strategy that will produce positive profits if rates rise. The inverse relationship between yields and bond prices suggests that this is equivalent to a strategy that will prove profitable if bond prices decline. *The appropriate strategy then is to be long puts on a debt instrument.* She decides to hedge by buying puts on T-bond futures. These puts have three months to expiration. She uses the same DV01 model used to determine the hedge ratio when she was hedging in futures. Thus, she concludes that she would need puts covering about $22 million of underlying T-bonds. As it happens, each option covers one T-bond futures contract and each futures contract covers $0.1 million, so she needs to buy 220 options. For these options, the CFO pays a premium of 1¼ per hundred dollars of face value (1.25 percent of par). The total cost of the options is therefore $275,000, which she pays up-front.

The payoff profile for these options, with the price of the underlying asset expressed as the yield-equivalent on the firm's bonds, rather than as a dollar price (horizontal axis), is depicted in Exhibit 14.18. This reexpression of the T-bond price as a corporate yield equivalent is necessary to allow us to combine the risk and payoff profiles. Notice that this reexpression makes the payoff profile of a long put look like the payoff profile of a long call. This is simply another reflection of the inverse relationship between prices and yields.

Exhibit 14.18
Payoff Profiole—Long T-Bond Put

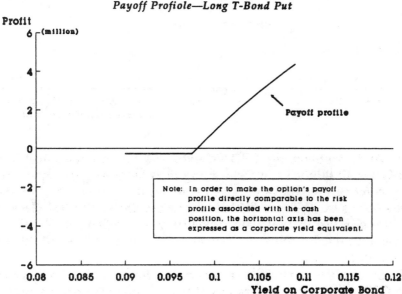

By combining the firm's risk profile, depicted in Exhibit 14.15, with the payoff profile from its long hedge in puts, depicted in Exhibit 14.18, we can quickly visualize the residual risk exposure associated with the hedged position. This is depicted in Exhibit 14.19.

Compare the residual risk profile from the option hedge (Exhibit 14.19) with the residual risk profile from the futures hedge (Exhibit 14.17). Notice that the futures hedge insulates the firm from any movement in interest rates whether that movement is

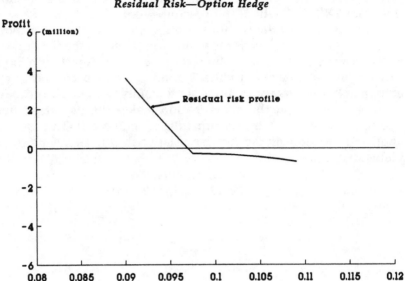

Exhibit 14.19
Residual Risk—Option Hedge

favorable or unfavorable. The option hedge protects the firm from increases in interest rates but still allows the firm to benefit from decreases in interest rates. Thus, if rates decline between the time the board authorizes the sale of new debt and the time of the actual public offering of that debt, the firm will enjoy lower financing costs than the current 9.75 percent. On the other hand, the preservation of the opportunity to benefit from a decline in rates has a cost to the firm. This cost is the up-front premium the firm pays to the option writer.

Notice the slight dip in the right side of the residual risk profile depicted in Exhibit 14.19. This dip reflects the fact that the size of this option hedge is *not* adjusted as the yield changes. The performance of the hedge can be improved by periodically adjusting the size of the hedge to take into account the changing DV01s. This issue was discussed in Chapter 12 and we do not consider it further here.

The option hedging strategy employed above can just as easily be used to hedge exchange-rate risk, equity-price risk or commodity-price risk. The appropriate strategy, i.e., buying puts, buying calls, writing puts, writing calls, straddles, spreads, and so on, will depend on the nature of the firm's exposure. This is best visualized, as argued above, with graphic depictions of the firm's risk profile.

Cash Settled Options

The original call and put options, like the original futures contracts, provided for the physical delivery of the underlying asset. In the case of futures, the delivery occurs during the contract's delivery month with the specific time of delivery left to the discretion of the contract seller. In the case of options, the delivery occurs only if the option holder, the long, elects to exercise the option. With American options, exercise can occur at any time. With European options, exercise is limited to the exercise period. However, just as deliverable futures contracts are rarely delivered, options are rarely exercised. Instead, parties with open positions in options make offsetting trades, called **closing trades.** That is, a party that had sold an option buys an identical option. He or she is now long and short an identical instrument. The clearing house then scratches one long and one short—thereby terminating the trader's position.

Shortly after the introduction of cash settlement futures on stock indexes, futures exchanges persuaded the CFTC to allow trading in options on futures, called **futures options** on a trial basis. The experiment was successful and was later made permanent. Futures options now trade on most futures exchanges. The purpose of writing options on futures is to allow the option writer, in the case of a call, or purchaser, in the case of a put, to deliver a standardized unit of underlying asset (the futures contract) should the long elect to exercise the option. With the introduction of options on stock-index futures, we had an option that, if exercised, resulted in the delivery of a futures contract that was then cash settled. It was a short step from this type of option to an option that was written directly on a stock index and settled in cash at the end of the option's life. Such options do not require an explicit decision on the part of the long to exercise the option. Instead, the option writer pays the option holder a sum equal to the amount that the option is in-the-money or zero, whichever is greater, at the time of the option's expiration.

Cash settled options written directly on stock indexes quickly supplanted options on stock-index futures. They also paved the way for other forms of cash settled options including rate caps and rate floors, which we take up in the next chapter.

Summary

Options are contracts that grant their purchaser the right but not the obligation to do something. Most often this is the right to buy or sell some number of units of some underlying asset. In the case of cash settled options, the "right" is the right to receive a cash payment. Options have limited lives. If not exercised by the end of its life, an option expires and is worthless. Options that can be exercised at any time are called American options and options that can only be exercised during a limited period are called European options.

Traditional options include calls and puts. Call options grant their holders the right to buy some number of units of the underlying asset as the options' strike price, while put options grant their holders the right to sell some number of units of the underlying asset at the options' strike price. For the right that an option conveys, the option purchaser pays the option writer an up-front fee called the option premium.

Options are attractive as speculative instruments because they provide the speculator with considerable leverage while strictly limiting downside risk. They are also attractive to hedgers because they provide a way to protect from adverse price movements while still preserving the opportunity to benefit from favorable price movements. The payoff profiles associated with options are somewhat more complex than those associated with futures and forward contracts. Further, these instruments can be combined in a great many ways to create a myriad assortment of unique profit structures and this, as much as anything else, is the source of their appeal to financial engineers.

Option valuation models are exceedingly complex. Most such models were derived as variants of the original Black/Scholes model. Even those that were not formulated as variants bear a strong resemblance to the Black/Scholes model.

The value of an option consists of two parts. The first is called intrinsic value and it can be defined with the aid of a MAX function. In other words, the intrinsic value is the amount by which an option is in-the-money or zero, whichever is greater. The second component of option value is called time value. Time value represents the option's potential to acquire more intrinsic value before it expires.

While all early options allowed for the physical delivery of the underlying asset, many options introduced in recent years are specifically designed to be cash settled. Cash settlement in options is a very attractive feature and greatly reduces the machinery necessary to handle an exercise. It also paved the way for multi-period options.

Endnotes

[1]The reader interested in the mathematics of option pricing models should consider several of the following: Marshall (1989), Ritchken (1987), Cox and Rubinstein (1985), and Jarrow and Rudd (1983). The reader interested in the mathematics of stochastic calculus should see Shimko (1991) and Ritchken (1987).

[2]*A-Pack*, described in the notes to Chapter 3, is a fairly typical example of the type of inexpensive microcomputer-based software that employs the Black/Scholes model for option valuation.

[3]For a more detailed examination of these option pricing models, their evolution and empirical testing, see the references and suggested readings to this chapter.

[4]For a more thorough development of each of these strategies as well as the formulas for the computation of their payoff profiles, see Marshall (1989), Chapters 17 through 20.

References and Suggested Readings

Ball, C. and W. Torous. "On Jumps in Common Stock Prices and Their Impact on Call Option Pricing," *Journal of Finance*, 40 (1985), pp. 155-173.

Ball, C. and W. Torous. "Futures Options and the Volatility of Futures Prices," *Journal of Finance*, 41 (1986), pp. 857-870.

Black, F. "The Pricing of Commodity Contracts," *Journal of Financial Economics*, 4 (1976), pp. 167-179.

Black, F. and M. Scholes "The Pricing of Options and Corporate Liabilities," *Journal of Political Economy*, (May/June 1973), pp. 637-59.

Bodurtha, R. and N. Gonedes. "Tests of the American Option Pricing Model on the Foreign Currency Options Market," *Journal of Financial and Quantitative Analysis*, 22 (1987), pp. 153-167.

Borensztein, E. and M. Dooley. "Options on Foreign Exchange and Exchange Rate Expectations," *International Monetary Fund Staff Papers*, 34 (1987), pp. 643-680.

Cox, J.C. and M. Rubinstein. *Options Markets*, Englewood Cliffs, NJ: Prentice Hall, 1985.

Jarrow, R.A. and A. Rudd. *Option Pricing*, Homewood, IL: Irwin, 1983.

Marshall, J.F. *Futures and Option Contracting: Theory and Practice*, Cincinnati, OH: South-Western, 1989.

Merton, R. "Option Pricing When Underlying Stock Returns are Discontinuous," *Journal of Financial Economics*, 3 (1976), pp. 125-144.

Ogden, J. and A. Tucker. "Empirical Tests of the Efficiency of the Currency Futures Options Market," *Journal of Futures Markets*, 7 (1987), pp. 695-703.

Ritchey, R. "Call Option Valuation for Discrete Normal Mixtures," *Journal of Financial Research*, 13 (1990), pp. 285-296.

Ritchken, P. *Options: Theory, Strategy, and Applications*, Glenview, IL: Scott, Foresman, 1987.

Shastri, K. and K. Wethyavivurn. "The Valuation of Currency Options for Alternative Stochastic Processes," *Journal of Financial Research*, 10 (1987), pp. 283-293.

Shimko, D.C. *Continuous-Time Asset Valuation in Finance: A Primer*, Miami, FL: Kolb Publishing, 1991.

Chapter 15

Multiperiod Options: Caps, Floors, Collars, Captions, Swaptions, and Compound Options

Overview

The instruments we will be discussing in this chapter are similar to the instruments we discussed in Chapter 14 in that they are also options. They differ, however, in that the options discussed in this chapter are multiperiod options or options on multiperiod instruments. In particular, we will be looking at multiperiod interest rate options including interest rate caps, interest rate floors, and interest rate collars. We will also discuss options on interest rate caps, called captions, and options on swaps, called swaptions. Finally, we will discuss compound options.

Multiperiod options are a fairly new product of financial engineering. Nevertheless, they have already proven very successful. When we wrote the first draft of this chapter about a year ago, the next two sentences read "It is exceedingly likely that the logic underlying the multiperiod interest rate options engineered in recent years will be applied in other areas. For example, it is surely only a matter of time before multiperiod currency options and multi-period commodity options are developed." Since writing those lines, multiperiod currency options have been introduced and multiperiod commodity options are about to be introduced. While we do not go into these two forms of multiperiod options in this chapter, their structures are analogous to the multiperiod interest rate options that we do examine.

Multiperiod options are particularly interesting because they are easily combined with other instruments, such as swaps, to engineer interesting payoff profiles and to achieve very specialized solutions to financial problems. We will look at some of the ways that options can be combined with swaps later in this chapter. As in the last chapter, we do not discuss option pricing formulas. The interested reader is advised to see the references to this chapter and the references to the previous chapter.[1]

Interest Rate Caps (Caps)

From the perspective of the hedger, cash settled options, like those written on stock indexes, are limited in their usefulness to those situations in which the hedger is concerned about fluctuations in prices over a short span of time. Think of this span as a single period. In other words, a single cash settlement will terminate the option on its expiration date. But suppose that the firm has a risk exposure that spans multiple periods, one following another. Such a situation might, for instance, occur if the firm is paying a semi-annual floating rate of interest on its long-term debt and is concerned about a rise in rates.

Theoretically, this exposure can be hedged by stringing together a series of single-period interest rate options—one expiring every six months. But this is impractical for two reasons. First, it assumes that each contract delivery month will be sufficiently liquid to enter a contract without substantial liquidity costs. Second, it assumes that options with every required delivery month into the very distant future are currently available. Both assumptions fail. In practice, only the front one or two contract months tend to be liquid—if indeed any are liquid—and conventional calls and puts are almost never written with expiration dates more than a year into the future, although exchange traded long-dated calls and puts have recently been introduced.

The solution involves special over-the-counter options traded in dealer markets. These options are called **interest rate caps** and

interest rate floors. We begin with interest rate caps, known, more simply, as **caps**. The writer of a cap pays the cap holder each time the contract's **reference rate** is above the contract's **ceiling rate** on a settlement date. By this structure, a cap provides a multiperiod hedge against increases in interest rates. It is important to note that even though caps are multiperiod options, the full premiums are ordinarily paid up front.

Most cap dealers, like most swap dealers, are commercial and investment banks. Dealers both buy and sell caps and profit, as usual, from a spread between the bid price and the ask price. The cap premium takes the form of a percentage of the notional principal on which the cap will be written. For example, consider a dealer making a market in 3-year 6-M LIBOR caps with a strike price (**cap rate**) of 8 percent. The dealer might bid 1.28 percent and offer 1.34 percent. That is, the dealer will write a cap for a premium of 1.34 percent and buy a cap for a premium of 1.28 percent. The difference between the bid and ask, 0.06 percent (6 basis points), is the dealer's bid-ask spread.

Before considering the uses of caps, let's take a few moments to examine the structure of a cap and the settlement procedures more carefully. The dealer and the dealer's customer enter an agreement in which they specify a term for the cap (such as two years or five years), a reference rate (such as three-month LIBOR, six-month LIBOR, or three-month T-bill), a **contract** or **ceiling rate** which serves as the cap's strike price and that is sometimes called the **cap rate**, the cap's **notional principal**, and the **settlement dates**. The term of the cap is called its **tenor**. On the first settlement date, the cap writer pays the cap holder a sum determined by Equation 15.1. This sum is recalculated on the calculation date that precedes each settlement date. If the dealer is the cap writer, the dealer will pay the customer any amount due. If the dealer is the cap holder, the customer will pay the dealer any amount due.

$$\text{Dealer Pays} = D \times \text{MAX[Reference} - \text{Ceiling, 0]} \times NP \times LPP \quad (15.1)$$

In Equation 15.1, D denotes a dummy variable that takes the value +1 if the dealer is the cap seller and –1 if the dealer is the cap purchaser; MAX denotes the "MAX function" described in Chapter 14, NP denotes the notional principal, and LPP denotes the length of the payment period. The value LPP will depend on the choice of reference rate and the frequency of payments. For example, LIBOR is quoted actual over 360. Thus, LPP for six-month LIBOR will typically be between 181 over 360 (181/360) and 184 over 360 (184/360). If the calculation results in a positive value (which can only happen if the dealer is the cap writer), then the dealer pays the client. If the calculation results in negative value (which can only happen if the dealer is the cap purchaser), then the client pays the dealer. If the calculation produces the value zero, then no payments are made.

We can use Equation 15.1 to determine the payoff profile for a cap. The payoff profile is drawn for a single settlement date, but it looks the same for each settlement date covered by the cap. Such a payoff profile appears, from the cap purchaser's perspective, in Exhibit 15.1.

Exhibit 15.1
Payoff Profile for a Cap Purchaser
(Per Settlement Period)

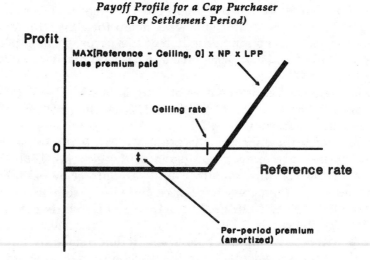

Notice that the cap's payoff profile looks identical to that for the long calls discussed in Chapter 14. But this is misleading. A call option usually depicts *price* rather than *rate* on the horizontal axis. If price is substituted for rate on the horizontal axis of the cap's payoff profile, the payoff profile actually looks like that of a long put on a debt instrument. The reason for this is that rates (yields) and prices are inversely related. This demonstrates that caps are analogous to put options for purposes of developing hedge positions and can accurately be described as multiperiod puts. (Nevertheless, because of the shape of the payoff profile, they are sometimes described as multiperiod calls).

Since the cap is a multiperiod option and the premium for this option is paid up front in a single lump sum, the payoff profile must amortize the premium to be truly representative. Suppose, for example, that a four-year semiannual cap can be purchased for 1.85 percent of the notional principal. Then the premium must be prorated by way of a standard amortization formula. We use Equation 15.2 for this purpose.

$$\text{Per period cost} = \text{Total Premium} + \text{PVAF} \qquad (15.2)$$

where PVAF denotes the *present value annuity factor* given by Equation 15.3.

$$\text{PVAF} = \frac{1 - (y / m)^{-nm}}{y / m} \qquad (15.3)$$

In Equation 15.3, y is the annual yield (discount rate), n is the term of the cap (in years), and m is the number of payment periods per year. For example, suppose that y is 8.00 percent. Then Equation 15.3 yields a PVAF of 6.7327 and Equation 15.2 yields 0.2748. We conclude that the per period value of the premium is 0.2748 percent. This 0.2748 percent is the amortized single period premium for the cap depicted in Exhibit 15.1.

We have chosen here to express the cap premium on a per period basis—in this case a period is six months in length. It is also quite common to express the cap premium as an **effective annual percentage cost**. The per-period cost can be reexpressed as an effective annual percentage cost using Equation 15.4.

$$\text{Effective Annual Percentage Cost} = (1 + \text{PPC})^m - 1 \qquad (15.4)$$

The per period cost is denoted PPC, which is obtained from Equation 15.2. In this example, the effective annual percentage cost is 0.55 percent. It is very useful for the financial engineer to express the premium paid for the cap as an effective annual percentage cost, particularly when he or she is trying to compare alternative financing strategies. In such cases, the financial engineer must reduce all costs to a single effective per-annum rate called **all-in-cost**. (We examine all-in-cost and consider its calculation in Chapter 23.)

The following example shows an interest rate cap at work. Suppose that it is currently 15 February 1993. A firm in need of a 5-year interest rate cap on 6-M LIBOR approaches a cap dealer. The firm and the dealer agree to a ceiling rate of 10.00 percent, notional principal of $50 million, and settlement dates of 15 August and 15 February. The firm pays the dealer the up-front fee for writing the cap. Assume the cap commences immediately and the calculation dates are some set number of days prior to each settlement date. The calculation date is simply the day on which the parties determine how much, if anything, is to be paid on the subsequent settlement date. The amount is determined by the spot value of the reference rate on the **fixing date**. The fixing date serves the same role in caps that the reset date serves in swaps.

Now suppose that the reference rate (6-M LIBOR) at the time of rate setting for the first payment is 10.48 percent. Since the reference rate exceeds the ceiling rate, the dealer must make a payment to the firm. The amount of this payment is determined by Equation 15.1. Substituting the values +1 for D, 10.48 percent for the reference rate, 10.00 percent for the ceiling rate, $50 million for the notional principal, and 181/360 for the *LPP*, we obtain a payment of $120,667. The full set of payments to the firm on this particular cap might look something like that depicted in Table 15.1. (In Table 15.1, the indicated values for the reference rate are for illustration purposes only and do not represent actual rates on any specific dates.)

Table 15.1
The Series of Payments On the Cap

Payment Date	Value of the Reference Rate	Value of the Ceiling Rate	LPP	Payment
15 Aug 1993	10.48	10.00	181/360	$120,667
15 Feb 1994	9.89	10.00	184/360	0
15 Aug 1994	9.24	10.00	181/360	0
15 Feb 1995	8.56	10.00	184/360	0
15 Aug 1995	9.78	10.00	181/360	0
15 Feb 1996	10.18	10.00	184/360	46,000
15 Aug 1996	10.94	10.00	182/360	237,611
15 Feb 1997	12.34	10.00	184/360	598,000
15 Aug 1997	11.08	10.00	181/360	271,500
15 Feb 1998	9.67	10.00	184/360	0
				$1,273,778

Since caps are multiperiod options, the simplest way to price a cap is to decompose it into the actual series of single-period options to which it is equivalent. This series of single-period options is sometimes called a **strip**. The fair value of each of the options in the strip can then be determined by using an appropriate single-period option pricing model. The sum of these fair values is the fair value of the cap. The dealer would then add (or subtract) a sum to this fair value to obtain the price at which it would sell (or buy) such a cap. As noted earlier, the difference between the dealer's bid and ask prices is just another bid-ask spread.

The factors that influence the value of a cap are the same as the factors that influence the value of any option. They include the current level of interest rates, the ceiling rate (strike price) of the cap, the volatility of the reference rate, the current level of the reference rate, and the time to each cash settlement. With this special kind of option, however, we must also consider the tenor of the cap. The longer the tenor, the more valuable the cap.

Caps are priced as a percentage of the notional principal. Thus a cap, like the one above, that the dealer priced at 1.85 would require an up-front payment by the dealer's customer of $925,000. On this particular cap, the dealer ultimately paid out a total of $1,273,778. There was no way, of course, to know in advance what the total payout would be. It could easily have been much less than $925,000 and it also could easily have been much more.

There are many uses for interest rate caps but the most common is to impose an upper limit to the cost of floating-rate debt. For example, suppose a firm raises debt capital by issuing a five-year floating rate note paying six-month LIBOR plus 80 basis points. The firm's management decides that it can handle an annual interest expense up to 10.8 percent but cannot afford to go above 10.8 percent. To limit the potential interest expense on this floating rate note, the firm buys the cap described above from the dealer. Any time six-month LIBOR exceeds 10 percent, the firm must pay more than 10.8 percent to its lenders. But, with the cap in place, the dealer will pay the firm a sum equal to the excess over the firm's 10.8 percent cost and, therefore, the firm's net interest expense on its floating rate note is limited to a maximum of 10.8 percent. On the other hand, when LIBOR is below 10 percent, the firm is paying less than 10.8 percent to its lenders and so it does not need offsetting payments from the dealer. These cash flows are illustrated in Exhibit 15.2.

Financial engineers often combine interest rate caps with interest rate swaps and/or currency swaps. This produces **rate-capped swaps**. Consider a simple example. A firm wants rate-capped float-

Exhibit 15.2
Interest Flows: Cap Dealer, Firm, and Lenders

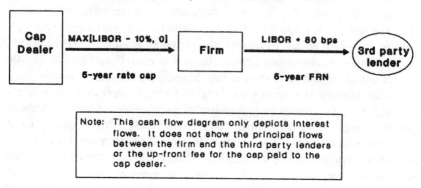

Note: This cash flow diagram only depicts interest
flows. It does not show the principal flows
between the firm and the third party lenders
or the up-front fee for the cap paid to the
cap dealer.

ing-rate debt but the firm has a comparative advantage in the fixed-rate market. It can thus reduce its borrowing cost if it borrows at a fixed rate, swaps its fixed-rate payments for floating-rate payments with a swap dealer, and then caps its floating-rate payments to the swap dealer with an interest rate cap. The interest payment flows associated with these transactions are depicted in Exhibit 15.3. For obvious reasons, there are economies of scale for swap dealers who also make markets in rate caps. The swap/cap dealer depicted in Exhibit 15.3 happens to be a commercial bank.

Exhibit 15.3
Interest Flows on a Rate-Capped Swap

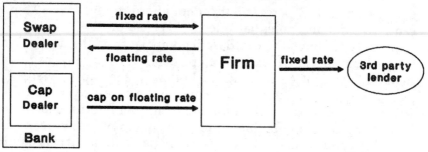

Unlike swaps, which are generally not freely assignable, caps are assignable by their holder. That is, the owner of a cap can sell or otherwise transfer the cap to another party. This assignability is important. For example, it is not unusual for a financial engineer to structure an intermediate- to long-term floating-rate financing for a client firm by employing a commercial paper rollover strategy. The firm for which this strategy is developed, however, may want to cap its floating rate, so the engineer adds an interest rate cap with the six-month commercial paper rate as the reference rate. Should, at some point, the firm decide that it no longer needs the financing (perhaps it has disposed of the assets supported by the financing), it would simply not roll over its outstanding paper upon the paper's maturity. But, while the floating-rate financing has terminated, the cap, for which the firm expended resources, continues to exist despite the fact that the firm no longer has a need for it. A cap, like any option, will have at least some value until such time as it expires. By allowing the firm to assign the cap, the firm can recapture this value. As a practical matter, most cap dealers will buy back a cap at its current fair value less a small discount. We should note that caps *are not* assignable by the writer without the approval of the owner.

Before moving on to rate floors, let's examine one last issue involving interest rate caps that end users must consider: What ceiling rate should an end user purchase? That is, after the reference rate is decided, say six-month LIBOR, at what rate for six-month LIBOR should the ceiling (strike) be set? Should it be 9 percent, 10 percent, or 11 percent? The lower the ceiling, the greater the likelihood that the cap owner will receive payments from the dealer and the greater these payments will be. Obviously, the lower the ceiling rate, the more attractive is the cap from the purchaser's perspective. But, as usual, there is no "free lunch." The lower the ceiling rate, the greater the price the dealer is going to demand for the cap. The question then becomes, how much protection does the end user require and how much is the end user prepared to pay for this protection? We will not try to answer this question yet. As we will see shortly, there are other courses of action that can be pursued to reduce the cost of a cap. This brings us logically to the subject of interest rate floors.

Interest Rate Floors (Floors)

An **interest rate floor** or, more simply, a **floor**, is a multiperiod interest rate option identical to a cap except that the floor writer pays the floor purchaser when the reference rate drops *below* the contract rate, called the **floor rate**. Let's again assume that the dealer is the seller of the option and a customer of the dealer is the purchaser. In this case, the dealer will pay the customer a cash sum, based on a settlement formula, whenever the reference rate falls below the floor rate. The cash settlement formula, which is repeated on each settlement date, is given by Equation 15.5.

$$\text{Dealer Pays} = D \times \text{MAX[Floor} - \text{Reference, 0]} \times NP \times LPP \qquad (15.5)$$

Notice that Equation 15.5 is almost identical to Equation 15.1 except that we have reversed the positions of the strike price (ceiling rate in the case of the cap and floor rate in the case of the floor) and the reference rate in the formula. All other terms are identical. The payoff profiles associated with Equation 15.5 are depicted in Exhibit 15.4. Observe that the payoff profiles are identical to those for the call options that we described in Chapter 14—but only after we recognize that we are using a *rate* in lieu of a *price* on the horizontal axis. Clearly, a floor is a multiperiod call option. (Because of the shape of the payoff profile, however, floors are sometimes described as multiperiod put options.)

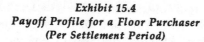

Exhibit 15.4
Payoff Profile for a Floor Purchaser
(Per Settlement Period)

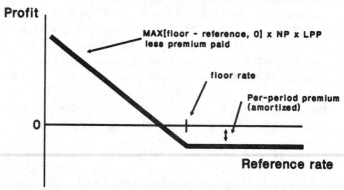

The premium depicted in the single-period payoff profile for the floor, like the premium depicted in the single-period payoff profile for the cap, is an amortized single-period equivalent for the full premium paid up front at the time of the floor purchase. The amortized value of this premium is found in an identical fashion to that for the cap by using Equations 15.2 and 15.3 and this per-period cost can be converted to an effective annual percentage cost using Equation 15.4.

Interest rate floors have been described as the "mirror image" of interest rate caps. But this is technically not correct. The same kind of confusion often arises with calls and puts. The payoff profile for a long call is not the mirror image of the payoff profile for a long put. The mirror image of a long call is a short call and the mirror image of a long put is a short put. This is a direct result of the fact that option trading is, in the language of economics, a zero-sum game. That is to say, the profits to the winners are equal to the losses to the losers. The counterparty to a call purchaser is not a put purchaser. It is a call writer. Similarly, the counterparty to a put purchaser is a put writer. The final proof that long cap payoff profiles and long floor payoff profiles are not mirror images is the readily apparent fact that there is no theoretical limit to how high a reference rate can go, but there is an absolute limit to how low a reference rate can go.

Just as with interest rate caps, financial engineers find many uses for interest rate floors. The most common usage is to place a floor on the interest income from a floating-rate asset. Let's consider a simple case: An insurance company has obtained funds by selling 7.00 percent 10-year fixed-rate annuities. These annuities constitute fixed-rate liabilities. Because the insurance company's managers believe that interest rates are going to rise, they decide to invest the proceeds from the sale of the annuities in floating-rate assets (six-month T-bills) that are currently yielding 7.25 percent. Management's plan is to sell the floating-rate assets after rates rise and then invest the funds in fixed-rate assets.

While management's plan seems quite rational—*fix interest costs now by the sale of the annuities while interest rates are low, invest in floating-rate assets until rates rise, and then move to fixed-rate assets*—management still runs the risk that its interest rate projections might prove wrong. To deal with this risk, a financial engineer suggests the purchase of an interest rate floor. The firm buys a 10-year floor with a floor rate of 7.00 percent and the six-month T-bill rate as the reference rate. For this floor, the firm pays an up-front premium of 2.24 percent, which is equivalent to an annual percentage cost of 0.34 percent at a discount rate of 7 percent (compounded semi-annually). The firm is now protected from declines in rates. The full structure of this strategy is depicted in Exhibit 15.5.

As it happened, management's interest rate projections proved wrong—at least for a time. Rates declined and stayed below the floor rate for four years. During this time, the insurance company received payments from the floor dealer. These payments made it possible for the insurance company to meet its obligations to the holders of its annuity policies. About four and a half years after the commencement of the floor, interest rates began to rise and about five years after the commencement of the floor, the insurance company converted its floating-rate assets into five-year fixed-rate assets yielding 8.375 percent. At the same time, the insurer sold what remained of the floor back to the dealer for 0.82 percent. While the firm held it, the floor performed exactly as required. It spared the insurance company serious financial damage by guaranteeing a minimum return on its floating-rate assets.

Exhibit 15.5
Interest Flows: Floor Dealer, Firm & Annuity Holders

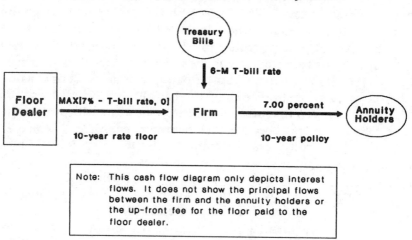

Like interest rate caps, interest rate floors can be, and often are, married to swaps.

The examples we used above to illustrate the cap and the floor both involved end users who were purchasers of these interest rate options. Not all end users will be purchasers. One interesting situation, in which the end user is a floor seller, involves a combination of a cap and a floor known as a **collar**. We consider this type of interest rate option in the next section.

Interest Rate Collars (Collars)

An interest rate collar is a combination of a cap and a floor in which the purchaser of the collar buys a cap and simultaneously sells a floor. Collars can be constructed from two separate transactions (one involving a cap and one involving a floor) or they can be combined into a single transaction. A collar has the effect of locking the collar purchaser into a floating rate of interest that is bounded on both the high side and the low side. This is sometimes called **locking into a band** or **swapping into a band.**

Consider an example: Suppose that a firm holds fixed-rate assets that are yielding 10 percent. These assets are funded with floating-rate liabilities tied to the prime rate. The current rate on these liabilities is 8 percent and the firm wants to cap the cost at 9.5 percent (called a **prime cap**). But, as it happens, the cap dealer wants an up-front premium which translates into an effective annual percentage cost of 0.5 percent for the prime cap. The firm feels that this is too high a price to pay. But, as it happens, the firm discovers that it can sell a prime floor with a floor rate of 7 percent for a premium equivalent to an effective annual percentage return of 0.45 percent. Since the firm is the seller of the floor it receives the premium. The firm decides to buy the cap and sell the floor—effectively purchasing a collar.

From the firm's perspective, its annual costs are now bounded between 7 percent and 9.5 percent. Since its interest revenue exceeds its interest cost, it has locked in a source of net revenue for the firm, although the amount of the revenue can vary within the bounds dictated by the collar. When prime rises above 9.5 percent, the dealer pays the firm the difference. When prime falls below 7 percent, the firm pays the dealer the difference. The payoff profile for the interest rate collar is depicted in Exhibit 15.6 and the cash flow diagram is depicted in Exhibit 15.7.

Exhibit 15.6
Payoff Profile for a Collar Purchaser
(Per Settlement Period)

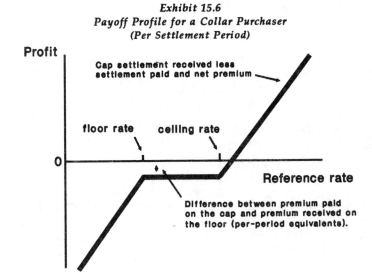

Exhibit 15.7
An Interest Rate Collar at Work

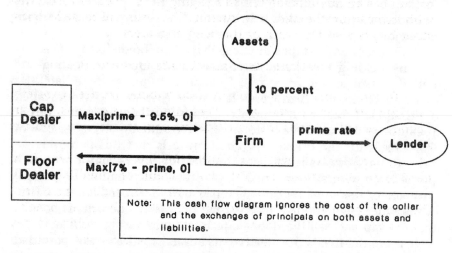

Note: This cash flow diagram ignores the cost of the collar and the exchanges of principals on both assets and liabilities.

By entering a collar, the firm is able to place an interest rate cap on its floating-rate liabilities while simultaneously reducing the cost of the cap with the premium received from the sale of the floor. The cost to the firm, of course, is the payouts the firm must make to the floor dealer should the reference rate fall below the floor rate. This potential payout by the firm in a low-rate environment is often of less concern then its uncapped payouts in a high-rate environment and, consequently, the collar is considered an attractive way to cap floating-rate debt.

Just as financial engineers often combine caps and floors with swaps, so also can collars be combined with swaps. Such a combination is called a **collar swap** or **mini-max swap**. The cash flow diagrams for a collar swap are depicted in Exhibit 15.8.

Exhibit 15.8
A Collar Swap at Work

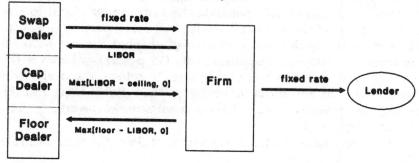

A dealer making markets (**running a book**) in caps, floors, and collars has an obvious interest in hedging the exposures associated with its positions in these instruments. The design of these hedging strategies is also the work of financial engineers.

Miscellaneous Interest Rate Options

To complete our look at multiperiod options, we need to briefly consider a few miscellaneous types of interest rate options. In particular, we will discuss the participating cap, the caption, and the swaption.

A **participating cap** is structured for the end user who is in need of an interest rate cap but who is unable or unwilling to pay the up-front cost of the cap. The end user could reduce the cost of the cap by entering into a collar, but the collar reduces the benefits from a decline in rates and the end user may not be willing to pay this price. One solution, the participating cap, is for the purchaser to pay the dealer a portion of the difference between the reference rate and the ceiling rate when the reference rate is below the ceiling rate and for the cap writer to pay the cap purchaser the usual full difference between the reference rate and the ceiling rate when the reference rate is above the ceiling rate. The payment formula for the participating cap appears as Equation 15.6.

$$\text{Dealer Pays} = D \times [\text{MAX}[RR - CR, 0] + (-PF \times \text{MAX}[CR - RR, 0])] \times NP \times LPP \qquad (15.6)$$

Here, RR denotes the reference rate, CR denotes the ceiling rate, and PF denotes the percentage factor. All other notation is the same as that used earlier for caps and floors.

Let's consider a simple case. A firm in need of a five-year cap on a floating-rate liability tied to one-year LIBOR approaches a cap dealer. The firm wants its rate capped at 10 percent on notional principal of $40 million. The dealer agrees to sell such a cap for an up-front premium of 2.75 percent. The firm cannot afford to pay such a large up-front fee so the dealer suggests a participating cap. The firm will pay the dealer 30 percent of the difference between the reference rate and the ceiling rate (10 percent) whenever the reference rate is below the ceiling rate. In return, the dealer will pay the firm the full difference between the reference rate and the ceiling rate whenever the reference rate exceeds the ceiling rate. The firm agrees.

One year later, on the first settlement date, the reference rate (one-year LIBOR) stands at 9.42 percent. Plugging the values into Equation 15.6, we obtain the sum –$70,566.67. Since this value is negative, the firm is paying the dealer. This calculation is repeated for each settlement period for five years.

Dealer Pays = +1 × [MAX[9.42% – 10.00%, 0] +
              (–30% × MAX[10.00% – 9.42%, 0])]
              × $40 million × 365/360
            = –$70,566.67

The second special type of interest rate option is actually an option on an option. Technically, it is a call option on a cap. This type of interest rate option, called a **caption**, was introduced in the mid 1980s. The term *caption* is a registered servicemark of Marine Midland Bank.

The question that immediately occurs is why an option on an option? The answer is surprisingly simple. Sometimes a firm wants to lock in the *right* to interest rate risk protection but it is not really sure that it will need the protection, or, the firm may feel that a better alternative may become available if it waits a while. In these situations, financial engineers will suggest a caption or a caption-like instrument.

Consider an example: The CFO of a firm is considering a seven-year floating-rate financing. He will be making a pitch to the firm's board for permission to go ahead. The CFO knows that the board will be concerned about the firm's exposure on a floating-rate financing and so the firm will need an interest rate cap. The CFO's bank, which makes markets in options, assigns a financial engineer to work with the CFO. This engineer suggests a 10.00 percent interest rate cap currently available for an up-front premium of 2.25 percent. The CFO does not know if the board will approve his funding plans and so he cannot commit immediately. The board will decide in two weeks. But by the time the board does approve the plan, the cost of the cap may have risen. To deal with this problem, the financial engineer suggests an option on the cap that is good for three weeks. For this option, the CFO agrees to pay the bank a premium of say 0.15 percent.

If the board approves the funding proposal, the CFO can notify the bank that he is exercising the firm's option on the cap. The bank then commits to a cap on the original terms, i.e., an up-front fee of 2.25 percent. If the board rejects the funding plan, the CFO lets the option on the cap expire.

To see the other use for an option on a cap, suppose that the board approves the funding plan but, in the intervening two weeks, the reference rate has declined considerably so that the same cap can be purchased for 1.95 percent. Should the CFO exercise the option on the cap? Clearly not. If he does, he will pay a premium of 2.25 percent. He can just as easily negotiate a new cap at a premium of only 1.95 percent. Thus, even though the board approves the funding plan, the CFO lets the option expire.

Just as a bank can make a market in options on caps, so can it also make a market in options on floors. These are not nearly as widely used as options on caps, however, and so we will not address them.

The final type of option we will consider in this section is the swaption. A **swaption** is an option on a swap. Such options can be written on interest rate swaps, currency swaps, commodity swaps, and equity swaps. (Equity swaps are discussed in Chapter 25.) The concept is nearly identical to an option on a cap. The end user and the swap dealer agree to the terms of a swap. The end user, however, cannot or does not want to make an immediate commitment to the swap. At the same time, the end user cannot afford to take the chance that the market will evolve unfavorably between now and the time when the end user can commit. To lock in the terms of the swap, the end user agrees to purchase a swaption from the swap dealer. Thus, the dealer guarantees the terms of the swap for some period of time—perhaps one month, for example—during which the end user can choose to exercise the swaption or simply let it expire. As always, the end user will be required to pay a premium for the swaption. This premium is lost whether the end user chooses to exercise the swaption or not.

Monetizing Embedded Options

In Chapter 10, the authors suggested a number of strategies that their hypothetical client firm, XYZ Corporation, could employ to hedge its strategic exposures and/or to adjust its short-term financial position. Among these were suggestions to purchase interest rate options and to enter interest rate and currency swaps to hedge certain exposures. At one point, the authors pointed out that XYZ had some embedded options in some of its asset/liability/equity positions. The authors suggested that current earnings might be enhanced by "monetizing the embedded options."

Because that discussion preceded our look at swaps and options, the reader was probably puzzled by the authors' meaning when they said "monetize the embedded options." That should no longer be the case. If a firm holds embedded options in its assets, in its liabilities, or in its equity accounts, the firm can write options (single or multiperiod depending on the nature of the embedded options) that offset the embedded options. Because the selling firm holds offsetting options, the firm can be viewed as writing covered options. The value of the embedded options, which would otherwise accrue to the firm over a period of time, is converted to an immediate monetary value by the firm's act of writing offsetting options. This is what the authors meant by "monetizing the embedded options."

It is important to appreciate that monetizing embedded options does not provide a free lunch. It merely transforms future value to present value. If markets are efficient at pricing options, the net gain in value will, generally, be small. However, the timing and/or the tax benefits can be sizeable depending on the nature of the embedded options, the volatility of the firm's earnings, and the firm's tax status (pending tax credits, tax loss carry forwards, etc.)

Compound Options

Compound options are options on options. The only explicit example of such an option that we have considered thus far is the caption. This option on a cap is a clear case of an option on an option, but less subtle forms of compound options exist as well.

Many financial instruments which were not designed to be options in the sense of representing an explicit *right without obligation* can nevertheless be viewed as options. The explanation for this is a bit complex and the reasoning is a bit intricate. But it is worth examining because it provides important insights into the market's valuation process.

Consider the case of a corporate bond that is not default free. The corporate bond is issued by the firm and represents an obligation of the firm. But, the firm is owned by its shareholders and it is, therefore, an obligation of the shareholders. If the firm defaults on its bond, then the shareholders surrender the firm to the firm's creditors. The firm's shareholders thus have an option. They can service their debt by making the required payments or they can surrender the firm to its creditors. Now, suppose that the bond has N years to maturity and pays an annual coupon. Denote these coupon payments by C_i where $i = 1,2,3,...,N$. There is also a final payment representing repayment of principal. Denote this payment by P_N.

Now, at time 1, the payment C_1 is due. The shareholders have the option to pay or to default. If they pay, then they acquire a new option. That is, they acquire the option to pay C_2 at time 2 or to default at time 2. If the shareholders do not pay, then they have allowed their "option to pay" to expire and they do not acquire a new option. If the shareholders do pay, then with each payment they make, they acquire a new option. Thus, with each payment, the exercise of the option to pay the required amount due brings the shareholders a new option and thus each option, barring the last, may be viewed as an option on an option. In this sense, a corporate bond is a compound option. This is illustrated in Exhibit 15.9.

Exhibit 15.9
A Risky Bond as a Compound Option

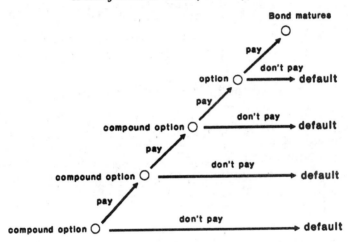

There are many other subtle examples of compound options that have been discussed in the literature. For example, it can be argued that common stock itself is a compound option, that standard operating leases are compound options, and that life insurance is a compound option.[2]

Consider the case of a standard operating lease. The lessee and the lessor enter a lease agreement allowing the lessee to use the lessor's asset(s). The lessor cannot recoup the asset prior to the end of the lease agreement unless the lessee fails to make the required lease payments in a timely manner. Thus, with each lease payment, the lessee is exercising an option to acquire another option—namely whether or not to make the next lease payment.

The life insurance example is also easily argued. Consider the case of a renewable term life insurance policy. If the insured makes the required payments, then he or she acquires the right, but not the obligation, to renew the contract for the next term. Thus, the decision to pay a premium constitutes an option on an option.

In closing this chapter on options, we should stress that there are very clear economies of scale for dealers that make markets in swaps to also make markets in related risk-management instruments. It is not surprising then that swap dealers also make markets in forward contracts, caps, floors, collars, options on caps, options on floor, and swaptions. Financial engineers can piece these instruments together and couple them with traditional capital market instruments, such as stocks and bonds, to achieve fascinating financial structures.

Summary

Interest rate caps and interest rate floors are multiperiod options that can be used for multiperiod hedging. A similar result can be obtained using a strip of single-period puts or a strip of single-period calls. Recognition of this latter relationship is the key to understanding the pricing of caps and floors. The primary use of caps is to place a ceiling on the cost of floating-rate liabilities and the primary use of floors is to place a lower limit on revenue received from floating-rate assets.

It is very important when costing an interest rate option to reexpress the premium as an effective annual percentage cost. This allows the cost of one financing or risk management alternative to be objectively compared to others. The conversion of a multiperiod option premium to an effective annual percentage cost is a relatively simple exercise in time value arithmetic.

Caps and floors can be combined to produce collars and other special configurations. They can also be combined with swaps to produce rate-capped swaps and rate-floored swaps. Sometimes, it is useful to buy an option on a cap, called a caption, or an option on a swap, called a swaption.

Captions are one type of compound options but there are many others as well. The key to seeing this is to think of other "nonoption" instruments in an option context. When viewed in this way, risky bonds, common stock, leases, and life insurance policies can all be seen to be compound options.

Dealers in swaps find that there are economies of scale to be enjoyed if they also make markets in caps, floors, collars and other interest rate options. It is not surprising then that such institutions try to maintain a broad line of risk management instruments and employ financial engineers capable of making the instruments work for their client firms.

Endnotes

[1] The reader interested in the mathematics of option pricing models should consider several of the following: Marshall (1989), Ritchken (1987), Cox and Rubinstein (1985), and Jarrow and Rudd (1983).

[2] The pricing of compound options has been examined by Geske (1977, 1984). Geske's also developed a model for valuing compound options, but its applicability is somewhat limited and we do not consider it here. These options are discussed in Ritchken (1987).

References and Suggested Readings

Black, F. and M. Scholes. "The Pricing of Options and Corporate Liabilities," *Journal of Political Economy* (May/June 1973), pp. 637-59.

Cox, J.C. and M. Rubinstein. *Options Markets*, Englewood Cliffs, NJ: Prentice Hall, 1985.

Degler, W. "Selecting a Collar to Fit Your Expectations," *Futures Magazine*, 18(3) (March 1989).

Geske, R. "The Valuation of Corporate Liabilities as Compound Options," *Journal of Financial and Quantitative Analysis*, 12 (November 1977), pp. 541-52.

Geske, R. and H. Johnson. "The Valuation of Corporate Liabilities as Compound Options: A Correction," *Journal of Financial and Quantitative Analysis*, 19 (June 1984), pp. 231-32.

Haghani, V.J. and R.M Stavis. "Interest Rate Caps and Floors: Tools for Asset/Liability Management," Bond Portfolio Analysis Group, Salomon Brothers (May 1986).

Fall, W. "Caps Vs Swaps Vs Hybrids," *Risk*, 1(5) (April 1988).

Jarrow, R.A. and A. Rudd *Option Pricing*, Homewood, IL: Irwin, 1983.

Marshall, J.F. *Futures and Option Contracting: Theory and Practice*, Cincinnati, OH: South-Western, 1989.

Ritchken, P. *Options: Theory, Strategy, and Applications*, Glenview, IL: Scott, Foresman, 1987.

Tompkins, R. "The A-Z of Caps," *Risk*, 2(3) (March 1989).

Chapter 16

Fixed Income Securities

Overview

This chapter examines the cash markets for fixed income securities. Fixed income securities are those private and public sector issues that meet any one of three criteria: (1) pay a fixed sum each period, (2) pay a sum to be determined by a formula, or (3) guarantee a fixed sum (or formula amount) upon maturity. The first criterion allows for traditional fixed rate debt and preferred stock; the second criterion allows for floating rate debt; and the third criterion allows for zero coupon bonds.

The fixed income securities markets are one of the favorite stomping grounds of financial engineers. As a result, these markets have witnessed dramatic innovations over the last decade. To get a flavor of this innovation, one need only examine some of the thousands of tombstones published in the financial press each year. In order to understand these innovations, however, one must first be familiar with the basic instruments that have long been the mainstay of the capital and money markets. The purpose of this chapter is to provide an overview of the various fixed income securities markets. Specifically, we will look at the markets for U.S. government debt, corporate debt and preferred stock, mortgage debt, and the Eurodollar/Eurobond market.

In the next chapter, we look more specifically at some of the recent innovations in the structure of the markets and the instruments that trade in the markets.

Primary versus Secondary Markets

In any discussion of securities, we need to distinguish between the primary and secondary markets. The primary market is the market through which the initial distribution and sale of securities takes place. The proceeds of these sales, less distribution costs, are funneled through to the issuer. The secondary market is the market in which existing holders (investors) transfer their claims on an issuer to other investors. These transactions result in a change of ownership of the securities but do not generate any additional proceeds for the issuer.

The market for U.S. government debt includes the debt of various U.S. government agencies. Our primary interest, however, is in the direct debt of the U.S. Treasury. The Treasury issues debt instruments in order to finance current budget deficits and to carry the national debt. The market is very liquid and the instruments are relatively homogeneous. The primary market for Treasury debt is made by the Federal Reserve Bank of New York which holds periodic auctions. Participating in this auction process are some forty primary government securities dealers. These dealers purchase the debt for resale to other intermediary institutions and for resale to investors. These government securities dealers, aided by brokers and smaller securities dealers, also make the secondary market in Treasury securities.

The market for corporate debt includes an array of debt instruments. Some have long maturities while others have very short maturities. Some issues are of high quality while others are of very low quality. For these reasons, the market for corporate debt is less homogeneous than the market for Treasury debt. It is also considerably less liquid, although the degree of liquidity varies considerably by issuer and by issue. The primary market for most corporate debt is made by investment banks acting in the role of underwriters. Some corporate issuers, however, place short term debt directly with investors. The secondary market consists of two parts: an OTC dealer-type market for wholesale transactions (large denomination) and an exchange-type market for retail transaction (small denomination). The latter market is made by the New York Stock Exchange.

The mortgage market is a classic example of financial engineering at work. For many decades, mortgages were routinely held until maturity by the institutions that originated them. During the last two decades however, it has become common practice to pool mortgages and issue security interests in the pools. This process of **securitization** has since been applied to other types of debt. There are actually two levels at which we can think of the primary market in mortgages. At the first, we have the originating financial institutions that approve loan applications and fund borrowers. At the second level, we have the various organizations that distribute the pooled securities. The distribution of pooled securities is a cooperative effort of the organizations that guarantee the pools and the dealers that purchase them for resale.

The Eurobond/Eurodollar market originated in London in the early 1960s as a way to put U.S. dollars, held outside the United States, back to work. After a slow start, the Eurobond/Eurodollar market grew rapidly and, today, it is a centerpiece of the world financial system. Both the primary and secondary markets for Eurobonds are made by investment banks and commercial banks. The Eurodollar market is primarily an interbank market.

The Cash Market for U.S. Treasury Debt

The United States Treasury routinely issues Treasury bills (T-bills), Treasury notes (T-notes), and Treasury bonds (T-bonds) in its effort to finance the ongoing needs of the United States government. These instruments are sold at periodic auctions held by the Federal Reserve Bank of New York. The funds are used to refund existing debt, called **refunding**, and to raise new money. The principal bidders at Treasury auctions are **primary government securities dealers**. They enter competitive bids for the securities and then resell the securities to the ultimate investors. As already noted, the Federal Reserve and the primary government securities dealers make the primary market for Treasury securities. Government securities dealers, including the primary government securities dealers, also make an active secondary market in Treasuries. They buy and sell in an effort to profit from the difference between their bid and ask prices.[1] Most government securities dealers are commercial banks or investment banks and most engage in a variety of other activities as well.

The government securities market is the least regulated of all securities markets. For this reason, this market has been the market of choice for those interested in experimentation and innovation. For example, the government securities market gave rise to the first widely accepted zero coupon products and also gave birth to the repo/reverse market. (These recent innovations are discussed in Chapter 17.)

The Instruments

Treasury bills are issued in maturities of three months (13 weeks or 91 days), six months (26 weeks or 182 days), and one year (52 weeks or 364 days). In addition, the Treasury occasionally issues very short-term **cash management** bills to cover funding gaps. Unlike conventional notes and bonds, T-bills do not pay periodic interest coupons. Instead, they are sold at a discount from face value and redeemed at face value. The interest is then the amount of the discount. For this reason, these instruments are correctly viewed as short-maturity zero coupon bonds.

Since 1977, T-bills have been issued exclusively in **book-entry form.** This means that there are no physical certificates evidencing ownership. Instead, ownership is evidenced by entries in a computer data file. The computer data file constitutes the "book." At present, T-bills represent about 40 percent of all outstanding Treasury debt. Interest on T-bills is exempt from state and local taxes, but the interest is subject to federal income taxation.

T-bill yields are not quoted on the same basis as bond yields. Instead, yields on bills are quoted on a **bank discount basis** (also known as **discount basis** and, sometimes, as **bank basis**). The bank discount yield (BDY) understates the true yield relative to the conventional yield measure for bonds. To see this, we will consider a quick example: Suppose that a newly issued 26 week (182 day) T-bill having a face value of $100,000 is sold to yield 9 percent BDY. The amount of discount is calculated using the actual number of days (actual) in the life of the bill but assuming the year has only 360 days. The precise formula for determining the amount of discount is given by Equation 16.1 in which *DD* denotes the amount of dollar discount, and *FV* denotes the face value of the bill.

$$DD = FV \times BDY \times \frac{Actual}{360}$$

(16.1)

In this example, the calculation is:

$$DD = 100,000 \times 9\% \times \frac{182}{360}$$

$$= 4,550$$

The investor purchasing this $100,000 six-month T-bill would actually pay $95,450. This purchase price (or present value) is obtained by deducting the amount of discount from the face value of the bill. This relationship is given in Equation 16.2.

$$\text{Purchase price} = FV - DD \qquad (16.2)$$

As already noted, a T-bill is simply a short-term zero coupon bond. In this example, the T-bill may be viewed as a zero coupon bond purchased for $95,450 and redeemed 182 days later for $100,000.

The bank discount yield understates the true yield for two reasons. First, the bank discount yield calculates the amount of discount on the basis of the bill's face value even though the investor actually pays a price that is less than face value. Second, interest is paid on all days (182 in this example) even though the daily interest rate assumes that the year only has 360 days.

Note and bond yields are quoted on the basis of what is called a **bond equivalent yield** (BEY). Bond equivalent yields are also known as **coupon equivalent yields**. In the jargon of the market, this is called **bond basis** and it is the yield to maturity that equates the present value of the instrument's cash flows to its current price when the yield is stated on the assumption of semiannual compounding. The discount yield may be converted to a bond equivalent yield (BEY) when the bill has a maturity of six months or less by Equation 16.3. Notice that the bond equivalent yield employs actual days over 365 while the discount yield uses actual over 360.

$$BEY = \frac{365 \times BDY}{360 - (BDY \times Actual)} \qquad (16.3)$$

Using Equation 16.3, the BEY on the bill in our earlier example is found to be 9.56 percent. Another way to get this same result *when the T-bill is precisely six months from maturity* is to treat the bill as a zero coupon bond and exploit a simple present value/future value relationship. The necessary relationship is given as Equation 16.4

$$FV = PV \times (1 + k) \qquad (16.4)$$

where *FV* is $100,000, *PV* is $95,450 and *k* is the periodic discount rate. Solving for *k* yields 4.76689 percent. But this discount rate represents a period of only 182 days. To reexpress the rate on the basis of 365 days, we must multiply by 365 over 182. This adjustment produces a bond equivalent yield of 9.56 percent. A more general formulation that will make an accurate BDY to BEY conversion for T-bills having *any* number of days to maturity is provided in an appendix to this chapter.

The difference between the discount yield and bond yield measures is clearly quite substantial. Such a difference in yield measures cannot be ignored in strategies designed to arbitrage across maturities or across instruments. For example, it would not be illogical to employ an arbitrage strategy requiring one to be long an instrument yielding 9.20 percent (discount basis) and short an instrument yielding 9.50 percent (bond basis). The uninitiated, however, would clearly think it foolish to hold an asset yielding 9.20 percent at a cost of 9.50 percent. Such exploitable situations are ready made for the talents of financial engineers.

By convention, bond equivalent yields assume semiannual compounding. As a result, they are not equivalent to effective annual rates of return. An effective annual rate of return is often called a **simple rate of interest** and it is the clearest, most direct way to compare alternative investment opportunities. An effective annual rate of return (ROR) can be obtained from a bond equivalent yield using Equation 16.5.

$$ROR = (1 + \frac{BEY}{2})^2 - 1 \qquad (16.5)$$

In the case of the T-bill used in the example above, the effective annual rate of return is found to be 9.79 percent. The calculation is depicted below.

$$ROR = (1 + \frac{0.0956}{2})^2 - 1$$

$$= 9.79 \text{ percent}$$

Thus, a 182-day T-bill with a quoted yield of 9 percent, using the customary bank discount basis, provides an investor with an effective annual rate of return 9.79 percent.

The conversion from discount basis to bond basis for bills that have maturities greater than six months (182 days) is considerably more complex than Equation 16.3.[2] Those involved in the trading of these instruments, however, need not concern themselves with the actual calculations; traders invariably have computer-based analytics at their disposal that provide the converted values. As already noted, Appendix 1 to this chapter provides one method of making the BDY to BEY conversion for T-bills of any maturity. As a side point, while it is customary to quote bond equivalent yields on the assumption of semiannual compounding, there are times when a different compounding frequency is called for. This is acceptable provided that the user specifies the frequency. For example, one-month bond basis, three-month bond basis, or annual bond basis call for a bond equivalent yield stated on the assumption of twelve compoundings, four compoundings, and one compounding per year, respectively. The procedure for converting semiannual bond basis to another compounding frequency is given in Appendix 2 to this chapter.

While the conversion of discount yields to bond equivalent yields makes T-bills and coupon bearing securities more directly comparable, a different conversion is necessary to make T-bills comparable to interest-bearing money market instruments, such as certificates of deposit and LIBOR, which are quoted on a **money market basis,** sometimes called a **yield basis.** The yield itself is called a **money market yield.** In this case, our goal is to make the yield on a discount instrument, stated actual over 360, equivalent to the yield on an interest-bearing instrument, which is also stated actual over 360. The problem is that an instrument quoted on a discount basis pays interest on the full-face value *even though the purchaser only pays the discount price* to get the instrument. An instrument quoted on a money market basis also pays interest on the full face value but, in these cases, the *purchaser really does pay the full face value* to get the instrument. The money market yield (MMY) is obtained from the bank discount yield using Equation 16.6.

$$MMY = \frac{360 \times BDY}{360 - (BDY \times actual)} \tag{16.6}$$

The 9 percent bank discount yield we used in our previous example is equivalent to a money market yield of 9.43 percent. The calculation is as follows:

$$MMY = \frac{360 \times 0.09}{360 - (0.09 \times 182)}$$

$$= 9.43 \text{ percent}$$

The different conventions used for quoting yields on different instruments is very important in the pricing of such risk management instruments as futures, swaps, and forward rate agreements. For example, in a typical fixed-for-floating interest rate swap, the

floating-rate is usually tied to LIBOR—the rate of interest on interbank lendings of Eurodollar deposits. LIBOR is quoted as a money
market yield, actual over 360. On the other hand, the fixed-rate
side of a swap is usually quoted on a bond equivalent basis and,
hence, actual over 365. The different conventions used for quoting
fixed and floating rates becomes particularly important when pricing
off-market swaps and the different conventions for quoting yields on
money market instruments becomes very important when pricing basis
swaps. (**Basis swaps** are floating-for-floating rate swaps in which the
two rates are tied to different money market instruments.)

Treasury notes and Treasury bonds both carry semiannual coupons and are often referred to, collectively, as **coupons** to distinguish
them from the Treasury's discount instruments. Treasury notes are
sold with original maturities from two to ten years. More specifically, they are sold in original maturities of two, three, four, five,
seven and ten years. There is a regular issue cycle for each of these
maturities. For example, 2-year notes are issued monthly and 4-year
notes are issued quarterly. Treasury bonds have original issue maturities of 30 years. The issue of 20-year bonds was discontinued
in 1986. Treasury bonds are issued quarterly as part of the Treasury's
quarterly refunding cycle.

Because notes are issued frequently and in different maturities,
there are multiple issues of similar maturity at any given time. For
example, a five-year original maturity note has a four-year maturity
after one year. Of course, a new four-year note also has a four-year
maturity. The most recently issued of any given maturity is considered the current issue. The current issues are the most liquid
and trading in them is active. Trading in all maturities greater than
10 years is active. Many investors and traders prefer to be in actively
traded issues in order to be assured of the liquidity necessary to exit
positions quickly and cost effectively. The actively traded issues (most
current issues of any given maturity) are called the **on the runs**. The
demand for the on the runs is greater than the demand for **off the
run** securities and traders pay a premium to be in the on the runs.
Consequently, investors who buy coupon Treasuries with the intention
of holding them to maturity will generally do better by buying off
the run securities. Coupons with less than a year to maturity tend to
be very illiquid. For this reason, those with an interest in trading
short-maturities are much more inclined to trade bills.

Treasury note and bond yields are quoted as bond equivalents.
While secondary market trading takes place in terms of price (as a

percentage of par value), the auctions are held in terms of yield. The Treasury announces a new auction at least one week in advance and then solicits competitive bids. Bidders submit secret bids to two decimal places, e.g., 8.63 percent, and the quantities desired. The Treasury then awards the issue to the lowest yield bidder first and progresses upward until the full issue is sold. The highest accepted bid (which translates to the lowest accepted price) is called the **stop out bid**, or, when translated to a price, the **stop out price**. The Treasury then sets the issue's coupon to the nearest one-eighth of a percentage point so that the average price paid is as close to par as possible without exceeding par. Each successful bidder is then charged a price that corresponds to its bid and the bond's coupon. Some bidders will pay a premium, others a discount, and some will pay par. The difference between the average bid and the stop out bid is called the **tail**.

Noncompetitive bids for small denomination bidders are accepted at Treasury auctions. All noncompetitive bidders pay the average competitive bid price.

The secondary market in Treasuries is quite active except as noted above. Bills trade in terms of yield but notes and bonds trade in terms of price. On the run bid-ask spreads tend to be very narrow; one thirty-second is typical and one sixty-fourth is not unusual. Off the run spreads are considerably greater, often running to an eighth (1/8) or more.

The Cash Market for Corporate Debt and Preferred Stock

Like the United States Treasury, financial and nonfinancial corporations (including banks) in the United States issue large quantities of debt. These issues include both long and short maturities and both fixed- and floating-rate instruments. The type of instrument issued will depend on the nature of the issuer (bank or nonbank), the length of time the funds are needed, the type of collateral available, the type of interest rate desired (fixed or floating), and the all-in cost of the different financing alternatives available. In this section, we examine fixed-rate and floating-rate securities, beginning with the former.

Fixed-Rate Instruments

The intermediate- to long-term fixed-rate instruments include notes and bonds. The short-term fixed-rate instruments include commercial paper and certificates of deposit.

Notes and bonds are intermediate- to long-term promissory notes of issuing corporations. Notes have original maturities of 10 years or less and bonds have original maturities of more than 10 years (20 or 30 years is typical). Short-maturity issues are often not callable but long-maturity issues usually are. For the remainder of this section, we will use the term *bond* to include both bonds and notes.

Issuers are most likely to call a callable issue after interest rates have declined. In these cases, the funds necessary to retire the issue can be obtained by issuing new debt at the prevailing lower interest rates. Recall from Chapter 8 that callable bonds expose their holders to call risk. To protect investors from a call accomplished with proceeds obtained from a new issue of debt securities, bond indentures often contain **refunding restrictions** which specifically bar the issuer from calling the bond with funds from this source. It is important for investors in corporate bonds to distinguish between protections from call and protections from refunding. The former is an absolute protection from a call while the latter is only protection from a call accomplished via funding from new debt issues.

Bonds are classified with respect to a number of characteristics. These include the issuer, the purpose of the issue, the type of security pledged on the issue, the method of interest payment, and the method of repayment. Bond rating agencies distinguish between types of issuers, which are lumped into several major categories. For example, Moody's lists four categories: public utilities, transportations, industrials, and banks and financial corporations. Each of these categories can be more finely divided. For example, public utilities can be divided into gas distribution companies, electric power companies, telephone companies, and so on. Even finer subdivisions are possible. Electric utilities, for example, can be divided into nuclear based and nonnuclear based.

The title of a bond often gives a clue to the issuer's purpose in issuing the bond, but title alone is not a reliable indicator. Some bonds issued to raise funds that will be used to retire an existing debt issue (refunding) or to change the mix of debt to equity in the firm's capital structure (debt-for-equity swaps). Other issues are used to finance specific acquisitions or other forms of corporate investment. Sometimes, the purpose is to raise funds for discretionary corporate purposes—having an available war chest for corporate takeovers, for example.

Bonds are also classified by the type of security pledged by the issuer. Security can take the form of a pledge of real property, a pledge of personal property, or a guarantee by another entity. Bonds secured by real property are called **mortgage bonds.** In a mortgage bond, the issuer grants the bondholders a first-mortgage on some or all of its property. Such bonds are often issued as part of a series, with the holders of each series having an equal claim to the mortgaged property in the event of default. Some bond indentures allow for new series to be issued and added to the first-mortgage, others do not. Not all series need have the same maturity and, often, multiple series, each with its own maturity, are issued simultaneously. Bonds secured by personal property, securities and inventory for example, are called **collateral trust bonds.** The personal property constitutes the collateral.

Some bonds are guaranteed by another entity. For example, an issuer with a weak credit rating might persuade a firm with a strong credit rating to guarantee its debt. The issue then gets the rating of the guaranteeing entity which reduces the coupon necessary to sell the issue at par. This kind of guarantee is quite common in parent/subsidiary relationships. Not surprisingly, such bonds are called **guaranteed bonds.** When no security or guarantee is available, the issue is called a **debenture.** In the event of default, the debenture holders become general creditors of the issuer. At times, corporate issuers will sell **subordinated debentures.** In the event of default, claims by holders of these instruments are satisfied only after the claims of general creditors have been satisfied. To reduce the coupon necessary to sell debentures and subordinated debentures, issuers will often make such instruments convertible to other assets—usually some number of shares of the issuer's common stock. These are called **convertible debentures.**

Bonds may be **bearer bonds** or **registered bonds.** The ownership of bearer bonds is evidenced by the physical securities. The owner of the bond collects interest by clipping the appropriate coupon and sending it to the designated paying agent. For this reason, bearer bonds are sometimes called **coupon bonds.** Neither the issuer nor the issuer's agent keeps a record of the ownership of bearer bonds. Registered bonds may be **fully registered** or **registered as to principal only.** The issuer, or issuer's agent, keeps continuous track of the ownership of fully registered bonds and sends the coupon payments and principal repayment without any action on the part of the bondholder. When registered as to principal only, the holder must still send the appropriate coupon in order to collect interest.

While most bonds require the periodic payment of fixed amounts of interest (the coupon) and any failure to pay the coupon in full or on time constitutes a default, there is an exception. The exception is income bonds. **Income bonds** provide for a fixed coupon, but the issuer, under terms specified in the indenture, can elect not to pay a coupon, without triggering default, upon the occurrence of certain events. In this sense, these bonds are very much like preferred stock. Missed coupon payments may be cumulative or noncumulative. An income bond is **cumulative** if missed coupons must be paid at a later date. If not, the bond is **noncumulative**.

Bondholders typically expect their principal to be repaid at the time of the bond's maturity. Most longer-term corporate bonds, however, are callable: That is, the issuer has reserved the right to demand that the bond be returned in exchange for the call price stipulated in the bond's indenture. The call price is usually the bond's par value plus a **call premium**. At one time, the call premium was routinely set at one year's interest, but, today, the call premium is usually set on a sliding scale and grows smaller as the bond approaches maturity. Interest stops accruing on bonds that have been called, so holders of called bonds have a financial incentive to turn them in immediately. Call features are often associated with **sinking fund provisions.** When sinking funds were first introduced, they most often provided that the issuer would periodically place funds in escrow in order to assure that the issuer would have sufficient funds on hand to retire the issue at maturity. Today, sinking fund provisions typically require the orderly retirement of the issue over its life. This usually means retiring a specified minimum portion of the issue each year. This can be accomplished in either of two ways: The issuer can provide sufficient funds to the trustee and the trustee will randomly select bonds to call, or, the issuer can purchase the bonds in the open market and tender these bonds to the trustee. The latter course is preferable from the issuer's perspective when the bonds are trading below the call price.

There is a difference between a **serial bond** and a bond that is retired by periodic calls. When a bond is callable, no holder knows if his or her bond will be called and, if so, when that call will occur. In a serial bond, the bond is divided into a number of series each with a specific maturity date and a specific coupon.

Thus, the purchaser of a serial bond can specify which series he or she wants and thereby know, quite precisely, when that bond will be redeemed (assuming that it is not also callable).

As already noted, the primary market for public offerings of corporate debt is made by investment banks acting in the role of **underwriter**. The underwriter buys the issue from the issuing firm at a discount from the **offering price**. The underwriter then sells the issue to investors, at the offering price, either directly or through a **syndicate** established for this purpose. From the issuer's perspective, the difference between the issue's par value and the proceeds actually received represents a **flotation cost**.[3] This is not, however, the only cost associated with a debt issue. The issuing firm is also required to bear some miscellaneous expenses and these miscellaneous expenses must be included when considering the total cost of floating a new debt issue.

The secondary market for domestic (U.S.) corporate bonds consists of two parts—an exchange market and an over-the-counter (OTC) market—both of which are centered in New York City. The New York Stock Exchange lists a great many specific bond issues and trading in these issues does take place on a floor of the New York Stock Exchange designated for this purpose. The bulk of bond trading however is made in an OTC dealer market by several dozen investment banks. Some regional firms also make a market in bonds but not on the same scale as the New York investment banks. The dealers provide quotes, which include both bid and ask (offer) prices. They stand ready to buy or sell at any time and they make their income from the bid-ask spread. Dealers usually keep their inventories hedged against interest-rate risk.

While individual investors do purchase corporate bonds, the bulk of investment activity is on the part of **institutional investors**. Institutional investors include insurance companies, mutual funds, pension funds, and so on. Such investors often have very specific maturity needs and bonds fit these needs quite well. The market made by bond dealers is largely a **wholesale market**. That is, it is a market for large denomination trades with narrow bid-ask spreads and, consequently, appeals to institutional investors. The exchange-based trading is largely a **retail market**. That is, it is a market for small denomination trades with wider bid-ask spreads. It appeals to small investors.

The liquidity of bond issues is measured by the volume of trading in the issue and by the size of the bid-ask spread. As a general rule, the greater the volume of trading, the narrower will be the spread.

Banks issue intermediate- and long-term debt in order to leverage up their returns. Bank regulators count such issues as part of a bank's capital for purposes of meeting capital requirements. Regulators, however, prefer equity capital to debt capital as a cushion against bank losses.

Our discussion of the intermediate- and long-term debt issues of domestic corporations applies equally well to banks. When we get to the short-term markets, however, there is a significant difference. Corporations issue short-term liabilities called **commercial paper** while banks and other depository institutions issue short-term liabilities called **certificates of deposit**. While both of these instruments are lumped together under the general heading of money market instruments, we will look at them separately.

Commercial paper is an unsecured promissory note with a maturity of 270 days or less.[4] For a long time, commercial paper, like T-bills, was sold at a discount from face value. Increasingly, however, commercial paper is marketed with add-on interest. In either case, the yield is quoted on a bank discount basis.

Commercial paper is issued both by industrial corporations and by financial corporations. **Industrial paper** is issued through a handful of commercial paper dealers who sell the paper to institutional investors. Financial corporations place most of their paper directly, but some finance company paper is placed through dealers. The largest firm engaged in the direct placement of its own commercial paper is General Motors Acceptance Corporation or GMAC and, consequently, GMAC's paper rates are important industry benchmarks.

Commercial paper is an effective financing tool for firms with investment grade ratings when funds are only needed for a short period of time. Interestingly, however, commercial paper is also used as the foundation of an intermediate- to long-term financing strategy. In such a strategy, a firm issues commercial paper with the intent of refunding the paper by periodically rolling the paper over. For example, a firm might need funds for four years. Rather than issue a four-year note, the firm might choose to issue six-month paper and then roll this paper over seven times, with six-month maturities each time, until the funding need terminates.

There are several good reasons why a firm might choose to finance with successive short-term **rollovers** rather than a single intermediate-term note issue. First, when the yield curve is upward sloping, the normal situation, the short end of the yield curve offers the lowest rates. Thus, short-term financing is cheaper than intermediate-term financing. If the yield curve does not change, each successive paper issue will cost the firm less than the coupon on an intermediate-term note. Second, the flotation costs for paper are a small fraction of the flotation costs for note and bond issues. For example, a four-year note issue might involve a discount to the underwriter of 4.5 percent of the offering price. On commercial paper, this might be as little as one-eighth of one percent per year. Over a four-year period, this translates to only one-half of one percent. Third, the amount of finance needed might change periodically. With an intermediate-term note issue, the issuer might find itself overfinanced if some or all of the assets the financing supports are prematurely liquidated. In the case of commercial paper, the firm can easily reduce the amount of funding on subsequent rollovers. A final reason for employing a series of paper rollovers instead of a single fixed-rate note issue involves the nature of the assets supported by the financing. If the assets' return is responsive to changes in interest-rates, so that return rises when rates rise and return falls when rates fall, then a series of paper rollovers might be a better match than intermediate- or long-term financing by way of a note or bond. Each time the paper is rolled over, the issuer agrees to pay the then prevailing rate on paper of the given maturity. While the rate is fixed for the life of the paper, it is better viewed as floating over the life of the entire financing. That is, in our example, the series of rollovers can be viewed as a four-year financing in which the rate is reset every six months. If the assets are interest-rate responsive and the supporting liabilities are also interest-rate responsive, then the issuer has a natural interest-rate hedge.

The user of the commercial paper rollover strategy is of course, subject to the risk that rates might rise before the next rollover. If the assets are not interest-rate responsive, then the user of the paper rollover strategy is exposed to considerable interest-rate risk. For example, suppose that a firm sells six-month paper at 7.5 percent and uses the proceeds to purchase three-year automobile receivables yielding 9.9 percent after costs. If the yield curve does not change at all, then each new rollover resets the firm's cost of funds at 7.5 percent. But suppose that the yield curve shifts sharply upward in response to a tightening in monetary policy and the next paper issue is sold at 10.4 percent. The return on the receivables is now below the firm's cost of funds. The interest-rate risk posed by long-term financing using the commercial paper with rollover strategy can be eliminated by coupling the strategy with a fixed-for-floating interest rate swap or by the purchase of an interest rate cap. (These strategies have already been discussed so we will not go into them here.)

The yield on paper is always higher than the yield on T-bills of similar maturity. The spread reflects the small, but ever present, risk of default that can occur on paper and a modest difference in the tax treatment of the interest earned on these money market instruments (T-bill interest is exempt from state income tax while paper interest is not). While the yields on T-bills and commercial paper may be different, they do track each other rather closely—but not perfectly. Historically, however, paper rates have been some-what more volatile than T-bill rates.

Unlike T-bills, there is no active secondary market in commercial paper and purchasers generally hold it to maturity. Nevertheless, both dealers and direct placers generally guarantee liquidity by standing ready to buy back their paper at any time.

The bank counterpart of commercial paper is negotiable certificates of deposit otherwise known as CDs. A CD is a receipt from a bank for funds deposited at the bank for a specific period of time and at a specific rate of interest. CDs have maturities of at least seven days and can run to several years. Original issue maturities of less than thirty days are, however, not very common. Similarly, original issue maturities of more than one year are also uncommon.

CDs are issued by all major money center banks and many regional banks as well. Yields are somewhat higher than T-bills of similar maturity. There is a viable secondary market for the CDs of well-established issuers but, for most issues, the bid-ask spreads are considerably greater than those in the more homogeneous T-bill market.

Banks can achieve long-term financing via CDs using the same type of rollover strategy we described for issuers of commercial paper. The strategy is often used, by both banks and thrifts, to finance long-term fixed-rate assets such as conventional mortgages. This gives rise to interest-rate risk and makes these institutions logical candidates for risk-management programs.

Before leaving this section, it is worth considering the degree to which the various money market rates track one another. We have already indicated that the tracking or, in statistical terms, the "correlation," is not perfect. Exhibit 16.1 depicts 36 weekly observations for the T-bill rate, the commercial paper rate, and the CD rate (all 3-month maturities) for a selected period in the mid 1980s. The vertical axis has been expanded to make it easier to distinguish between the three interest-rate paths.

Exhibit 16.1
Comparative Money Market Rates

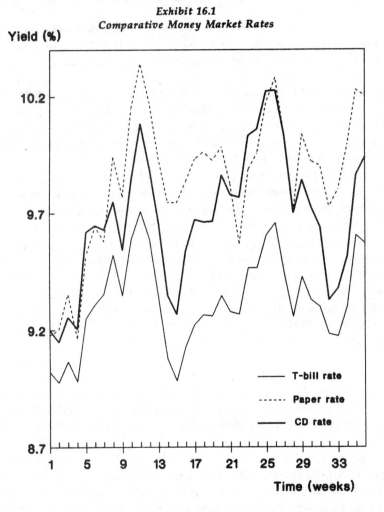

Notice in Exhibit 16.1 that the three curves do track each other closely, but the spread between them is not fixed. The fluctuation in the spread is the source of a special kind of risk called basis risk. Preferred stock is the last category of fixed income securities that we will review in this section. As its name suggests, **preferred stock** is a class of equity that endows its owners with certain preferences over common stockholders. For this reason, preferred stock is sometimes referred to as senior equity.

Preferred stock is, in many ways, similar to debt. Nevertheless, it is equity. Unlike common stock, preferred stock ordinarily pays a fixed dividend. This fixed dividend may be stated as a percentage of the par value of the stock or as a fixed dollar amount. Regardless, preferred shareholders are entitled to receive the full amount of their dividend before the common stockholders receive any dividend at all.

In addition to their first claim on dividends, preferred shareholders also have a claim on assets that comes before that of common shareholders in the event of liquidation. But, the claims of preferred shareholders are subordinate to those of debt holders. Thus, preferred stock occupies a niche between that of debt and that of common stock equity.

Most preferred stock is cumulative. This means that if management elects not to pay the preferred dividend when it is due, then the dividend accumulates and the full accumulation must be paid before any dividends are paid on any preferred stock junior to the issue in question and before any dividends are paid to common shareholders. Other financial restrictions on management also typically come into play when preferred dividends are in arrears. A less restrictive variation on the cumulative feature is **cumulative-to-the-extent-earned.** In this case, unpaid dividends on the preferred stock only accumulate to the extent that the firm has sufficient earnings to pay them but elects not to do so. This latter variation, however, is rare.

Because the preferred dividend is ordinarily fixed, preferred stock is often described as nonparticipating. This term reflects the fact that the preferred shareholders do not participate in the financial good fortunes of the firm should the firm's earnings increase. This is the price that preferred shareholders pay for the security of their fixed dividend and their senior position.

While preferred stock is very much like debt, the size of the market is much smaller. For example, there are about four times as many public corporations having publicly issued corporate debt as there are corporations having publicly issued preferred stock. What's more, the issuers tend to be concentrated in the electric utility industry. For example, during the 1980s, approximately 75 percent of the outstanding preferred stock issues and about 65 percent of the outstanding preferred stock par value was issued by this one industry. The reason for this was explained in an earlier chapter. In brief, the dividends paid by one corporation to another are largely exempt from federal taxation at the level of the recipient corporation. Thus, low-tax industries attract corporate investors. The earnings of the electric company can be passed to the preferred shareholders who then enjoy some tax-sheltered income.

Preferred stock may be **voting** or **nonvoting.** Nonvoting preferred shareholders do not have the right to vote on matters of interest to the shareholders. This right is reserved for common shareholders. While most preferred stock is nonvoting, some issues do grant the preferred shareholders voting rights. Still other issues grant the preferred shareholders **contingent voting rights.** In these cases, the preferred shareholders have a voting right if and only if they are not paid their dividends in full.

Preferred stock is most often issued when the issuing corporation believes that this method of raising capital is the cheapest or most flexible of the alternatives available to it. But, if interest rates decline, the outstanding preferred may subsequently prove costly. To handle such a development, the issuing corporation will insist on the inclusion of one or more provisions to allow for the redemption of the stock. These include provisions to call the stock, redemption by a sinking fund, or conversion into common stock. Indeed, it is not uncommon for an issuer to include both a call provision and a conversion provision. In such a situation, the issuer can force the preferred holders to convert their preferred stock into common stock or face a call. This strategy, called a **forced conversion,** only works, of course, when the conversion value is greater than the call price.

A great many specialty provisions and features for preferred stock have been engineered in recent years. These include all kinds of interesting attachments to the preferred stock, such as warrants and other sweeteners.

Floating-Rate Instruments

We have already demonstrated how short-term fixed-rate instruments, such as commercial paper and certificates of deposit, can be rolled over to provide intermediate- to long-term financing that has a floating-rate character. Although each short-term instrument pays a fixed rate, the rate is revised with each rollover and, in this sense, the overall financing strategy has a floating rate. An alternative way to achieve a floating rate on an intermediate- to long-term financing is to issue a single, intermediate- to long-term, instrument with a floating-rate coupon. Floating-rate debt, also sometimes called variable-rate debt or adjustable rate debt, is an obligation in which the interest rate is periodically reset in response to changing market conditions. These corporate instruments are called, collectively, **floating rate notes,** and are known by the buzzwords **FRNs** and **floaters.** Banks also issue floating rate securities called **floating-rate CDs.** We will explain these instruments together.

Floating rate notes are bond-type debt instruments that have floating-rate coupons rather than the fixed-rate coupons that characterize more conventional long-term debt instruments. The term floating rate note is often used generically to mean any type of debt security in which the coupon is adjusted periodically to reflect changes in the rate to which the coupon is pegged. These periodic adjustments may be made very frequently, say monthly, or only occasionally, say once every several years or so. For example, a floating rate note with a four-year maturity might have its coupon reset every six months. A one-year floating-rate CD might have its interest rate reset once a month.

As used more narrowly, the term floating rate note is taken to mean an intermediate- to long-term debt security whose interest rate is pegged to a short-term rate or rate index and adjusted frequently—more than once a year. For example, the rate to which these instruments' coupons are pegged might be the prime rate, the 26-week T-bill rate, or a six-month commercial paper index.

Floating rate notes originated in Europe. They first appeared in the United States in 1973. The U.S. market for FRNs grew rapidly thereafter and, for a time, demand for these new instruments far exceeded the quantities offered.[5]

By offering a floating rate note, a corporate issuer can achieve nearly the same outcome as if it had employed the commercial paper rollover strategy. For example, a corporation with a top investment grade rating can sell a four-year note with a floating rate tied to the rate on top tier six-month commercial paper. Every six months the coupon is reset for the following period. The coupon rate is reset, on predetermined reset dates, to the rate prevailing on those dates for top tier six-month paper.

What factors should a firm consider when choosing between

a floating rate note and a paper rollover strategy? There are a several important considerations. First, the firm should compare the rate at which it can issue paper to the rate at which it can issue a floating rate note. While the rates will generally be close, they will not necessarily be identical. Purchasers of the notes are committing their funds for an extended period of time and may demand a premium to compensate for a possible deterioration of the issuer's creditworthiness over the life of the instrument. Second, the issuer should compare the flotation costs associated with the financing alternatives. Finally, commercial paper is a short-term liability and, therefore, not always counted as part of the issuer's capital. A note with a maturity greater than one year, on the other hand, is counted as part of the issuer's capital. The firm's long-term-debt-to-total-capitalization ratio and other measures of financial leverage can, therefore, be affected by the choice of financing alternatives.

Another way to achieve floating-rate financing is for the firm (or bank) to issue an intermediate-term fixed-rate note and then employ a fixed-for-floating interest rate swap strategy to convert this fixed-rate obligation to a floating-rate obligation. This latter possibility will be considered in more detail in later chapters. Again, the same factors mentioned above must be considered when the issuer chooses among the available alternatives. It would, of course, help greatly if we could reduce the choice to a single quantifiable value. All-in cost is the value most often used for this purpose.

All-in cost is the total cost of a financial transaction including the interest expense, front-end and/or underwriting fees, periodic servicing fees, etc. This cost is typically stated as a per annum rate and can be thought of as the mirror image of an internal rate of return. Consider an example: A domestic corporation provides variable rate financing to purchasers of its products. In order for the corporation to provide financing to one of its larger customer, it needs to raise $20 million of new capital. To hedge interest-rate risk, the corporation would prefer floating-rate financing to fixed-rate financing. The corporation considers the all-in cost of two financing alternatives.

The first alternative is to sell $20 million of floating rate notes. The corporation estimates that the notes can be sold at par if it offers a coupon equal to the 26-week T-bill rate plus 1.5 percent. Suppose that the all-in cost, including the cost of underwriting the issue, is determined to be the T-bill rate plus 1.85 percent.

The second alternative is to sell $20 million of fixed-rate notes and then to swap this fixed-rate debt into floating-rate debt. Suppose that the fixed-rate debt can be sold at par with a coupon of 9.25 percent, and that this can be swapped for six-month LIBOR plus 0.25 percent. Finally, suppose that six-month LIBOR is almost perfectly correlated with the 26-week T-bill rate and that six-month LIBOR averages 0.5 percent over the 26-week T-bill rate. Given this, this form of floating-rate financing will cost the firm the 26-week T-bill rate plus 0.75 percent. After including the underwriting costs of the fixed-rate note issue and any front-end fees for the interest rate swap, suppose that the all-in cost from this latter financing alternative is determined to be the 26-week T-bill rate plus 1.15 percent. After comparing the all-in costs of the two alternatives, the corporation in this example chooses the fixed-rate note issue coupled with an interest-rate swap.

We have deliberately avoided a careful examination of the cash flows and the calculation of all-in cost in this brief presentation of this cost-comparing approach. We will, however, take a very careful look at these cash flows and the calculation of all-in cost in Chapter 23.

All floating rate debt must specify an objectively measurable market-determined rate—often called a benchmark or reference rate—to which the instrument's rate can be pegged. Further, this rate must not be easily manipulated by interested parties. Common benchmarks include the CD rates (one month, two months, etc.), prime rate, T-bill rates (one month, two months, etc.), Fed funds rate, commercial paper rates, the Twelfth District cost of funds, and, of course, LIBOR.

The Cash Market for Mortgage Debt

A mortgage is a loan secured by real property such as a building or land. In the residential mortgage market, the subject of this section, the borrower approaches a mortgage lender for a loan. If approved, the lender provides sufficient funds for the purposes of the borrower (usually funds to purchase the property) and the borrower signs a document agreeing to repay the loan, together with interest, according to some payment schedule. Since most mortgage lending involves amortization of the loan principal, the payment schedule is sometimes called an **amortization schedule**. The document constitutes the **mortgage**. The borrower is called the **mortgagor** and the lender is called the **mortgagee**. The mortgage must be serviced; that is, mortgage payments must be collected and recorded, real estate taxes must be collected and passed along to the appropriate taxing jurisdictions, and foreclosure proceedings must be instituted in the event of a default.

In a conventional mortgage, which is becoming increasingly rare, the mortgage rate is fixed for the life of the mortgage and the mortgage payments are all of equal size. For the latter reason, these mortgages are often called **level-payment mortgages.** Payments on residential mortgages are usually made monthly, but other payment frequencies are possible. Mortgages amortize over their lives so that each payment includes both interest and principal. Since each payment includes some repayment of principal, the mortgage balance (the remaining principal) gets progressively smaller with each payment. This makes conventional mortgages self-amortizing forms of debt. Conventional mortgages typically have a term of 30 years but shorter terms are not uncommon. Since each payment includes some principal, each subsequent payment must include less interest since the mortgage balance declines with each payment. If each payment is the same size but the interest component is declining, the principal component must get larger with each payment. Portions of a typical mortgage amortization schedule appear in Exhibit 16.2.

Exhibit 16.2
Conventional Mortgage Amortization Schedule

Payment Number	Total Payment	Principal Component	Interest Component	Principal Balance
1	1,755.15	88.48	1,666.67	199,911.52
2	1,755.15	89.22	1,665.93	199,822.30
3	1,755.15	89.96	1,665.19	199,732.33
.	.	.	.	.
180	1,755.15	390.84	1,364.31	163,326.60
.	.	.	.	.
251	1,755.15	704.51	1,050.64	125,371.88
.	.	.	.	.
358	1,755.15	1,712.10	43.05	3,453.35
359	1,755.15	1,726.37	28.78	1,726.98
360	1,741.37	1,726.98	14.39	0.00

Notes: Starting principal on loan $200,000
   Mortgage rate 10.00 percent
   Term 30 years, monthly payments

Source: *A-Pack: An Analytical Package for Business*

As can be seen in Exhibit 16.2, the early mortgage payments are mostly interest while the latter mortgage payments are mostly principal. Mortgagors are usually permitted to make payments on their mortgages in excess of that which is required. Such excess payments are called **prepayments** and are credited directly against the mortgage balance.

In recent years, mortgage lenders have been discouraging borrowers from taking out conventional fixed-rate mortgages in favor of **adjustable rate mortgages**, known colloquially as **ARMs**. There are many variants of ARMs but they all share one common characteristic—the mortgage rate may change in response to changing market conditions. To persuade borrowers to take these mortgages, the originating institution often provides an artificially low mortgage rate for the first year or so. This initial low rate is aptly described as a **teaser rate**. Following the period in which the rate is artificially held below market, the rate adjusts to a market level. Thereafter the rate periodically adjusts to keep pace with market conditions. Such mortgages often have **caps** on each rate revision as well as **life-time caps**. These caps are intended to protect the mortgagor from excessive changes in mortgage rates.

ARMs are themselves a product of financial engineering but the engineering did not stop with adjustable rates. Indeed, financial engineers have been active in the mortgage markets and have produced an interesting assortment of mortgage variants including graduated payment mortgages, graduated equity mortgages, pledged account mortgages, shared appreciation mortgages, and reverse annuity mortgages. While these latter mortgages represent relatively small segments of the overall mortgage market, they are nevertheless interesting in that they are indicative of the kind of innovative thinking characteristic of financial engineers.

Graduate payment mortgages (GPMs) differ from traditional level-payment mortgages in that not all the payments are the same size even though the interest rate is fixed over the life of the mortgage. The payments start out at a low level and then, at one or more points in time, adjust to a new higher level for some period of time. At some point however, the payments become equal for the remainder of the mortgage. There are a number of variants on this basic theme, but the principal involved is fundamentally the same. The payment schedules associated with GPMs are such that they usually involve a period of **negative amortization**. Negative amortization implies that the mortgage principal (loan balance) increases because the loan payment fails to cover the periodic interest—at least during the early years.

Graduated equity mortgages (GEMs) are the purest form of graduated payment mortgages. In such mortgages, the interest rate is fixed for the life of the mortgage but the monthly payment grows larger each and every month. Such mortgages can be structured so that the payments increase by a fixed dollar amount each month or by a fixed percentage amount each month.

Pledged account mortgages (PAMs) are an interesting example of financial engineering at work. From the mortgagor's (borrower's) perspective they resemble graduated payment mortgages in that the payments get larger over time; but, from the mortgagee's (lender's) perspective they resemble traditional level payment mortgages. This dichotomy is achieved by placing a sum of money (usually part or all of the down payment) in a special account that is used as collateral on the mortgage and which can only be used to pay down the mortgage. The mortgagor now makes a payment which is below that required on the traditional level payment mortgage with the difference made up by a contribution from the pledged account. Thus, the mortgagee receives the same sum that would be received had the mortgage been of the traditional level-payment variety.

Shared appreciation mortgages (SAMs) were first engineered in the early 1980s. They were developed in an effort to provide an alternative to the high mortgage rates then prevailing which had been brought about by a long period of accelerating inflation. Such mortgages are characterized by a rate of interest substantially below the market rate and a provision for the mortgagee to share in the profits resulting from any increase in the value of the property either upon the maturity of the mortgage, the sale of the property, or some other specified time.

All of the nontraditional mortgages we have considered thus far were engineered to make mortgages more accessible to young home buyers who often have insufficient current income to carry a conventional home mortgage. The last type of nontraditional mortgage we will consider was designed to service a very different clientele. These mortgages are called **reverse annuity mortgages (RAMs)** and are designed for homeowners with substantial equity in their homes. In these mortgages, the mortgagee (lender) makes periodic annuity-type payments to the mortgagor (homeowner/borrower) and the mortgagor repays this series of loans with a single lump-sum payment at the end. This cash flow pattern is the reverse of that typical in all other types of mortgages and, hence, the name. Reverse annuity mortgages are ideal for elderly people with substantial equity in their homes who require additional income to make ends meet. The reverse annuity mortgage allows these homeowners to monetize the equity in their home. With each payment they receive from the mortgagee, the homeowner's equity declines.

Mortgage lending was, at one time, a very routine affair. Using customer deposits as their primary source of funds, banks and thrifts originated mortgages that they then placed in their portfolios. These mortgages were serviced by the originating institution and held by that same institution until maturity. Of course, with its funds tied up in existing mortgages, the institution was unable to originate additional mortgages until either (1) it had collected sufficient repayments from existing mortgagors, or (2) attracted additional deposits.

In an effort to add liquidity to the secondary mortgage market, Congress sponsored the creation of several organizations, the last of which was the **Government National Mortgage Association (GNMA)**, more popularly known by its nickname **Ginnie Mae**, which was created in 1968. Since 1970, GNMA has provided a vehicle for the pooling and guaranteeing of mortgages. The GNMA guarantee covers the full and timely payment of both interest and principal. Once pooled and guaranteed, undivided interests in the pools, called **passthrough certificates** or **participation certificates,** are sold to investors.

Variations of the basic mortgage passthrough are also issued by other federally sponsored organizations including the Federal Home Loan Mortgage Corporation (FHLMC), nicknamed Freddie Mac, and the Federal National Mortgage Association (FNMA), nicknamed Fannie Mae, and by a number of private parties—usually large commercial banks. The nature of the guarantee provided by these organizations varies. FHLMC, for example, guarantees the timely payment of interest and the ultimate, but not necessarily timely, payment of principal. Private issuers of passthroughs may or may not purchase payment guarantees (insurance). The rest of our mortgage-oriented discussion will concentrate on GNMA passthroughs.

The pooling process separates the mortgage from the mortgage servicing function. The mortgage originator may keep the servicing rights or may sell them to another institution. The servicing rights have value because of a fee collected by the servicing agent. For example, in the GNMA pool, the servicing fee is set at 44 basis points (calculated on the principal balance) that is deducted from the mortgage interest. Six additional basis points are paid as a fee (premium) to GNMA for its guarantee. Together, these deductions total 50 basis points (one-half of one percent). Thus, a 10.75 percent mortgage coupon will return, if sold at par, 10.25 percent to investors in the passthroughs. This rate is called the **passthrough rate**.

In addition to the revenue derived from mortgage servicing fees, the mortgage originator also derives profit from the points it charges the borrower to originate the mortgage. A **point** is defined as one percent of the mortgage principal. The funds made available by the sale of the mortgages can be used to originate additional mortgages which, in turn, produces additional revenue from points collected on the new originations and from new servicing fees.

The pooling of mortgages, whether government sourced or privately sourced, has dramatically transformed the mortgage market. It is now routine for banks and thrifts to originate mortgages, pool them, and sell off the pools (either keeping the servicing rights for themselves or selling the servicing rights to another institution). While the pools themselves are large ($1 million dollars is the minimum size and most are considerably larger), the passthroughs can be purchased in denominations as small as $25,000. Thus, they appeal to many private investors. The structure of the passthrough market is depicted in Exhibit 16.3.

Exhibit 16.3
Interest Flows in GNMA Passthroughs
(conventional mortgages)

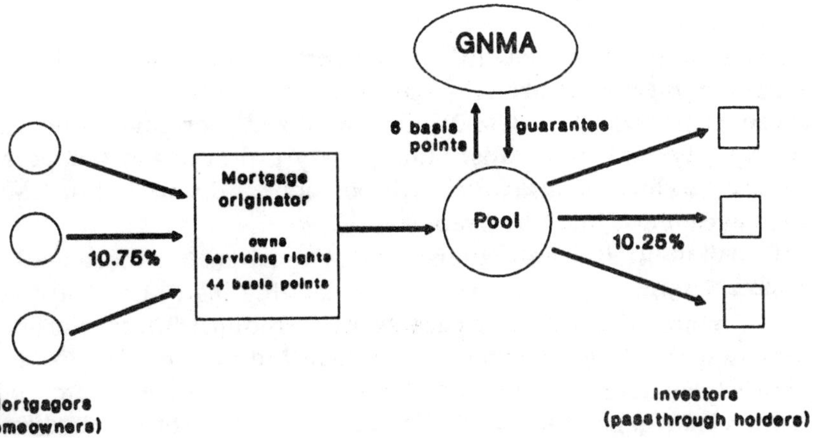

Because mortgage passthroughs represent undivided claims on the mortgage pool—meaning that each passthrough owner holds a *pro rata* claim to all interest and principal repayments—the investor in passthroughs is subject to both reinvestment risk and substantial prepayment risk. Further, if the investor sells the passthroughs prior to their maturities, he or she is also exposed to considerable interest-rate risk. The source of the interest-rate risk is the same as for any other debt instrument and, therefore, we do not discuss it further. The reinvestment risk and the prepayment risk, however, require a little more explanation. Recall that mortgages are amortizing forms of debt. That is, the investor receives periodic payments that include principal as well as interest. Since the periodic payments on amortizing debt are larger than the periodic payments on non-amortizing forms of debt, the reinvestment risk is greater on passthroughs than on coupon-bearing Treasury and corporate bonds. The prepayment risk stems from the fact that the mortgagors have the right, which they frequently exercise, to prepay all or part of the mortgage balance. That is, they may pay back the principal before they are required to do so. These prepayments are passed along to the holders of the passthroughs who must then reinvest. Prepayments occur for a variety of reasons including the sale of the home, a sudden availability of funds for the homeowner, the death of the homeowner, or a refinancing of the mortgage in response to lower interest rates. The last of these reasons accounts for the greatest number of prepayments on mortgages that are written during periods of high interest rates. A great deal of research has gone into modeling prepayment behavior.[6]

From the beginning, the prepayment risk problem has been a bane to investors. In June of 1983, in an effort to address this problem, investment banks, led by the First Boston Corporation and Salomon Brothers, introduced **collateralized mortgage obligations,** commonly known as **CMOs.** Collateralized mortgage obligations were a dynamic innovation and quickly captured a major portion of the mortgage market. We will postpone a discussion of CMOs, however, until the next chapter.

While a large percentage of newly originated mortgages are sold off soon after origination, most lending institutions still keep some mortgages in their investment portfolios. These mortgages are supported by customer deposits, including the CDs discussed earlier. For these lending institutions, interest rate mismatches between mortgage assets and CD liabilities are a very real concern.

Other holders of mortgage portfolios are also exposed to the various forms of mortgage related risk and the management of these risks has attracted a great deal of attention by financial engineers in recent years. We postpone discussion of this work, however, until a later chapter.

The International Debt Markets

When talking about the international debt markets, we must distinguish between domestic issues and foreign issues. Domestic issues are debt issues of governments, corporations, and other entities, sold within the country of the issuer and in the currency of the issuer. Dollar denominated U.S. Treasury bonds and U.S. corporate bonds sold in U.S. markets are examples of U.S. domestic issues. German government and German corporate bonds denominated in deutschemarks and sold in Germany are domestic deutschemark issues. Foreign issues are debt issues sold in one country and currency by an issuer of another country. Deutschemark denominated bonds sold by a U.S. corporation in Germany or dollar denominated bonds sold by a German corporation in the U.S. are examples of foreign issues. For purposes of a consistent framework for discussion, we will assume throughout the remainder of this section that the domestic market is the United States.

We often distinguish between issues denominated in dollars, called **U.S.-pay,** from issues denominated in other currencies, called **foreign-pay.** The prices of U.S.-pay issues respond to changes in U.S. interest rates and the prices of foreign-pay issues respond to changes in foreign interest rates. We will begin this section with a discussion of U.S.-pay foreign bonds.

In the early 1960s, a small market in U.S.-pay and foreign-pay bonds began to develop in London. This market became known as the **Eurobond market.** Eventually, trading in Eurobonds spread to other European centers and, still later, spread to countries outside of Europe. Despite the extension of the market to non-European countries, the market for these bonds continued to be called the Eurobond market. The Eurobond market grew rapidly during the 1970s and exploded in the 1980s. This explosive growth is largely explained by the ready availability of currency swaps beginning in the early 1980s. Indeed, today, the bulk of the funds raised through the sale of Eurobonds are swapped into other currencies—a spillover effect of the amazing success of the swap product.

Since its inception, the Eurobond market has been dominated

by U.S.-pay issues. This has changed somewhat in the last few years but dollar-pay bonds still account for more than 50 percent of the total new-issue volume. German-pay bonds are the next most important and now account for upwards of 15 percent of new-issue volume.

U.S.-pay Eurobonds are often called **Eurodollar bonds.** They share three characteristics: (1) they are denominated in U.S. dollars; (2) they are underwritten by an international syndicate; and (3) they are sold at issue to investors outside the United States. Because the bonds are sold outside the United States, they are exempt from registration with the Securities and Exchange Commission (SEC). There are no comparable registration requirements for debt issues sold in the Eurobond market. The absence of registration requirements and the costly due diligence investigation that precedes registration, suggests that there can be a cost advantage to offerings made outside the U.S. Once a Eurodollar issue has become **seasoned,** however, U.S. investors can purchase the issue in the secondary market. A bond is seasoned once it has traded for a sufficiently long period of time (at least 90 days) following completion of distribution.

While most domestic U.S.-pay bonds carry a semiannual coupon, Eurodollar bonds, and most foreign-pay bonds, carry an annual coupon. Thus, a conversion is necessary to make the yield quotes on Eurobonds comparable to the yield quotes on domestic bonds. The mathematics for this conversion is discussed in Appendix 2 to this chapter.

Issuers of Eurodollar bonds include U.S. issuers who prefer to raise dollars outside the United States, non-U.S. issuers who have a need for dollars, and U.S. and non-U.S. issuers who raise dollars in the Eurodollar bond market and then swap these dollar liabilities into liabilities denominated in other currencies.

In recent years, an increasing number of foreign entities in need of dollar financing have chosen to sell their bonds in the U.S. capital markets rather than the Eurobond market. These U.S.-pay bonds are called **Yankee bonds.** There are counterparts to Yankee bonds issued in many major capital markets. For example, the bonds of non-Japanese entities issued in the Japanese capital markets are called **Samurai bonds** and non-British bonds issued in the United Kingdom are called **bulldogs.**

The market of choice for issuing debt will depend principally on the comparative costs of alternative issuing arenas. Some issuers may hold a comparative advantage in one market while others may hold a comparative advantage in another market.

Foreign-pay Eurobonds, like U.S.-pay Eurobonds, are underwritten by an international syndicate that sells them in a number of international markets. The issuing entity may or may not be domiciled in the country and currency of issue. For example, a German firm may issue deutschemark bonds but a British firm may also issue deutschemark bonds.

While U.S.-pay issues have long dominated the Eurobond market, deutschemark issues, as already noted, are also a major component of this market. Floating rate notes are very popular in the Eurobond markets, irrespective of the currency of denomination, but they are particularly popular among investors in deutschemark issues.

At the short-end of the maturity spectrum, there is a very big market for short-term Eurodollar deposits. A Eurodollar deposit is a time deposit, denominated in dollars, that is held in a bank outside the United States. London is the principal center of the Eurodollar market. Banks acquire these deposits by issuing Eurodollar CDs. These Eurodollar CDs are purchased by other banks and by corporations—often U.S. corporations.

Eurodollar deposits are actively borrowed and lent among major banks both in Europe and elsewhere. London banks quote an important interest rate for interbank lending of these deposits. This rate, known as the London Interbank Offered Rate, or LIBOR, is always understood to be a dollar-based rate unless specifically indicated otherwise.[7] LIBOR is routinely quoted for one-month through twelve-months, but three-months, six-months, and twelve-months are generally the most active.

Summary

The largest debt market in the world is the market for U.S. Treasury debt. The major instruments trading in these markets are bills, notes, and bonds. T-bills have short maturities, are sold at a discount from face value, and trade in terms of yield with yield quoted on a bank discount basis. T-notes and T-bonds are coupon bearing securities that trade in terms of price. Yields on these instruments are quoted on a bond basis. Treasury debt is very homogeneous with a near continuum of maturities ranging from a few days all the way out to thirty years. The market for Treasury securities, which is made by government securities dealers, is largely unregulated.

The U.S. corporate (financial and nonfinancial combined) debt market is very heterogeneous. Nonbank institutions issue short-term debt in the form of commercial paper while banks issue short-term debt in the form of certificates of deposit. These same corporations issue a variety of intermediate- to long-term forms of debt that include both fixed-rate and floating rate notes and fixed-rate bonds. These instruments sometimes have substantial collateral backing and at other times lack collateral altogether. The primary market for corporate notes and bonds is made by investment banks acting as underwriters and the secondary market is made by bond dealers, although some exchange trading does occur.

The mortgage market was a rather humdrum affair until the introduction of mortgage passthroughs. Most newly originated mortgages created today are pooled with other mortgages for eventual sale as passthroughs or for conversion into CMOs. The pooling process separates the mortgage debt from the mortgage servicing rights. A mortgage originator will often find it advantageous to sell off the mortgages but to keep the servicing rights to the mortgages. The last decade has witnessed a major shift from conventional level-pay mortgages to various forms of adjustable rate mortgages.

The Eurobond market has grown to become a mainstay of the world financial system. Bonds denominated in any currency can be sold in the Eurobond market. U.S.-pay bonds have long dominated this market and continue to do so, but German-pay and other foreign-pay bonds have become an increasingly important segment of this market. There are advantages to selling U.S.-pay bonds outside the United States. One of the most important of these is the avoidance of a time consuming and expensive registration with the Securities and Exchange Commission. The Eurobond market's growth was stimulated by the advent of swaps. It is now quite routine to raise capital by selling bonds in one currency and then immediately swapping the proceeds from the sale into another currency. Thus, the Eurobond markets provide an efficient mechanism to tap the capital markets of the world in order to raise funds at the least possible cost.

Endnotes

[1]In all dealer activity, the bid price is the price the dealer will pay to buy a security. The ask or asked price, also known as an

offer, is the price at which the dealer is willing to sell the security. The difference between the higher ask price and the lower bid price is called the bid-ask spread. Note, when securities are traded on the basis of yield (as is the case with T-bills), the bid will be higher than the ask. This is a reflection of the inverse relationship between prices and yields.

[2]The reader interested in the conversion of discount yields to bond equivalent yields should see Fage (1986), Chapter 1. One way to convert T-bill yields of any term to bond equivalent yields is to first convert the T-bill yield to a simple rate of interest and then convert this simple rate of interest to a semiannual bond equivalent yield. The procedure is described in Appendix 1 to this chapter.

[3]The offering price will usually be at or close to par. The securities, however, may be sold for less than the offering price but never for more than the offering price. From the underwriter's perspective, the difference between the offering price and the proceeds paid to the issuer is called the **underwriter's discount.**

[4]Commercial paper with a maturity greater than 270 days is rare because any publicly offered issue with a maturity greater than 270 days must be registered with the SEC. This registration, and the accompanying due diligence investigation conducted by the underwriting team, is time consuming and expensive.

[5]The first documented public offering of floating rate notes in the U.S. is attributed to Mortgage Investors of Washington, which offered, on 1 November 1973, $15 million of Floating Rate (eight percent to twelve percent) Senior Subordinated Notes due 1 November 1980. For a more detailed discussion of the history of floating-rate debt, see Wilson (1987). For a discussion of the role of FRNs in financial engineering, see Smith (1988).

[6]Carron (1988) provides a very good starting point for anyone interested in mortgage prepayment models.

[7]For example, there is deutschemark LIBOR, usually denoted DEM LIBOR, that represents the interest rate in London for loans involving deutschemark deposits held with London banks.

References and Suggested Readings

Carron, A. *Prepayment Models for Fixed and Adjustable Rate Mortgages,* New York: First Boston, Fixed Income Research (August 1988).

Fabozzi, F.J and I.M. Pollock (eds.). *The Handbook of Fixed Income Securities*, 2d ed., Homewood, IL: Dow Jones-Irwin, 1987.

Fage, P. *Yield Calculations*, Credit Swiss First Boston Research, October 1986.

First Boston Corporation, *High Yield Handbook (1989)*, High Yield Research Group, The First Boston Corporation, January 1989.

Gelardin, J. "A Complex Market for Floating Rate Notes," *Euromoney*, 17-19 (January 1986).

Madura, J. and C. Williams. "Hedging Mortgages with Interest Rate Swaps vs Caps: How to Choose," *Real Estate Finance Journal*, 3:1 (Summer 1987), pp. 90-96.

Smith, D.J. "The Pricing of Bull and Bear Floating Rate Notes: An Application of Financial Engineering, *Financial Management*, 17(4) (Winter 1988).

Stigum, M. *The Money Market*, revised ed., Howewood, IL: Dow Jones-Irwin, 1983.

Wilson, R.S. "Domestic Floating-Rate and Adjustable-Rate Debt Securities," in *Handbook of Fixed Income Securities*, F.J. Fabozzi and I.M. Pollack, eds., 2d ed., Homewood, IL: Dow Jones-Irwin, 1987.

Appendix 1
Conversion of Bank Discount Yields to Bond Equivalent Yields

A very straightforward and intuitive way to convert bank discount yields (BDY) to bond equivalent yields (BEY) is to first convert the BDY to a simple rate of interest (also known as an effective annual rate of return). This simple rate of interest can then be converted to its BEY equivalent. The complete process takes five steps.

Step 1:

Calculate the dollar amount of the discount using Equation 16.1.

$$DD = FV \times BDY \times \frac{Actual}{360} \tag{16.1}$$

Step 2:

Calculate the present value of the T-bill using Equation 16.2.

$$PV = FV - DD \tag{16.2}$$

Step 3:

Calculate the periodic discount rate k using Equation 16.4 or its equivalent below.

$$k = \frac{FV}{PV} - 1 \tag{16.4}$$

Step 4:

Convert the periodic discount rate k to a simple rate of interest, denoted here by r, using Equation 16.A.1.

$$r = (1 + k)^a - 1 \tag{16.A.1}$$

$$\text{where } a = \frac{365}{Actual}$$

Step 5:

Convert the simple rate of interest to a semiannual bond equivalent yield using Equation 16.A.2.

$$BEY = 2 \times [(1 + r)^{1/2} - 1] \tag{16.A.2}$$

The calculation is complete at this step and you now have the bond equivalent yield stated in its conventional form as a semiannual rate.

Appendix 2
The Restatement of Bond
Equivalent Yields

While it is customary to quote bond yields on the assumption of semiannual compounding, the rate can be stated on any other compounding frequency one desires. The most frequent requirement, other than semiannual, is for a quote on an annual bond basis, but one month and three months are also occasionally called for. For this reason, a ready formula to move freely between different compounding frequencies is useful. This is given below.

$$r_m = m \times \left[\left(1 + \frac{r_z}{z} \right)^{z/m} - 1 \right]$$

r_z: is the rate quoted on a compounding frequency of z times per year.

r_m: is the desired quote on a compounding frequency of *m* times per year.

Chapter 17

Recent Debt Market Innovations

Overview

In the last chapter, we examined the fixed income securities markets with specific emphasis on the domestic markets for Treasury securities, corporate securities, and residential mortgage debt. We also briefly examined the international markets with our look at Eurocurrency instruments. Our discussion of these markets had a two-fold purpose. The first was to provide a somewhat traditional overview of the various types of fixed-income securities and the purposes of their issue. An appreciation of these markets is essential to understanding the fixed-income component of the capital and money markets that have long been, and which continue to be, the primary mechanism for the allocation of financial resources in market-based economies. The second purpose was to lay a foundation on which financial engineers can build. While not our primary intent, we did consider a number of recent engineering developments in the last chapter including such innovations as floating-rate debt, various forms of nontraditional residential mortgages, and the emergence of a more global view among issuers of fixed-income securities.

In this chapter, we will take a brief look at some recent innovations in the fixed-income markets that have done a lot to alter the financial landscape. All of these innovations are the work of financial engineers but many would not have been possible without an accommodative regulatory environment. The innovations discussed in this chapter are singled out because they (1) were of monumental significance, (2) set the stage for other innovations that followed, or (3) set the stage for innovations that, we believe, will follow. Specifically, in this chapter, we will look at the emergence of zero coupon securities, collateralized mortgage obligations, repurchase agreements, junk bonds, economic and legal defeasance, and shelf registration.

Zero Coupon Securities

The engineering of zero coupon securities is undoubtedly one of the most interesting innovations of the last fifteen years. While simple in design, these instruments are a very useful vehicle for achieving portfolio return objectives, hedging complex risk exposures, and engineering a wide variety of synthetic instruments. Zero coupon securities, particularly those derived from conventional Treasury debt issues, have a number of unique properties of particular interest to financial engineers and these properties are worth elaborating. We begin, however, with definitions and an historic overview.

A **zero coupon bond**, or **zero**, is a debt instrument that is sold at a deep discount from face value. As the name implies, these instruments do not pay periodic coupons. Instead, interest accrues via a gradual rise in the value of the instruments as they approach maturity. At maturity, zeros are redeemed for full face value. Actually, zero coupon instruments are not as new as widely believed. The U.S. Treasury has long issued discount instruments of short maturity. The best known of which are 13-week T-bills, 26-week T-bills, and 52-week T-bills. These instruments are just as surely zero-coupon products as are the longer-maturity instruments to which the term is more often applied.

Although the advent of Treasury-based zero coupon products gave a major boost to the general market for zero coupon bonds, corporate experimentation and municipal experimentation in zeros had occurred earlier. The volume of this early corporate and municipal activity was minimal and we do not consider it further. We would be remiss, however, if we failed to point out that municipal zeros offer many of the benefits of Treasury-based zeros (discussed below) with the added benefit of providing tax sheltered income.

Zero coupon munis have, consequently, become an important factor in the municipal bond market.

The first zero-coupon products involving Treasury securities and having a maturity greater than one year were actually derivative products and not Treasury securities at all. These were introduced in 1982 by Merrill Lynch, which called its product **Treasury Investment Growth Receipts,** or **TIGRs.** The creation of TIGRs was a three stage process. First, Merrill Lynch purchased conventional coupon-bearing Treasury securities and removed the coupons—thereby separating the coupons and the final redemption payment into separate cash flows. Second, these individual cash flows, each corresponding to a different maturity, were then used to created irrevocable trusts with a custodial bank. As the final step, the custodial bank issued shares in the trusts. These shares were the TIGRs that Merrill Lynch then marketed to its clients. Although the TIGRs were not themselves issues of the Treasury, they were fully collateralized by Treasury obligations and nearly equivalent to Treasuries in terms of default risk.[1]

To understand the appeal of Treasury-based zeros, we need a brief review of the various forms of risk to which a holder of a fixed income security is exposed. These risks, which were more fully discussed in Chapter 8, include interest rate risk, default risk, reinvestment risk, call or prepayment risk, and purchasing power risk. Interest rate risk is the risk that the value of a security will change after its purchase in response to changes in interest rates generally and the instrument's yield more specifically. This risk is most often measured with the aid of duration. Interest rate risk is of greatest concern to holders of fixed-income securities who might have to sell the security prior to its maturity.

Default risk is the risk that the issuer of the security will default on its financial obligations so that the holder of the instrument does not receive full payment of interest and/or principal in a timely fashion. It is generally accepted that the debt-rating agencies provide very good relative estimates of default risk, but empirical evidence has shown that the market does an excellent job of assessing default risk on its own.[2]

In conventional fixed-income securities markets (i.e., absent zeros), interest rate risk can be managed in several ways. The first is to match the maturity of the instrument to the investor's investment horizon. This maturity/horizon matching approach, however poses a reinvestment risk problem. This is the risk that the periodic coupons received will be reinvested at rates which differ from the yield prevailing on the bond at the time of its purchase. Fluctuations in the reinvestment rate create the potential for terminal wealth to differ from expectations and therefore constitute a form of risk. The second way to manage interest rate risk is to invest only in instruments having a maturity shorter than that of the investor's horizon and then to roll over into other instruments also of short maturity with the final rollover having a maturity date identical to the investor's horizon. This approach is particularly useful if the investor's horizon is uncertain or if the investor feels that a liquidation prior to the expected horizon is likely. By investing in short-maturity instruments, interest rate risk is minimized because short maturity instruments are less rate sensitive to interest rate fluctuations. The final approach using conventional instruments is to purchase an instrument having a maturity greater than the investor's horizon but then to hedge the interest rate risk in futures, forwards, or some other derivative instrument.

While the three approaches to managing interest rate risk can all be used to reduce risk exposure, none are perfect. The reason is simple: the ever present reinvestment risk. In the first strategy (maturity/horizon matching), the periodic coupons must be reinvested. In the second strategy (short-term rollovers), while the maturity proceeds of each rollover are known at the time of the instrument's purchase, the reinvestment rate on the next rollover is not known in advance and, hence, the reinvestment risk problem is amplified. The final approach (hedging), also fails to address the reinvestment risk problem.

The strategies described above have other failings as well. For example, the rollover strategy will produce a suboptimal return in an upward sloping yield curve environment and the hedging approach may involve a cost to the hedger.

Just as the interest rate risk management problem can be handled in several ways, the default risk problem can also be managed in several ways. The simplest way is to invest in securities having an extremely low risk of default individually. This would certainly include obligations of the U.S. Treasury but might also include investment grade corporate and municipal issues. An alternative approach is hold a diversified portfolio of low-grade debt issues. While the securities in the portfolio may individually be high risk, the overall portfolio will tend to be of lower risk. This does not completely eliminate default risk, but the excess yield on these instruments—which can be though of as a **default risk premium**—should be, in an efficient market, just sufficient to compensate the holder for the default risk he or she bears. Interestingly, there is empirical evidence to indicate that, in practice, the return on speculative grade debt of the junk bond variety has actually provided a return in excess of a fair default risk level for extended periods (see Chapter 8 for some empirical evidence of this).

Call (or prepayment) risk is the risk that the investor is repaid the loan principal, in whole or in part, prior to the expected date. This risk may be viewed as a form of reinvestment risk because proceeds received earlier than expected must be reinvested at the then prevailing rate. There is the added complication, however, that the time of repayment is itself unknown at the time of the instrument's purchase.

Treasury instruments are ideal for the management of both interest rate risk and default risk. First, they are available in every conceivable maturity from a few days out to 30 years and they are very liquid. This means that any investor can easily find an issue with a maturity that matches his or her investment horizon and can acquire the issue at minimal transaction costs. Second, Treasuries are as close to default free as any instrument can get and, so, the investor can disregard default risk. In addition, while some Treasury issues are callable, most are not.

Despite these appealing features, conventional Treasury issues still expose their holders to substantial reinvestment risk. It is this risk that zeros remove. By definition, a zero does not pay a periodic coupon and, consequently, there is no reinvestment risk for the investor who matches the bond's maturity to his or her horizon. Thus, the purchaser of zero coupon Treasuries who matches maturity and horizon is freed from interest rate risk, default risk, and reinvestment risk. The only other type of risk—purchasing power risk—does not disappear with zeros. Purchasing power risk is the risk that the terminal proceeds will have more or less purchasing power than expected because of unforeseen changes in the rate of inflation. It is possible to engineer zeros having a terminal value indexed to inflation, but inflation indexed bonds are not yet popular in the U.S. Such bonds have, however, found a welcome home in the European markets.

In addition to their risk management uses, zero coupon derivatives also afforded interesting tax benefits. At the time of their introduction, the tax code provided for the taxation of interest when received. Consequently, because zeros pay all of their interest at maturity, the taxation of the interest on zeros was deferred. Deferral of taxation, while not as attractive as tax-exemption, is desirable because it allows the investor to enjoy the use of the funds that would otherwise have been paid to the taxing jurisdiction. Note that this tax treatment no longer applies. The current rules governing the tax treatment of zero coupon and other original issue discount instruments are described in the appendix to this chapter.

Given the many benefits of zeros to investors, it is not surprising that Merrill Lynch's TIGRs soon had competition as other investment banks created their own zero coupon Treasury derivatives. These products, which traded under various acronyms, called trademarks, included such names as CATS, LIONs, COUGARs, DOGs, and EAGLEs, to mention just a few. The secondary market for each of these proprietary products was rather illiquid since the only dealer for each product was the investment bank that created it. In an effort to address this problem, a group of government securities dealers, led by The First Boston Corporation, created a generic Treasury-based zero coupon product called **Treasury Receipts**.

The risk management uses and the tax benefits of zeros combined to make these derivative products very attractive to investors and they quickly became popular. Although the tax benefits were eliminated by changes in the tax law that became effective in 1982, the instruments remained popular and by 1985 the par value of outstanding zeros reached $100 billion. For the investment banks, the incentive for creating zero coupon products was two-fold. First, the investment bank purchased a bond, stripped it to create a series of zeros, and then sold these zeros to the public. The investor benefits afforded by zeros were reflected in their price so that the series of zeros that could be created from a conventional bond had a collective value that exceeded that of the bond.

The U.S. Treasury was a major beneficiary of the popularity of Treasury-based zero coupon products. The demand for the zeros created a demand for the bonds that are the raw material for making zeros. This demand for strippable bonds by investment banks and other government securities dealers drove up the prices and drove down the yields on these issues. The Treasury then benefited from the lower yields. Nevertheless, until June of 1982, the Treasury objected to the stripping of bonds and actively tried to dissuade investment banks from engaging in the practice. The Treasury's objections were based on the tax deference opportunities made possible by zeros. With the change in the tax law noted earlier, the Treasury dropped its objections and, in 1984, the Treasury created its own program for stripping bonds. The program, called **Separate Trading of Registered Interest and Principal of Securities (STRIPS)**, allowed the stripping of specially designated note and bond issues. The program proved popular and was later extended to allow the stripping of all noncallable coupon issues with original maturities of 10 years or more. These zero coupon bonds are direct obligations of the U.S. Treasury and, hence, completely default free. All such securities are held in book-entry form.

Zeros and Conversion Arbitrage

The creation of zero coupon bonds from conventional bonds is a classic example of **conversion arbitrage.** In conversion arbitrage, an instrument (or group of instruments) with a given set of investment characteristics is converted into an instrument (or group of instruments) that has a different set of investment characteristics. The most important of these investment characteristics is the amount and the size of the cash flows, but other characteristics can be important as well. Included among these are the risk and tax characteristics of the cash flows. A general model of conversion arbitrage appears as Exhibit 17.1.

Exhibit 17.1
Conversion Arbitrage

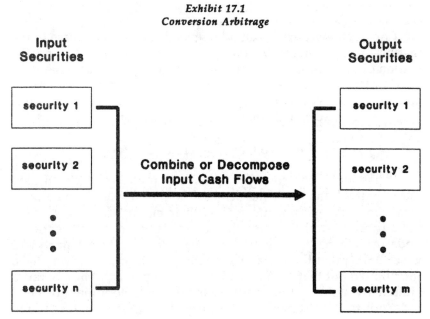

Zero coupon bond generation from conventional bonds is illustrated in Exhibit 17.2. The reader should verify that the conversion arbitrage model is satisfied in the creation of zeros.

Exhibit 17.2
Zero Coupon Bond Creation

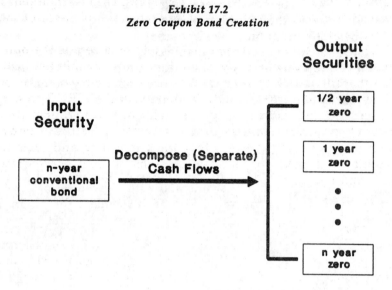

Conversion arbitrage can take several forms. In the case of the creation of zero coupon bonds from conventional bonds (and the creation of multiclass mortgage-backed securities discussed later in this chapter) the conversion arbitrage takes the form of **maturity intermediation**—a service long performed by financial institutions in their more traditional role of borrower/lender.

The Zero Coupon Yield Curve

It has long been common practice to plot the yields on debt instruments against their maturities. The plot of yields on conventional Treasury instruments against their maturities is now called the **conventional yield curve.** If the plot is based on conventional bonds trading near par value, it is sometimes called a **par yield curve.** Both practitioners and academicians alike, however, have long pointed out that such a yield curve is imprecise at best because it implicitly assumes that maturity is the sole determinant of yield on default-free instruments. In an early effort to rectify this failing, analysts began to plot a yield-to-duration curve for conventional Treasury instruments. The argument in favor of such a plot is that duration is a better measure of a debt instrument's interest-rate sensitivity than is its maturity. As appealing as this argument is, the yield-to-duration plot never supplanted the well-established conventional yield curve.

This is where zeros come in. The yield on a zero is the purest measure of the demand/supply conditions for loanable funds of a given maturity since each zero provides a single payment at one and only one point in time. The introduction of the STRIPS program produced a well-defined and highly standardized zero coupon product with a continuum of maturities. An interesting feature of zeros—which is unique to zeros—is that their maturity and duration (Macaulay duration) are identical. As such, a yield curve drawn with respect to zero coupon bonds is a pure depiction of the demand/supply conditions for loanable funds across a continuum of durations *and* maturities. Not surprisingly, the **zero coupon yield curve**, sometimes called a **spot yield curve**, has become an important analytical tool in both financial analysis and financial engineering. A plot of a zero coupon yield curve and a conventional yield curve as they existed at the close on September 13, 1990 are depicted in Exhibit 17.3. (Note that we have not scaled the time axis.)

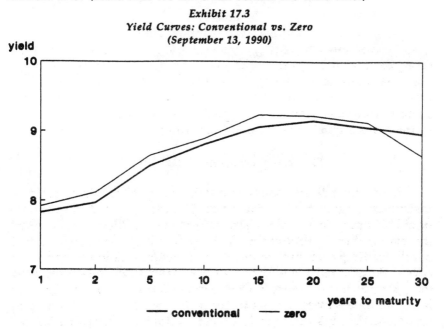

Exhibit 17.3
Yield Curves: Conventional vs. Zero
(September 13, 1990)

The zero coupon yield curve plotted in Exhibit 17.3 was generated by direct observation on U.S. Treasury STRIPS, that is, the zero coupon bonds created by stripping conventional Treasuries. The zero coupon bonds used to generate this yield curve are not as liquid as the conventional bonds from which they were created. This fact has led to the argument that the spot yield curve is not necessarily representative of the true zero coupon yield curve. To deal with this situation, those who have a use for a reliable zero coupon yield curve have developed a simple arithmetic method for backing an implied zero coupon yield curve out of the par yield curve. This procedure, sometimes called **bootstrapping,** can be used to obtain an implied zero coupon yield curve for Treasuries, an implied zero coupon yield curve for corporates, an implied zero coupon yield curve for municipals, or an implied zero coupon swaps curve. The latter is widely used today for marking swap portfolios to market, sometimes called **repricing.**

The procedure for generating an implied zero coupon yield curve needs to be explained. Let's suppose that we have six-month, twelve-month and eighteen-month conventional bonds trading near par (we will assume for illustration that they are all trading at par). These bonds are listed in Table 17.1 together with the implied zero coupon yields.

Table 17.1
Implies Zero Coupon Yields

Maturity (years)	Coupon rate	Periodic coupon	Conventional Yield	Implied Zero Coupon Yield
0.5	8.000	4.0000	8.000%	8.000%
1.0	8.250	4.1250	8.250	8.255
1.5	8.375	4.1875	8.375	8.384

We know that a yield is the discount rate that equates the present value of the future cash flows to the current market price of the bond. In this approach, all the cash flows are assumed to be discounted at the same rate—the bond's yield to maturity. But, the bond can also be viewed as a series of zero coupon bonds. If viewed this way, then the individual cash flows should each be discounted at the yield applicable to the maturities on the individual cash flows. Thus, the two present value models depicted in Equation 17.1 should produce the same market price.

$$\Sigma\ CF_t \cdot (1 + (y_t / 2))^{-t} = \Sigma\ CF_t \cdot (1 + (k / 2))^{-t} = \text{Price} \qquad (17.1)$$

In this model, the value CF_t is the cash flow to be received in period t; $t=1$ for the cash flow to be received in six months, $t=2$ for the cash flow to be received in twelve months, and $t=3$ for the cash flow to be received in eighteen months. The values y_t are the corresponding zero coupon yields for cash flows to be received at time t, $t=1,2,3$. The value k is the yield to maturity on the instrument. Now, since the bond with six months to maturity has already paid all cash flows but the last, its yield to maturity is also the zero coupon yield for a six-month zero. Thus, y_1 is 8.000 percent. We can use this information to "back out" the implied one-year zero coupon rate by using the twelve month conventional bond. The calculation, which makes use of the left-hand side of 17.1 is shown below:

$$4.125 \cdot (1 + .04000)^{-1} + 104.125 \cdot (1 + (y_2 / 2))^{-2} = 100$$

With a little arithmetic, we can solve for y_2, which is 8.255 percent. The reader should verify this. Now that we know the six-month implied zero coupon rate and the twelve-month implied zero coupon rate, we can use this information to get the eighteen-month implied zero coupon rate. The calculation is shown below:

$$4.1875 \cdot (1.0400)^{-1} + 4.1875 \cdot (1.041275)^{-2} + 104.1875 \cdot (1 + (y_3 / 2))^{-3} = 100$$

The reader should convince himself or herself that y_3 is approximately 8.384 percent. The same procedure is then used to get all implied zero coupon yields out to the limit of the maturities on the conventional issues.

Zeros in Financial Engineering

Zero coupon bonds and zero coupon yield curves have become two of the most important tools of financial engineers. There are good reasons for this. As discussed above, a zero coupon bond entitles its holder to a single payment at a prespecified point in time. Both the initial purchase price and the cash flow at maturity are known at the time of purchase. By stringing together an appropriate assortment of zeros, a financial engineer can replicate the cash flow pattern of any of a great many conventional and nonconventional forms of debt. Alternatively, very complex financial structures can be decomposed into elemental components and the cash flows associated with these elemental components can then be valued with the zero coupon yield curve.

For example, the process by which zeros are created can be reversed and the conventional Treasury bond can be recreated. Such a strategy would be profitable if conventional bonds of some maturity are priced above the cost of creating one via the assembly of zeros. The financial engineer can also use this process to duplicate the cash flow pattern of mortgage debt, or amortizing corporate debt involving a grace period, and so on. This process is depicted in Exhibit 17.4.

Exhibit 17.4
Financial Engineering with Zeros

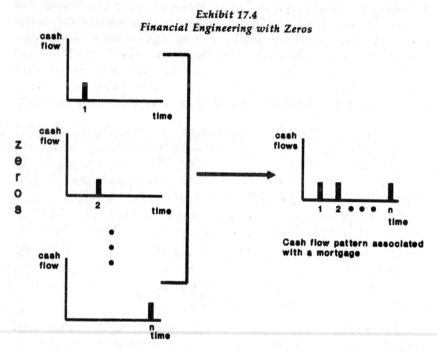

Cash flow pattern associated with a mortgage

Multiclass Mortgage-Backed and Asset-Backed Securities

While the financial engineering that led to the introduction of mortgage passthrough certificates added considerable liquidity to the mortgage market, the appeal of passthrough certificates is nevertheless limited by the **single class** nature of the instruments. That is, the pool arrangement allows for the passthrough of all interest and principal repayments to investors on a *pro rata* basis. Thus, all investors in the same passthrough instrument hold identical securities with identical cash flows, identical maturities, and identical rights. This single-class structure does not suit the needs of all potential mortgage investors.

Financial engineers set to work on the problem and eventually created a multiclass mortgage-backed instrument, called a collateralized mortgage obligation or CMO, that qualified for debt treatment under the existing tax code. The type of financial engineering embodied in the CMO product is very similar to that embodied in zero coupon bonds and is best described as maturity intermediation.

CMOs quickly captured a significant portion of the mortgage market. The instrument was adaptable and many variants soon evolved. The CMO product, however, had certain drawbacks. For example, it did not qualify for **flow-through** tax treatment and added considerable debt to the balance sheet of issuing institutions. A desire to remove the debt from the balance sheet eventually led the issuing institutions to develop grantor trust and owner trust structures. These structures, however, were less than ideal. They limited the issuer's flexibility and gave rise to other potentially adverse tax consequences.

The deficiencies of the CMO product under then existing tax law eventually led to inclusion of special provisions in the Tax Reform Act of 1986 (TRA) for the creation of a CMO-like product that qualified for flow-through tax treatment. Specifically, the legislation allowed for the creation of **Real Estate Mortgage Investment Conduits** or REMICs. Since their introduction, REMICs have partially supplanted CMOs as the operational vehicle for generating multiclass mortgage-backed securities from single-class mortgages.

Collateralized Mortgage Obligations

The creation of passthrough certificates by issuing undivided interests in mortgage pools was the first example of a class of instruments that became known as **mortgage-backed securities**— known colloquially as **mortgage-backs** (MBs). These instruments, and the streamlining of the process by which they are created, served to transform the sedentary mortgage market into an active competitor in the capital markets. From the investor's perspective, the guarantee that accompanies many passthroughs provides a degree of safety that comes close to that of holding Treasury debt. Yet, passthroughs typically afford a higher return.

Unlike long-term Treasury issues and most corporate issues, mortgage debt is amortizing. This means that the holder of mortgage debt receives payments (cash flows) that contain principal as well as interest. The precise size of the cash flows will depend on the type of mortgage involved, but the principle is the same regardless. The payments on nonamortizing Treasury and corporate debt, on the other hand, consist of interest only until the final payment. Upon maturity, the full principal is repaid in a single lump-sum (sometimes called a bullet).

The cash flow streams of nonamortizing Treasury debt and amortizing mortgage debt are compared in Exhibits 17.5 and 17.6. The mortgage flows depicted in Exhibit 17.6 are for conventional level-payment types of mortgages.

Exhibit 17.5
Nonamortizing Conventional Debt

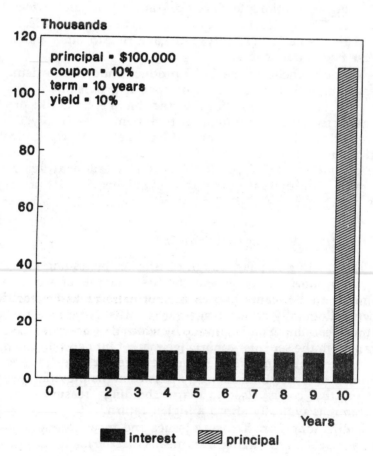

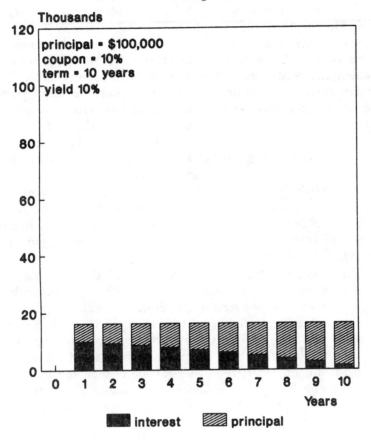

Exhibit 17.6
Amortizing Debt

For some investors, the cash flow patterns associated with mortgage debt are preferred to the cash flow patterns associated with nonamortizing debt. Retired persons seeking a regular monthly check to supplement their retirement income, for example, are quite likely to view passthroughs as attractive assets to hold. But this is not the case for all investors. Indeed, for some investors, passthroughs are very unattractive.

All other things being equal, the holder of a passthrough certificate will receive larger cash flows than will the holder of a nonamortizing form of debt. If the holder has no immediate need for these cash flows, then the reinvestment risk problem emerges. Further, because the flows are large, the reinvestment risk problem is amplified. To make matters worse, mortgagors have the right to prepay their mortgages and they often do. Unexpected prepayments are passed on to the passthrough holders who are then forced to find alternative investments.

In an effort to address these concerns, financial engineers at the First Boston Corporation and Salomon Brothers developed collateralized mortgage obligations or CMOs in June of 1983. CMOs were a dynamic innovation and quickly captured a major portion of the mortgage market. From a financial engineering perspective, CMOs are another example of conversion arbitrage. The investment bank purchases mortgage passthroughs (or whole mortgages) and then issues special bonds that are collateralized by the mortgages (hence the name). The bonds are divided into a series of distinct groups called **tranches.** The cash flows on the different tranches are different and, hence, the CMO structure allows a single-class instrument (the mortgage or pass through) to be transformed, via maturity intermediation, into a multiclass instrument (the CMO).

In the basic or plain vanilla CMO, each tranche is entitled to receive a *pro rata* share of interest, just as with a passthrough, *but only one tranche at a time receives principal.* For example, at the beginning, only the first tranche receives principal. This tranche, called the **fastest-pay tranche,** receives all principal collected by the servicers, whether paid on time or prepaid, until all of the tranche's principal has been amortized. The tranche is then retired and the second tranche becomes the fastest-pay tranche. The number of tranches on any one CMO may be as few as four or as many as ten or more. The structure of the CMO, using passthroughs or whole mortgages as the collateral source, is depicted in Exhibit 17.7 for a four-tranche situation.

Many variants of the basic CMO have evolved since this product was first introduced. Some have structures considerably more complex than that depicted in Exhibit 17.7. For example, there are CMOs in which more than one tranche receives principal at a time, there are zero coupon-like CMO tranches, and there are CMOs based on adjustable-rate mortgages. Consider, for example, zero coupon-like CMOs. On these CMOs, one or more of the **tranches** take the form of accrual bonds. An accrual bond, also called an **accretion bond** or a **Z-bond,** is a deferred interest obligation resembling a zero coupon bond. The accrual bond does not receive any interest or principal until such time as the preceding tranches are fully

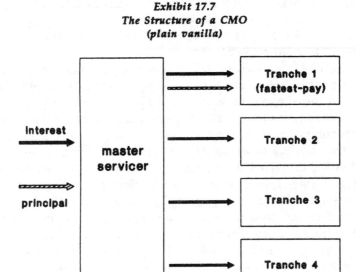

Exhibit 17.7
The Structure of a CMO
(plain vanilla)

retired. In the interim, the interest that would normally flow to the tranche accrues. Once all preceding tranches are retired, the accrual bond receives interest and principal in the usual way. The accrual bond structure is depicted in Exhibit 17.8 with the fourth tranche being the one and only accrual bond in this particular case.

While the CMO does not completely eliminate prepayment risk, it does greatly reduces it. The structure of the tranches guarantees that the first tranche will have a very short life, that the second tranche will have a somewhat longer life, that the third tranche will have a still longer life, and so on. Thus, a long-term instrument—the mortgage or passthrough—is used to create a series of distinct instruments, the tranches, that have short, intermediate, and long lives. The investor can pick the tranche that most closely mirrors his or her needs. Because investors can purchase need-specific securities and, hence, have less risk than that associated with whole mortgages or passthroughs, they are willing to pay a little more for these instruments. The collective value of the CMO tranches can then be more than the value of the mortgages (or

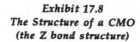

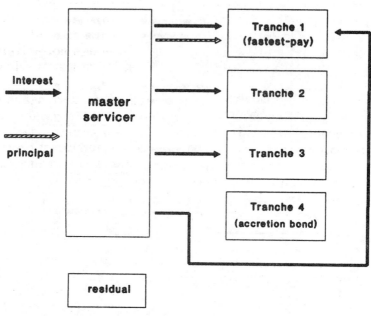

Exhibit 17.8
The Structure of a CMO
(the Z bond structure)

passthroughs) used to create them. This value difference is the source of a large portion of the investment bank's profit. The investment bank also makes the secondary market in CMOs, acting as a dealer, and derives profit from the bid-ask spread.

CMOs, particularly those with accrual bond tranches, give rise to residuals—which are another interesting feature of the product. Consider, for example, a situation in which the accrual bond holders have been promised a return of 9.00 percent. Now suppose that the reinvestment rate on the proceeds received by the grantor trust (into which the mortgage collateral has been placed) exceeds 9.00 percent. Then, upon the retirement of the final tranche, there will be excess value. This excess value is called the residual. Of course, if the reinvestment rate averaged less than 9.00 percent, the residual would be negative. To deal with this latter possibility, the CMO trustee uses very conservative reinvestment rate assumptions and overcollateralizes the CMO bonds. These precautions assure that the residual will be positive but the amount is still uncertain.

The CMO issuer can retain the residual or can sell it to an investor willing to bear the risk of the uncertain terminal value. The latter course has become the general, although not universal, rule. By selling the residual up-front, the CMO issuer is relieved of this source of uncertainty.

As already noted, CMOs are indirect claims on mortgage assets. Legally, they represent claims on the CMO issuer (or grantor trust) and are, hence, liabilities of the CMO issuer. (or grantor trust). The CMO issuer (or grantor trust) holds a separate and direct claim on the mortgage assets. For reasons already noted, there are inefficiencies associated with the CMO structure which the REMIC legislation sought to address.

Real Estate Mortgage Investment Conduits

Real Estate Mortgage Investment Conduits or REMICs were made possible by special provisions in the Tax Reform Act of 1986. The REMIC structure is nearly identical to that of the CMO and, in this sense, a REMIC may be viewed as an extension of the CMO. The REMIC takes advantage of the tax code provisions which grant the multiclass securities flow-through tax treatment without the need for owner trusts. The resultant securities are nevertheless off-balance sheet for accounting purposes. The off-balance sheet treatment offers considerable economic benefits for issuers including reduced capital requirements.

The REMIC legislation also clarified the tax rules for calculating original-issue discounts—a longstanding problem with CMOs. It also addressed, for the first time, the treatment of market discounts and premiums and thus removed several clouds that had hung over the MB market.

REMICs (and CMOs) can be developed in several ways. One way is for a financial institution (such as an investment bank) to buy whole mortgages or passthroughs and then use these to create its own REMIC/CMO products. Alternatively, mortgage bankers, thrifts, and commercial bankers that originate mortgages may develop their own REMICs and/or CMOs. In this latter scenario, the securities are developed and distributed with the aid of investment bankers serving in their traditional role as underwriters. Some of the larger mortgage bankers have gone this latter route. Additionally, smaller originators who lack the volume to efficiently generate their own MBs can "rent" an existing conduit, i.e., sell their mortgages to another institution with an established market presence and a volume sufficient to exploit the economies of scale. As a result, relatively few issuers have filed registration statements but those who have tend to be high volume originators.

The issuance of CMOs and REMICs requires filing and registration with the Securities and Exchange Commission. This entails considerable delay in any offering and considerable expense for the requisite due diligence investigation. The process however has been streamlined in recent years by the advent of another product of financial engineering—**shelf registration**. We examine this issue shortly.

Asset-Backed Securities

The fundamental logic in the engineering behind collateralized mortgage obligations is not specific to mortgages. Given the success of the CMO product, it is not surprising then that financial engineers soon looked for other payment streams that could benefit from the collateralization, often called **securitization**, process. A number of such payment flows have since been used as collateral on debt issues. These later debt issues are now known, collectively, as **asset-backed securities** or, more simply as **asset-backs (ABs)**. The term *asset-backed securities* refers to any securities backed by loans, leases, or installment contracts on personal property. Personal property is all property other than real estate and would include such things as computers and automobiles.

While any payment stream can be used to back a debt issue, the most frequently used are automobile receivables. The structure of asset-backed securities is similar to that of mortgage-backed securities. They may be a single-class instruments like mortgage passthroughs or multiclass instruments like CMOs.

As with mortgage-backed securities, the main risk to the holders of asset-backs is the prepayment risk associated with early prepayment of principal. Lack of knowledge concerning prepayment and reinvestment adds to the investor's uncertainty and makes it difficult to estimate the instrument's yield and effective maturity. These uncertainties will, of course, be reflected in an instrument's yield.

Defeasance

Closely related to the notion of asset-backing of securities are the concepts of economic defeasance and legal defeasance. Economic defeasance is the process of removing debt from a balance sheet by depositing U.S. Treasury securities into an **irrevocable trust**. An irrevocable trust is a trust that cannot be altered or terminated by its creator without the consent of the beneficiaries. Economic defeasance allows a firm to remove debt from its balance sheet for reporting purposes without triggering a tax event. Legal defeasance goes one step beyond economic defeasance by rendering the debt indenture null and void. As a result, legal defeasance not only removes the debt for reporting purposes but also triggers a tax event.

In the context of an issuer's debt obligations, defeasance involves the acquisition of a riskless portfolio of bonds such that the cash flows on the bonds are at least sufficient to pay the interest and the principal on the debt defeased. Consider a simple case. A corporation sells a 30-year mortgage bond having a face value $50 million and paying a semiannual coupon of 6.75 percent. The firm uses the proceeds to fund a new plant. Suppose that ten years later, after interest rates have risen, the bond is priced to yield 10.25 percent and has an aggregate market value of $35.24 million. The firm is cash heavy and would like to eliminate its debt. Unfortunately, management believes that an effort to buy-back its bond in the market will cause a significant run-up in price and will result in a taxable event—both of which it would like to avoid. The solution is an economic defeasance.

As it happens, noncallable Treasury bonds of similar maturity (20-years) and, coincidentally, carrying an identical semiannual coupon of 6.75 percent are priced to yield 10.00 percent. The firm could purchase $50 million (face value) of these T-bonds at a cost of $36.06 million. The T-bonds are then placed in an irrevocable trust with the interest and principal on the T-bonds used to meet the obligations on the firm's bond issue. The firm's $50 million bond liability is now defeased at a cost of $36.02 and the firm can remove the $50 million dollar liability represented by the bond from its balance sheet. The gain ($50 million – $36.06 million) is amortized over the remaining 20 years.

Defeasance can be employed to remove liabilities stemming from almost any type of debt (excluding floating rate debt and convertible debt). Whether the firm benefits from economic defeasance will depend on (1) the impact on the firm's financial statements, and (2) the economic merits of the transactions. The latter are a function of the size of the interest payments defeased, the after-tax reinvestment income on the defeasance portfolio (T-bonds) if any, and the cost of the defeasance portfolio after consideration of the tax consequences of the transactions.

A firm is a likely candidate for defeasance when (1) the firm has low-coupon debt on its books, (2) needs to reduce its use of leverage, (3) anticipates a decline in interest rates, and/or is (4) cash heavy. Importantly, economic defeasance should not concern the holders of the firm's debt because it does not trigger a tax event, there is no change in the debt's rating, there are no changes in the cash flows to the bondholders, and the issuer is still bound by the bond indenture.

Legal defeasance has the additional benefit for the issuer of removing all restrictive covenants of the defeased debt. For example, under economic defeasance, the firm described in the example above could not dispose of the assets backing its bond. Such a disposition is specifically prohibited by the bond's indenture. Once the bond has been legally defeased, however, the assets can be disposed of in any manner management sees fit. The downside of legal defeasance is that legal defeasance results in a taxable event for the debt defeaser. For the holders of the debt, however, legal defeasance is attractive because legally defeased debt receives a top investment-grade rating.

The Repo/Reverse Market

A **repo** or, more precisely, a **repurchase agreement** (also known as an **RP**), is the simultaneous sale and repurchase of a security for different settlement dates. A **reverse** or, more precisely, a **reverse repurchase agreement,** is the mirror image of a repo. That is, a reverse is the simultaneous purchase and sale of a security for different settlement dates. Not surprisingly, repos and reverses are two sides of the same transactions and which term applies depends on whether one is the seller or purchaser on the first settlement date.

Repos and reverses are nothing more than short-term loans collateralized by the underlying security. They are used to obtain short-term funding, to invest short-term cash balances, and to obtain securities for use in short sales.

Repos originated in the market for U.S. government securities. The largely unregulated nature of this market made it a fertile ground for the type of innovative thinking characteristic of financial engineers. As one would expect, in most early repos the underlying securities were T-bills and T-notes but, with the passage of time, all forms of securities have come to be used as the collateral on these transactions.

Consider first the repo market from the perspective of the borrower. The borrower sells securities with the promise to repurchase them at a later date at a specific price. The borrower/seller thus assumes all interest rate risk associated with the securities. The difference between the selling price and the agreed repurchase price represents the interest on the loan. Thus, a securities dealer holding temporarily unneeded securities can sell them to an investor under a repurchase agreement. The selling dealer might, for example, sell $20 million (face value) six-month bills to an investor for $19,199,200 with a promise to repurchase the bills three days later at a price of $19,212,400. The difference between the selling price and the repurchase price, $13,200 in this case, represents interest paid by the selling dealer to the investor for a three-day loan. The motivation of the selling dealer is the short-term loan it receives at a very low interest rate.

Consider the transaction from the perspective of the lender. The lender buys the securities with the promise to sell them back. The lender might be another dealer in need of securities or a corporate treasurer with excess cash to invest. The lender/purchaser has a very secure investment. First, the loan is fully collateralized (usually over collateralized); and, second, the borrower has assumed all interest rate risk associated with a change in the market value of the collateral.

The repo market is attractive to investors for several reasons. First, this market provides a ready means for investing surplus funds for very short periods of time. Indeed, a large volume of repos are done on an overnight basis, called **overnight repos.** Rates on overnight repos are usually lower than the Fed funds rate. While this is very low, it is still better than no return for the investor who lacks access to the Fed funds market. Second, by rolling over overnight repos, the investor can effectively manage surplus funds when the available quantity of surplus funds is uncertain from day to day.

Repos can also be done for longer terms. A repo of 30 days or more is called a **term repo.** Interest rates on term repos generally rise with the length of the term. Although the overnight repo market is very liquid, the term repo market is considerably less so.

We mentioned that securities dealers often engage in reverse repos in order to obtain securities. The usual motivation for a securities dealer doing a reverse is to obtain securities to deliver on its short sales. That is, when a securities dealer sells securities it does not own, it must borrow the securities in order to make the required delivery. The reverse market is a very effective way to acquire the securities for such sales.

Junk Bond

Junk bonds, also known as **high yield** and as **speculative grade, bonds** having a less-than-investment grade rating. For many decades, such bonds were difficult if not impossible to issue. Those that did exist were usually not issued as such but rather were issued as investment grade and subsequently deteriorated to speculative grade (with a concomitant rise in yield). Such issues are often termed **fallen angels.**

There are two distinct ways that a bond acquires a speculative grade rating. In the first, the issuer's credit standing, based on its historical performance and measured against other issuers, is below investment grade—as in the case of the fallen angels. The second applies to those firms who simply lack a financial history. (Prior to gaining access to the junk bond market, such firms were compelled to borrow from banks or to raising money through private placements—both of which often resulted in significant restrictive covenants that limited management maneuverability.)

There are a number of reasons that the high yield market was difficult for sellers of junk bonds to enter. First, many money managers managing fixed-income portfolios are barred from investing in any security having a less-than-investment-grade rating. Second, the inherent default risk associated with holding junk bonds can be dramatically reduced by diversification, but diversification requires a large universe of similar type securities from which to pick. The inability of issuers to issue such securities limited the ability of investors to diversify junk portfolios. Third, the junk markets tended to be thin and, hence, illiquid.

The nature of the junk bond market began to change when, in the mid-1970s, the investment banking firm of Drexel Burnham Lambert (Drexel) demonstrated, by way of detailed studies, that the yields required on speculative grade securities were excessive relative to their actual default rates.[3] These studies purported to showed that long-term investors in diversified junk portfolios would have fared consistently better in year-to-year returns *even with some defaults* than investors in investment-grade debt. Given this evidence, Drexel concluded that new issues of "high yield" securities should be salable and undertook to develop this market. In the beginning, the buyers of the high yield debt were individuals and a few high-yield mutual funds. But, these were later joined by other holders of fixed-income portfolios including insurance companies, pension funds, banks, and savings and loan associations.

The development of the junk bond market was aided by the work of one of the most amazing financial engineers of the 1980s— Michael Milken. Milken, who worked for Drexel, realized that the junk market was a perfect vehicle by which to raise the funds necessary for takeovers and leveraged buyouts. The strategy, while varied, usually developed as follows: The suitor would identify a target firm having assets (less liabilities) with a market value in excess of the market value of the target's outstanding stock. With the aid of Milken and Drexel, the suitor would sell junk bonds to raise cash very quickly. This would then be used as the war chest to acquire the target firm. Some, or all, of the firm's assets would then be sold and the proceeds used to retire the junk issue of the suitor—often at a handsome premium for the holders of the junk.

Under Milken and Drexel, the market for junk grew rapidly and other major investment banks were soon drawn in. Drexel maintained its dominance in the junk bond market in part by making liquid markets in all of the issues it underwrote as well as many of the issues underwritten by other investment banks. (The remarkable success of this financial engineering—in terms of the growth of the market for junk issues—was depicted in Exhibit 8.7 of Chapter 8.)

The story of Milken and Drexel in the junk bond financing of takeovers and LBOs has, unfortunately, a sad end. During the course of his inspiring rise in the ranks of investment bankers, Milken committed a number of violations of securities law to which he pleaded guilty. The firm of Drexel Burnham Lambert also pleaded guilty to several felony counts, resulting in fines that bankrupted the firm. The combined fines levied against Milken and Drexel totalled over a billion dollars. Despite his demise, Milken's rise represents one of the premier demonstrations of what innovative financial engineering can accomplish and he remains a legend among those in the industry.

Shelf Registration

It has long been a primary function of investment banks to underwrite corporate securities. The traditional underwriting process involves regulation by information and is a product of the Securities Act of 1933. The Act requires that underwriters conduct a **reasonable investigation** on behalf of the investors or be responsible for its absence. The underwriter must conduct its own investigation and must disclose all material facts. This principle has come to be known as **due diligence**.

The underwriting process involves a number of steps. These include (1) the selection of an underwriter by the issuer, (2) the due diligence investigation, (3) preparation of the preliminary registration filing with the Securities and Exchange Commission (SEC), (4) formation of the underwriting syndicate, (5) negotiation of the terms of the offering, (6) fixing the price of the offering, (7) registration statement and prospectus printed in quantity (after acceptance by SEC), (8) public offering, publication of the tombstone, and distribution of the securities, (9) payment to the issuer by the underwriter.

Of the functions performed for the issuer by the underwriter, the most important are preparation of the necessary filings, the pricing of the issue, and the guarantee of the issue's sale (if applicable). The latter involves a transfer of pricing risk from the issuer to the underwriter. The services provided by underwriters do not come cheaply. In fact, the underwriter's gross spread, i.e., the difference between the price to the public and the proceeds to the issuer, can run as high as four or five percentage points—but tend to be less for larger issues and for better quality issues. Nevertheless, several percentage points is not at all uncommon and the investigation and registration process are very time consuming.

Securities registration with the SEC only applies to securities having a maturity longer than 270 days. Thus, securities with a shorter maturity are exempt. This exemption from registration led to the growth of the commercial paper market. While paper can be issued with maturities up 270 days, 30 days, 60 days, 90 days and 180 days are far more common. Because paper offerings are exempt from registration, funds can be raised through this vehicle both quickly and cheaply. For example, the typical dealer fee for handling paper is 1/8 of a percentage point per dollar per year. Thus, 180-day paper can be distributed at a cost of about 1/16 of a percentage point.

The lower cost of issuing commercial paper gave birth to various strategies designed to exploit this short-term market. The most common is to issue paper having a short maturity and then rolling this paper over each period to give it a long-term character. By coupling the strategy with a swap, the interest rate can be fixed (or nearly so)—assuming no change in the quality of the issuer's rating.

In March of 1982, in an effort to reduce the cost and the time associated with bringing a longer-term issue to market, the SEC approved **rule 415**, popularly known as **shelf registration**. Shelf registration allows a firm to file an issue with the SEC and then to bring the issue out in stages as (1) the funds raised by the issue's sale are actually needed, and/or (2) windows of opportunity open. The filing is good for two years (barring material changes in the facts bearing on the issue). Thus, a potential issuer can file a registration statement and then sit back and use it if and when the need arises or attractive opportunities develop. Once in place, the shelf registration allows a new issue to be brought out very quickly. When a decision is made to use the filing, the issuer can put that portion of the securities it wishes to sell up for competitive bid by potential underwriters and dramatically reduce the underwriter's gross spread. This is acceptable to the underwriter since no time is wasted and no expense is incurred with respect to either a due diligence investigation or registration.

In the nine months following the approval of rule 415 (i.e., the remainder of 1982), shelf registration captured 29 percent of the new issue volume. For the full year of 1983, shelf registration captured 37 percent of new issue volume and, for the full year of 1984, shelf registration captured 47 percent of new issue volume. While initially viewed as experimental, rule 415 was deemed a success and made permanent on December 31, 1984. It has since become the issuance route of choice.

The merits of shelf registration become readily apparent when shelf registration is viewed in conjunction with some of the other products of financial engineering discussed earlier in this chapter. For example, consider the issuance of CMOs and REMICs by a major mortgage banker, such as GMAC Mortgage Securities, Inc. (GMAC), in the absence of a shelf registration option. To justify the expense of the due diligence and registration filings for a CMO or REMIC issue, GMAC must develop a large enough asset base (mortgages) to back a sufficiently large issue of CMO/REMIC securities. This may mean holding mortgage assets longer than desirable or paying inflated prices to acquire outside originations. Once the registration process is complete, the securities must be offered quickly—irrespective of the current market conditions and possibly to the detriment of the issuer. With shelf registration, on the other hand, the CMO and/or REMICs can be issued in much smaller quantities as mortgage assets are developed and the issuance can be managed to take advantage of those "windows of opportunity" noted earlier.

Floating Rate Preferred Stock and Reverse Floating Rate Debt

The last two special topics we will touch on in this chapter are simple extensions of other forms discussed in the preceding chapter and earlier in this chapter. One is adjustable rate preferred stock and the other is reverse floating-rate debt.

Floating rate preferred stock is any preferred stock on which the dividend rate is periodically reset or adjusted according to some well-defined rule. Quite a number of variant forms of floating rate preferred have been engineered in recent years. These include **adjustable rate preferred (ARPS), convertible adjustable preferred (CAPS), and single-point adjustable rate preferred (SPARS)** to mention just three. Adjustable rate preferred stock has been the most popular. In this form, the rate is periodically reset (usually quarterly) to a fixed spread over the highest point on the Treasury yield curve. For example, the spread might be 50 basis points over the yield curve. Thus, if, on the reset date, the highest yielding Treasury security is yielding 8.72 percent, the preferred stock dividend rate would be set to 9.22 percent and paid on the stock's par value.

Convertible adjustable rate preferred stock is identical to adjustable rate preferred stock except that it is putable to the issuer on the stock's quarterly reset date (quarterly anniversary). The convertibility feature of CAPS is, however, quite different from that associated with conventional convertible preferred stock. In the latter case, the conversion ratio is fixed. With CAPS, the conversion ratio is reset quarterly to equate it with the stock's par value and the issuer can elect to pay par or to convert to common. Since the value of these alternatives is the same, there is no strong economic preference for one over the other.

Single point adjustable preferred resets periodically, like adjustable preferred, but the dividend rate is reset to a specific reference rate such as three-month T-bill or three-month LIBOR. As with adjustable rate preferred stock, the dividend rate may be set to a spread over the reference rate and this spread is stated in terms of basis points, e.g., three-month T-bill plus 80 basis points.

Reverse floating rate debt, called **reverse floaters,** work the same way as regular floating rate debt in the sense that the rate is periodically reset based on some reference rate. But, in this case, the rate adjustment is in the opposite direction of the movement in the reference rate. This requires that the coupon be stated in terms of the difference between a constant and the reference rate. For example, the rate might be stated as 18 percent less three-month LIBOR. If LIBOR is 8 percent, the reverse floater pays 10 percent. If LIBOR rises to 10 percent, the reverse floater pays 8 percent.

Reverse floaters are useful for a variety of financial engineering purposes including offsetting the risk inherent in a firm's floating rate assets and/or floating rate liabilities. (This usage was suggested by the authors of Chapter 10 in their examination of a hypothetical firm's strategic exposures.) An interesting characteristic of this type of debt instrument is that it is more interest-rate sensitive than conventional fixed rate debt. (We leave it to the reader to figure out why this must be so.)

Summary

A great many of the financial engineering innovations of the last decade and a half have involved the manipulation of traditional forms of fixed-income securities and the creation of new forms. Many of these innovations represent variations on existing themes, but some represent bold breaks with tradition.

Some of the more important fixed-income innovations of the last fifteen years were the introduction of zero coupon bonds, multi-class mortgage-backed and asset-backed securities; the development of the repo/reverse market; the advent of debt defeasance; the emergence of a broad-based junk bond market; simplified procedures for the issuance of securities; and the creation of variant forms of preferred stock and reverse floating rate debt.

The creation of zero coupon bonds, multiclass mortgage-backed securities, and asset-backed securities all involve a process we have chosen to call conversion arbitrage. The latter two innovations are also examples of the securitization of assets. Zero coupon bonds have a number of attractive features and have captured a large part of the Treasury market. The zero coupon yield curve has become an important tool in assessing the demand and supply conditions for debt of specific maturities and has become an important tool in pricing some derivatives—most notably interest rate swaps. Zero coupon bonds are important to financial engineers because the proper combination of zeros can replicate the cash flow stream of a great number of other instruments.

The repo/reverse market provides a mechanism for short-term financing of dealer inventories, a vehicle for the short-term investment of excess cash, and a source of securities for short sales.

Defeasance is a strategy by which a firm can eliminate debt from its balance sheet. The defeaser purchases Treasury debt providing a cash flow stream that exactly matches is liabilities. The Treasury securities are then transferred to a trust and the debt is defeased.

The junk bond market has increased access to the capital markets for firms that would otherwise lack sufficient financial history to tap these markets. It has also provided a powerful vehicle for the financing of takeovers and leveraged buyouts.

The issuance of securities has been enhanced by the introduction of shelf registration. Shelf registration allows a firm to file a registration statement with the SEC and then to tap that filing as windows of opportunity appear or as the need arises. The filing is good for two years and has reduced flotation costs for the firms that use it.

Many other financial innovations have occurred in the fixed-income markets. Two of these are floating rate preferred stock and reverse floating rate debt. Floating rate preferred stock is preferred stock on which the dividend rate is adjustable. The rate is usually tied to some interest rate index. Reverse floating rate debt is debt on which the interest rate varies inversely with some interest rate index.

Endnotes

[1]While default risk is near zero in this structure, there remains the possibility that the custodial bank might fail. Should the custodial bank fail, the holders of the TIGRs might experience delays and legal costs in enforcing their claims.

[2]For discussion and/or empirical evidence with respect to market assessments of default risk versus bond ratings, see Ederington (1985), Ederington, Yawitz and Roberts (1987), Gentry, Whitford and Newbold (1988), Hsueh and Kidwell (1988), Liu and Moore

(1987), Ogden (1987), Perry, Liu and Evans (1988), Reilly and Joehnk (1982), Sorensen (1980).

[3]The empirical evidence presented by Drexel's junk bond chief, Michael Milken, was later shown to be incomplete. While junk bonds outperformed low risk bonds for extended periods, they did not do so for all periods as some investors claim to have been led to believe. See *The Wall Street Journal* (November 20, 1990), "Milken Sales Pitch On High Yield Bonds Is Contradicted by Data."

References and Suggested Reading

Carron, A. *Prepayment Models for Fixed and Adjustable Rate Mortgages*, New York: First Boston, Fixed Income Research (August 1988).

Davidson, L.S. and J.M. Finkelstein. "Variable Rate Financial Instruments' Impact upon Monetary Policy and Stability," *Mid-Atlantic Journal of Business*, 25(4) (February 1989).

Ederington, L.H. "Classification Models and Bond Ratings," *Financial Review*, 20(4) (1985), pp. 237-262.

Ederington, L.H., J.B. Yawitz, and Brian E. Roberts. "The Informational Content of Bond Ratings," *Journal of Financial Research*, 10(3) (1987), pp. 211-226.

Fabozzi, F.J and I.M. Pollock (eds.). *The Handbook of Fixed Income Securities*, 2d ed., Homewood, IL: Dow Jones-Irwin, 1987.

First Boston Corporation, *High Yield Handbook (1989)*, High Yield Research Group, The First Boston Corporation, January 1991.

Fisher, L., I.E. Brick and F.K.W. Ng. "Tax Incentives and Financial Innovation: The Case of Zero-Coupon and Other Deep-Discount Bonds," *Financial Review*, 18(4) (1983), pp. 292-305.

Gentry, J.A., D.T. Whitford, and P. Newbold. "Predicting Industrial Bond Ratings with a Probit Model and Funds Flow Components," *Financial Review*, 23(3) (1988), pp. 269-286.

Hsueh, L.P. and D.S. Kidwell. "Bond Ratings: Are Two Better than One?" *Financial Management*, 17(1) (1988), pp. 46-53.

Kovlak, D.L. "What You Should Know About Repos," *Management Accounting*, 67(11) (1986), pp. 52-56.

Liu, P. and W.T. Moore. "The Impact of Split Bond Ratings On Risk Premia," *Financial Review*, 23(1) (1987), pp. 71-86.

Ogden, J.P. "Determinants of the Ratings and Yields on Corporate Bonds: Tests of the Contingent Claims Model," *Journal of Financial Research*, 10(4) (1987), pp. 329-340.

Perry, L.G., P. Liu and D.A. Evans. "Modified Bond Ratings: Further Evidence on the Effects of Split Ratings on Corporate Bond Yields," *Journal of Business Finance and Accounting*, 15(2) (1988), pp. 231-242.

Reilly, F.K. and M.D. Joehnk. "The Association Between Market-Determined Risk Measures for Bonds and Bond Ratings," *Journal of Finance*, 31(5) (1976), pp. 1387-1403.

Rollins, T.P., D.E. Stout and D.J. O'Mara "The New Financial Instruments," *Management Accounting*, 71(9) (March 1990).

Sorensen, E.H. "Bond Ratings Versus Market Risk Premiums," *Journal of Portfolio Management*, 6(3) (1980), pp. 64-69.

Smith, D.J. and R.A. Tagart "Bond Market Innovations and Financial Intermediation," *Business Horizons*, 32(6) (November/December 1989).

Wertz, W.F. and A. Donadio. "Collateralized Mortgage Obligations," *The CPA Journal*, 57(11) (1987), pp. 68-71.

Appendix
Taxation of Zero Coupon Bonds

Bonds that are sold at issue for less than their redemption value are called, collectively, **original-issue discount bonds.** Zero coupon bonds are the clearest example of such original-issue discount bonds. The current tax law provides for the taxation of the interest earned, but not paid, on these bond's using accretion rules. The rules are different for bond's issued prior to July 2, 1982 than for bonds issued on-or-after July 2, 1982. For purposes of computing taxable interest, bonds issued before this date amortize the discount using straight-line rules while bonds issued on-or-after this date amortize the discount using a constant yield method. The constant yield method employs the yield to maturity prevailing *at the time the instrument was purchased*. Let's contrast these two approaches by way of a complete example (we will work in six month intervals).

Suppose that we buy a zero coupon bond with three years to maturity. For simplicity, suppose that we purchase the bond on January 1st. At the time we purchase the bond its yield (bond basis with semiannual compounding) is 10 percent. The bond has a maturity value (redemption value) of $100,000. Given the bond's yield, its price at purchase is $74,621.54. How would the interest accrue for tax purposes if the bond was issued before July 2, 1982 and how would it accrue if the bond was issued on-or-after July 2, 1982?

For the bonds issued before July 2, 1982, the original-issue discount accrues using a straight-line method. That is, we take the discount and divide by six (since there are two periods per year and the bond has three years to maturity). The calculation is (100,000 − 74,621.54) ÷ 6 = $4229.74. Thus, each six-month period we accrue $4229.74 of interest on which tax must be paid during the year of accrual. To avoid confusion as to the value of the bond for purposes of computing capital gains, should we elect to sell the bond, we must adjust the bond's basis for the accrued interest. The adjustment requires that we add the accrued interest to the previous period's basis to get the new basis, which is called the **adjusted basis.** This is summarized in Table 17.2.

Table 17.2
Accretion Calculations For Zero-Coupon Bonds
Issued Before July 2, 1982

Period	Time	Repo-table Interest	Adjusted Basis
1	0.5	4229.74	78,851.28
2	1.0	4229.74	83,081.02
3	1.5	4229.74	87,310.76
4	2.0	4229.74	91,540.50
5	2.5	4229.74	95,770.24
6	3.0	4229.74	100,000.00

If the same bond was issued on-or-after July 2, 1982, the accretion rules would be different. Specifically, each period we would multiply the previous period's adjusted basis by one-half the yield to maturity. The product is the accrued interest on which tax is due. Since the yield to maturity is 10 percent, each six month period we would multiply the previous adjusted basis by 5 percent. The product is then added to the previous period's adjusted basis to get the new adjusted basis. This is illustrated in Table 17.3.

Table 17.3
Accretion Calculations For Zero-Coupon Bonds
Issued On or After July 2, 1982

Period	Time	Previous Basis	Yield	Reportable Interest	Adjusted Basis
1	0.5	74,621.54	10%	3,731.08	78,352.62
2	1.0	78,352.62	10	3,917.63	82,270.25
3	1.5	82,270.25	10	4,113.51	86,383.76
4	2.0	86,383.76	10	4,319.19	90,702.95
5	2.5	90,702.95	10	4,535.15	95,238.10
6	3.0	95,238.10	10	4,761.90	100,000.00

Suppose now that you sold the bond for $91,450 after two years. If the bond was subject to the before July 2, 1982 rules, the capital gain would be -$90.50 (a capital loss). This sum is obtained by deducting the adjusted basis, $91,540.50, from the sale price $91,450. If the bond was subject to the on-or-after July 2, 1982 rules, the capital gain would be $747.05, which is obtained in the same way. It is readily apparent that the constant yield rules (post July 1, 1982 issues) result in a more attractive tax situation since less of the income is taxed earlier (more is taxed later). As we argued in earlier chapters, tax deference is preferred because it allows us to exploit the time value of money.

Chapter 18

Equity and Equity-Related Instruments

Overview

In this chapter, we are going to examine (1) equity instruments and equity related instruments, (2) the creation and distribution of equity instruments, and (3) the role of equity in the issuer's capital structure. The equity instruments we will consider include proprietorships, partnership interests, and common stock. The equity related instruments we will consider include equity options and warrants, subscription rights, index futures and options, and American depository receipts. We start with a brief examination of the forms of equity.

This chapter is the shortest in this section on instruments. This is not, however, to say that the instruments discussed in this chapter are any less important or any less interesting than others we have discussed. Indeed, just the opposite. Without equity there is no foundation on which to build the kind of organization which makes use of so many of the tools and strategies developed by financial engineers. And, common stock—giving every man and woman the opportunity to own a part of corporate America—may itself be regarded as the first truly revolutionary financial engineering innovation. The fact that this innovation took place hundreds of years ago does not, in any sense, diminish its significance.

457

This is the last chapter on instruments in their "pure" form. In the next and final chapter of this section on instruments, we consider hybrid securities.

Forms of Equity in the United States

Regardless of its form, equity represents an ownership interest in a business entity. This ownership interest is often described as **a residual interest** because the claims of the equity owners on the assets of the enterprise are subordinate to all other claims including the claims of all secured creditors, general creditors, and subordinated creditors. In the case of common stock, the claims are also subordinate to the claims of preferred stock holders. (Preferred stock was discussed in Chapters 16 and 17 and we do not consider it again in this chapter.)

The principal forms of equity are common stock, partnership interests, and proprietorship interests. Common stock represents an equity interest in a business entity organized and chartered as a corporation under the laws of the state in which it is domiciled. Partnership shares represent ownership interests in a business entity organized as a general or limited partnership. Proprietorships represent ownership of business enterprises organized as sole proprietorships. Sole proprietorships are not a major topic of this book, but they are the starting point to understanding partnerships and, consequently, we need to say a few words about them. We begin with proprietorships, then look at general partnerships, corporations, and, finally limited partnerships—in that order.

Proprietorships

A proprietorship or, more correctly, a sole proprietorship, is a business entity having one and only one owner. This form of business enterprise is the easiest to create. In most states within the United States, no special forms need to be filed to bring such a business into existence unless the owner chooses to operate the business under an assumed name. The term **assumed name,** simply means a name other than the legal name of the owner himself or herself and has no sinister implications. For example, if Joe Smith operates a carpet cleaning business under the name "Joe Smith," no special registration of the business is usually required. If, on the other hand, Joe Smith wants to operate his business under the name "Best Carpet Cleaning," then Joe must register the name of his business since he is operating under an assumed name.

The nature of any business can be such that local ordinances may require special permits, licenses, or periodic inspections for the protection of the firm's employees and the general public. But, these are operating considerations and not requirements for the mere existence of the business.

Besides the ease of creation, sole proprietorships have several advantages over other forms of business organization. In particular, the sole proprietor has full control over all managerial decisions and is not responsible to anyone but himself or herself. From a purely legal perspective, the business is indistinguishable from its owner. For this reason, the business profit (loss) is not taxed separately but, rather, is included in the personal income of the owner. If the owner is actively involved in the business, then any losses attributable to the business can be used to offset other income of the sole proprietor. This means that there is no double taxation of the income generated by the business as *is* the case with the corporate form of business organization. It also means that tax benefits, including the sheltering effects of noncash expenses such as depreciation, depletion, and amortization of assets can be passed along directly to the firm's owner.

On the downside, because the owner and the business are indistinguishable, the owner is personally liable for any obligations of the business. This can prove costly in the event of a judgement against the firm or a dissolution of the business. Furthermore, the one-owner structure of a sole proprietorship can make it very difficult to raise capital. Lenders want to see significant equity in the business and, if the sole proprietor does not have sufficient personal funds to invest in the business, lenders will be reluctant to provide financing.

General Partnerships

Partnerships are very similar to sole proprietorships except that there are multiple owners. In a general partnership, each partner is individually and severally liable for the obligations of the business. This means that creditors can seek what is due them from any partner individually or from the partners as a group. As a general rule, creditors can be expected to go after the "deep pockets."

The creation of a general partnership is similar to the creation of a sole proprietorship in that no special filings are necessary except to operate under an assumed name. The partners should, however, have a partnership agreement detailing the financial obligations of the various partners, the areas of decision authority, the division of profits, and any other matters bearing on the relationship among the partners. This is not a legal requirement however. Special permits and licenses may be required as dictated by local ordinances.

The tax treatment of partners is identical to that of sole proprietors except that each partner is only responsible for the taxes due on his or her share of the partnership income and can only take his or her share of partnership losses as a charge against other income. The Tax Reform Act of 1986 (TRA) dramatically changed the tax code regarding which partnership losses may be charged against other income and which may not. In general, the law distinguishes between active and passive income. Active losses can always offset other income, but the use of losses on passive income to offset other income is more limited.

Partnerships increase the ability to raise capital because there are more sources of equity—each partner is a potential source of equity. In addition, because each partner is individually liable for the obligations of the partnership, lenders are more inclined to provided debt financing than they are to a sole proprietorship. The partnership structure also allows for the inclusion of more managerial expertise among the owners because the partnership may include owners possessing different skills.

The downside is that the partnership structure diminishes the control of the business for each individual partner relative to the proprietorship structure. Further, the partners are liable for all actions of the firm whether or not they actively participated in the decisions leading to those actions—even if they were completely unaware of the actions. Finally, the death or withdrawal of a partner dissolves the partnership unless special provisions for dealing with such an event have been included in the partnership agreement.

Corporations

Corporations are quite different from proprietorships and partnerships. Whereas proprietorships and partnerships are indistinguishable from their owners, corporations are legal entities in and of themselves and are clearly distinguishable from their owners. Owners may freely transfer their equity interests, represented by shares of common stock, to others without any direct effect on the corporation itself.

In the corporate structure, the owners surrender control of the firm to professional management. Although the managers bear a fiduciary obligation to the firm's owners, the separation of management from ownership can result in less than optimal performance on the part of management, which is tempted to substitute its own objectives for those of the owners. The difference between the firm's value when management optimizes the owners' interests and the firm's value when management substitutes its own interests is called **agency costs**. Financial engineers have found agency costs a fertile ground for their unique talents during the last decade. Indeed, many corporate takeovers and leveraged buyouts are justified on the basis of reducing agency costs.

There are a number of benefits to the corporate form of organization. First, because ownership is diverse and ownership interests are easily transferred, it is relatively easy for successful corporations to raise equity capital. Further, the individual owners are not liable for the debts of the corporation. Thus, under a worst case scenario, the owners may lose their full investment in the corporation but no more than that. This limited liability and the ease of access to equity capital have long been the major attractions of the corporate form of business organization.

The downside to the corporate form of business organization, other than the agency cost problem already noted, is that the corporation's earnings are taxed twice. They are first taxed as corporate income at the firm's corporate income tax rate. Then, when the dividends are distributed, the dividend income is taxed again as personal income of the recipients. An additional drawback is that losses suffered by the firm cannot be passed directly along to the firm's owners to be used to offset income from other sources—although losses on the sale of the stock itself can be used to offset gains on the sale of other assets.

Limited Partnerships

Limited partnerships are business organizations that attempt to capture the best of the partnership form of business organization and the best of the corporate form of business organization. One or more of the partners are designated as general partners and they, and only they, are empowered to make managerial decisions. The other partners are designated limited partners and have no managerial decision-making authority. This explains the origin of the term *silent partner* sometimes used to describe limited partners. (The term *silent partner* has other usages as well and has never been a technically correct label for limited partners.)

The general partners are individually and severally liable for the obligations of the partnership but the limited partners have no liability for the obligations of the partnership in excess of their share of the firm's capital. This structure allows the partnership to sell limited partnership shares in a fashion very similar to the way common stock is sold, which increases the partnership's access to equity capital. At the same time, creditors' claims on the personal assets of the general partners allows access to debt capital.

Limited partnerships receive the same tax treatment as general partnerships. That is, the partnership income is not taxed at the level of the partnership. Instead, the partnership income is divided up on a *pro rata* basis whether or not the partnership income is distributed. The partners pay personal taxes on their shares of the partnership income. Prior to the Tax Reform Act of 1986, partnership losses were deductible against other income of the limited partner. This tax treatment inspired a great many tax-sheltered limited partnership deals designed to generate losses for the limited partners. Such partnerships developed for purposes of real estate investment, farming, cattle ranching, leasing, oil drilling, and other areas. Some of these had legitimate economic motivation but others were nothing more than tax avoidance schemes. Not surprisingly, the Treasury department objected to businesses formed for no other purpose than creating losses for the wealthy, and economists objected to the diversion of productive resources to nonproductive ends. Several steps were eventually taken to weaken the opportunity for using limited partnerships as vehicles for tax avoidance and these provisions were later incorporated into the revised tax code. The opportunity to create tax avoidance limited partnerships has, consequently, been greatly reduced—but not entirely eliminated.

The flexibility of the limited partnership form of business organization has resulted in this form of business organization becoming the form of choice in much financial engineering. Even without the tax-avoidance opportunities formerly afforded by the partnership structure, financial engineers find that the limited partnership structure is ideal for certain purposes.

An interesting financial engineering innovation involving limited partnerships took place in 1981 when Apache Petroleum Company formed the first **master limited partnership**.[1] A master limited partnership is a limited partnership whose partnership interests are traded, like stock, on an organized exchange. The partnership interests themselves are called **units**. To qualify as a master limited partnership, the partnership must conform to applicable state laws concerning limited partnerships, must have a large number of partners, and must have a high asset value.

The master limited partnership retains the tax benefits of partnerships but with the limited liability and ease of ownership entry and exit associated with a corporation. Between 1981 and 1986 more than thirty such master limited partnerships were created—most in the minerals extraction industries, particularly the energy industry.

The rest of our discussion centers around the corporate form of organization and so the equity interests we consider take the form of common stock. Nevertheless, much (but not all) of what we have to say on the subject of equity is equally applicable to the other forms.

Equity-Related Securities

Equity-related securities are any securities which represent a claim on equity or whose value is, in some way, related to that of equity. There are a number of forms of equity-related instruments including convertible debt, equity options, warrants, subscription rights, pooled investment vehicles, index futures and option contracts, and American depository receipts. Convertible debt has already been described in Chapter 16 and, so, we do not take it up in this chapter. Convertible debt, however, can be considered a form of hybrid security and, as such, fits the model discussed in the next chapter. We also do not say much about index futures and index options because futures and options have been adequately described in Chapters 14 and 15.

Equity Options

Equity options include call and put options on common stock and are often referred to as "stock options." We discussed call and put options more generally in Chapter 14 and it would be redundant to repeat that entire discussion. One example should suffice: Consider an option described as a "110 IBM July call." This is a call option on IBM stock expiring on the third Friday in July and having a strike price of $110. The option covers 100 shares (a round lot) and, in this particular case, trades on the Chicago Board Options Exchange (CBOE). Like all stock options traded in the United States, this option is of the American type—i.e., it can be exercised at any time before expiry. Also, like most stock options in the United States, this option has a maximum life of nine months.

Stock options have been trading in the United States since the early 1970s. They are included here among equity-related instruments because their price is a function of the price of the underlying equity and because they can be exercised to acquire or dispose of the underlying equity instrument. Despite their relationship to the underlying equity, stock options are not created by the issuer of the underlying equity. In fact, virtually anyone can create a stock option by simply writing (selling) it.

Financial engineers have developed sophisticated options trading strategies. While a single naked option position is very risky, a portfolio consisting of some long calls, some short calls, some long puts, and some short puts can have a very low risk character. Such strategies are the product of those financial engineers which we earlier described, in market parlance, as the "quant jocks."

In the type of option strategy alluded to above, the portfolio managers attempt to identify overvalued and undervalued options. The most critical, but unobservable, determinant of an option's value is the volatility of the price of the underlying asset. While historic volatility is a good starting point, considerable evidence exists that historic volatilities are not always indicative of future volatilities. Thus, the decision as to whether an option is undervalued or overvalued is largely a question of whether or not the market is properly assessing future volatility. At any rate, in such a strategy, the overvalued options are written (sold)—whether they are calls or puts, and the undervalued options are purchased—again whether they are calls or puts. However, even if a purchased option is undervalued, the position is still risky because the market price of the underlying asset may, at any time, change in an unfavorable way. The same is true for an overvalued option that has been written. But, by balancing the options purchased and the options written this risk can be dramatically reduced. In the extreme, the strategy can take on a near riskless arbitrage character.

Stock options are sometimes used in takeover strategies. That is, the suitor purchases call options on the target company. When enough such options have been purchased and enough stock has been positioned to trigger the require notice to the SEC, the options are exercised and the stock acquired. This strategy can reduce the cost of a takeover for the suitor firm. This use of options however is neither new nor particularly innovative and so we do not pursue it further.

Equity Warrants

Equity warrants are similar to call options on stock in the sense that they grant the holder the right without the obligation to buy the underlying stock from the warrant grantor. They differ from stock options, however, in several ways. First, warrants are issued by the corporation whose stock represents the underlying asset. Second, they do not necessarily cover 100 shares of stock. Third, they have very long lives—three to ten years is typical. Fourth, they are not necessarily exercisable during their entire lives—the exercise period may be more limited. Fifth, they are often issued in conjunction with (attached to) other issues of the corporation—most often debt or preferred stock—but are generally **detachable**. That is, once the debt or stock with the warrants has been purchased, the warrants can be detached and sold separately from the debt or preferred stock.

Equity warrants benefit the issuer by reducing the coupon necessary to sell debt or preferred stock. They benefit the investor by providing an equity **kicker**. Sometimes common stock will be sold in **units** with a unit defined as some number of common shares and some number of warrants. For example, a unit might consist of three shares and two warrants with each warrant covering one share.

Warrants are also used as a method of compensation for key employees and in an effort to motivate employees to work in the best interests of the firm's shareholders—an effort to reduce agency costs. They are also often used in restructuring deals and to sell additional issues of stock above the current market price. Investors find warrants attractive because, like stock options, they offer considerable leverage; warrants have the added feature of having much longer lives than stock options. Warrants can also be used as hedging instruments by speculators who short the stock and cover themselves by purchasing warrants.

Subscription Rights

Many corporate by-laws require that any new issues of stock not dilute the equity interest of existing stock holders. Indeed, many states require this provision in the corporate charter. In such situations, the corporation must offer its existing shareholders the right to purchase a percentage of the new issue equal to the percentage of the stock they currently own before this opportunity is presented to nonshareholders. To make the purchase of the new stock attractive to the existing shareholders, the corporation will issue **subscription rights** to existing shareholders. A subscription right grants the owner of the subscription right the right, but not the obligation, to buy some number of shares of the new stock issue at a fixed price called the **subscription price**. Subscription rights are only good for a short period of time.

It is readily apparent from the definition of a subscription right that such a right represents an option—although a very short lived one. Because options have value and the owner of the rights can sell them, they are a salable option and trade as such.

Pooled Investment Vehicles

A pooled investment vehicle is any arrangement by which assets are pooled and equity interests in the pool of assets are sold to investors. Mutual funds, representing open-end investment companies, are the best known of such vehicles for obtaining an equity interest in corporations. In such funds, the fund's share value is determined as a *pro rata* share of the fund's net asset value (NAV). The fund's NAV is determined as the market value of the firm's holdings less the firm's liabilities.

There are many other forms of pooled investment vehicles including closed-end investment companies and accumulation units (often used in pension funds)—both of which are equity-related. But, there are also non-equity mutual funds including bond funds and money market funds. There are also passthrough claims to mortgage pools and real estate investment trusts (REITs). Some of these latter instruments have been discussed elsewhere in this book and we do not take them up again. The general structure of a pooled investment vehicle is described in Exhibit 18.1.

Exhibit 18.1
Pooled Investment Vehicle

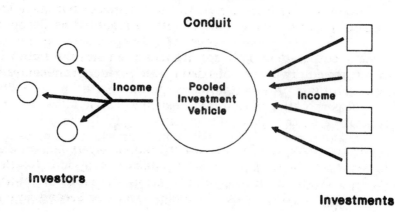

Index Futures and Index Options

Futures contracts and options contracts have been described in Chapter 12 and Chapters 14 and 15 respectively. There is no need to repeat the basic description of these instruments here, but a few words about the index form of these instruments is appropriate and necessary to understanding some of the strategies which we will discuss in the next section of this book.

Index futures contracts are futures contracts written on a stock index, bond index, or other index. Our interest is in the stock indexes. There are futures written on a number of stock indexes, both domestic and foreign. The more popular domestic index futures are the Standard & Poor's 500 Index (S&P), the Major Market Index (MMI), and the New York Stock Exchange Composite Index (NYSE Index). All such contracts are cash settled. That is, if they are not offset by their maturity date, the longs and shorts simply settle in cash, based on a final mark-to-market tied to the value of the cash index at the time of the final settlement.

Index futures have become very important in a great number of strategies developed in recent years by industrious financial engineers. The more interesting of these strategies include whole-market investing and the very controversial portfolio insurance and program trading strategies. (We discuss these strategies in the next section of this book.)

Index options are of two types. The first represents an option on an index futures contract. These options are deliverable. The deliverable asset is the underlying index futures (which is a cash settled instrument). The second type are options on the index itself. Such options are not exercisable in the usual sense. Instead, the options are settled in cash for their fair value in the same way that index futures are settled—irrespective of whether or not the holder chooses to exercise. Such options must be regarded as European type in the sense that the options are only exercisable at the end of the option's life, even though the exercise takes the form of a cash settlement. Index options have also played prominently in various controversial strategies.

Foreign Securities

For many decades most U.S. portfolio managers bought only U.S. corporate stocks. There were a number of reasons for this. First, the institutional brokerage firms, which double as investment bankers, generally did not handle foreign securities. Second, foreign issuers issuing their securities outside the United States are not required to register their securities with the Securities and Exchange Commission and many portfolio managers feared recrimination should it later develop that the issuances were in some way flawed by U.S. standards. Third, structural differences including time zones, operational systems, settlement procedures, language barriers, excessive transactions fees, and ineffectual legal recourse, combined to make foreign investment unattractive. Finally, the ownership of foreign securities exposes the American investor to exchange rate risk. Not only must dividends be exchanged but so also must the proceeds from any subsequent sale of the securities.

As foreign equity markets evolved and the financial industry became increasingly globalized, financial engineers looked for ways to make foreign securities more accessible to U.S. investors. In time, they hit upon the owner trust. That is, a commercial bank purchases a large number of shares of the foreign security and deposits these securities into a trust established for that purpose. The bank then issues single-class securities representing interests in the trust. These securities are called **American depository receipts (ADRs)**. The ADRs themselves are U.S. securities and trade in the U.S. markets in the usual way.

While the performance of the ADRs and the underlying foreign securities should be similar, since the value of the ADR is derived from that of the underlying foreign security, the relationship will not necessarily be one for one. There are two reasons for this. First, one ADR does not necessarily correspond to one share of the underlying stock. The ratio can be any number chosen by the trustee bank that issued the ADRs. Second, there are a limited number of the ADRs and their value is determined by the supply/demand conditions in the U.S. market. Thus, the ADRs can sell at a premium, or at a discount, to the underlying asset. Nevertheless, arbitrage pressure should keep the values from straying too far from one another.

Because of the structure of ADRs it is important for the American investor to understand that ownership of an ADR is not the same as ownership of the foreign security. Instead, the ADR represents an ownership interest in a trust. The trust, on the other hand, owns the underlying securities. Thus, the investor's claim on the foreign security is an indirect claim.

The ADR vehicle for investment in foreign equities is an efficient structure for most American investors and it has become quite popular.

As foreign equity markets evolved, some experienced extraordinary growth rates in values. During the same time, American portfolio managers were coming to realize the benefits of asset allocation strategies and, in particular, tactical asset allocation strategies that weight a portfolio among various classes of securities—of which foreign securities often make up at least one class. For example, an equities portfolio manager may hold a diversified portfolio of stocks with 20 percent in Japanese securities and 80 percent in American securities. If the portfolio manager's analytical techniques lead him or her to the conclusion that the Japanese equity markets will outperform the American equity markets, the portfolio manager will shift holdings from American equities to Japanese equities—yet still maintain a diversified portfolio of individual securities. The manager might, for example, increase the portfolio's holdings of Japanese securities to 70 percent and decrease the portfolio's holdings of American securities to 30 percent.

The phenomenal performance of some nations' equities markets over the last several decades has led to the creation of **country-specific equity mutual funds** for American investors. For example, there are Japanese funds, Korean funds, and Taiwanese funds. There are also funds that are not nation specific but rather region specific. For example, there are European funds, Asian funds, and Pacific Rim funds. More broadly based are the fully international funds that pass under such general labels as "international" funds, "global" funds, and "world-wide" funds. Each of these developments is a financial engineering extension of the fundamental process of collective investing as represented by the **conduit theory** of pooled ownership—undoubtedly one of the most successful financial engineering innovations of all time.

Equity Distribution

The issuance of equity, whether it be an initial public offering (IPO) or just a new issue of an existing publicly held firm's common stock (PO) is a complicated affair. The process is the same for equity as it is for debt and was described in the last chapter. In brief, the investment banker, acting in the capacity of an underwriter, contracts with the firm to handle the necessary due diligence investigation, the filing of the registration statement with the SEC, and the printing of the registration statement and the prospectus. The same, or a different, underwriter then negotiates the actual terms of the offering (price and quantity) and whether the underwriting will take the form of an **absolute purchase,** in which the underwriter assumes all risk, or a **best efforts** offering, in which the issuer bears the risk. The underwriter also develops the **distribution syndicate** with itself as the **lead underwriter** or as a co-leader of the underwriting.

The gross spread from the underwriting is divided among the lead underwriters, syndicate members, and secondary distributors via a complex formula which guarantees the lead underwriter a dominant share. As an alternative to the negotiation of the terms of the offering, the issuer can put the issue up for competitive bid and invite any investment bankers it chooses to submit bids.

An important new development in corporate underwritings is the re-emergence of commercial banks. In the early 1930s, investment banking and commercial banking activities were separated by the passage of the **Glass-Steagall Act.** But, in the 1980s, banking authorities concluded that the motivation for portions of that Act had been negated by the evolution of the industry and the development of effective risk management tools and techniques. On the basis of this, limited underwritings of corporate securities by commercial banks were again permitted. The degree of commercial bank involvement has subsequently expanded. It now appears only a matter of time before commercial banks become full participants in the underwriting and distribution of corporate securities.

The reintroduction of commercial banks into corporate underwriting has had the beneficial effect, from the end user's perspective, of reducing the underwriter's spread and, hence, the flotation costs to the issuer. At the same time, the introduction of shelf registration has also dramatically reduced the cost of floating new issues. Together, these events have dramatically improved the cost effectiveness and the efficiency of public offerings.

As a side point, the players in the market are ranked yearly and pride themselves on their position in what are called the **league tables.** The league tables for corporate underwritings (including both equity and debt issues) are published in such magazines as *Institutional Investor* and are eagerly awaited by all in the industry. The domestic and global league tables for 1990 appear as Exhibit 18.2. The league tables report the total dollar value handled by each major underwriter, the percentage of the total dollar value of all corporate public offerings, and the number of offerings handled. They also provide the rank for the previous year for comparative purposes.

Exhibit 18.2
The Corporate Underwriting Leaders

A summary of the top firms according to full credit to lead manager.

1989	1990		$ Volume (millions)	No. of issues
1	1	Merrill Lynch Capital Markets	$55,754.3	726
2	2	Goldman Sachs	40,743.2	474
3	3	First Boston	33,051.4	524
4	4	Salomon Brothers	32,667.1	375
5	5	Morgan Stanley	31,272.4	325
10	6	Kidder Peabody	22,066.0	672
6	7	Lehman Brothers	20,331.9	444
7	8	Bear Stearns	20,010.0	538
9	9	Prudential-Bache Capital Funding	13,449.5	335
11	10	Donaldson, Lufkin & Jenrette	6,172.7	294

Source: IDD Information Services, Inc. & Institutional Investor

The Role of Equity in the Corporate Capital Structure

Equity is an essential ingredient in any corporation. Although legal entities in and of themselves, corporations are nevertheless owned, and this ownership takes the form of common stock. The stockholders provide the start up capital, make decisions through their voting powers that profoundly affect the path the corporation takes, and elect members of the board of directors. The board of directors, in turn, appoint the executive and operating officers which manage the day-to-day business of the corporation.

The owners' objective is, of course, to maximize the market value of their holdings. This can, and usually does, require a mix of equity and debt capital. Capital is loosely defined as the sum of long-term debt and equity. Debt capital allows the firm to operate on a larger scale than would be possible with equity capital alone and thereby increases the potential returns to the shareholders. On the other hand, debt capital gives rise to an interest expense that must be paid in full and on time. Debt capital is, therefore, a source of financial leverage. The more debt the firm holds, relative to its equity, the more leverage the firm has.

Financial leverage is usually measured with the aid of **leverage ratios**. The most widely used of these ratios are the **debt ratio** (total debt divided by total assets), the **debt-to-equity ratio** (total debt divided by equity), and **long-term-debt-to-total-capitalization ratio** (long-term debt divided by the sum of the firm's debt and equity capital). These ratios are closely watched by rating agencies, lenders, shareholders, and others with an interest in the firm's performance. While it is seriously debated in the academic literature, practitioners generally maintain that there is an optimal capital structure, i.e., a value-maximizing balance between the use of debt and equity in a firm's capital structure.[2] This balance, on the other hand, varies from firm to firm and from time to time and is thus a serious issue for the financial engineer.

Summary

Equity is a necessary ingredient in any business enterprise. The form the equity takes depends on the ownership form of the business. The popular forms of business organization are the sole proprietorship, the general partnership, the limited partnership, and the corporation. Financial engineers have found many interesting uses for the limited partnership form but these uses have been severely restricted by recent changes in the tax code.

In addition to equity itself, there are also a number of equity-related instruments including equity options, warrants, stock-index futures, stock-index options, subscription rights, and pooled investment vehicles. With the maturing of the foreign equity markets, foreign equity has become an increasingly important component of the equity universe and many financial engineers have found uses for foreign equity in their portfolios. Indeed, many of the asset allocation strategies now marketed place considerable emphasis on foreign equity.

The underwriting process for equity is the same as for debt. Underwriters' shares of the underwritings market for both debt and equity are periodically reported in what are called "league tables." Those involved in this end of financial engineering pay close attention to their standing. The mix of equity and debt in a firm's capital structure determines the degree of financial leverage employed by the firm. The less equity, relative to debt, the greater the firm's leverage.

Endnotes

[1]For an economic analysis of master limited partnerships, see Collins and Bey (1986).

[2]The argument that capital structure is irrelevant to the value of the firm was first made by Modigliani and Miller (1958). This conclusion, which was based on arbitrage arguments and employed a number of unrealistic assumptions inspired one of the great debates in the finance literature. For a review of some of this literature see Chen and Kim (1979), more recently, see Durand (1989), Gordon (1989), and Weston (1989)

References and Suggested Reading

Aggarwal, R. and P. Rivoli. "Fads in the Initial Public Offerings Market," *Financial Management*, 19(4) (1990), pp. 45-57.

Chen, A.H. and E.H. Kim "Theories of Corporate Debt Policy: A Synthesis," *Journal of Finance*, 34, (May 1979), pp. 371-384.

Collins, J. M. and R.P. Bey. "The Master Limited Partnership: An Alternative to the Corporation," *Financial Management*, 15(4) (1986), pp. 5-14.

Durand, D. "Afterthoughts on a Controversy with MM, Plus New Thoughts on Growth and the Cost of Capital," *Financial Management*, 18(2) (1989).

Gordon, M.J. "Corporate Finance Under the MM Theorems," *Financial Management*, 18(2) (1989).

Jensen, M.C. and C.W. Smith "Stockholder, Manager, and Creditor Interests: Applications of Agency Theory," in *Recent Advances in Corporate Finance*, E.I. Altman and M.G. Subrahmanyam, eds., Homewood, IL: Irwin, 1985.

Modigliani, F. and M.H. Miller "The Cost of Capital, Corporation Finance and the Theory of Investment," *American Economic Review*, 48 (June 1958), pp. 261-297.

Netter, J. and A. Poulsen. "State Corporation Laws and Shareholders: The Recent Experience," *Financial Management*, 18(3) (1989), pp. 29-40.

Weston, J.F. "What MM Have Wrought," *Financial Management*, 18(2) (1989).

Chapter 19

Hybrid Securities

Bidyut Sen

Overview

This is the final chapter dealing with financial instruments. It has, quite appropriately, been put off to the end because it deals with hybrid securities. **Hybrid securities** can be defined as securities that combine more than one **elemental market** in their structure. The definition of an elemental market is temporal because markets are constantly evolving to higher degrees of complexity. At any point in time, therefore, the distinction between an elemental security and a hybrid security will be somewhat arbitrary.

For purposes of this text, we shall define elemental securities as those securities whose performance is derived from a *single* variable of return. That is, a return might be interest based, commodity based, equity based, or foreign-exchange based, *but it is based on only one*. For example, a pure debt instrument which provides a return from interest rates in a single currency is an elemental security. Similarly, a share of common stock is an elemental security because its return is based solely on the performance of the firm in which the stock represents an equity interest.

Another way of defining elemental securities and distinguishing them from hybrid securities would be on the basis of existing trading markets. Generally speaking, an instrument that has a deep

Bidyut Sen is a Managing Director of Morgan Stanley and Company, Inc. and heads the Worldwide Structured Derivatives Group. He has been involved in derivative products throughout his career and pioneered several kinds of hybrid securities.

Table 19.1
Elemental and Hybrid Securities

Elemental Securities	Hybrid Securities
1. 5-year fixed rate bond denominated in U.S. dollars.	1. 5-year fixed rate bond with interest in U.S. dollars and principal payable in Japanese yen.
2. 3-year forward exchange contract for yen in dollars.	2. 2-year floating rate note principal redemption tied to the value of the S&P 500 index.
3. S&P Index futures contract.	3. Convertible bond with interest in deutschemarks and conversion price in dollars.

trading market where an efficient bid and offer price is available from many market makers is an elemental instrument. For example, a simple interest rate swap is U.S. dollars is an elemental instrument. The market for such swaps is broad and at any point in time provides efficient bid and offer prices from several market makers. Similarly, a forward foreign exchange contract would be an elemental instrument even though it could be described as a combination of a spot foreign exchange rate and the interest differential between two currencies. Table 19.1 lists some well known securities with a categorization as hybrid or elemental.

It should be clear from the above definitions and examples that the distinction between hybrid securities and elemental securities is somewhat vague and will be constantly changing. This is to be expected as we are dealing with markets that are evolving to higher and higher degrees of complexity. As the complexity of financial instruments increases, it can be expected that the elemental security of tomorrow is the hybrid security of yesterday. In any case, the precise definition of a hybrid security is not very important. It is far more important to understand the process by which complex financial instruments are created from simpler financial instruments—a process that has been called a "LEGO" approach to financial engineering or a "building block" approach to financial engineering.[1] It is also important to understand the role played by hybrid securities in the market. In other words, what are the reasons for their coming into being and how are they created?

Types of Hybrid Securities

Broadly speaking, hybrid securities span four major elemental markets. These are interest rate markets, foreign-exchange markets, equities markets, and commodities markets. Combinations of any two or more of these markets can create a hybrid. In addition, each of the elemental markets can be subdivided into narrower markets. For example, the interest rate market consists of dollar-denominated instruments, yen-denominated instruments, deutschemark-denominated instruments, and so on; the commodities markets consist of gold, copper, wheat, cattle, and so on. A combination involving two subsets of the same elemental market can also create a hybrid.

The elemental markets defined above can be combined in several different ways. In addition, by superimposing optional features on these various combinations, we can create a virtually limitless number of variants. This process is illustrated in Exhibit 19.1.

The process by which a typical variant is created and then bought and sold is highly complex but is driven by the most basic economic forces—supply and demand. In the next few sections of this chapter, we will examine hybrids that combine different elemental markets in the broader sense described above. Before proceeding, however, it would help to have a better picture of the various ways that hybrid securities may be categorized and the evolution of derivative and hybrid securities. These are offered, without comment, as Exhibits 19.2 and 19.3, respectively.

Exhibit 19.1
Constructing New Hybrid Securities

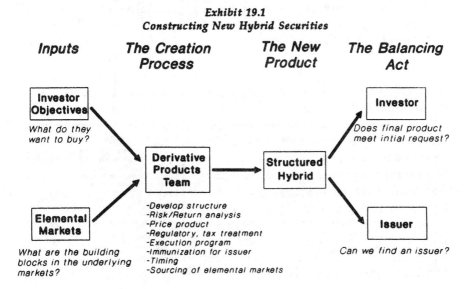

Inputs	The Creation Process	The New Product	The Balancing Act

Investor Objectives
What do they want to buy?

Elemental Markets
What are the building blocks in the underlying markets?

Derivative Products Team
-*Develop structure*
-*Risk/Return analysis*
-*Price product*
-*Regulatory, tax treatment*
-*Execution program*
-*Immunization for issuer*
-*Timing*
-*Sourcing of elemental markets*

Structured Hybrid

Investor
Does final product meet intial request?

Issuer
Can we find an issuer?

Exhibit 19.2
Types of Stuctured Hybrid Securities

Security Linkage: Access Opportunities in Other Markets

Currency-Linked Bonds	Commodity-Linked Bonds	Equity-Linked Bonds	Yield Curve-Linked Bonds	Interest-Rate-Linked Bonds	Portfolio Repackaging

Security Structure: Type of Linked Payments

Principal Repayment-Linked	Coupon Payment-Linked	Both Principal Repayment and Coupon Payment Linked

Derivative Form: Method of Embedding Linkage

Options-Oriented	Futures-Oriented	Forwards-Oriented	Swap-Oriented

Distribution: Method of Sale

Public Issues	Private Placements	Offshore Issues

Exhibit 19.3
The Recent Evolution of Derivative and Hybrid Securities
(selective components)

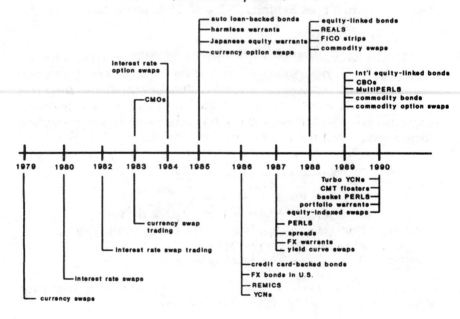

Interest-Rate/Foreign-Exchange Hybrid

A good example of an interest-rate/foreign-exchange hybrid is a dual currency bond. In its simplest form, a dual currency bond is a fixed rate bond with interest payments denominated in one currency and principal payments at redemption denominated in another currency. For example, consider a 5-year bond with a coupon of 12 percent payable annually in U.S. dollars. The principal redemption at maturity is equal to the U.S. dollar equivalent of 1,197.60 Australian dollars (AUD), equivalent to 1,000 U.S. dollars (USD) at the time of issue. Table 19.2 shows the **total return** profile for the investor for various values of USD/AUD exchange rates.

Table 19.2
Total Return Profile on Dual Currency Bond

USD/AUD at Maturity	Redemption Value in USD	Internal Rate of Return
0.60	718.56	7.12%
0.70	838.32	9.32
0.80	958.08	11.33
0.90	1,077.84	13.20
1.00	1,197.60	14.93
1.20	1,437.13	18.10

Interest-Rate/Equity Hybrid

An interest-rate/equity hybrid would combine an interest rate element and an equity element in the overall return for the security. Consider a three-year bond issued with a dollar-denominated fixed rate of interest of 10 percent per annum paid annually and a redemption value upon maturity tied to an equity index. For example, the redemption value might be tied to the major market index (MMI) as follows:

$$R = \$1000 + \left(1000 \times \frac{MMI_m - MMI_0}{MMI_0} \right) \tag{19.1}$$

R: Redemption value at maturity (in dollars).
MMI_0: The value of the MMI at the time of issuance. (Assume a value of 500.)
MMI_m: The value of the MMI at maturity.

Table 19.3 shows the total return profile for the investor for various maturity values of the MMI index.

Table 19.3
Total Return on Equity-Linked Bond

MMI$_m$	Redemption Value	Internal Rate of Return
300.0	600.00	(3.86%)
400.0	800.00	3.57
500.0	1,000.00	10.00
600.0	1,200.00	15.72
700.0	1,400.00	20.90

The basic equity-linked index formula given by Equation 19.1 above can be modified to create any number of possible variants. In the example, the total return increases as MMI increases and decreases as MMI deceases. An investor may desire the benefit of the upside of the market—but not wish to be penalized by the downside. In other words, the investor wants a synthetic call on the equity market. The redemption formula for such a security, which makes use of the MAX function described in the Chapter 14, could be as follows:

$$R = \text{MAX}[\$1000, \text{Equation 19.1 above}] \qquad (19.2)$$

All other things being equal, we would not expect the second equity-linked hybrid, with its embedded synthetic call, to provide the same coupon rate as the first equity-linked hybrid. The reason is simple, the option component (synthetic call) provides additional value: We can get as much total return on the upside as we can with the first variant but we cannot lose as much on the downside. We do not get value without giving value and the "giving of value" will, most likely, take the form of a lower coupon.

Several additional variants on this theme are possible. For example, the investor might be willing to give up the upside on the MMI index. In this case, the redemption formula could be given by Equation 19.4 in which the MIN function is the opposite of the MAX function.

$$R = \$1000 - \left(1000 \times \frac{\text{MMI}_m - \text{MMI}_o}{\text{MMI}_o} \right) \qquad (19.3)$$

$$R = \text{MIN}[\$1,000, \text{Equation 19.3 above}] \qquad (19.4)$$

Using similar reasoning to that above, it should be obvious that the coupon on this instrument would be higher than the 10 percent coupon on the first equity-linked hybrid. In this case, the investor may be viewed as having sold a synthetic call option. Exhibit 19.4 contrasts the payoff profiles for these three equity-linked hybrids on the assumptions that the instruments are held to maturity. The payoff profiles are expressed with the value of the MMI as the determining variable.

Financial engineers commonly use the major market index as the basis for equity-linked hybrids because the index is heavily capitalized and very liquid. Other equity indexes that are frequently used for the same purpose are the S&P 500, the Nikkei 225, the FTSE index, and the DAX index.

Currency/Commodity Hybrid

In a currency/commodity hybrid, the total return on the hybrid security is a function of the elemental return on a foreign exchange rate and the elemental return on the price of a commodity such as oil. For example, consider a two-year security with a fixed coupon of 9 percent per annun paid annually in U.S. dollars with a redemption value indexed to oil as per Equation 19.5.

$$R = \$1000 + \left(1000 \times \frac{P_m - P_o}{P_o} \right)$$

(19.5)

P_m: Yen price of a barrel of oil at maturity
P_o: Yen price of a barrel of oil at issuance
    (Assume P_o = ($35 × 132.00 JPY/USD) = JPY 4,620

Exhibit 19.4
Comparative Payoff Profiles
Equity-Linked Debt Hybrids

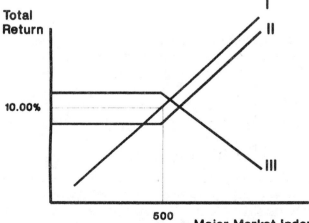

Table 19.5 depicts sample values from the total return profile for various JPY/USD exchange rates and oil prices at maturity. Because of the multiple sources of return on a hybrid, it is not possible to draw a two-dimensional payoff profile for a hybrid unless we hold all sources of return, except one, constant. Exhibit 19.5 illustrates the effect of changing oil prices on total return with the JPY/USD exchange rate held constant at 132:1 and Exhibit 19.6 illustrates the effect of a changing JPY/USD exchange rate with the dollar price of oil held constant at $35 per bbl.

Table 19.5
Total Return Payoff for Currency/Commodity Hybrid

JPY/USD	Oil Price USD Bbl.	Oil Price JPY Bbl.	Redemption Formula (USD)	Internal Rate of Return
100.00	10.00	1,000	216.45	(39.96%)
120.00	30.00	3,600	779.22	(2.16%)
140.00	50.00	7,000	1,515.15	31.27%
160.00	10.00	1,600	346.32	(29.29%)
180.00	30.00	5,400	1,168.83	16.79%
200.00	50.00	10,000	2,164.50	54.72%

Exhibit 19.5
Total Return Profile: Oil Component
(currency/commodity hybrid)

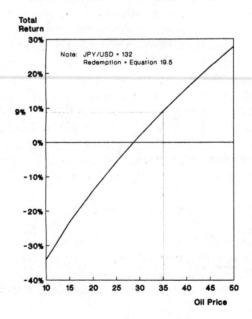

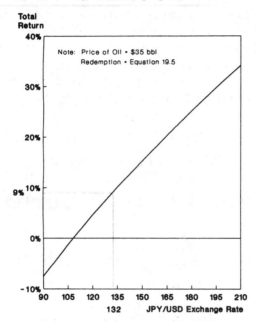

Exhibit 19.6
Total Return: Currency Component
(currency/commodity hybrid)

As with other hybrid structures, there are many different possible combinations of commodity, interest rate and foreign exchange elements. And, of course, we can create a great many hybrids with synthetic option components. Investors may desire to sell off the upside potential of oil prices for a higher coupon rate or, alternatively, they may elect to retain the upside and accept a lower coupon rate.

Two excellent examples of hybrid securities are the "11% Reverse Principal Exchange Rate Linked Securities Due May 19, 1992," otherwise known as "Reverse PERLS" issued by Ford Motor Credit Company and the "Oil Principal Indexed Syndicated Loan" of Sinochem International Oil Company Limited. The tombstones for these offerings appear as Exhibits 19.7 and 19.8.

Investor Motivation

We have defined hybrid securities as securities that combine more than one elemental market within a single structure. We have also defined elemental markets as those that have a high degree of liquidity and several market makers. Given our definitions, it fol-

Exhibit 19.7
Ford's Reverse PERLS Offering

U.S. $100,000,000
(Face Amount)

**Principal Repayable at Maturity in an Amount Equal to U.S. $200,000,000
Minus the U.S. Dollar Equivalent of Yen 13,920,000,000**

Ford Motor Credit Company

11% Reverse Principal Exchange Rate Linked Securities[SM]
(Reverse PERLS[SM]*) Due May 19, 1992*

Price 99.625% and Accrued Interest

---

*Copies of the Prospectus and the related Prospectus Supplement may be obtained
in any State from the undersigned in compliance
with the securities laws of such State.*

MORGAN STANLEY & CO.
Incorporated

May 12, 1987   *Principal Exchange Rate Linked Securities and PERLS
are service marks of Morgan Stanley & Co. Incorporated.*

Exhibit 19.8
Sinochem's Oil-Linked Offering

This announcement appears as a matter of record only

US$50,000,000
Oil-Linked Financing

Sinochem International Oil (Hong Kong) Company Limited

guaranteed by

China National Chemicals Import & Export Corporation

Lenders

BANQUE NATIONALE DE PARIS
CANADIAN IMPERIAL BANK OF COMMERCE
CREDIT LYONNAIS, HONG KONG BRANCH
GIROZENTRALE UND BANK DER OSTERICHISCHEN SPARKASSEN AKTIENGESELLSCHAFT
NMB POSTBANK GROEP N.V., HONG KONG BRANCH
WESTDEUTSCHE LANDESBANK GIROZENTRALE, HONG KONG BRANCH

Agent

BANQUE NATIONALE DE PARIS

The undersigned acted as arranger of the above transaction.

MORGAN STANLEY INTERNATIONAL

May 13, 1991

lows that investors should be able to combine the elemental markets on their own to create the desired hybrid security. Although this is true in theory, investors often prefer to be presented with a fully formed hybrid security as an investment choice. An investor's preference for a packaged hybrid security is based on the classic "make or buy" decision. Although it might be technically possible for an investor to create the hybrid instrument by piecing together the components himself or herself, it might not be possible to do so in the most cost efficient manner. This is a complex issue involving a number of dimensions.

Pricing Efficiency

It might be possible for the investor to obtain the hybrid return required in a cost efficient manner by finding the right kind of issuer. That is, an issuer who has a natural need to create the opposite exposure on the liability side of his balance sheet. The investor's exposure would appear on the asset side of his balance sheet. For example, an investor might be interested in a fixed interest rate investment with the redemption value tied to the price of oil. At the same time, an oil producer might desire a liability that has a fixed rate of interest and the principal redemption tied to the price of oil, a commodity owned by the issuer. By designing a hybrid security, the opposite requirements of the issuer and the investor can be met without using the elemental markets. This will usually result in better pricing efficiency and lower transaction costs.

Regulatory/Policy Constraints

Certain investors might be prevented from creating a hybrid security by themselves due to regulatory constraints or internal policy constraints. For example, an institutional investor wishing to invest in an interest-rate/equity hybrid might have a policy restricting investments to AAA credits. It would, therefore, be appropriate to design a hybrid security which could be issued as an AAA security. The alternative of creating the hybrid investment by combining the elemental components on one's own might not be feasible because of the absence of suitable AAA credit parties capable of, or willing to, provide each of the necessary elements.

Market Access

Not all investors have full access to all the elemental markets or can obtain the most efficient pricing in the various markets. For example, many retail investors who wish to invest in a fixed rate investment with a component of return tied to the stock market would not be able to create the required hybrid investment on their own because of difficulties involved in accessing the stock-index futures market. Additionally, even for those who are able to access this market, the pricing available to them might not be attractive for the investment size of their choice. A hybrid security packaged by professional financial engineers who have full access to the various elemental markets might be the preferred alternative.

Market Expertise

In the simplest description, a hybrid security is composed of two or more elemental securities. This does not, however, mean that creating a hybrid security is as simple as throwing together the elements that comprise the hybrid security. The packaging and pricing of a hybrid security very often requires a high degree of expertise in the various elemental markets and also require experience and insight into the interrelationships among the elements. These are requisite skills of the financial engineer. Investors understand that this financial engineering expertise might not always be available in-house and, therefore, must be bought in the marketplace. They do so by purchasing the fully formed hybrid security.

Desire to Deal with a Single Party

The investor who assembles a hybrid security on his or her own must deal with multiple parties. For example, one party might provide a currency component, another might provide an interest rate component, and still another might provide an equity component. The performance of each party must be monitored and any failures to perform must be dealt with immediately by the investor. A preformed hybrid, on the other hand, requires the monitoring of only one instrument and only one party. This can be more efficient and less time consuming.

Issuer Motivation

There are two broad reasons why an issuer could be interested in issuing a hybrid security. The most common reason is to exploit an arbitrage available in the markets to lower its cost of funds. For example, an issuer might issue a hybrid security but simultaneously hedge the various exposures inherent in the security such that the net result is a straight borrowing at a lower cost than that which is otherwise available to him. This is one of the principal uses for swaps, for example. You will recall from Chapter 13 that swaps are widely used to convert floating-rate obligations into fixed-rate obligation and to convert obligations in one currency into obligations in other currencies.

The second reason is to create a liability exposure desired by the issuer based on assets owned by the company. For example, a company which has a portion of its assets in oil might want to issue a bond where the redemption value depends on the price of oil at maturity. Such a liability would be a natural hedge for the oil assets owned by the corporation. Let's consider a concrete example of each of these motivations from the issuer's perspective.

Arbitrage Transactions

In an arbitrage transaction the issuer's motivation is straight-forward. All the hybrid exposures inherent in the security should be hedged such that the net effect is a simple borrowing in the currency desired by the issuer. In order to go through the mechanics of structuring the bond issue and the related hedges, the issuer requires a certain amount of savings from its normal cost of funds. For example, assume an AAA issuer wishes to raise $100 million on a floating-rate basis for a five-year term. Assume further that the firm could raise this money by issuing a dollar denominated floating rate note paying LIBOR + 20 bps. However, the firm could, as an alternative, sell a dual currency bond. The bond would be sold for $100 million (in yen but immediately converted to dollars at the spot rate of 140 JPY/USD) and the firm would pay a 12 percent USD coupon with payments made annually. Redemption would be made in yen with the same number of yen payable at the end as received at the beginning.

To convert the fixed-rate borrowing to the desired floating-rate borrowing, the firm would enter a fixed-for-floating interest rate swap as fixed-rate receiver (floating-rate payer). Suppose that such a swap is available and would require that the firm pay LIBOR in exchange for 12 percent, both paid annually. At the same time, the firm enters into some sort of five-year forward FX contract with a forward exchange rate of 140 JPY/USD to immunize itself from the exchange rate risk associated with the yen redemption at maturity. This hybrid is depicted in Exhibit 19.9.

Exhibit 19.9
Using Hybrids to Lower Financing Costs

Alternative 1: Straight Borrowing

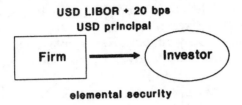

elemental security

Alternative 2: Hybrid with Conversions

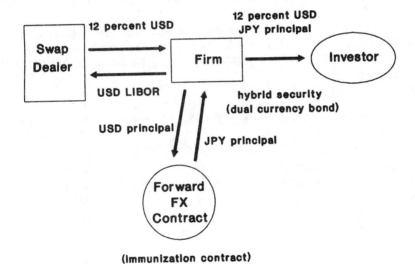

(Immunization contract)

Notice that the firm achieves the desired five-year floating rate financing at a cost of LIBOR. This is a full 20 basis points per year better than if it had borrowed floating rate directly. While 20 basis points may not seem like very much, on principal of $100 million it amounts to $200,000 a year for five years. At a 12 percent discount rate, this savings has a present value of about $721,000.

Nonarbitrage Transactions

In a nonarbitrage transaction the issuer enters into the transaction with the knowledge that it will create some sort of risk exposure for the firm. The issuer is willing to accept this exposure because it offsets an opposite exposure that the firm already has. The existing exposure may be due to the business activities the firm is involved in or it may be due to certain assets the firm owns.[2] For example, consider an oil company that is contemplating borrowing money on a fixed-rate basis for a five-year term. The company could do a five-year bond issue in which the redemption amount for a $1,000 bond is given by Equation 19.6.

$$R = MAX\left[1000, 1000 + \left(1000 \times \frac{P_m - P_o}{P_o}\right)\right] \qquad (19.6)$$

P_o denotes the price of oil at the time of the bond's issue and P_m is the price of oil at the time of the bond's maturity. Assume that P_o is $20.

The investor enjoys the upside of risky oil prices but does not have the downside risk. Table 19.6 provides the selected values from the payoff profile at redemption as a function of the price of oil at maturity.

Table 19.6
Selected Payoff Values for the Bond's Redemption

P_m	Redemption Amount
$40.00	$2,000
30.00	1,500
20.00	1,000
15.00	1,000
10.00	1,000

Since the investor only has upside potential on the price of oil and is protected from downside risk, he or she would be expected to accept a lower coupon on the security. From the issuer's viewpoint the situation is quite different. To start with, the issuer has a lower coupon than would be required on a straight bond issue. If the price of oil goes up, then the redemption value of the borrowing goes up. However, since the oil company owns oil as part of its asset base, the benefit from a higher oil price offsets the higher amount that he has to pay investors upon redemption. From the issuer's perspective, the firm has written a covered call.

In general, issuers can take advantage of various types of assets to issue hybrid securities that include a specific exposure. It is possible that an issuer could be willing to issue an unhedged security even if it does not own an asset with the opposite exposure position. The issuer could simply believe that oil prices have peaked and, consequently, there is a higher probability that prices will be lower in the future. In such cases, the issuer has decided that the lower coupon on its borrowing more than compensates for the risk of higher prices in the future.

Summary

The financial engineer's task in the area of hybrid securities is to create securities having new structures, price the new securities properly, assist in selling issuers and investors on the transaction, and lastly, execute the transaction. In order to be effective, the hybrid-security specialist must have a broad range of expertise. It is absolutely necessary for him or her to be familiar with the characteristics of all the elemental markets that will be used. The financial engineer must also understand the relationships among the various markets and the objectives of both the investors and the issuers. This requires expertise in the areas of corporate finance, international capital markets, asset/liability management, tax and accounting rules and a variety of related areas. Finally, the hybrid-security specialist should be able to execute the complete transaction. In order to do this, it is necessary for him or her to understand the actual workings of all the elemental markets that will be used.

Endnotes

[1]See Smithson (1987) for example. Note, LEGO is an exclusive trademark of INTERLEGO A.G. of Denmark.

[2]As examples of this, recall the various exposures uncovered in our examination of the financial statements of XYZ Corporation in Chapter 10. You might want to go back and glance through that chapter again after finishing this one.

References and Suggested Readings

Briys, E. and M. Crouchy. "Creating and Pricing Hybrid Foreign Currency Options," *Financial Management*, 17(4) (1988), pp. 59-65.

Chance, D.M. and J.C. Broughton. "Market Index Depository Liabilities: Analysis, Interpretation, and Performance," *Journal of Financial Services Research*, 1 (1988), pp. 335-352.

Chen A.H. "Puttable Stock: A New Innovation in Equity Financing," *Financial Management*, 17 (Spring 1988), pp. 27-37.

Chen, A.H. and J.W. Kensinger. "An Analysis of Market Index Certificates of Deposit," *Journal of Financial Services Research*, 4 (1990), pp. 93-110.

Chen, A.H. "Creating Contingent Liabilities: Master Craftsmanship in Financial Engineering," *Game Plans for the '90s*, Chicago: Federal Reserve Bank of Chicago, 1990.

Commodity Futures Trading Commission. Regulation of Hybrid Securities, *Federal Register*, 54 (January 1989).

Davis, R. "Are Indexed Oil Instruments Also Commodity Options?" *Commodity Law Letter*, (July/August 1986).

Finnerty, J.D. "Security Innovation: Where is the Value Added?" *Financial Management Collection* (Winter 1988), pp. 1-7.

Gynn, R. and J.J. Tindall. "Intermarket's 1987 Hybrid Debt Innovations Directory, *Intermarket* 4 (August 1987), pp. 42-46.

King, T.E. and A.K. Ortegren. "Accounting for Hybrid Securities: The Case of Adjustable Rate Convertible Notes," *Accounting Review*, 63(3) (1988), pp. 522-535.

Knight, L.G., R.A. Knight and J. Robertson. "Tax Status of Hybrid Securities, *The CPA Journal*, 58(9) (1988), pp. 44-50.

Ross, S.A. "Institutional Markets, Financial Marketing, and Financial Innovation," *Journal of Finance*, 44 (1989), pp. 541-556.

Smith, D.J. "The Pricing of Bull and Bear Floating Rate Notes: An Application of Financial Engineering," *Financial Management*, 176 (1988), pp. 72-81.

Smithson, C. "A LEGO Approach to Financial Engineering," *Midland Corporate Finance Journal* (Winter 1987), pp. 16-28.

Chapter 20

Asset/Liability Management

Overview

While asset/liability management is applicable to any organization's balance sheet, the subject is, without doubt, of greatest interest to depository institutions, nonbank financial corporations, and multinational corporations. Depository institutions include commercial banks, savings and loan associations, mutual savings banks, and credit unions (the latter three are collectively called thrifts). Nonbank financial corporations include insurance companies, pension funds, finance companies, mortgage banks, brokerage firms, and investment banks. Both the depository institutions and the nonbank financial corporations are primarily concerned with the return on their portfolios and the risk associated with holding those portfolios. For both types of organization, a principal source of earnings is the difference between interest received and interest paid, and the source of the risk is primarily the volatility of these same interest rates. Multinational corporations, which can include commercial banks and investment banks, have the additional problem of exchange-rate risk from holding assets denominated in one currency that are funded by liabilities denominated in another currency. Even when the currencies of the assets and the liabilities are matched there will usually be some residual translation exposure associated with financial statement consolidation.

We introduced asset/liability management in Chapter 7 as one of the conceptual tools of financial engineers. In that same chapter, we also introduced other conceptual tools associated with risk management including insurance and hedging. We went to the trouble of differentiating between asset/liability management and hedging despite the fact that they are very closely related activities and can be viewed as substitutes for, or as complements to, one another—depending on the purpose and the context. We also demonstrated that asset/liability management techniques include techniques for managing interest-rate risk and exchange-rate risk. In this chapter, we are going to look more closely at some of the more sophisticated asset/liability management techniques that have been introduced in recent years with a focus on interest-rate risk management. The reader is forewarned that, in this chapter, we blur the distinction between asset/liability management and hedging. We will, however, take a more detailed look at hedging in the next chapter.

Asset/liability management is a particularly complex subject having a great many dimensions. Consequently, we cannot possibly consider all asset/liability management strategies and issues in this one chapter. Indeed, one could easily devote several large books to this subject. The reader interested in asset/liability management in the context of the treasury function of a commercial bank should check the references and suggested readings section at the end of this chapter.[1] We would also mention that a number of the other strategies discussed in the following chapters, particularly those dealing with asset allocation issues, can themselves be viewed as extensions of asset/liability management.

The Evolution of Asset/Liability Management

Asset/liability management has changed a great deal over the last several decades. Consider, for example, the approach taken by depository institutions up until the early 1960s. Until that time, these institutions derived the bulk of their funding from customer deposits, long-term debt, and equity. The terms on the deposit accounts (demand and/or time deposits) were fixed (by Regulation Q). As a result, an institution's short-term funding mix was determined, primarily, by decisions made by the institution's depositors. Institutions, for example, could not attract depositors from outside their immediate geographic region by offering higher rates. In such an environment, there was very little art or science involved in liability management and the principal focus was on asset management. That is, the institution's treasury department used the funds provided by depositors (over which it had little control) to structure an asset portfolio that was appropriate for the given liability portfolio. A portion of the firm's assets would be set aside as noninterest earning reserves (deposits at the Fed) and the remainder would be invested in loan and securities portfolios. Any excess reserves would be lent in the Fed funds market until they were needed for some other purpose.

During the period when the strategy above was applicable, the deposit taking industries were highly regulated—implying limited competition—and interest rates were relatively stable (by recent standards). In such an environment, the management of the asset portfolio was a rather routine affair requiring relatively little day-to-day attention.[2] But all that began to change in the early 1960s when the demand for funds from corporate customers of New York money center banks began to outstrip those banks' traditional funding sources. To address this problem, Citibank introduced the **negotiable certificate of deposit**. This instrument was exempt from Regulation Q (provided that the amount of the deposit was at least $100,000 and that the term of the deposit was at least 14 days). Citibank's experiment was a major success and was soon copied by other depository institutions. The new instrument, by bypassing Regulation Q, provided an improved means for allocating funds to those end uses where the value was the greatest.

With the advent of CDs, banks had a tool by which to manipulate the mix of liabilities that supported their asset portfolios and it soon became apparent that the game would henceforth be one of active management of asset and liability portfolios, as opposed to the management of the asset portfolio alone. The first asset/liability strategies to develop were strategies for the management of **interest margin**. Interest margin is the difference between the interest received on earning assets and the interest paid on liabilities. Interest margin can be expressed in terms of dollars or as a percentage of earning assets. Interest margin management led to the concept of the gap and, subsequently, to **gap management.** Closely related to the notion of interest margin is the notion of **spread**. The spread, as the term is used in banking, is the difference between the percentage return earned on assets and the percentage cost paid on liabilities.

As time went on, asset/liability management became progressively more aggressive and complex. This was a response to increasingly volatile interest rates, the introduction of money market mutual funds, the development of overseas markets as both funding and lending sources, the introduction of significant competition in the U.S. markets by both domestic and foreign lending institutions, major new developments in risk management theory, the development of new risk management instruments, new outlets for asset sales, the gradual erosion of the effectiveness of antiquated regulations, and, eventually, the deregulation of financial services. Let's consider the effect of just two of these factors: the volatility of interest rates and the advent of money market mutual funds.

As we demonstrated in Chapter 2, most prices, including interest rates and exchange rates, experienced a dramatic increase in volatility beginning in the mid 1970s. Interest rates, in particular, not only became more volatile but also rose significantly in the latter 1970s and reached post war highs in the early 1980s. Consider just one additional bit of evidence of this increased volatility. In both the decades of the 1950s and the 1960s, there were a total of 16 changes in the prime rate of interest. In the 1970s, there were 139 changes in the prime rate of interest. The pace accelerated even more as we moved into the early 1980s. For example, between October 1979 and December 1980, the prime rate changed about 50 times. From August 1979 to January 1980, the prime rate rose from 11 percent to 20 percent before dropping back to just under 12 percent and then rising again to over 21 percent.[3]

Although they retreated from their record levels of the early 1980s, interest rates nevertheless remained high by historic standards throughout the 1980s. The sharp increase in the level and the volatility of interest rates, more than anything else, rung the death knell for the old way of doing business. As short-term interest rates rose, depository institutions learned the meaning of the old maxim "never borrow short to lend long." By committing themselves to long-term assets paying low fixed rates of interest—such as thirty year mortgages at rates of 6 to 8 percent during the 1950s and 1960s and only slightly higher rates during the early 1970s—these institutions, particularly the savings and loan associations, found themselves locked in the proverbial "no win" situation by the late 1970s. To make matters worse, their traditional source of low-cost financing—the demand and time deposits—dried up as savers gradually turned to more lucrative, equally liquid, unregulated alternatives. The process of **disintermediation** had begun.

Disintermediation is the process by which the traditional

customers of depository institutions, small savers, pull their funds out in order to earn higher returns elsewhere. The main driving force behind the disintermediation process was the **money market mutual fund,** first introduced in 1973. Money market funds were an interesting innovation. They demonstrate how financial engineers often take an old idea and revolutionize it with just a little twist. (After the fact, the benefits are plainly visible to all and everyone asks themselves why they did not think of it first.)

Money market mutual funds sell their shares to small investors and then pool the funds for subsequent investment—just like any traditional mutual fund. The difference, however, is that money market mutual funds invest exclusively in low-risk short-maturity money market instruments. The return from the money market instruments is then paid out to the shareholders, less a small management fee. Most often, the price per share is held constant at $1, dividends are paid frequently, usually daily, and credited monthly. Soon after money market funds were introduced, the funds added a check writing privilege—another innovation—which further enhanced their attractiveness as a bank alternative.

When first introduced, money market funds attracted very little attention largely because interest rates were still relatively low and the incremental gains were not sufficient for most investors to part with their locally accessible and "insured" bank and thrift deposits. But, as the 1970s wore on and interest rates rose to ever higher levels, the incremental benefits of switching to money market funds grew greater. Eventually, the disintermediation process became a nightmare for the depository institutions as hundreds of billions of dollars left banks and thrifts for a new home in the money market funds. The money market funds then purchased certificates of deposit from banks and thrifts. The banks and thrifts were then forced to pay significantly higher market rates. Before long, depository institutions, particularly the thrifts, found themselves paying higher rates on their short-term liabilities than they were earning on their long-term assets. It didn't take a genius to see that this was a sure route to bankruptcy.

Some institutions responded to the new environment by, quite simply, ignoring it. Hoping, it would seem, that time alone would solve the problem when rates returned to their historic levels. Unfortunately, time did not solve the problem and many of these institutions later engaged in desperate attempts to return to profitability by making high-risk/high-yield investments with depositors' money. For many, this strategy backfired—contributing to the financial disaster that befell the thrift industry in the late 1980s. In hindsight, it is easy to see that the government encouraged this process by failing to adjust deposit insurance premiums for the relative riskiness of the assets held by depository institutions.[4]

Fortunately, others were not so sanguine. They moved to improve their management skills; sent employees to training programs in the new methods and instruments for managing assets, liabilities, and risks; and hired skilled financial engineers to assist in their institutions' revitalization. At the same time, investment bankers recognized the potential to market a valuable new product— asset/liability management strategies, and devoted considerable energies to developing them. In the end, these engineers created a number of useful tools, some of which we will discuss later.

The Foundation Concepts

There are five foundation concepts to understanding all asset/liability management strategies. They are liquidity, term structure, interest rate sensitivity, maturity composition, and default risk. We consider each of these briefly.

Liquidity is loosely defined as the ease with which assets can be converted to cash. Liquidity is particularly important to deposit-taking institutions because depositors may suddenly withdraw funds, thereby necessitating a need for liquidity. Cash must be raised quickly to meet any such liquidity demands. There are two dimensions to liquidity as the term pertains to assets. The first is maturity liquidity. An asset is said to be liquid if it will mature in a very short period of time. For example, Fed funds and overnight repos are very liquid instruments for the simple reason that they automatically turn into cash in a single day. Multi-year commercial loans, on the other hand, are very illiquid assets. It is sometimes useful to array assets along a liquidity continuum in order to better appreciate this aspect of liquidity. Such a continuum is depicted in Exhibit 20.1.

Exhibit 20.1
The Maturity Liquidity Continuum

most liquid   **least liquid**

| Fed funds overnight repos | call money | short-term loans T-bills | notes term loans | mortgages | bonds |

The second dimension to liquidity is marketability. An asset is liquid if it can easily be sold in the secondary market without a major price concession. For example, a Treasury security is always readily marketable and, hence, very liquid. A junk bond, on the other hand, can be very difficult to sell (depending on market conditions) without a significant price concession.

All other things being equal, less liquid assets provide a greater rate of return than do more liquid assets. Thus, there is a trade-off between liquidity and profitability.

The second foundation concept is that of **term structure**. At any given point in time there is a relationship between debt instrument yields and those instruments' maturities. This relationship can be depicted via the familiar yield curve. We discussed the notion of a yield curve and the various explanations for the shape of the yield curve in Chapters 8 and 17. Such a relationship can be drawn for any group of securities having a similar credit rating (default free, AAA, BBB, junk, etc.). The shape of the yield curve and the asset/liability manager's expectations about the future shape of the curve will play a significant role in his or her strategy.

The third factor is **interest-rate sensitivity**. There are two distinct ways to look at interest-rate sensitivity. Most often, we use the term interest-rate sensitivity to describe the degree to which an instrument's price will change when the instrument's yield (a reflection of the current market rate) changes. In this context, we can measure interest-rate sensitivity with any of the tools discussed in Chapter 8 including duration, the yield value of a 32nd, or the dollar value of a basis point. Indeed, in our earlier discussion of asset/liability management in Chapter 7, we examined the role of duration in the management of asset and liability portfolios.

The second way to look at interest-rate sensitivity is to focus on the variable or floating-rate assets and liabilities. These instruments are interest-rate sensitive in the sense that, as market rates rise, the return on the interest-sensitive assets and the cost of the interest-sensitive liabilities will also rise. In this usage, the degree of interest sensitivity is determined by the degree to which an instrument's interest rate adjusts and the speed of this adjustment. This is the sense in which we use the term *interest-sensitive* in our later discussion of gap management.

The fourth factor important in asset/liability management strategies is **maturity composition**. The maturities of assets and liabilities can be matched or unmatched. If the maturity and the interest-rate sensitivity of an asset and a liability are matched, then the institution has a **spread lock** on that portion of the principals that are also matched. For example, suppose that a bank holds $8 million of a three-year fixed-rate asset returning 14 percent. These assets are funded by $6 million of a three-year fixed-rate liability, having a cost of 12 percent, and $2 million of three-month CDs. The bank has a spread lock on $6 million of assets with a spread of 2 percent. We could achieve a similar result holding floating-rate assets returning, for example, LIBOR plus 2 percent if those assets are funded by liabilities with a cost of LIBOR flat.

Maturity composition and term structure interact to determine interest-rate sensitivity. Consider a simple case. Suppose a financial institution can both borrow and lend for either 180 days or 360 days. The borrowing and lending opportunities are detailed below in Table 20.1 together with the 180-day rate expected to prevail 180 days out. We will assume that the institution borrows at LIBOR and lends at LIBOR + 1.5% (Note: these rates are not intended to be realistic. They are provided only to demonstrate the concepts involved.)

Table 20.1
Maturity Composition — Managing the Spread

Current Rates	Lending	Borrowing (LIBOR)	Spread
180 days	14.5%	13.0%	1.5%
360 days	15.5%	14.0%	1.5%
Expected 180 day rate 180 days from now	14.0%	12.5%	1.5%
6x12 FRA	FRA + 1.5%	FRA = 13.5%	

Alternative Strategies:

1. Borrow for 180 days at 13.0 percent and lend for 180 days at 14.5 percent. This strategy earns a known spread of 1.5 percent for 180 days.
2. Borrow for 360 days at 14 percent and lend for 360 days at 15.5 percent. This strategy also earns a known spread of 1.5 percent for 360 days.
3. Borrow for 180 days at 13 percent and lend for 360 days at 15.5 percent. Then, refund the lending for the remaining 180 days at the prevailing 180-day rate. This strategy produces a spread

of 2.5 percent for the first 180 days and an *expected* spread of 3 percent for the next 180 days. This strategy is risky because the realized cost of funds and the expected cost of funds 180 days out may diverge significantly.

4. Borrow for 180 days at 13 percent and lend for 360 days at 15.5 percent. Simultaneously enter a "6 x 12" forward rate agreement (FRA) to lock in a 180-day rate 180-days from now. This strategy guarantees a spread of 2.5 percent for the first 180 days and guarantees a spread of 2 percent for the second 180 days. This strategy represents an application of hedging to asset/liability management. While it reduces uncertainty, the hedge also adds a cost. In this case, the cost is the difference between the expected spread of 3 percent without the hedge and the known spread of 2 percent with the hedge. Thus, the total cost of the hedge is 1 percent during the second 180 days.

5. An intermediate strategy between (3) and (4) above would involve a 360-day lending at 15.5 percent coupled with a 180-day borrowing at 13 percent and the purchase of a single-period interest-rate cap with a ceiling rate of 13.5 percent and pegged to LIBOR (the rate at which the institution would actually borrow funds).

The point of reviewing the various possible strategies above, and these are only a few of many strategies possible, is to demonstrate the flexibility and the complexity of modern asset/liability management and the implications for interest margin and the spread associated with different strategies.

The final factor playing a role in asset/liability management is default risk. Recall that default risk is the risk that the debtor will be unable to repay the loan principal and/or interest. Financial institutions, particularly commercial banks, serve a very useful function in assessing borrower risks and in pooling those risks. Depositors at these institutions, in general, lack the expertise or time to evaluate borrowers' creditworthiness. A portion of a bank's spread must therefore be viewed as compensation for risk bearing and credit assessment. An institution's spread can always be increased by making higher-risk loans and/or investing in lower-grade securities.

The Changing Face of Liquidity Management

As noted above, in earlier days, asset/liability management concentrated on asset management and one of the principal concerns was always liquidity. Since depositors at financial institutions (depository institutions specifically) could withdraw funds on relatively short notice, managers had to plan for sufficient liquidity to meet these potential withdrawals. At some institutions, withdrawals by depositors occur with some regularity—such as when commercial accounts draw down their deposits to meet payrolls or when retail accounts are tapped during Christmas shopping seasons. At other institutions, such as those in farm belt communities, there is a more extended seasonality which coincides with production and harvest cycles. The liquidity needs made necessary by depositor behaviors of these types had to be planned for through asset management. That is, management had to hold assets of sufficient liquidity that the institution could liquidate the assets to meet withdrawal demands. In the case of the predictable patterns described above, assets with appropriate maturity liquidity could be used to meet the liquidity needs. Nevertheless, there always remained an unpredictable element in deposit withdrawals and good liquidity management required planning for the unexpected. Most depository institutions met this type of liquidity need by holding some cash equivalent assets. These include T-bills and other short-term, readily marketable, securities.

Liquidity management changed dramatically after the introduction of certificates of deposit. These instruments gave financial institutions a tool by which to manage their liquidity on the liability side. For example, a sudden withdrawal of deposits could be offset by the quick issue of negotiable CDs. By managing liquidity on the liability side of the balance sheet, the institution could reduce its holdings of low-return cash equivalents in favor of higher-return, longer-maturity, less liquid assets. Not surprisingly, depository institutions' holdings of cash and cash-equivalent assets declined dramatically over the next two decades. For example, at the start of the 1960s, bank holdings of cash and securities represented about 50 percent of total bank assets, with loans making up about 45 percent. By 1980, cash and securities comprised only 30 percent of total bank assets while loans had risen to almost 60 percent. The ability to manage liquidity on the liability side of the balance sheet was later enhanced further by the introduction of the repo/reverse market. (Discussed in Chapter 17.)

The CD approach to managing depository institution liquidity was soon replicated on the corporate side with the introduction of commercial paper. (Commercial paper was discussed in Chapter 16). In addition, corporations found the repo/reverse market a very attractive vehicle by which to invest excess cash and preserve their liquidity.

Margin Management (The Role of the Gap)

The essence of modern asset/liability management, in achieving the long-run goal of wealth maximization, is efficient and effective management of interest margins and spreads. Both of these concepts are linked to the institution's income statement. Also important is the concept of the gap.

The gap may be defined as (1) the dollar difference between a financial institution's floating-rate assets and floating-rate liabilities, or (2) the dollar difference between an institution's fixed-rate liabilities and fixed-rate assets. By these definitions, gap is best understood as a balance sheet concept. In this definitional structure, interest-sensitive assets and liabilities are defined as those having floating-rates of interest.

The simplest margin management strategy is a simple spread-lock strategy. In such a strategy, the institution's asset/liability management group would look to lock-in a spread by matching both the type and the maturity of its assets and liabilities. Thus, all fixed-rate assets would be funded by fixed-rate liabilities and all floating-rate assets would be funded by floating-rate liabilities. This strategy is relatively safe, barring loan and securities defaults, but it will not necessarily produce spreads sufficient to cover the institution's overhead expenses. Examples of these types of strategies include strategies (1) and (2) in Table 20.1. As already noted above, the spread can be increased by holding higher-risk assets, but this exposes the institution to greater default risk.

A more aggressive strategy involves **gap management**. In gap management the institution varies the gap in response to its expectations about the future course of interest rates and the shape of the yield curve. The basic strategy is to increase the gap when interest rates are expected to rise and to decrease the gap (negative gaps included) when interest rates are expected to fall. Since the gap is the difference between floating-rate assets and floating-rate liabilities. An increase in the gap will increase the spread when rates rise since the return on the variable-rate assets will rise but the cost of the fixed-rate liabilities used to fund the assets will not rise. The reverse argument applies when rates fall. Strategy (3) in Table 20.1 is an example of a gap management strategy employing such forecasts.

There are a number of problems in applying the basic gap management strategy outlined above. First, gap management assumes that the future direction of interest rates can be predicted.

Financial institutions expend a great deal of time and energy attempting to make such predictions. But a prediction is always just that—a prediction—and it can prove wrong. Faulty forecasts can lead to an unexpected narrowing of the spread or an unexpected widening of the spread. Thus, there is a trade-off between the spread to be earned and the risk to be borne. The wider the gap (in a rising rate market) the greater the potential spread but also the greater the spread variability. This trade-off is depicted in Exhibit 20.2.

Exhibit 20.2
Gap vs. Spread

Expectation: rising rate market

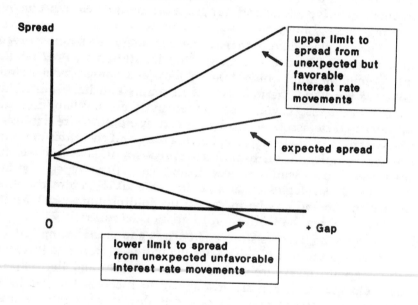

The second historical problem with gap management is that it took considerable time to alter the character of an institution's assets and/or liabilities. One did not just dump fixed-rate term loans made to corporate clients, for example, and invest the proceeds in short-term prime loans (the interest on which fluctuates with the prime rate). Established relationships would be damaged and relationships are a key to successful banking. The final problem with gap management concerns the very ability to alter the gap. Through the 1970s for example, one could only alter the gap if opportunities for appropriate types of lending and borrowing were available. Such opportunities were determined by the current state of the world and by the competitive pressures of the marketplace.

All of the old problems with gap management enumerated above disappeared during the 1980s as a consequence of financial engineering. Consider, for example, the impact of the risk management instruments discussed in Chapters 12 through 15. These included forward rate agreements, futures, swaps, and single-period and multi-period options. These instruments dramatically altered the landscape for asset/liability managers. The asset/liability manager can create positive gaps in rising interest-rate markets or create negative gaps in falling interest-rate markets and then hedge the resultant exposures. (These were Strategies (4) and (5) presented in Table 20.1.) They can also transform the character of their assets and/or liabilities by entering into appropriately structured swaps. For example, a bank treasurer carrying floating-rate assets funded by fixed-rate liabilities (a large positive gap) can quickly alter the character of the liabilities by entering into a fixed-for-floating rate swap with his institution as fixed-rate receiver. While the swap transaction is off-balance sheet, the character of the liabilities may now be regarded as floating. Thus, the gap is reduced. No longer are there the delays associated with altering the mix of the institution's individual assets and/or liabilities. Nor does one need to be overly concerned about the market opportunities to acquire the type of assets one wants—all one really needs are liquid derivative product markets.

The development of the risk management instruments mentioned above has greatly enhanced the flexibility and the opportunities for the asset/liability manager but it has also dramatically increased the competitive pressures and narrowed the interest margins and spreads available. The new products have also increased the level of sophistication required of asset/liability managers. Indeed, as recently witnessed on a wide scale in the thrift industry, failure to employ the available risk management tools in strategies appropriate to one's institution can lead to serious charges of mismanagement and, in extreme cases, to charges of criminal fraud.

The Investment Banker in Asset/Liability Management

In an effort to carve out new product niches, a number of investment banks developed strategies to assist financial institutions in the management of their portfolios.[5] Most of these strategies were developed in the late 1980s. Some worked well and others can only be described as failures. Undoubtedly, new strategies will appear as the 1990s progress and some of the old strategies will fall by the wayside. It would be instructive to look at a few of the strategies that are marketed under the general umbrella of asset/liability management techniques. In particular we will briefly describe **total return optimization** and **risk-controlled arbitrage**. The reader is reminded that many other strategies can be included under the umbrella of asset/liability management and some of these are discussed, albeit in other contexts, in later chapters.

Total Return Optimization

Total return optimization employs tools from the management sciences, such as linear programming, in an effort to determine the optimal mix of assets given a set of constraints and a variety of yield curve projections. This particular application of financial engineering is another excellent example of the contributions made by the academic community to many of the financial innovations of the last decade because most management science techniques were developed by academicians. It also demonstrates the role of the quant jock in developing customer services (as opposed to developing in-house trading strategies).

In total return optimization strategies, the total return to be maximized consists of the interest (coupons), the reinvestment income, and the change in market value of the assets. The constraints, sometimes called **portfolio attributes**, can include such things as liquidity requirements, durations, industry sector specifications, default risk levels, tax treatment of income, and obligations to hold minimum quantities of specific entities' debt (often necessitated by relationships with existing customers).

It might help for us to consider a simple example. Suppose that a client has five debt securities available to include in a portfolio. These are (1) Treasury bills, (2) Treasury bonds, (3) state bonds, (4) local municipal bonds, and (5) corporate bonds. Assume that the interest income earned on the T-bills and T-bonds is exempt from state and local taxes; the interest earned on the state bonds is exempt from federal and state taxes; the interest earned on the local municipal bonds is exempt from all taxes; and the interest earned on the corporate bonds is not exempt from any taxes. The federal tax rate is 26 percent, the state tax rate is 12 percent, and the local tax rate is 3 percent. For purposes of this example, we will treat applicable tax rates as though they are additive.[6] For example, if the interest income is subject to both federal and state taxes, then the applicable tax rate is 26 percent plus 12 percent for a total of 38 percent.

Suppose now that the client's objective is to maximize the total *after-tax* rate of return on its portfolio of debt securities. Under the first scenario, yields are not expected to change and, therefore, neither are prices. Our goal is to determine the optimal weights for the five securities to be included in the portfolio. If there were no constraints on our selections, we would simply calculate the after-tax rate of return on each security and then commit all the client's funds to that one security. But, as it happens, there are a number of constraints. Suppose, for example, that no more than 32 percent of the portfolio can be invested in any one security but that at least 12 percent must be invested in T-bills. Second, no more than fifty percent of the portfolio can be invested in state and local securities combined. Third, the portfolio's duration cannot exceed 7.2. Fourth, the weighted-average term to maturity (a crude measure of liquidity) cannot exceed 12. Finally, the portfolio weights must sum to unity and short positions are not permitted.

The individual securities' durations, maturities, and before- and after-tax yields appear in Table 20.2. The after-tax rate of return on a security is found by multiplying the before-tax rate by $(1-t)$ where t denotes the applicable tax rate.

Table 20.2
Relevant Security Characteristics

Security	Before-Tax Return	Applicable Tax Rate	After-Tax Return	Duration	Maturity
(1) T-bills	6.55%	26%	4.847%	0.5	0.5
(2) T-bonds	9.30%	26%	6.882%	8.8	18.5
(3) State	8.30%	3%	8.051%	9.9	19.4
(4) Municipal	7.65%	0%	7.650%	5.6	7.3
(5) Corporate	12.44%	41%	7.340%	7.6	24.4

This particular problem lends itself to a linear programming solution. A linear programming problem is any problem having three parts: First, there must be a linear objective function (linear with respect to the control variables). Second, there must be a set of linear constraints which can take the form of greater than or equal to (≤), less than or equal to (≥), or strict equality (=). The control variables cannot take on negative values. The control variables, in this particular case, are the weights to be assigned to the different securities.

The problem has a total of ten constraints. The first five require that the individual securities each have a weight of no more than (less than or equal to) 32 percent. The sixth requires that security 1 be weighted at least 12 percent. The seventh requires that securities 3 and 4 have a combined weighting of 50 percent or less. The eighth requires that the weighted duration of the portfolio be less than or equal to 7.2, and the ninth requires that the weighted maturity of the portfolio be less than or equal to 12. The final constraint is that the weights must sum to 1. The non-negativity constraints (no short sales) do not ordinarily need to be specified as they are an assumed condition in linear programming. We will use the notation w_i to denote the ith control variable (in this case the weight on the ith security). The full model then looks like that below where r_p denotes the overall after-tax return on the portfolio.

Maximize $r_p = 4.847\,w_1 + 6.882\,w_2 + 8.051\,w_3 + 7.650\,w_4 + 7.340\,w_5$

subject to:

$$1.00\,w_1 + 0.00\,w_2 + 0.00\,w_3 + 0.00\,w_4 + 0.00\,w_5 \leq 0.32$$
$$0.00\,w_1 + 1.00\,w_2 + 0.00\,w_3 + 0.00\,w_4 + 0.00\,w_5 \leq 0.32$$
$$0.00\,w_1 + 0.00\,w_2 + 1.00\,w_3 + 0.00\,w_4 + 0.00\,w_5 \leq 0.32$$
$$0.00\,w_1 + 0.00\,w_2 + 0.00\,w_3 + 1.00\,w_4 + 0.00\,w_5 \leq 0.32$$
$$0.00\,w_1 + 0.00\,w_2 + 0.00\,w_3 + 0.00\,w_4 + 1.00\,w_5 \leq 0.32$$
$$1.00\,w_1 + 0.00\,w_2 + 0.00\,w_3 + 0.00\,w_4 + 0.00\,w_5 \geq 0.12$$
$$0.00\,w_1 + 0.00\,w_2 + 1.00\,w_3 + 1.00\,w_4 + 0.00\,w_5 \leq 0.50$$
$$0.50\,w_1 + 8.80\,w_2 + 9.90\,w_3 + 5.60\,w_4 + 7.60\,w_5 \leq 7.20$$
$$0.50\,w_1 + 18.50\,w_2 + 19.40\,w_3 + 7.30\,w_4 + 24.40\,w_5 \leq 12.00$$
$$1.00\,w_1 + 1.00\,w_2 + 1.00\,w_3 + 1.00\,w_4 + 1.00\,w_5 = 1.00$$

and

$$w_1, w_2, w_3, w_4, w_5 \geq 0$$

Any good linear programming software can be used to solve for the control variables in this model.[7] The solutions, which we invite the reader to verify, are as follows:

Security	Optimal Weighting
T-bill	17.3 percent
T-bond	32.0 percent
State	18.0 percent
Local Municipal	32.0 percent
Corporate	0.7 percent

Using the weights above and assuming the yield curve projection proves correct, the weighting scheme above yields an after-tax return of 6.989 percent. *No other weighting scheme can produce a greater after-tax rate of return and still satisfy all of the constraints.*

This example, while unrealistically simple, serves to illustrate the logic in total return optimization. In more realistic applications, the yield curve scenario would be varied, and a great many more securities would be included in the universe from which the portfolio is to be built. The approach lends itself to an efficient assessment of the sensitivity of total return to changes in the constraining values. For example, we might ask how the total return would change if the duration constraint was relaxed, or we might ask how total return would change if the maximum investment in any one security was reduced, and so on.

Risk Controlled Arbitrage

Risk controlled arbitrage is an effort to maximize the interest spread by purchasing high-yield assets and funding these assets at the lowest possible cost. The assets purchased can be corporate loans (such as secured bank acquisition loans which are described in Chapter 22), whole mortgages, mortgage passthroughs, mortgage backed securities such as CMOs and REMICs, and so on. The funding source will usually be the repo market or fed funds as these are usually the cheapest sources for borrowers in a position to use these markets. (The securities acquired on the asset side are the same securities used as the collateral on the repo side.) The strategy will employ a swap to convert the floating character of the repo liabilities into a fixed-rate liability which closely matches the character and the principal of the assets.

The structure would work as follows: The institution engages in a reverse repo to secure funding (30 or 90 day term repos are most common). The funds obtained are used to purchase the higher yielding asset. The institution then enters a fixed-for-floating interest rate swap with itself as fixed-rate payer. The floating rate of the swap is tied to the repo rate or some other short-term rate (say one-month or three-month LIBOR). The combination of the reverse repos and the interest-rate swap create a synthetic fixed-rate obligation. The full structure, using three-month LIBOR on the floating-rate side of the swap, is depicted in Exhibit 20.3.

Exhibit 20.3
Risk Controlled Arbitrage

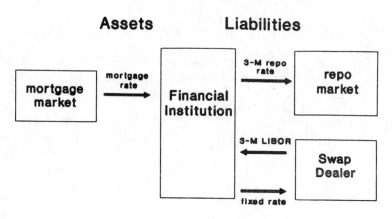

The structure depicted in Exhibit 20.3 is not risk free. First, there is default risk on the higher-yielding assets held, particularly if these take the form of corporate loans or securities, and, second, there is the basis risk associated with the mismatch of the two floating rates. Nevertheless, the strategy is relatively low risk in the sense that the interest-rate risk has been eliminated by the use of the swap. For obvious reasons, the strategy can be viewed as an arbitrage between the capital markets (corporate loans, securities and mortgages) and the money markets (the repo sourced financing).

When amortizing assets are used for the high-yield assets employed in the strategy, which is often the case, it is necessary for the swap dealer and the institution employing the strategy to agree on the amortization schedule and the pre-payment assumptions. This is particularly critical if the assets are mortgages or mortgage-backed securities. In these cases, the swap principal must also embody the same amortization schedule and prepayment assumptions. The prepayable nature of the assets, however, poses an additional risk to the user of the strategy. No matter how much effort is put into the preparation of the prepayment estimates, they can never hope to exactly capture the actual prepayment flows and, therefore, there is some residual prepayment risk.

Summary

Asset/liability management is the art and science of choosing the best mix of assets for the firm's asset portfolio and the best mix of liabilities for the firm's liability portfolio. While asset/liability management is important to all firms, it is particularly critical for financial institutions.

For a long time it was taken for granted that the liability portfolio of such firms was beyond the control of the firm and so management concentrated its efforts on choosing the asset portfolio mix. This changed dramatically during the 1970s and the 1980s as new instruments and strategies emerged giving the firm a much freer hand over the makeup of its liabilities.

There are five key concepts in understanding asset/liability management strategies. These are liquidity, term structure, interest-rate sensitivity, maturity composition, and default risk. Many strategies are based on gap management and interest margin. The gap is defined as the dollar difference between floating-rate assets and floating-rate liabilities and is best viewed as a balance sheet concept. Interest margin is the difference between the rate earned on earning assets and the rate paid on liabilities. Interest margin is best viewed as an income statement concept.

In recent years financial engineers working for investment banks have developed sophisticated asset/liability management strategies. Some of these strategies incorporate advanced tools from the quantitative side of the management sciences. These investment banks then market these strategies as "advisement services" to financial institutions. Two of the strategies that became popular are total return optimization and risk controlled arbitrage.

Endnotes

[1] In particular, the sophisticated reader might want to consider *Banker's Treasury Management Handbook*, edited by B.F. Binder (1988).

[2] Savings and loan associations, for example, originated mortgage loans which they then carried until the mortgages were fully amortized. Banks also made mortgage loans but concentrated more heavily in commercial loans. In both cases, however, the loans were usually carried by the originator until they matured.

[3] For a fuller discussion of the late 1970s early 1980s behavior of the prime rate, see Johnson and Johnson (1985).

[4] See Markowitz (1991), Kaufman (1991), Kane (1986, 1987),

Ronn and Verma (1986), Buser, Campbell and Glenn (1984), Sharpe (1978), Gibson (1972),

[5]We use the term "investment banks" loosely here to describe function rather than organization. Many commercial banks in recent years have taken on a lot of the traditional investment banking functions and work described in this section falls into that category.

[6]This is a simplification. Federal, state, and local taxes are not additive in determining the total applicable tax rate. As a general rule, state and local taxes are deductible in arriving at taxable federal income.

[7]We used *A-Pack*. *A-Pack* is discussed in Chapter 3.

References and Suggested Reading

Binder B.F. *Banker's Treasury Management Handbook*, Boston: Warren, Gorham & Lamont, Inc., 1988.

Brodt, A.I. "Optimal Bank Asset and Liability Management with Financial Futures," *Journal of Futures Markets*, 8(4) (1988), pp. 457-482.

Buser, S.A., A.H. Chen, and E.J. Kane. "Federal Deposit Insurance, Regulatory Policy, and Optimal Bank Capital," *Journal of Finance*, 36(1) (1981), pp. 51-60.

Campbell, T.S. and D. Glenn. "Deposit Insurance in a Deregulated Environment," *Journal of Finance*, 39(3) (1984), pp. 775-785.

Gibson, W.E. "Deposit Insurance in the United States: Evaluation and Reform," *Journal of Financial and Quantitative Analysis*, 7(2) (1972), pp. 1575-1594.

Goodman, L.S. and M.J. Langer. "Accounting for Interest Rate Futures in Bank Asset-Liability Management," *Journal of Futures Markets*, 3(4) (1983), pp. 415-428.

Johnson, F.P. and R.D. Johnson *Commercial Bank Management*, New York: Dryden Press, 1985.

Kane, E.J. "Appearance and Reality in Deposit Insurance: The Case for Reform," *Journal of Bank Finance*, 10(2) (1986), pp. 175-188.

Kane, E.J. "No Room for Weak Links in the Chain of Deposit Insurance Reform," *Journal of Financial Services Research*, 1(1) (1987), pp. 77-111.

Kaufman, G.G. "A Proposal for Deposit Insurance Reform that Keeps the Put Option Out-of-the-Money and Taxpayers In-the-Money," presented at a Symposium on Innovative Financial Instruments and Developments in Financial Services, Hofstra University, 1991.

Litzenberger, R.H. and O.M. Joy. "Target Rates of Return and Corporate Asset and Liability Structures Under Uncertainty," *Journal of Financial and Quantitative Analysis*, 6(2) (1971), pp. 675-686.

Marcus, A.J. and I. Shared. "The Valuation of FDIC Insurance Using Option-Pricing Estimates," *Journal of Money, Credit and Banking*, (November 1984), pp. 446-460.

Markowitz, H.M. "Markets and Morality, Or Arbitragers Get No Respect," Robert Weintraub Memorial Lecture at Baruch College's Center for the Study of Business and Government, reprinted in the *Wall Street Journal* (May 14, 1991).

Sharpe, W.F. "Bank Capital Adequacy, Deposit Insurance, and Security Values," *Journal of Financial and Quantitative Analysis*, 13(4) (1978), pp. 701-718.

Ronn, E.I. and A.K. Verma. "Pricing Risk-Adjusted Deposit Insurance: An Option Based Model," *Journal of Finance* (September 1986), pp. 871-895.

Chapter 21

Hedging and Related Risk Management Techniques

Anthony F. Herbst, Dilip D. Kare, and John F. Marshall

Overview

We defined a hedge in Chapter 7 as a position taken as a temporary substitute for a later cash position or to offset the risk associated with a current cash position. Most hedging involves positions in derivative instruments. Which hedging instrument is most appropriate in a given situation will depend on (1) the risk profile associated with the cash position to be hedged; (2) the type of risk the hedger would like to hedge against (all risk or just downside risk, for example), (3) the cost of hedging with the different hedging instruments at the point in time when the hedge is put on, and (4) the effectiveness of the different hedging instruments in the context of the need at hand.

There are many complex issues involved in hedging. Some of these issues have been addressed in Chapter 7 and others have been

Tony Herbst is Professor of Finance and C.R. and D.S Carter Chairholder at the University of Texas at El Paso. Dilip Kare is Associate Professor of Finance at the University of North Florida. Jack Marshall is Professor of Finance at St. John's University, New York. This chapter is based, in part on earlier work of the authors, Herbst, Kare and Marshall (1990a) and Herbst, Kare and Marshall (1990b).

introduced elsewhere in this book. Nevertheless, we need to consider hedging more thoroughly given its importance in so much of financial engineering. Indeed, in many people's minds, financial engineering and risk management are synonymous. (We, of course, take a broader view of financial engineering.)

In the way of review, we have already seen that all business organizations are exposed to various strategic risks. It is necessary for financial managers to identify the risks, quantify the risks, and hedge the risks if the cost of doing so is not too great. We demonstrated in Chapter 10 how corporations can use their financial statements as a starting point in identifying their strategic exposures. We have also shown how price risks, which are not company specific, can be translated into company-specific profit risks with the aid of risk profiles and statistical techniques. Finally, we have seen how the payoff profiles associated with hedges can offset the risk profiles associated with cash positions. The residual risk, called **basis risk,** is then the risk which remains as a result of imperfections in the hedge.

The importance of hedging in a volatile price environment is difficult to overstate. One of the saddest things to witness is the demise of an otherwise efficient producer or service provider as a consequence of adverse price movements over which it had no control. This kind of thing is often seen in the agricultural community when a bumper crop causes harvest prices to fall below a farmer's cost of production. Indeed, it was this very situation which led to the creation of the Chicago Board of Trade and the introduction of commodity futures in the 1860s. More recent examples have involved the financial community. A large part of the problem experienced by the thrift industry in recent years traces its origins to the volatility of interest rates. Similarly, a large part of the U.S. industrial sector's problems in recent years trace their origins to volatility in exchange rates.

The importance of understanding hedging became glaringly obvious recently in the case of Franklin Savings Corporation of Kansas. The Resolution Trust Corporation, which handles bankrupt thrifts, seized Franklin in a dispute over how paper losses and offsetting paper gains from hedges should be reported for accounting purposes. By their failure to understand Franklin's fully hedged strategy for locking in a spread, the regulators forced Franklin into technical violations of the federal capital requirements and then seized it. In a September 1990 ruling, a federal judge handed Franklin back to its former officials. Unfortunately, the failure of the regulators to understand Franklin's strategy resulted, in the words of *The Wall Street Journal*, in "maximum disruption, maximum cost to the taxpayers, and maximum risk to the financial system" [WSJ, September 7, 1990].

In this chapter, we will consider the cost of a hedge, the determination of hedge ratios, the influence of the hedge ratio and the hedge structure on hedge effectiveness, the use of baseline instruments in the management of an ongoing hedging operation, some recent improvements suggested by hedging theory, a **building block** approach to the design of a hedge structure, some issues in risk management that are expected to be of importance in the 1990s, and some miscellaneous risk management techniques. We will not elaborate on the uses of specific risk management instruments because that has already been done when each type of instrument was introduced in earlier chapters.

Hedge Ratios and Their Use

The concept of a hedge ratio is, paradoxically, both straightforward and complex. The definition is simple. A hedge ratio is nothing more than the number of units of the hedging instrument necessary to hedge one unit of the cash position. The complexity, as we will demonstrate shortly, is in the subtleties, rather than in the definition.

The calculation of the appropriate, or optimal, hedge ratio is different for different types of hedging instruments. We will concentrate here on the calculation of hedge ratios in futures hedging. The earliest thinking on the subject of hedge ratios was to assume that one unit of cash commodity could be hedged with one unit of futures. This 1:1 hedge ratio is today called, quite appropriately, the **naive approach**. The naive hedge ratio was long used and produced good results for *some* cash positions hedged in *some* futures. But it produced poor results for others.

In the early 1960s, Johnson (1960) and Stein (1961) took a portfolio approach to hedging arguing that the goal of hedging was to minimize the variance of the profit associated with the combined cash and futures position. This led to the use of regression analysis in determining the risk minimizing hedge ratio. At the time of their work, Johnson's and Stein's methodology could only be applied to the hedging of traditional commodities—as financial futures had not yet been introduced. Empirical tests on historical price data soon established the superiority of the Johnson/Stein approach with the result that the naive approach came to be regarded as both wrong and indicative of a lack of sophistication on the part of those who use it. After the introduction of financial futures in the 1970s, Ederington (1979) extended the Johnson/Stein methodology to the hedging of financial positions.

In the Johnson/Stein/Ederington (JSE) methodology, the spot price is regressed against the futures price using an ordinary least squares regression. A nearly equivalent, but theoretically superior, approach is to regress the change in the spot price against the change in the futures price. The differencing interval is usually one day. That is, the regression looks like that in Equation 21.1.

$$S = a + b \cdot F + u \qquad (21.1a)$$

or $$\Delta S = a + b \cdot \Delta F + u \qquad (21.1b)$$

where $\Delta S = S(t) - S(t-1)$ and $\Delta F = F(t,T) - F(t-1,T)$

The value u represents the error or residual term in the regression. The slope of the regression line, b, is the *minimum variance hedge ratio* and the value a is the intercept term, which is usually ignored. (In the case of a regression on the difference, a is usually close to zero.)

Despite the improvement in the effectiveness of hedges afforded by the JSE methodology, a number of problems remain. The most important of these involve violations of the assumptions underlying the regression technique. Specifically, the regression technique assumes that the relationship between the regressor variable (S) and the explanatory variable (F) is stable. This implies that the expected basis is the same regardless of when the observation on it is made. But, in fact, the relationship between the spot price and the futures price is usually not stable. For example, in a direct hedge—a hedge employing a futures contract in which the underlying asset is *exactly* the same as the cash position to be hedged—including the location of delivery—the futures price *must* converge to the spot price so that the basis vanishes at the time of delivery. The basis, it will be recalled, is the difference between the spot price and the futures price. The difference between the assumed behavior of the basis and the actual behavior of the basis is depicted in Exhibit 21.1.

For storable commodities, including most financials, the basis is explained by the cost of carry. That is, the futures price should equal the spot price plus the full cost of carry. The full cost of carry

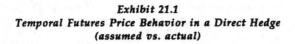

Exhibit 21.1
Temporal Futures Price Behavior in a Direct Hedge
(assumed vs. actual)

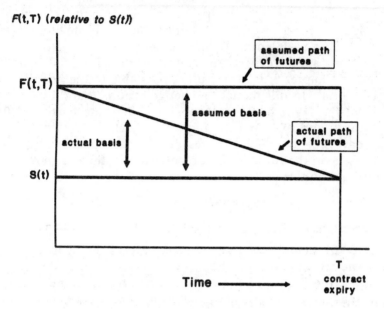

includes the interest cost of carrying the cash asset, the storage cost of holding the cash asset, less any convenience yield provided by the asset. That is, the futures price is related to the spot price by Equation 21.2.

$$F(t,T) = S(t) \cdot [1 + r(t,T) + w(t,T) - c(t,T)] \qquad (21.2)$$

In Equation 21.2, the value $r(t,T)$ is the periodic interest rate, and the values $w(t,T)$ and $c(t,T)$ are the periodic storage cost and convenience yield, respectively, both stated as a percentage of the spot price $S(t)$. As time passes and the current time t approaches expiry T, the cost of carry $[r(t,T) + w(t,T) - c(t,T)]$ converges to zero and hence the basis must vanish.

A second assumption of the regression technique is that the error terms are serially uncorrelated. But, it has been shown that, for at least some commodities, the error terms are serially correlated. This is attributable to the behavior of the basis over time.[1]

In the 1980s, a number of studies addressed the weaknesses

of the regression method for estimating hedge ratios.[2] Some of these pointed up the failings and others offered possible remedies and/or introduced alternative hedge ratio estimation techniques. Some of the new techniques were group specific in the sense that they work well for specific types of price risk but are not applicable to others. The dollar value basis point (DV01) model (of which the duration ratio model is a special case) is an example of this. The DV01 model, discussed in Chapter 8, is only really applicable to the hedging of interest-rate risk. In this model, the hedge ratio is found by taking the ratio of the DV01 of the cash position, dividing by the DV01 of the futures, and then multiplying by the yield beta βy obtained from a regression of yield changes on the cash position against yield changes on the futures instrument. That is, the hedge ratio is given by Equation 21.3.

$$HR = \frac{DV01_c}{DV01_f} \times \beta_y$$

(21.3)

The DV01 model has a lot of nice features. First, it requires the periodic recalculation of the relevant DV01s. This adjusts for the fact that the DV01s of the cash and futures are continuously changing but not necessarily at equal rates. The yield beta should also be periodically re-estimated. The yield beta is not likely to change very much over short periods of time—particularly for intermediate and long maturity cash positions and intermediate and long maturity futures. In general, this would surely include debt instruments having maturities of five years or more.

The DV01 model has become the mainstay of the financial community in search of an efficient hedging methodology for their many cash positions. The approach allows the financial institution to convert all of its cash positions to one common benchmark. Once so converted, the degree to which the various cash positions represent natural hedges for one another can be ascertained and the net exposure determined. *It is only the net exposure then that needs to be hedged in futures.* This approach is particularly useful for bond traders, fixed-income securities dealers, and market makers in swaps.

Consider a simple application for bond traders. Imagine a bond trader who looks for undervalued and overvalued bonds. The trader purchases undervalued bonds and sells (short) overvalued bonds. Such traders are sometimes called *value traders* or *relative value traders*. The proceeds from the short sales are used to cover the cost of the purchases. Any residual financing needed is obtained via transactions in the repo market. When the bond values correct, the positions are lifted. The trader usually has some net risk because the price sensitivities of the different bonds are not the same and, hence, the long and short positions are not perfectly offsetting *even if the dollar value of the long positions exactly equals the dollar value of the short positions.* It is therefore possible for the trader to correctly identify and purchase undervalued bonds and to correctly identify and sell overvalued bonds and yet to lose money because of an unanticipated shift in the yield curve. It is these unexpected shifts in the yield curve which the value trader seeks to hedge.

To demonstrate the mechanics of this operation let's suppose that a 15-year XYZ bond offering a semiannual coupon of 97⁄8 percent is priced to yield 9.875 percent. The bond trader estimates that it should yield only 9.640 percent. Thus, the bond is undervalued (reflecting the inverse relationship between yield and price). The trader buys $10 million face (par) value of the bond. At the same time, the trader identifies a 7-year ABC bond offering a semiannual coupon of 8¼ percent priced to yield 8.25 percent. The trader estimates that the yield should be 8.48 percent. Thus, the bond is overvalued. The trader sells $10 million face value of the bond. Since the coupon rates and the yields are the same for both bonds, the bonds are currently priced at par and the proceeds from the short sale of the ABC bond are just sufficient to pay for the XYZ bond (the bonds for the short sale are obtained by the appropriate transactions in the repo market). The problem is to determine the trader's net risk exposure—if any.

We start by calculating the DV01s of the two bonds, the DV01 of some benchmark futures contract (we will use the T-bond futures contract for this purpose) and the yield betas for the two bonds. As it happens, the DV01 of the XYZ bond is 0.077369 and the DV01 of the ABC bond is 0.052366. (You can easily prove this to yourself with a little arithmetic.) Suppose that the DV01 of the futures contract is 0.098755.[3] Next suppose that the yield beta for the XYZ bond is 0.54 and the yield beta for the ABC bond is 0.59. This information is summarized in Table 21.1.

Table 21.1

Risk Management Report

Bond	Position	Market Value	DV01	βy	HR	BE
XYZ 15-year	+10 M	+10 M	0.077369	0.54	0.42306	+4.2306M
ABC 7-year	−10 M	−10 M	0.052366	0.59	0.31285	−3.1285M
	0	0				+1.1021M

The hedge ratios in Table 21.1 are obtained by taking the DV01 of the cash position, dividing by the DV01 of the futures, and then multiplying the resultant quotient by the yield beta. We see that the XYZ bond has a hedge ratio of 0.42306. This implies that it takes 0.42306 dollars of T-bond futures to hedge $1 of XYZ bond. Another way of saying this is that $0.42306 of T-bonds is **risk equivalent** to $1 of XYZ bonds. Multiplying this hedge ratio by the size of the XYZ position yields the **baseline equivalent** (BE) of $4.2306 million. The baseline equivalent is interpreted as the size of a T-bond position that is risk equivalent to the $10 million long position in XYZ bonds. Similar interpretations are applied to the ABC bond values.

Once all bond positions have been converted to baseline equivalents, we can sum them to obtain the net exposure. In this case we find that the overall exposure is equivalent to a *long* position in $1.102 million of face value T-bonds. Since we will hedge in T-bond futures and each T-bond futures contract has a face value of $0.1 million, this means that the trader needs a hedge consisting of about 11 futures contracts. It is important to reiterate a point made earlier: The long and short positions can be dollar-for-dollar offsetting (as they are in this example) and yet the risks may not be dollar-for-dollar offsetting (as they are not in this example).

Recent Improvements in Hedging Theory

The ultimate test of a hedge's effectiveness is the degree to which it reduces the variance of the hedger's profit. The reduction in the variance of the hedger's profit is, in turn, a function of the degree of correlation between the futures price and the spot price and the hedge ratio employed. The use of the DV01 for the hedging of interest-rate risk has improved hedge effectiveness relative to both the naive model and the regression model. The reason for this improvement is that the DV01 adjusts for the changing relationship between the DV01 of the cash position and the DV01 of the futures instrument. This particular technique, however, is not applicable to the hedging of other types of price risk.

In an effort to improve the effectiveness of hedging price risks more generally, a number of academic researchers have proposed techniques that take into account the convergence property of futures and the cost of carry explanation for the basis. While we may be biased, we believe that some of the most significant improvements in hedging theory in recent years are due to the work of Herbst,

Kare and Marshall (1990a, 1990b), henceforth HKM, and Herbst and Marshall (1990). The former studies concentrate on improvements in the hedge ratio for direct and cross hedges respectively, and the latter concentrates on increasing the degree of correlation between the spot price and the futures hedge by diversifying the futures hedge.

In order to understand the improvements suggested by this recent work, it is necessary to distinguish between direct hedges and cross hedges. A direct hedge employs a futures contract which is written on an underlying asset which is identical in all ways—including the location of delivery—to the cash position which is the subject of the hedge. A cross hedge is a hedge written on anything else. Thus, a futures contract written on winter wheat is only a direct hedge for cash winter wheat that will be delivered in the same market as the futures contract. For winter wheat to be delivered in a geographically different cash market, the hedge is still a cross hedge. In some cases, the nature of the market and the nature of the cash position to be hedged are such that the hedge is always direct. The hedging of a currency position in a currency futures contract on the same currency is an example of such a hedge. Currency transactions are normally settled by simple bookkeeping entries and each unit of a currency is identical to each other unit of that currency.[4] Thus, a long position in yen futures is a direct hedge for a short cash position in yen irrespective of the delivery location.

We will review the improvements suggested by the research mentioned above in three stages. First, we will consider the HKM improvements in the calculation of hedge ratios in the context of a direct hedge. Then we will examine HKM's extension to cross hedges. Finally, we will examine the benefits from diversification associated with the composite approach to cross hedging suggested by Herbst and Marshall.

The Convergence Adjustment In Direct Hedges

As already noted, the traditional JSE regression approach to determining the optimal hedge ratio implicitly assumes a stable relationship between the futures price and the spot price. In the case of a direct hedge, however, it is clearly apparent that the relationship is not stable. Instead, the futures price converges to the spot price as the futures contract approaches expiry. This behavior is explained by Equation 21.2 which is repeated below as Equation 21.4 with the time subscripts on r, w, and c suppressed.

$$F(t,T) = S(t) \cdot [1 + r + w - c] \qquad (21.4)$$

Recall that in Equation 21.4 r, w, and c are the interest rate, the storage cost, and the convenience yield, respectively, all stated as a percentage of the spot price. As noted earlier, the cost of carry is $[r + w - c]$. We can now annualize this cost of carry and state it as a continuously compounded rate. Denote this rate by y. Finally, denote the length of time until contract expiry by τ (tau) where τ is stated as a fraction of a year. For example, if a contract has 45 days to expiry, then τ is 45/365.

With these adjustments, the relationship between the futures price and the spot price can be expressed in the form given by Equation 21.5 or 21.6.

$$F(t,T) = S(t) \cdot e^{y\tau} \qquad (21.5)$$

$$S(t) = F(t,T) \cdot e^{-y\tau} \qquad (21.6)$$

From Equation 21.6 it is clear that the hedge ratio, denoted h is the term $e^{-y\tau}$. The hedge ratio h makes it very clear that the optimal futures hedge is a function of the time to contract expiry τ and not independent of the time to expiry as implied by the JSE model.

Two problems remain. The first is to show that the HKM hedge ratio is estimatable. The second is to show that the HKM hedge ratio performs better than the traditional hedge ratio.

We begin by dividing both sides of Equation 21.6 by $F(t,T)$ and then take natural logarithms of both sides. This yields Equation 21.7.

$$\ln(S(t) / F(t,T)) = -y\tau \qquad (21.7)$$

Equation 21.7 can be estimated using its regression form. This is given by Equation 21.8.

$$\ln(S(t) / F(t,T)) = z + d\tau + v \qquad (21.8)$$

Where z is the intercept term (expected to be zero), d is the slope term and the estimate of $-y$, and v is an allowance for error. From the observed values $S(t)$, $F(t,T)$, and τ, the value of d is easily estimated and, once estimated, the best available estimate of the optimal hedge ratio is given by $e^{d\tau}$.

There are a number of advantages to using the HKM approach over the traditional JSE approach in determining the optimal hedge ratio. First, as shown above, the HKM approach explicitly takes the effect of a futures contract's maturity into consideration and this has been shown to be an important but long neglected factor in hedging theory. Second, the HKM approach can be estimated from just a few data points using the most recent observations. (The JSE approach requires considerably greater amounts of historic data.) Finally, the HKM approach allows for a changing hedge ratio over time while the JSE approach does not.

The remaining issue is whether or not the HKM hedge ratio performs better than the traditional JSE hedge ratio. To answer this question one needs to define performance. It has long been the practice to define a hedge's performance in terms of its effectiveness. Effectiveness is the degree to which the hedge reduces the variance of return (profit) relative to no hedge. The residual profit variance is a linear function of the variance of the basis that remains once the hedge has been placed. Thus, the test reduces to the question of whether or not the variance of the hedger's basis when employing a HKM hedge ratio is less than the variance of the hedger's basis when employing a JSE hedge ratio. HKM employed this logic in comparing the effectiveness of the two hedge ratios for six currencies for which futures contracts trade on the International Monetary Market (IMM). These were the British pound, the Canadian dollar, the French franc, the German mark, the Japanese yen, and the Swiss franc.

While past practice has routinely tested the effectiveness of a hedge on the same data sample as that used to estimate the hedge ratio, HKM argued for a more stringent test. They divided their data sample into two nonoverlapping but consecutive parts. They used the first data sample to develop the JSE and HKM hedge ratios. They then employed these hedge ratios in the calculation of the JSE basis and the HKM basis using the second data sample.[5] Finally, they calculated the variances of the two bases and compared them by way of standard statistical tests. For five of the six currencies the hypothesis of no difference in variance could be rejected at a 1 percent level of significance in favor of the alternative hypothesis of lower variance with the HKM hedge ratio. For the Canadian dollar, the two performed identically. This latter result is explained by the fact that the cost of carry for the Canadian dollar was approximately zero. It is not difficult to see that in such a case the HKM and JSE hedge ratios will produce the same result. For any nonzero cost of carry, the HKM hedge ratio should, and apparently does, perform better.

An Extension to Cross Hedges

The improvements in hedging theory described in the preceding section are clearly applicable in the case of direct hedges. But the question remains as to whether or not they are applicable to cross hedges. This is extremely important as most real world hedges take the form of cross hedges. Fortunately, the extension is very straightforward.

We begin by deleting, for economy of notation, the time subscripts from $S(t)$ and $F(t,T)$ and add a commodity subscript. We will use the subscript 1 to denote the underlying commodity on which a futures contract is written and the subscript 2 to denote the cash position commodity (which is the subject of the hedge). That is, F_1 denotes the futures contract written on commodity 1, S_1 is the spot price of commodity 1, and S_2 is the spot price of the cash position commodity. Now, for whatever reason, suppose that a direct hedge on commodity 2 is not available and so the hedger with a cash position in commodity 2 must hedge in the futures on commodity 1. Our goal is to determine the hedge ratio for this cross hedge.

Recall the hedge ratio for the direct hedge given by Equation 21.6 and repeated below without the time subscripts but with the commodity subscripts as Equation 21.9.

$$S_1 = F_1 \cdot e^{-y\,\tau} \tag{21.9}$$

Now, assuming a linear dependence between the spot price for commodity 1 and the spot price for commodity 2, we can define the functional relationship between them, in regression form, as Equation 21.10. Note that the convergence problem between a futures price and spot price does not come into play in this regression since we are looking at two spot prices.

$$S_2 = a + b \cdot S_1 + u \tag{21.10}$$

The value b is easily estimated by a regression of S_2 on S_1. Now, substituting for S_1 the value given by Equation 21.9 we get Equation 21.11a.

$$S_2 = a + b \cdot F_1 \cdot e^{-y\,\tau} + u \tag{21.11a}$$

Rearranging terms, we obtain Equation 21.11b.

$$S_2 = a + (b \cdot e^{-y\,\tau}) \cdot F_1 + u \tag{21.11b}$$

We now see that the term $(be^{-y\tau})$ is the hedge ratio. Notice that if the cost of carry, denoted y, is identically zero, then the term $e^{-y\tau}$ reduces to 1 and the hedge ratio reduces to b which is precisely the JSE hedge ratio b given by Equation 21.1. (This implies that the traditional JSE approach to determining the hedge ratio is a special case of the HKM approach.) Thus, we see that the HKM approach to estimating the hedge ratio for a direct hedge is directly extendable to a cross hedge.

Composite Hedging

Hedging theory routinely assumes that producers hedge all output and that they hedge in a single hedging instrument.[6] The assumption that producers hedge all output is tantamount to the assumption that producers are so risk averse that they seek maximum protection *irrespective of the cost of the hedge* or, alternatively, that hedging is *costless*. Neither of these assumptions is likely to hold.

In fact, many producers practice selective hedging. In selective hedging, producers hedge only a fraction of their output. The fraction hedged may range from no output hedged at all to all output hedged. The fraction actually hedged will depend on the effectiveness of the available hedge alternatives, the cost of hedging (which embodies the producer's forecast of the future spot price), and the producer's degree of risk aversion.

As important as the decision to hedge and how much output to hedge are, they are not the primary focus of this discussion.[7] Our interest here is in how to ascertain the best instrument in which to hedge when more than one hedging instrument is available. It is easily shown that the optimal hedging instrument is not dependent on the fraction of output to be hedged.[8] Therefore, no harm is done by assuming complete hedging for purposes of illustration.

For lack of a better term, a hedge consisting of a single hedging instrument, such as a single futures contract series, is called a **simple hedge.** A hedge consisting of multiple hedging instruments, such as multiple futures series, is called **composite hedge.** A simple hedge may be viewed as a special case of a composite hedge. The mathematics of composite hedging was introduced by Marshall (1989) and extended by Herbst and Marshall (1990). In essence, composite hedging links the risk reduction which accompanies portfolio diversification with the risk reduction inherent in hedging.

The mathematics of composite hedging is complex but not overly formidable and it readily lends itself to computer solutions.

The logic in composite hedging is very straightforward. Portfolio theory long ago established that a portfolio consisting of a number of securities is less risky than a portfolio consisting of just one. It also demonstrated that the risk associated with holding a security consists of two distinct parts which became known as systematic risk and unsystematic risk. This distinction is important because unsystematic risk is reduced by diversification and, with sufficient diversification, completely vanishes. Systematic risk, on the other hand, is not reduced by diversification. An important implication of these behaviors is that the portfolio manager should thoroughly diversify his or her portfolio in order to eliminate the unsystematic component of risk.

Composite hedging achieves greater risk reduction than simple hedging by exploiting the reduction in unsystematic risk that accompanies diversification. Unlike the securities portfolio however, the composite hedge cannot achieve complete elimination of unsystematic risk because there are relatively few good cross hedges (futures) to employ in any one composite hedging situation. The number is typically two or three and only occasionally reaches four. The fact that composite hedging cannot completely eliminate the unsystematic risk component in hedging, however, should not prevent the producer from considering this approach. The most significant decrease in unsystematic risk occurs in the earliest stages of diversification and so a composite hedge consisting of just two or three different futures may offer significant benefits. We will illustrate the procedure here but readers seriously interested in the logic and application of composite hedging should consider the reference material at the end of this chapter.

We begin by determining the risk-minimizing hedge ratio for each of the available cross hedges. We then adjust each futures position so that one unit of "adjusted" futures equals the hedge ratio number of units of the raw futures. That is, suppose that the optimal hedge ratio is f. (As you might expect, we prefer the HKM methodology for obtaining f, in which case $f = b \cdot e^{-y\tau}$, but the mathematics of composite hedging is applicable regardless of the method used to obtain f.) For example, suppose that it is found that the optimal hedge ratio is 2:1 when hedging in type A futures. Then, *one unit* of hedging instrument consists of two units of type A futures. Once the futures instrument has been redefined or adjusted in this way, the basis, which we will denote by B, can be defined as $S - f \cdot F$. The variance of this basis is, of course, the basis risk. The advantage of redefining the hedge instrument in this way is that it forces a hedge ratio of 1:1—which simplifies the later mathematics.

The effectiveness of a hedge is defined as 1 minus the ratio of the variance of the basis (basis risk), denoted σ_B^2, to the variance of the spot price (price risk), denoted σ_P^2 (Equation 21.12). This value is the **coefficient of determination**, denoted ρ^2 (rho squared), and it is the square of the correlation coefficient between the spot price and the adjusted futures. It is a precise measure of the percentage of the price risk eliminated by the hedge. The value must lie in the range 0 to 1.

$$\rho^2 = 1 - \frac{\sigma_B^2}{\sigma_p^2} \tag{21.12}$$

The reader may recall from Chapter 7 that the basis risk is related to the price risk by Equation 21.13. Equation 21.12 is easily obtained by manipulating Equation 21.13.

$$\sigma_B^2 = (1 - \rho^2) \cdot \sigma_p^2 \tag{21.13}$$

Now suppose that there are n different futures available for hedging some specific cash position. Denote the ith "adjusted" futures by $\hat{F}_i$ where the adjustment is as described earlier. That is $\hat{F}_i = f_i F_i$, where f_i denotes the hedge ratio for the ith hedging instrument. The ith basis is then defined as $B_i = S - \hat{F}_i$. Finally, let the covariance of the ith and jth bases be denoted $\sigma_{i,j}$. When i and j are the same such that $\sigma_{i,j} = \sigma_{i,i}$ then the covariance becomes a variance. The variance of the composite hedge basis, denoted σ_c^2, is then given by Equation 21.14.

$$\sigma_c^2 = \sum_i^n \sum_j^n w_i \cdot w_j \cdot \sigma_{i,j} \tag{21.14}$$

In Equation 21.14 the weights on the individual futures making up the composite hedge, denoted w_i, must sum to one for the hedge to be complete. Indeed, the composite hedge variance equation (21.14) is predicated on the assumption of complete hedging. In cases of incomplete hedging (hedging less than 100 percent of production), the variance term is somewhat more complex.

To see how composite hedging may benefit the producer, let's consider a simple example. (This particular application was developed by one of the authors for an agricultural commodities producer.) Suppose that a producer has three futures (adjusted) in which to hedge. Call these 1, 2, and 3. Suppose that the cost of hedging (described in the next section) is the same for all the futures, and so the only factor in making the hedge selection decision is the hedge's effectiveness. The hedge effectiveness, as we have already argued, is measured by the coefficient of determination. The closer this value is to one (1) the better is the hedge. Now suppose that the producer has measured the hedge effectiveness for each of the three futures. These are reported in Table 21.2 together with the variance of the spot price (measured in cents per unit) and the variance of the basis. Remember that the variance terms are squared values.

Table 21.2
Comparative Hedge Effectiveness

Futures	Hedge Effectiveness	Variance of the Basis	Spot Price
1	85.3%	180	1225
2	86.0%	172	1225
3	84.2%	194	1225

On the strength of this evidence, obtained from the historical performance of the three bases, the producer selects futures contract #2 as the hedging instrument. But suppose now that the producer's financial engineer takes the firm's historic bases data and computes the covariances of the three bases. The covariances of the bases appear in Table 21.3.

Table 21.3
Covariance Matrix of the Bases

Futures	Futures 1	2	3
1	180	32	26
2	32	172	44
3	26	44	194

The financial engineer now employs Equation 21.14 to determine the variance of a composite hedge's basis. While the outcome will depend on the weights assigned to each component of the hedge, we will just look at the outcome of an equally weighted composite hedge.[9] The calculation is illustrated below. It yields a variance of 83.3.

$$\sigma_c^2 = \sum_i^n \sum_j^n w_i \cdot w_j \cdot \sigma_{i,j} \qquad (21.14)$$

$$= (\tfrac{1}{3})^2 \cdot 180 + (\tfrac{1}{3})^2 \cdot 32 + (\tfrac{1}{3})^2 \cdot 26$$

$$+ (\tfrac{1}{3})^2 \cdot 32 + (\tfrac{1}{3})^2 \cdot 172 + (\tfrac{1}{3})^2 \cdot 44$$

$$+ (\tfrac{1}{3})^2 \cdot 26 + (\tfrac{1}{3})^2 \cdot 44 + (\tfrac{1}{3})^2 \cdot 194$$

$$= 83.3$$

If the composite hedge has a basis variance of 83.3, then the hedge effectiveness, using Equation 21.12, is 93.2 percent. This is a considerable improvement over the best of the three simple hedges which was 86 percent. These outcomes are compared, on the assumption of equally costly hedges, in Exhibit 21.2. (When the available simple hedges are not equally costly, the set of efficient hedges has the familiar concave shape characteristic of efficient portfolio frontiers when plotted in risk/return space.)

Composite hedging has many applications. The example above

Exhibit 21.2
Composite Hedge Effectiveness

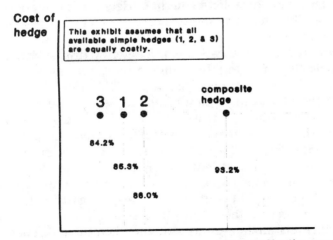

Cost of hedge

This exhibit assumes that all available simple hedges (1, 2, & 3) are equally costly.

3   1   2   composite hedge

84.2%

85.3%   93.2%

86.0%

Hedge effectiveness

illustrates an application in traditional commodities. A producer (or user) of wheat can hedge in wheat futures on several different futures exchanges or a livestock producer can hedge in several different meat and/or poultry contracts. For example, a sheep rancher might desire a direct hedge in sheep futures. Unfortunately, none exist in the United States, making a direct hedge unavailable. The rancher can create a cross hedge by hedging in cattle or hog futures. Neither, by itself, is a very effective hedge, but together they may be quite good. As another example, consider the bond trader hedging his corporate bonds in T-bond futures. (This example was used earlier in this chapter.) Instead of hedging in T-bond futures, the trader could hedge in T-note futures. But, because of nonparallel shifts in the yield curve, it may be more effective to use a composite hedge consisting of both T-bond and T-note futures. As a final example, consider a banker in need of a hedge on a 60-day forward 90-day CD commitment. That is, the banker needs to issue a 90-day CD 60 days from now in order to fund a loan. The banker wants to hedge the cost of the loan. The banker could hedge in T-bill futures or Eurodollar futures, or the banker could formulate a composite hedge consisting of both. (Commercial paper issuers can hedge their paper offerings in the same way.) The only way to know if the composite hedge is superior to the simple hedge is to, in the language of financial engineering, run the numbers.

The Cost of Hedging

Academicians have long sought to determine if there is a cost to hedging. The idea that there should be a cost to hedging was first postulated by Keynes (1930) who argued, in the context of futures hedges, that an excess of short hedging (by commodity producers) over long hedging (by commodity users) creates a need for speculators. The role of the speculator, in this view, is to bear the risks that the producers cannot afford to bear or are unwilling to bear. But, speculators, he reasoned, would not be willing to bear producers' risks unless they, the speculators, were compensated for doing so. Thus, there is the implication that hedgers must compensate speculators for the speculators' risk-bearing services.[10] A different view holds that speculators do not perceive themselves as passive risk bearers but, rather, as active forecasters. Under this view, speculators earn their profit from successfully predicting subsequent price movements and positioning themselves in such a fashion as to reap the benefits.

Early evidence suggested that futures prices are accurate predictors of subsequent spot prices.[11] As such they do not embody the sort of risk premium necessary for there to be a cost to hedging. That is, for there to be a cost to hedging, the futures price must embody a risk premium which accrues to the speculators (who are net long) and is paid by the hedgers (who are net short). More recent evidence, employing improved empirical technique, however, has demonstrated, that futures prices do indeed embody a risk premium and that this results in a transfer of wealth from large hedgers to large speculators. At the same time, the evidence also suggests that large speculators also derive benefits from successful forecasting. This profit, it appears, is earned at the expense of small speculators.[12]

It is important to realize that the passive risk bearing and active forecasting theories as to the source of speculative profits are not mutually exclusive. It is perfectly logical to believe that an excess of hedging on one side of the market will inflate or depress futures prices relative to the expected future spot price. The speculators then identify these mispricings and take positions to exploit them. In the process, they perform the required risk bearing. The cost of a hedge for a short hedger, stated on the basis of per unit of cash commodity hedged, is the difference between the adjusted futures price currently expected to prevail at the time the hedge is lifted and the current adjusted futures price. This is given by Equation 21.15.

$$\text{Cost of Hedge} = f \cdot (E[F(L,T)] - F(t,T)) \qquad (21.15)$$

The time subscripts in Equation 21.15 are interpreted as follows: $E[F(L,T)]$ denotes the current expectation of the futures price to prevail at the time the hedge is lifted (L) for a futures contract that expires at time T; $F(t,T)$, as before, denotes the current futures price for a futures contract that expires at time T; f, again, denotes the hedge ratio.

The point to recognizing that there may be a cost to hedging is in distinguishing between an effective hedge and an efficient hedge. A hedge is **effective** to the degree that it reduces risk. As explained above, we can measure effectiveness with the aid of a coefficient of determination. But, the most effective hedge is not necessarily the best hedge. A hedge which is more effective than another may be inferior to the less effective hedge if the cost of hedging in the more effective hedging instrument is greater than the cost of hedging in the less effective instrument. For example, suppose that one hedge is 89 percent effective and that another is 87 percent effective. Suppose further that the more effective hedge has a cost of $0.08 per unit hedged while the less effective hedge has a cost of only $0.03 per unit hedged. Then the less effective hedge may still be better. An **efficient** hedge is that hedge which, for any given cost, provides the greatest risk reduction. Not surprisingly, the most efficient hedges are often composite hedges.

The Building Block Approach to Hedging

This chapter has examined a number of important concepts relevant to those financial engineers who would design hedging strategies for their own firms or for others. We have argued that it is important to (1) employ analytically correct methodology in determining the optimal hedge ratio, (2) adjust the size of a hedge to reflect the minimum-risk hedge ratio, (3) measure and compare the effectiveness of alternative hedge instruments, (4) consider the possibility of composite hedging and the benefits derivable from that approach, and (5) measure and compare the cost of alternative hedges in an effort to eliminate inefficient hedges. In earlier chapters we demonstrated the importance of (1) identifying strategic price risks, (2) developing risk profiles and converting these to statistical measures of exposure, (3) determining whether an exposure is single period or multiperiod in nature, (4) determining the type of risk to be hedged (all risk or just downside risk), (5) determining the desired form of the residual risk profile, (6) identifying strategies to obtain the desired residual risk profile, and (7) comparing the costs of the alternative strategies to achieving the desired residual risk profile.

It might appear that some of our objectives in this chapter and some of our objectives in earlier chapters are the same. For example, item 5 discussed in this chapter (comparing the cost of alternative hedges) and item 7 discussed in earlier (and subsequent) chapters (comparing the cost of alternative strategies) seem very much the same. But this is not really so. Item 5 in this chapter concerns the cost of alternative hedges of the same type (all futures for example) while item 7 from earlier chapters concerns the cost of alternative strategies using different types of instruments. It is often possible to accomplish the same objective using different instruments. For example, by employing an appropriate combination of single-period options, we can **replicate** or **synthesize** a futures contract. A forward contract can also accomplish the same objective as a futures contract.

We can synthesize a swap with an appropriate strip of futures, with a strip of forwards, or with an appropriate strip of futures-like option combinations. The point is that different strategies can generate identical payoff profiles and, hence, can produce nearly identical hedge outcomes. If all markets were perfectly efficient at all times, then the cost of these equivalent, but alternative, strategies would be the same. But markets are not always perfectly efficient and, at any given point in time, one strategy might be less costly to employ than another. We explore trading techniques designed to exploit the relative cheapness and richness of alternative strategies in the next chapter when we take up arbitrage and synthetic instruments.

We have considered many different instruments that can be used to hedge various types of price risks. We have considered futures, options, forwards, and swaps. These are the essential building blocks available to a financial engineer in the design of a risk management program. By combining these instruments with the underlying cash position, we can manipulate a firm's risk exposure in an infinite variety of ways. There are three widely used ways to visualize this building block approach: (1) by way of risk and payoff profiles; (2) by way of boxed cash flow diagrams; and (3) by way of time line cash flow diagrams. We illustrated the use of risk and payoff profiles in Chapter 7 and we illustrated the use of boxed cash flow diagrams in Chapter 13. The former is depicted again in Exhibit 21.3 using call options as the hedging instrument and the latter is depicted again in Exhibit 21.4 using swaps as the hedging instrument.

Each of these approaches to visualizing the consequences of a hedge strategy has its uses, but which is most useful in a particular situation depends on the financial engineer's purpose. The same is true of the third approach which we introduce here. This is the time line cash flow approach and it consists of a time line with cash inflows and outflows depicted by upward and downward bars or arrows. (We will use the arrow form here although the bar form is at least equally popular.) Such a cash flow diagram is depicted in Exhibit 21.5. We should mention that the meanings we have attached to various arrows are not universally employed and the reader should check the user's key when consulting other sources.

Cash flows that are certain are indicated by solid arrows and cash flows that are uncertain are indicated by dashed arrows. A

Exhibit 21.3
Visualization: The Risk/Payoff Profile Approach

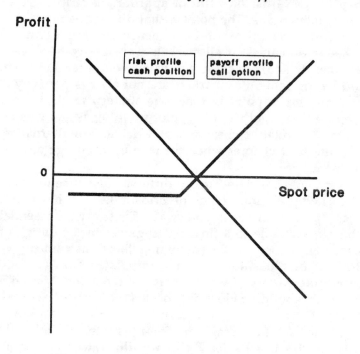

Exhibit 21.4
Visualization: The Boxed Cash Flow Diagram Approach

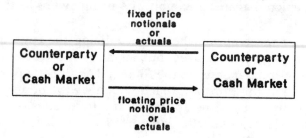

callable bond, for example, has an uncertain cash flow—depending on whether or not the bond issuer chooses to exercise the call feature. A fixed-rate instrument's cash flows are depicted by arrows of equal length and a floating-rate instrument's cash flows are depicted by

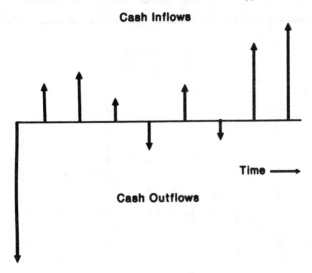

Exhibit 21.5
Visualization: The Time Line Cash Flow Approach

Cash Inflows

Time ⟶

Cash Outflows

arrows of varying length. Examples of each of these are illustrated in Exhibit 21.6.

The time line cash flow approach can also be used to depict

Exhibit 21.6
Time Line Cash Flows and Their Meanings

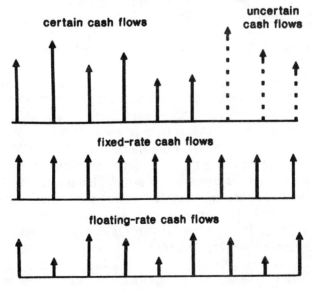

certain cash flows

uncertain cash flows

fixed-rate cash flows

floating-rate cash flows

multi-currency flows by either changing the color or the form of the arrow. For example, the filled arrows in Exhibit 21.7 depict dollar inflows and the hatched arrows depict deutschemark out-flows.

Exhibit 21.7
Representations of Multiple Currencies

dollar inflows

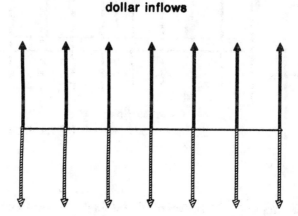

deutschemark outflows

By combining the cash flows associated with the cash position with the cash flows associated with the hedge position, we can achieve considerable insight into the performance of a hedge. Consider a simple example. Suppose a firm holds a five-year fixed-rate bond that is callable after three years. The note affords a semiannual coupon of 12.8 percent. The firm finances this note at the 182-day commercial paper rate. The cash flows associated with the note and the firm's commercial paper positions are depicted in Exhibit 21.8. All cash flows after three years are depicted with dashed arrows as they will not occur if the note is called after three years (in which case the commercial paper will not be rolled over).

Now suppose that the firm enters into a five-year interest rate swap (callable after three years) as fixed-rate payer and floating-rate receiver. (Note, a callable swap is a swap in which the fixed-rate paying party has the right to terminate the swap prior to its normal

Exhibit 21.8
Cash Flows on Cash Positions (Interest Only)

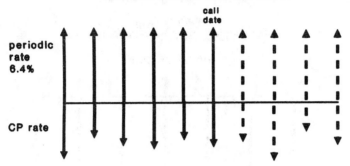

termination date.) The purpose of the swap is to hedge the firm's note and commercial paper positions. The floating-rate leg is tied to the commercial paper index and the coupon is set at 11.6 percent. These cash flows are depicted in Exhibit 21.9.

By combining all the cash flows in Exhibit 21.8 and 21.9 we

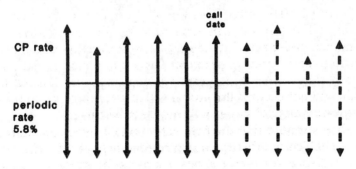

Exhibit 21.9
Cash Flows on Interest Rate Swap

get a clear visual picture of the net cash flows from the hedged position. These are depicted in Exhibit 21.10. Observe that the firm's residual position is a series of certain cash flows at the semiannual rate of 1.2 percent (periodic rate 0.6 percent).

Exhibit 21.10
Net Cash Flows on Hedged Position

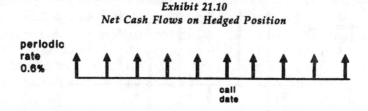

Regardless of the approach we choose to use to depict the outcomes of a hedge, the same building block logic applies. We start with a graphical or mathematical picture of our current risk exposure. We then overlay this picture with the cash flows associated with the various hedging instruments we are considering and we examine the form of the residual or *net* cash flows. By overlaying the cash positions with hedge positions constructed from futures and/or options and/or swaps, and by varying the delivery months and the strike prices, we can manipulate the risk exposure in a great many ways. This kind of analysis is greatly facilitated by spreadsheets and by software packages specifically designed to graphically simulate the net effects of combining positions.[13]

Miscellaneous Risk Management Issues and Instruments

Financial engineers continue to display their resourcefulness in developing new products and new product variants to better fit the needs of the end users of risk management services. Dealers in swaps have expanded their product lines to include forward rate agreements and all forms of single-period and multi-period interest rate and exchange rate options and they remain ready and, indeed, eager, to innovate. Futures and options exchanges too have become more innovative. The exchanges recognize that the over-the-counter products offered by commercial and investment banks compete directly with their traditional product lines. Yet, at the same time, the over-the-counter markets also complement and enhance the use of the exchange-traded futures and options as dealers maneuver to hedge their own positions.[14]

As an example of this innovation, consider recent risk management developments in the mortgage-related markets. We have already demonstrated how mortgage investing has been enhanced by various types of conversion arbitrage such as mortgage passthrough certificates, CMOs, and REITs. These instruments have made it possible for investors to take a position in this important market segment. Further, the latter two instruments have made it possible to manage, at least to some degree, the prepayment risk associated with holding mortgage portfolios. More recent products of financial engineering have further enhanced the risk management opportunities in these markets. For example, swap dealers have introduced mortgage swaps and the Chicago Board of Trade has revised mortgage-backed futures. Both of these instruments can be used to replicate a mortgage portfolio earnings stream without the need to hold mortgage assets. They can also be used to hedge mortgage portfolios from variations in earnings. Consider, for example, a mortgage swap.

In a mortgage swap, cash flows based on a group of GNMA mortgage-backed securities are exchanged for a floating rate of interest—usually LIBOR based. Upon the termination of the swap, a final cash settlement is made based on the change in the market value of the mortgages. For a party who pays the floating rate and receives the fixed rate, the swap is quite similar to holding a fixed-rate mortgage portfolio. The swap position has the added advantage, however, of being off-balance sheet. For the fixed-rate payer, the mortgage swap is equivalent to a short position in an index of mortgages and, therefore, can offset the risk associated with holding actual mortgages.

Critical in mortgage hedging, as one might expect, is the prepayment pattern on the mortgages. Most mortgage-backed instruments attempt to deal with this by incorporating a prepayment assumption. The standard prepayment assumption, called the **PSA** (Public Securities Association) **standard prepayment model**, is most often used for this purpose.[15] Mortgage swaps, on the other hand, use the actual prepayment experience of the index pool in determining the amortization of the principal on the swap. We will consider mortgage swaps again when we consider synthetic securities.

As a second example of the ongoing engineering in risk management consider just three very recent innovations in the over-the-counter options market: (1) path-dependent options, (2) look-back options, and (3) option-linked loans.[16] **Path-dependent options** are cash-settled options in which the payoff is based on an average value of the underlying asset over some period of time as opposed to the customary settlement based on the value of the underlying asset at the time of the option's expiry. These kinds of options are useful for hedging a multi-period exposure with a single-period option. Consider, for example, a cruise line that purchases 10 million gallons of fuel oil over the course of one year. The firm wants to hedge the cost of its fuel oil because it revises its cruise rates only once a year. The fuel is purchased gradually over the one year period with prices dependent on current market conditions. A path-dependent oil cap with a strike price of $0.80 would guarantee that the firm's *average* fuel cost would not exceed $0.80 a gallon over the course of the year. These types of options can also be useful to multinationals looking to hedge the translation exposure associated with their balance sheets. Such translations are typically made at the average exchange rate prevailing over the course of the year.

Look-back options are cash settlement options that are settled on the basis of the highest (or lowest) price of the underlying asset to prevail over the course of the option's life. That is, at the time of expiration, we "look back" over the option's life to determine the highest (or lowest) price to prevail and then cash settle based on that price. Obviously, such options command a higher premium than options which settle based on the value of the underlying asset at the time of expiry. Look-back options, to date, have largely been used as speculative tools rather than hedging tools.

Option-linked loans are loans denominated in one currency but in which the borrower writes options into the loan allowing the lender to redenominate into a different currency. These types of options can allow a firm to borrow floating rate at sub-LIBOR and can be used to hedge a borrowing in one currency that is serviced by revenue in another currency (as in the case of a dual currency loan).

Hedging and asset/liability management will undoubtedly continue to be the dominant forms of financial risk management through the 1990s and beyond. But other forms of risk management are also important. Diversification is one important means of dealing with risk, credit enhancement is another, overcollateralization is a third, and assignment is a fourth. We will say a few words about each before closing this chapter.

The principles underlying the risk-reducing powers of **diversification** have been thoroughly discussed elsewhere in this text and we will not dwell on them except to reiterate a few pertinent points. First, diversification is an excellent and nearly costless way to eliminate the unsystematic components of risk inherent in most financial positions. One of the best examples of this is the credit risk inherent in loan portfolios and bond portfolios. For example, while junk bonds are individually high risk, diversified junk bond portfolios—in which no single component represents more than a few percent of the overall portfolio—have outperformed far more conservative portfolios for extended periods even after allowing for losses due to default. This suggests that the risk-premiums on junk bonds may have been excessive.

Credit risk can also be reduced by **credit enhancement**. All credit enhancement techniques offer the lender an alternative means of collecting the interest and principal due the lender in the event that the borrower defaults. The most common method involves the purchase of a bank guarantee. In these cases, a lender has recourse to the bank guarantor in the event that the borrower is unable to meet its commitments to the lender. This method was widely used in the late 1980s by Japanese borrowers who needed to tap the Euromarkets to obtaining financing but who were not well enough known to borrow in those markets without back-up guarantees.

Overcollateralization is a risk mitigating method that has been discussed elsewhere in this book but is worth a brief second look. It is possible, by overcollateralization, to convert high risk loans or instruments into low risk loans or instruments. This concept has long been employed in mortgage lending in which the maximum lendable sum is always set at some percentage below the appraised value of the property used as collateral. But, it is only in recent years that the concept has been extended to the securities markets. Overcollateralization is used in both the securitization of mortgages and other assets (such as corporate receivables). Most recently, it has been used to convert the risk character of junk bonds. For example, in August 1990, The First Boston Corporation repackaged $245 million of low-rated bonds and produced securities having a rating of double A. These **collateralized bond obligations** (CBOs), as they are called, are similar in structure to CMOs. That is, the First Boston Corporation purchased $245 million of low-rated bonds and then issued multiclass instruments (similar to CMO tranches) against them. Two of the classes were heavily overcollateralized thereby securing a favorable rating. The third tranche was far riskier—entitling its owners to receive any excess from the overcollateralization of the first two classes.

The final method of risk reduction is **assignment.** In assignment, the holder of a position transfers both the rights and obligations associated with that position to a third party. By assigning a position to another party, the risk associated with holding that position is transferred to the acquiring party. This particular approach to risk management is widely used in the insurance industry where it is called **reinsurance.** Insurers will often write policies far beyond their own risk-bearing capabilities but then assign the policy to a larger insurance firm or farm out portions of the policy to a number of smaller insurers. Holding the full policy would defeat the insurer's efforts at diversification—a vital tool in the management of the insurer's risks. Through the reinsurance strategy, the insurer is able to offer a full range of insurance services including large policies and, at the same time, not take all of the associated risks onto its own books.

This look at hedging is not meant to be exhaustive and, indeed, cannot be so. Hedging is both an art and a science and thousands of financial engineers have devoted their careers to this complex subject. One could easily devote an entire text to any one of the hedging instruments and hedging techniques discussed in this book.

Summary

Hedging is the art of managing price risks by taking offsetting positions in derivative instruments. Hedges can be constructed from futures, forwards, options, and swaps. Once a hedging instrument has been selected, the hedger must ascertain the risk minimizing hedge ratio. A hedge ratio is the number of units of the hedging instrument necessary to hedge one unit of the cash instrument. Not surprisingly, much of hedging theory has been devoted to the subject of hedge ratio calculation. The earliest thinking was a 1:1 ratio. This was later shown to be naive and was replaced by a regression approach. Most recently, hedge ratio calculation has been improved by the explicit recognition of convergence of the futures price and the cash price and by the diversification benefits that accompany composite hedging.

As much as we would like to believe that hedging is costless, in fact, it often is not. This suggests that there may be a trade-off between the cost of hedging and hedge effectiveness. Critical to appreciating this trade-off is the realization that some hedges are efficient and some are not. An efficient hedge is a hedge that provides maximum risk reduction per unit cost.

Modern hedging practice takes a building block approach. That is, after determination of the firm's risk profile, the hedger builds a hedge structure using the various derivative instruments to manipulate the shape of the risk profile. Various types of cash flow diagrams and payoff profiles are used to help visualize this process.

In recent years, a number of miscellaneous risk management tactics and instruments have been introduced. These include instruments to hedge mortgage debt, various new types of options, credit enhancements, overcollateralization, and assignment. Each of these has specific uses and should be of interest to the financial engineer working in risk management.

Endnotes

[1]The presence of serial correlation among the regression residuals in a JSE estimation of a hedge ratio has been shown by Herbst, Kare, and Caples (1989).

[2]Examples of this work include Franckle (1980), Grammatikos and Saunders (1983), Herbst, Kare, and Caples (1989), Castelino (1990), and Malliaris and Urrutia (1989)

[3]The calculation of the futures contract DV01 has been glossed over here and in earlier usages in this book. The futures DV01 is the DV01 of the underlying deliverable asset—in the case of a T-bond futures, the deliverable instrument is a T-bond. The calculation is complicated, however, by the fact that T-bond futures are multi-instrument deliverable. That is, more than one T-bond issue may be used as the delivery instrument on any one futures contract. The CBOT attempts to equalize the different delivery instruments by incorporating a conversion factor for each instrument. Nevertheless, at any point in time, one deliverable T-bond issue will be the *cheapest-to-deliver*. To calculate the DV01 of the futures contract, one starts by determining the cheapest-to-deliver bond. The DV01 of the cheapest-to-deliver bond is then calculated. Finally, the DV01 of the cheapest-to-deliver bond is divided by the conversion factor for that bond (as published by the CBOT). The resultant value is the futures DV01.

[4]While it seems implausible, there are occasional exceptions to this rule. For example, some countries have employed dual cur-

rency systems in an effort to control the flow of capital. In such a system, there is one exchange rate for sanctioned foreign exchange transactions and a different exchange rate for non-sanctioned exchanges.

[5]This approach distinguishes between *ex post* and *ex ante* hedge ratios. It is, after all, not possible in practice to hedge a price risk after the fact. Why then should one test hedge ratio performance as if one could hedge after the fact? By using an *ex ante* approach, hedge performance can be judged in a far more realistic applications-type setting.

[6]We use the term "producer" in a very general sense to include any firm that adds value through production, conversion, storage, or transport of a commodity or a financial instrument.

[7]For a more thorough discussion of the relationship between the quantity hedged and the cost of hedging, see Marshall (1989), Chapter 7.

[8]This is an application of the separation theorem of portfolio theory.

[9]To determine the set of efficient composite hedges that may be created from a set of simple hedges we can use the same quadratic programming techniques used to determine the efficient set of portfolios that can be generated from a given universe of securities.

[10]This set of assumptions and the consequent conclusions together make up what has historically been called **normal backwardation**. Implicit in this theory is the assumption of a secular uptrend in futures prices.

[11]For a review of this literature, see Marshall (1989), Chapter 8.

[12]Maddala and Yoo (1990) provide recent evidence and also review earlier work in this area in their paper. In particular, their work supports the findings by Houthakker (1957) and Rockwell (1967).

[13]The larger commercial and investment banks have generally chosen to develop their own risk management software packages. There are, however, off-the-shelf packages available to aid in the measurement and visual depiction of cash flow patterns and risk and payoff profiles. One of the earliest of such packages was the LIFFE *Risk Manager*, published by the London International Financial Futures Exchange in 1985. This particular simulator is limited to LIFFE traded futures and options.

[14]For example, at the time of this writing, the CBOT was preparing to introduce "swap futures" and "swap options." These instruments are intended to provide a hedging vehicle for swap dealers.

[15]The PSA model was introduced in 1985 and is based on frequently observed patterns of prepayments. The PSA model is a variation of the SMM, or single monthly mortality, model developed by First Boston Corporation in 1978.

[16]These terms are borrowed from Brady and King (1989). Other terms will surely appear in time to describe these instruments.

References & Suggested Reading

Brady, S. and P. King. "The Options Explosion", *Euromoney, Special Supplement*, London: Euromoney, 1989.

Castelino, M.G. "Minimum-Variance Hedging with Futures Revisited," *The Journal of Portfolio Management*, 16(3) (1990).

Castelino, M.G., J.C. Francis, and A. Wolf. "Cross-Hedging: Basis Risk and Choice of the Optimal Hedging Vehicle, *Financial Review*, 26(20) (1991), pp. 179-210.

Ederington, L.H. "The Hedging Performance of the New Futures Markets," *Journal of Finance*, 34(1) (1979).

Franckle, C. "The Hedging Performance of the New Futures Market: Comment," *Journal of Finance*, 35(5) (1980).

Grammatikos, T. and A. Saunders. "Stability and the Hedging Performance of Foreign Currency Futures," *Journal of Futures Markets*, 3(3) (1983).

Herbst, A.F., D.D. Kare, and S.C. Caples. "Hedge Effectiveness and Minimum Risk Hedge Ratios in the Presence of Autocorrelation: Foreign Currency Futures," *Journal of Futures Markets*, 9(3) (1989).

Herbst, A.F., D.D. Kare, and J.F. Marshall. "A Time Varying, Convergence Adjusted Hedge Ratio Model," Working Paper, Department of Economics and Finance, The University of Texas at El Paso (August 1990a).

Herbst, A.F., D.D. Kare, and J.F. Marshall. "Direct Hedging and Cross Hedging: A Theoretical, Time-Varying Convergence Adjustment,"Working Paper, Department of Economics and Finance, The University of Texas at El Paso (August 1990b).

Herbst, A.F. and J.F. Marshall. "Effectiveness, Efficiency, and Optimality in Futures Hedging: An Application of Portfolio Theory," in *The Swaps Handbook: Swaps and Related Risk Management Instruments*, by K.R. Kapner and J.F. Marshall, New York: The New York Institute of Finance, 1990.

Houthakker, H.S. "Can Speculators Forecast Prices?" *The Review of Economics and Statistics* (May 1957).

Johnson, L.L. "The Theory of Hedging and Speculation in Commodity Futures," *Review of Economic Studies*, 27(3) (1960).

Keynes, J.M. *A Treatise on Money*, vol 2, London: Macmillan, 1930.

Maddala, G.S. and J. Yoo. "Risk Premia and Price Volatility in Futures Markets," Working Paper #205, Center for the Study of Futures Markets (1990).

Malliaris, A.G. and J. Urrutia. "Test of Random Walk of the Hedge Ratio and Measuring Hedge Effectiveness for Stock Indexes and Foreign Currency Futures Contracts," Chicago: Working Paper 89-08, Loyola University, 1989.

Rockwell, C.S. "Normal Backwardation, Forecasting and the Returns to Commodity Futures Traders, *Food Research Institute Studies*, 7 (supplement) (1967).

Stein, J. "The Simultaneous Determination of Spot and Futures Prices," *American Economic Review*, 51(5) (1961).

Wall Street Journal, editorial page "The Franklin Fiasco" (September 7, 1990).

Chapter 22

Corporate Restructuring and the LBO

Vipul K. Bansal and Robert Yuyuenyongwatana

Overview

Few financial engineering activities have attracted as much attention as has corporate restructuring. **Corporate restructuring** is an umbrella term that includes mergers and consolidations, divestitures and liquidations, and various types of battles for corporate control. At its most general level, the term corporate restructuring can and has been used to mean almost any change in operations, capital structure, and/or ownership, that is not part of the firm's ordinary course of business.

Our interest in restructuring focuses on the financial engineering involved. In particular, we want to know if restructuring generates value gains for shareholders (both those who own the firm before the restructuring and those who own the firm after the restructuring), how these value gains might be achieved, and the sources of the value gains. It is the perception of value gains, after all, that motivates the corporate restructuring, and it is the financial engineering which makes the restructuring possible.

Vipul Bansal and Robert Yuyuenyongwatana are Assistant Professors of Finance in the Graduate School of Business at St. John's University, New York.

We are going to focus most of our conversation on issues involving ownership and control. This leads logically to the subject of leveraged buyouts: both those by corporate outsiders and those by corporate insiders. While corporate mergers, consolidations, takeovers, and acquisitions have historically occurred in waves lasting from five to ten years and going at least as far back as the late 1800s, the leveraged buyout is unmistakably a product of the 1980s. It was during the 1980s that many of the new tools which made leveraged buyouts possible, including high yield or junk bonds, found favor. The 1980s also witnessed a more accommodating regulatory environment and a tax environment more conducive to capital formation and corporate restructuring.

We will begin this chapter with a brief examination of the various activities which fall under the corporate restructuring umbrella. Following this, we will focus more narrowly on the issues of going private and the role of the leveraged buyout in achieving this private status. We will then address the value concerns noted above. We will close the chapter with a brief look at the financial engineers that put the deals together.

Corporate Restructuring

The term corporate restructuring encompasses three distinct, but related, groups of activities: **expansions**—including mergers and consolidations, tender offers, joint ventures, and acquisitions; **contraction**—including sell offs, spin offs, equity carve outs, abandonment of assets, and liquidation; and **ownership and control**—including the market for corporate control, stock repurchase programs, exchange offers, and going private (whether by leveraged buyout or other means). All of these activities involve financial engineering. Some, such as leveraged buyouts, are often practiced by firms that specialize in this activity and which have their own financial engineers on board. These firms include such big names as Kohlberg, Kravis, Roberts and Forstmann Little, but increasingly also include LBO funds. Others are accomplished with the aid of financial engineers working for investment banks. Still others, indeed most, involve both groups.

The financial engineers that work for investment banks and which specialize in corporate restructurings most often work out of merger and acquisition (M&A) departments. As a general rule, an investment bank's M&A department tends to have a great deal of autonomy vis-a-vis the rest of the organization. Nevertheless,

M&A must work closely with the bank's other areas including the capital markets group, the corporate finance group, and the merchant banking group. Each of these latter groups has a role to play if a deal, particularly a contested one, is to be successful.

We will briefly look at each of the three major categories of restructuring in the sections which follow, beginning with expansions.

Expansions

Expansions include mergers, consolidations, acquisitions, and various other activities which result in an enlargement of a firm or its scope of operations. There is a lot of ambiguity in the usage of the terms associated with corporate expansions. For example, there are legal distinctions between those corporate combinations which constitute mergers and those which constitute consolidations. Technically, a **merger** involves a combination of two firms such that only one survives. Mergers tend to occur when one firm is significantly larger than the other and the survivor is usually the larger of the two. A **consolidation,** on the other hand, involves the creation of an altogether new firm owning the assets of both of the first two firms—and neither of the first two survive. This form of combination is most common when the two firms are of approximately equal size. Despite this legal distinction, however, the terms *merger* and *consolidation* are often used interchangeably to describe any combination of two firms.

A merger can take the form of a horizontal merger, a vertical merger, or a conglomerate merger. A **horizontal merger** involves two firms in similar businesses. The combination of two oil companies, or two solid waste disposal companies, for example, would represent horizontal mergers. A **vertical merger** involves two firms involved in different stages of production of the same end product or related end products. The combination of a waste removal and a waste recycler or the combination of an oil producer and an oil refiner would be examples of vertical mergers. A **conglomerate merger** involves two firms in unrelated business activities. The combination of an oil refiner and a solid waste disposal company would be an example of a conglomerate merger. These distinctions can be important in understanding the sources of value in business combinations.

Not all business expansions lead to the dissolution of one or more of the involved firms. For example, **holding companies** often seek to acquire equity interests in other firms. The target firm may or may not become a subsidiary of the holding company (50+ percent ownership) but, in either case, continues to exist as a legal entity. The **joint venture**, in which two separate firms pool some of their resources, is another such form that does not ordinarily lead to the dissolution of either firm. Such ventures typically involve only a small portion of the cooperating firms' overall businesses and usually have limited lives.

The term **acquisition** is another ambiguous term. At the most general, it means an attempt by one firm, called the **acquiring firm**, to gain a majority interest in another firm, called the **target firm**. The effort to gain control may be a prelude to a subsequent merger, to establish a parent subsidiary relationship, to break-up the target firm and dispose of its assets, or to take the target firm private by a small group of investors.

There are a number of strategies that can be employed in corporate acquisitions. In the **friendly takeover,** the acquiring firm will make a financial proposal to the target firm's management and board. This proposal might involve the merger of the two firms, the consolidation of the two firms, or the creation of a parent/subsidiary relationship. The existing shareholders of the target firm would receive cash or stock of the acquiring firm, or, in the case of a consolidation, stock in the new firm, in exchange for their stock in the target firm. In a friendly takeover, management of the target firm usually retain their positions after the acquisition is consummated.

At the other extreme is the hostile takeover. A **hostile takeover** may or may not follow a preliminary attempt at a friendly takeover. For example, it is not uncommon for an acquiring firm to embrace the target firm's management in what is colloquially called a **bear hug**. In this approach, the acquiring firm's board makes a proposal to the target firm's board. The target firm's board is required to make a quick decision on the acquiring firm's bid. The target firm's board may also be apprised of the acquiring firm's intent to pursue a tender offer if the target firm's board does not approve the bid. In such a situation, the acquiring firm looks to replace the noncooperating directors. The alternative to the bear hug is for the acquiring firm to appeal directly to the target firm's shareholders without any preliminary proposal to the target firm's board. Whether made explicit or not, it is understood that, in a hostile takeover, current management can expect to be replaced by management of the acquiring firm's choosing.

The same M&A departments that advise acquiring firms on takeovers also advise target firms on defenses against takeovers. These specialists have engineered a number of strategies which often have bizarre nicknames such as **shark repellents** and **poison pills**— terms which accurately convey the genuine hostility involved. In this same vain, the acquiring firm itself is often described as a **raider**. One such strategy is to employ a **target block repurchase** with an accompanying **standstill agreement**. This combination is sometimes described as **greenmail**. That is, the target firm agrees to buy back the acquiring firm's stake in the target firm's stock (the target block repurchase) at a premium to the current market price of that stock. In return, the raider is required to sign an agreement to the effect that neither the raider nor groups controlled by the raider will acquire an interest in the target firm for some specified period of time (the standstill agreement).

Other defenses against hostile takeovers include **leveraged recapitalizations** and **poison puts** (versions of the "shark repellant" and "poison pill" strategies alluded to above). The leveraged recapitalization, or **recap**, strategy was developed by Goldman Sachs in 1985 in an effort to fend off an attempted takeover of Multimedia, Inc. The strategy is also known as a **leveraged cash-out (LCO)**. In this strategy, the firm borrows heavily (issues debt) and uses the funds obtained from the issuance of debt to pay outside shareholders a large one-time cash dividend. At the same time, the firm pays its inside shareholders (managers and employees) their dividend in the form of additional shares of stock. This has two simultaneous effects: First, it increases the target firm's use of leverage and thereby decreases its attractiveness to the acquiring firm—as the latter might have planned its own **leveraging up** of the target firm's assets. Second, the strategy concentrates stock in the hands of insiders thereby making it more difficult for an outsider to gain a controlling interest. Leveraged cash-outs bear more than surface similarities to leveraged buy-outs in that both involve the use of a great deal of financial leverage in order gain control. We will return to this point later.

Corporate takeovers and other forms of change in effective control often result in a deterioration of the target firm's creditworthiness. This can be extremely costly to bondholders and other creditors of the firm. One way to deal with this is to grant debtholders protective poison put covenants which allow the debt holders to put the debt they hold back to the corporation or the acquiring firm in the event of a transfer of control. This can be extremely costly to the acquiring firm and, hence, decreases the attractiveness of the target. While it would seem that poison puts are a genuine form of investor protection, this is not necessarily the case. Such puts often grant the bondholders the right to put the bonds *if and only if* the takeover is hostile and, can, as such, exempt friendly takeovers and management buy-outs—even if they originate as a response to an earlier hostile takeover attempt. Whether it be friendly or hostile, a takeover can cause credit deterioration and, thus, the poison puts may be more for the protection of current management than for the protection of the debtholders.

A very appealing defensive measure against a hostile takeover attempt is for the target firm's management to seek a white knight. A **white knight** is a second acquiring firm with which the target firm can negotiate a more favorable and "friendly" takeover. An alternative to the white knight is for management itself to attempt a takeover—usually through a management-led leveraged buyout. A management-led leveraged buyout is sometimes called an **management buyout (MBO)**.

There are several advantages to a friendly takeover relative to an unfriendly one. First, the target firm's resources are not wasted in an effort to fend off the acquiring firm. Second, there is a greater chance that the management of the combination will have a more harmonious working relationship and more easily meld the operations of the two firms. Finally, employee morale, the importance of which is often underestimated, is less likely to suffer in a friendly takeover than in an unfriendly one.

Contractions

Contraction, as the term implies, results in a smaller firm rather than a larger one. If we ignore the abandonment of assets, occasionally a logical course of action, corporate contraction occurs as the result of disposition of assets. The disposition of assets, sometimes called **sell-offs**, can take either of three broad forms: **spin-offs**, **divestitures**, and **carve-outs**. Spin-offs and carve-outs create new legal entities while divestitures do not.

In a spin-off the parent company transfers some of its assets and liabilities to a new firm created for that purpose. The shareholders of the original firm are then given shares in the new firm on a proportional basis to their ownership in the original firm. After the sell-off, the original shareholders have the same equity interest but now divided between two separate entities. The share-holders are then free to transfer their stock or to keep it, as they see fit. By creating a new firm with its own assets, its own management, and separate ownership, the spin-off represents a genuine transfer of control. This was the approach taken when American Telephone & Telegraph (AT&T) was broken up into a group of individual regional phone companies.

There are a number of variations on the spin-off including the **split-off** and the **split-up**. In a split-off, some of the shareholders are given an equity interest in the new firm in exchange for their shares of the parent company. In a split-up, all the assets of the parent company are divided up among spin-off companies and the original parent ceases to exist. Spin-offs, regardless of their form, may be and have been described as stock dividends. It is important to observe that in all forms of spin-offs, the parent company receives no cash from its transfer of assets to the new firm(s).

In contrast to the no-cash transfer of assets in a spin-off, a **divestiture** involves an out and out sale of assets, usually for cash consideration. That is, the parent company sells some of the firm's assets for cash to another firm. In most cases, the assets are sold to an existing firm so that no new legal entity results from the transactions.

An equity **carve-out** is a form of contraction intermediate between a spin-off and a divestiture. It does bring cash to the original firm, but it also disperses assets and ownership in the assets to non-owners of the original firm. In this arrangement, the original firm forms a new firm and transfers some of the original firm's assets to the new firm. The original firm then sells equity in the new firm. The purchasers of this equity may or may not be the same as the owners of the original firm. Like a divestiture, an equity carve-out brings cash to the firm and, like a spin-off, the equity carve-out creates a new legal entity.

22.2.3 *Ownership and Control*

The third major area encompassed by the term corporate restructuring is that of ownership and control. Actually, this is closely related to both expansion activities and contraction activities. For example, a hostile takeover is effected by acquiring ownership and wresting control from the current board. Similarly, once ownership and/or control have been wrested from the current board, the new management will often embark on a full or partial liquidation strategy involving the sale of assets. Despite this overlap, however, our concern in this section is not so much with expansion or contraction, but rather with strategies intended to transfer ownership and/or control to a new group.

Let's first consider some steps that might be taken by current management to make the transfer of ownership and/or the transfer of control more difficult. One strategy often employed involves the adoption of antitakeover amendments to the corporate bylaws in order to make an acquisition more difficult and more expensive. Some common attempts include (1) staggering the terms of the members of the board so that an acquiring firm must wait a considerable period before replacing a sufficient number of board members to get its way; (2) supermajority voting provisions applied to matters involving merger—such as requiring a 75 or 80 percent favorable vote; and (3) providing current management with **golden parachutes**. The latter are sizeable termination payments made to current management in the event that management is terminated following a change in the control of the firm.

Current management starts off with a considerable advantage over dissident shareholders. First, as a general rule, management nominates new board members who are often rubber stamped by the majority of the firm's shareholders. The board, in turn, reappoints management. But, dissident shareholders are not without weapons of their own. One such weapon is the **proxy contest**. In a proxy contest, dissident shareholders attempt to secure the proxies of other shareholders in an effort to install their own people on the board and to lessen the control of the incumbents. Proxy contests are often used by major shareholders who lack a controlling interest but who nevertheless wield enough weight as to have a reasonable prospect of attracting sufficient proxies to swing a vote. Proxy fights, per se, do not involve a transfer of ownership but they do involve an effort to alter control of the firm.

The alternative to gaining, or retaining, control via proxy battles is to alter the very structure of ownership. We have already considered the more traditional ways by which ownership is passed to new parties via the merger or consolidation of firms but the really unique development of the 1980s was the advent of the leveraged buyout. The leveraged buyout preserves the integrity of the firm as a legal entity but consolidates ownership in the hands of a small group. We look at leveraged buyouts more closely in the next section.

Going Private: The Leveraged Buyout

While corporate restructurings are not new, they do tend to occur in waves. The 1980s experienced a major wave. The restructuring wave of the 1980s witnessed all the traditional forms of restructuring including mergers, acquisitions, consolidations, spin-offs, divestitures, and proxy battles. But it also saw the advent of a major new trend. In the 1980s, many large publicly traded firms went private and most employed a similar strategy called a leveraged buyout or LBO.

A number of economic and financial factors converged to make the leveraged buyout an attractive concept. All that was lacking was the means. The advent of junk bonds, bridge financing, venture capital firms, and merchant banking, all of which are products of financial engineering, provided those means. We begin with a look at the economic and financial factors that created an environment conducive to going private. We then consider the various means enumerated above, and, finally, we consider the sources of value that leveraged buyouts seek to capture.

The Economic and Financial Environment

A period of prolonged and accelerating inflation began in the 1960s and continued until the early 1980s. This extended period of inflation had the effect of dramatically reducing the ratio of the market value of U.S. corporations to the replacement cost of those corporations' assets. The ratio of market value to replacement cost of assets is sometimes called the **q-ratio.** When the q-ratio is less than one, it is cheaper to buy capacity by acquiring a going firm than it is to build capacity by purchasing real assets on one's own. Over the period from 1965 to 1981, the average q-ratio of American industrial corporations declined from about 1.3 to about 0.5.[1] The q-ratio did not start to rise again until 1982 when a bull market in U.S. equities began.

The inflation also had the effect of reducing the average corporation's real leverage. This occurred because both the interest and principal on preexisting debt was not indexed for inflation. Thus, in real terms, the inflation reduced both the amount of real debt on corporate balance sheets and the cost of servicing this debt. The unintentional decline in the pre-1980s use of leverage created an opportunity in the 1980s for corporate managers to enhance equity returns by leveraging up the firm or, more accurately, releveraging the firm. Any firm which failed to leverage up on its own became a potential target for a takeover by others who would leverage up once they had control.

Restructuring activity was also stimulated by a succession of favorable changes in tax law. One piece of legislation was particularly conducive. This was the Economic Recovery Tax Act (ERTA) of 1981. ERTA permitted old assets to be **stepped up,** for depreciation purposes, upon purchase by another firm and for the higher basis to be depreciated at an accelerated rate. It also enhanced the role of **Employee Stock Ownership Plans (ESOPs)** by making deductible both the interest and the principal on money borrowed from banks to purchase company stock for these plans. A subsequent change in the tax law increased bank willingness to lend for this purpose by allowing banks to deduct one-half the interest they received on these ESOP loans.

While not the consequence of new legislation, it also became clear in the 1980s that the government had adopted a more permissive attitude toward horizontal and vertical business combinations. This new attitude stimulated interest in exploiting production and marketing efficiencies made possible by product and market extensions.

The final economic factor setting the climate in the 1980s was real economic growth. In the end, a merger, a consolidation, or a leveraged buyout can only be successful if (1) its assets can be disposed of at a profit, or (2) the ongoing concern that has been acquired has healthy cash flows. Beginning in 1982, corporate earnings grew rapidly and nearly continuously throughout the decade. This earnings strength was sufficient to convince many that successful deals could be engineered.

The Tools for Going Private

While the economic climate in the 1980s was undoubtedly right for a wave of mergers and consolidations, leveraged buyouts, in which a small group of investors acquires most or all of a firm's outstanding equity and then takes the firm private, required new and very special financing tools. These tools soon appeared and were put to work quite aggressively. Most of these tools were engineered by investment banks but are often coupled with **secured acquisition loans** from banks. In addition to the bank-sourced acquisition loans, the principal tools are junk bonds, private placements, bridge financing, venture capital, and merchant banking.

Junk bonds are perhaps the most controversial of the tools used in leveraged buyouts. These bonds were described in Chapter 18 and represent high-yield/high-risk investments. They were pioneered by Michael Milken of the investment banking firm of Drexel Burnham Lambert and soon propelled Drexel to **bulge-bracket status** in the investment banking industry.[2] Other investment banks soon followed Drexel's lead into the high-yield market. By 1989, the $200+ billion junk bond market consisted of more than 2,000 issues representing some 800 companies in 100 industries.[3]

Many issues of junk bonds have a **reset provision** or belong to a category of **deferred-payment instruments.** These are designed to enhance the bond yields to the investors—but at a higher cost to the issuers. A reset provision forces the issuer to increase the interest rate it pays to the bondholders if the bond fails to trade at or above par by a stipulated date.

The two most frequent deferred-payment securities are the **payment-in-kind (PIK)** and a type of zero-coupon bond. A PIK holder receives additional bonds in lieu of cash payments up until the **cashout date** when the investor receives more interest payments from holding more bonds. In the zero coupon bond, an investor buys the bond at a discount (typically about 35 to 40 percent) and begins collecting interest after several years into the life of the bond.

Private placements represent issues of debt that are not offered to the general public. Instead, they are placed with a small group of institutions such as insurance companies, pension funds, and other sophisticated investors who do not need the protection afforded by registration with the Securities and Exchange Commission. All other things being equal, the holders of privately placed debt generally receive a higher return than do the holders of publicly offered debt. Nevertheless, private placements can be less costly to the issuer (since the costly registration process is avoided). Furthermore, private placements can be effected much more quickly since the due diligence investigation required for registration can be dispensed with.

Private placements and junk bond offerings differ from secured bank acquisition loans in that the former are typically unsecured and subordinated forms of debt. On the other hand, as debt holders, these investors have a senior claim to that of shareholders. Because they stand between the secured debt of the banks and the very risky residual claims of the shareholders, private placements and junk bonds used to finance leverage buyouts are often called mez-

zanine money. In addition to a higher rate of interest than that payable on the secured debt, the providers of mezzanine money often also receive a portion of the equity—called an **equity kicker.**

In **bridge financing,** the investment bank makes a loan to the buyout group as an interim financing until more permanent financing can be arranged. While the investment bank earns interest on its bridge financing, its primary motivation in providing bridge financing is usually the M&A advisement fees and the underwriting fees that it receives from its other involvements in the deal. These fees are far more likely to be earned if the deal can be closed before other parties have a chance to counter the buyout group's bid or the target firm has the chance to adopt defensive strategies that can make the buyout more costly. The bridge loan allows the deal to be effected far more quickly and, therefore, with a greater probability of success. The investment bank's intent is to retire the bridge loan as quickly as possible and remove it from its books. But, deals can go bad and the investment bank can get stuck with the loan. The Campeau Corporation's default in the late 1980s on its obligations after its successful takeover of Allied Stores, Inc. left its investment banker, The First Boston Corporation, with sizeable losses on its bridge financing to Campeau.

Venture capital firms can play several roles in a leveraged buyout. First, they can take and hold a portion of the privately placed debt. Second, they can act as members of the buyout group— taking a portion of the equity. It is not uncommon and, indeed, is rather typical for venture capital firms to take both debt and equity in the target firm. By definition, venture capital firms specialize in taking substantial risks in their effort to earn substantial rewards. Some have been immensely successful.

The last tool mentioned above is that of merchant banking. **Merchant banking** is a relatively new endeavor for investment banks. In merchant banking, the investment bank takes a portion of the target firm's equity on its own books. That is, the investment bank becomes an equity partner in the leveraged buyout. In merchant banking, the investment bank puts its own money at risk in the deal and it plays a very high stakes game. This is far more risky than making bridge loans which are intended to be retired quickly.

Sources of Value in a Leveraged Buyout

In a typical leveraged buyout, the acquiring group consists of a small number of persons or organizations. This group, using the financing tools described in the preceding section, acquires all or nearly all of the outstanding stock of the target firm and then takes the target firm private. The buyout group may or may not include current management of the target firm. If it does, the buyout is sometimes described as a management buyout or MBO. Nevertheless, it is still a leveraged buyout and we will not distinguish between nonmanagement LBOs and MBOs.

Once the LBO has been completed. The firm, now private, might continue to operate in its original form or it might sell-off some or all of its assets. If it continues to operate, it might go public again after a few years or it might be sold privately to a new group of investors in a second leveraged buyout. As odd as these latter courses may seem, they are not unusual paths for an LBO to take. If the LBO owners' intent in going public again or in selling to a new LBO group is to get their money out, the strategy is called **cashing out**. Cashing out in an LBO does not imply that the firm is in trouble (as it often does in sales of securities by managers in more traditional corporate structures). It only implies that the extraordinary returns possible with an LBO cannot continue without a re-leveraging of the firm. This will become clearer later after we run through a complete example.

In order for the acquiring group to gain a controlling interest in the target firm, they must make a **tender offer** for the firm's stock. The only exception to this is if enough of the firm's stock already rests in a few hands and those holders can be persuaded to become parties to the LBO. In all other cases, the acquiring group must bid for the stock at a premium to its current market price. The fact that successful LBOs often involve bids at premiums ranging to fifty percent or more of the market price prevailing just before the takeover was launched and the fact that the buyout group expects to profit handsomely from taking the firm private lead one to wonder about the source(s) of value in an LBO. How can it be, after all, that current shareholders can be bought out at a price significantly above market (thus receiving excess value) and the buyers subsequently also earn significant profits unless (1) the current market price significantly understates the current value of the firm, (2) some value is created by taking the firm private, or (3) value is transferred to the selling shareholders and the buyout group from other interested parties.

No issue has been more thoroughly discussed and more carefully examined in corporate restructurings than the sources of value.

There is a good reason for this. Market efficiency was long an accepted tenet of academic theory. This theory, which was discussed in Chapter 9, holds that all competitive markets price assets efficiently. In its purest form, the theory implies that a stock's current market price accurately reflects the value of all relevant information concerning the firm. Thus, if the source of the value in an LBO is simply a mispricing of the firm's stock, then the market could not have been efficient to begin with. While evidence developed during the 1980s has demonstrated that markets may not be as efficient as once believed, the evidence does not support mispricings on the scale necessary to justify LBOs at the kinds of premiums they typically command. The source of the value must, therefore, lie with one of the other two explanations. We should not ignore the possibility, however, that managers may possess superior information to that possessed by the firm's shareholders.

Let's first consider the possibility that the act of taking the firm private creates value. How might this be so? There are several possible ways in which value may be created. The first harks back to the agency problem we discussed in Chapter 18. The agency problem, you will recall, stems from the separation of ownership and control. That is, in a typical, publicly held corporation, management and ownership are vested in different groups of people. Theory holds that management will, at all times, make decisions and act in the best interests of the owners for whom they work. After all, managers are agents of the owners. But practice will often differ from theory and managers may be inclined to make suboptimal decisions particularly if they perceive benefits to themselves from doing so. Indeed, they may even do this unconsciously while convincing themselves that they are acting in the best interests of the shareholders. Suboptimal decisions can take many forms and range from the obvious—such as excessive perks for management—to the not so obvious—such as keeping unproductive assets rather than admit to an earlier mistake. The difference in the firm's value when the owners are the managers and the firm's value when the owners are not the managers represents the agency cost. By taking the firm private, ownership and control become one and the same. This eliminates, or greatly reduces, the agency costs and the reduction in agency costs is the source of the value gain associated with the LBO.

Another argument made for why going private can add to a firm's value concerns efficiency. There are several dimensions to the efficiency argument. The first is decision-making efficiency. That is to say, the managers do not have to engage in extensive and time-consuming studies, prepare detailed reports, and provide volumes of evidence to a skeptical board before making a decision to either launch a major new project or to terminate an existing one. Further, for those decisions involving approval of the firm's shareholders, the managers do not have to convince a diverse body of shareholders and wait for the annual meeting before gaining approval to take the firm in a new direction. The inefficiencies in the decision-making process introduced by the separation of ownership and control decrease the value of the firm which often loses the ability to move quickly in response to rapidly changing circumstances surrounding the decision in question. Another efficiency issue involves the publication of sensitive information. A publicly held firm is required to publish certain types of information which can include competitively sensitive material. A nonpublic firm has no such requirement. In addition, the nonpublic firm does not have to absorb the expense associated with periodic filing and compliance matters that are required of a publicly held firm. A final argument, which also sometimes passes under the efficiency label, involves production and portfolio efficiencies. For example, some LBO deals involve specialized LBO firms.[4] In deals of this type, there can be synergistic benefits such that the sum of the parts is greater than the whole, and there can be the risk-reduction benefits that accompany diversification.

The last potential source of value gain from going private involves tax benefits. This particular benefit unquestionably exists. First, the asset step-up for depreciation purposes which was discussed earlier—in the context of takeovers more generally—applies equally to leveraged buyouts. Second, the tax savings that accompanies the payment of interest (relative to dividends) is considerable in leveraged buyouts since the source of the leverage is the considerable debt that is employed. Finally, there are the benefits, also detailed earlier, that are associated with ESOPs. It is not surprising, therefore, that ESOPs play a significant role in many LBOs.

The value gains associated with an LBO which were discussed above are all, with the possible exception of the tax benefits, positive explanations for the value gains achieved by the prebuyout and post-buyout shareholders. The tax benefits can be construed, on the other hand, as either positive or negative depending on one's viewpoint. The alternative, but not mutually exclusive, explanation for the value gains to shareholders is decidedly more negative in nature. This view holds that the gains achieved by the shareholders come at the expense of other interested parties—particularly the firm's debtholders. That is, the gains to the shareholders are earned at the expense of others having a legitimate stake in the fortunes of the firm. For this reason, the value gain is described as a **wealth transfer**.

In addition to the firm's pre-buyout debtholders, others with a pre-existing stake in the firm—sometimes described collectively as **stakeholders**—include the firm's employees, preferred stockholders, suppliers, and federal and local government. The latter derive tax revenues from the profits of the firm and the payroll taxes of the employees. The loss of tax revenue was included in the value creation argument and we do not consider it again. The stake of the firm's employees takes the form of career commitments and pension benefits. It is not unusual, for example, for new owners of a firm to seek a more favorable arrangement with the firm's workers or to trim excess employees. On the other hand, the employees can also be major beneficiaries of leveraged buyouts as the new owners often see it in their own best interests to give the employees an even greater stake in the fortunes of the firm—a potentially useful motivating tool. The real issue then is the effect of the buyout on the firm's debtholders and we concentrate the remainder of our discussion on this group.

The prebuyout debtholders of the firm may have protective covenants which are activated in the event of a change in control or the issuance of additional debt. But, then again, they may not. The new debt, issued to finance the leveraged buyout, undoubtedly is not good for the prebuyout debtholders. The firm's increased use of leverage makes it that much more risky. All other things being equal, the increase in the riskiness of the firm reduces the creditworthiness of the firm and the market price of the firm's outstanding debt can be expected to reflect this decrease in creditworthiness. This is particularly likely to be the case if the new debt used to finance the leveraged buyout is not subordinated to the prebuyout debt or if it has a shorter duration than the prebuyout debt.

The empirical evidence on the wealth transfer hypothesis as the explanation for the value gain by shareholders in a leveraged buyout is mixed. Some studies have shown no significant loss of value to debtholders[5] while others have shown statistically significant losses to debtholders.[6] In no case, however, has a study been able to show that the cumulative losses to the debtholders are equal to or greater than the cumulative gains to shareholders. One may conclude from this that while wealth transfer is a possible, indeed probable, explanation for some of the value gains to shareholders, it is not sufficient in and of itself to account for all the gains.

It seems reasonable that all of the explanations offered for the value gains to shareholders in leveraged buyouts contain an element of truth and constitute parts of the total explanation. That is, the value gains to shareholders are partly a consequence of wealth transfer, and partly the result of efficiency gains, tax benefits, better information, and a reduction in agency costs. In any case, empirical evidence suggests that LBOs do create gains for the parent-companies' shareholders. Furthermore, LBO firms tend to exhibit superior performance after the leveraged buyout.[7]

Critics of LBOs argue that a leveraged buyout can (1) cause layoffs of the target firm's employees as the new management/owners streamline the firm's operations, (2) damage the debt markets resulting in higher costs for debt capital all around, (3) force post-LBO management to concentrate on short-term goals, e.g., to service the firm's debt by reducing the advertising and research and development budgets to the detriment of long-term growth, and (4) result in bankruptcies due to the firms' inability to service their debts. All of these, it is further argued, serve to reduce the nation's ability to compete globally and adversely affect the economy.[8]

Increasingly, there are legislative pressures and court rulings to curb the excesses of leveraged buyouts. The primary target for legislations is the tax deductibility of borrowings specifically undertaken to finance these deals. In 1986, the courts began applying a legal concept known as **fraudulent conveyance** to LBOs that resulted in bankruptcies. Using fraudulent conveyance arguments, the courts can order a return of part of the proceeds from an already-completed LBO transaction to the unsecured creditors if it can be reasonably shown that there was an intent to defraud creditors. This might occur, for example, if the loan proceeds are used to buyout existing shareholders rather than to continue to operate the firm. An example of such an action involved the Chapter 11 proceedings of Revco.[9]

A Typical Leveraged Buyout

It might be instructive to consider the entire process involved in a typical leveraged buyout. The example we present is hypothetical and not meant to describe any particular LBO but rather to capture the essence of the process by incorporating elements that tend to be rather typical. Capturing the essence requires simplification—hopefully without loss of too much realism.

At the end of 1985, the balance sheet of XYZ Corporation showed current assets of $4 million, depreciable fixed assets of $12 million, and nondepreciable fixed assets of $2 million. The depreciable assets had been fully depreciated but were still in good and quite usable condition. The replacement cost of these assets was estimated at about $10 million. The firm had current liabilities of $1.5 million, long-term debt of $2.5 million, and common stock equity (including retained earnings) of $2 million. There were 1 million shares of common outstanding. The balance sheet is given in Exhibit 22.1.

Exhibit 22.1
XYZ Corporation

Balance Sheet — 1985
(all values in millions)

ASSETS				LIABILITIES & EQUITY		
Current assets				Current liabilities		
cash	0.20			accruals	0.25	
marketable securities	1.55			accounts payables	0.75	
inventory	1.75			notes payable	0.50	
receivables	0.50					1.50
		4.00		Long term debt		2.50
Fixed assets						
depreciable	12.00			Equity		
less cum dep	(12.00)			common stock	0.50	
net	0.00			retained earnings	1.50	
nondepreciable	2.00					2.00
		2.00				
Total assets		6.00		Total Liabilities & equity		6.00

The firm's sales were very stable and its earnings had been very consistent. Given this, management suggested that the firm increase its use of debt and decrease its use of equity capital. This was rejected by the firm's board on the grounds that the firm's shareholders are too conservative to take kindly to a dramatic increase in leverage. At the time, the firm's short-term notes had a cost of 10 percent and its long-term debt had a cost of 12 percent. As a result, 1985's interest expense was $0.35 million. The firm's profit and loss statement for 1985 appears as Exhibit 22.2.

Exhibit 22.2
XYZ Corporation

Profit & Loss — 1985
(all values in millions)

Sales	$15.00
Cost of goods sold	8.00
Gross profit	7.00
Selling and administrative	5.50
Operating profit before depreciation	1.50
Depreciation	0.00
Operating profit	1.50
Interest expense	0.35
Earnings before taxes	1.15
Taxes (40 percent)	0.46
Earnings after taxes	0.69

Cash flow = earnings after taxes + depreciation
= $0.69 million + $0.00 million
= $0.69 million

In 1985, the firm's earnings per share (EPS) were $0.69 and the firm's stock was selling at about $8 a share or about 11.6 times earnings. Management had long believed that it could improve the firm's performance if freed from the dictates of the overly conservative board. Management, however, had been reluctant to attack the board's conservatism too aggressively out of fear of losing their jobs. Instead, in lieu of the better salaries and bonuses that might accompany better performance, management had settled for various perks including such things as unnecessarily lavish offices and substantial fringe benefits. In late 1985, partly in response to rumors that a takeover attempt by a rival firm was in the works, management secured the services of a leading investment bank in the hopes of taking the firm private. On the advise of the investment bank, the management group set up a shell corporation to act as the legal entity making the acquisition. This company was called XYZ Holdings.

With the aid of its investment banker, XYZ Holdings made a tender offer at $12 a share (17.4 times earnings) for all the stock of XYZ Corporation. In the end, XYZ Holdings' bid was successful and all the stock was purchased at $12 a share (deemed a fair value by the firm's investment bank). The two firms were then merged with the XYZ Holdings representing the surviving entity.

The acquisition cost to XYZ Holdings was $12 million ($12 per share × 1 million shares). Of this, $5 million was raised with the aid of a secured bank-acquisition loan, at a cost of 12 percent, and $4 million was raised through the sale of junk bonds, at a cost of 18 percent. The investment bank took a 40 percent equity stake by putting up $1.2 million of its own money and the management group put up the remaining $1.8 million. Management retained a buyout option with the investment bank to acquire the investment bank's equity after 5 years at a price which would afford the investment bank an annual compound return of about 40 percent. (This translates to a price of about $6.45 million.)

Upon taking control, XYZ Holdings stepped-up the depreciable basis of the acquired assets to $10 million. The revised balance sheet is given in Exhibit 22.3.

Exhibit 22.3
XYZ Holdings

Balance Sheet (revised) — 1985
(all values in millions)

ASSETS			LIABILITIES & EQUITY		
Current assets			Current liabilities		
cash	0.20		accruals	0.25	
marketable securities	1.55		accounts payables	0.75	
inventory	1.75		notes payable	0.50	
receivables	0.50				1.50
		4.00			
			Long term debt		11.50
Fixed assets					
depreciable	10.00		Equity		
less cum dep	(0.00)		common stock	3.00	
net		10.00	retained earnings	0.00	
nondepreciable		2.00			3.00
		12.00			
Total assets		16.00	Total Liabilities & equity		16.00

The new owners immediately moved their offices to less expensive quarters and took other steps to reduce the firm's overhead expenses. The net effect was to reduce the firm's selling and administrative expenses by $1.5 million a year. Management was also in a position to recoup taxes paid in previous years by XYZ Corporation. A decision was made to depreciate the firm's depreciable assets using accelerated methods in order to enhance cash flow. The firm used all cash flow over the first four years to retire its debt. Its higher-cost junk bonds were retired first. A portion of the cash flow in the fifth year was used to retire debt bringing debt back to the level it stood at before the buyout. The earnings of XYZ holdings over the next five years appear in Exhibit 22.4 together with the projections for the sixth year (1991). The sixth year's earnings were considered sustainable with an 80 percent dividend payout.

Exhibit 22.4
XYZ Holdings

Profit & Loss
(all values in millions)

	1986	1987	1988	1989	1990	1991*
Sales	$15.00	$15.00	$15.00	$15.00	$15.00	$15.00
Cost of goods sold	8.00	8.00	8.00	8.00	8.00	8.00
Gross profit	7.00	7.00	7.00	7.00	7.00	7.00
Selling and administrative	4.00	4.00	4.00	4.00	4.00	4.00
Operating profit before dep	3.00	3.00	3.00	3.00	3.00	3.00
Depreciation	2.50	2.50	2.25	2.00	0.75	0.00
Operating profit	0.50	0.50	0.75	1.00	2.25	3.00
Interest expense	1.67	1.35	0.99	0.72	0.46	0.35
Earnings before taxes	(1.17)	(0.85)	(0.24)	0.28	1.79	2.65
Taxes (40 percent)	(0.47)	(0.34)	(0.10)	0.11	0.72	1.06
Earnings after taxes	(0.70)	(0.51)	(0.14)	0.17	1.07	1.59
Dividend	0.00	0.00	0.00	0.00	0.00	1.27
Cash flow:	1.80	1.99	2.10	2.17	1.82	1.59
Debt remaining:						
Short term (10%)	0.50	0.50	0.50	0.50	0.50	0.50
Long-term Bank (12%)	7.50	7.50	5.61	3.44	2.50	2.50
Bonds (18%)	2.20	0.21	0.00	0.00	0.00	0.00
Cumulative retained earnings	(0.70)	(1.21)	(1.35)	(1.18)	0.64	0.96

*projected

At the end of five years, management exercised its right to buy out the investment bank's equity interest in the firm at the agreed price of $6.45 million. Management then took the firm public again in, what is called, a **secondary initial public offering** or **SIPO** and sold its equity interest at 15 times projected 1991 earnings. This brought the management group $23.85 million before flotation costs and $22.25 million afterward. After deducting the $6.45 million paid to the investment banking partner, the management team was left with $15.80 million on its initial investment of $1.8 million. This translates to an average annual compound rate of return of about 54 percent.

Let's consider for a moment the sources of the gains generated by this LBO. First, there were tax benefits from stepping-up the acquired assets of the firm, from the deductibility of the interest on the funds used to finance a large portion of the original purchase, and from the carryback of losses in 1986, 1987, and 1988. Second, there was a reduction in agency costs, apparent from the cost cutting in 1986 when management gave up some of its perks (the fancy offices and some fringe benefits). There were also the benefits afforded by the management group's extensive use of leverage—which is not as high risk as it might first seem if we take into consideration the stability of the firm's earnings and expenses.

The Investment Bank in an LBO: The Financial Engineer At Work

Notice in our hypothetical LBO described in the preceding section that it was not necessary for XYZ Holdings (the post-buyout firm) to exhibit a significant immediate improvement in earnings in order for the LBO to produce great value for the buyout group. Indeed, the buyout actually resulted in a sharp deterioration in after-tax earnings for the first four years. The key to understanding the viability of a leveraged buyout is clearly not profit but, rather, cash flow. Cash flow is the sum of earnings after taxes and noncash expenses. (Noncash expenses include such things as depreciation, depletion, and the amortization of intangible assets.)

The financial engineers who do the preliminary analysis and who, in the end, structure the deal, concentrate their energies on understanding the size, source, and stability of the target's cash flows. The cash flows will be used to reduce debt, acquire other assets (possibly other firms), and/or to pay large cash dividends to the shareholder group. The engineer's job is largely one of analyzing the cash flows and structuring a deal that can best exploit the cash flows. This leads to such issues as (1) how sensitive are the cash flows to changes in the underlying assumptions (sales growth, for example), (2) how much can the buyout group pay for the firm and still hope to make their target return, (3) what kinds of debt and how much debt can the firm support, (4) should an ESOP structure be employed and, if so, how aggressively, and (5) at what point should the buyout group—including the investment bank itself—look to cash out.

The leveraged buyout is a fascinating application of financial engineering as it brings together many elements of theory (the conceptual tools) and many of the new instruments (the physical tools) developed over the last fifteen years. It also demonstrates the importance of tax and accounting rule changes as well as the influence of the regulatory environment in determining the shape and form of the products of the engineer's work.

Summary

The 1980s bore witness to a decade of aggressive mergers, acquisitions, and takeovers. The hands of financial engineers were all over these corporate restructurings. Working within M&A teams at investment banks, the financial engineers find and exploit value. This value is split between those who hold the target firm's stock before the restructuring, those who hold the target's stock after the restructuring, and the investment bank that structures the deal. A portion of this value comes from a reduction in agency costs—which can only be applauded. But, a portion may come at the expense of other stakeholders in the firm. The latter raises serious questions that have yet to be fully resolved.

The leveraged buyout activity of the 1980s took many publicly held firms private. The principal instruments used to accomplish this were junk bonds, private placements, bridge financing, venture capital, and merchant banking. All of these are tools in the bag of the modern financial engineer.

Endnotes

[1]See Weston, Chung, and Hoag (1990), Chapter 16.

[2]The bulge-bracket firms are the top tier of the investment banking industry and are distinguished from the rest of the industry by their size and market presence. The term "bulge-bracket" derives from the tendency for these firms' names to "bulge" on **tombstones**—i.e., the published advertisements of public offerings which appear regularly in the financial press.

[3]See Farrel (1989), pp. 85.

[4]Examples of LBO specialist firms include Kohlberg, Kravis, Roberts & Company and Forstmann Little and Company.

[5]See Lehn and Poulsen (1988) for example.

[6]See Travlos and Cornett (1990) for example.

[7]See Bull (1989) and Hite and Vetsuypens (1989).
[8]See Gart (1990) and Waddel (1990).
[9]See Kolod (1990) and Michel and Shaked (1990).

References and Suggested Reading

Bull. I. "Financial Performance of Leveraged Buyouts: An Empirical Analysis," *Journal of Business Venturing,* 4 (July 1989), pp. 263-279.

Farrel, C. "The Bills are Coming Due," *Business Week* (September 11, 1989).

Gart, A. "Leveraged Buyouts: A Re-Examination," *Advanced Management Journal,* 55 (Summer 1990), pp. 38-46.

Hite, G.L. and M. Vetsuypens. "Management Buyouts of Divisions and Shareholder Wealth," *Journal of Finance,* 44 (1989), pp. 953-970.

Kolod, A. "LBO as Fraudulent Transfers," *Real Estate Finance,* 7 (Fall 1990), pp. 35-39.

Lehn, K. and A. Poulsen. "Leveraged Buyouts: Wealth Created or Wealth Redistributed?" in M. Weidenbaum and K. Chilton, eds., *Public Policy Towards Corporate Takeovers,* New Brunswick, NJ: Transaction Publishers, 1988.

Michel, A. and I. Shaked. "The LBO Nightmare: Fraudulent Conveyance Risk," *Financial Analysts Journal* (March/April 1990), pp. 41-50.

Travlos, N.C. and M.M. Cornett. "Going Private Buyouts and Determinants of Shareholder Returns, *Journal of Accounting, Auditing and Finance,* 1990.

Waddell, W.M. "Leveraged Buyouts: Clever Leveraging or Badly Bet Debt?," *Secured Lender,* 46 (November/December 1990), pp. 34-40.

Weston, J.F., K.S. Chung, and S.E. Hoag. *Mergers, Restructuring, and Corporate Control,* Englewood Cliffs, NJ.: Prentice Hall, 1990.

Chapter 23

Arbitrage and Synthetic Instruments

Overview

In this chapter, we are going to examine two areas that are extremely important in financial engineering: arbitrage and synthetic instruments. These topics are closely related to each other and also closely related to hedging. It should not surprise the reader therefore that much of what we have to say in this chapter will bear a close resemblance to hedging theory. When a concept from hedging theory is directly applicable to arbitrage and/or the creation of synthetic instruments, we will sometimes refer back to earlier chapters rather than repeat ourselves. This will avoid redundancy and economize on space and time.

Arbitrage is an activity with a long history. It involves two or more simultaneous transactions in different markets in order to take advantage of price discrepancies between them. As simple as this definition is, however, arbitrage is anything but a simple activity. There are many different forms of arbitrage and some of them involve the use of synthetic instruments. Strategies involving the use of synthetic instruments are often quite complex and reach to the limits of the financial engineer's talents.

Synthetic instruments, often called **synthetic securities,** are not, in and of themselves, securities at all. Rather, they are cash flow streams, formed by combining or decomposing the cash flow streams from one set of instruments, which replicate the cash flow streams of another set of instruments. Because the cash flow streams **replicate** or **synthesize** the cash flow streams of the real instruments (securities), the synthesized cash flow streams can be regarded as synthetic instruments (securities).

In this chapter we are going to examine the different forms of arbitrage, the logic and principles that underlie arbitrage, the process of synthetic securities creation, examples of different types of synthetic securities and their uses, the often overlooked qualitative differences between real and synthetic instruments, the role played by absolute and relative valuation in synthetic securities creation and in arbitrage, and various other issues pertaining to these important activities.

Arbitrage: From the Ancient to the Modern

As already noted, arbitrage involves simultaneous transactions in two or more markets in order to exploit price or value discrepancies between the markets. There are many different forms of arbitrage. The most intuitively obvious form involves the purchase of a commodity in one market and the simultaneous sale of the same commodity in a different market. The commodity is purchased in the lower-priced market (where it is said to be **cheap**) and sold in the higher-priced market (where it is said to be **rich**). The **arbitrager**, sometimes spelled arbitrageur, seeks to profit from the price discrepancy between the markets. This form of arbitrage is called **spatial** or **geographic arbitrage** and is one of the earliest forms of arbitrage. Indeed, in a sense, it is the foundation on which most merchant activity rests.

In order for spatial arbitrage to be profitable, the price discrepancy between the two markets must be sufficiently great to cover the transaction and transportation costs involved. Let's suppose, for example, that commodity can be moved between market 1 and market 2 at a transportation cost of $T_{1,2}$ and that the combined transaction cost involved in buying and selling the commodity is $R_{1,2}$. Then spatial arbitrage is only profitable if the price of the commodity in the higher-priced market is more than $T_{1,2} + R_{1,2}$ *greater* than the price of the commodity in the lower-priced market. When a sufficiently large price discrepancy does develop, arbitragers will quickly act to exploit it. But, by buying commodity in the cheap market, they tend to bid the price higher in that market. And, by selling in the rich market, they tend to drive the price lower in that market. In the end, the aggregate effect of arbitrage is to bring the two markets back into balance.

If there are no artificial barriers to trade, the activities of the spatial arbitragers described above should ensure that the prices of the same commodity in two different markets never deviate by more than the cost of transportation and transaction. Indeed, this thinking led to the development of a theory of geographic market equilibrium now known as the **law of one price**. The law of one price states that the price in market i, denoted P_i, and the price in market j, denoted P_j, are related as defined by Equation 23.1.

$$P_i = P_j + Z_{i,j} \tag{23.1}$$

where $\qquad -(T_{i,j} + R_{i,j}) \leq Z_{i,j} \leq (T_{i,j} + R_{i,j})$

In Equation 23.1, $Z_{i,j}$ is a stochastic bounded by the cost of transportation and transaction. In plain English, this means that the price in market i can be as high as $P_j + (T_{i,j} + R_{i,j})$ or as low as $P_j - (T_{i,j} + R_{i,j})$ without giving rise to profitable arbitrage opportunities.

The law of one price can be generalized to allow for different currencies. For example, if the price of the commodity in market i is stated in currency i and the price in market j is stated in currency j, then the law of one price must also reflect the exchange rate between currency i and currency j. If we denote this exchange rate by $E_{i,j}$, then the law of one price is given by Equation 23.2.

$$P_i = P_j \cdot E_{i,j} + Z_{i,j} \tag{23.2}$$

Equation 23.2 is interpreted as follows. The price of the commodity in market i stated in currency i must be equal to the price in market j in currency j times the exchange rate of currency i for currency j. $Z_{i,j}$ is the same stochastic observed earlier stated in terms of currency i.

The law of one price can be expanded to allow for commodities that are different but that are convertible into each other. For example, gold trades on some exchanges in 95 percent purity but on other exchanges in 99 percent purity. Thus, the 95 percent purity standard of the one market is not deliverable against the 99 percent purity standard of the other market. But, at some expense, 95 percent gold can be converted to 99 percent gold by resmelting the gold and removing some of the nongold alloy. Let's denote this conversion cost by $C_{i,j}$. Equation 23.2 then becomes 23.3.

$$P_i = P_j \cdot E_{i,j} + Z_{i,j} \qquad (23.3)$$

where $\qquad -(T_{i,j} + R_{i,j} + C_{i,j}) \leq Z_{i,j} \leq (T_{i,j} + R_{i,j} + C_{i,j})$

Another type of arbitrage that has long been practiced is **temporal arbitrage,** sometimes called **carrying-charge arbitrage.** It is only applicable for storable commodities. In this form of arbitrage the market in which the commodity is bought and the market in which it is sold differ temporally rather than spatially. For example, an arbitrager observes that the commodity for immediate (spot) delivery can be purchased for $P_i(t)$ and sold for later (forward) delivery for $F_i(t,T)$. As argued in Chapter 21, the difference between $F_i(t,T)$ and $P_i(t)$ should be equal to the cost of carry (our notation is a little different here). That is, $F_i(t,T)$ and $P_i(t)$ should be related by Equation 23.4 where $G_i(t,T)$ denotes the cost of carry which is defined as the interest cost plus the storage cost less any convenience yield.

$$F_i(t,T) = P_i(T) + G_i(t,T) \qquad (23.4)$$

Just as Equation 23.3 is the spatial equilibrium condition, Equation 23.4 is the temporal equilibrium condition. That is, at any value for $F_i(t,T)$ greater or less than the right-hand side of Equation 23.4 a profitable arbitrage opportunity arises (ignoring transaction costs). If $F_i(t,T)$ were greater than the right-hand side of Equation 23.4, the arbitrager would buy spot commodity and sell commodity for forward delivery. If $F_i(t,T)$ is less than the right-hand side of Equation 23.4, then the arbitrager would short the spot commodity and buy commodity for forward delivery (assuming the spot commodity is shortable).

The spatial equilibrium condition and the temporal equilibrium conditions represented by Equations 23.3 and 23.4, respectively, can be combined to provide a more general equilibrium condition that can explain both spatial and temporal price relationships. This is given by Equation 23.5.

$$F_i(t,T) = P_j(t) \cdot E_{i,j}(t) + G_i(t,T) + Z_{i,j} \qquad (23.5)$$

where $\qquad -(T_{i,j} + R_{i,j} + C_{i,j}) \leq Z_{i,j} \leq (T_{i,j} + R_{i,j} + C_{i,j})$

Whenever deviations from the pricing suggested by Equation 23.5 occur, an opportunity for profitable arbitrage arises. If arbitrage does not correct these deviations, it is often taken as *prima facie* evidence of the existence of some sort of trade barrier.

While Equation 23.5 was derived in the context of commodities, it is equally applicable to financial commodities including securities. Thus, the equation is capable of explaining the creation of zero-coupon bonds from conventional bonds, the creation of collateralized mortgage obligations from whole mortgages, the creation of swaps from forwards, and the creation of all the various forms of synthetic securities and many of the trading strategies that have recently appeared on the financial landscape. It is not surprising then that Equation 23.5 is the workhorse of those involved in arbitrage and the creation of synthetic instruments. It allows one to identify whether or not a given arbitrage opportunity is profitable whether one is arbitraging across space (spatial arbitrage), time (temporal arbitrage), or instruments (conversion arbitrage).

There are two forms of arbitrage that are not captured by Equation 23.5. These are arbitrage across risk and tax arbitrage. Insurance is an example of the former and preferred stock issued by low-tax corporations and held by high-tax corporations is an example of the latter. Recall that insurers take on many individually large risks and, through the pooling of these risks, dramatically reduce them. This is also the kind of risk abatement common in other forms of diversification. That is, through the proper structuring and diversification of a portfolio, very risky individual positions can be held with very little overall risk. If the parties bearing the individual risks are willing to pay a sufficiently large premium to be relieved of them, then the arbitrage can be profitable. We have discussed the benefits of diversification and other methods of risk abatement in earlier chapters and we will not dwell on them again here. Tax arbitrage is addressed separately in Chapter 24 so we will not dwell on that form of arbitrage here either.

In academic circles, arbitrage is often described as a profitable business activity involving no investment and no risk. Indeed, when using this definition, we often make our meaning clear by specifying **academic** or **pure** arbitrage. The academic definition assumes that all transactions, including both the purchase and sale, can be transacted simultaneously and that the positions can be financed entirely from loans (no equity). This academic view is so strongly held that academicians often define an **efficient market** as *one that does not give rise to profitable arbitrage opportunities.*

In practice, real world arbitrage generally cannot be effectively conducted without some, at least temporary, investment and it is rarely completely risk free. For example, suppose that an arbitrager spots an exploitable market mispricing. He attempts to profit by buying in the cheap market and selling in the rich market. If the two transactions can be effected simultaneously by saying "done" to the selling party and "done" to the buying party, then there is no transaction risk. But in practice it will usually happen that the transactions are only *near* simultaneous. That is, a split second passes between the buying and the selling transactions. It is possible that one of the opposing parties may withdraw his or her bid or offer before the second transaction can be effected. In such situations, the arbitrager winds up with a naked position (either long or short) and must either cover it or liquidate it quickly—even if this results in a loss. It is also possible that, even if both sides of the arbitrage are effected simultaneously, that one of the parties may default. Many potentially profitable arbitrage opportunities have gone sour as a consequence of a default. Given these realities, a better definition of arbitrage might be "a business transaction undertaken to earn a low-risk profit on little investment by exploiting a pricing discrepancy between two or more markets."

Synthetic Securities

As noted in the overview, a synthetic security is a cash flow stream created from a combination or a decomposition of the cash flows associated with a set of instruments that exactly replicates the cash flow stream associated with a real instrument. For example, if we can duplicate the cash flow stream of instrument i by combining the cash flow streams of instruments j and k, then we have effectively replicated instrument i. The combination of j and k that gives rise to the cash flows that mimic instrument i constitute a synthetic instrument i.

Most, but not all, synthetic securities involve the use of derivative instruments including futures, forwards, options, and swaps. Sometimes the goal is to create a synthetic instrument and sometimes the goal is to create a synthetic derivative instrument. Sometimes the synthesized instrument has a real counterpart and sometimes it does not. Consider, for example, two of the first synthetic instruments—**synthetic puts** and **synthetic zeros.** These two instruments are illustrative in that the first is created by combining several instruments and represents a synthetic derivative instrument and the second is created by decomposing an instrument and represents a synthetic instrument.

Let's begin with the synthetic put. In the early 1970s the Chicago Board Options Exchange (CBOE) was created and approved to trade a limited number of listed call options on individual common stocks. At about the same time, the first complete option pricing model (Black/Scholes) was published which allowed for the valuation of these instruments.[1] At the time the CBOE was created, the exchange argued that options would allow holders of equity positions to hedge those positions. While this argument is correct, it is more true for put options than for call options. (Recall that a put option grants its holder the right to sell the underlying asset.) Thus, the holder of a long position in a stock might like to hold a long position in a put option to hedge against downside risk. Despite this, for a number of years, the CBOE limited its listings to call options.

In an effort to use option valuation arithmetic to value put options, academic theorists discovered, using arbitrage theory, that there is a fundamental relationship between the value of a call option and the value of a put option. This relationship became known as the **put/call parity theorem**.[2] It has two fundamental uses. First, it can be used to value a put option once the value of a call option is known and, second, it can be used to formulate a synthetic put option. The relationship is given by Equation 23.6.

$$P(t,T) = C(t,T) - A(t) + S \cdot B(t,T) \qquad (23.6)$$

In Equation 23.6, $P(t,T)$ denotes the current (time t) fair value of a put option that expires at time T, $C(t,T)$ denotes the current fair value of a call option that expires at time T, $A(t)$ denotes the current price of the underlying asset, S is the strike price of both the call and the put options, and $B(t,T)$ is the current value of a $1 risk-free discount bond that matures at time T. Equation 23.6 also says that the combination of a long position in one call option (covering one unit of the underlying asset), a short position in one unit of the underlying asset, and a long position in S dollars of the discount bond is *exactly equivalent* to holding a long position in a put option on one unit of the underlying asset.

This contention is worth proving as it provides important insights. The easiest way to demonstrate the value equivalence is by payoff profiles (sometimes called profit diagrams). Recall that, in the case of options, payoff profiles are usually drawn for the option at the time of the option's expiration. Let's begin by asking what a real put option's payoff profile should look like. We can refer to Chapter 14 for this. The payoff profile for a put option is depicted in Exhibit 23.1.

Exhibit 23.1
Payoff Profile for Long Put

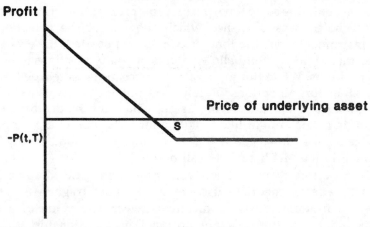

Now let's consider the payoff profiles for the three components of the synthetic put. That is, let's look at the payoff profile for the real long call, the short position in the underlying asset, and the long position in the discount bond as of the time of the option's expiry. These payoff profiles are depicted in Exhibits 23.2, 23.3, and 23.4 respectively.

Exhibit 23.2
Payoff Profile for Long Call

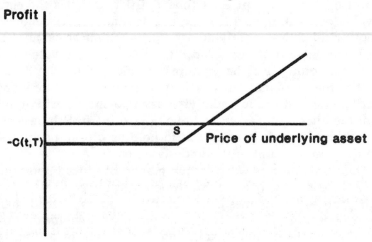

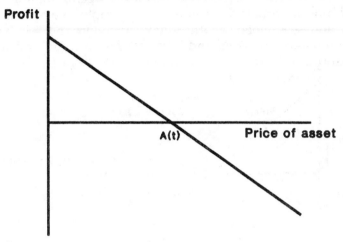

Exhibit 23.3
Payoff Profile for Short Position in Asset

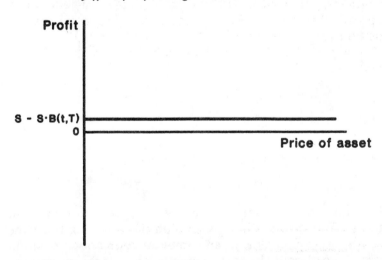

Exhibit 23.4
Payoff Profile for Long Position in Risk-Free Instrument

While none of the component payoff profiles looks even re-
motely similar, by itself, to the put's payoff profile, a very different
picture emerges when they are combined. This is depicted in Exhibit
23.5. This explains why many involved in financial engineering are
often heard to say that the art of financial engineering is the creation

of a whole that is greater than the sum of the parts. As one respected engineer put it to us, "...it is very much like seeing unique forms created from very ordinary materials. For example, one person looks at wood and sees wood, another looks at nylon and sees nylon, still another looks at wood and nylon and sees wood and nylon. But the engineer looks at wood and nylon and sees a tennis racket" (Ken Leong, Bank of Tokyo).

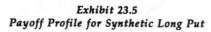

Exhibit 23.5
Payoff Profile for Synthetic Long Put

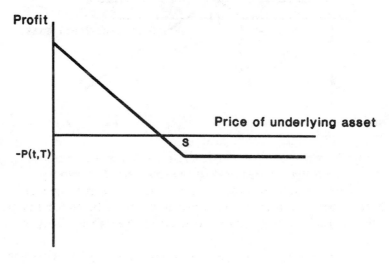

Equation 23.6 also suggests that a synthetic asset can be created from an appropriate combination of put and call options. For example, we can rearrange Equation 23.6 to get 23.7.

$$A(t) = C(t,T) - P(t,T) + S \cdot B(t,T) \tag{23.7}$$

This implies that the combination of a long position in a call option and a short position in a put option (both having the same strike price S) are equivalent, when combined with a long position in S dollars of the discount bond, to a long position in the underlying asset. We can demonstrate this by examining the payoff profile associated with the net flows on this combination of instruments. This is depicted in Exhibit 23.6.

The strategy will prove superior to a real long position in the underlying asset if (1) the call is cheap, (2) the put is rich, or (3)

Exhibit 23.6
Payoff Profile: Synthetic Long Position in Underlying Asset

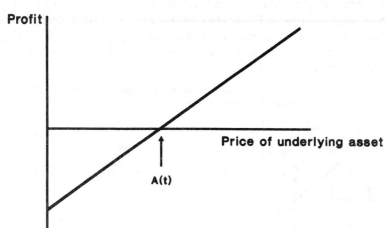

both. As a final point, if the underlying asset is a futures contract so that the options are options on futures, then the strategy above produces a synthetic futures contract. As for assets generally, a synthetic futures will prove superior to a real futures for any purpose that a real futures might be used if the call is cheap or the put is rich.

While both the creation of a synthetic put and the creation of a synthetic futures involves a combination of a number of instruments, some synthetics are created by the decomposition of a single instrument. The early zero coupon bonds are an example of this type of synthesis. You will recall from our discussion of zeros in Chapter 17, that a zero coupon bond is simply a bond that provides its holder with one and only one cash flow. Such a bond trades at a discount from its face value until such time as the bond matures. In the creation of the early zeros, the investment bank or other arbitrager purchased a conventional bond and then separated the individual future coupon payments and corpus (principal) redemption. These were sold separately, by way of various trust arrangements, to investors as zero coupon bonds. This process is illustrated, using the arrow cash flow technique, in Exhibit 23.7. Notice that, when decomposed, each cash flow has taken on the character of a zero coupon bond. In addition, each zero has properties that the conventional bond did not possess. As proof of this, consider duration. The duration of a conventional bond is always shorter than its maturity. The duration of a zero, on the other hand, is identical to its maturity.

Exhibit 23.7
Synthesizing a Strip of Zeros from a Conventional Bond

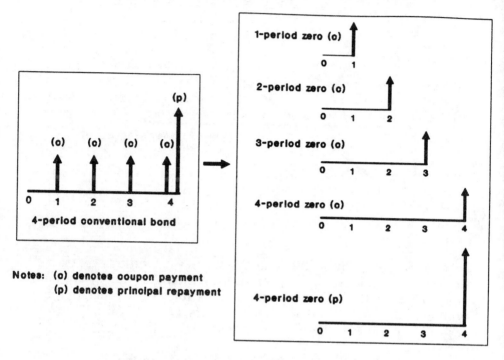

Notes: (o) denotes coupon payment
       (p) denotes principal repayment

The zero coupon bonds described above are **synthetic zeros** in the sense that they were not issued by the issuer as zero coupon bonds. This does not make them any less *real* than bonds issued by their issuer as zeros, but it does distinguish between the origin of real securities and the origin of synthetic securities.

Synthesizing Derivatives

Many of the over-the-counter derivative instruments that have appeared in recent years can be synthesized from other derivative instruments. For example, multiperiod options, such as caps and floors, can be synthesized from a strip of single-period put or single-period call options. Similarly, a short-dated swap (up to two or three years) can be synthesized from a strip of Eurodollar futures contracts.

This ability to synthesize a product is very important to a dealer in the instruments because it provides a mechanism by which to hedge the dealer's unmatched offerings. For example, the swap dealer that enters a two-year interest rate swap as fixed-rate payer can temporarily match his book by creating a synthetic short-dated swap from Eurodollar futures. Specifically, the dealer would purchase an appropriate strip of Eurodollar futures. This strip of futures would create a cash flow pattern nearly identical, in terms of its present value, to that which would be achieved with a matched swap. The dealer's goal in the purchase of the strip of futures is to hedge his swap book, but the point is unchanged, synthetic derivatives are useful to market makers in derivatives.

The Cash-and-Carry Synthetic

A **cash-and-carry** transaction involves the purchase of an instrument and the simultaneous sale of a futures contract (or other derivative) against it in order to create a synthetic short-term instrument. Such synthetic short-term instruments are created in order to earn low-risk short-term rates.

Let's take a simple example to illustrate the concept. Suppose that the 20.5-year Treasury bond carries a coupon of 8.00 percent and is currently priced at 93 16/32. At this price, the instrument provides a yield to maturity of 8.684 percent (bond equivalent or BEY). The instrument is deliverable against the six-month forward T-bond futures with a conversion factor of 1.000. That is, $100,000 face value of this bond is deliverable per futures contract. At the time of delivery, the bond itself will have a maturity of 20 years. The futures contract is priced at 93 2/32. What is the return to an investor who buys the bond and sells the futures?

To answer this question we need to ask how much the investor will earn from the transactions. First, the investor will receive a coupon payment of $4 in six months. This represents one half of the annual 8 percent coupon. Second, the investor is going to sell the instrument (deliver on the futures contract) for 93.0625 (92-2/32). Thus, in six months, the investor will have 97.0625. Since the investor has value at the end of 97.0625 at a current cost of 93.50 (93-16/32), the investor's return is 7.62 percent (semiannual bond equivalent yield). The calculation, which follows, is simple in this case because the holding period is exactly one-half of a year.

$$BEY = \left(\frac{97.0625}{93.5000} - 1\right) \times 2 = 7.62 \text{ percent}$$

It is important to appreciate that while the investor has purchased a T-bond, which is a long-term instrument, the forward sale of the bond, through the medium of the futures contract, gave the overall position a short-term character (a synthetic T-bill). As such, the position earns a short-term rate, 7.62 percent in this case, and *not* the long-term rate, 8.684 percent, embodied in the bond's price. The upshot is that the cash-and-carry strategy creates a synthetic short-term investment which provides a short-term return.

It is important to appreciate that the creation of a short-term synthetic from a long-term instrument will return a short-term rate and not a long-term rate. For example, at the time we observed the market prices used in this example, the 182-day T-bill rate was quoted at 7.24 percent (bank discount yield). Of course, bank basis and bond basis are not directly comparable without first making a conversion. As it happens, the bond equivalent yield for this T-bill is 7.619 percent. This is virtually identical to the return from the synthetic.

Why did the synthetic T-bill return the same rate as the real T-bill? The answer is simple. If markets price assets efficiently, then all equivalent assets should return the same rate. Of course, as we argued in Chapter 9, market efficiency is itself a consequence of the intensive exploitation of the markets by speculators and arbitragers. This does not, however, mean that opportunities to earn excess returns never arise. In fact, they do and quite often. As we also argued in Chapter 9, it is inconsistent to believe that markets can be perfectly efficient at all times. If they were, arbitragers and speculators would be unable to earn a fair return for their efforts and would withdraw from the markets. But if they withdraw from the markets, how could the markets continue to be efficient?

A synthetic T-bill can also be created by applying the cash-and-carry strategy to other assets. For example, we could buy stocks and sell stock index futures or we could buy corporate bonds and sell T-bond futures. These strategies are somewhat more complex than the Treasury cash and carry for a number of reasons. In the case of stock-index futures, the trader must build a portfolio of stocks which mimics the cash index underlying the futures contract. Further, the cash position must be liquidated independently of the futures contract since stock-index futures are not deliverable (they are cash settled). The calculations are complex but the opportunities also tend to be greater. Indeed, this strategy is often executed on a massive scale and is called **cash/index arbitrage** or **program trading**. (We discuss program trading in Chapter 25.)

In the case of a corporate cash and carry, i.e., buy corporate bonds and sell T-bond futures (since there are no corporate bond futures), the strategy produces a synthetic short-term instrument, but the yield is not as certain as it is with the Treasury cash and carry. The reason is that the corporate bond is not deliverable against the T-bond futures. Instead, the arbitrager would sell the corporate bond and offset the futures contract just before the futures contract was due to be delivered. But, since the corporate bond yield does not track the T-bond yield perfectly, there is a positive variance to the return from such a strategy. This is essentially a manifestation of basis risk even though the futures position was not undertaken as a hedge. This particular form of basis risk is sometimes called a **quality spread risk**. Because it is not riskless, the corporate cash and carry often offers a greater short-term return than the Treasury cash and carry.

Whether a cash and carry strategy is superior to a real short-term instrument depends on whether the futures to be used are cheap or rich. When they are cheap, the cash and carry strategy will be unattractive. When they are rich, the cash and carry strategy will be attractive. When properly priced, which, all other things being equal, we would expect to be the normal situation, the two strategies should produce identical returns. As an historic observation, money market investors would have done consistently better during most of 1981 and most of 1982 by investing in synthetic T-bills. During this period, T-bond futures were rich. The opposite was true during 1983 and most of 1984. Since 1984, there has been less consistency so that futures are sometimes rich and sometimes cheap but neither tends to prevail for a long period of time.

The lesson in this is that portfolio managers should evaluate all of their alternatives before selecting (or constructing) their investment vehicle. Clearly, the prohibitions against trading futures that are often imposed on such managers, out of a mistaken belief that such instruments are purely speculative, are misplaced. It also points up the importance of distinguishing once again between relative value and absolute value. At any point in time, there are a multitude of investment values available. At some points in time these values are greater than at other points in time in an absolute sense. For example, we might find that at one point in time T-bills return 8 percent and at another point in time T-bills return 10 percent. All other things being equal, the return during the second point in time is better in an absolute sense. On the other hand, at any given point in time, the investor's goal must be to select from among relative values. That is, if the real T-bill rate is 8.00 percent and the synthetic T-bill rate is 8.20 percent, then the synthetic T-bill provides better relative value.

Cash and Carry in Arbitrage: Enhancing Portfolio Return

We have demonstrated how the cash-and-carry strategy can be used to create synthetic T-bills. We have also argued that, if markets were always efficient, synthetic T-bills should return the same rate as real T-bills. In practice, however, synthetic securities sometimes offer a greater return and sometimes offer a lower return than real securities due to imperfections in the markets. We now focus on how arbitragers can enhance portfolio returns with synthetic instruments.

While portfolio managers, particularly money market portfolio managers, should compare the returns on real T-bills to the returns on synthetic T-bills, the problem is a little different for the arbitrager. Arbitragers, by definition, attempt to finance their positions. That is, the very large positions which they take and carry are taken with borrowed funds. Today, these positions are most often financed in the repo market and this is the key to understanding how arbitrage enhances portfolio returns.

Recall the example we used to illustrate the Treasury cash-and-carry strategy in the preceding section. That is, the arbitrager can buy the 20.5 year T-bond and sell the T-bond futures to create a synthetic T-bill thereby earning a certain return of 7.62 percent. This rate is identical to the 7.62 (7.619) percent return on real T-bills. It would appear that the arbitrager could invest equally profitably in either market. But, this is not necessarily the case. The real question is what is the **repo rate** at which the two positions can be financed.

To illustrate this issue, suppose that the T-bonds can be financed in the repo market at 7.34 percent and the T-bills can be financed in the repo market at 7.42 percent. That is, under current market conditions, the arbitrager can purchase T-bonds and then use them as collateral in the repo market to obtain the funding used to purchase the bonds at a cost of 7.34 percent. Also under current market conditions, the arbitrager can purchase T-bills and use them as collateral in the repo market to obtain the funding needed to purchase the bills at 7.42 percent. In this case we have the following situation:

Strategy	Repo Rate	Return	Net Profit
Cash and Carry	7.34	7.62	28 bps
Buy T-bills	7.42	7.62	20 bps

Under this scenario, the cash and carry (synthetic T-bill) is the superior investment for the arbitrager since it returns 8 basis points (bps) more than the real T-bill. At this point it is worth noting that while 28 basis points might not seem like very much—after all it is only a little more than one quarter of one percentage point—it is actually a very handsome return for an investment that is riskless and requires almost no investment of the arbitrager's own funds. For example, suppose that the trade involves $10 million of synthetic bills and only requires $50,000 of the arbitrager's own money. The strategy would return $14,000 over the course of six months. This translates to a per annum return of 56 percent (compounded semi-annually) on the arbitrager's investment. Not so insignificant a return as it first seemed!

Let's take this example just a little further. Suppose that the real T-bill returns 7.66 percent while the synthetic T-bill returns 7.62 percent. All the other information is the same as above. For a money market portfolio manager, there is no question that the real T-bill offers greater relative value (7.66 percent versus 7.62 percent). But, for the arbitrager, the synthetic T-bill offers greater relative value (28 bps versus 24 bps). Clearly, for the arbitrager, the repo rate, which represents the financing cost, cannot be ignored. It is for this reason that the term **implied repo rate** is used to describe the return on the synthetic security. As such, it is the financing rate at which the arbitrager would break even. In the example just used, the implied repo rate is 7.62 percent.

Creating Synthetic Long Bonds

Just as we can use a cash-and-carry strategy to create a synthetic short-term instrument, so can we also create a **synthetic long bond**. In this particular case, we would buy a three-month T-bill together with T-bond futures. The strategy requires us to equate the volatility of the bill/futures position with the volatility of the **target bond**, i.e., the real bond we are attempting to synthesize. Once we have done this, the risk level from holding the bill/futures position is identical (or very nearly so) to the risk associated with holding the target bond. The choice then becomes, again, one of relative values. If the futures are cheap, the synthetic bond will return more than the real bond. If the futures are rich, the real bond will return more than the synthetic bond.

The key to the synthetic long bond strategy is to equate volatilities. We have already discussed the tools for measuring this volatility in our several discussions of risk and hedging in Chapters 6, 7 and 21. As you would expect, most arbitragers use the dollar value of a basis point, or DV01, model to measure these volatilities. Let's consider a simple example. Suppose that the target bond (the one we wish to replicate) will have a DV01 of $0.0765 at the time the futures contract matures and the T-bond futures has a DV01 of $0.0684. (Both DV01s are stated per $100 of face value.) The yield beta is 1.000. How many futures having a face value of $0.1 million does it take to replicate a $50 million position in the target bond assuming that the target bond has a current market value of $47.5625 million?

The procedure to obtain the solution is described below.

Step 1: **Determine the Hedge ratio**

$$\text{Hedge ratio} = \frac{0.0765}{0.0684} \times 1$$

$$= 1.1184$$

Step 2: **Determine the face value of the futures position**

$$\text{Face value of futures} = \text{Hedge ratio} \times \frac{\text{Face value of}}{\text{position to be replicated}}$$

$$= 1.1184 \times \$50 \text{ million}$$

$$= \$55.92 \text{ million}$$

Step 3: **Determine the number of futures contracts needed**

$$\text{Number of futures} = \frac{\text{Face value of futures needed}}{\text{Face value of one futures}}$$

$$= \frac{55.92}{0.1} \approx 559$$

We conclude from this calculation that to replicate a $50 million long position in the target bond, we would purchase a three month cash bill having a current market value of $47.5625 million and 559 bond futures maturing in three months. Unlike the synthetic short-term instrument, however, we cannot tell in advance how the synthetic bond investment will perform since we do not know what is going to happen to yields. But, we can conduct **what if** analysis. What if analysis is sometimes called **scenario analysis** and sometimes called **sensitivity analysis**. We usually begin by assuming no change in yields and compare the return on the target real bond and the synthetic bond. We then repeat the calculation assuming a rise of some number of basis points and again assuming a decline of some number of basis points. As a practical matter, the difference between the performance of the real bond and the synthetic bond under the assumption of no change in yields and the difference between the performance under any other reasonable yield change scenario will not be much different. Thus, if the synthetic bond outperforms the real bond under the assumption of no yield change, it will also outperform the real bond under other yield change assumptions.

The ability to synthesize financial instruments undoubtedly makes the portfolio manager's job more complex and more challenging. The portfolio manager can no longer simply invest in one type of instrument. He or she must now track all possible ways of replicating that instrument. If there were just one way to replicate an instrument this would not be too difficult a task; but, in fact, there can be dozens of different ways to replicate the same instrument. While the challenge is great, the rewards can be too. The portfolio manager which routinely searches the spectrum of alternatives before committing funds can potentially add return to the portfolio without adding risk.

Using Swaps to Synthesize Positions

While financial engineers have long known that (1) put options can be synthesized from call options, the underlying assets, and the risk-free asset (the synthetic put), (2) zero-coupon bonds can be synthesized from conventional bonds, and (3) futures contracts can be synthesized by combining put and call options (a synthetic futures), no one anticipated the kind of synthetic securities that would be made possible by the introduction of swaps.

When properly structured and combined with appropriate cash positions it is possible to use swaps to replicate the cash flow stream associated with virtually any financial instrument. We have already considered examples of this in Chapter 15 when we looked at swaps. Specifically, we have seen how a fixed-for-floating interest rate swap can be used to convert a floating-rate financing, such as a commercial paper rollover strategy, into fixed-rate debt. We have seen how a financial obligation denominated in one currency can be converted to an obligation in another currency. And we have seen how swaps can be used to convert a floating commodity price in one currency to a fixed price in another currency. We will use this section to explore a few other possibilities.

Synthesizing a Dual Currency Bond

A **dual currency bond** is a bond which is sold and redeemed in one currency with coupon payments in another currency. The cash flows for such an instrument are depicted in Exhibit 23.8 using the arrow approach. The exhibit depicts a dual currency bond in which the principal is in dollars and the coupon payments are in deutschemarks.

Exhibit 23.8
The Cash Flows on a Dual Currency Bond
(deutschemark/dollar)

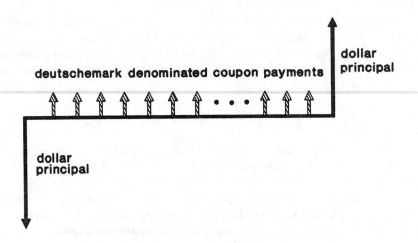

Such a bond can be synthesized by taking an ordinary Treasury or corporate bond and entering an appropriately structured currency swap. To make this work, we will need a fixed-for-fixed currency swap. The swap will be amortizing (the level payment variety) and written without an initial exchange of principals. (A fixed-for-fixed currency swap can itself be synthesized by combining a fixed-for-floating currency swap with a fixed-for-floating interest rate swap.

Exhibit 23.9
The Cash Flows on a Conventional Dollar Bond

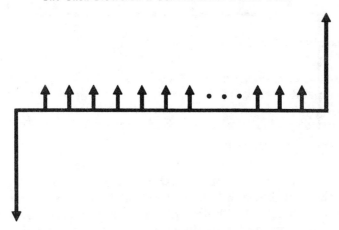

This combination is sometimes called a circus swap.) The cash flows from the ordinary U.S.-pay bond are depicted in Exhibit 23.9 and the cash flows on the swap are depicted in Exhibit 23.10. The combined cash flows are depicted in Exhibit 23.11.

Exhibit 23.10
Level Payment Amortizing Currency Swap
(with no initial exchange of principals)

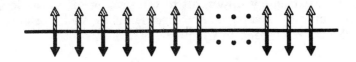

Exhibit 23.11
Combined Cash Flows: Bonds and Swap
(synthetic deutschemark/dollar dual currency bond)

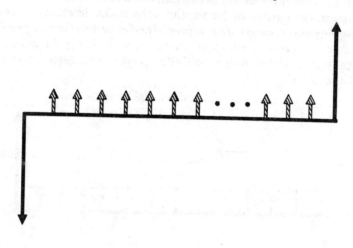

It is readily clear that the cash flows in Exhibit 23.11 are identical to the cash flows in Exhibit 23.8. Thus, the dual currency bond has been synthesized. Whether or not it is profitable to synthesize a dual currency bond will depend on whether, by doing so, the investor in need of such a bond can earn a return greater than that on a real dual currency bond having equal risk. Arbitragers too can be expected to play in dual currency bonds. Imagine for example, that an arbitrager can issue dollar/deutschemark dual currency bonds at a coupon of 7.50 percent. The funds obtained from the issuance of the bond can then be invested in a U.S.-pay investment grade corporate bond and converted, by way of the currency swap to an 8.25 percent dollar/deutschemark dual currency bond. The arbitrager then earns 75 basis points more on its dual currency assets than it pays on its dual currency liabilities.

The swap pricing issue has been ignored in this example. Clearly, it is extremely important to the pricing of synthetic securities that employ swaps. For a discussion of swap pricing, the reader should refer back to Chapter 13.[3]

Synthesizing a Foreign-Pay Zero

Suppose that a Japanese investor would like to hold yen-pay

zero coupon bonds. Can such a bond be synthesized from a U.S. Treasury zero? The answer is yes. The investor would buy the Treasury zero and then enter two separate swaps. The first swap is a zero coupon interest rate swap in which the investor is the zero coupon payer floating-rate receiver. The second swap is a yen/dollar zero coupon currency swap in which the investor is the zero coupon yen receiver and floating-rate dollar payer. The cash flows appear in Exhibit 23.12.

Exhibit 23.12
Components of a Synthetic Foreign-Pay Zero

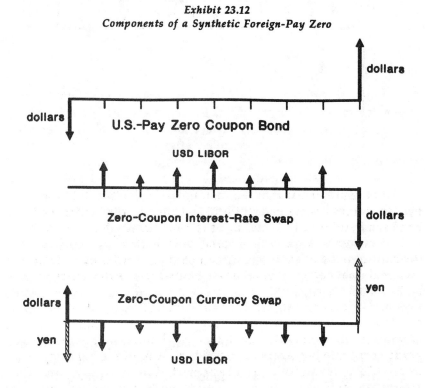

The net cash flows from these transactions, after the cancellation of all offsetting transactions, appear as Exhibit 23.13. Notice that the end result is a synthetic yen-pay zero coupon bond.

Assuming that yen-pay zeros are available to this investor as real instruments, the investor would compare the return offered by the real yen-pay zero and the synthetic yen-pay zero and select that which offers the better return, assuming risk levels to be equivalent. If, on the other hand, real yen-pay zeros are unavailable, then the investor in need of a yen-pay zero must synthesize one.

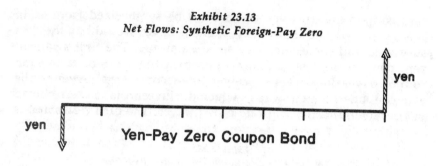

Exhibit 23.13
Net Flows: Synthetic Foreign-Pay Zero

Synthetic Equity

In the late 1980s Bankers Trust, a leader in financial innovation, undertook to offer an array of risk management products, including options and swaps, that were based on equity cash flow streams but which were otherwise modeled after the over-the-counter options and swaps that had become so popular in interest rate and exchange rate risk management. These options and swaps allow investors to replicate equities positions. The strategy proved extremely successful for Bankers Trust which earned over $100 million in 1989 alone from the sale of these instruments.[4]

Some of Bankers Trust's new equity derivatives are similar to the equity options and index futures that have traded on exchanges for some years. But, they tend to be larger in denomination and longer-term. Because they trade over the counter, they can also be tailored to meet the idiosyncratic needs of the end users. They allow the end user to create synthetic equity, to hedge equity positions, and to earn equity returns without taking equity on its books. They also allow users to take large equity stakes with minimal transaction costs, and they afford some unique opportunities for equity speculation. While not the primary justification for their existence, these equity derivatives can, in some cases, also allow an end user to circumvent local taxes, investment restrictions, and margin requirements.

Let's consider a simple application of an equity swap. Suppose that a pension fund has $1 million to invest in equity for three years. Rather than invest in equity directly the pension fund decides to invest indirectly by synthesizing equity from a fixed-rate note and an equity swap. The pension fund purchases a $1 million face value three-year corporate note offering an annual coupon of 9 percent and currently priced at par. At the same time, the pension fund enters into an equity swap with an equity swap dealer. The swap calls for the pension fund to pay the swap dealer 8.5 percent annually in exchange for the swap dealer paying the pension fund the return on the S&P 500. Both payments will be calculated on the basis of $1 million of notional principal. Importantly, the swap dealer pays the pension fund when the equity return (S&P 500) is *positive* but the pension fund pays the swap dealer when the equity return is *negative*. (This latter payment is in addition to the 8.5 percent it pays the swap dealer on the fixed rate leg of the swap.) The cash flows are illustrated in Exhibit 23.14.

Exhibit 23.14
Components of One Form of Synthetic Equity

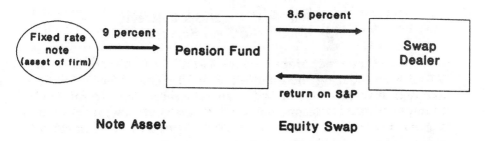

It is readily obvious that this strategy results in a return to the pension fund equal to the S&P 500 return plus 50 basis points. It is also obvious that the net effect is to create the equivalent of an equity position for the pension fund. Nevertheless, due to the off-balance sheet nature of the swap, the pension fund only shows its note asset on its balance sheet.

Equity swaps can also be used to construct synthetic asset allocation strategies. For example, an idea that has recently gained favor is to write equity swaps, like the one above, which pay the *higher* of the return on two different stock indexes. Such an equity swap might pay the higher of the S&P 500 index (a U.S. stock index) or the Nikkei 225 index (a Japanese stock index). There are, of course, no free lunches in synthetic securities. As we would expect, an equity swap offering the higher of two different stock index returns will require a higher fixed rate on the fixed-rate leg than would an equity swap that paid on the basis of one index only.

We will have more to say about equity and equity-related strategies, including asset allocation, in Chapter 25. Many of the strategies discussed in that chapter can be synthesized with the use of equity swaps and other equity derivatives now offered in an over-the-counter setting by firms like Bankers Trust.

As with financial engineers generally, the financial engineers involved in the new equity derivatives cannot afford to rest on their laurels. New equity derivatives will surely appear with the same innovative thinking and speed that has characterized fixed-income derivatives.

Qualitative Differences Between Synthetic and Real Securities

It would be inappropriate for us to discuss synthetic securities without considering the qualitative differences between synthetic and real securities. We defined a synthetic security as a combination of instruments or a decomposition of an instrument which produces a cash flow pattern which is identical to or nearly identical to a real instrument. This is in essence a **quantitative** definition. That is, if the cash flows are equal quantitatively, then the two instruments are equivalent. This overlooks what can be important **qualitative** differences.

Qualitative features include such things as the likelihood that a cash flow pattern may change on one instrument and not another, the jurisdiction for litigating an instrument in the event of a default, the difficulty of tracking the returns from the instrument, the amount and type of documentation needed to fully effect and to enforce a transaction, any lags involved in the receipt of payments, the length of time it takes to put a deal together, any variation margins that might be required (typical of synthetics involving futures), and whether a position is *on* balance sheet or *off* balance sheet.

Let's consider just one such qualitative factor to make the point. Suppose that a firm wants to raise five-year fixed-rate money. The funds would be used to finance an investment opportunity expected to return an annual compound rate of 16 percent. The firm is considering four alternative financing scenarios. First, it could issue a five-year fixed-rate note. If it does so, the firm can expect to pay 12 percent if it goes the public offering route. This will also involve an up front flotation cost of 3 percent. Together with the miscellaneous fees involved, the total package has an all-in cost of 13.8 percent and will take three months to put together. Alternatively, the firm's investment bank can do a private placement but the note will carry a coupon of 13.75 percent. When the issuance and administrative costs are considered, the all-in cost of this alternative is 14.0 percent. Because the financing is a private placement, no registration with the SEC is required and the financing can be in place in just seven days. The third alternative is to issue a floating rate note. The firm's bankers feel such a note could be issued at CP plus 100 basis points (where CP is the commercial paper rate on top grade paper). The flotation costs will be 3 percent and the issue can be distributed in about three months. With the administrative costs, the all-in cost of this alternative is CP plus 225 basis points. The FRN can be converted to a fixed-rate obligation using a fixed-for-floating interest rate swap. In such a swap, the swap dealer will pay the firm the commercial paper rate on top grade paper and the firm will pay the swap dealer 11.25 percent. The end result is that this financing alternative has an all-in cost of 13.50 percent. Finally the firm can issue six-month commercial paper at the commercial paper rate (top grade) plus 50 basis points. With the various administrative and issuance costs, this translates to CP plus 80 basis points. The spread over CP might change, however, should the firm's credit quality change. The financing would be given a long-term character by rolling over every six months for five years and it would be converted to fixed rate using the same swap described above. The all-in cost of this alternative is 12.05 percent. The financing could be in place in seven days.

When all is said and done, the four financing alternatives presented here have identical cash flow patterns (except for the size). Exhibit 23.15 depicts the interest flows (on an all-in basis) for the four

Exhibit 23.15
Interest Payments on Fixed-Rate Financing

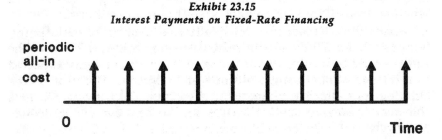

alternatives. The principal flows are not depicted. If there were no qualitative differences between the financing alternatives, the selection would be simple. Choose the alternative that can be effected at least cost. This is, of course, the commercial paper with rollover and swap conversion strategy which has an all-in cost of 12.05 percent. But, there *are* qualitative differences. These are summarized in Table 23.1.

Table 23.1
Identifying Qualitative Differences

| Alternative | Description | Cost | Qualitative Considerations | |
			issue time	cost may rise
1	Fixed rate issue (public)	13.80%	3 months	No
2	Fixed rate issue (private)	14.00%	7 days	No
3	FRN with swap	13.50%	3 months	No
4	CP with rollover with swap	12.05%	7 days	Yes

We see that there are two important qualitative differences between these financing alternatives. One is the time necessary to put the financing in place and the second is the possibility of an increase in the cost of the financing. The only two strategies that can be directly compared, because the qualitative factors are the same, are numbers 1 and 3. Of these two, alternative 3 has the lower cost, and, so, alternative 1 can be rejected. The choice then comes down to balancing the qualitative differences with the cost savings. If speed is the ultimate criteria—perhaps the very attractive investment opportunity might be lost if it is not seized immediately—then the choice comes down to alternatives 2 and 4. If, on the other hand, the firm's management is extremely risk averse so that they would not take the chance of any increase in their borrowing costs, then the choice might come down to alternatives 2 and 3.

The upshot of these closing remarks is that qualitative differences between real instruments and synthetic instruments and qualitative difference amongst different synthetic instruments simply cannot be ignored. To ignore the qualitative differences is to open the door to unpleasant surprises that may develop later.

We have repeatedly made reference to the concept of all-in cost in this chapter and elsewhere in this book. All-in cost is defined and the procedure for calculating it are discussed in the appendix to this chapter.

Summary

Arbitrage is the simultaneous transacting in two or more markets in order to exploit price discrepancies among the markets. While spatial arbitrage is the most intuitive form of arbitrage, arbitrage across time, securities, risk, and taxes are also very important.

Synthetic securities are cash flow streams, formed by combining or decomposing the cash flow stream from a set of other securities, which replicate the cash flow streams of real securities. By combining the appropriate combination of instruments and derivative instruments it is possible to synthesize the cash flows of virtually any security. The question of whether or not it is better to hold a real security or a synthetic security is different for an investor than it is for an arbitrager. For an investor, the issue is which instrument provides the higher rate of return. For the arbitrager, the issue is which instrument provides the greater spread over its implied repo rate.

One of the most important tools in creating synthetic instruments and in arbitraging across securities is the swap. Swaps can be used tailor a cash flow stream in an unlimited number of ways. It is not surprising that swaps have become the tool of choice for many financial engineers.

It is important to consider the qualitative difference between real securities and synthetic securities before choosing one alternative over another. If one ignores the qualitative differences, one runs the risk of a nasty surprise later.

Endnotes

[1]This is not technically correct. The first call options listed on the CBOE were American-type options on payout assets while the Black/Scholes model was designed to value European-type options on non-payout assets. The Black/Scholes model gave rise to other option pricing models. Some of the latter were useful for valuing American-type stock options. See Black and Scholes (1973).

[2]The put/call parity theorem given here is for European-type options written on non-payout assets. The derivation of this relationship including a discussion of the arbitrage theory that gives rise to it is provided in Marshall (1989), Chapter 17. The put/call parity theorem was first derived by Stoll (1969) and extended shortly thereafter by Merton (1973).

[3]For a more thorough discussion of swap pricing than that presented in Chapter 15, see Kapner and Marshall (1990).
[4]See Hansell (1990).

References & Suggested Reading

Asay, M. and C. Edelsburg. "Can a Dynamic Strategy Replicate the Returns of an Option?," *Journal of Futures Markets*, 6(1) (1986), pp. 63-70.

Black, F. and M. Scholes. "The Pricing of Options and Corporate Liabilities," *Journal of Political Economy* (May 1973), pp. 637-659.

Hansell, S. "Is the World Ready for Synthetic Equity?" *Institutional Investor* (August 1990).

Leland, H.E. "Option Pricing and Replication with Transaction Costs," *Journal of Finance*, 40(5) (1985), pp. 1283-1301.

Kapner, K.R. and J.F. Marshall. *The Swaps Handbook: Swaps and Related Risk Management Instruments*, New York: New York Institute of Finance, 1990.

Kopprasch, R.W., C.L. Johnson, A.H. Tatevossian. *Strategies for the Asset Manager: Hedging and the Creation of Synthetic Assets*, Salomon Brothers, Inc., Bond Portfolio Analysis Group.

Marshall, J.F. *Futures and Option Contracting: Theory and Practice*, Cincinnati: South-Western Publishing Company, 1989.

Merton, R.C. "The Relationship Between Put and Call Option Prices: Comment," *Journal of Finance*, 28 (1973), pp. 183-184.

Rubinstein, M. and H.E. Leland. "Replicating Options with Positions in Stock and Cash," *Financial Analysts Journal*, 37(4) (1981), pp. 63-72.

Singleton, J.C. and R. Grieves. "Synthetic Puts and Portfolio Insurance Strategies," *Journal of Portfolio Management*, 10(3) (1984), pp. 63-69.

Stoll, H. "The Relationship Between Put and Call Option Prices," *Journal of Finance*, 24 (May 1969), pp. 801-824.

Partridge-Hicks, S. and P. Hartland-Swann *Synthetic Securities*, London: Euromoney Publications, 1989.

Appendix
All-In Cost

We have repeatedly referred to the all-in cost associated with financing opportunities. It is worth a few moments of our time to consider this concept a little more carefully.

It can be extremely difficult for a financial manager presented with multiple financing alternatives to choose among them without first having a conceptual tool with which to reduce the costs to some common denominator. There are a number of approaches that have been suggested over the years, but none has proved superior to the concept of all-in cost, also called **effective annual percentage cost.** The term all-in cost implies that this calculation considers *all* costs associated with a financing, not just the explicit interest costs. Other, less obvious, costs include such things as flotation costs (underwriters' fees, etc.) and miscellaneous administrative expenses.

The concept is much easier for the beginner to understand if he or she is already familiar with the concept of internal rate of return. An all-in cost is the cost-side equivalent of the revenue-side notion of internal rate of return. Internal rate of return, often denoted IRR, is a concept familiar to most modern financial managers. It is defined as the discount rate that equates the present value of all the future cash flows from an investment with the investment's initial cost. In equation form, the IRR is the value k, which solves Equation 23.A.1. In Equation 23.A.1, $CF(t)$ denotes the cash flow at time t, n is the number of periods of cash flow involved, and k is the discount rate.

$$Cost = \sum_{t=1}^{n} CF(t) \cdot (1+k)^{-t} \qquad (23.A.1)$$

Internal rate of return is used to convert cash flow revenue streams to a percentage return basis. The technique assumes each cash flow received can be reinvested to earn the same rate. While this assumption may in practice be violated, it does not, for the reasons discussed in Chapter 5, detract from the usefulness of the approach.

Let's briefly review the concept of internal rate of return. Suppose that, for an initial cash outlay (cost) of $500, we can receive positive cash flows (revenues) each year for the next three years. Each cash flow is received at the end of the year involved. The first cash flow will be $200, the second will be $300, and the third will be $150.

Table 23.A.1
Cash Flow Stream

time	Cash Flow	Type
0	($500)	cost
1	200	revenue
2	300	revenue
3	150	revenue

The solution to the IRR equation is found using an iterative approach. That is, we select a value for k and plug it into Equation 23.A.1. If the right-hand side (the sum of the present values) is greater than the left-hand side (the cost), then the discount rate was too low. If the right-hand side is less than the left-hand side, then the discount rate was too high. By successively trying different values for k, we can determine the IRR to any degree of accuracy we desire. The IRR calculation is available on most modern financial calculators and many spreadsheet packages. In this particular case, the value of k that satisfies the equation is 14.923 percent. We therefore conclude that the investment's internal rate of return is 14.923 percent.

The only difference between an internal rate of return and an all-in cost is that, in an internal rate of return, the cash outflows precede the cash inflows from the investment, whereas, in an all-in cost, the cash inflows precede the cash outflows of the financing. But, since one party's liability is another party's asset, it follows that one party's internal rate of return is another party's all-in cost. With this understanding, the solution is simple. First, calculate the firm's initial proceeds from a financing (the revenue) and then calculate each subsequent cash outlay (cost). When all the cash flows have been generated, we simply reverse all the signs, that is, we treat the initial proceeds as the initial cost and we treat the subsequent cash outflows as cash inflows (revenues). Once the signs have been changed, we can compute the internal rate of return in the usual manner and call it an all-in cost.[1] It would certainly help to consider an example.

All-In Cost: An Example

Suppose that the Gremlin Corporation needs to raise $20 million of seven-year debt capital. The firm's financial managers would like a fixed rate of interest and they are considering two financing alternatives. Management has no strong preference for the structure of the financing. Consequently, the sole objective is to minimize the firm's cost of funds as measured by the "all-in cost."

Alternative 1:

The firm would issue a straight fixed-rate note (nonamortizing). The firm's investment bank has told the firm that the note can be sold at par if the firm is willing to pay a semiannual coupon of 12¾ percent. The investment bank would offer the note to the public at par (100) with 97½ going to the firm. The difference represents the flotation costs of the issue. The firm would also bear the administrative costs of servicing the issue. These costs amount to $41,000 every six months payable at the same time as the coupon.

Alternative 2:

The firm would issue $20 million of six-month commercial paper through a commercial paper dealer. Every six months new paper would be sold and the proceeds used to pay off the maturing paper. This strategy would involve an initial issue and then thirteen rollovers (refundings). The paper dealer would charge 1/16 of a point for each issue to handle the distribution. This would be payable at the time of issue. The firm has an excellent credit rating and would pay the going rate on investment-grade paper. For purposes of this example, we will suppose that the commercial paper rate for investment-grade paper has averaged 50 basis points over LIBOR. To convert this floating-rate liability to a fixed-rate liability, the firm would enter a fixed-for-floating interest rate swap. The commercial paper dealer, which also makes a market in interest rate swaps, has offered a seven-year interest rate swap with itself as floating-rate payer. The firm would pay the dealer a semiannual rate of 12 percent and the dealer would pay the firm six-month LIBOR. Administrative costs will total $18,000 every six months payable at the time the paper is redeemed by the firm. There are no other costs.

The key to calculating the all-in costs of these two financing alternatives is to generate the full set of net cash flows. To generate the set of net cash flows, the precise amount and time of each cash inflow and each cash outflow must be determined. Once the full set of cash flows has been obtained, the all-in cost can be determined by using an internal rate of return program. There are, however, two special considerations: First, the cash flows are stated on a semiannual basis. Thus, the IRR generated will be a half-year IRR. The rate must still be annualized. Second, if we designate cash inflows as positive (+) values and cash outflows as negative (-) values, all the flows will have the opposite sign from that ordinarily used to generate an IRR. As noted earlier, this problem is solved by simply reversing the signs when entering the cash flows into the IRR program.

The first thing to do is to list all sources of "cash in" and all sources of "cash out." For Alternative 1, the "cash in" includes the proceeds from the sale of the seven-year fixed rate note. The "cash out" includes the underwriting fee (paid only once), the interest coupon paid semiannually, the administrative costs paid semiannually, and the final redemption. These individual flows, together with the resultant net flows, are depicted in Table 23.A.2.

Table 23.A.2
Cash Flows for Alternative 1

Cash Flows

Period	Proceeds	Underwriting costs	Interest	Adm	Redemp	Net Flow
0	20000000	–500000				19500000
1			–1275000	–41000		–1316000
2			–1275000	–41000		–1316000
3			–1275000	–41000		–1316000
.			.	.		.
.						
.						
13			–1275000	–41000		–1316000
14			–1275000	–41000	–20000000	–21316000

The flows for Alternative 2 are a bit more complex than the flows for Alternative 1. First, there is a new issue every six months and a redemption every six months. Second, there are two sets of interest flows—the interest flows on the paper and the interest flows on the swap. It is important to note that we don't need to concern ourselves with the unknown value "LIBOR" since the firm will pay

LIBOR plus 50 bps (the approximate paper rate) and receive LIBOR. The LIBORs cancel leaving a net cost of 50 bps (25 basis points every six months). The swap coupon is 12 percent paid in two semiannual installments ($1.2 million each). The full set of cash flows is depicted in Table 23.A.3.

Table 23.A.3
Cash Flows for Alternative 2

Cash Flows

Period	Proceeds	Underwriting costs	25 bps Interest	swap coupon Interest	Adm	Redemp	Net Flow
0	20000000	−12500				19987500	
1	20000000	−12500	−50000	−1200000	−18000	−20000000	−1280500
2	20000000	−12500	−50000	−1200000	−18000	−20000000	−1280500
3	20000000	−12500	−50000	−1200000	−18000	−20000000	−1280500
.		.		.		.	.
.		.		.	.	.	.
.		.	.	.		.	.
13	20000000	−12500	−50000	−1200000	−18000	−20000000	−1280500
14			−50000	−1200000	−18000	−20000000	−21268000

We are now ready to determine the all-in cost of the two financing alternatives. We reverse the signs of all the net cash flows above and then calculate the all-in cost as an internal rate of return. Alternative 1 is found to have a half-year all-in cost (AIC) of 6.863 percent. This half-year value can be translated to an effective annual percentage rate using Equation 23.A.2. This translation yields an all-in cost of about 14.20 percent. The same procedure applied to Alternative 2 produces an annual all-in cost of 13.22 percent.

$$\text{Effective annual percentage cost} = (1 + \text{AIC})^2 - 1 \quad (23.A.2)$$

The all-in cost calculations suggest that Alternative 2 is the better financing alternative. It accomplishes the same end result as Alternative 1 but saves the firm 98 basis points a year. It is important to note that we have ignored any qualitative differences between the two alternatives. We would be remiss if we failed to point out that qualitative differences will sometimes influence the financing decision.

While commercial paper is, by definition, short-term debt, the strategy of rolling the paper over every six months for a period of seven years coupled with an interest rate swap gives the strategy a long-term fixed-rate character and it is, therefore, best viewed as long-term debt.

The all-in cost approach discussed above is particularly useful when the firm is considering capping a floating-rate liability, placing a floor under a floating-rate asset, or wrapping a collar around a floating-rate liability. The reader should recall that the premiums paid to acquire interest rate caps, interest rate floors, and interest rate collars can be amortized to obtain their percentage annual cost equivalents. For example, suppose that a firm has priced a floating-rate financing and determined that the all-in cost is LIBOR + 1.25 percent. The firm would like to place a 10 percent cap on the floating rate so it also prices a 10 percent interest rate cap. Suppose that the cap has an annual percentage cost equivalence of 0.25 percent. We can now obtain the all-in cost of the capped floating rate financing by simply adding the 0.25 percent cost of the cap to the LIBOR + 1.25 percent cost of the financing to get an all-in cost of LIBOR + 1.50 percent but capped at 10.25 percent (10 percent plus cost of cap). The point, once again, is that the merits of alternative forms of financing can only be intelligently compared if we reduce all costs to a common denominator.

Endnote

[1]The software package that we used for calculating the all-in cost in the examples which follow, *A-Pack*, release 2.00, has an all-in cost option which automatically performs the sign changes described. It also annualizes the cost in those situations in which the cash flows occur more frequently than once a year. *A-Pack* is discussed in Chapter 3.

Chapter 24

Tax-Driven Deals

John S. Manna and Robert Willens

Overview

Those of us who practice financial engineering with respect to tax liability enjoy the ability most of the time to assess immediately the financial value of our work. The amount of dollars at risk often can be measured to the penny.

Tax laws are like the rules to a game. They are finite, though lengthy and complex. They are expressly made, though occasionally ambiguous. Once the rules are understood, a player can usually know exactly what his situation is, what his risks are, and how to manage those risks. The goals of the players are clear, i.e., to minimize tax liability, and it is possible to become an expert player through study and experience.

It is hard to imagine a financial deal which does not involve tax issues. If an item or right is purchased for resale, a potential taxable gain (or loss) is involved. The sale of many items involves the question of whether sales tax applies. The use of certain items may involve use taxes. The transfer of property by sale or otherwise raises the issue of whether transfer taxes, gift taxes or estate taxes might apply. Issuing corporate shares, making a mortgage, paying

John S. Manna is Assistant Professor of Business Law at Saint John's University, New York. Bob Willens is Senior Vice President with Lehman Brothers. He is also Certified Public Accountant (CPA).

rent under a lease, and buying real estate each involves the issue whether special taxes will apply to the transaction. If you are paid for the same work as an employee, as opposed to an independent contractor, different tax liabilities exist.

Tax issues can sometimes be the sole reason for making a particular deal. More commonly, though, tax issues influence how a deal is structured. In either case, such deals are said to be **tax driven.**

Tax driven deals require the involvement of financial engineers with skills and knowledge that differ greatly from other types of financial engineers. However, other types of financial engineers are often also needed because their skills and knowledge are essential to the nontax aspects of the deal. Such deals emphasize the complementary nature of the skills and knowledge base of different types of financial engineers.

The symbiosis of financial engineering relationships is the source of many financial engineering innovations. The combination of different financial engineering specializations in one group allows the group to go beyond the limits of each person's individual specialization and to devise new solutions which none of them could have achieved alone. The excitement of brainstorming such new solutions is one of the most enjoyable aspects of financial engineering.

This chapter introduces the reader to tax driven deals as a category of financial engineering. It does so by analyzing various tax driven deals in a manner which gives the reader an understanding of how the financial engineer views the problem and resolves it. The thinking process of the financial engineer is explained in sufficient detail to allow the reader to understand the approach taken by financial engineers and to adapt it in future situations. In some cases, we also consider the taxing authorities' responses to the efforts of the financial engineers. These responses are included to focus on the regulatory dialectic discussed earlier, i.e., the cat and the mouse game between financial engineers and regulatory and taxing authorities.

Each deal is analyzed by isolating the situation that exists, the tax dangers which are present, and a possible solution. While the deals may appear to be hypothetical, each one actually describes a deal which financial engineers already have implemented, although the dollar amounts and other numbers used in the chapter often are fictitiously inserted for simplicity or enhanced pedagogy.

Some deals, and the parties who made them, may be recognizable to the reader, but it is important to understand that these deals are reproducible and, consequently, they should be viewed generically.

Preventing A Hostile Takeover

Situation: Celene Corporation, a publicly traded corporation, is fearful that KEF Enterprises will make a hostile takeover of Celene because of Celene's strong asset base. To discourage such an attempt by KEF or others, Celene would like to dilute significantly the asset base and/or the stock ownership of Celene if any person makes a tender offer or acquisition of a certain percentage of Celene's stock. To accomplish this, Celene's lawyers advise that Celene should adopt a "poison pill" plan which gives Celene's current shareholders the right to buy preferred stock if such a tender offer or acquisition is made.

Danger: The granting of such poison pill rights to shareholders could be viewed by tax authorities as a dividend distribution of stock or property in a manner similar to a cash dividend. The issuance to shareholders of share-type certificates (or options) giving them the poison pill rights could be viewed as analogous to a dividend of stock, especially to the extent such rights are exercisable or separately tradeable from the common stock with respect to which they are distributed. This would ensure a finding by tax authorities that the poison pill rights are taxable. This would give rise to taxable income which must be reported by the shareholders who must pay taxes on this "income." Obviously, in such an event, the shareholders would be reluctant, if not hostile, to the poison pill plan.

An Engineered Solution: Poison pill plans should be adopted in a manner which creates **inchoate rights** which are an attribute of the underlying stock. No share-type certificates or other documents should be issued which would be exercisable or separately tradeable or have some value distinct from the underlying share certificate.

Responses: State tax authorities have begun challenging the nontaxable nature of poison pill plans which do not involve the issuance of share certificates. The federal government, however, has stated that such poison pill plans do not give rise to taxable income.

Recapitalization of the Firm

Situation: RUK Corporation is heavily in debt and needs to recapitalize. RUK's best available course of action is to exchange securities previously issued for senior notes. However, prospective purchasers of the senior notes will be reluctant to buy them unless RUK enhances the offer in a visible and tangible manner. To accomplish this, RUK is considering offering one of the following with the senior notes: cash rebates, market discount bonds, price protection warrants, or RUK common stock.

Danger: In a recapitalization, a gain derived from the value of property, other than securities, (commonly referred to as *boot*) received by the creditors is considered a realized gain for tax purposes. The creation of a taxable gain for investors should be avoided since it diminishes the value and attractiveness of the property offered to investors, requiring the recapitalizing corporation to offer more value than would otherwise be required to induce the investors to extend credit. The proposed cash rebate and other items, which clearly are not securities, would generate realized gains which usually are capital gains. The proposed market discount bonds, which are bonds acquired after their original issue at a price below their principal amount, are very similar in nature to a cash rebate and also would create realized gains. If the original security was also a market discount bond, the gain recognized in the recapitalization exchange is considered ordinary interest income to the extent of any accrued market discount associated with it.

Price protection warrants can provide noteholders with a specified dollar amount of downside protection against increases in prevailing interest rates, against deterioration in the issuing corporation's creditworthiness, or against other risks of loss. As such, realized gains would also be recognized to the extent of the value of the warrants.

An Engineered Solution: RUK's common stock is considered a security, so its inclusion in the offer could not generate a realized gain. However, RUK may want to offer alternative or additional non-gain items. A financial engineer would then be needed to formulate a new instrument, or to choose a security from existing types, and have RUK offer it to the holders of its senior notes.

The financial engineer must know the rules under which he or she works, since a gain could be realized if the financial solution is not a security. Various rules of thumb are applied to determine whether an instrument is a security. They include the following: (1) whether the instrument is essentially equity or debt based (an equity based instrument is a security, while debt is subject to the following factors); (2) the length of the instrument's term (the longer the term, the more likely that it is a security); (3) the likelihood of repayment on or before the maturity date (greater doubt regarding such repayment increases the chances that it is a security); (4) whether the instrument is secured (unsecured instruments are more likely to be securities); and (5) the investment grade of the instrument (the lower the grade, the more likely it is a security).

As described elsewhere in this book, the financial engineer could formulate a great many different types of securities that would satisfy the criteria for classification as a security.

Nonprofits: Tax on Unrelated Business Income

Situation: Starburst Corporation is a nonprofit organization which owns an extensive portfolio of investment instruments. Starburst's financial engineers have suggested that Starburst employ various risk management techniques to minimize risks to Starburst's portfolio. It is important to Starburst that the income from its investments remain untaxed, so Starburst has asked its financial engineers to look at the tax effect of using risk management techniques.

Danger: Nonprofit organizations include pension funds, churches, sports leagues, foundations, schools, trade associations, credit card companies and other tax-exempt organizations. Despite their tax exempt status, nonprofits can be taxed on what is called "unrelated business income." Unrelated business income is income from a business which is regularly carried on by the nonprofit but which is not substantially related to the execution or performance of the non-profit's tax-exempt purpose.

Investment property, which would normally fit within a nonprofit's tax-exempt purpose, generates unrelated business income if the property fits within the Internal Revenue Code's definition of "debt-financed" property. Since many of the risk management techniques employed by financial engineers involve some form of debt, it is important for Starburst's financial engineers to determine whether the IRS would view the investment property purchased through these techniques as debt-financed.

An Engineered Solution: To determine whether investment property is debt-financed, the IRS looks at whether the funds used to implement the risk management technique have been borrowed. If the funds were borrowed, this indicates a debt-financed nature. Another important factor is the intent of the nonprofit which purchased the investment property. If debt securities and swap arrangements are used to establish an inventory for sale to customers or regular buyers, they would be considered a debt-financed unrelated business.

When a nonprofit purchases investment property which involves debt, but for ordinary or routine investment activities undertaken in connection with the management of its securities portfolio, the investment property is not considered debt-financed. Assume Starburst makes an interest rate swap arrangement whereby the nonprofit purchases a floating-rate instrument and simultaneously agrees with the counterparty to make floating-rate payments and receive fixed-rate payments. If Starburst enters into this arrangement as part of an investment strategy designed to stabilize the returns on the floating-rate instrument, the property would not be considered debt-financed and would retain its tax-exempt nature.

Similarly, Starburst can employ currency swaps, short selling, index arbitrage and other risk management techniques which would be considered tax-benign nonprofit activities to the extent that Starburst's purposes remain the same.

Meeting the Need for Short-Term Financing

Situation: Slade Enterprises, Inc. needs to obtain short-term financing. Slade wants to avoid offering an instrument which federal tax authorities might view as a debt instrument. Slade desires to enhance the value of the instrument it issues to corporate investors. As it happens, Slade is in a very low tax bracket.

Danger: Notes, commercial paper, and other forms of debt with short terms fall squarely within the tax authorities' definition of debt instruments which can give rise to realized gain and thereby defeat Slade's purpose.

An Engineered Solution: Slade's financial engineers have suggested that some form of short-term preferred stock would suit Slade's purpose because such stock has a greater likelihood of being considered equity (as opposed to debt). Also, this would entitle Slade's corporate investors to a dividends-received deduction for dividends paid on the stock if the holding period for the stock is a minimum of 46 days.

Ancillary Danger: Slade liked the suggestion and asked the financial engineers to prepare a form of preferred stock which meets these requirements. Slade asked the engineers to further enhance the attractiveness of the stock to investors by giving investors an option to sell the stock. Slade's suggestion raised a problem for the financial engineers because a holder of the stock would not receive credit toward the 46-day holding period requirement for any day(s) on which the holder of the stock is insulated from market risk or possesses an option, or rights equivalent to an option, to sell the stock.

An Engineered Solution: Slade's financial engineers suggested auction-rate preferred stock with a 46-day holding period. Although such stock is a functional alternative to commercial paper and other short-term debt, it has strong elements of an equity security because the holder's rights are similar to those found in more traditional forms of preferred stock. For example, the holder has no right to receive a sum certain on demand or on a specified date (such right would be an element of negotiable instruments, which are considered debt in nature). Also, the holder's rights upon liquidation or in bankruptcy are subordinate to claims of creditors, as is the case with equity investments. Finally, the holder's receipt of dividends is dependent upon dividends being declared and paid out of legally available funds, a feature of equity investments.

The question still remains whether other elements of this technique may limit risk to the extent that it is considered a debt instrument in nature. For example, does the right to sell the stock at an auction amount to rights equivalent to an option to sell the stock, thereby making this a debt instrument in which gain is realized?

Neither the ability nor the expectation of the stockholder to sell the stock at an auction after the holding period constitutes a guaranteed, formal option to sell because of the possibility that the auction may fail if there is insufficient interest in the stock. Such failures have occurred on many occasions. Also, since the broker-dealer does not agree to guarantee the success of an auction, the possibility of a failed auction provides sufficient risk to allow the stockholder to satisfy the 46-day rule for a dividends-received deduction.

Ancillary Danger: Slade liked the creative, flexible approach of its financial engineers, but did not like confronting its investors with all of the risk inherent in a failed auction. Slade suggested that something be done to reduce the investors' perception of risk.

An Engineered Solution: Slade's financial engineers said that they could add a penalty rate to be paid by Slade to the stockholders in the event of an auction failure. This would show investors that Slade, the issuer, had a financial incentive to redeem the stock, thereby providing greater investor security.

Ancillary Danger: Slade was willing to maximize investor security by offering a penalty rate which was so high that investors would easily see that Slade had no choice but to redeem the stock. Such investor security would significantly increase the attractiveness of the stock to investors. However, Slade's financial engineers pointed out that while a significant penalty rate can exist without vitiating the required element of risk, a penalty rate which is so high that it virtually compels the issuer to redeem the stock eliminates the required element of risk. For this reason, Slade's financial engineers included a strong penalty rate which left an acceptable level of risk for the investors.

Bond Swaps

Situation: Telva Corporation is faced with a serious current need for funds. For various reasons, Telva plans to issue a bond which will be publicly traded. If certain events occur, as Telva expects, Telva might swap the bond in the future with a new bond which reduces the interest it must pay. The investor market has been amenable to such swaps under the proper circumstances, and Telva believes that a bond swap will work.

Danger: When a debt swap occurs, income, which is regarded as arising from the cancellation of the indebtedness, will be recognized for the debtor to the extent that the adjusted issue price of the old bond exceeds the issue price of the new bond (unless the debtor is bankrupt or insolvent). Looking ahead toward the issuance of the new bonds, Telva notes that, under present tax law, the issue price for tax purposes for publicly traded bonds is the initial trading price. The issue price for nonpublic debt instruments which provide for adequate stated interest is the stated principal amount of the bond. If the situation occurs for which Telva is planning, the adjusted issue price of its first bond, for tax purposes, will be significantly higher than the issue price of the new bond. This would produce a significant tax gain.

Undaunted, Telva changes its plan so that Telva will not swap bonds at all, but will instead issue only one bond. Telva is confident that, when the time is right, it will be able to persuade the bond-holders to reduce the interest. Unfortunately, the IRS does not require an actual physical exchange of bonds to find that a bond swap occurred. The change of material terms of an existing bond can be viewed as a de facto (or constructive) exchange of bonds which has the same negative tax effect that an actual bond swap would create. A reduction in a bond's principal or in its interest rate is considered a material change.

An Engineered Solution: Telva's financial engineers suggest that the problem be solved by including a clause in the original bond's indenture providing for the reduction in interest. This could work because changes to bond terms which would otherwise be material have been regarded as insufficient to constitute a constructive bond swap if they are contained in the original bond's indenture.

Responses: The IRS recently found that a taxable exchange of key executive life insurance policies occurred simply because the corporate owner of the policy changed the person whose life was insured under the policy. The original policy provided that the corporate owner of the policy could change the insured's identity since the purpose was to provide key-man insurance. However, the IRS, viewing the life of the insured as an item material to a life insurance policy (not surprisingly), found that this was a taxable exchange of policies even though the change arose only through an option provided for in the original document.

Financial engineers must be aware of the possibility of such an interpretation being applied to bond documents. Perhaps interest rate change options contained in original bond indentures can be distinguished successfully from changes of the insured in life insurance policies. The insured's life is the primary focus of the life insurance policy, whereas repayment of the principal could be viewed as the primary focus of a bond. Bond interest might be viewed as a less material aspect of the bond, perhaps similar to insurance premiums. Also, if the debt instrument is private, and the option was negotiated as part of the original document's negotiations, there is a stronger basis for finding that no de facto exchange occurred.

If such reasoning is successful, financial engineers will continue to produce such bonds in these situations. If not, a different approach must be developed, such as using a nonmaterial change (e.g., extension of the maturity date has been found to be non-material) in the bond, or the use of another instrument.

Self-liquidating Preferred Stock

Situation: Emerald Enterprises, Inc., a holding company, wants to acquire Earl Corporation, a public corporation, and merge Earl into Keo Corp., a subsidiary of Emerald. Emerald can afford to pay cash for a good portion of the shares of Earl; Emerald is willing to offer securities issued by it to acquire shares of Earl; and Emerald would like this reorganization to be a tax-free event to the extent possible. Emerald knows that if it offers Emerald securities to acquire Earl's shares, the securities must be very attractive to the shareholders of Earl to match the desirability of cash to many shareholders. Emerald is also concerned about unduly eroding its asset base.

Danger: Emerald's plan to increase and reorganize its holdings can be viewed by the IRS as a reorganization in which the shareholders of Earl, who receive Emerald's securities, realize a gain for tax purposes. If Emerald's securities are perceived as securities which will realize a tax gain, the securities would be less desirable and would probably trade at a discount thereby creating an effective yield exceeding securities that are similarly rated. This would make Emerald's sale of these securities more difficult and would require Emerald to place more value in the securities, causing a further erosion of its assets.

In order to qualify as a tax free reorganization, the securities offered must meet the "continuity of proprietary interest" test. This test would be satisfied if the value of the new securities is at least 45 percent of the sum of the amount of cash paid to Earl's shareholders plus the value of the new securities.

An Engineered Solution: Emerald's financial engineers propose that Emerald issue a new class of Emerald preferred stock which would be exchanged for 50 percent of Earl's shares, and that Emerald pay cash for the other 50 percent of Earl's shares. This meets the 45 percent requirement.

The financial engineers added some special features to make the preferred stock very attractive to Earl's shareholders. This maximized Emerald's ability to obtain Earl's shares with Emerald's preferred stock. The Emerald preferred will have an adjustable dividend rate that will be periodically reset at a fixed spread in excess of the yield curve. Also, the stock will be issued at $50 per share and will be redeemable after five years at a price not less than $50 per share although its liquidation value at such time would only be $5 per share, i.e., the preferred stock is self-liquidating but contains a built-in windfall.

Responses: The Internal Revenue Code was subsequently amended to impose new penalties on what it considers self-liquidating preferred stock. **Self-liquidating preferred stock** is considered preferred stock with a declining dividend rate (or with a dividend rate that can be reasonably expected to decline) and with an issue price that exceeds either its redemption price or its liquidation value.

Applying this test to Emerald's preferred stock we would find that the adjustable rate aspect of such stock means that it must be viewed as having a dividend rate that can be reasonably expected to decline. Also, Emerald's preferred issue price is clearly excessive over its $5 liquidation price, making certain that the new penalties would apply. Hence, a new opportunity for financial engineers.

The new penalties would involve application of the Code's extraordinary dividend rules to corporate shareholders of Emerald preferred. Corporate shareholders would forfeit the benefits of the 70 percent intercorporate dividends-received deduction regardless of the applicable holding period with respect to the underlying stock. The loss of the deduction is effected by a reduction in the basis of the preferred stock in an amount equal to the dividends-received deduction. This effectively causes the value of the dividends-received deduction to be taxed at the time the preferred stock is sold or otherwise disposed of.

Where Is a White Knight When You Need One?

Situation: Bannor Corporation is fearful of a hostile takeover by Satiuz Enterprises. Bannor has good relations with Delea Corporation, which is not interested in, or capable of, taking over Bannor.

Danger: Satiuz is preparing an attractive offer to Bannor's shareholders which provides a choice of excessive cash, or valuable securities involving no current tax gain. If Bannor does not act soon, the Satiuz offer will be so attractive that Bannor will be taken over and will lose its ability to act at all. Bannor must act in a manner which does not erode its asset base or expose itself to additional dangers.

An Engineered Solution: Bannor's financial engineers prepared a solution by which Bannor would issue to Delea convertible preferred stock possessing terms that are extremely favorable to Delea. These include an above-market dividend rate and a below-market conversion premium. Since such preferred stock is both sold and recorded at par value, no taxable gain is realized. Also, the dividends will not receive negative tax treatment as extraordinary dividends because they are issued, recorded, and sold at the same value (par value), fitting them within the meaning of qualified preferred dividends, and the basis of the preferred stock will not be reduced as long as the stock's actual rate of return does not exceed 15 percent.

Responses: The preferred stock which Bannor's financial engineers proposed is commonly called **whitemail** or **white squire preferred**. A Financial Accounting Standards Board (FASB) subcommittee which is charged with the responsibility of promulgating rules for distinguishing debt from equity is considering a change in the accounting rules for whitemail.

Whitemail stock is worth more than its par value because of its high dividend coupon. The value above par would be the present value of the stream of excess dividends. Some accountants propose that whitemail preferred shares be recorded at their true value, which would be the sum of the par value and the excess value. The issuer would then be viewed as receiving a combination of cash equal to the par value and an intangible asset equal to the excess value which would be called **takeover insurance**. Since takeover insurance is not a cognizable asset and is, by its nature and purpose, a form of management compensation, this asset would be charged to earnings in the year it comes into existence.

This possible accounting rule is analogous to other established accounting principles. Consider, for example, the portion of payments made to redeem greenmail stock which exceeds the value of such stock. Such excess payments will generally be charged to operations (rather than capitalized as part of the cost of Treasury stock) when an asset such as a standstill agreement, is acquired in exchange for the excess payment. If this approach is adopted by the IRS with respect to whitemail, the stock's issue price would exceed both its liquidation preference and its redemption price, giving rise to the negative tax effects the strategy was designed to avoid.

Renegotiating Debt

Situation: Roth Corporation has issued $10 million worth of publicly traded bonds. Each Bond has a $1000 face value. Due to recent economic difficulties, Roth is facing default on the bonds and bankruptcy if it cannot alter some of its obligations on the bonds by issuing a new bond or by modifying the terms of the original bond. The trading price of the bonds has dropped to $700.

Danger: If a tax gain is realized for the creditors or for the corporation, the benefits of the bond modification would be reduced, the cost would be dramatically increased, and the potential success of the effort would be jeopardized. For example, if this transaction were viewed by the IRS as a bond swap in which Roth (the debtor) realized cancellation of indebtedness income because Roth swapped $1000 bonds for an equal number of bonds worth only $700 each, a forgiveness of debt in the amount of $300 per bond, Roth would realize $3 million of such income. The tax effect on the financially strapped Roth would be devastating.

An Engineered Solution: Roth's financial engineers suggested the issuance of junk bonds to replace the current bonds. At the time in question, the issue price of a new bond exchanged for an existing bond is, for the debtor's tax purposes, the greater of the new bond's trading price and the adjusted issue price (usually the face amount) of the bond being retired. Therefore, the junk bonds would be issued at a face amount equal to the current bonds, avoiding any realized gain attributable to the face amount of the bonds. In reality, however, once the swap is made, the new junk bonds probably will begin trading at a price close to the $700 trading price of the old bonds. This reflects the true value of the junk bonds as opposed to their nominal face value. It also reflects the reality that the bondholders have lost $300 of the value of the original face amount of the old bonds. They will accept junk bonds only because it is a better alternative to the bankruptcy or insolvency of the corporation.

Responses: New IRS rules cause swaps of existing debt for new debt to generate cancellation of indebtedness income to the extent that the principal amount of the retired debt exceeds the IRS's new definition of the "issue price" of the new debt. If the new debt is a publicly traded junk bond such as Roth's, the issue price is equal to the bond's initial trading price *if* the bond begins trading within ten trading days of the exchange date.

Danger: In this case, since the initial trading price of the junk bonds would be $700, Roth would be burdened with $300 worth of realized gain for tax purposes. Worse, this bond swap will not generate a deductible loss for the bondholders stemming from the decline in value of the investment. Worse still, the bondholders will also have phantom taxable income because the junk bonds are regarded as issued with original issue discount equal to the excess of the new bond's principal amount over its initial trading price. This discount must be reported as income over the life of the junk bond.

An Engineered Solution: Financial engineers would suggest the use of nonpublic traded debt whenever possible in this situation. If the old bond is nonpublicly traded and the new junk bond can be issued as nonpublicly traded debt, cancellation of indebtedness will rarely arise. This is so because the issue price of the new nonpublicly traded bond is deemed to be its stated principal amount, rather than its fair value, if the new bond's interest is no less than the Treasury's borrowing rate for debt of a comparable term.

If a debtor cannot take advantage of the benefits of the tax rules applicable to nonpublicly traded debt, the debtor's best course of action might be the bankruptcy court. Where publicly traded bonds are swapped in a bankruptcy proceeding and the debtor transfers to bondholders more than a nominal amount of equity, cancellation of indebtedness income will not arise. The law regards stock equal to a mere 10 percent of the face amount of the retired debt as constituting more than a nominal or token amount of equity.

Taxes and Costs on Real Estate Transfers

Situation: The Sylberry Wine Division of Volinstaad Corporation, a research and development company, has developed a new wine called Sylberry wine. Initial studies show that it will be extremely well-received by the general public. The grape is a hybrid produced solely by Volinstaad in special vineyards which produce only the Sylberry grape. Volinstaad is developing a special logo, bottle and label for the product. Due to its R&D nature, Volinstaad is unable to manage a wine production and distribution business over the long term, so it does not wish to retain the Sylberry wine business. Rather, Volinstaad wants to use this business to generate a one-time capital gain to offset anticipated R&D losses in other areas, to pay dividends to anxious shareholders, and to fund other R&D projects that could be equally profitable. Volinstaad now seeks to acquire the real estate needed to grow and store large quantities of the grape over the next two years. Once these steps are implemented, Volinstaad anticipates that it will have applied $30 million of resources, of which $20 million would be real estate costs, and would be able to sell the entire business and its assets for $40 million (assuming no appreciation of the real estate).

Danger: The danger arises if Volinstaad handles this situation in the conventional manner, i.e., if Volinstaad buys the $20 million worth of real estate, implements its plan and sells the real estate and the other assets of its Sylberry Wine Division to the buyer. The transfer of the land would generate the following special costs and local taxes in the area in question:

$125,000	(.625%)	Title Insurance
$525,000	(2.625%)	Transfer Tax [2.625% if the land is worth $500,000 or more; 1.425% otherwise]
$412,500	(2.75%)	Mortgage Recording Tax [Assumes $15 million mortgage]
$ 80,000	(0.4%)	Filing of Deed
$600,000	(3%)	Points to bank and application fees
Total Special Costs:	$1,742,500	

A total of $1,742,500 in special expenses have been generated which could be targeted by the financial engineer.

An Engineered Solution: Volinstaad's financial engineer proposes that Volinstaad Corporation create a wholly owned susidiary corporation, the Sylberry Wine Corporation, which would own all of the real estate involved in the business. The Sylberry Wine Corporation would be sold to the eventual buyer, thereby eliminating the need to have an additional transfer and closing of the real estate. By avoiding the transfer and closing, Volinstaad would have avoided $1,742,500 worth of special expenses which would be direct savings to Volinstaad to the extent Volinstaad would have paid them. To the extent the buyer would have paid some of these expenses, the savings would be bargaining chips for Volinstaad. Volinstaad can use them to make the deal more attractive to a buyer or to persuade the buyer to pay Volinstaad for all or a portion of what the buyer would have paid on the conventional transaction. After all, Volinstaad still can transfer the real property to the buyer from the corporation, causing the buyer to incur the expenses. Volinstaad also has the advantage of offering existing financing to the buyer by selling the corporation, which should facilitate the deal.

Responses: A few tax authorities have tried to reduce the tax benefits of this solution. For example, some have provided that particular taxes, such as the transfer tax, would apply to the sale of shares of a corporation which is primarily a real estate owner. Exceptions such as these could affect the Sylberry Wine Corporation to the extent these special laws apply to them, but the other costs and taxes mentioned in this example generally are not affected by such special laws.

Variation for Special Transfer Tax Laws: Suppose the local tax authorities have passed a special transfer tax on real estate owned by a corporation whose shares are sold. Fine, they may get some tax out of the transfer, but Volinstaad still can reduce it by not holding all the land in one corporation. Volinstaad could purchase the land through separate corporations, each of which will buy parcels expected to have a market value less than $500,000 at the time of resale. This would reduce the future applicable transfer tax by approximately $240,000 if all parcels are less than $500,000 in value. Even if all of the parcels are worth more than $500,000 each, Volinstaad can subdivide each parcel to portions worth below $500,000 before taking title in the name of the separate corporations.

Real Property Taxes

Situation: Tuck Corporation wants to buy one hundred acres of industrial property as part of its expansion efforts. Tuck would build a small plant on approximately twenty acres and would expand over the next ten years, shifting its personnel and equipment to the new plant without disrupting its current operations. Tuck's Real Estate Department has located the following properties, which happen to be adjacent to each other in an area which is ideal for Tuck's expansion.

	Price
1. a 100 acre parcel of land, already zoned industrial	$5 million
2. a 250 acre parcel of land, zoned for farming	$6 million
3. a 40 acre parcel of land, already zoned industrial	$3 million

The first parcel is an exact match with what Tuck wants. The second property, a farm called Southbridge, also would meet Tuck's needs and its cost per acre emphasizes the relatively lower value of farmland. The owners of each of these properties are willing to allow Tuck to buy it for $1.5 million down (which is all that Tuck has available for this purpose). Tuck has learned that financing is available for the rest of the purchase price. Tuck is not interested in the third parcel because it would not fit within Tuck's expansion plans.

After a little investigating, Tuck learned that Southbridge can be subdivided and rezoned for industrial use without difficulty, and the excess acreage could then be sold at a profit. Tuck decided to pursue the larger property even though its funds and cash flow would have been stretched by the down payment and debt service required to buy the smaller less expensive first parcel. Unfortunately, the additional $120,000 per year debt service cost of Southbridge is not affordable to Tuck. Humbull Farms, the owner of Southbridge, then informs Tuck that Humbull is selling Southbridge despite Humbull's own urgent need for the farmland, because of Humbull's more urgent need for the $1.5 million down payment. A financial engineer at Humbull offers a possibility to Tuck: Tuck can buy Southbridge with a balloon purchase money mortgage from Humbull which would delay for 20 years the entire debt service on the additional $1 million price of this property. This offer is quite attractive to Tuck because it would not stretch Tuck beyond Tuck's cash flow limit and because Tuck surely would sell, develop, or use the excess acreage within the 20 years. Breathing a sigh of relief, Tuck's CEO approves the deal and signs the contract to buy Southbridge.

Danger: When the deal is announced in the papers, a friendly but rival CEO calls Tuck's CEO to congratulate him on the deal. The rival CEO says he would have liked to buy Southbridge himself, but his company could not afford the hike in real estate taxes which would go from $3000 per year to $93,000 per year once the property was sold to a non-farmer. Tuck had not realized the net real estate tax consequences of its plan and it cannot afford the $90,000 increase. Tuck's CEO now envisions insolvency for Tuck. Tuck's CEO approaches Humbull about cancelling the deal, but Humbull refuses, reminding Tuck that Humbull has its own problems, such as finding farmland and paying off its $1.5 million debt.

An Engineered Solution: A financial engineer for Tuck investigated the special $3000 farming assessment which was given to Humbull Farms as owner of the property. The engineer learned that this farm assessment also would apply to Tuck Corporation if Tuck farmed the land or leased it to a farmer who actively farmed it. The financial engineer proposed that Tuck rent the land to Humbull with a 10-year lease providing for rent of $10,000 per year, reserving an option for Tuck to subdivide and develop portions of the land for industrial use or sale with a corresponding *pro rata* decrease in the rent. Humbull agreed since it now regained the use of nearly all of the farmland it had sold, giving it more time to find new farmland. By this strategy Tuck converted a $90,000 annual expense to a $10,000 revenue gain for a net positive value of $100,000.

Summary

Most of the tax driven deals covered in this chapter involve tax risks related to corporate securities. This was done for purposes of introducing the concepts and methods of engineering tax-driven deals. As the last tax deals in the chapter show, the imaginative application of financial engineering techniques can be used to manage tax risks in many other areas directly related to the business investment. A financial engineer looks for the opportunity to apply his or her skills in any business situation which arises, especially in new situations or in situations overlooked by others.

There is a wide variety of types of taxes which create risks which can be effectively managed. An analysis of all such taxes is beyond the scope of this chapter. The reader should be aware that the opportunities for tax risk management are expanded from time to time by the continuous creation and modification of the various types of taxes. These opportunities are expanded further by the fact that every type of business deal, large or small, has tax ramifications.

The best financial engineers develop methods to identify the tax risks in a deal. They learn how to discover the alternative methods of accomplishing the deal and to evaluate the relative tax consequences of the alternatives. Finally, they learn how to incorporate in their analysis other nontax risks which arise and which must be managed. With so many variables, this leaves the financial engineer of tax-driven deals in a most exciting environment—one in which his or her effectiveness is limited only by his or her diligence, knowledge, experience, intelligence and creativity.

References & Suggested Reading

Barnea, A., R. A. Haugen and L. W. Senbet. "An Equilibrium Analysis of Debt Financing Under Costly Tax Arbitrage and Agency Problems," *Journal of Finance*, 36(3) (1981), pp. 569-581.

Dammon, R. M. and R. C. Green. "Tax Arbitrage and the Existence of Equilibrium Prices for Financial Assets," *Journal of Finance*, 42(5) (1987), pp. 1143-1166.

Givoly, D. and A. Ovadia. "Year-End Tax-Induced Sales and Stock Market Seasonality," *Journal of Finance*, 38(1) (1983), pp. 171-185.

Heaton, H. "On the Possible Tax-Driven Arbitrage Opportunities in the New Municipal Bond Futures Contract," *Journal of Futures Markets*, 8(3) (1988), pp. 291-302.

Hochman, S. and O. Palmon. "A Tax-Induced Clientele for Index -Linked Corporate Bonds," *Journal of Finance*, 43(5) (1988), pp. 1257-1263.

Lakonishok, J. and T. Vermaelen. "Tax-Induced Trading Around Ex-Dividend Days," *Journal of Financial Economics*, 16(3) (1986), pp. 287-319.

Litzenberger, R. H. and K. Ramaswamy. "Dividends, Short Selling Restrictions, Tax-Induced Investor Clienteles and Market Equilibrium," *Journal of Finance*, 35(2) (1980), pp. 469-482.

Miller, E. "Tax-Induced Bias in Markets for Futures Contracts," *Financial Review*, 15(2) (1980), pp. 35-38.

Robichek, A. A. and W. D. Niebuhr. "Tax-Induced Bias in Reported Treasury Yields," *Journal of Finance*, 25(5) (1970), pp. 1081-1090.

Schaefer, S. M. "Tax-Induced Clientele Effects in the Market for British Government Securities: Placing Bounds on Security Values in an Incomplete Market," *Journal of Financial Economics*, 10(2) (1982), pp. 121-159.

Chapter 25

Miscellaneous Equity-Based Strategies

Overview

In this chapter, we examine certain equity-based strategies developed by financial engineers over the last few decades. We also examine the purpose and the logic underlying these strategies. Specifically, we will consider dividend capture strategies, whole-market investing, asset allocation, portfolio insurance, program trading, and unbundling of stocks. Not all of these strategies have been successful and many are controversial but they all are products of industrious financial engineers and each is an example of the potential of the discipline to change the face of modern financial practice.

For the most part, this chapter has been structured to allow the individual chapter sections to be read independently. The exception is the section on asset allocation which should be read before the section dealing with portfolio insurance. The reader is expected to be familiar with the conceptual tools and the instruments that were discussed in Chapters 4 through 19.

Dividend Capture Strategies

Dividend capture strategies became a major contributor to stock market volume in the United States during the 1980s. On some days, dividend capture strategies could explain 30 percent or more of total trading volume on the New York Stock Exchange.

There are several different types of dividend capture strategies. We will briefly consider two of them. One involves dividend capture motivated by U.S. tax law and the other involves dividend capture motivated by Japanese law. We will examine the U.S. tax law motivated cases first.

Under current U.S. tax law, a recipient corporation that owns less than 20 percent of the equity of another corporation is entitled to a 70 percent exclusion of dividend income it receives from the paying corporation. If the recipient corporation owns less than 80 percent but at least 20 percent of the equity of the paying corporation, then the recipient corporation is entitled to an 80 percent dividend exclusion. Finally, if the recipient corporation owns 80 percent or more of the equity of the paying corporation, then the recipient corporation is entitled to a 100 percent dividend exclusion. This explains why some of the cases examined elsewhere in this book used an 80 percent dividend exclusion while others used a rate of 70 percent.

The dividend exclusion is the key to some dividend capture strategies. If we ignore certain legal requirements, we can readily see that a corporation could earn a dividend by purchasing another corporation's stock just before the stock's ex-dividend date and then selling the stock just after the ex-dividend date. All other things being equal, the stock price declines by the amount of the dividend on the ex-dividend date. Thus, the strategy results in dividend income and an equivalent capital loss. The dividends received would be 70 percent excludable from the recipient corporation's taxable income and the capital loss could be used to offset other capital gains of the firm.

To prevent the dividend exclusion rules from being abused, the law requires, as noted in Chapter 24, that the stock be held for a minimum of 46 days to qualify for the dividend exclusion. (Another example of the regulatory dialectic.) This holding period requirement exposes the purchasing corporation to considerable price risk. That is, the market value of the stock might change unfavorably during the holding period, resulting in a loss on the position.

The corporation, however, can get around this problem by employing hedging instruments and hedging techniques to make the positions almost riskless. It is easiest to do this by hedging the stock in stock options. We demonstrated in Chapter 23 that we can synthesize a position in an underlying asset by an appropriate combination of call options and put option on the underlying asset and a risk-free bond. For example, suppose that Ford Motor Company purchases the stock of IBM just before IBM goes ex-dividend. Ford is required to hold the IBM stock for 46 days, so it constructs a synthetic short position in IBM stock by writing calls, purchasing puts, and shorting the risk-free bond. The options used in the strategy are as near-to-the-money as possible.

Variations of this strategy might employ just call options or just put options in which the corporation uses the option deltas as the hedge ratios. This strategy, however, requires dynamic hedging in the sense that the sizes of the option positions must be periodically adjusted to reflect changing deltas. If properly monitored, these strategies can be nearly risk free. Alternatively, the corporation could hedge only the downside risk by purchasing real or synthetic puts in a 1-to-1 ratio to the number of shares held.

Now let's consider dividend capture motivated by Japanese law. Again, the purpose of the dividend capture strategy is to convert capital gain income into dividend income. This was important to Japanese pension funds during the 1980s because of a quirk in Japanese pension law. Pension programs in Japan were required to pay pensioners from current income (dividends and interest) as opposed to capital gain income. The motivation was, perhaps, to discourage pension programs from "trading the market" in search of short-term gains and, instead, to concentrate on long-term investment. During the 1980s, the pension funds, which held large portfolios of common stocks (both Japanese and American), experienced an unprecedented increase in the value of their portfolios. This was a consequence of the broadly based and prolonged bull market in equities in both countries. As a result, the pension funds reaped extraordinary capital gain income.

As nice as capital gain income is, it was not the form of income needed by the Japanese pension funds. The problem then became one of converting the gains to other forms of income. Securities settlement practices in the United States made this possible. Specifically, in the United States, stock transactions normally settle five business days following the transaction date. That is, the purchaser of stock becomes the legal owner of the stock for all corporate purposes five business days after he or she buys it. This can be regarded as the normal delivery period for *spot* transactions in stock in the U.S. But the rules also allow for transactions made on a special seller's option. A seller's option allows the seller of the security to specify, at the time of the transaction, a delivery period either shorter or longer than the normal five days. This is the key to understanding this type of dividend capture. Before demonstrating this, however, we need to review the normal dividend payment process.

The dividend decision—consisting of the amount of the dividend to be paid, the form the dividend will take, and the date the dividend will be paid—is made by the board of directors after consideration of input provided by shareholder representatives and financial officers of the corporation. The board of directors will declare a per share dividend, the date the dividend is to be paid (**dividend payment date**) and the **holder-of-record date** for purposes of determining who is entitled to receive the dividend. The actual date the dividend is announced is called the **dividend declaration date**.

The holder-of-record date is the key to understanding who gets the dividend. Only those holders of the corporation's stock on the holder-of-record date will be entitled to receive the dividend on the dividend payment date. But, to be a holder of record, one must have purchased the stock at least five business days prior to the holder-of-record date with normal five-day settlement. If the stock was purchased four days (or less) before the holder-of-record date, then the purchaser is *not* a holder of record on the holder-of-record date and is not entitled to receive the dividend on the dividend payment date.

To keep things fair, the dividend is removed from the stock, for trading purpose, four business days prior to the holder-of-record date. That is, the stock price is **marked down** by the amount of the dividend to be paid four days prior to the holder-of-record date. The mark-down day is called the **ex-dividend date.** Thus, an investor who purchases the stock before the ex-dividend date is entitled to receive the dividend and pays for this entitlement in the price of the stock. An investor who buys the stock on or after the ex-dividend date is not entitled to receive the dividend but that is all right because the investor pays a reduced price. These relationships are best illustrated diagrammatically. Exhibit 25.1 depicts the sequence of flows in terms of days.

Notice that the board of directors declares the dividend and announces its size several weeks before the payment date. This is

Exhibit 25.1
Stock Dividends: Relevant Dates

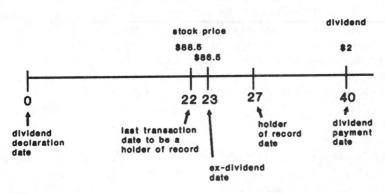

Time (in business days)

to give those who own the stock but who do not want to receive the dividend and those who do not own the stock but who do want to receive the dividend a chance to adjust their positions. The payment date is usually anywhere from three weeks to seven weeks after the declaration date. In the exhibit, the holder-of-record date occurs 27 business days after the declaration date. The actual dividend payment date is day 40. Now notice that a buyer of the stock on day 22 is a holder of record on day 27 but a buyer on day 23 is not a holder of record on day 27.

We are now ready to explain the dividend capture strategy. A Japanese pension fund learns that XYZ Corporation is going to pay a $2 per share dividend to holders of record on day 27. The Japanese fund identifies several multimillion share institutional holders of XYZ stock. The day before the ex-dividend date, XYZ stock happens to be priced at 88½. The Japanese fund approaches each institutional holder of XYZ stock with the following offer: The Japanese fund will buy the stock from the institution for 88½ on a normal settlement *on the condition that the institution will immediately buy the stock back for a price of 86⅜ on a six-day seller's option.* Thus, the purchase and sale are made simultaneously but with the purchase made on a normal five-day settlement and the sale made on a seller's option six-day settlement. Structurally, this two-part transaction is not much different from the repos often executed in the debt markets, although the motivation is quite different.

What is the effect of the transactions? The answer is simple and neat. The institutional seller keeps its stock but is not a holder of record on the holder-of-record date. The seller earns 2⅛ on the transaction (sale at 88½ and repurchase at 86⅜). The seller is not a holder of record for purposes of the dividend because it sold five business days before the holder-of-record date and the repurchase does not make it a holder of record again until six days later. Thus, the only day it is not a holder of record is on the holder-of-record date. The Japanese fund, on the other hand, is a holder of record *on the holder-of-record date and only on the holder-of-record date*. The Japanese pension fund is therefore entitled to receive the dividend of $2. Of course, it also suffers a capital loss of $2⅛. The capital loss offsets a portion of the capital gains on its portfolio from the run up in stock values and transforms those gains into dividend income that can be used to pay the pensioners, as required by Japanese law.

Both firms benefit from this transaction. The Japanese firm gets the conversion it needs and the American institutional investor makes a quick and riskless ⅛ point ($2⅛ gain less $2 divided) Of course, the transaction results in a cost to the Japanese firm equal to the ⅛ the American firm makes (and any transaction costs involved). But the need for the conversion justifies the cost.

An interesting feature of the two transactions that are involved in a dividend capture play is that the sale can actually appear on the official transaction tape before the purchase. It merely depends on which typist is the fastest. When the strategy first appeared and was not yet understood by the tape watchers, the transaction prices seemed, not surprisingly, bizarre.

The financial engineers that developed and executed these strategies worked for institutional brokerage firms that derived commissions from the deals. On these very large transactions, such commissions would typically be in the range of one cent to three cents per share.

Whole-Market Investing

The term **whole-market investing** was coined in 1983 by one of the authors of this book.[1] It describes an investment strategy designed to track the *whole market*, as defined by some proxy index. For this reason, it is sometimes described as **index investing.** Most often, the index of choice is the S&P 500, but it can just as easily be the Dow Jones Industrial Average (DJIA), the New York Stock Exchange Composite Index (NYSE Index), or any other well-defined index the investor chooses.

The logic underlying whole market investing grows out of efficient market theory. Efficient market theory, you will recall, holds that competitive markets continuously price assets efficiently. By efficiently, we simply mean correctly—i.e., prices accurately reflect all relevant available information. If markets are truly efficient, then the most elaborate and painstaking efforts to outperform the market, through technical or fundamental analysis of prices, can only be successful by pure chance. And, indeed, the efforts are less than likely to be successful when the transaction costs associated with an active management strategy are taken into consideration. This argument is supported by a number of well-documented studies which demonstrated that mutual funds that attempt to outperform the popular market averages (the usual yardstick of performance) are successful less than 50 percent of the time.[2] When adjusted for different degrees of systematic risk, they are successful even less often.

Reasoning that it is difficult, if not impossible, to consistently outperform an unmanaged index and that it is resource wasteful to try to do so—as a consequence of paying for analysts and absorbing transaction costs and management fees—some portfolio managers decided it was better to structure an equities fund to mimic the index. Structuring a fund in this way is a rather elementary example of financial engineering but one that has proven hugely successful. The engineer, a portfolio manager in this case, includes the same stocks in the fund as are included in the target index or, alternatively, picks stocks with similar betas and similar capitalizations to accomplish the same purpose. The engineering involved is a basic application of portfolio theory. Over time, such a fund should produce a return nearly perfectly correlated with that of the unmanaged index. Such funds have, in general, tracked the target indexes very well and have attracted many billions of dollars of investment.

The next step in the evolution of whole-market investing occurred in 1982 with the introduction of the first stock-index futures contract. These contracts made it possible to hold a single leveraged instrument whose performance, by design, would be perfectly correlated with the index on which it was written.[3] As leveraged instruments, these contracts gave the whole-market investor an opportunity to take leveraged speculative positions on the direction of the market at very small transaction costs and to play the market for the first time on the short side with the same ease as the long side. The downside, however, is that index futures are not a dividend source as are index funds.

The next step in the evolution of whole-market investing involved the introduction of stock-index options. These instruments made their appearance in 1983. The introduction of index options gave the whole-market investor the opportunity to employ considerable leverage, like futures, but to strictly limit downside risk. The first index options were written on index futures. Subsequently, cash settlement options written on the index itself were introduced. These soon supplanted the options on index futures and have been enormously successful in terms of trading volume.

Asset Allocation

Asset allocation has become an important topic area in investment analysis and a great deal of financial engineering talent has been devoted to it. In brief, asset allocation involves the distribution of funds among major classes of assets. It differs from traditional portfolio analysis in that the latter is primarily concerned with the behavior of return on a combination of individual assets *within* a given class of assets. Thus, portfolio analysis deals with the mix of stocks in a stock portfolio, the mix of bonds in a bond portfolio, and so forth. Asset allocation, on the other hand, involves the allocation of assets among portfolios of domestic stocks, bonds, money market instruments, real estate, foreign equities, and foreign bonds. In a very real sense, asset allocation often treats classes of assets (i.e., portfolios of assets) as though they were individual assets.

Asset allocation has its root in evidence developed during the 1980s that showed that different asset classes exhibit different risk/reward behaviors.[4] Some classes produce superior returns under certain states of the world and others produce superior returns under other states of the world. This evidence conflicts with the efficient markets hypothesis that gained favor in the 1970s. This is not to say that markets are not informationally efficient, only that, historically, they were not as informationally efficient as once believed.

By using regression and optimization techniques, asset allocators seek to discover which classes of assets perform better under which states of the world. They then shift funds between the classes to give more weight to those classes expected to perform better. The financial engineer plays two roles in asset allocation. First, the engineer must uncover historic patterns of behavior for the different classes of assets. Second, the engineer must devise a strategy to exploit these behaviors.

As with portfolio managers, some assets allocators are very conservative and others very aggressive. Some pursue relatively passive strategies and others pursue relatively aggressive strategies. Some asset allocation strategies are very judgmental in nature while others are very mechanistic. The mechanistic asset allocation strategies are often described as **dynamic asset allocation strategies**. The best known of these are those asset allocation strategies that (1) shift funds between stock and bond portfolios on the basis of historic patterns of performance, and (2) portfolio insurance strategies.

Families of no-load mutual funds, offering both stock funds and bond funds, usually allow investors to shift rapidly between these classes of assets, without becoming bogged down in such issues as which individual stocks and which individual bonds to include in the portfolio. Thus, the portfolio managers concentrate on which stocks to include in the stock and bond funds while the asset allocator concentrates on the mix between the stock fund and the bond fund.

In a statistical sense, the goal of asset allocation is to change the distribution of returns. This objective is most clearly visible in that dynamic asset allocation strategy called portfolio insurance. We consider portfolio insurance next.

Portfolio Insurance

Portfolio insurance is probably the most talked about of the dynamic asset allocation strategies. It was the early 1980s brainchild of two academicians.[5] In brief, the strategy attempts to assure a minimum rate of return on a portfolio without foreclosing on the opportunity to benefit from favorable movements in the markets.

The concept of portfolio insurance was first developed and applied in the management of pension portfolios. In pension portfolios, the beneficiaries can be divided into two distinct groups: those who have already retired and those who are still active (working). The retired workers (pensioners) are promised a nominal return and this is assured by immunizing the portfolio that will provide the promised future benefits. Cash flow matching or duration matching can be used for this purpose. This is a straightforward application of the asset/liability management techniques discussed in Chapter 20. The active workers, on the other hand, are promised a real rate of return. This is formulated as an **actuarial interest rate** and is used as the **target rate of return** by the asset allocators.

The asset allocator must earn the target rate as a minimum but a superior return is preferred. This calls for a strategy in which there is positive probability of earning returns above the actuarial target but zero probability that returns will fall below the actuarial target. This is depicted graphically in Exhibit 25.2.

Exhibit 25.2
Payoff Profile: Portfolio Insurance

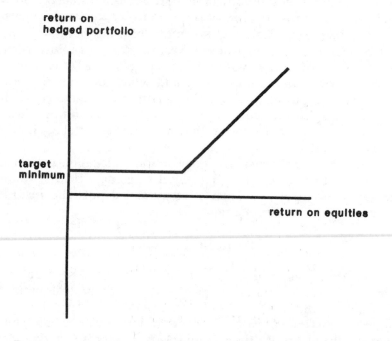

From our earlier examination of multiperiod options, it becomes apparent that the portfolio strategy involves replicating a payoff profile that is analogous to an interest rate floor. If our examination of financial engineering to this point has done nothing else, it has surely made it plain that any given payoff profile can be created in many different ways and this is certainly true of portfolio insurance.

One solution is to hold a portfolio of stocks or bonds and to buy put options on that portfolio. Another solution is to buy and hold riskless assets, such as T-bills, and to buy call options on a stock portfolio. Still another solution, and the one most frequently advocated, is to employ a dynamic asset allocation strategy which moves between stocks and T-bills. For example, suppose that T-bills return 8 percent and that the target rate for the portfolio is 3 percent. Now suppose that the asset allocator initially invests entirely in stocks. As it happens, the stock market declines by 5 percent within a few days. The asset allocator would now sell the stocks and use the proceeds to purchase T-bills. The T-bills can be held for the rest of the year and the portfolio manager achieves the required 3 percent return (8 percent less 5 percent).[6] At this point he returns to stocks— i.e., sells the T-bills and purchases equities. Suppose that, this time, the stocks rally over the next year by 20 percent with no significant interim pullbacks. Then the pension fund benefits fully from this move. If, on the other hand, the stocks decline again, then the asset allocator moves back to T-bills.

In a rising equities market, portfolio insurance will generally employ what is often described in other contexts as **trailing stops**. That is, the strategy might require liquidation of stocks after a 5 percent decline from any new high. Thus, with each new high achieved in the rising market, the trigger price for the portfolio insurance strategy rises as well. The strategy effectively replicates the payoff profile of the options alternative and is, therefore, appropriately viewed as a synthetic option.

There is one critical consideration we have ignored and this is transaction costs. Transaction costs consist of both explicit commissions and implicit market impact cost (one gets the bid price when one sells and pays the ask price when one purchases). These transaction costs can be considerable when a manager repeatedly liquidates and reacquires a diversified portfolio of stocks.

The solution to the transaction cost problem is to *keep* the portfolio of stocks and to sell a risk-equivalent number of stock-index futures contracts. The stock index futures contracts represent a hedge on the stock portfolio and explains why this approach to portfolio insurance is sometimes referred to as **dynamic hedging**. That is, after the market has declined by the specified percentage to trigger stock sales, the asset allocator sells a sufficient quantity of stock index futures to fully hedge the portfolio of stocks. This removes the risk of a further market decline but preserves the dividend flow from the stocks. As we will argue in the next section, if all assets are efficiently priced, the hedged stock portfolio should produce the risk-free (T-bill) rate. This strategy is considered superior to selling the stocks and buying the T-bills because transaction costs in liquid futures are much smaller—as a percentage of underlying value—than transaction costs in stocks.

The attractiveness of the portfolio insurance strategy was readily evident to managers of pension portfolios and many quickly became converts to dynamic asset allocation. Rather than attempt to manage the complex mathematics themselves, however, most chose to turn over the asset allocation function to outside managers. In this way, the pension fund portfolio manager could concentrate on what he or she did best—i.e., pick stocks to include in the portfolio—without concern for the portfolio insurance operation going on behind the scenes. Indeed, many portfolio managers felt it best that they not even know what the asset allocator was doing lest it bias his or her own stock selection decisions.

Portfolio insurance quickly became a mainstay service of investment bankers and competing private portfolio insurance operators. By the time of the 1987 stock market crash, estimates are that portfolio insurance strategies covered somewhere between sixty and eighty billion dollars of underlying stocks.

The flaw in portfolio insurance strategies only materializes when (1) a sufficiently large base of stock portfolios are similarly covered by this strategy, and (2) the equities market has experienced a prolong rise in value. The latter assures that all equity-based pension portfolios will be fully invested in equities. When these two conditions are simultaneously satisfied, then a sufficiently large decline in the equities market, for whatever reason, can trigger a wave of sales of stock index futures by portfolio insurers. This wave of sales can become so massive that futures prices drop to a significant discount to the value of the underlying stocks. This has two related effects. First, it means that many portfolio insurers will sell futures at the worst possible time—when the price is below its true equilibrium. Second, the discrepancy between fair value and market price will trigger another type of market activity sometimes described as **program trading** but more accurately described as **cash/futures arbitrage**. (We consider program trading in the next section.)

The portfolio insurance in place during the market collapse in October 1987 has received much of the blame for the depth and the breadth of that decline. The argument is that, by selling stock index futures into a declining market, the portfolio insurers exacerbated the market decline. The issue has been thoroughly studied in academic circles, market circles, and regulatory circles but universal agreement as to the extent of the impact has not yet been reached. Undoubtedly, however, portfolio insurance, with its policy of selling into a declining market, can only have served to amplify the speed at which the markets fell with concomitant losses for many of the pension funds employing the strategy. For many, portfolio insurance has been discredited—but this too is not universally agreed.

It is worth considering why portfolio insurance strategies might not work properly in rapidly declining markets. In theory, portfolio insurance requires a continuous distribution of market returns with instantaneous asset allocation adjustments as the market declines. But, markets actually move in discrete price jumps. When these jumps are small, portfolio insurance will work well. When the jumps are large, as they were during the market crash of October 1987, portfolio insurance will not work well and may fail completely to protect against losses. One must also expect that there will be a cost to this form of protection. Portfolio insurance seeks to replicate a put option. Real put options can be purchased at a cost known as the premium. The synthetic puts known as portfolio insurance should also be expected to be costly but their cost is much more difficult to assess. As with real puts, the cost of synthetic puts will be higher during volatile market periods.

Program Trading

Program trading means different things to different people and a number of different activities pass under the umbrella of the program-trading label. Some, for example, include portfolio insurance when talking about program trading and others include computer-driven technical trading systems. The generally accepted meaning, however, is cash/futures arbitrage in the stock market. This is the definition we are using here. In this form of trading, the trader buys stock index futures and sells stocks *or* sells stock-index futures and buys stocks when the price discrepancy between the cash and futures instruments is sufficiently great to provide a riskless return in excess of the riskless rate—after allowing for transaction costs. We have touched on program trading at several other points in this book but we have never looked at it in detail.

Program trading was developed by quantitatively sophisticated financial engineers—the classic "quant jocks" to whom we have referred many times.

Program trading was made possible by the introduction of stock-index futures, which occurred in 1982 when the Kansas City Board of Trade introduced a futures contract on the Value Line Composite Index. This was followed by futures contracts on the Standard & Poor's 500 Index and New York Stock Exchange Composite Index, and, later, by the Major Market Index—a surrogate for the Dow Jones Industrial Average. (The different methods for calculating stock indexes are discussed in an appendix to this chapter.)

The trick to understanding program trading is the pricing relationship between the futures price and the underlying spot index. The stocks that make up the index provide a return in the form of a dividend. This aggregate dividend can be expressed as a periodic dividend rate denoted $d(t,T)$. This dividend rate is the aggregate dividend payable between time t and time T stated as a percentage of the spot index price. We assume that the program trader can both borrow and lend at the risk-free rate (not completely unrealistic for the well-heeled players in the game). This periodic rate is denoted $r(t,T)$. The current value of the spot index is denoted $I(t)$ and the futures price at time t for the futures contract that matures at time T is denoted $F(t,T)$. Ignoring transaction costs, the arbitrage logic discussed in Chapter 23 dictates that the fair futures price is given by Equation 25.1.

$$F(t,T) = I(t)[1 + r(t,T) - d(t,T)] \qquad (25.1)$$

The logic of Equation 25.1 is as follows. The futures price at time T, denoted $F(T,T)$, will be settled in cash for the value of the index $I(T)$. Thus, they must converge. Because they must converge, the difference between the two can only be explained by the cost of carry. In this case, the cost of carry is the difference between the cost of the funds necessary to buy the underlying index, $r(t,T)$, and the dividend rate the index portfolio will return, $d(t,T)$. As the value $T - t$ grows shorter, the cost of carry, $r(t,T) - d(t,T)$, gets smaller until it completely vanishes at time T. This relationship is depicted graphically in Exhibit 25.3 on the assumption that there is no change in the spot index (for ease of representation).

The trading strategy dictated by this relationship follows directly. If the actual futures price exceeds the fair futures price, sell the futures and buy the spot index. If the actual futures price is below the fair futures price, sell the index (short) and buy the fu-

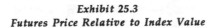

Exhibit 25.3
Futures Price Relative to Index Value

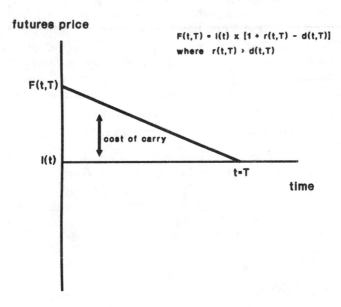

tures. If it is this simple, however, why do we need the quant jocks? The answer is that there is no "spot index" to buy or sell. The spot index is itself nothing more than a mathematical construct. One cannot buy the index, one can only buy the underlying stocks. The quant jock's job is to identify a set of stocks and a set of weightings representing a portfolio of stocks that can be quickly bought or sold and which possess the property that they, collectively, mimic the spot index. The simplest such portfolio to visualize is the set of stocks and the weights that are employed in the index itself. But, this set will not necessarily provide the most profitable opportunity. Thus, the program trader is continuously searching for a stock basket. Once identified, the basket must be acquired in its entirety very quickly with simultaneous transactions in futures. Consider this basket of stocks a "unit" of stock index.

The program trading strategy is complicated by the presence of transaction costs. That is, the purchase (or sale) of stocks and the sale (or purchase) of futures involves some transaction costs. This will include the market impact cost associated with executing the orders at market to ensure that they are indeed acquired very quickly. Transaction costs are minimized by employing a computer-based order-matching system. To date, the order-matching system of choice has been the **designated order turnaround (DOT) system** maintained by the New York Stock Exchange. As efficient as the DOT system is, however, it does not completely eliminate transaction costs. The transaction costs will be positive whether or not the program trader is the seller or purchaser of futures. Thus, in the presence of transaction costs, denoted by C, Equation 25.1 becomes 25.2.

$$F(t,T) = I(t)[1 + r(t,T) - d(t,T)] \pm C \qquad (25.2)$$

Equation 25.2 gives rise to a **no arbitrage window.** This window is depicted in Exhibit 25.4. As long as the futures price remains within the window, no profitable arbitrage is possible. When the futures price rises above the window, however, futures are sold and stocks are purchased. When the futures price drops below the window, futures are purchased and stocks are sold.

Exhibit 25.4
Program Trading: The No-Arbitrage Window

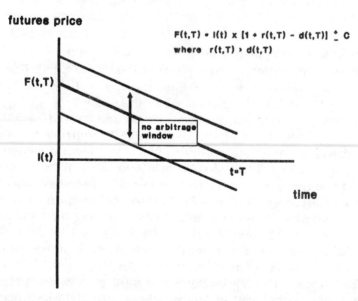

Program trading is practiced on such a wide scale that any opportunity for riskless profits quickly triggers massive movements of capital into or out of the stock market. For example, it is not unusual for billions of dollars to move in just a few minutes. This is often accompanied by a very sharp movement in equity prices and creates the appearance, at least, of increased equity-price volatility. It is now quite commonplace for sharp equity price movements to be "explained" in the financial press by the activities of the program trader.

Many people associate increased price volatility with a lessening of market efficiency. Others equate increased price volatility with manipulative speculation and conclude that program trading makes profits for large institutions at the expense of the small investor. Given these images, it is not surprising that program trading has received a great deal of criticism from many quarters—including some regulatory and some legislative bodies.

The bad press which program trading received led many brokerage firms to suspend their own program trading operations. This move was taken to preserve their goodwill with their customer base. Nevertheless, many brokerage firms have come back to program trading and the academic community, in general, is in accord with this decision.

It is hard to understand why program trading—a classic, although quantitatively complex, form of arbitrage—should decrease cash market efficiency when similar forms of arbitrage in other markets have been shown to increase price efficiency in those markets.[7] Indeed, to believe that program trading destabilizes stock prices flies in the face of an overwhelming body of sound scientific evidence.[8] How then can we explain the apparent increase in price volatility?

The evidence to date suggests that any increase in cash price volatility attributable to program trading is short-lived. That is, price changes measured over short periods of time (say fifteen minute intervals) are more extreme now than they were before the advent of program trading. At the same time, however, cash price changes measured over longer periods of time (say several days or a week) are no more volatile today than they were before the advent of program trading. Finally, it has been shown that stock-index futures prices lead the spot index by from fifteen to thirty minutes.[9] All of this evidence is consistent with an environment in which futures prices reflect information more quickly than the spot index and in which the value of information is transmitted to the underlying stocks via program trading.

There are several plausible explanations for why futures prices might respond more quickly than the underlying index to new information. One possibility is that the spot index cannot fully reflect the effects of new information until all the stocks in the index have had an opportunity to trade. But relatively few individual stocks are as liquid as the leading stock index futures. Thus, the delay in the trading of the individual stocks introduces a delay in the spot index's ability to reflect information. This argument is called the **nonsynchronous trading argument.** Another possible explanation is based on transaction costs. There is no doubt that a "unit" of the spot index is considerably more costly to trade than is a unit of stock index futures. Thus, transacting on information is more cost effective in futures than in stocks. We would expect that information traders would be cost driven to trade the futures rather than the stocks. Finally, there is the possibility that it may be easier to determine the market value of new information than the individual stock value of that same information. If so, traders would be tempted to register their opinions in the futures market first.

Whatever the explanation(s), the end result is that futures prices respond to new information more quickly than stock prices and this differential speed of response shows up as greater price volatility in index futures than in stocks. It also gives rise to price discrepancies between cash stocks and stock index futures. When a price discrepancy develops, program traders move to exploit it. By simultaneously buying (selling) the index futures and selling (buying) the underlying stocks, program traders cause the stock values and futures prices to pull closer together—a natural consequence of all arbitrage. This, in turn, transmits the informational value *and* the information-induced volatility to the spot index by way of the cash stocks. The equities market then experiences the increased volatility. Importantly, the stocks would, in time, fully reflect the value of information even in the absence of futures. The existence of futures merely speeds up the process. In the end, we experience an increase in short-run efficiency and an increase in short-run volatility. The longer-run, however, is largely unaffected.

Resource allocation in a market economy is guided by prices. It therefore follows that more efficient prices should lead to more efficient allocation of resources. This is a powerful argument in favor of allowing program trading to continue and, indeed, encouraging it. It also suggests that efforts to introduce various types of circuit breakers, such as trading halts and suspension of the DOT system, are misguided. It also argues against changes in the current margining system used in index futures trading.

The real problem with program trading concerns how it interacts with other forms of mechanized trading. In particular, program trading can easily interact with portfolio insurance strategies and technical trading systems. It is generally accepted that the interplay, although completely unintentional, between these various forms of trading has the potential to increase the magnitude of normal market adjustments and to cause these adjustments to go to extremes. Many consider this the explanation for the events of October 1987. According to this scenario, a deterioration in the **economic fundamentals** ended the longstanding bull market in stocks in August of 1987. This led to **topping action** in the eyes of technicians, who sold stocks and futures in response. The decline in stocks and futures triggered the portfolio insurers to sell large quantities of stock index futures. These sales caused a gap to open between stock index futures and cash stocks. The program traders then sold stocks and bought futures. This aggressive selling of stocks drove stock prices lower and reinforced the opinions of the technicians and the portfolio insurers, who then sold more futures. In the end, the selling pressure got out of hand and panic set in. While the validity of this scenario will long be debated, it undoubtedly contains elements of truth.

Unbundling Stocks

The success that financial engineers had with conversion arbitrage in the mortgage market, when they created multiclass mortgaged-backed instruments, such as CMOs, from single-class mortgages and passthroughs, and in the T-bond market, with the creation of zeros from conventional coupon bonds, led some of these innovators to look for ways to engineer value through the conversion of equity. One approach, generally regarded as a failure, was to try to decompose common stock into several distinct instruments. This decomposition of common stock is sometimes called **unbundling**. The concept was developed at Shearson Lehman in late 1988. In December of that year, a number of leading corporations, including American Express, Dow Chemical, Pfizer, and Sara Lee, attempted such a conversion.

In the unbundling process, a unit of common stock is transformed into three separate securities, a thirty-year bond that pays a fixed coupon equal to the stock's current dividend rate, a share of preferred stock that pays no initial dividend but which will pay a sum equal to any increase in dividends over the current dividend on common for thirty years, and an equity appreciation certificate which would pay its holder a sum equal the amount of equity appreciation, beyond some stated amount, at the end of the thirty-year period. This unbundling is illustrated graphically in Exhibit 25.5.

Exhibit 25.5
Unbundled Stock Unit

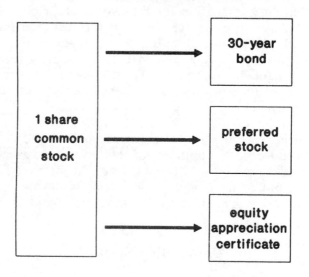

From the investor's perspective, the collective cash flows of the instruments created from the unbundling are identical to the cash flows associated with the common stock from which it is created. There are, however, several potential sources of added value. First, the individual components may appeal to investors to whom the stock units, as a whole, do not appeal in much the same way that the zeros created from a conventional bond can be more attractive than the conventional bond from which the zeros are created. The second source of value is one involving tax asymmetries. The dividends payable on the stock units are not tax deductible for corporate tax purposes. The interest obligation on the bond, however, is deductible. Thus, the after-tax cost of the bond component is less than the after-tax cost of a dividend of the same size. Finally, it was also argued that, with fewer shares outstanding, reportable earnings per share would be enhanced. This last argument however was debatable and eventually killed by the SEC which ruled that earnings per share must be calculated on the basis of all shares—whether whole or unbundled.

If unbundled stocks offered potential value enhancements, why did Shearson's experiment fail? There are several possible explanations. First, the stocks themselves had well-established markets and plenty of liquidity. It was not at all certain that this would be the case for the individual component securities. Second, the move sought to replace voting shares with nonvoting securities. Thus, the right to vote on matters of interest to the shareholders would be lost with the unbundled securities.

Voting rights are an important issue. It has been argued that voting rights have certain option characteristics.[10] When management is doing a good job, voting rights have little value because it would be silly to vote management out or to approve major changes in the firm's structure or businesses that management did not desire. But, voting rights have great value when management is performing poorly since voting rights grant the shareholders the opportunity to replace management or to dispose of the firm as they, in their collective wisdom, see fit. Thus, voting rights can have a positive value but never a negative value and, in this sense, are similar to options.

By not including voting rights among the unbundled securities, the conversion lost one of the sources of a stock's value and this, together with the liquidity concerns, might be sufficient to explain the poor reception unbundling received. On the other hand, this problem cannot be alleviated without a change in the law governing voting rights. Under most current state laws, voting rights cannot be separated from equity. There are precedents, however. In Germany, Switzerland, and some other European nations nonvoting equities, called **participation certificates**, do trade. And there are precedents for separate trading of voting rights. Such a situation occurred in France when the government privatized some industries. Nevertheless, any challenge to the traditional one-share-one-vote rule runs into immediate resistance.

Summary

Financial engineers have developed a number of equity-based strategies over the past decade. Some of these strategies are extensions of old themes while others serve altogether new and different purposes. We discussed a few of these strategies.

Dividend capture strategies, of which there are several types, are used to convert capital gain income into dividend income. In some cases, this conversion is motivated by the dividend exclusion rules in U.S. tax law. In these cases, the stock is purchased prior to the ex-dividend date and disposed of after the ex-dividend date. The stock must be held for a required period of time and, during this time, it is hedged. In other cases, the conversion is motivated by a quirk in Japanese pension law. In these cases, the strategy involves the purchase of the stock, under normal settlement, and the simultaneous sale of the stock, under extended settlement. Such a strategy is useful when one holds sizable capital gains while dividend income is, for whatever reason, preferred.

Whole-market investing, also known as index investing, is any investment strategy designed to replicate the performance of some market index. Index mutual funds were the first vehicle created for this purpose. During the last decade, index futures and index options extended the opportunities for whole-market investing. While not discussed in this chapter, equity swaps (discussed in Chapter 18) have also enhanced the opportunity for whole-market investing.

Asset allocation is the allocation of investment funds across various classes of assets. In a sense, it is portfolio theory applied on a grand scale. Many novel strategies fall under the umbrella of asset allocation including fixed income versus equity timing strategies and portfolio insurance. The latter seeks to replicate a put option on a stock portfolio by moving between stocks and risk-free assets.

Program trading, more accurately described as cash/futures arbitrage applied to stocks and stock-index futures, is a strategy that seeks to earn risk-free returns above the risk-free rate by exploiting price discrepancies between stocks and stock-index futures. Such a strategy can only work if futures and/or stocks are mispriced (rich or cheap). The basic strategy is an old one. The application to stocks, however, is new and quantitatively complex—requiring a live data feed, considerable data processing capability, and near instantaneous order execution.

The final strategy we considered is the unbundling of stock. In unbundling strategies, common stock is decomposed into a series of distinct cash flows. These include a long-maturity bond, a share of preferred stock which pays a dividend differential, and an equity appreciation certificate. Unbundling has not been received well by the markets. It is not clear, as of this writing, if this is because the bundle was mispriced or if the decomposition missed an important component—such as voting rights.

Endnotes

[1]See Marshall (1983).

[2]See, for example, Jensen (1968).

[3]This is not completely accurate. The futures price and the spot index must converge and, consequently, the correlation will not be perfect. This point has been argued in Chapter 21.

[4]There is evidence on both sides of this argument. The interested reader might want to consider Carman (1981), Chen (1987), Fong (1980), Kritzman (1980), Leibowitz (1987), Perold (1988), Sharpe (1987), and Solnik and Noetzlin (1982).

[5]See Rubinstein and Leland (1981).

[6]This is an oversimplification. After the loss of 5 percent, an 8 percent return only brings the portfolio to 102.6 percent of its original value. This is a compounding effect. The initial acceptable loss can, however, be set to adjust for this compounding effect.

[7]For a discussion of the price stabilizing effects of arbitrage and speculation in commodity markets, see Marshall (1989), Chapter 8.

[8]See, for example, Edwards (1988), Laatsche and Schwarz (1989), MacKinlay and Ramaswamy (1987), and Blume, MacKinlay and Terker (1989).

[9]Herbst, McCormack and West (1987), Cheung and Ng (1990), and Ng (1987).

[10]See Walmsley (1989).

References and Suggested Reading

Arnott, R. and F.J. Fabozzi. *Asset Allocation: A Handbook of Portfolio Policies, Strategies, and Tactics*, Chicago: Probus, 1988.

Arnott, R.D. "The Pension Sponsor's View Of Asset Allocation," *Financial Analysts Journal*, 41(5) (1985), pp. 17-19, 22-23.

Bauman, W.S. and C.H. McClaren. "An Asset Allocation Model for Active Portfolios," *Journal of Portfolio Management*, 8(2) (1982), pp. 76-86.

Benari, Y. "An Asset Allocation Paradigm," *Journal of Portfolio Management*, 14(2) (1988), pp. 47-51.

Blume, M.E., A.C. MacKinlay and B. Terker. "Order Imbalances and Stock Price Movements on October 19 and 20, 1987," *Journal of Finance*, 44 (1989), pp. 827-848.

Carman, P. "The Trouble with Asset Allocation," *Journal of Portfolio Management*, 8(1) (1981), pp. 17-22.

Chen, S. "Simple Optimal Asset Allocation under Uncertainty," *Journal of Portfolio Management*, 13(4) (1987), pp. 69-76.

Cheung, Y.W. and L.K. Ng. "The Dynamics of S&P 500 Index and S&P 500 Futures Intraday Price Volatilities," presented as the Spring Research Seminar, Chicago Board of Trade (May 1990).

Edwards, F. "Futures Trading and Cash Market Volatility: Stock Index and Interest Rate Futures, *Journal of Futures Markets*, 8 (1988), pp. 421-439.

Evnine, J. and R. Henriksson. "Asset Allocation and Options," *Journal of Portfolio Management*, 14(1) (1987), pp. 56-61.

Fong, H. Gifford. "An Asset Allocation Framework," *Journal of Portfolio Management*, 6(2) (1980), pp. 58-66.

Herbst, A.F., J. McCormack, and E. West. "Investigation of a Lead-Lag Relationship Between Spot Stock Indices and Their Futures Contracts," *Journal of Futures Markets*, 7 (1987), pp. 373-381.

Herbst, A.F., D.D. Kare, and J.F. Marshall. "A Time Varying, Convergence Adjusted Hedge Ratio Model," Working Paper (June 1990).

Jensen, M.C. "The Performance of Mutual Funds in the Period 1945-64," *Journal of Finance*, 23(2) (May 1968).

Kritzman, M. and J.C. Ryan. "A Short-Term Approach to Asset Allocation," *Journal of Portfolio Management*, 7(1) (1980), pp. 45-49.

Laatsche, F. and T. Schwarz. "Price Discovery and Risk Transfer in Stock Index Cash and Futures Markets," *Review of Futures Markets*, 7 (1989), pp. 273-289.

Leibowitz, M.L. "Liability Returns: A New Look at Asset Allocation," *Journal of Portfolio Management*, 13(2) (1987), pp. 11-18.

Leibowitz, Martin L. "Total Portfolio Duration: A New Perspective On Asset Allocation," *Financial Analysts Journal*, 42(5) (1986), pp. 18-29, 77.

MacKinlay, A.C. and K. Ramaswamy. "Index-Futures Arbitrage and the Behavior of Stock Index Futures Prices," *Review of Financial Studies*, 1 (1987), pp. 137-158.

Marshall, J.F. "New Opportunities for the Whole-Market Investor," *Review of Business*, 5(3) (Winter 1983), pp. 20-23.

Marshall, J.F. *Futures and Option Contracting: Theory and Practice*, Cincinnati: South-Western, 1989.

Ng, N. "Detecting Spot Price Forecasts in Futures Prices Using Causality Tests," *Review of Futures Markets*, 6 (1987), pp. 250-267.

Perold, A.F. and W.F. Sharpe. "Dynamic Strategies for Asset Allocation," *Financial Analysts Journal*, 44(1) (1988), pp. 16-27.

Rubinstein, M. and H. Leland. "Replicating Options with Positions in Stock and Cash," *Financial Analysts Journal*, 37 (1981).

Sharpe, W.F. "Integrated Asset Allocation," *Financial Analysts Journal*, 43(5) (1987), pp. 25-32.

Solnik, B. and B. Noetzlin. "Optimal International Asset Allocation," *Journal of Portfolio Management*, 9(1) (1982), pp. 11-21.

Walmsley, J. "Unbundling The World?" *Intermarket Magazine* (August 1989), pp. 48-49.

Appendix
The Calculation of Stock Indexes

There are a number of ways to calculate stock indexes but two are particularly common. These two are called **price weighting** and **value weighting**. Both involve arithmetic means. Also important is **geometric weighting**. The Dow Jones Industrial Average (DJIA) and the Major Market Index (MMI) are computed using price weighting. The New York Stock Exchange Composite Index (NYSE Composite) and the Standard and Poor's Index of 500 stocks (S&P 500) are examples of value weighted indexes. The Value Line Index (Value Line) is an example of a geometrically weighted index.

Price Weighting

Price weighted indexes are formed by simply summing the prices of the stocks in the index and dividing by an adjustment factor. Thus, a price weighted index (PWI) on day t is calculated as the sum of the prices on that day of the n stocks included in the index divided by some adjustment factor (AF).

$$PWI(t) = \frac{\Sigma P_i(t)}{AF}$$

Value Weighting

Value weighting is also called **capitalization weighting**. In this method, the price of each stock is multiplied by the number of outstanding shares of that stock. These products are then summed. Finally, the sum is divided by a base-period value. That is, the value weighted index (VWI) on day t is found by multiplying each stock's price on day t, denoted $P(t)$, by the number of outstanding shares, denoted $N(t)$, and then adding them all up. The sum is then divided by the base period value (BPV). Value weighting gives greater weight to more heavily capitalized companies.

$$VWI(t) = \frac{\Sigma N_i(t) \cdot P_i(t)}{BPV}$$

Geometric Weighting

Geometrically weighted stock indexes are calculated using geometric means rather than arithmetic means. That is, we form the product of all the return relatives for the n stocks included in the index. We then take the *nth* root of this product. Finally, we multiply the n'th root by the previous day's index value. For example, to calculate the geometrically weighted index (GWI) for day t, we would first divide the price of each stock on day t by its own price on day $t - 1$. These return relatives are then multiplied by each other. We then raise the product to the $1/n$ power. Finally, we multiply by GWI(t − 1).

$$GWI(t) = \left\{ \Pi \left[\frac{P_i(t)}{P_i(t-1)} \right] \right\}^{1/n} \times GWI(t-1)$$

Chapter 26

---

*Future Trends: Globalization
and Technology*

*For the financial services industry, globalization implies both a harmo-
nization of rules and a reduction of barriers that will allow for the
free flow of capital and permit all firms to compete in all markets.*[1]

Overview

The globalization of the capital markets has been driven by
technological advances in the areas of information processing and
telecommunications, the removal or liberalization of restrictions on
the cross border flow of capital, the deregulation of domestic capital
markets, the development of unregulated offshore markets, the explosive growth of derivative products that allow fluid movements
between currencies, and ever greater competition among these markets for a share of the world's transactions business. As we have
worked our way through this book we have seen how each of these
factors has helped to bring about an increasing integration of the
world's capital markets. In this chapter, we are going to briefly
recap these developments in an effort to put them in perspective.
We have included an excellent article by Christine Pavel of
Citibank (formerly of the Federal Reserve Bank of Chicago) and
John McElravey of the Federal Reserve Bank of Chicago as an appendix to this chapter. That article, which first appeared in *Economic
Perspectives* in May/June 1990, provides an excellent and detailed
examination of the globalization of the financial services industry.

We are also going to consider the developments now taking place and likely to soon take place as the globalization process continues. This involves areas of uniformity of regulation and market supervision, better access to all markets by all market participants, standardization of capital requirements, the economic integration of Europe and the opening of the U.S. banking system to interstate banking, and, finally, recent efforts to standardize the world's clearing and settlement systems. Throughout, we are going to focus our discussion on the role played by commercial and investment banks, as this is the level at which globalization is most directly felt and this is the level at which most financial engineering occurs.

The Meaning of Globalization

As the definition of globalization at the start of this chapter makes clear, **globalization** of the financial markets implies a harmonization of the rules and a reduction of the barriers that will allow the free flow of capital and permit all firms to compete in all markets. More simply put, globalization may be viewed as the increasing tendency of borrowers to ignore national boundaries when in need of financing and for lenders to ignore national boundaries when in search of attractive investment opportunities. The term **capital market integration** is sometimes used in lieu of the term globalization. (The term *capital market integration,* however, is often used more narrowly.)

There are those who view capital market integration as a step on the road to a universal currency and a single global capital market. Early efforts in this direction, which had limited applicability, were the SDR (special drawing rights) of the World Bank, and the ECU (European currency unit) of the European Economic Community or EEC. The single-currency global capital market yearnings are consistent with the modern view of our world as a global village. Despite these yearnings, however, a truly universal capital market is, at best, decades away and may, for political reasons, never fully develop. But partial integration, in which one can raise capital in many markets and move freely between currencies without exchange rate risk, is already here. The Euromarkets, for example, allow firms domiciled in one country to raise long-term capital in another country and to convert the currency denomination of that capital into any of a great number of other currencies without engendering exchange rate risk, if coupled with appropriately structured swaps. Shorter-term financial needs can be met in a similar fashion but can use futures and forwards instead of swaps to achieve the necessary conversions.

As far as capital market integration has come, it does not yet encompass all markets. The Eastern European countries, the Soviet Union, other formerly and presently centrally planned economies, and the world's LDCs are still largely segregated. Recent political events, however, may portend a more inclusive interaction in the not too distant future.

In a world of segregated capital markets, interest rates are determined in different countries independently of one another. Capital cannot move from low interest rate countries, where it has relatively little value, to high interest rate countries, where it has relatively greater value. In a perfectly integrated and efficient financial world, on the other hand, there would be only one interest rate for capital of a given character. In our present state of partial integration, interest rates in the different capital markets are determined interdependently. High rates in one country will be arbitraged against low rates in another country by movements of capital. While these transactions take place, for the most part, at the bank-to-bank (interbank) level, the consumer feels the impact in the form of his or her borrowing costs. The segregated capital markets, the completely integrated capital markets, the partially integrated capital markets, and the completely integrated capital markets are depicted diagrammatically as Exhibits 26.1, 26.2, and 26.3, respectively.

The actual degree of capital market integration can, in theory, be measured quite precisely. For example, one can measure the degree of statistical correlation between interest rates in various countries or the correlation between equity (stock market) returns in various countries. One would have to adjust, of course, for country-specific factors but, all other things being equal, the higher the degrees of correlation (and the shorter the intermarket response time) the more complete is the process of integration. It is well documented that the degrees of capital market correlation for the major western countries has increased dramatically over the last twenty years.

A Recap of Recent Developments Toward Financial Globalization

The present state of market integration is the result of the convergence of a number powerful factors. One of the first of these

Exhibit 26.1
Segregated Capital Markets

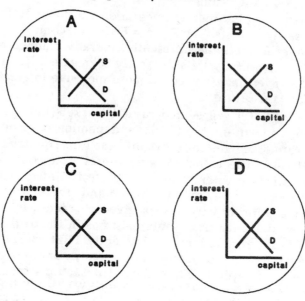

Exhibit 26.2
Partially Integrated Capital Markets

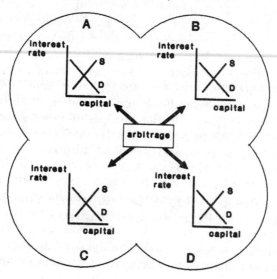

Exhibit 26.3
Completely Integrated Capital Markets

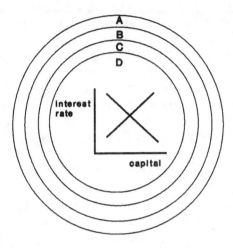

to appear was the development of the nearly unregulated Eu-romarkets. These markets originated in London but have since developed elsewhere. Nevertheless, London still dominates. Other important centers include The Bahamas, Singapore, Bahrain, Hong-kong, and, more recently, the United States and Japan. These off-shore markets allow players to raise funds or to invest funds outside of their domestic market. They are not subject to the kind of securities regulation and registration typical of many domestic markets (most notably the U.S. and Japan). This permits funds to be raised more quickly, at less cost, and with less disclosure of sensitive, competitively valuable, information.

The development of the Euromarkets was not, however, in and of itself sufficient to bring about globalization. While those who tapped the markets could raise funds outside of their own country, the most attractive opportunities were not necessarily denominated in the desired currency or have the desired form of interest (fixed verses floating). The advent of swaps changed this forever. The largely unregulated Euromarkets, when coupled with the swap's ability to convert almost any currency into almost any other currency quickly and inexpensively and to convert fixed rates into floating rates and vice versa, served, more than anything else, to make globalization possible. When combined with advances in telecommunications and data processing, these developments make it possible to search the world over for available financing opportunities and to execute the tedious calculations necessary to make these alternative opportunities directly comparable on an all-in cost basis. Thus, the unregulated nature of the Euromarkets, the fluidity made possible by swaps, and the access to information and the ability process it made possible by technology were the principal driving forces behind globalization.

Globalization also implies more perfect competition. In addition to the challenge posed by domestic competitors, globalization opens the door to foreign competitors as well. (Indeed, in a truly global environment no one is foreign. Rather, we are all residents of the same global village.) This intensifies competition and can leave firms that carry a greater regulatory burden at a significant disadvantage to firms less encumbered. Not surprisingly, globalization has contributed to a rethinking of regulation. In the United States, this rethinking has led to some relaxation of the old prohibitions against interstate banking, a gradual erosion of the separation of commercial banking and investment banking *a la* Glass-Steagall, the lifting of ceilings on interest rates, the introduction of shelf registration, and other forms of deregulation or more accommodative regulation. Parallel developments have taken place in other countries. The most notable example is the rapid deregulation of the financial services industry in the United Kingdom during the latter half of the 1980s. This deregulation was so broad and enacted with such speed that it became known as the **Big Bang**. A less well-known but still important case is that of Japan. Japan has begun to open its capital markets to foreign banks (it has also progressively allowed its residents greater freedom to invest and lend overseas). These banks have been granted securities licenses—something long desired by domestic Japanese banks but prohibited by Article 65, the Japanese equivalent of Glass-Steagall. While one would not expect Japanese banks to welcome the entry of foreign banks, the granting of securities licenses to foreign banks sets the stage for the demise of Article 65. Why, after all, should foreign commercial banks be permitted to deal in securities while domestic Japanese banks are not? Such competitive arguments for deregulation become quite powerful when market share begins to erode.

One of the most important developments on the road to the globalization of the world's capital markets is the economic liberalization and financial integration of the European Community scheduled for 1992 and already underway in earnest. Under the new rules, the EEC will issue a single license allowing banks domiciled in any EEC country to operate in any of the twelve EEC countries while governed by the banking rules of their home country.[2] This has important implications for the future shape of regulation. For example, banks domiciled in countries having more liberal banking laws will operate at a competitive advantage over those domiciled in countries having more restrictive banking laws. This suggests that pressure will inevitably develop toward greater uniformity of regulation but not necessarily for the elimination of regulation. Such an effort is already well advanced in so far as bank capital requirements are concerned. In 1987, bank supervisors and regulators met in Basle, Switzerland to develop more uniform measures of bank assets, risk exposures (including the regulation of off-balance sheet activity) and capital requirements. This effort led to a set of working principles and capital standards known as the **Basle Accord** and which has since been adopted by bank regulators, in whole or in part, in many countries including the United States. What is perhaps of equal importance to the new standards themselves is the clear signal the agreement sent that bank regulators and supervisors understand the global evolution of the financial marketplace and the need for uniformity in regulation and supervision.

For banks operating within the EEC but domiciled outside the EEC, the rules are a bit different and center around **reciprocity**. The general meaning of reciprocity is that non-EEC banks will be permitted to operate within the EEC on an equal footing to EEC banks on the expectation that the EEC banks will be granted similar treatment when operating in the non-EEC market.

Despite the enlightened thinking involved in the admission of foreign banks into the U.S. capital markets, prohibitions against interstate banking continue. In 1927, Congress passed the **McFadden Act** which prohibited banks from branching across state lines and permitted federally chartered banks within a state to branch within the state only to the same extent as state chartered banks in that state. As of this writing, about a dozen or so states, mostly in the Midwest, permit only unit banking; that is, no branches at all are allowed. Another dozen or so states allow only limited intrastate branching.

The prohibitions against interstate banking within the United

States have been slow in coming down. Indeed, what relaxation of the prohibitions that have occurred have come about on a case-by-case basis in response to the thrift industry crisis rather than by means of an outright lifting of the prohibitions through legislation at the federal level. Nevertheless, the economies of scale that characterize the commercial banking industry make full interstate banking and broad consolidation within the industry inevitable.

Other globalization trends that are underway include a breakdown in the separation of commercial banking and investment banking activities. While many factors have contributed to the demise of Glass-Steagall in the United States and Article 65 in Japan, the two most important are global competition and the development of efficient risk management instruments and techniques (primarily derivative products and hedging techniques). These developments have rendered obsolete the historic justification for separation of these two activities.

Development of New Markets and Market Linkages

The competition offered by the increasing globalization of the capital markets has led to a number of new market developments worthy of some mention. In recent years, there have been concerted efforts to improve the efficiency of and the access to traditional capital markets in many countries. For example, until recently the West German capital markets consisted of a fragmented system of eight stock exchanges. Access to the exchanges was controlled by a number of large German banks (which held a monopoly on brokerage and offered loans to their client firms at attractive rates). This structure limited corporate access to the equities markets and ensured the banks of control over their client firms' access to equity capital and loans. But, over the last few years, the banks have worked together to increase access and to provide computer linkages between the various exchanges. This has increased transactional efficiency and reduced transaction costs. The stock exchanges have reorganized their listing system for this purpose. It has also made it easier for corporations to become listed on stock exchanges.

Another important development has been the explosive growth of futures and options exchanges. The market for these derivative products had long been dominated by the United States with only a few exchanges operated elsewhere. But, in recent years, futures and options markets have been introduced or expanded throughout

Europe and Asia. These markets tend to trade contracts having a global-finance appeal such as Eurodollars, U.S. Treasuries, and currencies. Among the more interesting of the developments in these markets has been the establishment of linkages between exchanges operating in different countries and different time zones. These linkages allow traders who have taken a position in a derivative instrument to offset that instrument on another exchange. This increases access by allowing a trader to take or to offset a position during hours when its domestic exchange is closed. The first such linkage, introduced a few years ago, involved the Singapore International Monetary Exchange (SIMEX) and the International Monetary Market (IMM), an affiliate of the Chicago Mercantile Exchange. The SIMEX, like the IMM, trades Eurodollar futures and currency futures. The SIMEX designed its contracts to exactly replicate those of the IMM. As a result, by mutual agreement, contracts opened on either exchange can be offset on the other.

With an appropriate ring of futures exchanges and linkages around the world, 24 hour trading becomes possible. Such trading is occurring in T-bond futures. A trader can take a position at any time and offset a position at any time. This type of access becomes increasingly important in a world in which economic and financial events happening in one part of the world have immediate consequences for financial markets elsewhere in the world. Linkages are, of course, made possible by efficient and inexpensive telecommunications and would not be possible without the instant access provided by such telecommunications.

A second way to create 24 hour trading involves expanding the hours in which exchanges operate. This can be done in two ways. One is to extend the hours in which the trading floor is open. Some exchanges have pursued this course by extending regular hours or by adding evening sessions. The second way is by executing trades through a central computer without the need for humans on the floor of the exchange. Such a system can be operated during the hours in which the exchange floor is closed. Both of the major Chicago exchanges have developed and implemented such systems. As originally envisioned, such systems are intended to augment the human activity on the floor of the exchange; but many people believe that such systems will eventually replace trading on the traditional floor. Several arguments can be made in favor of such computer assisted order matching. First, such a system, if properly designed, guarantees that a trader has simultaneous access to all orders currently on the "floor" and will get the best fill possible. Computer matching can speed order execution, reduce execution costs, and produce a much more accurate audit trail than human face-to-face order matching. Such a system can also allow a trader to operate from any location in the world as efficiently as if he or she were physically present on the trading floor. As with 24 hour trading made possible via exchange linkages, 24 hour trading via after-hours order matching is made possible by advances in technology. Without the development of very fast microprocessors and telecommunications equipment, such trading would still be a far away dream.

Recent Advances in Settlement and Clearing

The integration of the world's capital markets coupled with the economic expansion of the 1980s and the increased emphasis on asset allocation strategies by portfolio managers has led to an enormous increase in the volume of cross-border securities transactions. For example, the volume of this activity increased over ten fold during the last decade. This has placed a great strain on those involved in the processing of these transactions.

While operations areas have increased their use of automation, allowing them to process larger transaction volumes, there has been relatively little impact on the timeliness and accuracy of international settlement which has long been notorious for fails.[3] The root cause of this problem is that each country continues to operate with its own set of rules concerning settlement procedures. The differences can be enormous. For example, in Germany, corporate securities are settled two business days after transaction. In the United States, corporate securities are settled five business days after transaction. In France, securities are settled once a month. This lack of standardization increases the cost and decreases the accuracy of matching trades and transferring securities and funds. In addition, the greater the time between transaction and settlement, the greater the risk that one party will default.

In the late 1980s, an international organization known as the **Group of Thirty,** or **G-30,** attempted to address these problems. In the process, they developed a set of recommendations for standardizing the clearance and settlement of international securities transactions. The recommendations of G-30 are enumerated in Box 1 below in which day "t" denotes the transaction date.

Box 1⁴

1. Comparisons should be established between direct market participants (brokers, exchange members) by day t+1.
2. Indirect market participants should be members of a positive-affirmation comparison system by 1992.
3. Each country should have a central securities depository (CSD, used to immobilize securities) by 1992.
4. Each country should implement a netting system by 1992, unless volume is low enough to permit otherwise.
5. A delivery versus payment system should be in place by 1992.
6. Payment in same-day funds should be adopted.
7. Rolling settlement should be adopted. No later than 1990, final settlement by t+5 should be the rule. The ultimate goal is t+3 by 1992.
8. Securities lending as a means of expediting settlement should be encouraged.
9. The numbering of securities and message codes should be

The Group of Thirty's recommendations are an attempt to coordinate and to accelerate the evolution of worldwide financial markets in response to the changing nature of international trading. The general consensus is that the recommendations of G-30 will go a long way toward achieving that objective.

Globalization, Financial Engineering, and Monetary Policy

While globalization is for most a positive financial development, it is a source of concern for those who would make monetary policy. There are a number of reasons for this. First, globalization of the capital markets reduces the monetary authorities' control over the availability of credit. If, for example, the Federal Reserve attempts to limit credit availability by raising interest rates, capital immediately flows into the United States in order to exploit the higher interest rates vis-a-vis the rest of the world. This is a consequence of the mobility of capital which is itself a consequence of the financial engineering we have repeatedly stressed. Second, the use of floating-rate financing coupled with risk management techniques renders many borrowers immune to changes in interest rates, at least in the short run. Thus, the timing of the effects of changes in monetary policy are less certain.

Other aspects of financial engineering have also lessened the effectiveness of monetary policy. For example, many of the recent financial engineering innovations have created liquid secondary markets for formerly illiquid assets. This has rendered old definitions of monetary aggregates—the traditional measures of money supply—less reliable and less meaningful. The repo market and the securitization of receivables are two obvious examples.

Spreadsheeting and Modeling: The Role of the Microcomputer

In our many discussions of the uses of technology in financial engineering, we have repeatedly made reference to telecommunications and data processing. Much of the latter has long been the purview of the mainframe computer. But financial engineering has been greatly aided by the advent of the microcomputer. The development of the Apple II and the IBM PC probably did more for the advancement of financial engineering in a shorter period of time than all the powerful mainframes throughout their considerably longer history. These machines, when coupled with revolutionary easy-to-use modeling software, such as spreadsheets, took computing power and placed it in the hands of financially oriented and very innovative minds. There is no doubt that the complex analysis and number crunching that are the heart and soul of much of financial engineering would not have been possible without these remarkable aids.

Given the importance of financial modeling, it is not surprising that a working knowledge of microcomputers and spreadsheets are a prerequisite part of the knowledge base of the modern financial engineer. The student of financial engineering should appreciate this importance as he or she maps out a program of study.

Toward a New World

As we approach the end of this book, we cannot help but look back admiringly at the work of financial engineers and to simultaneously look forward with excitement at the innovations yet to come. If our review of financial engineering has done nothing else, it has made it very clear that small, sometimes innocuous, innovations can, cumulatively and over time, change the shape of the world. The financial world today is clearly a very different place from what it was a decade ago. We would be very naive to believe that it will not be a very different place again a decade from now.

As the capital markets move toward ever greater integration, we look forward to a world in which policy decisions are better coordinated and the interrelationships between the world's economies are better understood. We can bet that financial engineers will play prominently in that which is yet to be just as surely as they did in that which has been.

Summary

The trend toward globalization of markets has been relentless. Globalization implies a harmonizing of the rules and a reduction of the barriers to the free flow of capital among nations. Once segregated capital markets have become, at least partially, integrated. The trend is evident in commercial banking, investment banking, in regulation, in settlement and clearing practices, in market linkages, in automated trading systems, and on and on. Nevertheless, some resistance remains. The most noticeable resistance is in the United States where prohibitions against interstate banking remain in effect.

The globalization of the markets has had the effect of weakening the hand of the monetary authorities in the making of monetary policy. Various financial engineering activities have contributed to this effect. However unintentional, the lessoning of monetary control should be of concern to policy makers. The new world will undoubtedly demand more coordination of policy at an international level if it is to be effective.

Endnotes

[1]Pavel and McElravey [1990].

[2]We would be remiss not to point out that some have questioned whether or not the economic and financial integration of the European Community will actual lead to globalization. Some have argued that it may, in fact, lead to a crystallization of a deutschemark dominated currency sector isolated from the dollar sector and the yen sector. Only time will tell.

[3]DeGennaro and Pike [1990].

[4]Ibid.

References and Suggested Reading

Pavel, C. and J.N. McElravey. "Globalization in the Financial Services Industry," *Economic Perspectives*, Federal Reserve Bank of Chicago, 14(3) (May/June 1990).

DeGennaro, R.P. and C.J. Pike "Standardizing World Securities Clearance Systems," *Economic Commentary*, Federal Reserve Bank of Cleveland (April 1990).

"Clearance and Settlement Systems in the World's Securities Markets, Group of Thirty, London (March 1989).

Chappe, T. "Global Finance: Causes, Consequences and Prospects for the Futures, *Global Finance Journal*, 1(1) (Fall 1989).

Financial Times, "International Settlement and Custody" (September 3, 1990), Section III.

Appendix

Globalization in the financial services industry

The pace has been most rapid at the wholesale, bank-to-bank and bank-to-multinational level; at the retail customer level, globalization will soon quicken, particularly in Europe.

Christine Pavel and John N. McElravey

Globalization can be defined as the act or state of becoming worldwide in scope or application. Apart from this geographical application, globalization can also be defined as becoming universal. For the financial services industry, this second meaning implies both a harmonization of rules and a reduction of barriers that will allow for the free flow of capital and permit all firms to compete in all markets.

This article looks at how global the financial services industry already is, and will likely become, by examining the nature and trends of globalization in the industry. It will also draw lessons from global nonfinancial industries and from recent geographic expansion of banking firms within the United States.

Financial globalization is being driven by advances in data processing and telecommunications, liberalization of restrictions on cross-border capital flows, deregulation of domestic capital markets, and greater competition among these markets for a share of the world's trading volume. It is growing rapidly, but primarily at the intermediary, rather than the customer, level. Its effects are felt at the customer level mainly because prices and interest rates are influenced by worldwide economic and financial conditions, rather than because direct customer access to suppliers has increased. However, globalization at the customer level will soon become apparent, at least in Europe after 1992, when European Community banking firms will be allowed to cross national borders.

Trends in other industries and lessons from interstate banking in the United States suggest that as financial globalization progresses, financial services will become more integrated, more competitive, and more concentrated. Also, firms that survive will become more efficient, and consumers of financial services will benefit considerably. Reciprocity is likely to be an important factor for those countries not already part of a regional compact, as it has been for interstate banking to proceed in the United States.

International commercial banking

The international banking market consists of the foreign sector of domestic banking markets and the unregulated offshore markets. It has undergone important structural changes over the last decade.

Like domestic banking, international banking involves lending and deposit taking. The primary distinction between the two types of banking lies in their customer bases. Since 1982, international lending and deposit taking have both been growing at roughly 15 percent annually. At year-end 1988, foreign loans and foreign liabilities at the world's banks each totalled more than $5 trillion. The extent, nature, and growth of international banking, however, are not the same in all countries.

When she wrote this article, Christine Pavel was an economist at the Federal Reserve Bank of Chicago. She is now an assistant vice president at Citicorp North America Inc. John N. McElravey is an associate economist at the Federal Reserve Bank of Chicago.

Figures 1 and 2 show the ten countries whose banks have the largest shares of foreign banking assets and liabilities. Combined, these ten countries account for nearly three-quarters of all foreign assets and liabilities. Nearly half of all foreign banking assets and liabilities are held by banks in the United Kingdom, Japan, the United States, and Switzerland, up from 47 percent in 1982. This increase is almost entirely due to the meteoric rise in foreign lending by Japanese banks.

Perhaps the most notable event in international banking has been the rapid growth of Japanese banks. This extraordinary growth can be traced to deregulation in Japan, as well as to its banks' high market capitalization, the country's high savings rate, and its large current account surplus. Japanese foreign exchange controls and restrictions on capital outflows were removed in 1980. This allowed the banks' industrial customers to go directly to the capital markets for financing. The loss of some of their best customers, along with deposit rate deregulation and stiffer competition from other types of institutions, reduced profits.[1] To improve their profitability and to service Japanese nonfinancial firms that had expanded overseas, Japanese banks moved into new markets abroad. While a large part of the business of Japanese banks abroad is with

Japanese firms, Japanese banks have been very successful lending to foreign industrial firms because of a competitive advantage conferred by a more favorable regulatory environment. Japan's capital requirements have been relatively easy, allowing banks to hold assets at 25 to 30 times book capital.[2] Japan's share of all foreign assets and liabilities rose from 4 percent in 1982 to more than 14 percent in 1988, surpassing the U.S. and second only to the U.K.

While many banks have significant international operations, only a few are truly international in scope. More than one-half of the total banking assets and liabilities in Switzerland, nearly one-half of total banking assets and liabilities in the United Kingdom, and over one-quarter of total banking assets and liabilities in France are foreign. In contrast, less than 25 percent of the balance sheets of German, Japanese, and U.S. banks consist of foreign assets and liabilities.

The United Kingdom and Switzerland have long been international financial centers. For more than 100 years Swiss bankers have been raising loans for foreigners. The largest Swiss banks, in fact, try to maintain a 50–50 split between their foreign and domestic assets for strategic and marketing reasons.[3] Deregulation, or the lack of regulation in some cases.

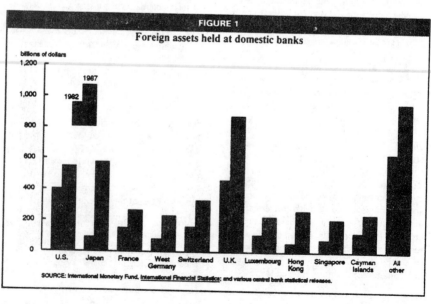

FIGURE 1

Foreign assets held at domestic banks

billions of dollars

SOURCE: International Monetary Fund, *International Financial Statistics*; and various central bank statistical releases.

and the restructuring of the British financial system have made London a powerful international financial center. More than half of all banking institutions in the U.K. are foreign-owned, and 59 percent of all assets of banks in the U.K. are denominated in foreign currency.[4]

At the aggregate level, the proportion of bank assets that are claims on foreigners is roughly equivalent to the proportion of liabilities that are claims of foreigners. This is not true of individual countries. Some countries' banks lend more to foreigners than they borrow from them. Foreign assets of German banks are almost twice the size of foreign liabilities, and Swiss banks hold about 34 percent more foreign assets than liabilities. For banks in these countries, the combination of international orientation and their country's high domestic saving rates makes them strong net lenders. Banks in the United States, Japan, and France, however, have more foreign liabilities than foreign assets, although in each case the difference is less than 5 percent.

U.S. banks have not always been net foreign borrowers. In 1982, foreign deposits at U.S. banks accounted for less than 13 percent of total liabilities, while foreign assets accounted for over 20 percent of total assets. Foreign deposits at U.S. banks have more than doubled over the 1982–87 period, growing far

more rapidly than domestic deposits. Foreign assets increased only 37 percent over that time and more slowly than domestic assets. This is due largely to the reduction in LDC lending and to the writing down of LDC loans by U.S. banks.

Foreign deposit growth also outpaced domestic deposit growth at Japanese banks. In 1982, foreign deposits accounted for 9 percent of total liabilities, and by 1987, they accounted for 18 percent. Similarly Japanese banks booked foreign assets about twice as fast as domestic assets over the 1982–87 period.

Offshore banking centers

A considerable portion of international banking activity occurs in unregulated offshore banking centers commonly known as the Euromarkets.[5] The Euromarkets, unlike the domestic markets, are virtually free of regulation. Euromarkets consist of Eurocurrency deposits, Eurobonds, and Euro-commercial paper. Eurocurrency deposits are bank deposits denominated in a foreign currency, and account for 86 percent of banks' foreign-owned deposits.

The development of Eurocurrency deposits marked the inauguration of the Euromarket in the mid-1950s. Eurocurrency deposits grew at a moderate rate until the mid-1960s when they began to grow more rapidly.[6] At that

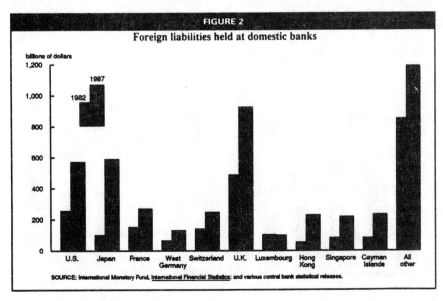

FIGURE 2

Foreign liabilities held at domestic banks

billions of dollars

SOURCE: International Monetary Fund, *International Financial Statistics*; and various central bank statistical releases.

time, the U.S. government imposed severe controls on the movement of capital, which "deflected a substantial amount of borrowing demand to the young Eurodollar market."[7] These U.S. capital controls were dismantled in 1974, but the oil crisis of the 1970s helped to fuel the continued growth of the Eurocurrency market. The U.S. oil embargo made oil-exporting countries fearful of placing their funds in domestic branches of U.S. banks. In the late 1970s and early 1980s, high interest rates bolstered the growth of Eurocurrency deposits, which are free of interest-rate ceilings and not subject to reserve requirements or deposit insurance premiums. From 1975 to 1980, Eurocurrency deposits grew over threefold.

Since 1980, Eurocurrency deposits have continued to grow quite rapidly, reaching a gross value of $4.5 trillion outstanding in 1987 and a net value of nearly $2.6 trillion (net of interbank claims). Eurodollar deposits, however, have not grown as rapidly. During the early 1980s, Eurodollars represented over 80 percent of all Eurocurrency deposits outstanding, but by 1987, they represented only 66 percent (see Figure 3). The declining importance of Eurodollar deposits can be explained, at least partially, by the decline in the cost of holding noninterest-bearing reserves against domestic deposits in the United States.[8]

Many Eurocenters have developed throughout the world. They have developed where local governments allow them to thrive, i.e., where regulation is favorable to offshore markets. Consequently, some countries with relatively small domestic financial markets, such as the Bahamas, have become important Eurocenters. Similarly, some countries with major domestic financial markets have no or very small offshore markets. In the United States, for example, the offshore market was prohibited until 1981 when International Banking Facilities (IBFs) were authorized.

Japan did not permit an offshore market to develop until late in 1986. Until then the "Asian dollar" market consisted primarily of the Eurocenters of Singapore, Bahrain, and Hong Kong. Now Japan's offshore market is about $400 billion in size, over twice as large as the U.S. offshore market, but still smaller than that in the United Kingdom.[9]

The interbank market

The international lending activities of most banks, aside from the money centers, are concentrated heavily in the area of providing a variety of credit facilities to banks in other countries. Consequently, a large proportion of banks' foreign assets and liabilities are claims on or claims of foreign banks. Eighty percent of all foreign assets are claims on other banks.[10] This ratio varies somewhat by country; however, since 1982, it has been increasing for all the major industrialized countries.

Similarly, nearly 80 percent of all banks' foreign liabilities are claims of other banks.[11] In Japan, 99 percent of all foreign liabilities at banks are deposits of foreign banks. Swiss banks are the exception, where only 28 percent of foreign liabilities are claims of banks.

The Swiss have a long history of providing banking services directly to foreign corporate and individual customers, which explains their relatively low proportion of interbank claims. A favorable legal and regulatory climate aided the development of a system that caters to foreigners, especially those wishing to shelter income from taxes. Confidentiality is recognized as a right of the bank customer, and stiff penalties can be imposed on bank officials who violate that right. In effect, no information about a client can be given to any third party.[12]

Since a very large portion of foreign deposits are Eurocurrency deposits, it is no surprise that about half of all Eurocurrency deposits are interbank claims. Eurocurrency

FIGURE 3

Eurocurrency deposits

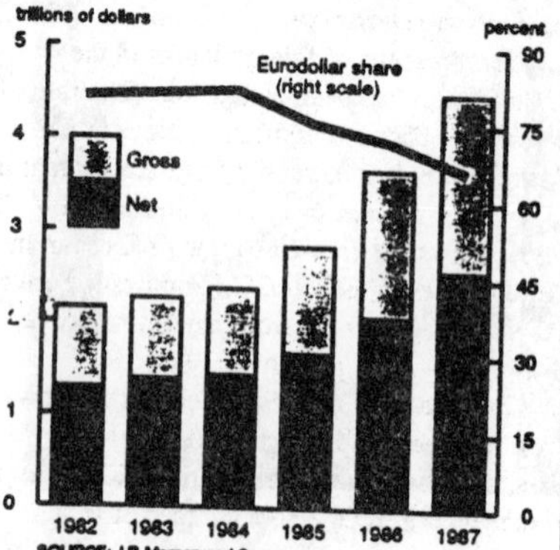

trillions of dollars / percent

Eurodollar share (right scale)

Gross

Net

1982 1983 1984 1985 1986 1987

SOURCE: J.P. Morgan and Co.

deposits are frequently re-lent to other, often smaller, banks in the interbank market.[13]

The Japanese have become very large borrowers in the interbank market in response to domestic restrictions on prices and volumes of certain activities. Japanese banks operating overseas have been funding their activities by borrowing domestically (from nonresidents) in one market (e.g., the U.K.), and lending the funds through the interbank market to affiliates in other countries (e.g., the U.S.).[14]

Foreign exchange trading

Foreign exchange (forex) trading is another important international banking activity. Informal estimates place daily foreign exchange trading at $400 billion.[15] Like the loan markets, forex markets are primarily interbank markets. The primary players involved in the United States are the large money center and regional commercial banks, Edge Act corporations, and U.S. branches and agencies of foreign banks. Forex trading also involves some large nonbank financial firms, primarily large investment banks and foreign exchange brokers. However, according to the Federal Reserve Bank of New York's *U.S. Foreign Exchange Market Survey* for April 1989, 82 percent of the forex trading volume of banks was with other banks. Foreign exchange trading in New York grew at about 40 percent annually since 1986 to reach more than $130 billion by April 1989. In contrast, foreign trade (imports plus exports) has been growing at only about 6 percent annually since 1982 (3 percent on an inflation-adjusted basis).

The German mark is the most actively traded currency, followed by the Japanese yen, British pound, Swiss franc, and Canadian dollar. Since 1986, however, the German mark has lost some ground to the Japanese yen and the Swiss franc.[16]

The explosion of forex trading can, at least partly, be explained by the high rate of growth in cross-border financial transactions. Capital and foreign exchange controls were reduced or eliminated in a number of countries during the 1980s.

An international banking presence

There are several ways that commercial banks engage in international banking activities—through representative offices, agencies, foreign branches, and foreign sub-sidiary banks and affiliates. In addition, in the United States, commercial banks may operate International Banking Facilities (IBFs) and Edge Act corporations, which unlike the other means, do not involve a physical presence abroad. The primary difference among these types of foreign offices centers on how customer needs are met (often because of regulation). For example, agencies of foreign banks are essentially branches that cannot accept deposits from the general public, while branches, as well as subsidiary banks, can offer a full range of banking services.

U.S. branches and agencies of foreign banks devote well over half of their assets to loans, about the same proportion as the domestic offices of U.S. commercial banks. U.S. commercial banks, however, hold a much larger proportion of their assets in securities and a much smaller proportion in customer's liability on acceptances.[17] This latter situation reflects the international trade financings of U.S. foreign offices.

U.S. offices of foreign banks compete with domestic banks primarily in commercial lending and, to a lesser extent, in real estate lending.[18] However, a significant portion of the commercial loans held at U.S. offices of foreign banks were purchased from U.S. banks, rather than originated by the foreign offices themselves.[19]

Both U.S. offices of foreign banks and domestic offices of U.S. commercial banks primarily fund their operations with deposits of individuals, partnerships and corporations (IPC).[20] Offices of foreign banks currently gather 23 percent of these deposits from foreigners, and nearly all of these deposits are of the nontransaction type.

The presence of foreign banks in the United States has been increasing. The ratio of foreign offices to domestic offices in the United States has increased from 2.8 percent in 1981 to 4.4 percent in 1987. Similarly, the ratio of assets of foreign banking offices in the United States to assets of U.S. domestic banks has increased over 5 percentage points since 1981 to nearly 21 percent in 1987.[21]

The presence of U.S. banks abroad, however, has been falling since 1985. At that time, U.S. banks operated nearly 1,000 foreign branches.[22] Similarly, the number of U.S. banks with foreign branches peaked at 163 in 1982 and began to fall in 1986. By 1988, the number of banks with foreign branches had fallen to 147. On an inflation-adjusted basis, total assets of foreign branches of U.S. banks fell 12 percent since 1983 to $506 billion in 1988. The number of IBFs and Edge Act Corporations has also been waning. Edge Acts numbered 146 in 1984 and were down to 112 by 1988.[23] This retrenchment reflects the lessening attractiveness of foreign operations as losses on LDC loans have mounted.

Implications of Europe after 1992

The presence of foreign banking firms in European domestic markets will likely increase over the next few years as the 12 European Community states become, at least economically, a "United States of Europe." The EC plans to issue a single license that will allow banks to expand their networks throughout the Community, governed by their home country's regulations.[24]

Since banking powers will be determined by the rules of the home country, banks from countries with more liberal banking laws operating in countries with more restrictive banking laws will have an advantage over their domestic competitors. Consequently, the most efficient form of banking will prevail. Countries with more fragmented banking systems will need to liberalize for their banks to compete with banks from countries with universal banking.

While reciprocity will not be important for nations within the EC, it will be an issue for banks from countries outside the EC, especially those from Japan and the U.S. As financial services companies in Europe begin to operate with fewer restrictions, there will be competitive pressure on the U.S. and Japan to remove the barriers between commercial and investment banking. To be most efficient, firms operating in various markets want similar powers in each market. The EC, as previously noted, solved this problem with a Community banking license. Thus, the EC's efforts at regulatory harmonization may hasten the demise of Glass-Steagall in the U.S. and Article 65 in Japan.[25]

The implications for European banking will be similar to the experience in the United States following the introduction of interstate banking in the early to mid-1980s. Since that time, the U.S. commercial banking industry has been consolidating on nationwide, re-

gional, and statewide bases through mergers and acquisitions. Acquiring firms tend to be large, profitable organizations with expertise in operating geographically dispersed networks, while targets tend to be smaller, although still relatively large firms, in attractive banking markets. Large, poorly-capitalized firms will also find themselves to be potential takeover targets.

What these lessons imply for Europe in 1992 is that the largest and strongest organizations with the managerial talent to operate a geographically dispersed organization will become Europe-wide firms, while smaller firms will have a more regional focus and others will survive as niche players. In addition, just as different state laws have slowed the process of nationwide banking in the United States, language and cultural barriers will slow the process in Europe as well. The overall result of a more globally integrated financial sector in Europe, and elsewhere, will be that the organizations that survive will be more efficient, and customers will be better served. Also, it is very likely that the 1992 experience will improve European banks' ability to compete outside of Europe.

Size is not, and will not be, a sufficient ingredient for survival. In general, firms in protected industries, such as airlines, tend to be inefficient. Large banking organizations based in states with restrictive branching and multibank holding company laws tended to be less efficient than their peers in states that allow branches and, therefore, more competition. In addition, commercial banking organizations that operated in unit banking states had little expertise in operating a decentralized organization, and tended to focus primarily on large commercial customers. Consequently, these banking firms have not acquired banks far from home.

The process of consolidation has already begun within European countries and within Europe as firms prepare for a single European banking market. Unlike the Unites States' experience of outright mergers and acquisitions, however, the European experience centers on forming "partnerships." Partnerships have been formed Europe-wide, even though the most recent directive on commercial banking permits branching, because of the difficulties in managing an organization that spans several cultures and languages. Apparently, financial services firms want to get their feet wet first, rather than plunge into European banking and risk drowning before 1992 arrives. But also, until regulations among countries become more uniform, partnerships and joint ventures allow financial firms to arbitrage regulations.

The formation of partnerships and joint ventures is not only a European phenomenon. Indeed, U.S. firms have entered into such agreements with European and Japanese companies. For example, Wells Fargo and Nikko Securities have formed a joint venture to operate a global investment management firm, and Merrill Lynch and Société Générale are discussing a partnership to develop a French asset-backed securities market.

The experience of nonfinancial firms suggests that this arrangement can be a good way to establish an international presence. For example, in 1984, Toyota and General Motors entered into a joint manufacturing venture in California. Through this venture, the Japanese were able to acquaint themselves with American workers and suppliers before opening their own plants in the U.S. Since then, Toyota has opened two more manufacturing plants on its own in North America, and there is speculation in the auto industry that they will buy GM's share of the joint venture once the agreement ends in 1996.[26]

Another case of international expansion through joint ventures can be found in the petroleum industry. Oil companies from some oil-producing countries have been quite active in recent years buying stakes in refining and marketing operations in the United States and Europe. These acquisitions give producers an outlet for their crude in important retail markets, and refiners get a reliable source. Saudi Arabia purchased a 50 percent stake in Texaco's eastern and Gulf Coast refining and marketing operations in November 1988. The state-owned oil companies from Kuwait and Venezuela have joint ventures with European oil companies as well.[27] If joint ventures between financial services firms are as successful as nonfinancial ones have been, then global financial integration will benefit.

International securities markets

International securities include securities that are issued outside the issuer's home coun-

try. Some of these securities trade on foreign exchanges. Issuance and trading of international securities have grown considerably since 1986, as has the amount of such securities outstanding.

Greater demand for international financing is stimulating important changes in financial markets, especially in Europe. Regulations and procedures designed to shield domestic markets from foreign competition are gradually being dismantled. London's position as an international market was strengthened by the lack of sophistication of many other European markets. Greater demand for equity financing in Europe has been encouraged by private companies, and by governments privatizing large public-sector corporations. These measures to deregulate and, therefore, improve the efficiency, regulatory organizations, and settlement procedures are a response to competition from other markets, and the explosion of securities trading in the 1980s.[28]

It is estimated that the world bond markets at the end of 1988 consisted of about $9.8 trillion of publicly issued bonds outstanding, a nearly $2 trillion increase since 1986.[29] At year-end 1988, two-thirds of all bonds outstanding were obligations of central governments, their agencies, and state and local governments. This figure varies considerably across countries. Over two-thirds of bonds denominated in the U.S. dollar and the Japanese yen are government obligations, but less than one-third of bonds denominated in the German mark are government obligations, and only 10 percent of bonds denominated in the Swiss franc represent government debt.[30]

The international bond market includes foreign bonds, Eurobonds, and Euro-commercial paper. Foreign bonds are bonds issued in a foreign country and denominated in that country's currency. Eurobonds are long-term bonds issued and sold outside the country of the currency in which they are denominated. Similarly, Euro-commercial paper is a short-term debt instrument that is issued and sold outside the country of the currency in which it is denominated.

The Japanese are the biggest issuers of Eurobonds because it is easier and cheaper than issuing corporate bonds in Japan. Japanese companies issued 21 percent of all Eurobonds in 1988.[31] Ministry of Finance (MOF) regulations and the underwriting oligopoly of the four largest Japanese securities firms keep the issuance cost in the domestic bond market higher than in the Euromarket. The ministry would like to bring this bond market activity back to Japan, so it has been slowly liberalizing the rules for issuing yen bonds and samurai bonds (yen bonds issued by foreigners in Japan). So far, the impact of these changes has been small.[32]

International bonds accounted for almost 10 percent of bonds outstanding at the end of 1988 and over three-quarters are denominated in the U.S. dollar, Japanese yen, German mark and U.K. sterling (see Figure 4). These countries represent four of the largest economies and financial markets in the world.

The importance of international bond markets has increased considerably for many countries. As Table 1 shows, international bonds account for nearly half of all bonds denominated in the Swiss franc and over one-third of all bonds denominated in the Australian dollar. International bonds account for over 21 percent of bonds denominated in the British pound, up dramatically from less than 1 percent in 1980. The rise in importance of international bonds for these currencies can, at least in part, be explained by the budget surpluses in the countries in which these currencies are denominated and, therefore, the slower growth in the debt obligations of these countries' governments.

The value of world equity markets, at $9.6 trillion in 1988, is about equal to the value of world bond markets. Three countries—the United States, Japan, and the United Kingdom—account for three quarters of the total capitalization on world equity markets, and they account for nearly half of the 15,000 equity issues listed on the world's stock exchanges (see Figure 5).

American, Japanese, and British equity markets are the largest and most active. American and British markets are very open to foreign investors, but significant barriers to foreign competitors still exist in Japan.

Stocks have, historically, played a relatively minor role in corporate financing in many European countries. Various regulatory and traditional barriers to entry made these bourses financial backwaters. The stock exchanges in Switzerland, West Germany, France, and Italy have only recently taken steps to modernize in order to compete against exchanges in the U.S. and the U.K. It was estimated that about 20 percent of daily trad-

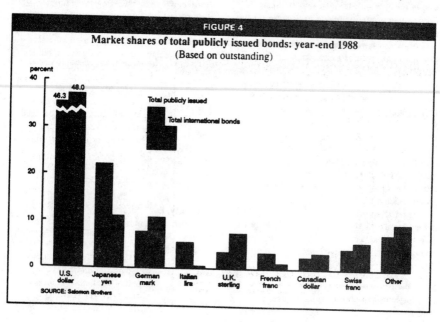

FIGURE 4

Market shares of total publicly issued bonds: year-end 1988
(Based on outstanding)

SOURCE: Salomon Brothers

TABLE 1			
International shares of the world's major bond markets (Percent based on outstanding)			
	1980	1985	1988
U.S. dollar	4.4	8.8	10.5
Japanese yen	1.6	3.2	5.0
German mark	12.6	11.2	14.2
U.K. sterling	0.9	9.4	21.3
Canadian dollar	3.1	5.5	13.7
Swiss franc	27.3	42.3	49.2
Australian dollar	n.a.	9.5	36.2
SOURCE: Salomon Brothers			

ing in French equities was done in London in 1988.[33] French regulators hope that their improvements will lure some of that trading back to Paris.

West German equity markets, until recently, provided a good illustration of the kinds of barriers that keep stock exchanges small, inefficient, and illiquid. Access to the stock exchange was effectively controlled by the largest banks, which have a monopoly on brokerage. Under this arrangement, small firms were kept from issuing equity, thus remaining captive loan clients. Large German firms have traditionally relied more heavily on bank credit and bonds than on equity to finance growth. The integration of banking and commerce in Germany has contributed to this reliance. German banks, "through their equity holdings, exert significant ownership control over industrial firms."[34]

The fragmented structure of the West German system, which consists of eight independent exchanges each with its own interests, also helped check development. Over the last several years, though, rivalries between the exchanges have been somewhat buried, and they have been working to improve their integration and cooperation. One way is through computer links between exchanges to facilitate trading. A transaction that cannot be executed immediately at one of the smaller exchanges can be forwarded to Frankfurt to be completed. Overall, German liberalization efforts have been moderately successful, adding about 90 new companies to the stock exchange between 1984 and 1988.[35]

Active institutional investors, such as pension funds, which have a major position in the U.S. markets, have no tradition in the German equity market. Billions of marks in pension funds are on the balance sheets of German companies, treated as long-term loans from employees.[36] Freeing these funds in a deregulated and restructured market could have a profound effect on Germany's domestic equity markets.

Issuance of international securities

The issuance of international securities was mixed in 1988. Issuance of international bonds was relatively strong, while issuance of international equities, at $7.7 billion in 1988, was off considerably from 1987, but almost triple 1985 issuance.[37]

The contraction of international equities was driven by investors, and reflects their caution. Following the stock market crash in October 1987, portfolio managers reportedly focussed, and have continued to focus, on low-risk assets and on domestic issues.[38] Lower volatility of share prices on the world's major

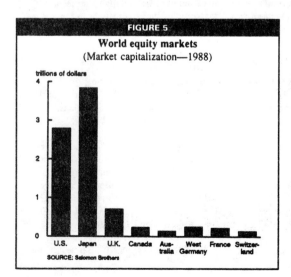

FIGURE 5

World equity markets
(Market capitalization—1988)

trillions of dollars

U.S. Japan U.K. Canada Australia West Germany France Switzerland

SOURCE: Salomon Brothers

exchanges, however, would likely aid a re-bound in the appetite for and in the issuance of international equities.

Some important structural changes took place in international financial markets between 1985 and 1987. A sharp increase in issuance for the U.K. translated into substantially greater market share of international equity issuance, from 3.7 percent in 1985 to 33.0 percent in 1987. This increased share of international activity reflects the deregulation and restructuring of the London markets that occurred in the fall of 1986, improving their place as an international marketplace for securities. Even with the retrenchment in 1988, London maintained its leading role, with twice the issuance of second-place U.S.[39]

Over this same three-year period, Switzerland's international equity issuance translated into a substantially smaller market share, falling from 40.7 percent to 6.0 percent. This sharp decline in market share, from undisputed leader to fourth, reveals Switzerland's failure to keep pace with deregulation in other countries. For years, a cartel system dominated by its three big banks has set prices and practices in the stock markets. It is only recently that competition from markets abroad has forced the cartel to liberalize its system.[40]

In contrast to the international equities markets, issuance of international bonds was very strong in 1988, following a sharp contraction in 1987 entirely due to a 25.5 percent decline in Eurobond issuance.[41] Eurobonds account for about 80 percent of international bond issues, and nearly two-thirds of all international issues are denominated in three currencies—the U.S. dollar, Swiss franc, and the Deutschemark. Nearly 60 percent of international bonds are issued by borrowers in Japan, the United Kingdom, the United States, France, Canada, and Germany.

The long-time importance of the United States and the U.S. dollar in the international bond market has been dwindling. In 1985, 54 percent of all Eurobonds were denominated in U.S. dollars, but by 1988 only 42 percent were in U.S. dollars.

Similarly, U.S. borrowers issued 24 percent of all international bonds in 1985, but issued only 8 percent in 1988. The impetus behind this decline lies in part with the investors who prefer low-risk securities and are leery of U.S. bonds because of the perceived increase in "event risk" associated with restructurings and leveraged buyouts. Also, no doubt, developments such as the adoption of Rule 415 by the Securities and Exchange Commission (shelf registration) have encouraged U.S. firms to issue domestic securities by making it less costly to do so.

Trading in international securities

The United States is a major center of international securities trading. Foreign transactions in U.S. markets exceed U.S. transactions in foreign markets by a ratio of almost 7 to 1. This is a result of several factors. The United States has the largest and most developed securities markets in the world. U.S. equity markets are virtually free of controls on foreign involvement. SEC regulations on disclosure dissipate much uncertainty concerning the issuers of publicly listed securities in the United States while less, or inadequate, regulation in other countries makes investments more risky in those foreign markets. The market for U.S. Treasury securities has also been very attractive to foreign investors. In fact, large purchases of these securities by the Japanese have helped finance the U.S. government budget deficit.

Both foreign transactions in U.S. markets and U.S. transactions in foreign markets have been increasing at a very rapid pace. Foreign transactions in U.S. equity securities in U.S. markets plus such transactions in foreign equities in U.S. markets grew at almost 50 percent annually to exceed $670 billion in 1987.[42] Foreign transactions in U.S. stocks on U.S. equity markets have been increasing faster than domestic transactions; in 1988, foreign transactions accounted for 13 percent of the value of transactions on U.S. markets, up from 10 percent in 1986 (see Table 2).

Foreign transactions have increased in securities markets abroad as well; however, they have not, in general, kept pace with domestic trading. Consequently, foreign transactions as a percentage of all transactions has declined over the 1986-88 period for Japan, Canada, Germany, and the United Kingdom. Nevertheless, transactions by U.S. residents in foreign equity markets were estimated at about $188 billion in 1987, nearly 12 times as much as in 1982.[43]

TABLE 2		
Foreign transactions in domestic equity markets: Share of domestic trading (Percent of total volume)		
	1985	**1988**
Japan	8.7	6.5
Canada	29.5	21.6
Germany	29.9	8.7
U.S.	9.7	13.1
U.K.	37.3	20.8
France	38.0	43.5
Switzerland	4.6	6.3
SOURCE: Salomon Brothers		

Foreign transactions in U.S. bonds and foreign bonds in U.S. markets in 1988 increased to more than 13 times their 1982 level (see Figure 6). This trading boom was fueled mainly by growth in transactions for U.S. Treasury bonds, which accounted for about 84 percent of total foreign bond transactions in 1988, up from 63 percent in 1982. These transactions in U.S. Treasury bonds accounted for almost three-quarters of all foreign securities transactions in U.S. markets in 1988.

Bond transactions in other countries by nonresidents also increased dramatically. In Germany, for example, the value of such transactions increased by 300 percent over the 1985-88 period and now account for over half of the value of all transactions in German bond markets.[44] Foreign bond transactions by U.S. residents reached an estimated $380 billion in 1987, six times greater than the 1982 figure.

Derivative products

Globalization has affected derivative financial products in two ways. First, it has spurred the creation and rapid growth of internationally-related financial products, such as Eurodollar futures and options and foreign currency futures and options as well as futures and options on domestic securities that trade globally, such as U.S. Treasury securities. Trading hours on some U.S. futures and options exchanges have been expanded to support cross-border trading of underlying assets, such as Treasury securities. Second, globalization has lead to the establishment of futures and options exchanges worldwide. Once the exclusive domain of U.S. markets, especially in Chicago, financial derivative products are now traded in significant volumes throughout Europe and Asia.

The number of futures contracts on Eurodollar CDs and on foreign currencies as well as the number of open positions has increased rapidly (see Figure 7). The number of futures contracts on Eurodollar CDs traded worldwide increased almost 70 percent annually since 1983 to reach over 25 million in 1988. This compares with a 20 to 25 percent annual growth rate for Eurodollars.[45] Similarly, nearly 40 million futures and options contracts on various foreign currencies were traded worldwide in 1988, up from 14 million in 1983. This growth rate is roughly equivalent to that of forex trading.

The rapid increase in the volume of trading of internationally-linked futures and options contracts has largely benefited U.S. exchanges, which are the largest and sometimes the only exchanges where such products are traded. Nevertheless, the share of exchange traded futures and options volume commanded by the U.S. exchanges has dropped from 98 percent in 1983 to about 80 percent in 1988.

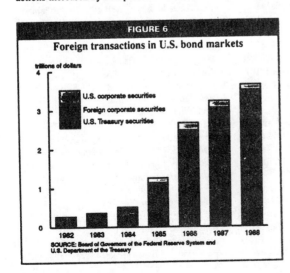

FIGURE 6

Foreign transactions in U.S. bond markets

trillions of dollars

■ U.S. corporate securities
Foreign corporate securities
U.S. Treasury securities

1982 1983 1984 1985 1986 1987 1988

SOURCE: Board of Governors of the Federal Reserve System and U.S. Department of the Treasury

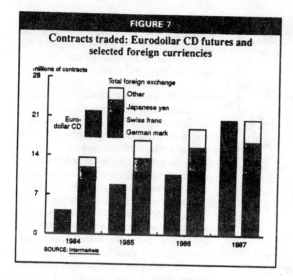

FIGURE 7

Contracts traded: Eurodollar CD futures and selected foreign curriencies

millions of contracts

Total foreign exchange
Other
Japanese yen
Euro-dollar CD
Swiss franc
German mark

1984   1985   1986   1987

SOURCE: Intermarkets

petition from London for business that the Germans felt should be in Frankfurt. LIFFE began trading futures on West German government bonds in September 1988, and, as of year-end 1989. it was the second most active contract on the exchange, trading about 20,000 contracts daily. It has been estimated that anywhere from 30 to 70 percent of this London-based trading is accounted for by the German business community.[50]

When an exchange is established, its product line usually includes a domestic government bond contract, a stock index futures contract, and, sometimes. a domestic/foreign currency futures or option contract.

These 18 percentage points were primarily lost to European and Japanese exchanges.

In the past four years, 20 new exchanges have been established, bringing the total to 72.[46] Many of these new exchanges are in Europe. In addition, foreign membership at many exchanges is considerable. For example, over two-thirds of LIFFE's (London International Financial Futures Exchange) membership is based outside of the United Kingdom.[47]

Two notable additions to futures and options trading are Switzerland and West Germany. The Swiss Options and Financial Futures Exchange (SOFFEX) was established in March 1988, and is the world's first fully-automated, computer-based exchange.[48] SOFFEX trades index options on the Swiss Market Index, which consists of 24 stocks traded on the three main stock exchanges in Geneva, Zurich, and Basle. Critics of the system contend that there is a lack of liquidity on the underlying stocks, thus limiting its effectiveness. Swiss banks control brokerage and can match trades internally with their own clients. This leaves a small amount for open trading on the exchange.[49]

The Germans will begin trading futures and options in 1990. The exchange will trade bond and stock-index futures, and options on 14 high-turnover German stocks. Trading will be executed entirely by computer, as on its Swiss counterpart. The main reason the government approved the new exchange was com-

Therefore. the number of contracts listed on foreign exchanges that compete with contracts on U.S. exchanges is small relative to the number of contracts traded throughout the world.

The U.S. exchanges' most formidable competitors are LIFFE and SIMEX (Singapore International Monetary Exchange). LIFFE competes with U.S. exchanges for trading volume in U.S. Treasury bond futures and options and in Eurodollar futures and options. SIMEX also competes for trading volume in Eurodollar futures as well as in Deutschemark and Japanese yen futures. But the SIMEX contracts are also complements to U.S. contracts in that a contract opened on the U.S. (Singapore) exchange can be closed on the Singapore (U.S.) exchange.

As shown in Figure 8, LIFFE commands less than 3 percent of trading volume in T-bond futures and options and Eurodollar options. Similarly, less than 3 percent of all Deutschemark futures trading occurs on SIMEX. LIFFE and SIMEX, however, are much more significant competitors for Eurodollar futures volume. SIMEX accounts for 7.5 percent of trading volume and LIFFE accounts for 6.5 percent.

Furthermore, in only three years. SIMEX managed to capture over 50 percent of the annual trading volume in the yen futures contract. The relatively greater success of SIMEX with the yen contract reflects the importance

14

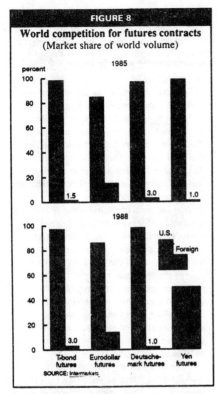

FIGURE 8

World competition for futures contracts
(Market share of world volume)

1985

1988

SOURCE: Intermarkets

of trading in the same time zone as one side of a foreign exchange transaction. In June 1989, a yen/dollar futures contract was launched in Tokyo, along with a Eurodollar contract. The experience of SIMEX suggests that the yen contract will attract market share away from SIMEX rather than from the CME because Singapore and Tokyo are in the same time zone. The above experiences suggest that once deutschemark futures begin trading on the German exchange, some proportion now traded in London will move to Germany.

24-hour trading

True 24-hour trading exists in only a few markets, and is most valuable for assets whose investors span several time zones. Major currencies are traded around the clock in at least seven major money centers. Precious metals, especially gold bullion, and oil, which trade in New York, London and Singapore, are traded 24 hours a day. U.S. Treasury bonds are traded around the clock as well, but overseas markets are thin. Twenty percent of the busi-

ness at the French futures exchange in Paris (Matif) is conducted outside of normal trading hours, indicating how important the extended hours can be.[51]

To a lesser extent, stocks of about 200 major multinational firms are traded in foreign markets as well as in their domestic markets, but foreign trading volume does not compare with that in domestic markets. One reason is that most information about a firm is revealed while domestic markets are open.

In preparation for the increase in round-the-clock trading and due to perceived competition from foreign exchanges, the National Association of Securities Dealers, the Chicago Mercantile Exchange, and the Chicago Board of Trade have made plans to extend their normal trading hours through computerized systems. The New York Stock Exchange is considering trading stocks electronically outside of normal trading hours, and the Cincinnati Stock Exchange and the CBOE are planning 24-hour electronic trading systems. The trading hours for foreign currency options on the Philadelphia Stock Exchange begin at 7:45 a.m. (Eastern Standard Time) to encompass more of the London business day.

International investment banking

As financial markets become more globally integrated, foreign investment banks are attempting to play larger roles in domestic markets. Overall, they are meeting with mixed results.

Foreign investment banks in the United States

Foreign-based investment banks have made some inroads into U.S. domestic capital markets. For the first time, two foreign firms ranked among the top ten advisers for U.S. mergers and acquisitions in the first quarter of 1989. Kleinwort Benson and S.G. Warburg, ranked sixth and seventh, respectively, according to the value of deals.[52] They placed ahead of Merrill Lynch and Kidder Peabody. No Japanese firms ranked among the top M&A advisers, although Fuji Bank of Japan has an ownership interest in Kleinwort Benson.

The Japanese are making a concerted effort to penetrate the U.S. investment banking market, but they have met with little success. The Big Four—Nomura Securities, Daiwa Securities, Nikko Securities, and Yamaichi

Securities Company—expanded in the United States in the mid-1980s, but have scaled back personnel due to unprofitable U.S. operations. Two of the Big Four—Nomura and Yamachi—have been trying to model their U.S. operations as identifiable Wall Street companies, and not just subsidiaries of Tokyo firms, by their appointment of Americans to head their U.S. operations. Nomura's strengths have been its primary dealership in U.S. government securities and U.S. stock trading unit, primarily for Japanese purchase. Nomura's weaknesses, however, are its lack of financial product development and its trading skills.

The Japanese have been more successful in U.S. derivative markets. In April 1988, Nikko Securities became the first Japanese securities firm to acquire a clearing membership at the Chicago Board of Trade (CBOT). Since then, fifteen others have joined the CBOT. The Chicago Mercantile Exchange (CME) has seventeen Japanese companies as members. Nikko, Daiwa, and Yamaichi are members of both the CBOT and CME. Recently, Nomura announced a cooperative agreement with Refco, one of the world's largest futures merchants. Consummation of the deal will assist Nomura in learning futures trading.

U.S. investment banks' activities abroad

Merger and acquisition activity has been slowing in the United States, prompting Wall Street firms to look to foreign markets. According to a 1988 survey, U.S. firms accounted for slightly more than half of all cross-border merger and acquisition activity. The most active U.S. investment banks were Shearson Lehman Hutton (57 deals), Goldman Sachs (46), and First Boston (34).[53]

U.S. investment banks represented about 12 percent of all mergers and acquisitions for European clients in 1988. The most active U.S. firms in this category were Security Pacific Group (37 deals), Shearson Lehman Hutton (26), and Goldman Sachs (22). Security Pacific has acquired two foreign investment banks, one Canadian and one British.[54]

U.S. firms expect to find some business in Asia as well. The newly formed investment bank, Wasserstein Perella, for example, recently dispatched merger and acquisition

teams to Japan to set up the Tokyo joint venture, Nomura Wasserstein Perella.

In the area of securities underwriting, U.S. firms are quite strong. Seven of the top ten underwriters of debt and equity securities worldwide are U.S. firms; however, only three U.S. firms rank among the top underwriters of non-U.S. securities. Merrill Lynch was the top underwriter of all debt and equity offerings worldwide during the first half of 1989.[55]

The strength of U.S. firms abroad lies primarily in Europe. Foreign securities firms in Tokyo have found it difficult to establish themselves. Thirty-six of the 51 Tokyo branches of foreign securities houses lost a total of $164 million for the six months ending March 1989.[56] As a result of these losses, many foreign firms have cut back their Tokyo operations, concentrating on a particular product or service. Twenty-two out of the 115 Tokyo stock exchange members are foreign firms. Another 29 foreign securities houses have opened branch offices in Tokyo. Nevertheless, the Big Four dominate the Tokyo exchange, accounting for almost 50 percent of daily business. The foreign firms account for only 4.5 percent of this daily business.[57]

Three American investment banks. Salomon Brothers, Merrill Lynch, and First Boston, have been able to develop profitable operations in the Tokyo market. All three American firms attribute their success in part to a well-trained staff, and to hiring Japanese college graduates to fill positions. Salomon posted a $53.6 million pretax profit as of March 31, 1989. It also made a $300 million capital infusion, which has helped to make Salomon a challenger to the Big Four in bond trading.[58]

The U.S. government has been pressuring for greater access for U.S. firms to Japanese capital markets since 1984. For instance, Japanese government securities are predominantly sold through closed syndicates, in which foreign firms account for only about 8 percent of the total. Change has been slower than foreign investment banks and governments would like, but some progress has been made. The Japanese sold 40 percent of its 10-year bonds at an open auction in April 1989.[59]

Conclusion

Financial markets and financial services are becoming more globally integrated. As businesses expand into new markets around the world, there is greater demand for financing to follow them. All major areas of international finance have grown far more rapidly than foreign trade in recent years. Trading of securities in U.S. markets by nonresidents, trading volume of foreign currency futures and options, and foreign exchange trading have been growing at 40 percent or more a year. This rapid growth of international financial transactions reflects the growth in cross-border capital flows.

The major markets for domestic as well as international financial services are the United States, Japan, and the United Kingdom, although it is beginning to make more sense to talk about the dominant markets as the United States, Japan, and Europe. The reduction of regulatory barriers and harmonization of rules among countries have allowed more firms to compete in more markets around the world. These markets are also competing against each other for a share of the world's trading volume.

Today, a very large part of financial globalization involves financial intermediaries dealing with other, foreign, financial intermediaries. Consequently, prices in one market are affected by conditions in other markets, but, with a few exceptions, of which commercial lending is the most notable, customers do not have direct access to more suppliers. Again, this could change as Europe moves toward economic and financial unification.

Lessons from industries such as automobiles and petroleum, as well as lessons from geographic expansion in the United States, indicate that the financial services industry will become more consolidated, with firms from a handful of countries garnering substantial market share. International joint ventures will be common and often precursors to outright acquisitions. For smaller firms to survive as global competitors, they will have to find and service a market niche.

As the financial services industry and financial markets become more globally integrated, the most efficient and best organized firms will prevail. Also, countries with the most efficient—but not necessarily the least—regulation will become the world's major international financial centers.

FOOTNOTES

[1]"Japanese Finance." Survey. *The Economist*, December 10, 1988, pp. 3 and 10.

[2]Ibid.

[3]Thomas H. Hanley, et. al., "The Swiss Banks: Universal Banks Poised to Prosper as Global Deregulation Unfolds," *Salomon Brothers Stock Research*, June 1986.

[4]See David T. Llewellyn. *Competition, Diversification, and Structural Change in the British Financial System*, 1989, unpublished xerox, p. 1.

[5]Christopher M. Korth. "International Financial Markets," in William H. Baughn and Donald R. Mandich, eds., *The International Banking Handbook*, Dow Jones-Irwin, 1983, pp. 9-13.

[6]During the Cold War, the U.S. dollar was the only universally accepted currency, and the Russians wanted to maintain their international reserves in dollars, but not at American banks for fear that the U.S government might freeze the funds. Therefore, the Russians found some British, French and German banks that would accept deposits in dollars. See Korth, p. 11.

[7]Christopher M. Korth. "The Eurocurrency Markets," in Baughn and Mandich, p. 26.

[8]Herbert L. Baer and Christine A. Pavel. "Does regulation drive innovation?," *Economic Perspectives*, Vol. 12, No. 2, March/April 1988, pp. 3-15, Federal Reserve Bank of Chicago.

[9]"Japanese banking booms offshore." *The Economist*, November 26, 1988, p. 87.

[10]*International Financial Statistics*, International Monetary Fund, various years.

[11]Ibid.

[12]This does not apply in criminal cases, bankruptcy, or debt collection. The disclosure of secret information to foreign authorities is not allowed, unless provided for in an international treaty. In such a case, which is an exception, the foreign authorities could obtain only the information available to Swiss authorities under similar circumstances. See Peat, Marwick, Mitchell & Co., *Banking in Switzerland*, 1979, pp. 35-6.

[13]Eurobanks have specific rates at which they are prepared either to borrow or lend Eurofunds. In London, this rate is known as LIBOR (the London Interbank Offer Rate). LIBOR dominates the Eurocurrency market.

[14]Henry S. Terrell, Robert S. Dohner, and Barbara R. Lowrey. "The Activities of Japanese Banks in the United

Kingdom and in the United States, 1980-88," *Federal Reserve Bulletin*, February 1990, p. 43.

[15]Michael R. Sesit and Craig Torres, "What if They Traded All Day and Nobody Came?," *Wall Street Journal*, June 14, 1989, p. C1.

[16]*U.S. Foreign Exchange Market Survey*, Federal Reserve Bank of New York, April 1989, pp. 5-7.

[17]"Report of Assets and Liabilities of U.S. Branches and Agencies of Foreign Banks," Table 4.30, *Federal Reserve Bulletin*, June 1989, Board of Governors of the Federal Reserve System; and *Annual Statistical Digest*, Board of Governors of the Federal Reserve System, Table 68.

[18]Ibid.

[19]*Senior Loan Officer Opinion Survey on Bank Lending Practices for August 1989*, Board of Governors of the Federal Reserve System.

[20]See footnote 17.

[21]*Annual Report*, Board of Governors of the Federal Reserve System, Banking Supervision and Regulation Section, various years; authors' calculations from Report of Condition and Income tapes, Board of Governors of the Federal Reserve System, various years.

[22]Ibid.

[23]Ibid.

[24]"European banking: Cheque list," *The Economist*, June 24, 1989, pp. 74-5.

[25]The Glass-Steagall Act is the law that separates commercial banking from investment banking in the U.S. Article 65 is its Japanese equivalent.

[26]James B. Treece, with John Hoerr, "Shaking Up Detroit," *Business Week*, August 14, 1989, pp. 74-80.

[27]*Standard and Poor's Oil Industry Survey*, August 3, 1989, p. 26.

[28]"European Stock Exchanges," *A supplement to Euromoney*, August 1987, pp. 2-5.

[29]Rosario Benvides, "How Big is the World Bond Market?—1989 Update" *International Bond Markets*, Salomon Brothers, June 24, 1989.

[30]Ibid.

[31]"Look east, young Eurobond," *The Economist*, September 16, 1989, pp. 83-4; "Japanese paper fills the void," *A supplement to Euromoney*, March 1989, p. 2.

[32]See *The Economist*, Sept. 16, 1989, pp. 83-4.

[33]"La grande boum," *The Economist*, October 1, 1988, pp. 83-4.

[34]Christine M. Cumming and Lawrence M. Sweet, "Financial Structure of the G-7 Countries: How Does the United States Compare?," *Federal Reserve Bank of New York, Quarterly Review*, Winter 1987/88, pp. 15-16.

[35]"Sweeping away Frankfurt's old-fashioned habits," *The Economist*, January 28, 1989, pp. 73-4.

[36]Ibid.

[37]*Financial Market Trends*, OECD, February 1989, pp. 85-6.

[38]Ibid.

[39]Ibid.

[40]"A smooth run for Switzerland's big banks," *The Economist*, June 17, 1989, pp. 87-8.

[41]*World Financial Markets*, J.P. Morgan & Co., November 29, 1988.

[42]"Foreign Transactions in Securities," Table 3.24, *Federal Reserve Bulletin*, June 1989, Board of Governors of the Federal Reserve System.

[43]Ibid.

[44]Various central bank statistical releases.

[45]The underlying instrument is worth $1 million.

[46]"US exchanges fight for market share," *A supplement to Euromoney*, July 1989, p. 9.

[47]Elizabeth R. Thagard, "London's Jump," *Intermarkets*, May 1989, p. 22.

[48]See *A supplement to Euromoney*, August 1987, p. 28.

[49]Ginger Szala, "Financial walls tumble for German investors," *Futures*, January 1990, p. 44.

[50]Ibid., p. 42.

[51]See Thagard, p. 23.

[52]Ted Weissberg, "Wall Street Seeks Global Merger Market: IDD's First-quarter M&A Rankings," *Investment Dealers Digest*, May 8, 1989, pp. 17-21.

[53]"The World Champions of M&A," *Euromoney*, February 1989, pp. 96-102.

[54]Ibid.

[55]Philip Maher, "Merrill Lynch Holds on to Top International Spot," *Investment Dealers Digest*, July 10, 1989, pp. 23-25.

[56]"Japan proving tough for foreign brokerage," *Chicago Tribune*, September 11, 1989, section 4, pp. 1-2

[57]Ibid.

[58]Ibid.

[59]Ibid.

Chapter 27

Legal Protections For Innovative Financial Products and Services

Peter K. Trzyna

Introduction and Overview

The financial industry is increasingly using intellectual property law to prevent competitors from offering similar or related financial products and services. Thus, when creating, underwriting, or marketing such products and services, companies should be aware of the legal protections available to themselves and to others. Copyrights, patents, unfair competition (misappropriation), and trademarks have all been used to protect securities, insurance, banking, and financial innovations.

A copyright protects original works of authorship from unauthorized reproduction. For example, reoffering circulars and stock market indexes have been accorded copyright protection through litigation. Financial instruments, prospectuses, underwriting documents, and advertising are copyrightable. In addition, computer programs used to create, value, manipulate, exchange, or otherwise

Peter K. Trzyna is a Washington, D.C. based patent attorney who has filed numerous patents, trademarks, and copyright applications involving financial products and services. He has authored and coauthored a number of articles on the use of intellectual property laws to protect financial products

support financial products are copyrightable. Art work on bank checks or stock certificates can also be protected by copyright.

A copyright protects the author's expression, but not the underlying idea being expressed. Thus, a copyright will not prevent a competitor from offering a similar financial product with independently authored documents. But a copyright can protect against the competitor's copying or deriving documents from those that are copyrighted.

Copyright ownership is an area of perennial conflict. Initially, the owner of the copyright is the author or the author's employer. Merely purchasing the work will not transfer the copyright; the copyright owner must sign an assignment of the copyright. Thus, if a company retains a law firm to draft financial documents and a computer consultant to write an accounting program, without signed copyright assignments, the law firm and the computer consultant will retain the copyrights and the exclusive rights to make copies and derivative works.

A patent grants the exclusive right to make, use, or sell a machine, process, article of manufacture, or composition of matter. An example of the use of a patent to gain an advantage in the financial industry involves computers and computer programs. If the financial product requires computer support, the exclusive right to use a computer system or any equivalent system can mean the exclusive right to the products themselves. Such an exclusive right can be obtained by a patent for a term of 17 years.

In a patent, the invention can be broadly defined. For example, the invention could include "data processing means" for handling automated aspects of a financial product—language that could cover essentially all computer hardware/software systems for the product.

If a competitor could not be secure a license for such a patent, it could be relegated to doing the computations by hand. But this may not always be feasible. For example, if the product required processing an extensive amount of data or providing up-to-the-minute computations like the value of the S&P 500, the competitor may be forced to withdraw from offering a competitive product for the 17 year term of the patent.

Many patents cover computer systems used to support financial products and services. Patents cover computer systems that do program trading, control pension benefit plans, automate insurance quotes and policy issuance, run stock and commodity exchanges, authorize credit card purchases, facilitate automated bank teller machines, implement mortgages, and compute securities payouts.

Successful patent litigation has involved the Merrill Lynch Cash Management System and the CollegeSure CD.

Patent litigation is often hard fought and expensive due to the possibility of a significant judgment. It is critical to obtain a legal opinion from a patent attorney whenever one might be infringing a known patent. If infringement is later found, a prior, contrary opinion from patent counsel will usually prevent the award of treble damages and attorney's fees.

Common law protections against unfair competition have protected labor, skill, and effort from misappropriation by a competitor. Standard & Poor's Corporation, Inc. and Dow Jones & Company, Inc. have successfully sued others for misappropriating their respective stock market indexes. However, the viability of this form of protection against unfair competition may have been undermined by recent court decisions.

A trademark or service mark protects a term or symbol identifying the source of goods or of services, respectively. In the financial industry, many marks have been federally registered, including the names of institutions, such as banks, brokers, insurance companies, and underwriters. The names of financial products, such as charge cards and securities, have also been registered. Successful trademark litigation has involved the STANDARD & POOR'S mark, for example.

Protecting a trademark limits the extent to which a financial product of one company can be associated with the product of another. Federal registration provides significant advantages. Nonetheless, a trademark will not prevent competitors from issuing similarly structured offerings under a distinctly different name.

The implications for both creators and competitors is clear. A variety of intellectual property protections is available to protect financial products and services. The protections are not mutually exclusive, and litigation typically involves a combination of copyright, patent, misappropriation, and trademark allegations.

For the creator of a new financial product, these protections can permit recovery of research and development costs and can provide a reward for creativity. Thus, those who create, underwrite, issue, and market financial products or services should take advantage of available protections.

For competitors, the exclusive rights pose significant risks. Court injunctions could require withdrawing the financial product from the market. In addition, damages (which a court can triple for some willful cases), attorney fees, costs and interest, and, under limited circumstances, criminal penalties, are also possible remedies for infringement. Thus, those who offer financial products and services that compete with new offerings should be alert to the legal protections that others might have.

What follows is a detailed discussion of the legal protections used in the financial industry.

Using a Copyright to Protect a Financial Product

A copyright protects against verbatim copying as well as preparing derivative works. A derivative work is one based in part on a preexisting work. Infringement includes the unauthorized copying, distributing, or displaying of a copyrighted work or a derivative thereof.

A copyright protects only the author's expression. It does not protect an idea, procedure, process, system, method of operation, concept, principle, or discovery embodied in the expression. Thus, there is no infringement where the only similarity between two works is an underlying idea.

A financial product was protected by a copyright in *Merritt Forbes & Co. v. Newman Investment Securities, Inc.*[1] Merritt Forbes & Co. ("Merritt Forbes"), a securities underwriter and marketer, registered a copyright for its reoffering circulars and supplements for tax-exempt municipal bonds. Merritt Forbes successfully sued Newman Investment Securities, Inc. and others ("Newman") for infringing the copyright by using substantially copied documents in an offering. The court expressly rejected Newman's argument that such documents are uncopyrightable.

What Can and Cannot Be Protected

One requirement for a copyright is proper subject matter. Copyright protection can be obtained for "original works of authorship fixed in any tangible medium of expression."[2] Literary, artistic, and graphic works exemplify works of authorship. There is no requirement of literary merit or qualitative value for a copyright. Thus, documents such as underwriting guidelines, a prospectus, an offering circular, a computer program, or an advertising brochure can be protected by a copyright. Art work on a bank check or a stock certificate also can be protected.

Another requirement for a copyright is originality (i.e., independent creation). The requisite originality may be missing where an expression is solely functional, for example, a statutory recitation or a list of ingredients or facts. However, one court found that a list of component stocks in an index was copyrighted and not a mere list of ingredients.[3]

In sum, copyright laws allow enough latitude for documents used with financial products to be written or artistically rendered so they will be protected by a copyright. However, not all financial documents are copyrightable, and the text in some otherwise copyrighted documents may be so functional that it is not protected.

How to Obtain Protection

A copyright exists from the moment the work is created, i.e., from the moment an expression is fixed in any tangible medium of expression. The protection lasts for 50 years plus the life of the author, or, if created by an independent contractor, either for 75 years from the first publication, or for 100 years from the date of creation, whichever ends first.

The following issues frequently arise in obtaining copyright protection.

Ownership. Initially, a copyright vests in the author, unless the author creates the work as an employee, in which case the copyright belongs to the employer, i.e., the work is "made for hire." To qualify as an author, one must actually create the work; merely setting specifications for the work is insufficient for even sharing the ownership. Thus, if a law firm, a computer consultant, or another independent contractor creates a work according to a client's specifications, the client will obtain only a copy of the work—not the copyright itself. The copyright owner retains its exclusive rights unless a copyright assignment is signed. Because the need for a signed copyright assignment is frequently overlooked, copyright ownership is an area of perennial conflicts.

Notice. Placing a copyright notice on the work is unnecessary. However, giving notice prevents a defense of innocent infringement, i.e., a claim that the document was copied without knowing that it is copyrighted. If proven, this defense could reduce an award of damages. Proper notice is useful for avoiding innocent infringements and this defense.

Proper forms of copyright notice are ©, the abbreviation "Copr.," or the word "Copyright," followed by the year of first publication, and the copyright owner's name. In addition, the phrase "All Rights Reserved" can be used to assure protection under the

Buenos Aires Convention, to which the United States and most Latin American countries belong. The notice should be located on the work where it is likely to be seen.

Registration. For works of U.S. origin, registration is unnecessary to preserve the copyright. However, registration (or a denial of registration) is a prerequisite for filing an infringement suit. Also, timely registration is required for an award of statutory damages and attorney fees. Registration is not timely if the infringement commenced either: (1) before the date of its registration, if the work is unpublished; or (2) after first publication and before registration, unless the copyright is registered within three months after the first publication.

Registration is seldom difficult; therefore, it is usually inexpensive. An application requires an executed two-page form, a nominal fee, and, for most documentary works, two copies. Other registration expenses are usually minimal. A Certificate of Registration usually issues within a few months, though an expedited procedure exists. Procedures also exist for preserving confidential information in applications and registrations for unpublished works.

Enforcement

A copyright infringement suit must be filed in federal district court. However, an action also can be brought in the International Trade Commission (ITC)[4] to exclude the importation of infringing goods. Presumably, this would include copyrighted financial documents. An ITC proceeding offers no monetary remedy, but it does offer the possibility of an exclusion order. The entire proceeding lasts between 12 and 18 months, though preliminary relief can sometimes be obtained within 90 to 150 days. The U.S. Customs Service provides enforcement. In either the court or the ITC, the plaintiff must prove, by a preponderance of the evidence: (1) ownership of a valid copyright and (2) infringement. A Certificate of Registration is prima facie proof of ownership of a valid copyright and all facts stated therein. Infringement is proven by showing that the defendant was exposed to the work and that there is a substantial similarity between the copyrighted work and the allegedly infringing work.

The owner of an infringed copyright may recover damages (actual damages or the infringer's profits) or may simply choose to receive statutory damages of $500 to $20,000 per infringement. If the infringement is unintentional, a court may reduce the award to as little as $200. However, if a court finds the infringement willful, it may increase damages up to $100,000. Preliminary and permanent injunctions are relatively easy to obtain. The Copyright Act also authorizes the impoundment and destruction of infringing articles and, for egregious cases, provides criminal sanctions.

Copyright infringement of a registered copyright for a document is a very efficient legal proceeding. That is, cases tend to involve simple evidence, e.g., the plaintiff opting for statutory damages to dispense with the damages portion of a trial. Damage awards, though usually modest in comparison with patent infringement awards, are often granted.

Advantages and Disadvantages

Some of the advantages of copyright protection are as follows: (1) it is inexpensive; (2) it is quickly obtained; (3) litigation is highly efficient; (4) injunctive relief is relatively easy to obtain; and (5) damages, though rarely overwhelming, are often awarded. A disadvantage is that the protection is limited; ideas are unprotected, and independent creation, even of an identical work, is a complete defense.

Comment

Copyright protection should be considered for significant original works and authorized derivative works, including financial documents. A copyright can at least protect against a competitor's offering a financial product by simply using essentially copied documents. Copyrights inhibit competitors from copying or deriving registration and proxy statements, underwriting guidelines, prospectuses, statements of additional information, annual reports, and advertising.

The copyright should be registered soon after the work is created. The potential benefits of registration usually outweigh its cost. Delaying registration can only impair enforcement. Also, a proper copyright notice should be used on protected works.

Further, caution should be exercised in deriving prospectuses, registration statements, and other financial documents from those of others, even when they bear no copyright notice. Copyright notice is not mandatory, and if the copyright has been registered, an injunction could be obtained for an infringement.

Finally, the need to distinguish between owning a copyright and owning a copy of the copyrighted work must be underscored.

Without a signed assignment, the copyright belongs to the author or the author's employer.

Using a Patent to Protect a Financial Product

A patent can indirectly protect a financial product by protecting computerized aspects of the product, and many aspects of the financial industry are computerized. In situations where a computer system is necessary to create, value, execute, document, exchange, or otherwise support the product, the patent owner can obtain the exclusive right to use the computer system or any equivalent system. Such a patent can effectively exclude others from selling an equivalent financial product for the 17-year term of the patent. As examples, the Merrill Lynch Cash Management System and the CollegeSure CD[5] were successfully protected by patent litigation.

Many patents involve financial products or services, a sampling of which follow.

Sample Securities Patents. As to securities, a device for computerized display of securities trading quotations is the subject of an expired patent.[6] A current patent[7] covers a system for carrying out a debt-for-debt exchange. The system computes face values for zero coupon bonds, generates documentation, and prints certificates. Another current patent[8] covers a system that controls an insurance program by determining premium charges and managing an investment portfolio. Still another patent[9] covers a system that determines the price to be charged for a note. The system issues a floating rate zero coupon note and determines the redemption value.

Patents control other aspects of the securities industry as well, including an automated stock exchange,[10] an international commodity trade exchange,[11] an automated securities trading system,[12] an automated investment system,[13] various cash management systems,[14] a securities valuation system,[15] and a renewable option accounting and marketing system.[16]

Sample Insurance Patents. A computer system that automatically provides insurance premium quotes and issues policies is patented.[17] A similar system specialized for insuring against weather conditions is also patented.[18] Further, a patent[19] covers a medical insurance claim verification and billing system having the capability of issuing a payment check or executing an electronic transfer of funds. Still another patent, now expired, covered a system that computes insurance and investment quantities.[20]

An insurance investment system that estimates the cost of a liability, the date on which the liability will occur, and the present value of each unit of insurance needed to yield the expected cost at maturity is patented.[21] A system that issues one-year renewable term insurance to fund the purchase of floating rate zero coupon notes also is patented.[22] The system projects an expected death benefit payment and calculates the annual insurance premium.

Sample Banking Patents. Many patents cover aspects of automated teller machines.[23] A system that debits and credits bank accounts based on payment coupons also is patented,[24] as is a computer system for administering mortgages.[25] Patents have also protected a system for projecting the impact of inflation indexed deposit and loan accounts on an institution's capital structure under various inflationary scenarios to select among different deposit accounts,[26] a method for determining interest rates,[27] and a computer system/calculator for maximizing interest earnings and providing payments from principal without interest penalty.[28]

Other Financial Patents. A data processing system that manages vehicle financing is protected by a patent.[29] Various patents cover systems that analyze, report, supervise, coordinate, or implement personal financial plans.[30] Visa International is not the only company to patent a charge card authorization system.[31] Yet another patent[32] protects a financial communications system that permits access to up-to-date savings plans, withdrawal information, benefit plans, and computes a variety of "what-if" scenarios. In addition, patents cover systems for managing pension benefits programs,[33] and even frequent flyer mileage is tracked by a patented system.[34] The Instinet financial database system also was patented.[35]

What Can and Cannot be Protected

Subject Matter. Patents are available for "any new and useful process, machine, manufacture, or composition of matter."[36] Because financial products are not within the categories of patentable subject matter, they are not patentable per se.

Computer programs are also considered unpatentable subject matter. Viewing computer programs as algorithms, courts have expressed fear that patents should not intrude on mental processes, methods of doing business, and other unpatentable subjects.[37]

However, a computer is patentable as a machine, and the computer does not cease to be a machine simply because it is running a computer program. Accordingly, courts have concluded that one can patent a computer in combination with a computer program,[38] regardless of whether the computer system is used to support financial products and services.

Merrill Lynch, for example, has patented its Cash Management System[39] and has successfully sued others for infringement of the patent.[40] The defendants moved to dismiss the suit, arguing that the Cash Management System was merely a method of doing business and a set of algorithms. The court, however, found that the patent claims defined a computer system and denied the motion. The defendants then settled the case, reportedly by paying royalties under patent licenses.

By patenting the computer system necessary to support a financial product, patent subject matter requirements can be satisfied and the product can be indirectly protected. Other companies seeking to market a competitive financial product may be relegated to doing the computations by hand.

New and Not Obvious. A patentable invention must be new and not obvious.[41] In the United States, making the invention known to the public or available for sale will start a one-year period during which an application must be filed.[42]

Even if the invention is new, it cannot be obvious at the time of the invention. For example, a mutual fund may be new in its particular composition; however, computerized aspects of a fund that differ from other funds only by the stocks held would be obvious. Nonetheless, the first computer programmed to compute the value of a mutual fund might not have been obvious when first invented.

Claims. A patent claim is a one-sentence definition of the invention that has been allowed by the Patent and Trademark Office (PTO). A claim defines the metes and bounds of an invention much like a description of land in a deed. If a claim is phrased so broadly that it includes unpatentable subject matter or technology that is old or obvious, then the claim may be invalidated by a court. A claim that is too narrow is of limited value because a competitor can design around the requirements of the claim to get the same result. Patents usually have numerous claims of decreasing scope so that, if some unknown prior art surfaces later and invalidates the broader claims, the narrower claims may survive. There is infringement if the requirements of at least one valid claim are satisfied. A representative patent claim is as follows:

Computerized Option Marketing

U.S. Patent No. 4,823,265

> *Claim 1. An automated renewable option accounting and marketing system comprising:*
>
> *first data storage means for storing data describing a holding in a renewable option in an underlying security;*
>
> *second data storage means for storing criteria under which the renewable option will be renewed;*
>
> *access means for accessing market and date data from which a determination can be made as to whether the renewal criteria has (sic) bee satisfied; and*
>
> *data processing means for processing said first data storage means data, said second data storage means data, and said market and date data such that the renewable option is renewed when the renewal criteria are satisfied.*

Claims are what make patent protection so powerful. The invention can be defined with phrases like **data processing means** and **computer means.** Such phrases are not limited to one computer, computer program, or computer system; they encompass essentially all computer systems that perform the specified function. Accordingly, a patent with broad claims could conceivably control automated aspects of a large class of financial products and services. Once, for example, a patent might have had claims with sufficient breadth to cover computerized aspects of mortgage-backed securities, whole life products, funds, or index-based products.

A single computer system could meet the terms of claims in several patents and, thus, could infringe all of them. Any system that lacks as much as one of the claim's requirements does not infringe that specific claim. However, infringement cannot be avoided by merely *adding* other features not recited in a claim.

Obtaining Protection

To obtain a patent, an application must be filed with the PTO. The application must describe how to make and use the best mode of the invention.

Prior to writing the application, it is often wise to conduct a search of the prior art. The search results may show that the invention is unpatentable or that the likely scope of protection would be too narrow. If the results suggest that it is reasonable to proceed, knowledge of the prior art also will be useful for drafting claims that maximize protection without including subject matter that is old or obvious.

Having a patent application drafted and filed (including filing fees and technical drafting) will likely cost substantially more than the cost for obtaining any other form of intellectual property protection. Further expenses will likely be incurred because, although a patent may issue directly, the usual case involves responding to at least one rejection by the PTO—e.g., because, in the Examiner's view, the invention defined in the claim is merely an obvious variation of prior technology.

A patent has a term of 17 years from the date of issuance, if periodic maintenance fees are paid. Getting a patent usually takes 18 to 25 months, or somewhat less if the PTO grants expedited processing. During its pendency, a patent application is confidential and provides no right of action against an infringer.

Enforcement

Whoever makes, uses, or sells the patented invention within the United States without authority is a direct infringer. Products made by a U.S.-patented process will also infringe. For example, a patented method for computing the value of a financial product would likely prevent sale or importation of the product itself. Infringement includes inducing or contributing to another's infringement. One can also infringe under a doctrine of equivalents. Under this doctrine, the literal requirements of a claim are interpreted to cover equivalent subject matter. Thus, a competitor's computer system that is not literally the same as that recited in any of the patent's claims would infringe nonetheless if it is an equivalent. For example, if a claim required a personal computer, the use of main frame computer could be viewed as an infringing equivalent.

Suit for patent infringement must be brought in federal court. If infringing goods (e.g., securities made by a U.S.-patented, computerized process) are imported, a patent owner can initiate an ITC proceeding to stop the importation. In either case, only a preponderance of the evidence is required to prove infringement.

In contrast, clear and convincing evidence is required to prove a patent invalid. The defendant can also raise the defenses of non-infringement, absence of liability for infringement, and unenforceability. Later independent creation of the patented invention is no defense.

Patent infringement litigation is usually complex, expensive, and lengthy, reflecting the prospect that a court will award a significant judgment. A court can enjoin further infringement and/or award damages (lost profits or a reasonable royalty), costs, and interest. For willful infringement, a court may award treble damages, attorney fees, and prejudgment interest. Thus, a competitor needing to use a patented computer system to support its product and unable to obtain a license to do so could be forced to withdraw the product.

A legal opinion on the validity and infringement of a patent should be obtained when there is reason to suspect that one might be infringing a patent. Courts can award treble damages and attorney fees for willful infringement. Willful infringement involves the knowing disregard of another's patent, for example, by infringing without having previously obtained an opinion from a patent attorney that the claims are either invalid or not infringed. Even if the claims appear to be valid and apparently would be infringed, it may be possible to design around the requirements of the claims. In view of the substantial penalties that are regularly awarded for willful patent infringement and the possibilities for avoiding such an award, it would be folly not to get an opinion of patent counsel.

Advantage and Disadvantages

The following are advantages of patent protection: (1) broad protection for 17 years; and (2) potent remedies. There also are disadvantages: (1) patent protection is more expensive to obtain than the other forms of protection; (2) protection exists only for patentable subject matter that is new and unobvious; (3) a patent is unenforceable until it issues; and (4) it is potentially expensive to enforce.

Comment

Patent protection offers the most promising means for obtaining exclusive rights to a type of financial product or service for a significant period of time. It should be considered particularly for innovative products and services that require computer support. Further, because patents can be obtained to protect other machines, articles of manufacture, processes, or improvements, in an industry such as the financial industry that is becoming ever more automated and standardized, patent protection should be used creatively.

Patents have the potential for causing the greatest reverberations in the financial industry. Competitors could well find themselves foreclosed from marketing a product or class of products for 17 years, or find themselves marketing such products only by paying royalties under a license. Courts are not timid about damage awards, and injunctive relief could require competitors to repurchase the financial products to remove them from the market.

As patents are becoming more common in the financial industry, companies should take increased care when deciding whether to compete with a new product or service. Again, the need for a company to get a validity/infringement opinion whenever it might be infringing a patent must be emphasized.

Using Unfair Competition Law to Protect a Security

Misappropriation is an amorphous form of unfair competition and can give rise to a common law or state statutory cause of action. Misappropriation litigation has been successful in protecting stock market indexes such as the Dow Jones Industrial Average and the Standard & Poor's 500.[43]

What Can and Cannot Be Protected

Three findings are necessary to prove misappropriation: First, that the plaintiff made a substantial investment of labor, skill, and effort to create a "thing" that a court can characterize as a kind of property right; second, that the defendant appropriated the thing at little or no cost, such that the court can characterize defendant's actions as "reaping where it has not sown;" and third, that the defendant injured the plaintiff by the misappropriation. Injury is proven by showing a diversion of profits from the plaintiff. The following cases (two of which involve financial services) relate to misappropriation law.

International News Service v. Associated Press[44]

Associated Press (AP) gathered news to be published by its member newspapers. When the news stories were released in the Eastern portion of the United States, International News Service (INS) wrote stories based on AP's uncopyrighted stories. INS then competed against AP in selling news stories on the West Coast. AP brought suit alleging that this was unfair competition. INS argued that once newspapers published the AP news without any copyright protection, the news became public property available for anyone to use for any purpose. Thus, INS could copy or rewrite it to sell to newspapers that were not members of AP.

The U.S. Supreme Court disagreed. The Court defined misappropriation as "taking material that has been acquired by complainant as the result of organization and the expenditure of labor, skill, and money, and which is salable by complainant for money."[45] The Court then found that INS's copying was:

> *an unauthorized interference with the normal operation of complainant's legitimate business precisely at the point where the profit is to be reaped, in order to divert a material portion of the profit from those who have earned it to those who have not; with special advantage to defendant in the competition because of the fact that it is not burdened with any part of the expense.*[46]

The Court concluded that even though the news was not copyrighted, the actions of INS constituted unfair competition.[47]

Standard & Poor's Corporation, Inc. v. Commodity Exchange, Inc.[48]

In the first case that has applied the *INS* decision to the financial industry, Commodity Exchange, Inc. (Comex) sought to market contract futures based upon the Comex 500 Stock Index—an index identical to the Standard & Poor's (S&P) 500. S&P sued Comex for misappropriation, federal and common law trademark infringement, false designation of origin, trademark dilution, copyright infringement, and other causes of action.

The district court[49] enjoined trading of the Comex 500 index-based product, based primarily on a finding of misappropriation. The U.S. Court of Appeals affirmed, reasoning that the use of the S&P 500 was a misappropriation.

Chicago Board of Trade v. Dow Jones & Co.[50]

The *INS* reasoning has also been applied to enjoin the Chicago Board of Trade (CBT) from determining the value of its own index-based securities product in the same way as the Dow Jones (Dow) Industrial Average. CBT sought a widely known stock market index to use as the basis for its financial product. When it could not get a license to use the Industrial Average, the CBT made a similar index and proposed to independently calculate it according to the published mathematical equation used by Dow. But the court ruled in Dow's favor:

> *The strong correlation of the Dow Jones Average to the general pattern of stock market activity is essential to the usefulness of the [Board's] Index contract as a hedging device, and it is*

> *that correlation which will give 'hedgers' confidence in the contract. That correlation exists solely as a result of Dow Jones' expertise, and has garnered considerable good will and respect for Dow Jones . . . . Thus the Board's use of the Dow Jones Averages is not a 'collateral' service . . . [and] the Board's conduct is within the boundaries of the doctrine of misappropriation.*[51]

How to Obtain Protection

In the future, misappropriation protection might not be as viable a means for protecting financial products because it might be deemed preempted by either the patent or copyright laws. Preemption by the federal patent law was successfully raised as a defense in *Bonito Boats, Inc. v. Thunder Craft Boats, Inc.*[52] Bonito Boats, Inc. (Bonito) sued Thunder Craft Boats, Inc. (Thunder Craft) for copying its boat hulls by a direct molding process. A Florida statute specifically prohibited such copying, arguably, a form of misappropriation. The U.S. Supreme Court found that the Florida law was preempted by federal law, which favors patentlike protection only for patentable subject matter. Thundercraft also raised the defense of federal preemption under the copyright laws because copyrights protect certain designs; however, the Court did not address the copyright law defense, having already decided the case based on the patent law. Therefore, the Court has not ruled on the question of whether state misappropriation protections covering copyrightable subject matter are federally preempted.

The *Chicago Board of Trade* case involved the use of a published mathematical equation applied to the prices of stocks in an index. It could be argued that Dow's list of stocks that make up the index is copyrightable subject matter or subject matter that is protectable only under federal law. Also, a computer system to compute the index is patentable, and the computer program is copyrightable — arguably, subject matter that is protectable only under federal law. If a court were to accept either argument, the kind of misappropriation suit brought by Dow might now be deemed preempted by federal law.

Enforcement

If misappropriation protection exists, it exists by virtue of state law. Thus, initially, state law will determine the availability of this cause of action, the legal requirements for proving a case of misappropriation, and the remedies available. Suit must be filed in state court, unless a basis exists for federal court jurisdiction (e.g., diversity). In theory, misappropriation could be alleged in an ITC proceeding. The plaintiff must prove misappropriation by a preponderance of the evidence. Though injunctions have been issued, courts seldom award damages, attorney fees, or costs.

Misappropriation litigation is likely to be expensive for several reasons. First, the law is vague and debatable. Second, there are no favorable legal presumptions, as there are for patents, federally registered trademarks, and registered copyrights. Third, a defense motion directed to whether federal law preempts misappropriation protection is likely to be raised before a court can even reach the merits of the case.

Advantages and Disadvantages

The following are advantages of protections against misappropriation: (1) it exists immediately (if at all); (2) it does not involve registration expenses; and (3) it lasts indefinitely. There are some disadvantages too, including that: (1) it might not exist in a given state or at all; (2) litigation is inefficient; (3) monetary damages, attorney fees, costs, interest, etc., are not likely to be awarded; and (4) it does not protect against independent creation or the copying of subject matter that is not unique. Nonetheless, misappropriation law has been successfully used to protect stock market indexes, and it may be viable for protecting other aspects of labor, skill, and effort.

Comment

Though vague in its parameters and uncertain in its viability, misappropriation law has its place. In some situations, this species of unfair competition law may be the only possibility for protecting a financial product. However, other forms of intellectual property protection may be more efficient and ultimately more reliable.

Using a Trademark or Service Mark to Protect a Security

Trademarks and service marks are legion in the financial industry. The Merrill Lynch bull and the Dreyfus lion are unmistakable symbols of their companies. Federal registrations have issued for DREXEL BURNHAM LAMBERT, FIDELITY INVESTMENTS, SALOMON BROTHERS, THE FIRST BOSTON CORPORATION,[53] and many other marks of financial institutions. Registrations have also issued for the financial services provided by such institutions, for example, CATS, DARTS, FASTBAC FIRST AUTOMOTIVE SHORT TERM BONDS AND CERTIFICATES.[54] Courts also have enforced the rights of those owning marks used in the financial industry.[55]

A trademark protects against another's use of a mark that is likely to cause confusion, mistake, or deceit. Thus, a trademark can be used to limit the extent to which a competitor's financial product can be associated with the creator's product.

Trademark protections supplement those provided by securities law. Section 35(d) of the Investment Company Act of 1940[56] prohibits a registered investment company from using certain terms in its company name or securities. The use of misleading terms, or those representing or implying that the security is guaranteed, sponsored, recommended, or approved by the United States, can be enjoined. General prohibitions against misrepresentation under section 10(b) of the Securities Exchange Act[57] may also prohibit a financial company from using a misleading term as the name of the company or its securities product.

A Variety of Trademark/Service Mark Protections

There are a number of means available to protect the names or symbols used in the financial industry. Common law protection may be available. In addition, it may be possible to register the trademark in one or more states. Federal registration of the mark on either the Principal Register or Supplemental Register offers further advantages. It may also be possible to obtain one registration as a trademark (for goods) and a second registration as a service mark (for services). Separate registrations for a name made of initials and for the words that make up the initials may offer broader protection.

Common Law Protection

Common law protection for a trademark is obtained by actual use of the mark to distinguish the goods or services of one seller from those of another. A mark may be any word, name, symbol, color, sound, device, design, picture, slogan, or any such combination. Marks signifying a seller's goodwill are generally known as **trademarks**. Technically, a trademark is used on goods, such as automated bank teller machines, and a **service mark** is used in association with services, such as underwriting. Together, such symbols are known as **marks**.

The service mark may be used by putting it on documents (e.g., underwriting guidelines) and offering the services for sale in association with the documents. When sales are made under a symbol that is recognizable to customers, the seller acquires certain exclusive rights. These rights include the right to prevent others from confusing the seller's customers by trading upon the mark of the seller's goodwill. To enforce this common law right, the seller must bring suit for unfair competition.

Not all names and symbols are protectable. A generic term is legally incapable of serving as a trademark because it is an ordinary name for the product, e.g., stocks and bonds. In contrast, if the name is fanciful or arbitrary, common law protection arises upon use of the mark. For example, in *Merritt Forbes & Co. v. Newman Investment Securities Inc.,*[58] the defendant was accused of infringing the following common law marks: TENDER OPTION PROGRAM, TENDER OPTION, and TOP's. The court prohibited suit on the first two claimed marks because they are generic terms, but allowed suit based on the TOP's mark.

State Protection of a Mark

Most states provide some kind of registration for marks used in the state, and the owner of the mark can get whatever additional protection is conferred by state statute. These rights range from rights of minimal legal significance (e.g., proof that on a certain day the registrant filed a claim that it was using a mark) to prima facie evidence of ownership of the mark.

Some states also prohibit dilution. Dilution is the use of another's mark in a manner that will erode the uniqueness of a famous mark. For example, one court held that THE GREATEST USED CAR SHOW ON EARTH diluted Ringling Brothers' THE GREATEST SHOW ON EARTH mark.[59] Unlike trademark infringement, dilution does not require proof of a likelihood of confusion.

State registration may be suited for marks used with financial products offered only in one state — for example, marks for a local realtor or state and municipal bonds or bond funds. If the mark is not used in commerce regulated by the federal government, e.g., interstate commerce, it usually will not qualify for federal registration.

Federal Trademark Registration

Depending on the particular mark and how it is used, a mark can be registerable on the Principal Register or on the Supplemental Register, as a trademark and/or a service mark, and as words and/or the initials of the words, as is discussed below.

Principal Register. The owner of a mark used in the commerce of the United States may apply to the PTO for federal registration of the mark. Federal registration on the Principal Register provides many substantive advantages[60] and is usually worth obtaining.

Federal registration usually allows the use of the mark in all states. Also, to recover profits and damages in an infringement action, a registrant may give notice of the registration by using the ® symbol, the phrase "Registered in the U.S. Patent and Trademark Office," or "Reg. U.S. Pat. & Tm. Off." It is illegal to use these notices *before* obtaining a federal registration. However, the symbols TM and SM (i.e., trademark or service mark) may be used at any time to claim ownership in a mark.

An application for registering a mark on the Principal Register does not require that the mark already be in use. All that is necessary is a bona fide intent to use the mark in the commerce of the United States. However, for the registration to issue, there must be actual use of the mark within four years of the application filing date. This "intent-to-use" procedure allows a company to secure priority rights in a mark before investing in advertising and marketing.

Certain marks cannot be registered on the Principal Register, and certain other marks cannot be federally registered at all. The PTO will refuse registration for a term or symbol that does not function as a mark, is offensive, or is likely to cause confusion with a prior mark of another.[61] However, a primarily descriptive mark will not be refused registration if, through use in commerce, the mark has become distinctive. A distinctive "secondary meaning" is presumed after five years of use that is substantially continuous and exclusive.

Supplemental Register. A mark that is ineligible for registration on the Principal Register, but not otherwise barred by federal law,[62] may be registered on the Supplemental Register. Registration on the Supplemental Register does not provide any of the advantages previously listed, except that it provides a basis for registration in some foreign countries and jurisdiction in federal courts.

Trademark and/or Service Mark. Securities products are intangibles. Thus, it is not clear that they are "goods" for the purpose of obtaining a federally registered trademark. Two cases have considered the question, but have reached opposite conclusions.[63] To avoid potential future objection, a service mark registration may be preferable. The PTO registered the CATS, DARTS, and FASTBAC service marks for the services associated with these financial products.

However, some marks may be used in association with goods and services, for example, a mark used on automated banking machines and in association with the banking services. Such marks can be registered as a trademark and as a service mark, thereby extending the areas of commercial activity explicitly covered in the federal registration.

One and/or Two Marks. It is not uncommon to register both initials and the words that the initials represent, for example, FASTBAC and FIRST AUTOMOTIVE SHORT TERM BONDS AND CERTIFICATES. Registering both, preferably in separate registrations, reflects the test for infringement: Is there a likelihood of confusion between the source of one seller's services under its mark and the source of another seller's services under the respective mark? It is arguable that FASTBAC is confusingly similar to FIRST AUTOMOTIVE SHORT TERM BONDS AND CERTIFICATES. But registering both removes any doubt and effectively increases the scope of protection by increasing the range of what would be confusingly similar.

Protecting a mark consisting of initials is separate from, but related to, protecting the words that the initials represent. For example, the words may be more descriptive than the initials and might not be registerable. Any combination of registrations may be used, but broader protection is probably afforded by separately registering both.

Obtaining Federal Trademark Registration. A federal trademark registration requires filing an application with the PTO. If the application is not opposed by a third party, obtaining the registration may cost several thousand dollars, depending on the complexity of the issues presented. The cost will be greater if a search is conducted, preferably before the mark is selected, to ensure that the mark is available for exclusive use. Obtaining a registration will likely take at least one year — or many months, if expedited processing is granted.

Preserving a federal registration does require sustained effort.

Failure to continue to use a mark or to enforce exclusive rights will result in the loss of rights. Additionally, between the fifth and sixth years after the registration issues, an affidavit of continued use must be filed, or else the registration will be canceled. The registrant can then also file for incontestable status if the mark has been used continuously without contest. Finally, to remain effective, a federal registration must be renewed every 10 years.

Enforcement

Trademark rights include the right to prevent others from confusing the seller's customers by trading upon the symbol, or a similar symbol, of the seller's good will. It is an infringement to use in commerce any reproduction, counterfeit, copy or colorable imitation of a registered mark with the sale, distribution, or advertising of any goods or services that is likely to cause confusion, or to cause mistake, or to deceive.

Suit for infringement of a U.S.-registered mark may be brought in state or federal court. An ITC proceeding also can be initiated to stop the importation of goods with an infringing mark. Suit for infringement of a state registration or a common law mark may be brought in state court and often in federal court too.

Enforcing a federal trademark registration is more efficient than litigation involving common law rights or a state registration lacking presumptive rights. A federal registration is prima facie evidence of ownership of a distinctive mark. In an infringement suit, the registrant need only prove by a preponderance of the evidence that the defendant's mark is likely to cause confusion. Defenses include prior right to the mark, abandonment by the registrant, noninfringement, unclean hands,[64] and, under some circumstances, latches and estoppel. Remedies include: an injunction; damages (defendant's profits and plaintiff's damages sustained), which may be tripled; and destruction of infringing articles. Damage awards are usually adequate.

Advantages and Disadvantages

Each form of trademark protection has its advantages and disadvantages. Common law protection has the potential advantage of not requiring the registration and maintenance expenses. If the financial product will be on the market for less than a year — the approximate amount of time normally required to secure a federal trademark registration — common law protection may be all that is necessary to meet business objectives. Thus, for example, one issue of short term notes may be ill suited for the long term protection of a trademark registration, but if the notes are regularly issued under the same name, federal registration of that name may be desirable.

A disadvantage of common law protection is that unfair competition law is not a well defined body of law; thus, there may be uncertainty about the ability to enforce common law trademark rights. Further, unlike an action for infringement of a federally registered trademark, a plaintiff lacks presumptive rights. With more evidence required, the litigation is often more expensive, and the likelihood of success is reduced. In addition, common law remedies are more limited than those provided by statute.

The advantages and disadvantages of state registration vary from state to state, but state registration can be useful under some circumstances. For example, a state registration usually issues in less time than a federal registration. Also, a state registration may be advantageous over common law protection, if there is no interstate commerce, which is necessary for a federal registration. However, a state registration is not well suited for commercial transactions conducted substantially outside the state(s) in which the mark is registered. Because the cost of preparing and filing an application for a state registration is about the same as that for a federal filing, and a federal registration offers broader protection, this approach is not favored for enduring products or products in interstate commerce.

Of all of the forms of trademark protection, federal registration is preferable because it offers significant presumptive rights at a nominal cost. Trademark/ service mark protection has the following advantages: (1) it vests immediately upon use or upon issuance with priority from the filing date of a proper "intent to use" application; (2) it protects against a likelihood of confusion among distinctive symbols used in association with goods and services; and (3) it tends to involve efficient litigation with reasonable remedies. The primary disadvantage is that it does not protect against similar financial products and services marketed under a distinctly different mark.

Comment

Care should be taken in selecting marks to ensure that they are available for use. In addition, consideration should be given to federal registration for marks used with financial products and services provided in the commerce of the United States for any substantial time. Thereafter, registrants should use the symbol. The marks can also be incorporated into the "image" of the company or product, such as the Merrill Lynch bull ("Merrill Lynch is bullish on America"), the Dreyfus Lion, etc. A mark can be used to great commercial advantage and to limit the extent to which a competitor's product can be associated with the creator's product.

Summary

In sum, the use of intellectual property law to protect financial products and services is a significant development in the financial industry, with consequences for both creators and competitors. For the creators, copyright, patent, misappropriation, and trademark protections are cumulative. In many circumstances, a combination of these protections can pose a formidable legal barrier to competitors in the U.S. or elsewhere in the world. The cost associated with obtaining and maintaining even the most aggressive combination of protections may not be excessive when compared with the market value of what is protected.

For competitors, an infringement of these protections poses the risks of business embarrassment and significant liability exposure. The potential also exists for having to withdraw a successful financial product from the market. Even having to withdraw and replace certain securities documents can be expensive. The need to be careful and thorough when offering competitive financial products should be recognized because the risks are now greater.

Whether any form of intellectual property protection for financial products or services will be worth the cost of obtaining it is a business decision that will reflect the particular circumstances in each case.[65] However, when creating, issuing, underwriting, or dealing in such products, companies should be alert to the intellectual property protections available to themselves and to others.

ENDNOTES

[1]*Merritt Forbes & Co. v. Newman Investment Securities, Inc.,* 604 F. Supp. 943 (S.D.N.Y 1985).

[2]17 U.S.C. §102 (1990).

[3]*Dow Jones & Co. v. Board of Trade of Chicago,* 546 F. Supp. 113 (S.D.N.Y 1982).

[4]22 U.S.C. §1337 (1990).

[5]*Paine, Webber, Jackson & Curtis, Inc. v. Merrill Lynch, Pierce, Fenner & Smith, Inc.,* 564 F. Supp. 1358 (D. Del. 1983); and *College Savings Bank v. Centrust Savings Bank,* S.D. Fla. Civ. No. 89-824 (April 2, 1989).

[6]Securities Quotation Apparatus, U.S. Patent No. 3,082,402, issued May 10, 1960, to J.R. Scantlin.

[7]Methods and Apparatus for Restructuring Debt Obligations, U.S. Patent No. 4,739,478, issued April 19, 1988 (assigned to Lazard Freres & Co.).

[8]Methods and Apparatus for Funding Future Liability of Uncertain Cost, U.S. Patent No. 4,642,768, issued February 10, 1987, to Peter A. Roberts.

[9]Method and Apparatus for Funding a Future Liability of Uncertain Cost, U.S. Patent No. 4,752,877, issued June 21, 1988 (assigned to College Savings Bank).

[10]Automated Stock Exchange, U.S. Patent No. 4,412,287, issued October 25, 1983, to Walter D. Braddock, III.

[11]International Commodity Trade Exchange, U.S. Patent No. 4,677,552, issued June 30, 1987, to H.C. Sibley, Jr.

[12]Automated Securities Trading System, U.S. Patent No. 4,674,044, issued June 16, 1987 (assigned to Merrill Lynch, Pierce, Fenner & Smith, Inc.).

[13]Automated Investment System, U.S. Patent No. 4,751,640, issued June 14, 1988 (assigned to Citibank).

[14]Securities Brokerage-Cash Management System, U.S. Patent No. 4,346,442, issued August 24, 1982 (assigned to Merrill Lynch, Pierce, Fenner & Smith).

Securities Brokerage-Cash Management System, U.S. Patent No. 4,376,978, issued March 15, 1983 (assigned to Merrill Lynch, Pierce, Fenner & Smith).

System and Method of Investment Management Including Means to Adjust Deposit and Loan Accounts for Inflation, U.S. Patent No. 4,742,457, issued May 3, 1988 (assigned to Trans Texas Holding Corporation).

Securities Brokerage-Cash Management System Obviating Float Costs by Anticipatory Liquidation of Short Term Assets, U.S. Patent No. 4,597,046, issued June 24, 1986 (assigned to Merrill Lynch, Pierce, Fenner & Smith).

[15]Securities Valuation System, U.S. Patent No. 4,334,270, issued June 8, 1982, to Frederic C. Towers.

[16]Renewable Option Accounting and Marketing System, U.S. Patent No. 4,823,265, issued April 18, 1989, to George E. Nelson.

[17]Computerized Insurance Premium Quote Request and Policy Issuance System, U.S. Patent No. 4,831,526, issued May 16, 1989 (assigned to The Chubb Corporation).

[18]Method of Determining the Premium for, and Writing a Policy Insuring Against, Specified Weather Conditions, U.S. Patent No. 4,766,539, issued August 23, 1988, to Henry L. Fox.

[19]Medical Insurance Verification and Processing System, U.S. Patent No. 4,491,725, issued January 1, 1985, to Lawrence E. Pritchard.

[20]Analog Computation of Insurance and Investment Quantities, U.S. Patent No. 3,634,669, issued January 11, 1969 (assigned to Aer-Flow Dynamics, Inc.).

[21]Methods and Apparatus for Funding Future Liability of Uncertain Cost, U.S. Patent No. 4,722,055, issued January 26, 1988 (assigned to College Savings Bank).

[22]Method and Apparatus for Insuring the Funding of a Future Liability of Uncertain Cost, U.S. Patent No. 4,839,804, issued June 13, 1989 (assigned to College Savings Bank).

[23]Automatic Transaction Machine, U.S. Patent No. 4,803,347, issued February 7, 1989 (assigned to Omron Tateisi Electronics Company).

Financial Data Processing System with Distributed Data Input Data Devices and Method of Use, U.S. Patent No. 4,914,587, issued April 3, 1990 (assigned to Chrysler First Info. Technologies, Inc.).

[24]Financial Data Processing System Using Payment Coupons, U.S. Patent No. 4,974,878, issued December 4, 1990 (assigned to Remittance Technology Corporation).

[25]System and Method for Implementing and Administering a Mortgage Plan, U.S. Patent No. 4,876,648, issued October 24, 1989, to Charles B. Lloyd.

[26]System and Method of Investment Management Including Means to Adjust Deposit and Loan Accounts for Inflation, U.S. Patent No. 4,742,457, issued May 3, 1988 (assigned to Trans Texas Holding Corporation).

[27]Method and System for Determining Interest Rates, U.S. Pa-

tent No. 4,194,242, issued March 18, 1980 (assigned to Patricia Ann Cotts, Nancy Fern Hamburger, Betty B. Robbins, William Norman Robbins).

[28]Apparatus for Maximizing Interest Earnings and Providing Payments From Principal Without Interest Penalty, U.S. Patent No. 4,232,367, issued November 4, 1980, to Robert H. Youden and Charles S. Robertson.

[29]Data Processing Methods and Apparatus for Managing Vehicle Financing, U.S. Patent No. 4,736,294, issued April 5, 1988 (assigned to The Royal Bank of Canada).

[30]System for the Operation of a Financial Account, U.S. Patent No. 4,953,085, issued August 28, 1990 (assigned to Proprietary Financial Products, Inc.).

[31]Transaction Approval System, U.S. Patent No. 4,908,521, issued March 13, 1990 (assigned to Visa International Services Association).

Card Authorization Terminal, U.S. Patent No. 4,874,932, issued October 17, 1989 (assigned to Omron Tateisi Electronics Company).

[32]Method and Apparatus for Benefit and Financial Communication, U.S. Patent No. 4,648,037, issued March 3, 1987 (assigned to Metropolitan Life Insurance Company).

[33]Pension Benefits System, U.S. Patent No. 4,750,121, issued June 7, 1988, to Gustavo M. Halley and Julio Yanes.

Self-implementing Pension Benefits System, U.S. Patent No. 4,969,094, issued November 6, 1990, to Gustavo M. Halley and Julio M. Yanes.

[34]Investment Management System with Travel Usage Funds Indexed to Customer Account Status, U.S. Patent No. 4,885,685, issued December 5, 1989 (L & C Family Partnership).

[35]Instinet Communication System for Effectuating the Sale or Exchange of Fungible Properties between Subscribers, U.S. Patent No. 3,573,747, issued April 6, 1971 (assigned to Institutional Networks Corporation).

[36]35 U.S.C. §101 (1990).

[37]*See* Barrett, Mathematical Algorithms and Computer Programs, 1106 TMOG 5-12 (Official Gazette of the United States Patent and Trademark office, Vol. 1106/No. 1, September 5, 1989).

[38]*Parker v. Flook*, 437 U.S. 584 (1978).

[39]U.S. Patent Nos. 4,346,442 and 4,376,978, footnote 15, *supra*.

[40]*Paine, Webber, Jackson & Curtis, Inc., v. Merrill Lynch, Pierce, Fenner & Smith, Inc.,* 564 F. Supp. 1358 (D. Del. 1983).

[41]35 U.S.C. §§102, 103. (1989).

[42]Most foreign nations require that the patent application be filed prior to such events. Thus, in order to secure patent protection in many foreign nations, the inventor must file a patent application prior to making the invention publicly available or placing the invention on sale.

[43]*Standard & Poor's Corp. v. Commodity Exchange, Inc.,* 683 F. 2d 704 (2d Cir. 1982); and *Board of Trade v. Dow Jones & Co.,* 108 Ill. App. 3d 681, 439 N.E.2d 526 (1982), *aff'd,* 98 Ill. 2d 109, 456 N.E.2d 84 (1983), respectively.

[44]248 U.S. 215 (1918).

[45]*Id.* at 239.

[46]*Id.* at 240.

[47]*INS* involved a federal common law action. In the subsequent decision of *Erie R.R. Co. v. Tompkins,* 304 U.S. 64, (1938), the U.S. Supreme Court concluded that suits could no longer be based on federal common law. Thereafter, misappropriation became a question of state common law. *Compare Loeb v. Turner,* 257 S.W.2d 800 (Tex. Civ. App., 1953) (arguably rejecting the INS doctrine as a matter of Texas law), with *Toho Company, Ltd. v. Sears, Roebuck & Co.,* 645 F.2d 788 (9th Cir. 1981) (recognizing an *INS* claim as common law unfair competition in California for which statutory remedies, including damages, are apparently available).

[48]683 F.2d 704 (2d Cir. 1982).

[49]*Standard & Poor's Corp. v. Commodity Exchange, Inc.,* 538 F. Supp. 1063 (S.D.N.Y. 1982).

[50]*Board of Trade v. Dow Jones & Co.,* 108 Ill. App. 3d 681, 439 N.E.2d 526 (1982), *aff'd,* 98 Ill.2d 109, 456 N.E.2d 84 (1983).

[51]439 N.E.2d at 534.

[52]____U.S. ____, 109 S. Ct. 971 (1989).

[53]DREXEL BURNHAM LAMBERT, U.S. Trademark Registration No. 1,243,129, registered June 21, 1983, by Drexel Burnham Lambert Group Inc.

FIDELITY INVESTMENTS, U.S. Trademark Registration No. 1,481,037, registered March 15, 1988, by FMR Corporation.

SALOMON BROTHERS and logo, U.S. Trademark Registration No. 911,433, registered April 13, 1971, by Salomon Brothers Inc.

THE FIRST BOSTON CORPORATION and logo, U.S. Trademark Registration No. 1,331,245, registered April 16, 1985, by The First Boston Corporation.

[54]CATS, U.S. Trademark Registration No. 1,369,433, registered November 5, 1985, by Salomon Brothers Inc.

DARTS, U.S. Trademark Registration No. 1,513,044, registered November 15, 1988, by Salomon Brothers Inc.

FASTBAC FIRST AUTOMOTIVE SHORT TERM BONDS AND CERTIFICATES and design, U.S. Trademark Registration No. 1,409,824, registered September 16, 1986, by Drexel Burnham Lambert Incorporated.

[55]See, e.g., *Merritt Forbes & Co. v. Newman Inv. Sec., Inc., Standard & Poor's Corp. v. Commodity Exchange, Inc.,* 683 F.2d 704 (2d Cir. 1982); and *Midwest Packaging Materials Co. v. Midwest Packaging Corp.,* 312 F. Supp. 134 (S.D. Iowa 1970).

[56]15 U.S.C. § 80a-34(d) (1990).

[57]15 U.S.C. § 77j(b) (1990).

[58]*Merritt Forbes & Co. v. Newman Inv. Sec., Inc.,* 604 F. Supp. 943 (S.D.N.Y. 1985).

[59]*Ringling Bros. Barnum & Baily Combined Shows, Inc. v. Celozzi-Ettleson Chevrolet, Inc.,* 6 U.S.P.Q.2d 1300 (N.D. Ill. 1987), *aff'd,* 855 F.2d 480 (7th Cir. 1988).

[60]Among the advantages of a federal registration on the Principal Register are: (1) *prima facie* evidence of the validity of the registration, registrant's ownership of the mark, and of registrant's exclusive right to use the mark in commerce in connection with the goods or services specified in the certificate; (2) the filing date of the application is a constructive date of first use of the mark in commerce (this gives registrant nationwide priority as of that date, except for certain prior users or prior applicants); (3) constructive notice of a claim of ownership (which eliminates a good faith defense for a party adopting the trademark after the registrant's date of registration); (4) *prima facie* right to expand use of the mark to all states and protectorates of the U.S.; (5) the possibility of incontestability, in which case the registration is conclusive evidence of the registrant's exclusive right, with certain limited exceptions, to use the registered mark in commerce; (6) the right to sue in federal court for trademark infringement; (7) the right to deposit the reg-

istration with the U.S. Customs Service in order to stop the importation of goods bearing an infringing mark; (8) availability of
criminal penalties and treble damages in an action for counterfeiting
a registered trademark; (9) remedies of the defendant's profits, plus
damages and costs, and under some circumstances, treble damages
and attorney's fees; and (10) treaty rights for efficiently securing
trademark rights in most foreign nations.

[61]More particularly, 17 U.S.C. § 1052 (1989) prohibits registration of the Principal Register of a mark or term that: (1) does not
function as a trademark to identify the goods or services as coming
from a particular source (e.g., the matter applied for is merely or-
namentation); (2) is immoral, deceptive or scandalous; (3) may dis-
parage or falsely suggest a connection with persons, institutions,
beliefs or national symbols, or bring them into contempt or disre-
pute; (4) consists of or simulates the flag or coat of arms or other
insignia of the United States, or a State or municipality, or any
foreign nation; (5) is the name, portrait or signature of a particular
living individual, unless he has given written consent; or is the
name, signature or portrait of a deceased President of the United
States during the life of his widow, unless she has given her consent;
(6) so resembles a mark already registered in the PTO as to be
likely, when applied to the goods of the applicant, to cause confusion, or to cause mistake, or to deceive; (7) is merely descriptive
or deceptively misdescriptive of the goods or services; (8) is primarily geographically descriptive or deceptively misdescriptive of
the goods or services of the applicant; or (9) is primarily merely a
surname.

[62]See items 1, 7, 8, or 9 in footnote 45, *supra.*

[63]*Midwest Packaging Materials Co. v. Midwest Packaging Corp.,*
312 F. Supp. 134 (S.D. Iowa 1970) (securities are goods); *The Side
Fund, Inc. v. New England Life Side Fund, Inc.,* Fed. Sec. L. Rep. (CCH)
¶92,860 (S.D.N.Y. Nov. 2, 1970) (A security is not goods or services).

[64]Unclean hands is an equitable defense whereby a court will
not grant relief to one who has engaged in unconscionable conduct.
For example, in *Trak Inc. v. Benner Ski KG,* 475 F. Supp. 1076 (D.
Mass. 1979), relief was denied because the plaintiff used the ® symbol without having obtained a federal registration.

[65]This chapter does not address mortgaging intellectual prop-

erty or tax aspects of researching, developing, licensing, maintaining, or transferring intellectual property. In a given case, particularly in mergers and acquisitions, these factors can be significant business considerations.

Index